READINGS IN
ORGANIZATIONAL BEHAVIOR

READINGS IN
ORGANIZATIONAL BEHAVIOR
Dimensions of
Management Actions

RICHARD C. HUSEMAN
ARCHIE B. CARROLL
University of Georgia

Allyn and Bacon, Inc.
Boston, London, Sydney, Toronto

Library of Congress Cataloging in Publication
Data
Main entry under title:

Readings in organizational behavior.

   Includes bibliographical references.
   1. Organizational behavior—Addresses, essays,
lectures. 2. Management—Addresses, essays,
lectures. I. Huseman, Richard C. II. Carroll,
Archie B.
HD58.7.R43   658.4   78-27060
ISBN 0-205-06515-5

Printed in the United States of America.

10 9 8 7 6 5 4 3 2   85 84 83 82

CONTENTS

PREFACE

Integrative Readings in Organizational Behavior: Dimensions and Management Actions brings together a number of readings on organizational behavior. Although only a small sampling of the available articles can be included in any one book, articles have been selected that contain a wide range of important ideas and at the same time are readable and practical.

The major objective of this book is to provide present and future managers with a conceptual framework for understanding behavior in organizations. The authors have drawn upon their experience as researchers and classroom teachers as well as their experience as trainers in numerous management development programs for practicing managers. As a result of these experiences, readings were selected for inclusion that stress a balance among ideas, concepts, management strategies, and empirical research, and were chosen from classic and modern sources.

This book is intended for use in courses in management, organizational behavior/theory, and human resource management. It is structured so that it can be used as the primary or supplementary text in the courses mentioned above. The text is also intended for use in both management development courses and short courses for practicing managers. Entire chapters may be emphasized for concentrated study in a particular area of organizational behavior or selected articles may supplement other instructional materials.

The authors would like to thank the writers whose articles make up the book, and have given specific recognition to each writer at the beginning of his contribution. We wish to express our appreciation to Elmore Alexander for his assistance and suggestions throughout this project. The contributions of Russell Driver and Martha Hollowell are also gratefully acknowledged. We also thank Jackie Ogletree for her time and patience in her efficient handling of many of the details associated with the project.

Richard C. Huseman
Archie B. Carroll

INTRODUCTION

In recent years the field of organizational behavior has moved away from an emphasis on simple description and prescription. The contemporary orientation is one moving toward an understanding and analysis of the interrelationships among the variables that comprise the total organizational system. This book attempts to build upon the latter concern by providing an integrative model or framework upon which to situate and conceptualize the numerous variables that come to bear on the behavioral encounters faced by managers and students of management.

In Part I the focus is on the major dimensions of organizational behavior. These are conceptualized as telescoping encounters between the individual, small and large groups, the formal organization itself, and the general environment or culture. Our purpose here is to develop an understanding of the characteristics and nature of the dimensions that need to be considered in understanding organizational behavior.

The readings in Part II are categorized by major management-initiated actions available to leaders in organizations—motivation, leadership, communication, MBO, organizational development, and managing change and conflict. Our purpose is to provide the reader with a number of selective insights and views concerning the management of organizational behavior. Though it is difficult to diagram accurately and completely the many concepts covered in both parts of the book, Figure 1 attempts to present the above-mentioned components in a useful framework. A closer look at each of the major parts of the model follows.

INDIVIDUAL LEVEL

It has long been held that the *individual* is the hub of concern in the field of organizational behavior. It should be stressed here that we are referring to human behavior in organizational settings, not the behavior of organizations per se. Thus, the individual is a necessary component in any behavioral situation—whether as an act in isolation, as a part of an

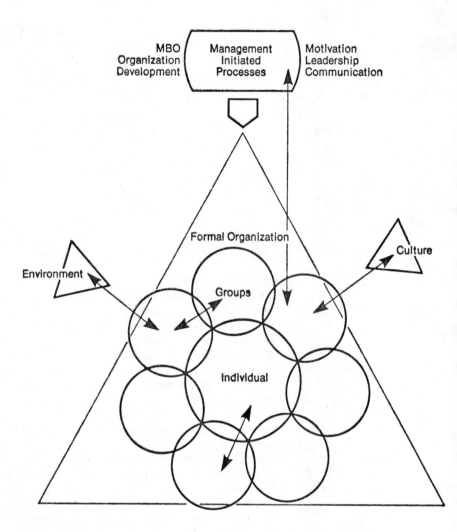

FIGURE 1. The Integrative Model of Organizational Behavior.

informal group, in response to the expectations of the formal organization, or environmentally induced pressures.

It is useful to pursue readings on various facets of the individual to help round out the fundamental nature of human beings. In this connection we present readings on the significant facets of individual behavior —perception, attitude formation, learning, and the nature of individual decision making. Rather than discuss human motivation at this point, we have chosen to treat motivation in the final part of the book, where it is dealt with in the context of management-initiated processes. Thus our approach is not one that addresses the question "*What is it* that motivates people?" but rather one that addresses the question "*How should management* motivate people?"

GROUP LEVEL

We next turn our attention in the integrative model to a focus on groups. Groups are defined as two or more individuals who band together, either informally or formally, for a common purpose. Relevant considerations here include a knowledge of the group's structure or anatomy, group processes or dynamics, and one of the frequent outcomes of group functioning —conflict. With consideration of the group, we widen our analysis, encompassing more than was possible with the sole focus on the individual.

ORGANIZATIONAL LEVEL

The focus of the model next moves to a consideration of the *formal organization* and its role in organizational behavior. Of particular interest here is how management creates order and system by stipulating a structure or arrangement of parts, the primary intention of which is to create a goal-directed mechanism for carrying out what the organization and its leaders see as the organization's purpose.

This structure manifests itself in the specification of authority, responsibility, and communication bonds or relationships. Additional ways in which this structure is seen include the relationships depicted on a typical organization chart, and the specification of job boundaries, scope, and responsibilities as seen in the job descriptions of organizational members. Of particular interest to our integrative model is the nature of the interface (point of contact) between the individual and the organization and its design, technology and structure. What we are generally interested in here is the impact the formal organization has on behavior within the organization.

ENVIRONMENTAL LEVEL

Expanding our direction, we next focus in the integrative model on *environment* and its influence on behavior. Quite technically this should include all facets of the environment—economic, political, technological, social, and so on. We have chosen to cast our attention on two major aspects: (*a*) how the environment's nature and turbulence impact on structure, which in turn affects behavior, and (*b*) how the social environment is assuming an ever more pervasive role in its impact on behavior in organizations. The latter area is of special concern because of recent revelations pointing out the impact of changing values on work attitudes, and the growing importance of and expectation for ethical behavior in the work place.

To this point we have identified all of the micro-to-macro components of the integrative model. The readings presented have been included because it was felt they effectively explored the nature and functioning of these parts of the model, and hence integrated these components into a cohesive socio-human system.

MANAGEMENT-INITIATED PROCESS

Feeding into this system—but at the same time an integral part of the system—is the last element of the integrative model: *management and its initiated processes* or actions. The articles constituting Part II deal with management-initiated efforts to understand, monitor, guide, and direct their organizations. Managers are the formal leaders assigned this task, and they employ a number of techniques or approaches in their efforts to keep the organization running smoothly, and moving toward its goals. In this part of the integrative model management is observed attempting to achieve its objectives through the use of specialized knowledge about motivation, power, leadership, communication, MBO, organization development, and the handling of change and conflict.

Through these efforts, management unifies the system into an integrated, goal-directed whole, that ideally (or, optimistically), maximizes the long-range use of the organization's resources. The readings included in this part of the book are intended to discuss ideas and concepts that have been shown to be effective over time in managing organizational behavior. By using the model as a conceptual framework, and the articles contained in the book as the substance, it is hoped that the manager and the student of management will understand and appreciate the usefulness of an integrative framework of organizational behavior, with its many dimensions and nuances, in bringing about more effective organizational performance both now and in the future.

PART I

DIMENSIONS OF ORGANIZATIONAL BEHAVIOR

INDIVIDUAL DIMENSIONS
OF BEHAVIOR

In this chapter we examine the first element of our integrative model of organizational behavior—the individual. It is appropriate that the individual is our first point of analysis in that an understanding of the determinants of individual behavior will provide a basis for understanding the other elements of organizational behavior. The readings in this chapter explain how the individual is involved in determining behavior patterns throughout the organization. It is by learning how individuals influence other elements of organizational behavior that insight is gained as to how organizational goals may best be accomplished. In this chapter we examine four areas of individual behavior: individual perception, attitude formation, learning, and individual decision making.

We first examine the role and influence of perception on behavior. In the article, "Perception: Some Recent Research and Implications for Administration" by Zalkind and Costello, the authors discuss the basic factors in the perceptual process. This classic article on perception covers such topics as the nature of the perceptual process, the formation of impressions, the characteristics of the perceiver and the perceived, situational and organizational influences on perception, and finally, the impact of perception on interpersonal adjustment.

"The Functional Approach to The Study of Attitudes," by Daniel Katz is a consideration of the four major functions that attitudes perform for the individual: the instrumental or adjustive function, the ego-defensive function, the value-expressive function, and the knowledge function. Katz sets forth the conditions necessary to arouse or modify attitudes according to the motivational basis of the attitude.

David Kolb in "Management and the Learning Process" explores the idea that a successful manager is characterized not by a particular body of knowledge, but by his ability to adapt and master the ever-changing demands made upon him. Thus, the manager's effectiveness is determined by his ability to learn. Kolb provides a four-stage learning cycle that illustrates how experience is translated into concepts that in turn are translated into guides in the choice of new experiences for the manager.

Finally, Chris Argyris identifies problems in the area of individual decision making in his article, "Interpersonal Barriers to Decision Making." He points out that the actual behavior of top executives during decision-making meetings is often inconsistent with their attitudes and prescriptions about effective executive action. Taken together, the articles in this chapter go a long way toward capturing the essence of the individual as a part of the total organizational model.

PERCEPTION: SOME RECENT RESEARCH AND IMPLICATIONS FOR ADMINISTRATION

SHELDON S. ZALKIND
AND
TIMOTHY W. COSTELLO

Management practice is being increasingly influenced by behavioral science research in the areas of group dynamics, problem solving and decision making, and motivation. One aspect of behavior which has not been fully or consistently emphasized is the process of perception, particularly the recent work on person perception.

In this paper we shall summarize some of the findings on perception as developed through both laboratory and organizational research and point out some of the administrative and managerial implications. We discuss first some basic factors in the nature of the perceptual process including need and set; second, some research on forming impressions; third, the characteristics of the perceiver and the perceived; fourth, situational and organizational influences on perception; and finally, perceptual influences on interpersonal adjustment.

NATURE OF THE PERCEPTUAL PROCESS

What are some of the factors influencing perception? In answering the question it is well to begin by putting aside the attitude of naïve realism, which suggests that our perceptions simply regis-

Reprinted with the permission of the *Administrative Science Quarterly*.

ter accurately what is "out there." It is necessary rather to consider what influences distort one's perceptions and judgments of the outside world. Some of the considerations identified in the literature up to the time of Johnson's 1944 review of the research on object perception (where distortion may be even less extreme than in person perception) led him to suggest the following about the perceiver:[1]

1. He may be influenced by considerations that he may not be able to identify, responding to cues that are below the threshold of his awareness. For example, a judgment as to the size of an object may be influenced by its color even though the perceiver may not be attending to color.
2. When required to form difficult perceptual judgments, he may respond to irrelevant cues to arrive at a judgment. For example, in trying to assess honesty, it has been shown that the other person's smiling or not smiling is used as a cue to judge his honesty.
3. In making abstract or intellectual judgments, he may be influenced by emotional factors— what is liked is perceived as correct.
4. He will weigh perceptual evidence coming from respected (or favored) sources more heavily than that coming from other sources.
5. He may not be able to identify all the factors on which his judgments are based. Even if he

is aware of these factors he is not likely to realize how much weight he gives to them.

These considerations do not imply that we respond only to the subtle or irrelevant cues or to emotional factors. We often perceive on the basis of the obvious, but we are quite likely to be responding as well to the less obvious or less objective.

In 1958, Bruner, citing a series of researches, described what he called the "New Look" in perception as one in which personal determinants of the perceptual process were being stressed.[2] Bruner summarized earlier work and showed the importance of such subjective influences as needs, values, cultural background, and interests on the perceptual process. In his concept of "perceptual readiness" he described the importance of the framework or category system that the perceiver himself brings to the perceiving process.

Tapping a different vein of research, Cantril described perceiving as a "transaction" between the perceiver and the perceived, a process of negotiation in which the perceptual end product is a result both of influences within the perceiver and of characteristics of the perceived.[3]

One of the most important of the subjective factors that influence the way we perceive, identified by Bruner and others, is *set*. A study by Kelley illustrated the point.[4] He found that those who were previously led to expect to meet a "warm" person, not only made different judgments about him, but also behaved differently toward him, than those who were expecting a "cold" one. The fact was that they simultaneously were observing the same person in the same situation. Similarly, Strickland indicated the influence of set in determining how closely supervisors feel they must supervise their subordinates.[5] Because of prior expectation one person was trusted more than another and was thought to require less supervision than another, even though performance records were identical.

FORMING IMPRESSIONS OF OTHERS

The data on forming impressions is of particular importance in administration. An administrator is confronted many times with the task of forming an impression of another person—a new employee at his desk, a visiting member from the home office, a staff member he has not personally met before. His own values, needs, and expectations will play a part in the impression he forms. Are there other factors that typically operate in this area of administrative life? One of the more obvious influences is the physical appearance of the person being perceived. In a study of this point Mason was able to demonstrate that people agree on what a leader should look like and that there is no relationship between the facial characteristics agreed upon and those possessed by actual leaders.[6] In effect, we have ideas about what leaders look like and we can give examples, but we ignore the many exceptions that statistically cancel out the examples.

In the sometimes casual, always transitory situations in which one must form impressions of others it is a most natural tendency to jump to conclusions and form impressions without adequate evidence. Unfortunately, as Dailey showed, unless such impressions are based on important and relevant data, they are not likely to be accurate.[7] Too often in forming impressions the perceiver does not know what is relevant, important, or predictive of later behavior. Dailey's research furthermore supports the cliché that, accurate or not, first impressions are lasting.

Generalizing from other research in the field, Soskin described four limitations on the ability to form accurate impressions of others.[8] First, the impression is likely to be disproportionately affected by the type of situation or surroundings in which the impression is made and influenced too little by the person perceived. Thus the plush luncheon club in which one first meets a man will dominate the impression of the man himself. Secondly, although impressions are frequently based on a limited sample of the perceived person's behavior, the generalization that the perceiver makes will be sweeping. A third limitation is that the situation may not provide an opportunity for the person perceived to show behavior relevant to the traits about which impressions are formed. Casual conversation or questions, for example, provide few opportunities to demonstrate intelligence or work characteristics, yet the perceiver often draws conclusions about these from an interview. Finally, Soskin agrees with Bruner and Cantril that the impression of the person perceived may be distorted by some highly individualized reaction of the perceiver.

But the pitfalls are not yet all spelled out; it is possible to identify some other distorting influences on the process of forming impressions. Research has brought into sharp focus some typical errors, the more important being stereotyping, halo effect, projection, and perceptual defense.

Stereotyping

The word "stereotyping" was first used by Walter Lippmann in 1922 to describe bias in perceiving peoples. He wrote of "pictures in people's heads," called stereotypes, which guided (distorted) their perceptions of others. The term has long been used to describe judgments made about people on the basis of their ethnic group membership. For example, some say "Herman Schmidt [being German] is industrious." Stereotyping also predisposes judgments in many other areas of interpersonal relations. Stereotypes have developed about many types of groups, and they help to prejudice many of our perceptions about their members. Examples of stereotypes of groups other than those based on ethnic identification are bankers, supervisors, union members, poor people, rich people, and administrators. Many unverified qualities are assigned to people principally because of such group memberships.

In a research demonstration of stereotyping, Haire found that labeling a photograph as that of a management representative caused an impression to be formed of the person, different from that formed when it was labeled as that of a union leader.[9] Management and labor formed different impressions, each seeing his opposite as less dependable than his own group. In addition, each side saw his own group as being better able than the opposite group to understand a point of view different from its own. For example, managers felt that other managers were better able to appreciate labor's point of view, than labor was able to appreciate management's point of view. Each had similar stereotypes of his opposite and

considered the thinking, emotional characteristics, and interpersonal relations of his opposite as inferior to his own. As Stagner pointed out, "It is plain that unionists perceiving company officials in a stereotyped way are less efficient than would be desirable.[10] Similarly, company executives who see all labor unions as identical are not showing good judgment or discrimination."

One of the troublesome aspects of stereotypes is that they are so widespread. Finding the same stereotypes to be widely held should not tempt one to accept their accuracy. It may only mean that many people are making the same mistake. Allport has demonstrated that there need not be a "kernel of truth" in a widely held stereotype.[11] He has shown that while a prevalent stereotype of Armenians labeled them as dishonest, a credit reporting association gave them credit ratings as good as those given other ethnic groups.

Bruner and Perlmutter found that there is an international stereotype for "businessmen" and "teachers."[12] They indicated that the more widespread one's experience with diverse members of a group, the less their group membership will affect the impression formed.

An additional illustration of stereotyping is provided by Luft.[13] His research suggests that perception of personality adjustment may be influenced by stereotypes, associating adjustment with high income and maladjustment with low income.

Halo Effect

The term halo effect was first used in 1920 to describe a process in which a general impression which is favorable or unfavorable is used by judges to evaluate several specific traits. The "halo" in such case serves as a screen keeping the perceiver from actually seeing the trait he is judging. It has received the most attention because of its effect on rating employee performance. In the rating situation, a supervisor may single out one trait, either good or bad, and use this as the basis for his judgment of all other traits. For example, an excellent attendance record causes judgments of productivity, high quality of work, and so forth. One study in the U. S.

Army showed that officers who were liked were judged more intelligent than those who were disliked, even though they had the same scores on intelligence tests.

We examine halo effect here because of its general effect on forming impressions. Bruner and Taguiri suggest that it is likely to be most extreme when we are forming impressions of traits that provide minimal cues in the individual's behavior, when the traits have moral overtones, or when the perceiver must judge traits with which he has had little experience.[14] A rather disturbing conclusion is suggested by Symonds that halo effect is more marked the more we know the acquaintance.[15]

A somewhat different aspect of the halo effect is suggested by the research of Grove and Kerr.[16] They found that knowledge that the company was in receivership caused employees to devalue the higher pay and otherwise superior working conditions of their company as compared to those in a financially secure firm.

Psychologists have noted a tendency in perceivers to link certain traits. They assume, for example, that when a person is aggressive he will also have high energy or that when a person is "warm" he will also be generous and have a good sense of humor. This logical error, as it has been called, is a special form of the halo effect and is best illustrated in the research of Asch.[17] In his study the addition of one trait to a list of traits produced a major change in the impression formed. Knowing that a person was intelligent, skillful, industrious, determined, practical, cautious, and warm led a group to judge him to be also wise, humorous, popular, and imaginative. When warm was replaced by cold, a radically different impression (beyond the difference between warm and cold) was formed. Kelley's research illustrated the same type of error.[18] This tendency is not indiscriminate; with the pair "polite–blunt," less change was found than with the more central traits of "warm–cold."

In evaluating the effect of halo on perceptual distortion, we may take comfort from the work of Wishner, which showed that those traits that correlate more highly with each other are more likely to lead to a halo effect than those that are unrelated.[19]

Projection

A defense mechanism available to everyone is projection, in which one relieves one's feelings of guilt or failure by projecting blame onto someone else. Over the years the projection mechanism has been assigned various meanings. The original use of the term was concerned with the mechanism to defend oneself from unacceptable feelings. There has since been a tendency for the term to be used more broadly, meaning to ascribe or attribute any of one's own characteristics to other people. The projection mechanism concerns us here because it influences the perceptual process. An early study by Murray illustrates its effect.[20] After playing a dramatic game, "Murder," his subjects attributed much more maliciousness to people whose photographs were judged than did a control group which had not played the game. The current emotional state of the perceiver tended to influence his perceptions of others; i.e., frightened perceivers judged people to be frightening. More recently, Feshback and Singer revealed further dynamics of the process.[21] In their study, subjects who had been made fearful judged a stimulus person (presented in a moving picture) as both more fearful and more aggressive than did nonfearful perceivers. These authors were able to demonstrate further that the projection mechanism at work here was reduced when their subjects were encouraged to admit and talk about their fears.

Sears provides an illustration of a somewhat different type of projection and its effect on perception.[22] In his study projection is seeing our own undesirable personality characteristics in other people. He demonstrated that people high in such traits as stinginess, obstinacy, and disorderliness, tended to rate others much higher on these traits than did those who were low in these undesirable characteristics. The tendency to project was particularly marked among subjects who had the least insight into their own personalities.

Research thus suggests that our perceptions may characteristically be distorted by emotions we are experiencing or traits that we possess. Placed in the administrative setting, the research would suggest, for example, that a manager frightened by rumored organizational changes might not only judge others to be more frightened than they were, but also assess various policy decisions as more frightening than they were. Or a general foreman lacking insight into his own incapacity to delegate might be oversensitive to this trait in his superiors.

Perceptual Defense

Another distorting influence, which has been called perceptual defense, has also been demonstrated by Haire and Grunes to be a source of error.[23] In their research they ask, in effect, "Do we put blinders on to defend ourselves from seeing those events which might disturb us?" The concept of perceptual defense offers an excellent description of perceptual distortion at work and demonstrates that when confronted with a fact inconsistent with a stereotype already held by a person, the perceiver is able to distort the data in such a way as to eliminate the inconsistency. Thus, by perceiving inaccurately, he defends himself from having to change his stereotypes.

CHARACTERISTICS OF PERCEIVER AND PERCEIVED

We have thus far been talking largely about influences on the perceptual process without specific regard to the perceiver and his characteristics. Much recent research has tried to identify some characteristics of the perceiver and their influence on the perception of other people.

The Perceiver

A thread that would seem to tie together many current findings is the tendency to use oneself as the norm or standard by which one perceives or judges others. If we examine current research, certain conclusions are suggested:

1. *Knowing oneself makes it easier to see others accurately.* Norman showed that when one is aware of what his own personal characteristics are he makes fewer errors in perceiving others.[24] Weingarten has shown that people with insight are less likely to view the world in black-and-white terms and to give extreme judgments about others.[25]

2. *One's own characteristics affect the characteristics he is likely to see in others.* Secure people (compared to insecure) tend to see others as warm rather than cold, as was shown by Bossom and Maslow.[26] The extent of one's own sociability influences the degree of importance one gives to the sociability of other people when one forms impressions of them.[27] The person with "authoritarian" tendencies is more likely to view others in terms of power and is less sensitive to the psychological or personality characteristics of other people than is a nonauthoritarian.[28] The relatively few categories one uses in describing other people tend to be those one uses in describing oneself.[29] Thus traits which are important to the perceiver will be used more when he forms impressions of others. He has certain constant tendencies, both with regard to using certain categories in judging others and to the amount of weight given to these categories.[30]

3. *The person who accepts himself is more likely to be able to see favorable aspects of other people.*[31] This relates in part to the accuracy of his perceptions. If the perceiver accepts himself as he is, he widens his range of vision in seeing others; he can look at them and be less likely to be very negative or critical. In those areas in which he is more insecure, he sees more problems in other people.[32] We are more likely to like others who have traits we accept in ourselves and reject those who have the traits which we do not like in ourselves.[33]

4. *Accuracy in perceiving others is not a single skill.* While there have been some variations in the findings, as Gage has shown, some consistent results do occur.[34] The perceiver tends to interpret the feelings others have about him in terms of his feelings towards them.[35] One's ability to perceive others accurately may depend on how sensitive one is to differences between people and also to the norms (outside of oneself) for judging them.[36] Thus, as Taft has shown, the ability to judge others does not seem to be a single skill.[37]

Possibly the results in these four aspects of person perception can be viewed most constructively in connection with earlier points on the process of perception. The administrator (or any other individual) who wishes to perceive someone else accurately must look at the other person, not at himself. The things that he looks at in someone else are influenced by his own traits. But if he knows his own traits, he can be aware that they provide a frame of reference for him. His own traits help to furnish the categories that he will use in perceiving others. His characteristics, needs, and values can partly limit his vision and his awareness of the differences between others. The question one could ask when viewing another is: "Am I looking at him, and forming my impression of his behavior in the situation, or am I just comparing him with myself?"

There is the added problem of being set to observe the personality traits in another which the perceiver does not accept in himself, e.g., being somewhat autocratic. At the same time he may make undue allowances in others for those of his own deficiencies which do not disturb him but might concern some people, e.g., not following prescribed procedures.

The Perceived

Lest we leave the impression that it is only the characteristics of the perceiver that stand between him and others in his efforts to know them, we turn now to some characteristics of the person being perceived which raise problems in perception. It is possible to demonstrate, for example, that the status of the person perceived is a variable influencing judgments about his behavior. Thibaut and Riecken have shown that even though two people behave in identical fashion, status differences between them cause a perceiver to assign different motivations for the behavior.[38] Concerning co-operativeness, they found that high status persons are judged as wanting to co-operate and low status persons as having to co-operate. In turn, more liking is shown for the person of high status than for the person of low status. Presumably, more credit is given when the boss says, "Good morning," to us than when a subordinate says the same thing.

Bruner indicated that we use categories to simplify our perceptual activities. In the administrative situation, status is one type of category, and role provides another. Thus the remarks of Mr. Jones in the sales department are perceived dif-

ferently from those of Smith in the purchasing department, although both may say the same thing. Also, one who knows Jones's role in the organization will perceive his behavior differently from one who does not know Jones's role. The process of categorizing on the basis of roles is similar to, if not identical with, the stereotyping process described earlier.

Visibility of the traits judged is also an important variable influencing the accuracy of perception.[39] Visibility will depend, for example, on how free the other person feels to express the trait. It has been demonstrated that we are more accurate in judging people who like us than people who dislike us. The explanation suggested is that most people in our society feel constraint in showing their dislike, and therefore the cues are less visible.

Some traits are not visible simply because they provide few external cues for their presence. Loyalty, for example, as opposed to level of energy, provides few early signs for observation. Even honesty cannot be seen in the situations in which most impressions are formed. As obvious as these comments might be, in forming impressions many of us nevertheless continue to judge the presence of traits which are not really visible. Frequently the practical situation demands judgments, but we should recognize the frail reeds upon which we are leaning and be prepared to observe further and revise our judgments with time and closer acquaintance.

SITUATIONAL INFLUENCES ON PERCEPTION

Some recent research clearly points to the conclusion that the whole process of interpersonal perception is, at least in part, a function of the *group* (or interpersonal) context in which the perception occurs. Much of the research has important theoretical implications for a psychology of interpersonal relations. In addition, there are some suggestions of value for administrators. It is possible to identify several characteristics of the interpersonal climate which have direct effect on perceptual accuracy. As will be noted, these are characteristics which can be known, and in some cases controlled, in administrative settings.

Bieri provides data for the suggestion that when people are given an opportunity to interact in a friendly situation, they tend to see others as similar to themselves.[40] Applying his suggestion to the administrative situation, we can rationalize as follows: Some difficulties of administrative practice grow out of beliefs that different interest groups in the organization are made up of different types of people. Obviously once we believe that people in other groups are different, we will be predisposed to see the differences. We can thus find, from Bieri's and from Rosenbaum's work, an administrative approach for attacking the problem.[41] If we can produce an interacting situation which is co-operative rather than competitive, the likelihood of seeing other people as similar to ourselves is increased.

Exline's study adds some other characteristics of the social context which may influence perception.[42] Paraphrasing his conclusions to adapt them to the administrative scene, we can suggest that when a committee group is made up of congenial members who are willing to continue work in the same group, their perceptions of the goal-directed behavior of fellow committee members will be more accurate, although observations of purely personal behavior (as distinguished from goal-directed behavior) may be less accurate.[43] The implications for setting up committees and presumably other interacting work groups seem clear: Do not place together those with a past history of major personal clashes. If they must be on the same committee, each must be helped to see that the other is working toward the same goal.

An interesting variation in this area of research is the suggestion from Ex's work that perceptions will be more influenced or swayed by relatively unfamiliar people in the group than by those who are intimates.[44] The concept needs further research, but it provides the interesting suggestion that we may give more credit to strangers for having knowledge, since we do not really know, than we do to our intimates, whose backgrounds and limitations we feel we do know.

The *organization,* and one's place in it, may also be viewed as the context in which perceptions take place. A study by Dearborn and Simon illustrates this point.[45] Their data support the hypothesis that the administrator's perceptions will often be limited to those aspects of a situation which relate specifically to his own department, despite an attempt to influence him away from such selectivity.

Perception of self among populations at different levels in the hierarchy also offers an opportunity to judge the influence of organizational context on perceptual activity. Porter's study of the self-descriptions of managers and line workers indicated that both groups saw themselves in different terms, which corresponded to their positions in the organization's hierarchy.[46] He stated that managers used leadership-type traits (e.g., inventive) to describe themselves, while line workers used follower-type terms (e.g., co-operative). The question of which comes first must be asked: Does the manager see himself this way because of his current position in the organization? Or is this self-picture an expression of a more enduring personal characteristic that helped bring the manager to his present position? This study does not answer that question, but it does suggest to an administrator the need to be aware of the possibly critical relationship between one's hierarchical role and self-perception.

PERCEPTIONAL INFLUENCES ON INTERPERSONAL ADJUSTMENT

Throughout this paper, we have examined a variety of influences on the perceptual process. There has been at least the inference that the operations of such influences on perception would in turn affect behavior that would follow. Common sense judgment suggests that being able to judge other people accurately facilitates smooth and effective interpersonal adjustments. Nevertheless, the relationship between perception and consequent behavior is itself in need of direct analysis. Two aspects may be identified: (1) the effect of accuracy of perception on subsequent behavior and (2) the effect of the duration of the relationship and the opportunity for experiencing additional cues.

First then, from the applied point of view, we can ask a crucial question: Is there a relationship between accuracy of social perception and adjustment to others? While the question might suggest a quick affirmative answer, research findings are inconsistent. Steiner attempted to resolve some of these inconsistencies by stating that accuracy may have an effect on interaction under the following conditions: when the interacting persons are co-operatively motivated, when the behavior which is accurately perceived is relevant to the activities of these persons, and when members are free to alter their behavior on the basis of their perceptions.[47]

Where the relationship provides opportunity only to form an impression, a large number of subjective factors, i.e., set, stereotypes, projections, etc., operate to create an early impression, which is frequently erroneous. In more enduring relationships a more balanced appraisal may result as increased interaction provides additional cues for judgment. In his study of the acquaintance process, Newcomb showed that while early perception of favorable traits caused attraction to the perceived person, over a four-month period the early cues for judging favorable traits became less influential.[48] With time, a much broader basis was used which included comparisons with others with whom one had established relationships. Such findings suggest that the warnings about perceptual inaccuracies implicit in the earlier sections of this paper apply with more force to the short-term process of impression forming than to relatively extended acquaintance-building relationships. One would thus hope that rating an employee after a year of service would be a more objective performance than appraising him in a selection interview—a hope that would be fulfilled only when the rater had provided himself with opportunities for broadening the cues he used in forming his first impressions.

SUMMARY

Two principal suggestions which increase the probability of more effective administrative action emerge from the research data. One suggestion is that the administrator be continuously aware of the intricacies of the perceptual process and thus be warned to avoid arbitrary and categorical judgments and to seek reliable evidence before judgments are made. A second suggestion grows out of the first: increased accuracy in one's

self-perception can make possible the flexibility to seek evidence and to shift position as time provides additional evidence.

Nevertheless, not every effort designed to improve perceptual accuracy will bring about such accuracy. The dangers of too complete reliance on formal training for perceptual accuracy are suggested in a study by Crow.[49] He found that a group of senior medical students were somewhat less accurate in their perceptions of others after a period of training in physician–patient relationships than were an untrained control group. The danger is that a little learning encourages the perceiver to respond with increased sensitivity to individual differences without making it possible for him to gauge the real meaning of the differences he has seen.

Without vigilance to perceive accurately and to minimize as far as possible the subjective approach in perceiving others, effective administration is handicapped. On the other hand, research would not support the conclusion that perceptual distortions will not occur simply because the administrator says he will try to be objective. The administrator or manager will have to work hard to avoid seeing only what he wants to see and to guard against fitting everything into what he is set to see.

We are not yet sure of the ways in which training for perceptual accuracy can best be accomplished, but such training cannot be ignored. In fact, one can say that one of the important tasks of administrative science is to design research to test various training procedures for increasing perceptual accuracy.

NOTES

1. D. M. Johnson, A Systematic Treatment of Judgment, *Psychological Bulletin,* 42 (1945), 193–224.
2. J. S. Bruner, "Social Psychology and Perception," in E. Maccoby, T. Newcomb, and E. Hartley, eds., *Readings in Social Psychology* (3d ed.: New York, 1958), pp. 85–94.
3. H. Cantril, Perception and Interpersonal Relations, *American Journal of Psychiatry,* 114 (1957), 119–126.
4. H. H. Kelley, The Warm–Cold Variable in First Impressions of Persons, *Journal of Personality,* 18 (1950), 431–439.

5. L. H. Strickland, Surveillance and Trust, *Journal of Personality,* 26 (1958), 200–215.

6. D. J. Mason, Judgements of Leadership Based upon Physiognomic Cues, *Journal of Abnormal and Social Psychology,* 54 (1957), 273–274.

7. C. A. Dailey, The Effects of Premature Conclusion upon the Acquisition of Understanding of a Person, *Journal of Psychology,* 33 (1952), 133–152.

8. W. E. Soskin, Influence of Information on Bias in Social Perception, *Journal of Personality,* 22 (1953), 118–127.

9. M. Haire, Role Perceptions in Labor-Management Relations: An Experimental Approach, *Industrial Labor Relations Review,* 8 (1955), 204–216.

10. R. Stagner, *Psychology of Industrial Conflict* (New York, 1956), p. 35.

11. G. Allport, *Nature of Prejudice* (Cambridge, Mass., 1954).

12. J. S. Bruner and H. V. Perlmutter, Compatriot and Foreigner: A Study of Impression Formation in Three Countries, *Journal of Abnormal and Social Psychology,* 55 (1957), 253–260.

13. J. Luft, Monetary Value and the Perception of Persons, *Journal of Social Psychology,* 46 (1957), 245–251.

14. J. S. Bruner and A. Taguiri, "The Perception of People," ch. xvii in G. Lindzey, ed., *Handbook of Social Psychology* (Cambridge, Mass., 1954).

15. P. M. Symonds, Notes on Rating, *Journal of Applied Psychology,* 7 (1925), 188–195.

16. B. A. Grove and W. A. Kerr, Specific Evidence on Origin of Halo Effect in Measurement of Morale, *Journal of Social Psychology,* 34 (1951), 165–170.

17. S. Asch, Forming Impressions of Persons, *Journal of Abnormal and Social Psychology,* 60 (1946), 258–290.

18. Kelley, *op. cit.*

19. J. Wishner, Reanalysis of "Impressions of Personality," *Psychology Review,* 67 (1960), 96–112.

20. H. A. Murray, The Effect of Fear upon Estimates of the Maliciousness of Other Personalities, *Journal of Social Psychology,* 4 (1933), 310–329.

21. S. Feshback and R. D. Singer, The Effects of Fear Arousal upon Social Perception, *Journal of Abnormal and Social Psychology,* 55 (1957), 283–288.

22. R. R. Sears, Experimental Studies of Perception, I. Attribution of Traits, *Journal of Social Psychology,* 7 (1936), 151–163.

23. M. Haire and W. F. Grunes, Perceptual Defenses: Processes Protecting an Original Perception of Another Personality, *Human Relations,* 3 (1958), 403–412.

24. R. D. Norman, The Interrelationships among Acceptance-Rejection, Self-Other Identity, Insight into Self, and Realistic Perception of Others, *Journal of Social Psychology,* 37 (1953), 205–235.

25. E. Weingarten, A Study of Selective Perception in Clinical Judgment, *Journal of Personality,* 17 (1949), 369–400.

26. J. Bossom and A. H. Maslow, Security of Judges as a Factor in Impressions of Warmth in Others, *Journal of Abnormal and Social Psychology,* 55 (1957), 147–148.

27. D. T. Benedetti and J. G. Hill, A Determiner of the Centrality of a Trait in Impression Formation, *Journal of Abnormal and Social Psychology,* 60 (1960), 278–279.

28. E. E. Jones, Authoritarianism as a Determinant of First-Impressions Formation, *Journal of Personality,* 23 (1954), 107–127.

29. A. H. Hastorf, S. A. Richardson, and S. M. Dornbusch, "The Problem of Relevance in the Study of Person Perception," in R. Taguiri and L. Petrullo, *Person Perception and Interpersonal Behavior* (Stanford, Calif., 1958).

30. L. J. Cronbach, Processes Affecting Scores on "Understanding of Others" and "Assumed Similarity," *Psychology Bulletin,* 52 (1955), 177–193.

31. K. T. Omwake, The Relation between Acceptance of Self and Acceptance of Others Shown by Three Personality Inventories, *Journal of Consulting Psychology,* 18 (1954), 443–446.

32. Weingarten, *op. cit.*

33. R. M. Lundy, W. Katovsky, R. L. Cromwell, and D. J. Shoemaker, Self Acceptability and Descriptions of Sociometric Choices, *Journal of Abnormal and Social Psychology,* 51 (1955), 260–262.

34. N. L. Gage, Accuracy of Social Perception and Effectiveness in Interpersonal Relationships, *Journal of Personality,* 22 (1953), 128–141.

35. R. Taguiri, J. S. Bruner, and R. Blake, On the Relation between Feelings and Perceptions of Feelings among Members of Small Groups," in Maccoby et al., *Readings in Social Psychology, op. cit.*

36. U. Bronfenbrenner, J. Harding, and M. Gallway, "The Measurement of Skill in Social Perception," in H. L. McClelland, D. C. Baldwin, U. Bronfenbrenner, and F. L. Strodtbeck, eds., *Talent and Society* (Princeton, N.J., 1958), pp. 29–111.

37. R. Taft, The Ability to Judge People, *Psychological Bulletin,* 52 (1955), 1–21.

38. J. W. Thibaut, and H. W. Riecken, Some Determinants and Consequences of the Perception of Social Causality, *Journal of Personality,* 24 (1955), 113–133.

39. Bruner and Taguiri, *op. cit.*

40. J. Bieri, Change in Interpersonal Perception Following Interaction, *Journal of Abnormal and Social Psychology,* 48 (1953), 61–66.

41. M. E. Rosenbaum, Social Perception and the Motivational Structure of Interpersonal Relations, *Journal of Abnormal and Social Psychology,* 59 (1959), 130–133.

42. R. V. Exline, Interrelations among Two Dimensions of Sociometric Status, Group Congeniality and Accuracy of Social Perception, *Sociometry,* 23 (1960), 85–101.

43. R. V. Exline, Group Climate as a Factor in the Relevance and Accuracy of Social Perception, *Journal of Abnormal and Social Psychology,* 55 (1957), 382–388.

44. J. Ex, The Nature of the Relation between Two Persons and the Degree of Their Influence on Each Other, *Acta Psychologica,* 17 (1960), 39–54.

45. D. C. Dearborn and H. A. Simon, Selective Perception. A Note on the Departmental Identifications of Executives, 21 (1958), 140–144.

46. L. W. Porter, Differential Self-Perceptions of Management Personnel and Line Workers, *Journal of Applied Psychology,* 42 (1958), 105–109.

47. I. Steiner, Interpersonal Behavior as Influenced by Accuracy of Social Perception, *Psychological Review,* 62 (1955), 268–275.

48. T. M. Newcomb, The Perception of Interpersonal Attraction, *American Psychologist,* 11 (1956), 575–586, and *The Acquaintance Process* (New York, 1961).

49. W. J. Crow, Effect of Training on Interpersonal Perception, *Journal of Abnormal and Social Psychology,* 55 (1957), 355–359.

THE FUNCTIONAL APPROACH TO THE STUDY OF ATTITUDES

DANIEL KATZ

The study of opinion formation and attitude change is basic to an understanding of the public opinion process even though it should not be equated with this process. The public opinion process is one phase of the influencing of collective decisions, and its investigation involves knowledge of channels of communication, of the power structures of a society, of the character of mass media, of the relation between elites, factions and masses, of the role of formal and informal leaders, of the institutionalized access to officials. But the raw material out of which public opinion develops is to be found in the attitudes of individuals, whether they be followers or leaders and whether these attitudes be at the general level of tendencies to conform to legitimate authority or majority opinion or at the specific level of favoring or opposing the particular aspects of the issue under consideration. The nature of the organization of attitudes within the personality and the processes which account for attitude change are thus critical areas for the understanding of the collective product known as public opinion.

Reprinted with the permission of the *Public Opinion Quarterly* and Daniel Katz.

EARLY APPROACHES TO THE STUDY OF ATTITUDE AND OPINION

There have been two main streams of thinking with respect to the determination of man's attitudes. The one tradition assumes an irrational model of man: specifically it holds that men have very limited powers of reason and reflection, weak capacity to discriminate, only the most primitive self-insight, and very short memories. Whatever mental capacities people do possess are easily overwhelmed by emotional forces and appeals to self-interest and vanity. The early books on the psychology of advertising, with their emphasis on the doctrine of suggestion, exemplify this approach. One expression of this philosophy is in the propagandist's concern with tricks and traps to manipulate the public. A modern form of it appears in *The Hidden Persuaders,* or the use of subliminal and marginal suggestion, or the devices supposedly employed by "the Madison Avenue boys." Experiments to support this line of thinking started with laboratory demonstrations of the power of hypnotic suggestion and were soon extended to show that people would change their attitudes in an uncritical manner under the influence of the prestige of authority and numbers. For example, individuals would accept or reject the same idea depending upon whether it came from a positive or a negative prestige source.[1]

The second approach is that of the ideologist who invokes a rational model of man. It assumes that the human being has a cerebral cortex, that he seeks understanding, that he consistently attempts to make sense of the world about him, that he possesses discriminating and reasoning powers which will assert themselves over time, and that he is capable of self-criticism and self-insight. It relies heavily upon getting adequate information to people. Our educational system is based upon this rational model. The present emphasis upon the improvement of communication, upon developing more adequate channels of two-way communication, of conferences and institutes, upon bringing people together to interchange ideas, are all indications of the belief in the importance of intelligence and comprehension in the formation and change of men's opinions.

Now either school of thought can point to evidence which supports its assumptions, and can make fairly damaging criticisms of its opponent. Solomon Asch and his colleagues, in attacking the irrational model, have called attention to the biased character of the old experiments on prestige suggestion which gave the subject little opportunity to demonstrate critical thinking.[2] And further exploration of subjects in these stupid situations does indicate that they try to make sense of a nonsensical matter as far as possible. Though the same statement is presented by the experimenter to two groups, the first time as coming from a positive source and the second time as coming from a negative source, it is given a different meaning dependent upon the context in which it appears.[3] Thus the experimental subject does his best to give some rational meaning to the problem. On the other hand, a large body of experimental work indicates that there are many limitations in the rational approach in that people see their world in terms of their own needs, remember what they want to remember, and interpret information on the basis of wishful thinking. H. H. Hyman and P. Sheatsley have demonstrated that these experimental results have direct relevance to information campaigns directed at influencing public opinion.[4] These authors assembled facts about such campaigns and showed con-

clusively that increasing the flow of information to people does not necessarily increase the knowledge absorbed or produce the attitude changes desired.

The major difficulty with these conflicting approaches is their lack of specification of the conditions under which men do act as the theory would predict. For the facts are that people do act at times as if they had been decorticated and at times with intelligence and comprehension. And people themselves do recognize that on occasion they have behaved blindly, impulsively, and thoughtlessly. A second major difficulty is that the rationality-irrationality dimension is not clearly defined. At the extremes it is easy to point to examples, as in the case of the acceptance of stupid suggestions under emotional stress on the one hand, or brilliant problem solving on the other; but this does not provide adequate guidance for the many cases in the middle of the scale where one attempts to discriminate between rationalization and reason.

RECONCILIATION OF THE CONFLICT IN A FUNCTIONAL APPROACH

The conflict between the rationality and irrationality models was saved from becoming a worthless debate because of the experimentation and research suggested by these models. The findings of this research pointed toward the elements of truth in each approach and gave some indication of the conditions under which each model could make fairly accurate predictions. In general the irrational approach was at its best where the situation imposed heavy restrictions upon search behavior and response alternatives. Where individuals must give quick responses without adequate opportunities to explore the nature of the problem, where there are very few response alternatives available to them, where their own deep emotional needs are aroused, they will in general react much as does the unthinking subject under hypnosis. On the other hand, where the individual can have more adequate commerce with the relevant environmental setting, where he has time to obtain more feedback from his reality testing, and where he has a number of realistic choices, his behavior will reflect the use of his rational faculties.[5] The child will often respond to the directive of the parent not by implicit obedience but by testing out whether or not the parent really meant what he said.

Many of the papers in this issue, which describe research and theory concerning consistency and consonance, represent one outcome of the rationality model. The theory of psychological consonance, or cognitive balance, assumes that man attempts to reduce discrepancies in his beliefs, attitudes, and behavior by appropriate changes in these processes. While the emphasis here is upon consistency or logicality, the theory deals with all dissonances, no matter how produced. Thus they could result from irrational factors of distorted perception and wishful thinking as well as from rational factors of realistic appraisal of a problem and an accurate estimate of its consequences. Moreover, the theory would predict only that the individual will move to reduce dissonance, whether such movement is a good adjustment to the world or leads to the delusional systems of the paranoiac. In a sense, then, this theory would avoid the conflict between the old approaches of the rational and the irrational man by not dealing with the specific antecedent causes of behavior or with the particular ways in which the individual solves his problems.

In addition to the present preoccupation with the development of formal models concerned with cognitive balance and consonance, there is a growing interest in a more comprehensive framework for dealing with the complex variables and for bringing order within the field. The thoughtful system of Ulf Himmelstrand, presented in the following pages, is one such attempt. Another point of departure is represented by two groups of workers who have organized their theories around the functions which attitudes perform for the personality. Sarnoff, Katz, and McClintock, in taking this functional approach, have given primary attention to the motivational bases of attitudes and the processes of attitude change.[6] The basic assumption of this group is that both attitude formation and attitude change must be understood in terms of the needs they serve and that, as these motivational processes differ, so too will the conditions and techniques for attitude change. Smith,

Bruner, and White have also analyzed the different functions which attitudes perform for the personality.[7] Both groups present essentially the same functions, but Smith, Bruner, and White give more attention to perceptual and cognitive processes and Sarnoff, Katz, and McClintock to the specific conditions of attitude change.

The importance of the functional approach is threefold. (1) Many previous studies of attitude change have dealt with factors which are not genuine psychological variables, for example, the effect on group prejudice of contact between two groups, or the exposure of a group of subjects to a communication in the mass media. Now contact serves different psychological functions for the individual and merely knowing that people have seen a movie or watched a television program tells us nothing about the personal values engaged or not engaged by such a presentation. If, however, we can gear our research to the functions attitudes perform, we can develop some generalizations about human behavior. Dealing with nonfunctional variables makes such generalization difficult, if not impossible.

(2) By concerning ourselves with the different functions attitudes can perform we can avoid the great error of oversimplification—the error of attributing a single cause to given types of attitude. It was once popular to ascribe radicalism in economic and political matters to the psychopathology of the insecure and to attribute conservatism to the rigidity of the mentally aged. At the present time it is common practice to see in attitudes of group prejudice the repressed hostilities stemming from childhood frustrations, though Hyman and Sheatsley have pointed out that prejudiced attitudes can serve a normative function of gaining acceptance in one's own group as readily as releasing unconscious hatred.[8] In short, not only are there a number of motivational forces to take into account in considering attitudes and behavior, but the same attitude can have a different motivational basis in different people.

(3) Finally, recognition of the complex motivational sources of behavior can help to remedy the neglect in general theories which lack specification of conditions under which given types of attitude will change. Gestalt theory tells us, for

example, that attitudes will change to give better cognitive organization to the psychological field. This theoretical generalization is suggestive, but to carry out significant research we need some middle-level concepts to bridge the gap between a high level of abstraction and particularistic or phenotypical events. We need concepts that will point toward the types of motive and methods of motive satisfaction which are operative in bringing about cognitive reorganization.

Before we attempt a detailed analysis of the four major functions which attitudes can serve, it is appropriate to consider the nature of attitudes, their dimensions, and their relations to other psychological structures and processes.

NATURE OF ATTITUDES: THEIR DIMENSIONS

Attitude is the predisposition of the individual to evaluate some symbol or object or aspect of his world in a favorable or unfavorable manner. Opinion is the verbal expression of an attitude, but attitudes can also be expressed in nonverbal behavior. Attitudes include both the affective, or feeling core of liking or disliking, and the cognitive, or belief, elements which describe the object of the attitude, its characteristics, and its relations to other objects. All attitudes thus include beliefs, but not all beliefs are attitudes. When specific attitudes are organized into a hierarchical structure, they comprise *value systems*. Thus a person may not only hold specific attitudes against deficit spending and unbalanced budgets but may also have a systematic organization of such beliefs and attitudes in the form of a value system of economic conservatism.

The dimensions of attitudes can be stated more precisely if the above distinctions between beliefs and feelings and attitudes and value systems are kept in mind. The *intensity* of an attitude refers to the strength of the *affective* component. In fact, rating scales and even Thurstone scales deal primarily with the intensity of feeling of the individual for or against some social object. The cognitive, or belief, component suggests two additional dimensions, the *specificity* or *generality* of the attitude and the *degree of differentiation* of the beliefs. Differentiation refers to the number of

beliefs or cognitive items contained in the attitude, and the general assumption is that the simpler the attitude in cognitive structure the easier it is to change.[9] For simple structures there is no defense in depth, and once a single item of belief has been changed the attitude will change. A rather different dimension of attitude is the *number and strength of its linkages to a related value system*. If an attitude favoring budget balancing by the Federal government is tied in strongly with a value system of economic conservatism, it will be more difficult to change than if it were a fairly isolated attitude of the person. Finally, the relation of the value system to the personality is a consideration of first importance. If an attitude is tied to a value system which is closely related to, or which consists of, the individual's conception of himself, then the appropriate change procedures become more complex. The *centrality* of an attitude refers to its role as part of a value system which is closely related to the individual's self-concept.

An additional aspect of attitudes is not clearly described in most theories, namely, their relation to action or overt behavior. Though behavior related to the attitude has other determinants than the attitude itself, it is also true that some attitudes in themselves have more of what Cartwright calls an action structure than do others.[10] Brewster Smith refers to this dimension as policy orientation[11] and Katz and Stotland speak of it as the action component.[12] For example, while many people have attitudes of approval toward one or the other of the two political parties, these attitudes will differ in their structure with respect to relevant action. One man may be prepared to vote on election day and will know where and when he should vote and will go to the polls no matter what the weather or how great the inconvenience. Another man will only vote if a party worker calls for him in a car. Himmelstrand's work is concerned with all aspects of the relationship between attitude and behavior, but he deals with the action structure of the attitude itself by distinguishing between attitudes where the affect is tied to verbal expression and attitudes where the affect is tied to behavior concerned with more objective referents of the attitude.[13] In the first case an individual derives satisfaction from talking about a problem; in the second case he derives satisfaction from taking some form of concrete action.

Attempts to change attitudes can be directed primarily at the belief component or at the feeling, or affective, component. Rosenberg theorizes that an effective change in one component will result in changes in the other component and presents experimental evidence to confirm this hypothesis.[14] For example, a political candidate will often attempt to win people by making them like him and dislike his opponent, and thus communicate affect rather than ideas. If he is successful, people will not only like him but entertain favorable beliefs about him. Another candidate may deal primarily with ideas and hope that, if he can change people's beliefs about an issue, their feelings will also change.

FOUR FUNCTIONS WHICH ATTITUDES PERFORM FOR THE INDIVIDUAL

The major functions which attitudes perform for the personality can be grouped according to their motivational basis as follows:

1. *The instrumental, adjustive, or utilitarian function* upon which Jeremy Bentham and the utilitarians constructed their model of man. A modern expression of this approach can be found in behavioristic learning theory.
2. *The ego-defensive function* in which the person protects himself from acknowledging the basic truths about himself or the harsh realities in his external world. Freudian psychology and neo-Freudian thinking have been preoccupied with this type of motivation and its outcomes.
3. *The value-expressive function* in which the individual derives satisfactions from expressing attitudes appropriate to his personal values and to his concept of himself. This function is central to doctrines of ego psychology which stress the importance of self-expression, self-development, and self-realization.
4. *The knowledge function* based upon the individual's need to give adequate structure to his universe. The search for meaning, the

need to understand, the trend toward better organization of perceptions and beliefs to provide clarity and consistency for the individual, are other descriptions of this function. The development of principles about perceptual and cognitive structure have been the contribution of Gestalt psychology.

Stated simply, the functional approach is the attempt to understand the reasons people hold the attitudes they do. The reasons, however, are at the level of psychological motivations and not of the accidents of external events and circumstances. Unless we know the psychological need which is met by the holding of an attitude we are in a poor position to predict when and how it will change. Moreover, the same attitude expressed toward a political candidate may not perform the same function for all the people who express it. And while many attitudes are predominantly in the service of a single type of motivational process, as described above, other attitudes may serve more than one purpose for the individual. A fuller discussion of how attitudes serve the above four functions is in order.

1. The Adjustment Function. Essentially this function is a recognition of the fact that people strive to maximize the rewards in their external environment and to minimize the penalties. The child develops favorable attitudes toward the objects in his world which are associated with the satisfaction of his needs and unfavorable attitudes toward objects which thwart him or punish him. Attitudes acquired in the service of the adjustment function are either the means for reaching the desired goal or avoiding the undesirable one, or are affective associations based upon experiences in attaining motive satisfactions.[15] The attitudes of the worker favoring a political party which will advance his economic lot are an example of the first type of utilitarian attitude. The pleasant image one has of one's favorite food is an example of the second type of utilitarian attitude.

In general, then, the dynamics of attitude formation with respect to the adjustment function are dependent upon present or past perceptions of the utility of the attitudinal object for the individual. The clarity, consistency, and nearness of rewards and punishments, as they relate to the individual's activities and goals, are important factors in the acquisition of such attitudes. Both attitudes and habits are formed toward specific objects, people, and symbols as they satisfy specific needs. The closer these objects are to actual need satisfaction and the more they are clearly perceived as relevant to need satisfaction, the greater are the probabilities of positive attitude formation. These principles of attitude formation are often observed in the breach rather than the compliance. In industry, management frequently expects to create favorable attitudes toward job performance through programs for making the company more attractive to the worker, such as providing recreational facilities and fringe benefits. Such programs, however, are much more likely to produce favorable attitudes toward the company as a desirable place to work than toward performance on the job. The company benefits and advantages are applied across the board to all employees and are not specifically relevant to increased effort in task performance by the individual worker.

Consistency of reward and punishment also contributes to the clarity of the instrumental object for goal attainment. If a political party bestows recognition and favors on party workers in an unpredictable and inconsistent fashion, it will destroy the favorable evaluation of the importance of working hard for the party among those whose motivation is of the utilitarian sort. But, curiously, while consistency of reward needs to be observed, 100 per cent consistency is not as effective as a pattern which is usually consistent but in which there are some lapses. When animal or human subjects are invariably rewarded for a correct performance, they do not retain their learned responses as well as when the reward is sometimes skipped.[16]

2. The Ego-Defensive Function. People not only seek to make the most of their external world and what it offers, but they also expend a great deal of their energy on living with themselves. The mechanisms by which the individual protects his ego from his own unacceptable impulses and from the knowledge of threatening forces from without, and the methods by which he reduces his anxieties created by such problems, are known as

mechanisms of ego defense. A more complete account of their origin and nature will be found in Sarnoff's article in this issue.[17] They include the devices by which the individual avoids facing either the inner reality of the kind of person he is, or the outer reality of the dangers the world holds for him. They stem basically from internal conflict with its resulting insecurities. In one sense the mechanisms of defense are adaptive in temporarily removing the sharp edges of conflict and in saving the individual from complete disaster. In another sense they are not adaptive in that they handicap the individual in his social adjustments and in obtaining the maximum satisfactions available to him from the world in which he lives. The worker who persistently quarrels with his boss and with his fellow workers, because he is acting out some of his own internal conflicts, may in this manner relieve himself of some of the emotional tensions which beset him. He is not, however, solving his problem of adjusting to his work situation and thus may deprive himself of advancement or even of steady employment.

Defense mechanisms, Miller and Swanson point out, may be classified into two families on the basis of the more or less primitive nature of the devices employed.[18] The first family, more primitive in nature, are more socially handicapping and consist of denial and complete avoidance. The individual in such cases obliterates through withdrawal and denial the realities which confront him. The exaggerated case of such primitive mechanisms is the fantasy world of the paranoiac. The second type of defense is less handicapping and makes for distortion rather than denial. It includes rationalization, projection, and displacement.

Many of our attitudes have the function of defending our self-image. When we cannot admit to ourselves that we have deep feelings of inferiority we may project those feelings onto some convenient minority group and bolster our egos by attitudes of superiority toward this underprivileged group. The formation of such defensive attitudes differs in essential ways from the formation of attitudes which serve the adjustment function. They proceed from within the person, and the objects and situation to which they are attached are merely convenient outlets for their expression.

Not all targets are equally satisfactory for a given defense mechanism, but the point is that the attitude is not created by the target but by the individual's emotional conflicts. And when no convenient target exists the individual will create one. Utilitarian attitudes, on the other hand, are formed with specific reference to the nature of the attitudinal object. They are thus appropriate to the nature of the social world to which they are geared. The high school student who values high grades because he wants to be admitted to a good college has a utilitarian attitude appropriate to the situation to which it is related.

All people employ defense mechanisms, but they differ with respect to the extent that they use them and some of their attitudes may be more defensive in function than others. It follows that the techniques and conditions for attitude change will not be the same for ego-defensive as for utilitarian attitudes.

Moreover, though people are ordinarily unaware of their defense mechanisms, especially at the time of employing them, they differ with respect to the amount of insight they may show at some later time about their use of defenses. In some cases they recognize that they have been protecting their egos without knowing the reason why. In other cases they may not even be aware of the devices they have been using to delude themselves.

3. The Value-Expressive Function. While many attitudes have the function of preventing the individual from revealing to himself and others his true nature, other attitudes have the function of giving positive expression to his central values and to the type of person he conceives himself to be. A man may consider himself to be an enlightened conservative or an internationalist or a liberal, and will hold attitudes which are the appropriate indication of his central values. Thus we need to take account of the fact that not all behavior has the negative function of reducing the tensions of biological drives or of internal conflicts. Satisfactions also accrue to the person from the expression of attitudes which reflect his cherished beliefs and his self-image. The reward to the person in these instances is not so much a matter of gaining social recognition or monetary rewards as of establishing his self-identity and confirming his notion of the sort of person he sees himself to be. The gratifications obtained from value expression may go beyond the confirmation of self-identity. Just as we find satisfaction in the exercise of our talents and abilities, so we find reward in the expression of any attributes associated with our egos.

Value-expressive attitudes not only give clarity to the self-image but also mold that self-image closer to the heart's desire. The teenager who by dress and speech establishes his identity as similar to his own peer group may appear to the outsider a weakling and a craven conformer. To himself he is asserting his independence of the adult world to which he has rendered childlike subservience and conformity all his life. Very early in the development of the personality the need for clarity of self-image is important—the need to know "who I am." Later it may be even more important to know that in some measure I am the type of person I want to be. Even as adults, however, the clarity and stability of the self-image is of primary significance. Just as the kind, considerate person will cover over his acts of selfishness, so too will the ruthless individualist become confused and embarrassed by his acts of sympathetic compassion. One reason it is difficult to change the character of the adult is that he is not comfortable with the new "me." Group support for such personality change is almost a necessity, as in Alcoholics Anonymous, so that the individual is aware of approval of his new self by people who are like him.

The socialization process during the formative years sets the basic outlines for the individual's self-concept. Parents constantly hold up before the child the model of the good character they want him to be. A good boy eats his spinach, does not hit girls, etc. The candy and the stick are less in evidence in training the child than the constant appeal to his notion of his own character. It is small wonder, then, that children reflect the acceptance of this model by inquiring about the characters of the actors in every drama, whether it be a television play, a political contest, or a war, wanting to know who are the "good guys" and who are the "bad guys." Even as adults we persist in labeling others in the terms of such character images. Joe McCarthy and his cause collapsed in fantastic fashion when the telecast of the Army hearings showed him in the role of the villain attacking the gentle, good man represented by Joseph Welch.

A related but somewhat different process from childhood socialization takes place when individuals enter a new group or organization. The individual will often take over and internalize the values of the group. What accounts, however, for the fact that sometimes this occurs and sometimes it does not? Four factors are probably operative, and some combination of them may be necessary for internalization. (1) The values of the new group may be highly consistent with existing values central to the personality. The girl who enters the nursing profession finds it congenial to consider herself a good nurse because of previous values of the importance of contributing to the welfare of others. (2) The new group may in its ideology have a clear model of what the good group member should be like and may persistently indoctrinate group members in these terms. One of the reasons for the code of conduct for members of the armed forces, devised after the revelations about the conduct of American prisoners in the Korean War, was to attempt to establish a model for what a good soldier does and does not do. (3) The activities of the group in moving toward its goal permit the individual genuine opportunity for participation. To become ego-involved so that he can internalize group values, the new member must find one of two conditions. The group activity open to him must tap his talents and abilities so that his chance to show what he is worth can be tied into the group effort. Or else the activities of the group must give him an active voice in group decisions. His particular talents and abilities may not be tapped but he does have the opportunity to enter into group decisions, and thus his need for self-determination is satisfied. He then identifies with the group in which such opportunities for ego-involvement are available. It is not necessary that opportunities for self-expression and self-determination be of great magnitude in an objective sense, so long as they are important for the psychological economy of the individuals themselves. (4) Finally, the individual may come to see himself as a group member if he can share in the rewards of group activity which includes his own efforts. The worker may not play much of a part in building a ship or make any decisions in the process of building it. Nevertheless, if he and his fellow workers are given a share in every boat they build and a return on the proceeds from the earnings of the ship, they may soon come to identify with the ship-building company and see themselves as builders of ships.

4. The Knowledge Function. Individuals not only acquire beliefs in the interest of satisfying various specific needs, they also seek knowledge to give meaning to what would otherwise be an unorganized chaotic universe. People need standards or frames of reference for understanding their world, and attitudes help to supply such standards. The problem of understanding, as John Dewey made clear years ago, is one "of introducing (1) *definiteness* and *distinction* and (2) *consistency* and *stability* of meaning into what is otherwise vague and wavering." [19] The definiteness and stability are provided in good measure by the norms of our culture, which give the otherwise perplexed individual ready-made attitudes for comprehending his universe. Walter Lippmann's classical contribution to the study of opinions and attitudes was his description of stereotypes and the way they provided order and clarity for a bewildering set of complexities.[20] The most interesting finding in Herzog's familiar study of the gratifications obtained by housewives in listening to daytime serials was the unsuspected role of information and advice.[21] The stories were liked "because they explained things to the inarticulate listener."

The need to know does not of course imply that people are driven by a thirst for universal knowledge. The American public's appalling lack of political information has been documented many times. In 1956, for example, only 13 per cent of the people in Detroit could correctly name the two United States Senators from the state of Michigan and only 18 per cent knew the name of their own Congressman.[22] People are not avid seekers after knowledge as judged by what the educator or social reformer would desire. But they do want to understand the events which impinge directly on their own life. Moreover, many of the attitudes they have already acquired give them sufficient basis for interpreting much of what they perceive to be important for them. Our already existing stereotypes, in Lippmann's language, "are an ordered, more or less consistent picture of the world, to which our habits, our tastes, our capacities, our comforts and our hopes have adjusted themselves. They may not be a complete picture of the world, but they are a picture of a possible world to which we are adapted." [23] It follows that new information will not modify old attitudes unless there is some inadequacy or incompleteness or inconsistency in the existing attitudinal structure as it relates to the perceptions of new situations.

The articles in this issue by Cohen, Rosenberg, Osgood, and Zajonc discuss the process of attitude change with respect to inconsistencies and discrepancies in cognitive structure.

DETERMINANTS OF ATTITUDE AROUSAL AND ATTITUDE CHANGE

The problems of attitude arousal and of attitude change are separate problems. The first has to do with the fact that the individual has many predispositions to act and many influences playing upon him. Hence we need a more precise description of the appropriate conditions which will evoke a given attitude. The second problem is that of specifying the factors which will help to predict the modification of different types of attitude.

The most general statement that can be made concerning attitude arousal is that it is dependent upon the excitation of some need in the individual, or some relevant cue in the environment. When a man grows hungry, he talks of food. Even when not hungry he may express favorable attitudes toward a preferred food if an external stimulus cues him. The ego-defensive person who hates foreigners will express such attitudes under conditions of increased anxiety or threat or when a foreigner is perceived to be getting out of place.

The most general statement that can be made about the conditions conducive to attitude change is that the expression of the old attitude or its anticipated expression no longer gives satisfaction to its related need state. In other words, it no

longer serves its function and the individual feels blocked or frustrated. Modifying an old attitude or replacing it with a new one is a process of learning, and learning always starts with a problem, or being thwarted in coping with a situation. Being blocked is a necessary, but not a sufficient, condition for attitude change. Other factors must be operative and will vary in effectiveness depending upon the function involved.

AROUSING AND CHANGING UTILITARIAN ATTITUDES

Political parties have both the problem of converting people with antagonistic attitudes (attitude change) and the problem of mobilizing the support of their own followers (attitude arousal). To accomplish the latter they attempt to revive the needs basic to old attitudes. For example, the Democrats still utilize the appeals of the New Deal and the Republicans still talk of the balanced budget. The assumption is that many people still hold attitudes acquired in earlier circumstances and that appropriate communication can reinstate the old needs. For most people, however, utilitarian needs are reinforced by experience and not by verbal appeals. Hence invoking the symbols of the New Deal will be relatively ineffective with respect to adjustive attitudes unless there are corresponding experiences with unemployment, decreased income, etc. Though the need state may not be under the control of the propagandist, he can exaggerate or minimize its importance. In addition to playing upon states of need, the propagandist can make perceptible the old cues associated with the attitude he is trying to elicit. These cues may have associated with them favorable affect, or feeling, though the related needs are inactive. For example, the fighters for old causes can be paraded across the political platform in an attempt to arouse the attitudes of the past.

The two basic conditions, then, for the arousal of existing attitudes are the activation of their relevant need states and the perception of the appropriate cues associated with the content of the attitude.

To change attitudes which serve a utilitarian function, one of two conditions must prevail: (1)

the attitude and the activities related to it no longer provide the satisfactions they once did, or (2) the individual's level of aspiration has been raised. The Chevrolet owner who had positive attitudes toward his old car may now want a more expensive car commensurate with his new status.

Attitudes toward political parties and voting behavior are often difficult to change if there is no widespread dissatisfaction with economic conditions and international relations. Currently, however, the polls show that even Republicans in the age group over sixty are worried about increased costs of medical care and the general inadequacy of retirement incomes. Thus many old people may change their political allegiance, if it becomes clear that the Democratic Party can furnish a program to take care of their needs.

Again the mass media play a role secondary to direct experience in changing attitudes directly related to economic matters. Once dissatisfaction exists, they can exert a potent influence in suggesting new ways of solving the problem. In the field of international affairs, mass media have a more primary role because in times of peace most people have no direct experience with other countries or their peoples. The threat of war comes from what they read, hear, or see in the mass media.

The area of freedom for changing utilitarian attitudes is of course much greater in dealing with methods of satisfying needs than with needs themselves. Needs change more slowly than the means for gratifying them, even though one role of the advertiser is to create new needs. Change in attitudes occurs more readily when people perceive that they can accomplish their objectives through revising existing attitudes. Integration of white and Negro personnel in the armed forces came to pass partly because political leaders and military leaders perceived that such a move would strengthen our fighting forces. And one of the powerful arguments for changing our attitudes toward Negroes is that in the struggle for world democracy we need to put our own house in order to present a more convincing picture of our own society to other countries. Carlson has experimentally demonstrated that discriminatory attitudes toward minority groups can be altered

by showing the relevance of more positive beliefs to such individual goals and values as American international prestige and democratic equalitarianism.[24]

Just as attitudes formed in the interests of adjustment can be negative evaluations of objects associated with avoidance of the harmful effects of the environment, so too can attitudes change because of unpleasant experiences or anticipation of harmful consequences. The more remote the cause of one's suffering the more likely he is to seize upon a readily identifiable target for his negative evaluation. Public officials, as highly visible objects, can easily be associated with states of dissatisfaction. Thus there is truth in the old observation that people vote more against the candidates they dislike than for the candidates they like. In the 1958 elections, in a period of mild recession, unemployment, and general uneasiness about atomic weapons, the incumbent governors (the more visible targets), whether Republican or Democratic, fared less well than the incumbent legislators.

The use of negative sanctions and of punishment to change utilitarian attitudes is more complex than the use of rewards. To be successful in changing attitudes and behavior, punishment should be used only when there is clearly available a course of action that will save the individual from the undesirable consequences. To arouse fear among the enemy in time of war does not necessarily result in desertion, surrender, or a disruption of the enemy war effort. Such channels of action may not be available to the people whose fears are aroused. The experiment of Janis and Feshback in using fear appeals to coerce children into good habits of dental hygiene had the interesting outcome of a negative relationship between the amount of fear and the degree of change. Lurid pictures of the gangrene jaws of old people who had not observed good dental habits were not effective.[25] Moreover, the group exposed to the strongest fear appeal was the most susceptible to counterpropaganda. One factor which helps to account for the results of this investigation was the lack of a clear-cut relation in the minds of the children between failure to brush their teeth in the prescribed manner and the pictures of the gangrene jaws of the aged.

The necessity of coupling fear appeals with clear channels of action is illustrated by a study of Nunnally and Bobren.[26] These investigators manipulated three variables in communications about mental health, namely, the relative amount of message anxiety, the degree to which messages gave apparent solutions, and the relative personal or impersonal phrasing of the message. The high-anxiety message described electric shock treatment of the psychotic in distressing detail. People showed the least willingness to receive communications that were high in anxiety, personalized, and offered no solutions. When solutions were offered in the communication, there was more willingness to accept the high-anxiety message.

The use of punishment and arousal of fear depend for their effectiveness upon the presence of well-defined paths for avoiding the punishment, i.e. negative sanctions are successful in redirecting rather than suppressing behavior. When there is no clearly perceptible relation between the punishment and the desired behavior, people may continue to behave as they did before, only now they have negative attitudes toward the persons and objects associated with the negative sanctions. There is, however, another possibility, if the punishment is severe or if the individual is unusually sensitive. He may develop a defensive avoidance of the whole situation. His behavior, then, is not directed at solving the problem but at escaping from the situation, even if such escape has to be negotiated by absorbing extra punishment. The attitudes under discussion are those based upon the adjustive or utilitarian function, but if the individual is traumatized by a fearful experience he will shift from instrumental learning to defensive reactions.

AROUSAL AND CHANGE OF EGO-DEFENSIVE ATTITUDES

Attitudes which help to protect the individual from internally induced anxieties or from facing up to external dangers are readily elicited by any form of threat to the ego. The threat may be external, as in the case of a highly competitive situation, or a failure experience, or a derogatory remark. It is the stock in trade of demagogues to exaggerate the dangers confronting the people, for instance, Joe McCarthy's tactics with respect to Communists in the State Department. Many people have existing attitudes of withdrawal or of aggression toward deviants or out-groups based upon their ego-defensive needs. When threatened, these attitudes come into play, and defensive people either avoid the unpleasant situation entirely, as is common in the desegregation controversy, or exhibit hostility.

Another condition for eliciting the ego-defensive attitude is the encouragement given to its expression by some form of social support. The agitator may appeal to repressed hatred by providing moral justification for its expression. A mob leader before an audience with emotionally held attitudes toward Negroes may call out these attitudes in the most violent form by invoking the good of the community or the honor of white womanhood.

A third condition for the arousal of ego-defensive attitudes is the appeal to authority. The insecurity of the defensive person makes him particularly susceptible to authoritarian suggestion. When this type of authoritarian command is in the direction already indicated by his attitudes of antipathy toward other people, he responds quickly and joyously. It is no accident that movements of hate and aggression such as the Ku Klux Klan or the Nazi Party are authoritarian in their organized structure. Wagman, in an experimental investigation of the uses of authoritarian suggestion, found that students high in ego-defensiveness as measured by the F-scale were much more responsive to directives from military leaders than were less defensive students.[27] In fact, the subjects low in defensiveness were not affected at all by authoritarian suggestion when this influence ran counter to their own attitudes. The subjects high in F-scores could be moved in either direction, although they moved more readily in the direction of their own beliefs.

A fourth condition for defensive arousal is the building up over time of inhibited drives in the individual, for example, repressed sex impulses. As the drive strength of forbidden impulses increases, anxiety mounts and release from tension is found in the expression of defensive attitudes. The deprivations of prison life, for example, build up tensions which can find expression in riots against the hated prison officials.

In other words, the drive strength for defensive reactions can be increased by situation frustration. Though the basic source is the long-standing internal conflict of the person, he can encounter additional frustration in immediate circumstances. Berkowitz has shown that anti-Semitic girls were more likely than less prejudiced girls to display aggression toward an innocent bystander when angered by a third person.[28] In a subsequent experiment, Berkowitz and Holmes created dislike by one group of subjects for their partners by giving them electric shocks which they thought were administered by their partners.[29] In a second session, subjects worked alone and were threatened by the experimenter. In a third session they were brought together with their partners for a cooperative task of problem solving. Aggression and hostility were displayed by subjects toward one another in the third session as a result of the frustration produced by the experimenter, and were directed more against the disliked partner than toward an innocuous partner.

Studies outside the laboratory have confirmed the principle that, where negative attitudes exist, frustration in areas unrelated to the attitude will increase the strength of the prejudice. Bettelheim and Janowitz found that war veterans who had suffered downward mobility were more anti-Semitic than other war veterans.[30] In a secondary analysis of the data from the Elmira study, Greenblum and Pearlin report that the socially mobile people, whether upward or downward mobile, were more prejudiced against Jews and Negroes than were stationary people, provided that the socially mobile were insecure about their new status.[31] Though it is clear in these studies that the situation frustration strengthens a negative attitude, it is not clear as to the origin of the negative attitude.

Most research on ego-defensive attitudes has been directed at beliefs concerning the undesirable character of minority groups or of deviants, with accompanying feelings of distrust, contempt, and hatred. Many ego-defensive attitudes, however, are not the projection of repressed aggression but are expressions of apathy or withdrawal. The individual protects himself from a difficult or demanding world and salvages his self-respect by retreating within his own shell. His attitudes toward political matters are anomic: "It does not make any difference to people like me which party is in power" or "There is no point in voting because I can't influence the outcome." Threat to people of this type takes the form of a complexity with which they cannot cope. Thus, they daydream when the lecturer talks about economic theories of inflation or the public official talks about disarmament proposals.

The usual procedures for changing attitudes and behavior have little positive effect upon attitudes geared into our ego defenses. In fact they may have a boomerang effect of making the individual cling more tenaciously to his emotionally held beliefs. In the category of usual procedures should be included increasing the flow of information, promising and bestowing rewards, and invoking penalties. As has already been indicated, punishment is threatening to the ego-defensive person and the increase of threat is the very condition which will feed ego-defensive behavior. The eneuretic youngster with emotional problems is rarely cured by punishment. Teachers and coaches know that there are some children who respond to censure and punishment by persevering in the forbidden behavior. But what is not as well recognized is that reward is also not effective in modifying the actions of the ego-defensive person. His attitudes are an expression of his inner conflicts and are not susceptible to external rewards. The shopkeeper who will not serve Negroes because they are a well-fixated target for his aggressions will risk the loss of income incurred by his discriminatory reactions.

Three basic factors, however, can help change ego-defensive attitudes. In the first place, the removal of threat is a necessary though not a sufficient condition. The permissive and even supportive atmosphere which the therapist attempts to create for his patients is a special instance of the removal of threat. Where the ego-defensive behavior of the delinquent is supported by his group, the social worker must gain a measure of group acceptance so as not to be perceived as a threat by the individual gang members. An objective, matter-of-fact approach can serve to remove threat, especially in situations where people are accustomed to emotional appeals. Humor can also be used to establish a nonthreatening atmosphere, but it should not be directed against the audience or even against the problem. Cooper and Jahoda attempted to change prejudiced attitudes by ridicule, in the form of cartoons which made Mr. Biggott seem silly, especially when he rejected a blood transfusion which did not come from 100 per cent Americans.[32] Instead of changing their attitudes, the subjects in this experiment found ways of evading the meaning of the cartoons.

In the second place, catharsis or the ventilation of feelings can help to set the stage for attitude change. Mention has already been made of the building up of tension owing to the lack of discharge of inhibited impulses. When emotional tension is at a high level the individual will respond defensively and resist attempts to change him. Hence, providing him with opportunities to blow off steam may often be necessary before attempting a serious discussion of new possibilities of behavior. Again, humor can serve this purpose.

There are many practical problems in the use of catharsis, however, because of its complex relationship to other variables. In his review of the experimental work on the expression of hostility Berkowitz reports more findings supporting than contradicting the catharsis hypothesis, but there is no clear agreement about the mechanisms involved.[33] Under certain circumstances permitting emotional outbursts can act as a reward. In a gripe session to allow individuals to express their complaints, group members can reinforce one another's negative attitudes. Unless there are positive forces in the situation which lead to a serious consideration of the problem, the gripe session may have boomerang effects. The technique often employed is to keep the group in session long enough for the malcontents to get talked out so that more sober voices can be heard. Catharsis may function at two levels. It can operate to release or drain off energy of the moment, as in the above description. It can also serve to bring to the surface something of the nature of the conflict affecting the individual. So long as his impulses are repressed and carefully disguised, the individual has little chance of gaining even rudimentary insight into himself.

In the third place, ego-defensive behavior can be altered as the individual acquires insight into his own mechanisms of defense. Information about the nature of the problem in the external world will not affect him. Information about his own functioning may have an influence, if presented without threat, and if the defenses do not go too deep into the personality. In other words, only prolonged therapy can help the psychologically sick person. Many normal people, however, employ ego defenses about which they have some degree of awareness, though generally not at the time of the expression of such defenses. The frustrations of a tough day at work may result in an authoritarian father displacing his aggression that night on his family in yelling at his wife, or striking his youngsters. Afterward he may recognize the cause of his behavior. Not all defensive behavior, then, is so deep rooted in the personality as to be inaccessible to awareness and insight. Therefore, procedures for arousing self-insight can be utilized to change behavior, even in mass communications.

One technique is to show people the psychodynamics of attitudes, especially as they appear in the behavior of others. Allport's widely used pamphlet on the A B C's of Scapegoating is based upon the technique.[34] Katz, Sarnoff, and McClintock have conducted experimental investigations of the effects of insightful materials upon the reduction of prejudice.[35] In their procedure the psychodynamics of prejudice was presented in the case history of a subject sufficiently similar to the subjects as to appear as a sympathetic character. Two findings appeared in these investigations: (1) Subjects who were very high in defensiveness were not affected by the insight materials, but subjects of low or moderate defensiveness were significantly affected. (2) The changes in attitude produced by the arousal of self-insight persisted for a longer period of time than changes induced by information or conformity pressures. In a further experiment Stotland, Katz, and Patchen found that involving subjects in the task of understanding the dynamics of prejudice helped arouse self-insight and reduce prejudice.[36] McClintock compared an ethnocentric appeal, an information message, and self-insight materials, with similar results.[37] There was differential acceptance of these influences according to the personality pattern of the subject. McClintock also found a difference in F-scale items in predicting attitude change, with the projectivity items showing a different pattern from the conformity items.

Of practical concern are four general areas in which insufficient attention has been paid to the ego-defensive basis of attitudes with respect to the role of communication in inducing social change:

1. Prejudices toward foreigners, toward racial and religious outgroups, and toward international affairs often fall into this category. The thesis of the authors of *The Authoritarian Personality* that the defenses of repression and projectivity are correlated with racial prejudice has seen more confirmation than disproof in spite of the fact that not all racial prejudice is ego-defensive in nature. In a review of studies involving the California F-scale, Titus and Hollander report investigations where positive correlations were obtained between high scores on authoritarianism and prejudice and xenophobia.[38]

Of course not all the variance in social prejudice can be accounted for by ego-defensiveness. Pettigrew has shown that a sample of Southern respondents was almost identical with a sample of Northern respondents on the F-scale measure of authoritarianism, but the Southern sample was much more negative toward Negroes with respect to employment, housing, and voting.[39]

Relations have also been found between authoritarianism and attitudes toward nationalism and internationalism. Levinson constructed a scale to give an index of internationalism which included such items as opinions about immigration policy, armaments, the get-tough with Russia policy, cooperation with Red China, our role in the UN, etc. This measure of internationalism correlated .60 with the F-scale.[40] A study by Lane in 1952 showed that a larger proportion of authoritarians than of equalitarians were against working toward a peaceful settlement of the Korean issue. The authoritarians either favored the bombing of China and Manchuria or else were for complete withdrawal.[41] And Smith and Rosen found such consistent negative relations between world-mindedness and the dimension of authoritarianism that they suggested in the interest of parsimony the two be considered as slightly

different aspects of the same basic personality structure.[42]

2. A related area of attitudes consists of opinions toward deviant types of personalities, e.g. delinquents, the mentally ill, Beatniks, and other nonconformers. The problem of the rehabilitation of the ex-convict or the discharged mental patient is sometimes impeded by the emotional attitudes of the public toward individuals with a record of institutionalization.

3. Attitudes toward public health measures, whether the fluoridation of the water supply of a community, the utilization of X-ray examinations for the prevention of disease, or the availability of information about birth control, often have their roots in unacknowledged anxieties and fears. Davis, for example, believes that opposition to fluoridation is not so much a matter of ignorance of the specific problem as it is a function of a deeper attitudinal syndrome of naturalism.[43] Governmental interference with natural processes is regarded as the source of many evils, and this general ideology is tinged with suspicion and distrust suggestive of defensive motivation.

4. Apathy toward political issues and especially toward atomic weapons may reflect a defensive withdrawal on the part of some people. The information officer of a government agency or the public relations officer in charge of a health campaign faces the difficult problem of changing public attitudes which may satisfy different needs for different people. To present information designed to show the dangerous situation we are in may be effective for some people but may prove too threatening for others. What is needed in such cases is research which will get at the reasons why people hold the attitudes they do. There are times when dramatically confronting the public with the dangers of a situation may be more effective strategy than a more reassuring approach. But there are also occasions when the first strategy will merely add to defensive avoidance. Gladstone and Taylor presented communications to their students, two of which were news stories from the *New York Times*.[44] One reported speeches made by Malenkov and Khrushchev about the peaceful intentions of the Soviet Union but its readiness to crush aggressors. The second news story reported British reactions to the American opinion

about the situation in Indo-China. A third communication concerned the H-bomb and its dangers. Students were previously tested on their susceptibility to being threatened. Those who were threat-prone tended to deny the truth of the points in the communications or to overlook them entirely. For these subjects the communications had no effect on existing attitudes.

The use of mass communication has been better adapted to supplying information and to emphasizing the advantages of a course of action than to changing defensive attitudes. A new field in communication to large publics is the creation of self-understanding, which so far has been pre-empted by personal advice columns. The specifics for this new development remain to be worked out, but they may well start with techniques based upon attitude research of the basic reasons for resistance to an objectively desirable program.

CONDITIONS FOR AROUSING AND CHANGING VALUE-EXPRESSIVE ATTITUDES

Two conditions for the arousal of value-expressive attitudes can be specified. The first is the occurrence of the cue in the stimulus situation which has been associated with the attitude. The liberal Democrat, as a liberal Democrat, has always believed in principle that an income tax is more just than a sales tax. Now the issue has arisen in his state, and the group in which he happens to be at the moment are discussing an increase in sales tax. This will be sufficient to cue off his opposition to the proposal without consideration of the specific local aspects of the tax problem. The second condition for the arousal of this type of attitude is some degree of thwarting of the individual's expressive behavior in the immediate past. The housewife occupied with the routine care of the home and the children during the day may seek opportunities to express her views to other women at the first social gathering she attends.

We have referred to voters backing their party for bread and butter reasons. Perhaps the bulk of voting behavior, however, is the elicitation of value-expressive attitudes. Voting is a symbolic expression of being a Republican or a Democrat.

Party identification accounts for more variance in voting behavior than any other single factor.[45] Though there is a minority who consider themselves independent and though there are minor shifts in political allegiance, the great majority of the people identify themselves as the supporters of a political party. Their voting behavior is an expression of this self-concept, and it takes a major event such as a depression to affect their voting habits seriously.

Identification with party is in good measure a function of the political socialization of the child, as Hyman has shown.[46] An analysis of a national sample of the electorate in 1952 by Campbell, Gurin, and Miller revealed that of voters both of whose parents were Democrats, 76 per cent identified themselves as Democrats, another 10 per cent as independent Democrats, and 12 per cent as Republicans.[47] Similarly, of those with Republican parents 63 per cent considered themselves Republican and another 10 per cent as independent Republicans. Attachment to party, Hyman suggests, furnishes an organizing principle for the individual and gives stability to his political orientation in the confusion of changing issues.

Even in European countries, where we assume greater knowledge of issues, political behavior is the symbolic expression of people's values. Members of the Labor Party in Norway, for example, are little more conversant with the stand of their party on issues than are voters in the United States. In fact, the policy of their party in international affairs and armament in recent years has been closer to the views of Conservative voters than to their own. Nevertheless, they consider themselves supporters of the party which reflects their general values.

The problem of the political leader is to make salient the cues related to political allegiance in order to arouse the voters who consider themselves party supporters to the point of expressing their attitudes by voting on election day. One technique is to increase the volume and intensity of relevant stimulation as the election approaches. If the relevant cues could be presented to each voter on election day—for example, a ballot box in his home—then the appropriate behavior would follow. But the citizen must remember on the given Tuesday that this is election day and that he must find time to go to the polls. The task of party organization is to try to remind him of this fact the weekend before, to call him that very day by phone, or even to call for him in person.

Again, two conditions are relevant in changing value-expressive attitudes:

1. Some degree of dissatisfaction with one's self-concept or its associated values is the opening wedge for fundamental change. The complacent person, smugly satisfied with all aspects of himself, is immune to attempts to change his values. Dissatisfaction with the self can result from failures or from the inadequacy of one's values in preserving a favorable image of oneself in a changing world. The man with pacifist values may have become dissatisfied with himself during a period of fascist expansion and terror. Once there is a crack in the individual's central belief systems, it can be exploited by appropriately directed influences. The techniques of brain washing employed by the Chinese Communists both on prisoners of war in Korea and in the thought reform of Chinese intellectuals were essentially procedures for changing value systems.

In the brain washing of Chinese intellectuals in the revolutionary college, the Communists took advantage of the confused identity of the student.[48] He had been both a faithful son and a rebellious reformer and perhaps even an uninvolved cynic. To make him an enthusiastic Communist the officials attempted to destroy his allegiance to his parents and to transfer his loyalty to Communist doctrines which could meet his values as a rebel. Group influences were mobilized to help bring about the change by intensifying guilt feelings and providing for atonement and redemption through the emotional catharsis of personal confession.

To convert American prisoners of war, the Communists made a careful study of the vulnerability of their victims. They found additional weaknesses through a system of informers and created new insecurities by giving the men no social support for their old values.[49] They manipulated group influences to support Communist values and exploited their ability to control behavior and all punishments and rewards in the situation. The direction of all their efforts, however, was to undermine old values and to supply new ones. The degree of their success has probably been exaggerated in the public prints, but from their point of view they did achieve some genuine gains. One estimate is that some 15 per cent of the returning prisoners of war were active collaborators, another 5 per cent resisters, and some 80 per cent "neutrals." Segal, in a study of a sample of 579 of these men, found that 12 per cent had to some degree accepted Communist ideology.[50]

2. Dissatisfaction with old attitudes as inappropriate to one's values can also lead to change. In fact, people are much less likely to find their values uncongenial than they are to find some of their attitudes inappropriate to their values. The discomfort with one's old attitudes may stem from new experiences or from the suggestions of other people. Senator Vandenburg, as an enlightened conservative, changed his attitudes on foreign relations from an isolationist to an internationalist position when critical events in our history suggested change. The influences exerted upon people are often in the direction of showing the inappropriateness of their present ways of expressing their values. Union leaders attempt to show that good union men should not vote on the old personal basis of rewarding friends and punishing enemies but should instead demand party responsibility for a program. In an experiment by Stotland, Katz, and Patchen there was suggestive evidence of the readiness of subjects to change attitudes which they found inappropriate to their values.[51] Though an attempt was made to change the prejudices of the ego-defensive subjects, individuals who were not basically ego-defensive also changed. These subjects, who already approved of tolerance, apparently became aware of the inappropriateness of some of their negative evaluations of minority groups. This second factor in attitude change thus refers to the comparatively greater appropriateness of one set of means than another for confirming the individual's self-concept and realizing his central values.

We have already called attention to the role of values in the formation of attitudes in the early years of life. It is also true that attitude formation is a constant process and that influences are continually being brought to bear throughout life which suggest new attitudes as important in implementing existing values. An often-used method is to make salient some central value such as the thinking man, the man of distinction, or the virile man, and then depict a relatively new form of behavior consistent with this image. The role of motivational research in advertising is to discover the rudimentary image associated with a given product, to use this as a basis for building up the image in more glorified terms, and then to cement the association of this image with the product.

AROUSING AND CHANGING ATTITUDES WHICH SERVE THE KNOWLEDGE FUNCTION

Attitudes acquired in the interests of the need to know are elicited by a stimulus associated with the attitude. The child who learns from his reading and from his parents that Orientals are treacherous will not have the attitude aroused unless some appropriate cue concerning the cognitive object is presented. He may even meet and interact with Orientals without identifying them as such and with no corresponding arousal of his attitude. Considerable prejudice in this sense is race-name prejudice and is only aroused when a premium is placed upon social identification. Since members of a minority group have many other memberships in common with a majority group, the latent prejudiced attitude may not necessarily be activated. Prejudice based upon ego-defensiveness, however, will result in ready identification of the disliked group.

The factors which are productive of change of attitudes of this character are inadequacies of the existing attitudes to deal with new and changing situations. The person who has been taught that Orientals are treacherous may read extended accounts of the honesty of the Chinese or may have favorable interactions with Japanese. He finds his old attitudes in conflict with new information and new experience, and proceeds to modify his beliefs. In this instance we are dealing with fictitious stereotypes which never corresponded to reality. In other cases the beliefs may have been adequate to the situation but the world has changed. Thus, some British military men formerly in favor of armaments have changed their attitude toward disarmament because of the char-

acter of nuclear weapons. The theory of cognitive consistency later elaborated in this issue can draw its best examples from attitudes related to the knowledge function.

Any situation, then, which is ambiguous for the individual is likely to produce attitude change. His need for cognitive structure is such that he will either modify his beliefs to impose structure or accept some new formula presented by others. He seeks a meaningful picture of his universe, and when there is ambiguity he will reach for a ready solution. Rumors abound when information is unavailable.

GLOBAL INFLUENCES AND ATTITUDE CHANGE

In the foregoing analysis we have attempted to clarify the functions which attitudes perform and to give some psychological specifications of the conditions under which they are formed, elicited, and changed. This material is summarized in the table on page 32. We must recognize, however, that the influences in the real world are not as a rule directed toward a single type of motivation. Contact with other peoples, experience in foreign cultures, group pressures, group discussion and decision, the impact of legislation, and the techniques of brain washing are all global variables. They represent combinations of forces. To predict their effectiveness in any given situation it is necessary to analyze their components in relation to the conditions of administration and the type of population toward which they are directed.

The Effect of Contact and Intercultural Exchange. Contact between peoples of different races, nations, and religions has been suggested as an excellent method of creating understanding and reducing prejudice. Research studies have demonstrated that such an outcome is possible but not that it is inevitable. People in integrated housing projects have developed more favorable attitudes toward members of the other race;[52] the same findings are reported from children's camps,[53] industry,[54] and army units.[55] But some studies report increased prejudice with increased contact.[56] Obviously, contact as such is not a statement of the critical variables involved.

Determinants of attitude formation, arousal, and change in relation to type of function

Function	Origin and Dynamics	Arousal Conditions	Change Conditions
Adjustment	Utility of attitudinal object in need satisfaction. Maximizing external rewards and minimizing punishments	1. Activation of needs 2. Salience of cues associated with need satisfaction	1. Need deprivation 2. Creation of new needs and new levels of aspiration 3. Shifting rewards and punishments 4. Emphasis on new and better paths for need satisfaction
Ego defense	Protecting against internal conflicts and external dangers	1. Posing of threats 2. Appeals to hatred and repressed impulses 3. Rise in frustrations 4. Use of authoritarian suggestion	1. Removal of threats 2. Catharsis 3. Development of self-insight
Value expression	Maintaining self identity; enhancing favorable self-image; self-expression and self-determination	1. Salience of cues associated with values 2. Appeals to individual to reassert self-image 3. Ambiguities which threaten self-concept	1. Some degree of dissatisfaction with self 2. Greater appropriateness of new attitude for the self 3. Control of all environmental supports to undermine old values
Knowledge	Need for understanding, for meaningful cognitive organization, for consistency and clarity	1. Reinstatement of cues associated with old problem or of old problem itself	1. Ambiguity created by new information or change in environment 2. More meaningful information about problems

Contact carries with it no necessary conditions for alleviating the internal conflicts of the ego-defensive. If anything, the immediate presence of hated people may intensify prejudice. For less defensive people, contact with other groups depends upon the cooperative or competitive nature of the interaction. Prejudice against a minority can increase in a community as the minority grows in numbers and competes successfully with the majority group. Contact has increased but so too has prejudice. On the other hand, the successful effects of integrating white and Negro soldiers during World War II occurred under conditions of joint effort against a common enemy. Sherif has experimentally demonstrated the importance of cooperation toward common goals in a camp situation.[57] First he created two antagonistic groups of boys, established the identity of each group, and placed them in a series of competitive and conflicting situations. As a result the two groups felt mutual dislike and held negative stereotypes of each other. The groups then were brought together for a picnic, but the antagonistic attitudes persisted; food was hurled back and forth between the two gangs. Finally, superordinate goals were created by sending all the boys on an expedition during which the water supply broke down. Group differences were forgotten as the boys worked together to solve the common problem. Favorable interactions continued after the incident.

Contact, then, can change adjustive attitudes in the direction of either more positive or more negative evaluations depending upon whether the conditions of contact help or hinder the satisfaction of utilitarian needs. Contact can also change attitudes which serve the knowledge function, provided that little ego defensiveness and little competitiveness are present. The usual negative stereotypes toward other groups are gross simplifications and exaggerations of the characteristics of large numbers of human beings. Contact will provide richer and more accurate information about other people and will show them to be very much like members of one's own group.

A special case of contact is experience in a foreign culture. Our cultural-exchange program is predicated upon the assumption that sending representatives of our nation abroad to teach, study, entertain, or work with the citizens of other countries and bringing their students, scientists, and representatives here will aid in international understanding and in mutually improved attitudes. The bulk of the research evidence supports this assumption. Reigrotski and Anderson have conducted one of the most extensive investigations in this area, involving interviews with sizable samples in Belgium, France, Holland, and Germany.[58] Foreign contact, as measured by visiting abroad and having friends and relatives abroad, was found to increase favorable images of other peoples and to make individuals more critical of their compatriots. But again we need to make more specific the conditions of such experiences as they relate to the motivations of the principles in the drama. The importance of such specification is documented by the findings of Selltiz, Hopson, and Cook, who interviewed some 348 foreign students in thirty-five colleges and universities in the United States shortly after their arrival and again five months later.[59] They found no relationship between amount of personal interaction with Americans and attitude change, and they suggest as one possible explanation that "other factors may be of overriding importance."

The importance of the utilitarian and value-expressive functions in attitude change through cross-cultural experience is indicated in the study of Watson and Lippitt of twenty-nine Germans brought here by the State Department for advanced study.[60] These visitors were interviewed while in the United States, shortly after their return to Germany, and six months after their return. They were eager to learn techniques which would help them with their own problems in areas where they regarded us as more expert. They were also willing to adopt new attitudes

which were implementations of their own value systems. At first they had negative evaluations of American patterns of child rearing. However, they placed a high value on individualism and were ready to learn how to be successfully individualistic. When they saw the relation of the American child-rearing practices to individualism they developed favorable attitudes toward these practices.

Perhaps the reason most of the evidence suggests positive outcomes from cross-cultural experiences stems from the selective nature of the people engaged in visiting and traveling. Students and visitors who come from abroad come for specific purposes related to their needs and values. They do not come for the ego-defensive purposes of venting their aggression on a scapegoat or expressing their superiority, though some may come to escape problems at home. Once the visitor is in a foreign country, however, many circumstances can arouse ego-defensiveness. He is in a strange world where his usual coping mechanisms are no longer successful. He lacks the customary social support of his group. He may be forced to accept a lower status than he enjoys at home. The wife of the American Fulbrighter, who bears the brunt of the adjustment problem, may become defensive and negative toward the host country. The status problem is often in evidence when Indian scholars who enjoy privilege and position in their own country are reduced to the lowly status of a first-year graduate student. Another interesting issue arises with respect to the status of the country of the visitor as perceived by the people he meets in the host country. Morris studied 318 foreign students at U.C.L.A. and noted that finding one's country occupying a low status in America did not matter so much unless there was a discrepancy between the status expected and the status accorded.[61] Thus, if the visitor expected a moderately low evaluation he was not upset when he encountered it. But if with the same expectation he met an even lower evaluation, he was affected. Of the visiting students who found that their national status was higher than anticipated, some 66 per cent held favorable attitudes toward the United States. Of those who experienced a relative loss in national status, only 38 per cent were favorable.

Group Influences. In any practical attempt to change attitudes, social support and group influence assume first importance. The power of the group over the individual, however, needs to be assessed carefully with respect to the dynamics of the influence exerted. The concept of *group identification* points to an emotional tie between the individual and the group symbols. This can be a matter of individual incorporation of group values as expressing his own inner convictions, as in the case of the dedicated union member. Or it can result from the insecure person's attachment to the strength of the group to compensate for his own weakness. The concept of *reference group* implies less emotional attachment and suggests that many people turn to particular groups for their standards of judgment. In this narrow sense the reference group has the function of helping to supply cognitive structure for the individual's uncertainties. Sherif's early experiments demonstrated that in ambiguous situations people would turn to the group norms for support.[62]

Whatever definition is used for terms to describe the relation between the individual and the group, groups do serve all three of the functions described above. They also serve the fourth function of aiding the individual in his utilitarian attempt to maximize satisfactions. He gains recognition and other rewards through becoming a good group member. Since all four basic motivations can be present in group settings, we need to know the function involved if we are to predict the effectiveness of various types of appeal from the group. The defensive person can be used by the group more readily than the person motivated by utilitarian needs, who is more likely to want to use the group for his own purposes. The man who has internalized the group's values can be moved markedly by group leaders in the direction of their attainment but may prove to be very resistant to leaders who attempt to move him in the opposite direction.

Control Over Behavior: Change Through Legislation. Attitudes can be expressed in overt action, but actions can also determine attitudes. Often behavior change precedes attitude change. People enter new groups, they take on new jobs, and in their new roles behave in a fashion appropriate to the expectations of those roles. In time they will develop attitudes supportive of the new behavior. Lieberman tested workers before and after their assumption of new roles as foremen and union stewards.[63] As workers they were very much alike in attitudes and beliefs. As foremen and stewards they quickly acquired the distinctive standards and values appropriate to the new roles.

Attitudes may change when people take on new roles for a number of reasons, but the two most likely causes are: (1) Both appropriate attitudes and appropriate behavior are necessary to receive the full rewards and anticipated benefits of the system the newcomers have entered. (2) It is confusing to have conflicting beliefs and behavior. Some people will maintain private attitudes at variance with their public behavior, but this becomes difficult if the public behavior has to be maintained fairly constantly.

The implications of the strategy of changing attitudes by requiring new behavior have long been recognized. Efforts are made, for example, to control juvenile delinquency by providing new recreational, educational, and social activities for teenagers; the critics in the group are given some responsibility for running these activities.

The use of legislation has been of special interest in the desegregation controversy. Its opponents contend that if change is to come about it should come about through education. Its advocates assert their belief in the efficacy of legislation. At least three conditions are important to the outcome of this debate: (1) Law in our culture is effective when directed against behavior and not against attitudes. We can legislate against specific discriminatory practices but not against prejudice as such. (2) Laws are accepted when the behavior is regarded as being in the public domain and not the private domain. People will not support measures directed at personal matters such as the length of women's skirts. (3) When the behavior is in the public domain, regulatory acts still may not work if they are not applied quickly and consistently. The basis of legal authority is in acceptance of what is properly legal. Hence if there is doubt, delay, and confusion in the administration of the law, with Federal authorities saying one thing and state authorities another, the legitimacy of the act is in question. Lack of powerful Federal legislation and a strong administrative enforcement program to implement the Supreme Court decision on desegregation gave local resistance a chance to form and to confuse the issue.

The problem of whether behavior is in the private or public domain is in good part a matter of public opinion and can be ascertained on borderline matters. Public schools, public housing, and government employment are, almost by definition, not in question. With respect to private housing there may be more of a question in the public mind, though it is recognized that the community has the right to pass zoning laws. Since people will resist legislation in what they regard as purely private matters, a survey of a representative sample of the public including both whites and Negroes can provide useful information.

Though legislation about desegregation can change behavior and the attitudes corresponding to it, the generalization to other attitudes and other forms of behavior is more difficult to predict.[64] The basic problem of the generalization of change will be considered in a later section.

Brain Washing. Though brain-washing methods are directed at changing the self-concept and its related values, they differ from other procedures by virtue of the complete control acquired over the individual. In a prisoner-of-war camp or in some institutions, the leaders have control over all information reaching their charges, all punishments and rewards, the composition of groups, and the formation of group life. Repressive methods and manipulation of people through reward and punishment are old devices. What is new in brain washing is the more thorough use of old procedures, on the one hand, and the development of techniques for controlling group life with respect to both its formal and informal structure, on the other—a perverted group dynamics, in fact.

Eight procedures can be identified from the experience of the Korean camps.[65] (1) Leaders or potential leaders were segregated from the other prisoners, making group resistance to the Communists more difficult. (2) All ties and informational support from home were removed through systematic censorship of letters and materials from the outside world. (3) Distrust of their fellows was created among the prisoners through the use of informers and suspicion of informers. Generally, when formal group controls are in operation, informal communication and informal standards develop to protect the lowly against the decision makers. With potential ringleaders already screened out of the group and with the inculcation of fear of communication with comrades, no effective informal group structure developed. (4) Group life was made available to the prisoners if they participated in activities prescribed by the Communists. If a unit of men all participated in a study group they could then take part in a ball game or other group sport. Pressure to conform and participate in the discussion session was thus generated among the men themselves. At a later stage, self-criticism in group sessions was encouraged under threat of withholding the reward of group games. (5) The first instances of real or distorted collaboration by prisoners were used with telling effect upon their fellows. A testimonial from a prisoner or a lecture by a collaborator destroyed any illusion of group resistance and, moreover, made it seem pointless for others to resist further. (6) The Communists paced their demands so that they required little from the prisoner in the early stages. Once he made some concessions it was difficult for him to resist making further ones. (7) The Communists always required some behavioral compliance from the prisoners, no matter how trivial the level of participation. (8) Rewards and punishments were carefully manipulated. Extra food, medicine, and special privileges were awarded for acts of cooperation and collaboration. Punishments were threatened for acts of resistance, but only imprisonment was consistently used as a penalty.

These techniques were, of course, carried out with varying degrees of thoroughness and effectiveness in the different camps and at different stages of the war. Unfamiliarity with American culture on the part of many Chinese leaders made for difficulties in breaking down informal group processes of the prisoners, some of whom would indulge in ridiculous caricature during the self-criticism session. The over-all effect of brain washing was not so much the production of active collaboration and of ideological conversion to the Communist cause as it was the creation of apathy and withdrawal. The environment was so threatening that the prisoners resorted to primitive defense mechanisms of psychological escape and avoidance. There is some evidence to indicate that this apathetic reaction resulted in a higher death rate, since many men refused to marshal their strength to combat the rigors of the situation.

Perhaps the two most important lessons of the Korean experience are (1) the importance of central values in sustaining the ego under conditions of deprivation and threat and (2) the necessity of maintaining some form of group support in resisting the powerful manipulations of an opponent.

GENERALIZATION OF ATTITUDE CHANGE

Perhaps the most fascinating problem in attitude change has to do with consequences to a person's belief systems and general behavior of changing a single attitude. Is the change confined to the single target of the attitude? Does it affect related beliefs and feelings? If so, what types of related belief and feeling are affected, i.e. on what does the change rub off? Teachers and parents, for example, are concerned when a child acquires an immoral attitude or indulges in a single dishonest act, for fear of the pernicious spread of undesirable behavior tendencies. Responsible citizens are concerned about the lawless actions of extremists in the South in combatting integration, not only because of the immediate and specific implications of the behavior but because of the general threat to legal institutions.

Research evidence on the generalization of attitude change is meager. In experimental work, the manipulations to produce change are weak and last for brief periods, sometimes minutes and at the most several hours. It is not surprising, therefore, that these studies report few cases of change which has generalized to attitudes other than the one under attack. Even in the studies on self-insight by Katz *et al.*, where the change in prejudice toward Negroes was still in evidence some two months after the experiment, there were no consistent changes in prejudice toward other

minority groups.[66] In real-life situations outside the laboratory, more powerful forces are often brought to bear to modify behavior, but again the resulting changes seem more limited than one would expect on an a priori logical basis. Integration of whites and Negroes in the factory may produce acceptance of Negroes as fellow workers but not as residents in one's neighborhood, or as friends in one's social group. Significant numbers of Democrats were influenced by the candidacy of Dwight Eisenhower to help elect him President in 1952 and 1956, but, as Campbell *et al.* have established, this change in voting behavior did not rub off on the rest of the Republican ticket.[67] Most of the Democratic defectors at the presidential level voted for a Democratic Congress. Nor did they change their attitudes on political issues. And the chances are that this change will not generalize to other Republican presidential candidates who lack Eisenhower's status as a national figure.

It is puzzling that attitude change seems to have slight generalization effects, when the evidence indicates considerable generalization in the organization of a person's beliefs and values. Studies of authoritarian and equalitarian trends in personality do find consistent constellations of attitudes. It is true that the correlations are not always high, and Prothro reports that, among his Southern subjects, there was only a slight relationship between anti-Semitism and Negro prejudice.[68] But studies of the generalization hypothesis in attitude structure give positive findings. Grace confirmed his prediction that the attitudes people displayed in interpersonal relations toward their friends and colleagues carried over to their attitudes toward international matters.[69] He studied four types of reaction: verbal hostility, direct hostility, intropunitiveness, and apathy. People characteristically giving one type of response in everyday situations would tend to respond similarly in professional and international situations. Stagner concluded on the basis of his empirical investigation of attitudes toward colleagues and outgroups that the evidence supported a generalization theory rather than a displacement of sublimation theory.[70] Confirmation of the generalization hypothesis comes from a Norwegian study by Christiansen in which reactions were classified on two dimensions: (1) threat-oriented versus problem-oriented and (2) outward-directed versus inward-directed. Thus, blaming oneself would be a threat-oriented, inwardly directed reaction. Christiansen found that (a) people tend to react consistently toward everyday conflict situations, (b) they react consistently to international conflicts, (c) there is a correlation between reactions to everyday conflicts and to international conflicts, and (d) this correlation is lower than the correlations among reactions to everyday conflicts and among reactions to international conflicts, respectively.[71]

Three reasons can be suggested for the failure to find greater generalization effects in attitude change:

1. The over-all organization of attitudes and values in the personality is highly differentiated. The many dimensions allow the individual to absorb change without major modification of his attitudes. A Democrat of long standing could vote for Eisenhower and still remain Democratic in his identification because to him politics was not involved in this decision. Eisenhower stood above the political arena in the minds of many people. He was not blamed for what his party did, as the Gallup polls indicate, nor did his popularity rub off on his party. In 1958, in spite of Eisenhower's urgings, the people returned a sizable Democratic majority to Congress. There are many standards of judgment, then, which pertain to content areas of belief and attitude. An individual uses one set of standards or dimensions for a political decision but will shift to another set when it is more appropriate.

2. The generalization of attitudes proceeds along lines of the individual's own psychological groupings more than along lines of conventional sociological categories. We may miss significant generalized change because we do not look at the individual's own pattern of beliefs and values. One man may dislike foreigners, but to him foreigners are those people whose English he cannot understand; to another person foreigners are people of certain physical characteristics; to a third they are people with different customs, etc.

People will utilize many principles in organizing their own groupings of attitudes: (a) the objective similarities of the referents of the atti-

tudes, (b) their own limited experiences with these referents, (c) their own needs, and (d) their own ideas of causation and of the nature of proper relationships. Peak has used the concept of psychological distance and difference between events in psychological space to describe attitude structure and generalization.[72]

The liberal-conservative dimension, for example, may be useful for characterizing large groups of people, but individuals may differ considerably in their own scaling of attitudes comprising liberalism-conservatism. Some conservatives can stand to the left of center on issues of the legal rights of the individual or on internationalism. Social classes show differences in liberal and conservative ideology, the lower socio-economic groups being more liberal on economic and political issues and the upper income groups more liberal on tolerance for deviants and on democratic values in interpersonal relationships. Stouffer found that during the McCarthy period the low-status groups were more tolerant, and other studies have shown more authoritarian values among these groups.[73]

3. Generalization of attitude change is limited by the lack of systematic forces in the social environment to implement that change. Even when people are prepared to modify their behavior to a considerable extent they find themselves in situations which exert pressures to maintain old attitudes and habits. The discharged convict who is ready to change his ways may find it difficult to find a decent job and his only friends may be his former criminal associates. It does not necessarily help an industrial firm to train its foremen in human relations if the foremen must perform in an authoritarian structure.

ASSESSMENT OF MOTIVATIONAL BASES OF ATTITUDES

If an understanding of the nature of attitudes and the conditions for their change depends upon a knowledge of their functional bases, then it becomes of first importance to identify the underlying motivational patterns. The traditional advertising approach is to give less attention to the research assessment of needs and motives and more attention to multiple appeals, to gaining public attention, and to plugging what seems to work. Multiple appeals will, it is hoped, reach some members of the public with an effective message. In political campaigns, there is more concern with gearing the approach to the appropriate audience. If the political party makes serious mistakes in its assessment of the needs of particular groups, it is not a matter of losing a few potential customers but of losing votes to the opposing party, and so losing the election. Political leaders are, therefore, making more and more use of public opinion polls and a number of the major candidates for high office enlist their own research specialists. So true is this that we may no longer have political conventions naming a dark-horse candidate for the presidency. If the leaders are not convinced by poll results that a candidate has a good chance to win, they are not likely to support him.

There are no reliable short-cuts to the assessment of the needs which various attitudes satisfy. Systematic sampling of the population in question by means of interviews or of behavioral observation is a necessity. A growing number of devices are becoming available to supplement the depth interview. Objective scales for determining personality trends, such as the F-scale or the Minnesota Multiphasic Inventory, have been widely used. Projective methods which call for the completion of sentences and stories or furnishing stories about ambiguous pictures are just beginning to be exploited. In a nationwide survey of attitudes toward public health, Veroff *et al.* successfully used a picture test to obtain scores for people with respect to their needs for achievement, for affiliation, and for power.[74] Methods for measuring motivation are difficult, but the basic logic in their application is essentially that of any research tool. If early abuses of these instruments do not prejudice the research field, they will in the future have almost as wide a use as the polls themselves. Moreover, polling methods can be adapted to measuring people's needs with indirect questions which have been validated against more projective tests.

In many situations inferences can be made about people's needs without elaborate measures. If farm income has fallen drastically in a given section of the country, or if unemployment has risen sharply in a certain city, obvious inferences can be drawn. The extent and depth of the dissatisfaction will be better known through adequate measurement.

Measures of the four types of motivational pattern discussed indicate wide individual differences in the extent to which the patterns characterize the person. Though all people employ defense mechanisms, there are wide differences in the depth and extent of defensiveness. And Cohen has shown that the need for knowledge varies even in a college population.[75] Subjects were assigned scores on their need to know by a questionnaire with forced-choice alternatives to a wide variety of hypothetical situations. One of three alternatives indicated a desire for more information. In the experimental situation which followed, one group was given fear-arousing communications about the grading of examinations and then given information about grading on the basis of the normal curve. Their need for information was thus aroused before the presentation of the information. A second group was given the information about grading on the basis of the curve and then given the fear-arousing communication. Measures were taken of the acceptance of the information at a subsequent period. The subjects who had scored low on need for knowledge were definitely affected by the order of presentation. When they received information before their anxieties had been aroused about grades, they were much less receptive than were the low-need scorers who had their anxieties aroused before they received the information. On the other hand, the subjects scoring high on the need to know were not affected by the order of the presentation. Their needs for knowledge were sufficiently strong that they were receptive to information without the specific need arousal of the experimental situation. In other words, the need to know, like other needs, varies in intensity among people as a characteristic of personality.

In spite of characteristic differences in the strength of needs and motives, we cannot predict attitude change with precision solely on the basis of measures of need. We must also have measures of the related attitudes. Knowledge of the need state indicates the type of goal toward which the individual is striving. But the means for reaching this goal may vary considerably, and for this reason we need to know the attitudes which reflect the evaluation of the various means. Farmers with depressed incomes may still vote for the Republican Party if they have confidence in Nixon's farm program. Some need patterns furnish more direct predictions than others. The defensive person who is extrapunitive will be high in prejudice toward outgroups. Even in this case, however, his prejudices toward specific outgroups may vary considerably.

THE FACTOR OF GENERAL PERSUASIBILITY

We have emphasized the fact that appeals to change attitudes must be geared to the relevant motivational basis of the attitude. An opposed point of view would be that there is a general personality characteristic of persuasibility according to which some people are easier to convince than others no matter what the appeal. Hovland and Janis have tested this hypothesis in a series of experiments.[76] In one investigation ten different communications were presented to 185 high school students. The communications ranged from logical arguments to fear-arousing threats on five topics, on both the pro and con sides of the issue. In general there was some tendency for the acceptance of the influence of one communication to be associated with the acceptance of other influences. Of the 45 correlation coefficients for the ten communications, 39 were positive but only 11 were significant at the .01 confidence level and only 6 were over .40. Though there may be some general susceptibility to influence, it is apparently not a potent factor and accounts for a small amount of variance in attitude change. For certain purposes, however, it deserves consideration, especially in situations where attitudes are not supported by strong motivational patterns.

SUMMARY

The purpose of this paper was to provide a psychological framework for the systematic consideration of the dynamics of public and private attitudes. Four functions which attitudes perform for the personality were identified: the *adjustive function* of satisfying utilitarian needs, the *ego-defensive function* of handling internal conflicts, the *value-expressive function* of maintaining self-identity and of enhancing the self-image, and the *knowledge function* of giving understanding and meaning to the ambiguities of the world about us. The role of these functions in attitude formation was described. Their relevance for the conditions determining attitude arousal and attitude change were analyzed. Finally, constellations of variables such as group contact and legislative control of behavior were considered in terms of their motivational impact.

NOTES

1. Muzafer Sherif, *The Psychology of Social Norms,* New York, Harper, 1936.

2. Solomon E. Asch, *Social Psychology,* New York, Prentice-Hall, 1952.

3. *Ibid.,* pp. 426–427. The following statement was attributed to its rightful author, John Adams, for some subjects and to Karl Marx for others: "those who hold and those who are without property have ever formed distinct interests in society." When the statement was attributed to Marx, this type of comment appeared: "Marx is stressing the need for a redistribution of wealth." When it was attributed to Adams, this comment appeared: "This social division is innate in mankind."

4. Herbert H. Hyman and Paul B. Sheatsley, "Some Reasons Why Information Campaigns Fail," *Public Opinion Quarterly,* Vol. 11, 1947, pp. 413–423.

5. William A. Scott points out that in the area of international relations the incompleteness and remoteness of the information and the lack of pressures on the individual to defend his views results in inconsistencies. Inconsistent elements with respect to a system of international beliefs may, however, be consistent with the larger system of the personality. "Rationality and Non-rationality of International Attitudes," *Journal of Conflict Resolution,* Vol. 2, 1958, pp. 9–16.

6. Irving Sarnoff and Daniel Katz, "The Motivational Bases of Attitude Change," *Journal of Abnormal and Social Psychology,* Vol. 49, 1954, pp. 115–124.

7. M. Brewster Smith, Jerome S. Bruner, and Robert W. White, *Opinions and Personality,* New York, Wiley, 1956.

8. Herbert H. Hyman and Paul B. Sheatsley, "The Authoritarian Personality: A Methodological Critique," in Richard Christie and Marie Jahoda, editors, *Studies in the Scope and Method of the Au-*

thoritarian Personality, Glencoe, Ill., Free Press, 1954, pp. 50–122.

9. David Krech and Richard S. Crutchfield, *Theory and Problems of Social Psychology,* New York, McGraw-Hill, 1948, pp. 160–163.

10. Dorwin Cartwright, "Some Principles of Mass Persuasion," *Human Relations,* Vol. 2, 1949, pp. 253–267.

11. M. Brewster Smith, "The Personal Setting of Public Opinions: A Study of Attitudes toward Russia," *Public Opinion Quarterly,* Vol. 11, 1947, pp. 507–523.

12. Daniel Katz and Ezra Stotland, "A Preliminary Statement to a Theory of Attitude Structure and Change," in Sigmund Koch, editor, *Psychology: A Study of a Science,* Vol. 3, New York, McGraw-Hill, 1959, pp. 423–475.

13. See pages 224–250 of this issue of the *Quarterly.*

14. See pages 319–340 of this issue of the *Quarterly.*

15. Katz and Stotland, *op. cit.,* pp. 434–443.

16. William O. Jenkins and Julian C. Stanley, "Partial Reinforcement: A Review and Critique," *Psychological Bulletin,* Vol. 47, 1950, pp. 193–234.

17. See pp. 251–279.

18. Daniel R. Miller and Guy E. Swanson, *Inner Conflict and Defense,* New York, Holt, 1960, pp. 194–288.

19. John Dewey, *How We Think,* New York, Macmillan, 1910.

20. Walter Lippmann, *Public Opinion,* New York, Macmillan, 1922.

21. Herta Herzog, "What Do We Really Know about Daytime Serial Listeners?" in Paul F. Lazarsfeld and Frank N. Stanton, editors, *Radio Research 1942–1943,* New York, Duell, Sloan & Pearce, 1944, pp. 3–33.

22. From a study of the impact of party organization on political behavior in the Detroit area, by Daniel Katz and Samuel Eldersveld, in manuscript.

23. Lippmann, *op. cit.,* p. 95.

24. Earl R. Carlson, "Attitude Change through Modification of Attitude Structure," *Journal of Abnormal and Social Psychology,* Vol. 52, 1956, pp. 256–261.

25. Irving L. Janis and Seymour Feshback, "Effects of Fear-arousing Communications," *Journal of Abnormal and Social Psychology,* Vol. 48, 1953, pp. 78–92.

26. Jum C. Nunnally and Howard M. Bobren, "Variables Governing the Willingness to Receive Communications in Mental Health," *Journal of Personality,* Vol. 27, 1959, pp. 38–46.

27. Morton Wagman, "Attitude Change and the Authoritarian Personality," *Journal of Psychology,* Vol. 40, 1955, pp. 3–24. The F-scale is a measure of authoritarianism comprising items indicative of both defensiveness and ideology.

28. Leonard Berkowitz, "Anti-Semitism and the Displacement of Aggression," *Journal of Abnormal and Social Psychology,* Vol. 59, 1959, pp. 182–188.

29. Leonard Berkowitz and Douglas S. Holmes, "The Generalization of Hostility to Disliked Objects," *Journal of Personality,* Vol. 27, 1959, pp. 565–577.

30. Bruno Bettelheim and Morris Janowitz, *Dynamics of Prejudice,* New York, Harper, 1950.

31. Joseph Greenblum and Leonard I. Pearlin, "Vertical Mobility and Prejudice," in Reinhard Bendix and Seymour M. Lipset, editors, *Class, Status and Power,* Glencoe, Ill., Free Press, 1953.

32. Eunice Cooper and Marie Jahoda, "The Evasion of Propaganda: How Prejudiced People Respond to Anti-prejudice Propaganda," *Journal of Psychology,* Vol. 23, 1947, pp. 15–25.

33. Leonard Berkowitz, "The Expression and Reduction of Hostility," *Psychological Bulletin,* Vol. 55, 1958, pp. 257–283.

34. Gordon W. Allport, *The Nature of Prejudice,* Cambridge, Mass., Addison-Wesley, 1954.

35. Daniel Katz, Irving Sarnoff, and Charles McClintock, "Ego Defense and Attitude Change," *Human Relations,* Vol. 9, 1956, pp. 27–46. Also their "The Measurement of Ego Defense as Related to Attitude Change," *Journal of Personality,* Vol. 25, 1957, pp. 465–474.

36. Ezra Stotland, Daniel Katz, and Martin Patchen, "The Reduction of Prejudice through the Arousal of Self-insight," *Journal of Personality,* Vol. 27, 1959, pp. 507–531.

37. Charles McClintock, "Personality Syndromes and Attitude Change," *Journal of Personality,* Vol. 26, 1958, pp. 479–593.

38. H. Edwin Titus and E. P. Hollander, "The California F-Scale in Psychological Research: 1950–1955," *Psychological Bulletin,* Vol. 54, 1957, pp. 47–64.

39. Thomas F. Pettigrew, "Personality and Sociocultural Factors in Intergroup Attitudes: A Cross-national Comparison," *Journal of Conflict Resolution,* Vol. 2, 1958, pp. 29–42.

40. Daniel J. Levinson, "Authoritarian Personality and Foreign Personality," *Journal of Conflict Resolution,* Vol. 1, 1957, pp. 37–47.

41. Robert E. Lane, "Political Personality and Electoral Choice," *American Political Science Review,* Vol. 49, 1955, pp. 173–190.

42. Howard P. Smith and Ellen W. Rosen, "Some Psychological Correlates of Worldmindedness and Authoritarianism," *Journal of Personality,* Vol. 26, 1958, pp. 170–183.

43. Morris Davis, "Community Attitudes toward Fluoridation," *Public Opinion Quarterly,* Vol. 23, 1959, pp. 474–482.

44. Arthur I. Gladstone and Martha A. Taylor, "Threat-related Attitudes and Reactions to Commu-

nication about International Events," *Journal of Conflict Resolution,* Vol. 2, 1958, pp. 17–28.

45. Angus A. Campbell, Philip Converse, Warren Miller, and Donald Stokes, *The American Voter,* New York, Wiley, 1960.

46. Herbert H. Hyman *Political Socialization,* Glencoe, Ill., Free Press, 1959.

47. Augus A. Campbell, Gerald Gurin, and Warren Miller, *The Voter Decides,* Evanston, Ill., Row, Peterson, 1954.

48. Robert J. Lifton "Thought Reform of Chinese Intellectuals: A Psychiatric Evaluation," *Journal of Social Issues,* Vol. 13, No. 3, 1957, pp. 5–20.

49. Edgar H. Schein, "Reaction Patterns to Severe, Chronic Stress in American Army Prisoners of War of the Chinese," *Journal of Social Issues,* Vol. 13, No. 3, 1957, pp. 21–30.

50. Julius Segal, "Correlates of Collaboration and Resistance Behavior among U.S. Army POW's in Korea," *Journal of Social Issues,* Vol. 13, No. 3, 1957, pp. 31–40.

51. Stotland, Katz, and Patchen, *op. cit.*

52. Morton Deutsch and Mary E. Collins, *Interracial Housing: A Psychological Evaluation of a Social Experiment,* Minneapolis, University of Minnesota Press, 1951.

53. Marian R. Yarrow, editor, "Interpersonal Dynamics in a Desegregation Process," *Journal of Social Issues,* Vol. 14, No. 1, 1958, pp. 1–63.

54. Allport, *op. cit.,* pp. 274–276.

55. Samuel A. Stouffer *et al., The American Soldier,* Vol. 1, Princeton, N.J., Princeton University Press, 1949, pp. 566–599.

56. Muzafer Sherif and Carolyn W. Sherif, *An Outline of Social Psychology,* rev. ed., New York, Harper, 1956, pp. 548–551.

57. Sherif and Sherif, *op. cit.,* pp. 287–331.

58. Erich Reigrotski and Nels Anderson, "National Stereotypes and Foreign Contacts," *Public Opinion Quarterly,* Vol. 23, pp. 515–528.

59. Claire Selltiz, Anna L. Hopson, and Stuart W. Cook, "The Effects of Situational Factors on Personal Interaction between Foreign Students and Americans," *Journal of Social Issues,* Vol. 12, No. 1, 1956, pp. 33–44.

60. Jeanne Watson and Ronald Lippitt, "Cross-cultural Experience as a Source of Attitude Change," *Journal of Conflict Resolution,* Vol. 2, 1958, pp. 61–66. Also, Jeanne Watson and Ronald Lippitt, *Learning across Cultures,* Ann Arbor, Mich., Institute for Social Research, Research Center for Group Dynamics, 1955.

61. Richard T. Morris, "National Status and Attitudes of Foreign Students," *Journal of Social Issues,* Vol. 12, No. 1, 1956, pp. 20–25.

62. M. Sherif, *Psychology of Social Norms, op. cit.*

63. Seymour Lieberman, "The Relationship between Attitudes and Roles: A Natural Field Experiment," University of Michigan, 1954, unpublished doctoral dissertation.

64. Stuart Cook, "Desegregation, A Psychological Analysis," *American Psychologist,* Vol. 12, 1957, pp. 11–13.

65. Schein, *op. cit.*

66. Stotland and Katz, *op. cit.*

67. Campbell, Converse, Miller, and Stokes, *op. cit.*

68. E. Terry Prothro, "Ethnocentrism and Anti-Negro Attitudes in the Deep South," *Journal of Abnormal and Social Psychology,* Vol. 47, 1952, pp. 105–108.

69. H. A. Grace, *A Study of the Expression of Hostility in Everyday Professional and International Verbal Situations,* New York, Columbia University Press, 1949.

70. Ross Stagner, "Studies of Aggressive Social Attitudes," *Journal of Social Psychology,* Vol. 20, 1944, pp. 109–120.

71. Bjorn Christiansen, *Attitudes towards Foreign Affairs as a Function of Personality,* Oslo, Norway, Oslo University Press, 1959.

72. Helen Peak, "Psychological Structure and Person Perception," in Renato Tagiuri and Luigi Petrullo, editors, *Person Perception and Interpersonal Behavior,* Stanford, Calif., Stanford University Press, 1958, pp. 337–352.

73. Samuel A. Stouffer, *Communism, Conformity and Civil Liberties,* New York, Doubleday, 1955.

74. Joseph Veroff, John W. Atkinson, Sheila C. Feld, and Gerald Gurin, "The Use of Thematic Apperception to Assess Motivation in a Nationwide Interview Study," *Psychological Monographs,* in press.

75. Arthur R. Cohen, "Need for Cognition and Order of Communication as Determinants of Opinion Change," in Carl Hovland *et al.,* editors, *The Order of Presentation in Persuasion,* New Haven, Conn., Yale University Press, 1957, pp. 79–97.

76. Carl I. Hovland and Irving L. Janis, editors, *Personality and Persuasibility,* New Haven, Conn., Yale University Press, 1959.

MANAGEMENT AND
THE LEARNING PROCESS

DAVID A. KOLB

Today's highly successful manager or administrator is distinguished not so much by any single set of knowledge or skills but by his ability to adapt to and master the changing demands of his job and career—by his ability to learn. The same is true for successful organizations. Continuing success in a changing world requires an ability to explore new opportunities and learn from past successes and failures. These ideas are neither new nor particularly controversial. Yet it is surprising that this ability to learn, which is so widely regarded as important, receives so little explicit attention from managers and their organizations. There is a kind of fatalism about learning. One either learns or he doesn't. The ability to consciously control and manage the learning process is usually limited to such schoolboy maxims as "Study hard" and "Do your homework."

Part of the reason for this fatalism lies, I believe, in a lack of understanding about the learning process itself. If managers and administrators had a model about how individuals and organizations learn, they would better be able to enhance their own and their organizations' ability to learn. This article describes such a model and attempts

© 1976 by the Regents of the University of California. Reprinted from *California Management Review*, volume XVIII, number 3, pp. 21 to 32, by permission of the Regents.

to show some of the ways in which the learning process and individual learning styles affect management education, managerial decision making and problem solving, and organizational learning.

THE EXPERIENTIAL
LEARNING MODEL

Let us begin with a model of how people learn, which I call the experiential learning model. The model is labeled "experiential" for two reasons. The first is historical, tying it to its intellectual origins in the social psychology of Kurt Lewin in the 1940s and the sensitivity training and laboratory education work of the 1950s and 1960s. The second reason is to emphasize the important role that experience plays in the learning process, an emphasis that differentiates this approach from other cognitive theories of the learning process. The core of the model is a simple description of the learning cycle—how experience is translated into concepts, which in turn are used as guides in the choice of new experiences (Figure 1).

Learning is conceived of as a four-stage cycle. Immediate concrete experience is the basis for observation and reflection. These observations are assimilated into a theory from which new implications for action can be deduced. These implications or hypotheses then serve as guides in acting

42

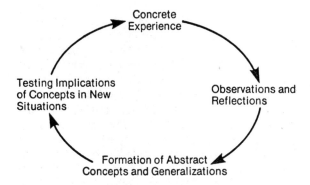

FIGURE 1. The experiential learning model.

to create new experiences. The learner, if he is to be effective, needs four different kinds of abilities —*concrete experience* (CE), *reflective observation* (RO), *abstract conceptualization* (AC), and *active experimentation* (AE). That is, he must be able to involve himself fully, openly, and without bias in new experiences (CE); he must be able to reflect on and observe these experiences from many perspectives (RO); he must be able to create concepts that integrate his observations into logically sound theories (AC); and he must be able to use these theories to make decisions and solve problems (AE).

Yet how difficult this ideal is to achieve! Can anyone become highly skilled in all of these abilities, or are they necessarily in conflict? How can one act and reflect at the same time? How can one be concrete and immediate and still be theoretical? Indeed, a closer examination of the four-stage learning model reveals that learning requires abilities that are polar opposites and that the learner, as a result, must continually choose which set of learning abilities he will bring to bear in any specific learning situation.

More specifically, there are two primary dimensions to the learning process. The first dimension represents the concrete experiencing of events at one end and abstract conceptualization at the other. The other dimension has active experimentation at one extreme and reflective observation at the other. Thus, in the process of learning one moves in varying degrees from actor to observer, from specific involvement to general analytic detachment.

Most cognitive psychologists see the concrete/abstract dimension as a primary dimension on which cognitive growth and learning occurs.[1-4] Goldstein and Scheerer suggest that greater abstractness results in the development of the following abilities: to detach our ego from the outer world or from inner experience; to assume a mental set; to account for acts to oneself, to verbalize the account; to shift reflectively from one aspect of the situation to another; to hold in mind simultaneously various aspects; to grasp the essential of a given whole—to break up a given into parts to isolate and synthesize them; to abstract common properties reflectively, to form hierarchic concepts; to plan ahead ideationally, to assume an attitude toward the more possible, and to think or perform symbolically.[5] Concreteness, on the other hand, represents the absence of these abilities, the immersion in and domination by one's immediate experiences.

Yet as the circular model of the learning process would imply, abstractness is not exclusively good and concreteness exclusively bad. To be creative requires that one be able to experience anew, freed somewhat from the constraints of previous abstract concepts. In psychoanalytic theory this need for a concrete, childlike perspective in the creative process is referred to as regression in service of the ego.[6] In his essay on the conditions for creativity, Bruner further emphasizes the dialectic tension between abstract detachment and concrete involvement.[2] For him the creative act is a product of detachment and commitment, of passion and decorum, and of a freedom to be dominated by the object of one's inquiry.

The active/reflective dimension is the other major dimension of cognitive growth and learning. As growth occurs, thought becomes more reflective and internalized, based more on the manipulation of symbols and images than covert actions. The modes of active experimentation and reflection, like abstractness/concreteness, stand in opposition to one another. Reflection tends to inhibit action and vice versa. For example, Singer has found that children who have active internal fantasy lives are more capable of inhibiting action for long periods of time than are children with little internal fantasy life.[7] Kagan has found, on the other hand, that very active orientations toward learning situations inhibit reflection and thereby preclude the development of analytic concepts.[8] Herein lies the second major dialectic in the learning process—the tension between actively testing the implications of one's hypotheses and reflectively interpreting data already collected.

INDIVIDUAL LEARNING STYLES

As a result of our hereditary equipment, our particular past life experience, and the demands of our present environment most people develop learning styles that emphasize some learning abilities over others. We come to resolve the conflicts between being active and reflective and between being immediate and analytical in characteristic ways. Some people develop minds that excel at assimilating disparate facts into coherent theories, yet these same people are incapable of or uninterested in deducing hypotheses from their theories. Others are logical geniuses but find it impossible to involve and surrender themselves to an experience, and so on. A mathematician may come to place great emphasis on abstract concepts, while a poet may value concrete experience more highly. A manager may be primarily concerned with the active application of ideas, while a naturalist may develop his observational skills highly. Each of us in a unique way develops a learning style that has some weak and some strong points.

For some time now I have been involved in a program of research studies aimed at identifying different kinds of learning styles and their consequences. The purpose of this research is to better understand the different ways that people learn and solve problems so that we can both make individuals aware of the consequences of their own learning style and of the alternative learning modes available to them, and improve the design of learning experiences to take into account these learning-style differences. In this work we have developed a simple self-description inventory, the Learning Style Inventory (LSI), which is designed to measure an individual's strengths and weaknesses as a learner. The LSI measures an individual's relative emphasis on the four learning abilities described earlier, concrete experience (CE), reflective observation (RO), abstract conceptualization (AC) and active experimentation (AE) by asking him, several different times, to rank in order four words that describe these different abilities. For example, one set of four words is "feeling" (CE), "watching" (RO), "thinking" (AC), and "doing" (AE). The inventory yields six scores, CE, RO, AC, and AE plus two combination scores that indicate the extent to which the individual emphasizes abstractness over concreteness (AC-CE) and active experimentation over reflection (AE-RO).

The LSI was administered to 800 practicing managers and graduate students in management to obtain a norm for the management population. In general these managers tended to emphasize active experimentation over reflective observation. In addition, managers with graduate degrees tended to rate their abstract learning skills higher.[9, 10] While the managers we tested showed many different patterns of scores on the LSI, we have identified four dominant types of learning styles that occur most frequently. We have called these four styles the converger, the diverger, assimilator, and accommodator. (The reason that there are four dominant styles is that AC and CE are highly negatively correlated as are RO and AE. Thus individuals who score high on both AC and CE or on both AE and RO occur with less frequency than do the other four combinations of LSI scores.)

The converger's dominant learning abilities are AC and AE. His greatest strength lies in the practical application of ideas. We have called this learning style the converger because a person with this style seems to do best in situations such as conventional intelligence tests, where there is a single correct answer or solution to a question or problem.[11] His knowledge is organized in such a way that, through hypothetical-deductive reasoning, he can focus it on specific problems. Hudson's research on this style of learning shows that convergers are relatively unemotional, preferring to deal with things rather than people.[12] They tend to have narrow technical interests and choose to specialize in the physical sciences. Our research shows that this learning style is characteristic of many engineers.

The diverger has the opposite learning strengths of the converger. He is best at CE and RO. His greatest strength lies in his imaginative ability. He excels in the ability to view concrete situations from many perspectives. We have labeled this style diverger because a person with this style performs better in situations that call for generation of ideas such as a "brainstorming" session. Hudson's work on this learning style shows that divergers are interested in people and tend to be imaginative and emotional.[12] They have broad cultural interests and tend to specialize in the arts. Our research shows that this style is characteristic of managers from humanities and liberal arts backgrounds. Personnel managers tend to be characterized by this learning style.

The assimilator's dominant learning abilities are AC and RO. His greatest strength lies in his ability to create theoretical models. He excels in inductive reasoning—in assimilating disparate observations into an integrated explanation. He, like the converger, is less interested in people and more concerned for abstract concepts, but he is less concerned with the practical use of theories. For him it is more important that the theory be logically sound and precise. As a result, this learning style is more characteristic of the basic sciences rather than the applied sciences. In organizations this learning style is found most often in the research and planning departments.

The accommodator has the opposite learning strengths of the assimilator. He is best at CE and AE. His greatest strength lies in doing things, in carrying out plans and experiments and involving himself in new experiences. He tends to be more of a risk taker than people with the other three learning styles. We have labeled this style accommodator because he tends to excel in situations where he must adapt himself to specific immediate circumstances. In situations where the theory or plans do not fit the facts, he will most likely discard the plan or theory. (His opposite style type, the assimilator, would be more likely to disregard or reexamine the facts.) The accommodator is at ease with people but is sometimes seen as impatient and "pushy." His educational background is often in technical or practical fields such as business. In organizations people with this

learning style are found in action-oriented jobs, often in marketing or sales.

These different learning styles can be illustrated graphically (Figure 2) by plotting the average LSI scores for managers in our sample who reported their undergraduate college major (only those majors with more than ten people responding are included). Before interpreting these data, some cautions are in order. First, it should be remembered that all of the individuals in the sample are managers or managers-to-be. In addition, most of these men have completed or are in graduate school. These two facts should produce learning styles that are somewhat more active and abstract than the population at large (as indicated by total sample mean scores on AC-CE and AE-RO, +4.5 and +2.9 respectively).

The interaction between career, high level of education, and undergraduate major may produce distinctive learning styles. For example, physicists who are not in industry may be somewhat more reflective than those in this sample. Second, undergraduate majors are described only in the most general terms. There are many forms of engineering or psychology. A business major at one school can be quite different than that at another. However, even if we take these cautions into consideration, the distribution of undergraduate majors on the learning style grid is strikingly consistent with theory.[9] Undergraduate business majors tend to have accommodative learning styles, while engineers on the average fall in the convergent quadrant. History, English, political science, and psychology majors all have divergent learning styles, along with economics and sociology. Physics majors are very abstract, falling between the convergent and assimilative quadrants. What these data show is that one's undergraduate education is a major factor in the development of his learning style. Whether this is because individuals' learning styles are shaped by the fields they enter or because of selection processes that put people into and out of disciplines is an open question at this point. Most probably both factors are operating—people choose fields that are consistent with their learning styles and are further shaped to fit the learning norms of their field once they are in it. When there is a mismatch between the field's learning norms and the individ-

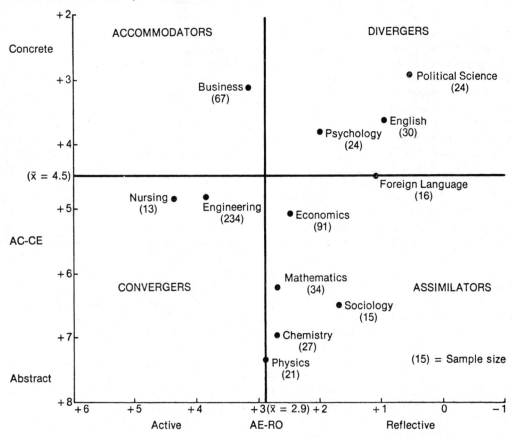

FIGURE 2. Average LS1 scores on Active/Reflective (AE-20) and Abstract/Concrete (AC-CE) by undergraduate college major.

ual's learning style, people will either change or leave the field. Plovnick's research indicates that the latter alternative is more likely the case.[13] He studied a major university physics department and concluded that the major emphasis in physics education was on convergent learning. He predicted that physics students who had convergent learning styles would be content with their majors, whereas physics majors who were divergent in their learning style would be uncertain of physics as a career and would take more courses outside of the physics department than their convergent colleagues. His predictions were confirmed. Those students who are not "fitted" for the convergent learning style required in physics tend to turn away from physics as profession.

These results pose something of an educational dilemma for the physics department. To contrib-

ute in physics today one must know many facts, so learning content is important; and this takes time, time that might be spent developing the convergent skills of divergers. So isn't it simpler to select (implicitly or explicitly) people who already possess these convergent experimental and theoretical skills? Perhaps, but in the process the creative tension between convergence and divergence is lost. The result of this process may be a program that produces fine technicians but few innovators.

Kuhn put the issue this way, "Because the old must be revalued and reordered when assimilating the new, discovery and invention in the sciences are usually intrinsically revolutionary. Therefore they **do demand** just that flexibility and open-mindedness that characterize and indeed define the divergent." [14] It just may be that one of the reasons why creative contributions in the sciences are made primarily by younger men is that the learning styles of older men have been shaped by their professional training and experience so that they adapt well to the inquiry norms of their profession, but the creative tension is lost.[15]

LEARNING STYLES AND MANAGEMENT EDUCATION

Differences in learning style create similar problems for management education. The manager who comes to the university for mid-career education experiences something of a culture shock. Fresh from a world of time deadlines and concrete, specific problems that he must solve, he is suddenly immersed in a strange, slow-paced world of generalities where the elegant solution to problems is sought even when workable solutions have been found. One gets rewarded here for reflection and analysis rather than concrete, goal-directed action. The manager who "acts before he thinks—if he ever thinks" meets the scientist who "thinks before he acts—if he ever acts."

Our research on learning styles has shown that managers on the whole are distinguished by very strong active experimentation skills and are very weak on reflective observation skills. Business school faculty members usually have the reverse profile. To bridge this gap in learning styles the management educator must somehow respond to pragmatic demands for relevance and the application of knowledge while encouraging the reflective examination of experience that is necessary to refine old theories and to build new ones. In encouraging reflective observation the teacher often is seen as an interrupter of action—as a passive, "ivory tower" thinker. Indeed, this is a critical role to be played in the learning process. Yet if the reflective observer role is not internalized by the students themselves, the learning process can degenerate into a value conflict between teacher and student, each maintaining that his is the right perspective for learning.

Neither the faculty nor student perspective alone is valid, in my view. Managerial education will not be improved by eliminating theoretical analysis or relevant case problems. Improvement will come through *integration of the scholarly and practical learning styles*. My approach to achieving this integration has been to apply directly the experiential learning model in the classroom.[10] To do this we created a workbook providing games, role plays, and exercises (concrete experiences) that focus on fifteen central concepts in organizational psychology. These simulations provide a common experiential starting point for managers and faculty to explore the relevance of psychological concepts for their work. In traditional management education methods the conflict between scholar and practitioner learning styles is exaggerated because the material to be taught is filtered through the learning style of the faculty member in his lectures or his presentation and analysis of cases. The student is "one down" in his own analysis because his data are second-hand and already biased.

In the experiential learning approach this filtering process does not take place because both teacher and student are observers of immediate experiences, which they both interpret according to their own learning styles. In this approach the teacher's role is that of a facilitator of a learning process that is basically self-directed. He helps students to experience in a personal and immediate way the phenomena in his field of specialization. He provides observational schemes and perspectives from which to observe these experiences. He stands ready with alternative theories and concepts as the student attempts to assimilate his observations into his own conception of reality. He assists in deducing the implications of the student's concepts and in designing new experiments to test these implications through practical, "real world" experience.

There are two goals in the experiential learning process. One is to learn the specifics of a particular subject. The other goal is to learn about one's own strengths and weaknesses as a learner— learning how to learn from experience. When the process works well, managers finish their educational experience not only with new intellectual insights, but also with an understanding of their own learning style. This understanding of learning strengths and weaknesses helps in the application of what has been learned and provides a framework for continuing learning on the job. Day-to-day experience becomes a focus for testing and exploring new ideas. Learning is no longer a special activity reserved for the classroom; it becomes an integral and explicit part of work itself.

LEARNING STYLES AND MANAGERIAL PROBLEM SOLVING

We have been able to identify relationships between a manager's learning style and his educational experiences, but how about his current behavior on the job? Do managers with different learning styles approach problem solving and decision making differently? Theoretically, the answer to this question should be yes, since learning and problem solving are not different processes but the same basic process of adaptation viewed from different perspectives. To illustrate this

point I have overlaid in Figure 3 a typical model of the problem-solving process on the experiential learning model.[16] In this figure we can see that the stages in a problem-solving sequence generally correspond to the learning-style strengths of the four major learning styles described previously. The accommodator's problem-solving strengths lie in executing solutions and initiating problem finding based on some goal or model about how things should be. The diverger's problem-solving strengths lie in identifying the multitude of possible problems and opportunities that exist in reality ("compare model with reality and identify differences"). The assimilator excels in the abstract model building that is necessary to choose a priority problem and alternative solutions. The converger's strengths lie in the evaluation of solution consequences and solution selection.

To date, two studies have been conducted to

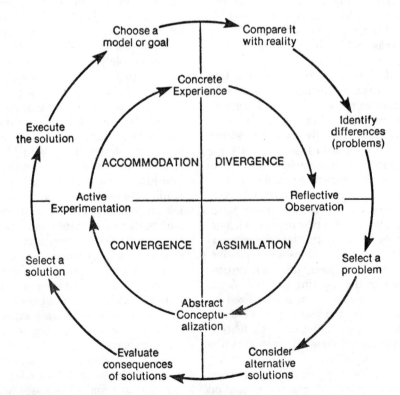

FIGURE 3. Comparison of the experiential Learning Model with a typical model of the problem solving process (after Pounds 1965).

discover whether there is anything to this theoretical model. The first study was conducted by Stabell in the trust department of a large Midwestern bank.[17] One aim of his study was to discover how the learning styles of investment portfolio managers affected their problem solving and decision making in the management of the assets in their portfolios. While his study involved only thirty-one managers, he found a strong correspondence between the type of decisions these managers faced and their learning styles. More specifically, he found that nearly all of the managers in the investment advisory section of the department, a high-risk, high-pressure job (as indicated by a large percentage of holdings in common stock, a large percentage of discretionary accounts, and a high performance and risk orientation on the part of clients) had accommodative learning styles (scoring very high on the AE and CE LSI scales). On the other hand, the men in the personal trust section, where risk and performance orientations were low and there were few discretionary accounts and fewer holdings in common stock, scored highest on reflective observation. This finding supports our earlier analysis that high-pressure management jobs develop and select for active experimentation learning skills and inhibit reflective observation learning skills.

Stabell was interested in whether he could identify differences, on the basis of their LSI scores, in the way managers went about making investment decisions. He focused his research on differences between managers with CE learning skills and AC learning skills. He asked these managers to evaluate the importance of the information sources they used in making decisions and found several interesting differences. First, CE managers cited more people as important sources (colleagues, brokers, and traders), while the AC managers listed more analytically oriented printed material as sources (economic analyses, industry and company reviews). In addition, it seemed that CE managers sought services that would give them a specific recommendation that they could accept or reject (a potential list), while the AC managers sought information they could analyze themselves in order to choose an investment. This analytic orientation of the AC managers is further illustrated by the fact that they tended to

use more information sources in their decisions than the CE managers. These data fit well with the learning/problem solving model in Figure 3. The concrete managers prefer go/no go implementation decisions based on personal recommendations, while the abstract managers prefer to consider and evaluate alternative solutions themselves.

The second study of the relationship between learning styles and managerial problem solving was a laboratory computer simulation of a production "trouble-shooting" problem where the problem solver had to determine which specific type of "widget" was failure-prone. This experiment, which is a modification of an earlier problem-solving experiment by Bruner and associates,[18] was conducted by Grochow as part of his doctoral dissertation.[19] His subjects for the experiment were twenty-two middle-level managers at MIT's Sloan Fellows program. Grochow was particularly interested in the different types of problem-solving strategies that assimilators and accommodators would use to solve this problem. He predicted that the accommodators would use a strategy that called for little complexity in use and interpretation, little inference from the data, and little cognitive strain in assimilating information, while assimilators would prefer a strategy that had the opposite characteristics—more complex use and interpretation and more assimilation strain and required inference. The former strategy, called successive scanning, was simply a process whereby the problem solver scans the data base of widgets for a direct test of his current hypothesis. It requires little conceptual analysis, since the current hypothesis is either validated or not in each trial. The latter strategy, called simultaneous scanning, is in a sense an optimal strategy in that each data point is used to eliminate the maximum number of data points still possible. This strategy requires considerable conceptual analysis, since the problem solver must keep several hypotheses in his head at the same time and deduce the optimal widget to examine in order to test these hypotheses.

The results of Grochow's experiment confirmed his hypothesis that accommodators would use successive scanning, while assimilators would use the more analytical simultaneous scanning strategy. He further found that managers with accommodative learning styles tended to show more inconsistency in their use of strategies, while the assimilative managers were quite consistent in their use of the simultaneous scanning strategy. The accommodative managers seemed to be taking a more intuitive approach, switching strategies as they gathered more data during the experiment. Interestingly, Grochow found no differences between accommodative and assimilative managers in the amount of time it took them to solve the problem. Though the two groups used very different styles, in this problem they performed equally well.

The results of both of these studies are consistent with the learning/problem-solving model. Managers' learning styles are measurably related to the way in which they solve problems and make decisions on the job and in the laboratory.

THE ORGANIZATION AS A LEARNING SYSTEM

Like individuals, organizations learn and develop distinctive learning styles. They do so through their transactions with the environment and through their choice of how to relate to that environment. This has come to be known as the "open systems" view of organizations. Since many organizations are large and complex, the environment they relate to becomes highly differentiated and diverse. The way the organization adapts to this external environment is to differentiate itself into units, each of which deals with just one part of the firm's external conditions. Marketing and sales face problems associated with the market, customers, and competitors. Research deals with the academic and technological worlds. Production deals with production equipment and raw materials sources. Personnel and labor relations deal with the labor market, and so on.

Because of this need to relate to different aspects of the environment, the different units of the firm develop characteristic ways of thinking and working together, different styles of decision making and problem solving. These units select and shape managers to solve problems and make decisions in the way their environment demands. In fact, Lawrence and Lorsch define organiza-

tional differentiation as "the difference in cognitive and emotional orientation among managers in different functional departments." [20]

If the organization is thought of as a learning system, then each of the differentiated units that is charged with adapting to the challenges of one segment of the environment can be thought of as having a characteristic learning style that is best suited to meet those environmental demands. The LSI should be a useful tool for measuring this organizational differentiation among the functional units of a firm. To test this we studied approximately twenty managers from each of five functional groups in a Midwestern division of a large American industrial corporation. [21] The five functional groups are described below, followed by my hypothesis about the learning style that should characterize each group given the environments to which they relate.

1. Marketing (n = 20). This group is primarily former salesmen. They have a nonquantitative, intuitive approach to their work. Because of their practical sales orientation in meeting customer demands, they should have accommodative learning styles—concrete and active.

2. Research (n = 22). The work of this group is split about evenly between pioneer research and applied research projects. The emphasis is on basic research. Researchers should be the most assimilative group—abstract and reflective, a style fitted to the world of knowledge and ideas.

3. Personnel/Labor Relations (n = 20). In this company men from this department serve two primary functions, interpreting personnel policy and promoting interaction among groups to reduce conflict and disagreement. Because of their people orientation these men should be predominantly divergers, concrete and reflective.

4. Engineering (n = 18). This group is made up primarily of design engineers who are quite production oriented. They should be the most convergent subgroup—abstract and active—although they should be less abstract than the research group. They represent a bridge between thought and action.

5. Finance (n = 20). This group has a strong computer/information-systems bias. Finance men,

given their orientation toward the mathematical task of information-system design, should be highly abstract. Their crucial role in organizational survival should produce an active orientation. Thus, finance group members should have convergent learning styles.

Figure 4 shows the average scores on the active/reflective (AE-RO) and abstract/concrete (AC-CE) learning dimensions for the five func-

tional groups. These results are consistent with the above predictions with the exception of the finance group, whose scores are less active than predicted; thus, they fall between the assimilative and the convergent quadrant.[21] The LSI clearly differentiates the learning styles that characterize the functional units of at least this one company. Managers in each of these units apparently use very different styles in doing their jobs.

But differentiation is only part of the story of

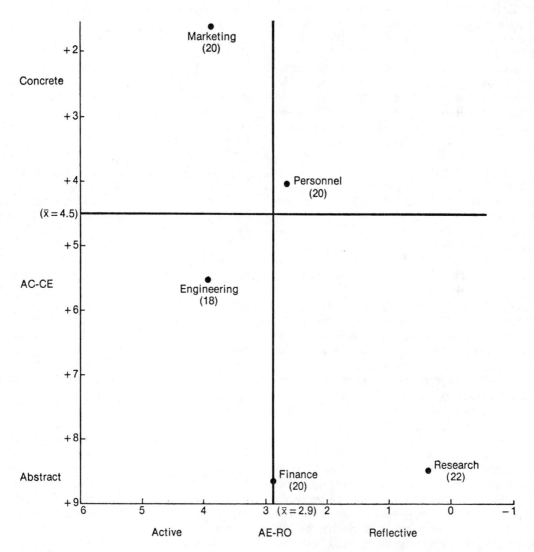

FIGURE 4. Average LS1 scores on Active Reflective (AE-RO) and Abstract/Concrete (AC-CE) by Organizational Function.

organizational adaptation and effectiveness. The result of the differentiation necessary to adapt to the external environment is the creation of a corresponding internal need to integrate and coordinate the different units. This necessitates resolving in some ways the conflicts inherent in these different learning styles. In actual practice this conflict gets resolved in many ways. Sometimes it is resolved through confrontation and integration of the different learning styles. More often, however, it is resolved through dominance by one unit over the other units, resulting in an unbalanced organizational learning style. We all know of organizations that are controlled by the marketing department or are heavily engineering-oriented, and so forth. This imbalance can be effective if it matches environmental demands in a stable environment; but it can be costly if the organization is called upon to learn to respond to changing environmental demands and opportunities.

One important question concerns the extent to which the integrative conflict between units is a function of managers' learning styles rather than merely a matter of conflicting job and role demands. To get at this question we asked the managers in each of the five functional units in the preceding study to rate how difficult they found it to communicate with each of the other four units. If integrative communication is a function of learning style, there should be a correspondence between how similar two units are in their learning style and how easy they find it to communicate. When the average communication difficulty ratings among the five units are compared with differences in unit learning styles, we find that in most cases this hypothesis is confirmed—those units that are most different in learning style have most difficulty communicating with one another.[22]

To test this notion more rigorously we did a more intensive study of communication between the two units that were most different in learning styles, marketing and research. To ascertain whether it was the manager's learning style that accounted for communication difficulty we divided managers in the marketing unit into two groups. One group had learning styles that were similar to those managers in research (assimila-

tors), while the other group had accommodative learning styles typical of the marketing function. The research group was divided similarly. The results of this analysis are shown in Figure 5. When managers have learning styles similar to another group they have little trouble communicating with that group. When style differences are great, communication difficulty rises. These results suggest that managers' learning styles are an important factor to consider in achieving integration among functional units.

MANAGING THE LEARNING PROCESS

To conclude, let us return to the problem we began with—how managers and organizations can explicitly manage their learning process. We have seen that the experiential learning model is useful not only for examining the educational process but also for understanding managerial problem solving and organizational adaptation. But how can an awareness of the experiential learning model and our own individual learning style help improve individual and organizational learning? Two recommendations seem important.

First, learning should be an explicit objective that is pursued as consciously and deliberately as profit or productivity. Managers and organizations should budget time to specifically learn from their experiences. When important meetings are held or important decisions made, time should be set aside to critique and learn from these events. In my experience all too few organizations have a climate that allows for free exploration of such questions as, What have we learned from this venture? Usually active experimentation norms dictate—We don't have time; let's move on.

Which leads to the second recommendation. The nature of the learning process is such that opposing perspectives, action and reflection, concrete involvement and analytical detachment, are all essential for optimal learning. When one perspective comes to dominate others, learning effectiveness is reduced in the long run. From this we can conclude that the most effective learning systems are those that can tolerate differences in perspective.

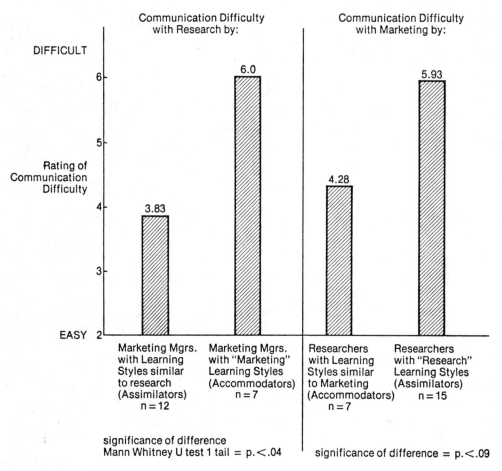

FIGURE 5. Communication difficulty between Marketing and Research as a function of Learning Style.

This point can be illustrated by the case of an electronics firm that I have worked with over the years. The firm was started by a group of engineers with a unique product. For several years they had no competitors and when some competition entered the market they continued to dominate and do well because of their superior engineering quality. Today is a different story. They are now faced with stiff competition in their original product area. In addition, their very success has caused new problems. They are no longer a small, intimate company but a large organization with several plants in the U.S. and Europe. The company has had great difficulty in responding to these changes because it still responds to prob-

lems primarily from an engineering point of view. Most of the top executives in the company are former engineers with no formal management training. Many of the specialists in marketing, finance, and personnel who have been brought in to help the organization solve its new problems feel like second-class citizens. Their ideas just don't seem to carry much weight. What was once the organization's strength—its engineering expertise—has become to some extent its weakness. Because engineering has flourished at the expense of the development of other organizational functions, such as marketing and the management of human resources, the firm is today struggling with rather than mastering its environment.

REFERENCES

1. John Flavell, *The Developmental Psychology of Jean Piaget* (New York: Van Nostrand Reinhold Co., 1963).
2. J. S. Bruner, *Essays for the Left Hand* (New York: Atheneum, 1966).
3. J. S. Bruner, *The Proces of Education* (New York: Vintage Books, 1960).
4. O. J. Harvey, David Hunt and Harold Schroder, *Conceptual Systems and Personality Organization* (New York: John Wiley, 1961).
5. K. Goldstein and M. Scheerer, "Abstract and Concrete Behavior: An Experimental Study with Special Tests," *Psychological Monographs* (1941), p. 4.
6. Ernst Kris, *Psychoanalytic Explorations in Art,* (New York: International Universities Press, 1952).
7. J. Singer, "The Importance of Daydreaming," *Psychology Today* (1968), pp. 18–26.
8. Jerome Kagan, Bernice L. Rosman, Deborah Day, Joseph Alpert, and William Phillips, "Information Processing in the Child: Significance of Analytic and Reflective Attitudes," *Psychological Monographs* (1964).
9. David A. Kolb, "Individual Learning Styles and the Learning Process," MIT Sloan School Working Paper No. 535-71, 1971.
10. David Kolb, Irwin Rubin and James McIntyre, *Organizational Psychology: An Experiential Approach* (Englewood Cliffs, N.J.: Prentice-Hall, 1971).
11. David Torrealba, "Convergent and Divergent Learning Styles," MS thesis, MIT Sloan School, 1972.
12. L. Hudson, *Contrary Imaginations* (Middlesex, England: Penguin Books Ltd., 1966).
13. M. S. Plovnick, "A Cognitive Ability Theory of Occupational Roles," MIT School of Management, Working Paper No. 524-71, Spring 1971.
14. Thomas Kuhn, *The Structure of Scientific Revolutions* (Chicago: University of Chicago Press, 1952).
15. H. C. Lehman, *Age and Achievement* (Princeton, N.J.: Princeton University Press, 1953).
16. William Pounds, "On Problem Finding," Sloan School Working Paper No. 145-65, 1965.
17. Charles Stabell, "The Impact of a Conversational Computer System on Human Problem Solving Behavior," unpublished working paper, MIT Sloan School, 1973.
18. J. S. Bruner, J. J. Goodnow and G. A. Austin, *A Study of Thinking* (New York: Wiley & Sons, 1956).
19. Jerrold Grochow, "Cognitive Style as a Factor in the Design of Interactive Decision-support Systems," Ph.D. thesis, MIT Sloan School, 1973.
20. Paul Lawrence and Jay Lorsch, *Organization and Environment* (Boston: Division of Research, Graduate School of Business Administration, 1967), p. 11.
21. F. Weisner, "Learning Profiles and Managerial Styles of Managers," S.M. thesis, Sloan School of Management, MIT, 1971. (I have reanalyzed Weisner's data for presentation here.)
22. "t" tests for significance of difference between groups on the abstract/concrete dimension yield the following one-tail probabilities that are less than 0.10. Marketing is more concrete than personnel ($p < 0.10$), engineering (< 0.05), research ($p < 0.005$), and finance ($p < 0.005$). Finance and research are more abstract than personnel (on both comparisons $p < 0.005$). On the active/reflective dimension, research is more reflective than marketing ($p < 0.05$), engineering ($p < 0.05$), and to a lesser extent finance ($p < 0.10$).

INTERPERSONAL BARRIERS TO DECISION MAKING

CHRIS ARGYRIS

- What are they?
- What damage do they do?
- What can be done to overcome them?

- The actual behavior of top executives during decision-making meetings often does not jibe with their attitudes and prescriptions about effective executive action.

- The gap that often exists between what executives say and how they behave helps create barriers to openness and trust, to the effective search for alternatives, to innovation, and to flexibility in the organization.

- These barriers are more destructive in important decision-making meetings than in routine meetings, and they upset effective managers more than ineffective ones.

- The barriers cannot be broken down simply by intellectual exercises. Rather, executives need feedback concerning their behavior and opportunities to develop self-awareness in action. To this end, certain kinds of questioning are valuable; playing back and analyzing tape recordings of meetings has proved to be a helpful step; and laboratory education programs are valuable.

These are a few of the major findings of a study of executive decision making in six representative companies. The findings have vital implications for management groups everywhere; for while some organizations are less subject to the

weaknesses described than are others, *all* groups have them in some degree. In this article I shall discuss the findings in detail and examine the implications for executives up and down the line. (For information on the company sample and research methods used in the study, see page 56.)

WORDS vs. ACTIONS

According to top management, the effectiveness of decision-making activities depends on the degree of innovation, risk taking, flexibility, and trust in the executive system. (Risk taking is defined here as any act where the executive risks his self-esteem. This could be a moment, for example, when he goes against the group view; when he tells someone, especially the person with the highest power, something negative about his impact on the organization; or when he seeks to put millions of dollars in a new investment.)

Nearly 95% of the executives in our study emphasize that an organization is only as good as its top people. They constantly repeat the importance of their responsibility to help themselves and others to develop their abilities. Almost as often they report that the qualities just mentioned—motivation, risk taking, and so on—are key characteristics of any successful executive system. "People problems" head the list as the most difficult, perplexing, and crucial.

NATURE OF THE STUDY

The six companies studied include: (1) an electronics firm with 40,000 employees, (2) a manufacturer and marketer of a new innovative product with 4,000 employees, (3) a large research and development company with 3,000 employees, (4) a small research and development organization with 150 employees, (5) a consulting-research firm with 400 employees, and (6) a producer of heavy equipment with 4,000 employees.

The main focus of the investigation reported here was on the behavior of 165 top executives in these companies. The executives were board members, executive committee members, upper-level managers, and (in a few cases) middle-level managers.

Approximately 265 decision-making meetings were studied and nearly 10,000 units of behavior analyzed. The topics of the meetings ranged widely, covering investment decisions, new products, manufacturing problems, marketing strategies, new pricing policies, administrative changes, and personnel issues. An observer took notes during all but 10 of the meetings; for research purposes, these 10 were analyzed "blind" from tapes (i.e., without ever meeting the executives). All other meetings were taped also, but analyzed at a later time.

The major device for analyzing the tapes was a new system of categories for scoring decision-making meetings.* Briefly, the executives' behav-

*For a detailed discussion of the system of categories and other aspects of methodology, see my book, *Organization and Innovation* (Homewood, Illinois, Richard D. Irwin, Inc., 1965).

ior was scored according to how often they—

...owned up to and accepted responsibility for their ideas or feelings;

...opened up to receive others' ideas or feelings;

...experimented and took risks with ideas or feelings;

...helped others to own up, be open, and take risks;

...did not own up; were not open; did not take risks; and did not help others in any of these activities.

A second scoring system was developed to produce a quantitative index of the *norms* of the executive culture. There were both positive and negative norms. The positive norms were:

1. *Individuality,* especially rewarding behavior that focused on and valued the uniqueness of each individual's ideas and feelings.
2. *Concern* for others' ideas and feelings.
3. *Trust* in others' ideas and feelings.

The negative norms were:

1. *Conformity* to others' ideas and feelings.
2. *Antagonism* toward these ideas and feelings.
3. *Mistrust* of these ideas and feelings.

In addition to our observations of the men at work, at least one semistructured interview was conducted with each executive. All of these interviews were likewise taped, and the typewritten protocols served as the basis for further analysis.

In short, the executives vote overwhelmingly for executive systems where the contributions of each executive can be maximized and where innovation, risk taking, flexibility, and trust reign supreme. Nevertheless, the *behavior* of these same executives tends to create decision-making processes that are *not* very effective. Their behavior can be fitted into two basic patterns:

Pattern A—Thoughtful, Rational, and Mildly Competitive. This is the behavior most frequently observed during the decision-making meetings. Executives following this pattern own up to their ideas in a style that emphasizes a serious concern for ideas. As they constantly battle for scarce resources and "sell" their views, their openness to others' ideas is relatively high, not because of a sincere interest in learning about the point of view of others, but so they can engage in a form of "one-upmanship"—that is, gain information about the others' points of view in order to politely discredit them.

Pattern B—Competitive First, Thoughtful and Rational Second. In this pattern, conformity to ideas replaces concern for ideas as the strongest norm. Also, antagonism to ideas is higher—in many cases higher than openness to ideas. The relatively high antagonism scores usually indicate, in addition to high competitiveness, a high degree of conflict and pent-up feelings.

Exhibit I summarizes data for four illustrative groups of managers—two groups with Pattern A characteristics and two with Pattern B characteristics.

Practical Consequences

In both patterns executives are rarely observed:

taking risks or experimenting with new ideas or feelings;

helping others to own up, be open, and take risks;

using a style of behavior that supports the norm of individuality and trust as well as mistrust;

expressing feelings, positive or negative.

These results should not be interpreted as implying that the executives do not have feelings. We know from the interviews that many of the executives have strong feelings indeed. However, the overwhelming majority (84%) feel that it is a sign of immaturity to express feelings openly *during decision-making meetings.* Nor should the results be interpreted to mean that the executives do not enjoy risk taking. The data permit us to conclude only that few risk-taking actions were *observed* during the meetings. (Also, we have to keep in mind that the executives were always observed in groups; it may be that their behavior in groups varies significantly from their behavior as individuals.)

Before I attempt to give my views about the reasons for the discrepancy between executives' words and actions, I should like to point out that these results are not unique to business organi-

---

EXHIBIT I. Management groups with Pattern A and Pattern B characteristics

	Pattern A				Pattern B			
Total Number of Units Analyzed *	Group 1 198		Group 2 143		Group 3 201		Group 4 131	
Units characterized by:	Number	Percent	Number	Percent	Number	Percent	Number	Percent
Owning up to own ideas and feelings	146	74	105	74	156	78	102	78
Concern for others' ideas and feelings	122	62	89	62	52	26	56	43
Conformity to others' ideas and feelings	54	27	38	26	87	43	62	47
Openness to others' ideas and feelings	46	23	34	24	31	15	25	19
Individuality	4	2	12	8	30	15	8	6
Antagonism to others' ideas and feelings	18	9	4	3	32	16	5	4
Unwillingness to help others own up to their ideas	5	2	3	2	14	7	4	3

* A unit is an instance of a manager speaking on a topic. If during the course of speaking he changes to a new topic, another unit is created.

zations. I have obtained similar behavior patterns from leaders in education, research, the ministry, trade unions, and government. Indeed, one of the fascinating questions for me is why so many different people in so many different kinds of organizations tend to manifest similar problems.

WHY THE DISCREPANCY?

The more I observe such problems in different organizations possessing different technologies and varying greatly in size, the more I become impressed with the importance of the role played by the values or assumptions top people hold on the nature of effective human relationships and the best ways to run an organization.

Basic Values

In the studies so far I have isolated three basic values that seem to be very important:

1. *The significant human relationships are the ones which have to do with achieving the organization's objective.* My studies of over 265 different types and sizes of meetings indicate that executives almost always tend to focus their behavior on "getting the job done." In literally thousands of units of behavior, almost none are observed where the men spend some time in analyzing and maintaining their group's effectiveness. This is true even though in many meetings the group's effectiveness "bogged down" and the objectives were not being reached because of interpersonal factors. When the executives are interviewed and asked why they did not spend some time in examining the group operations or processes, they reply that they were there to get a job done. They add: "If the group isn't effective, it is up to the leader to get it back on the track by directing it."

2. *Cognitive rationality is to be emphasized; feelings and emotions are to be played down.* This value influences executives to see cognitive, intellectual discussions as "relevant," "good," "work," and so on. Emotional and interpersonal discussions tend to be viewed as "irrelevant," "immature," "not work," and so on.

As a result, when emotions and interpersonal

variables become blocks to group effectiveness, all the executives report feeling that they should *not* deal with them. For example, in the event of an emotional disagreement, they would tell the members to "get back to facts" or "keep personalities out of this."

3. *Human relationships are most effectively influenced through unilateral direction, coercion, and control, as well as by rewards and penalties that sanction all three values.* This third value of direction and control is implicit in the chain of command and also in the elaborate managerial controls that have been developed within organizations.

Influence on Operations

The impact of these values can be considerable. For example, to the extent that individuals dedicate themselves to the value of intellectual rationality and "getting the job done," they will tend to be aware of and emphasize the intellectual aspects of issues in an organization and (consciously or unconsciously) to suppress the interpersonal and emotional aspects, especially those which do not seem relevant to achieving the task.

As the interpersonal and emotional aspects of behavior become suppressed, organizational norms that coerce individuals to hide their feelings or to disguise them and bring them up as technical, intellectual problems will tend to arise.

Under these conditions the individual may tend to find it very difficult to develop competence in dealing with feelings and interpersonal relationships. Also, in a world where the expression of feelings is not valued, individuals may build personal and organizational defenses to help them suppress their own feelings or inhibit others in such expression. Or they may refuse to consider ideas which, if explored, could expose suppressed feelings.

Such a defensive reaction in an organization could eventually inhibit creativity and innovation during decision making. The participants might learn to limit themselves to those ideas and values that were not threatening. They might also decrease their openness to new ideas and values. And as the degree of openness decreased, the capacity to experiment would also decrease, and fear of taking risks would increase. This would reduce the *probability* of experimentation, thus decreasing openness to new ideas still further and constricting risk taking even more than formerly. We would thereby have a closed circuit which could become an important cause of loss of vitality in an organization.

SOME CONSEQUENCES

Aside from the impact of values on vitality, what are some other consequences of the executive behavior patterns earlier described on top management decision making and on the effective functioning of the organization? For the sake of brevity, I shall include only examples of those consequences that were found to exist in one form or another in all organizations studied.

Restricted Commitment

One of the most frequent findings is that in major decisions that are introduced by the president, there tends to be less than open discussion of the issues, and the commitment of the officers tends to be less than complete (although they may assure the president to the contrary). For instance, consider what happened in one organization where a major administrative decision made during the period of the research was the establishment of several top management committees to explore basic long-range problems:

As is customary with major decisions, the president discussed it in advance at a meeting of the executive committee. He began the meeting by circulating, as a basis for discussion, a draft of the announcement of the committees. Most of the members' discussion was concerned with raising questions about the wording of the proposal:

- "Is the word *action* too strong?"
- "I recommend that we change 'steps can be taken' to 'recommendations can be made.' "
- "We'd better change the word 'lead' to 'maintain.' "

As the discussion seemed to come to an end, one executive said he was worried that the announcement of the committees might be interpreted by the people below as an implication "that the executive committee believes the organization is in trouble. Let's get the idea in that all is well."

There was spontaneous agreement by all executives: "Hear, hear!"

A brief silence was broken by another executive who apparently was not satisfied with the concept of the committees. He raised a series of questions. The manner in which it was done was interesting. As he raised each issue, he kept assuring the president and the group that he was not against the concept. He just wanted to be certain that the executive committee was clear on what it was doing. For example, he assured them:

- "I'm not clear. Just asking."
- "I'm trying to get a better picture."
- "I'm just trying to get clarification."
- "Just so that we understand what the words mean."

The president nodded in agreement, but he seemed to become slightly impatient. He remarked that many of these problems would not arise if the members of these new committees took an overall company point of view. An executive commented (laughingly), "Oh, I'm for motherhood too!"

The proposal was tabled in order for the written statement to be revised and discussed further during the next meeting. It appeared that the proposal was the president's personal "baby," and the executive committee members would naturally go along with it. The most responsibility some felt was that they should raise questions so the president would be clear about *his* (not *their*) decision.

At the next meeting the decision-making process was the same as at the first. The president circulated copies of the revised proposal. During this session a smaller number of executives asked questions. Two pushed (with appropriate care) the notion that the duties of one of the committees were defined too broadly.

The president began to defend his proposal by citing an extremely long list of examples, indicating that in his mind "reasonable" people should find the duties clear. This comment and the long list of examples may have communicated to others a feeling that the president was becoming impatient. When he finished, there was a lengthy silence. The president then turned to one of the executives and asked directly, "Why are you worried about this?" The executive explained, then quickly added that as far as he could see the differences were not major ones and his point of view could be integrated with the president's by "changing some words."

The president agreed to the changes, looked up, and asked, "I take it now there is common agreement?" All executives replied "yes" or nodded their heads affirmatively.

As I listened, I had begun to wonder about the commitment of the executive committee members to the idea. In subsequent interviews I asked each about his view of the proposal. Half felt that it was a good proposal. The other half had reservations ranging from moderate to serious. However, being loyal members, they would certainly do their best to make it work, they said.

Subordinate Gamesmanship

I can best illustrate the second consequence by citing from a study of the effectiveness of product planning and program review activities in another of the organizations studied:

It was company policy that peers at any given level should make the decisions. Whenever they could not agree or whenever a decision went beyond their authority, the problem was supposed to be sent to the next higher level. The buck passing stopped at the highest level. A meeting with the president became a great event. Beforehand a group would "dry run" its presentation until all were satisfied that they could present their view effectively.

Few difficulties were observed when the meeting was held to present a recommendation agreed to by all at the lower levels. The difficulties arose when "negative" information had to be fed upward. For example, a major error in the program, a major delay, or a major disagreement among the members was likely to cause such trouble.

The dynamics of these meetings was very interesting. In one case the problem to present was a major delay in a development project. In the dry run the subordinates planned to begin the session with information that "updated" the president. The information was usually presented in such a way that slowly and carefully the president was alerted to the fact that a major problem was about to be announced. One could hear such key phrases as:

- "We are a bit later than expected."
- "We're not on plan."
- "We have had greater difficulties than expected."
- "It is now clear that no one should have promised what we did."

These phrases were usually followed by some reassuring statement such as:

- "However, we're on top of this."
- "Things are really looking better now."
- "Although we are late, we have advanced the state of the art."
- "If you give us another three months, we are certain that we can solve this problem."

To the observer's eyes, it is difficult to see how the president could deny the request. Apparently he felt the same way because he granted it. However, he took nearly 20 minutes to say that this shocked him; he was wondering if everyone was *really* doing everything they could; this was a serious program; this was not the way he wanted to see things run; he was sure they would agree with him; and he wanted their assurances that this would be the final delay.

A careful listening to the tape after the meeting brought out the fact that no subordinate gave such assurances. They simply kept saying that they were doing their best; they had poured a lot into this; or they had the best technical know-how working on it.

Another interesting observation is that most subordinates in this company, especially in presentations to the president, tended to go along with certain unwritten rules:

1. Before you give any bad news, give good news. Especially emphasize the capacity of the department to work hard and to rebound from a failure.

2. Play down the impact of a failure by emphasizing how close you came to achieving the target or how soon the target can be reached. If neither seems reasonable, emphasize how difficult it is to define such targets, and point out that because the state of the art is so primitive, the original commitment was not a wise one.

3. In a meeting with the president it is unfair to take advantage of another department that is in trouble, even if it is a "natural enemy." The sporting thing to do is say something nice about the other department and offer to help it in any way possible. (The offer is usually not made in concrete form, nor does the department in difficulty respond with the famous phrase, "What do you have in mind?")

The subordinates also were in agreement that too much time was spent in long presentations in order to make the president happy. The president, however, confided to the researcher that he did not enjoy listening to long and, at times, dry presentations (especially when he had seen most of the key data anyway). However, he felt that it was important to go through this because it might give the subordinates a greater sense of commitment to the problem!

Lack of Awareness

One of our most common observations in company studies is that executives lack awareness of their own behavioral patterns as well as of the negative impact of their behavior on others. This is not to imply that they are completely unaware; each individual usually senses some aspects of a problem. However, we rarely find an individual or group of individuals who is aware of enough of the scope and depth of a problem so that the need for effective action can be fully understood.

For example, during the study of the decision-making processes of the president and the 9 vice presidents of a firm with nearly 3,000 employees, I concluded that the members unknowingly behaved in such a way as *not* to encourage risk taking, openness, expression of feelings, and cohesive, trusting relationships. But subsequent interviews with the 10 top executives showed that they held a completely different point of view from mine. They admitted that negative feelings were not expressed, but said the reason was that "we trust each other and respect each other." According to 6 of the men, individuality was high and conformity low; where conformity was agreed to be high, the reason given was the necessity of agreeing with the man who is boss. According to 8 of the men, "We help each other all the time." Issues loaded with conflict were not handled during meetings, it was reported, for these reasons:

• "We should not discuss emotional disagreements before the executive committee because when people are emotional, they are not rational."
• "We should not air our dirty linen in front of the people who may come in to make a presentation."
• "Why take up people's time with subjective debates?"
• "Most members are not acquainted with all the details. Under our system the person who presents the issues has really thought them through."

• "Pre-discussion of issues helps to prevent anyone from sandbagging the executive committee."
• "Rarely emotional; when it does happen, you can pardon it."

The executive committee climate or emotional tone was characterized by such words as:

• "Friendly."
• "Not critical of each other."
• "Not tense."
• "Frank and no tensions because we've known each other for years."

How was I to fit the executives' views with mine? I went back and listened to all the interviews again. As I analyzed the tapes, I began to realize that an interesting set of contradictions arose during many of the interviews. In the early stages of the interviews the executives tended to say things that they contradicted later; Exhibit II contains examples of contradictions repeated by 6 or more of the 10 top executives.

What accounts for these contradictions? My explanation is that over time the executives had come to mirror, in their behavior, the values of their culture (e.g., be rational, nonemotional, diplomatically open, and so on). They had created a culture that reinforced their own leadership styles. If an executive wanted to behave differently, he probably ran the risk of being considered a deviant. In most of the cases the executives decided to forgo this risk, and they behaved like the majority. These men, in order to live with themselves, probably had to develop various defenses and blinders about their acquiescence to an executive culture that may not have been the one they personally preferred and valued.

Incidentally, in this group there were two men who had decided to take the other route. Both men were viewed by the others as "a bit rough at the edges" or "a little too aggressive."

To check the validity of some of the findings reported, we interviewed the top 25 executives below the executive committee. If our analysis was correct, we knew, then they should tend to report that the members of the executive committee were low in openness to uncomfortable information, risk taking, trust, and capacity to deal with conflicts openly, and high in conformity. The results were as predicted (see Exhibit III).

EXHIBIT II. Contradictory statements.

During One Part Of the Interview an Executive Said:	Yet Later in the Same Interview He Said:
The relationship among the executive committee members is "close," "friendly," and based on years of working together.	I do not know how [my peers] feel about me. That's a tough question to answer.
The strength of this company lies in its top people. They are a dedicated, friendly group. We never have the kinds of disagreements and fights that I hear others do.	Yes, the more I think of it, the more I feel this is a major weakness of the company. Management is afraid to hold someone accountable, to say, "You said you would do it. What happened?"
I have an open relationship with my superior.	I have no direct idea how my superior evaluates my work and feels about me.
The group discussions are warm, friendly, not critical.	We trust each other not to upset one another.
We say pretty much what we think.	We are careful not to say anything that will antagonize anyone.
We respect and have faith in each other.	People do not knowingly upset each other, so they are careful in what they say.
The executive committee tackles all issues.	The executive committee tends to spend too much time talking about relatively unimportant issues.
The executive committee makes decisions quickly and effectively.	A big problem of the executive committee is that it takes forever and a day to make important decisions.
The members trust each other.	The members are careful not to say something that may make another member look bad. It may be misinterpreted.
The executive committee makes the major policy decisions.	On many major issues, decisions are really made outside the executive committee meetings. The executive committee convenes to approve a decision and have "holy water" placed on it.

Blind Spots

Another result found in all organizations studied is the tendency for executives to be unaware of the negative feelings that their subordinates have about them. This finding is not startling in view of the fact that the executive problem-solving processes do not tend to reward the upward communication of information about interpersonal issues that is emotionally laden and risky to communicate. To illustrate:

In one organization, all but one of the top executive committee members reported that their relationships with their subordinates were "relatively good to excellent." When asked how they judged their relationships, most of the executives responded with such statements as: "They do everything that I ask for willingly," and "We talk together frequently and openly."

The picture from the middle management men who were the immediate subordinates was different. Apparently, top management was unaware that:

EXHIBIT III. How the executive committee was rated by 25 executives below it.

Characteristic Rated	Number of Managers Rating the Committee as:		
	Low	Moderate	High
Openness to uncomfort-able information*	12	6	4
Risk taking	20	4	1
Trust	14	9	2
Conformity	0	2	23
Ability to deal with conflicts	19	6	0

* Three executives gave a "don't know" response.

71% of the middle managers did not know where they stood with their superiors; they considered their relationships as ambiguous, and they were not aware of such important facts as how they were being evaluated.

65% of the middle managers did not know what qualities led to success in their organizations.

87% felt that conflicts were very seldom coped with; and that when they were, the attempts tended to be inadequate.

65% thought that the most important unsolved problem of the organization was that the top management was unable to help them overcome the inter-group rivalries, lack of cooperation, and poor communications; 53% said that if they could alter one aspect of their superior's behavior, it would be to help him see the "dog eat dog" communication problems that existed in middle management.

59% evaluated top management effectiveness as not too good or about average; and 62% reported that the development of a cohesive management team was the second most important unsolved problem.

82% of the middle managers wished that the status of their function and job could be increased but doubted if they could communicate this openly to the top management.

Interestingly, in all the cases that I have observed where the president asked for a discussion of any problems that the top and middle management men present thought important, the problems mentioned above were never raised.

Rather, the most frequently mentioned problem (74% of the cases) was the overload problem. The executives and managers reported that they were overloaded and that the situation was getting

worse. The president's usual reply was that he appreciated their predicament, but "that is life." The few times he asked if the men had any suggestions, he received such replies as "more help," "fewer meetings," "fewer reports," "delay of schedules," and so on. As we will see, few of these suggestions made sense, since the men were asking either for increases in costs or for a decrease in the very controls that the top management used to administer the organization.

Distrust & Antagonism

Another result of the behavior patterns earlier described is that management tends to keep promotions semisecret and most of the actual reasons for executive changes completely secret. Here is an example from an organization whose board we studied in some detail over a period of two years:

The executives complained of three practices of the board about which the board members were apparently unaware: (1) the constant alteration of organizational positions and charts, and keeping the most up-to-date versions semiconfidential; (2) shifting top executives without adequate discussion with all executives involved and without clearly communicating the real reasons for the move; and (3) developing new departments with product goals that overlapped and competed with the goals of already existing departments.

The board members admitted these practices but tended not to see them as being incompatible with the interests of the organization. For example, to take the first complaint, they defended their practice with such statements as: "If you tell them everything, all they do is worry, and we get a flood of rumors"; "The changes do not *really* affect them"; and, "It will only cut in on their busy schedule and interrupt their productivity."

The void of clear-cut information from the board was, however, filled in by the executives. Their explanations ranged from such statements as "They must be changing things because they are not happy with the way things are going" to "The unhappiness is so strong they do not tell us." Even the executives who profited from some of these moves reported some concern and bewilderment. For example, three reported instances where they had been promoted over some "old-timers." In all cases they were told to "soft-pedal the promotion aspect" until the old-timers were diplomatically informed. Unfortunately, it took months to inform the latter men, and in some cases it was never done.

There was another practice of the board that produced difficulties in the organization:

Department heads cited the board's increasing intervention into the detailed administration of a department when its profit picture looked shaky. This practice was, from these subordinates' view, in violation of the stated philosophy of decentralization.

When asked, board members tended to explain this practice by saying that it was done only when they had doubts about the department head's competence, and then it was always in the interests of efficiency. When they were alerted about a department that was not doing well, they believed that the best reaction was to tighten controls, "take a closer and more frequent look," and "make sure the department head is on top of things." They quickly added that they did not tell the man in question they were beginning to doubt his competence for fear of upsetting him. Thus, again we see how the values of de-emphasizing the expression of negative feelings and the emphasizing of controls influenced the board's behavior.

The department heads, on the other hand, reported different reactions. "Why are they bothered with details? Don't they trust me? If not, why don't they say so?" Such reactions tended to produce more conformity, antagonism, mistrust, and fear of experimenting.

Still another board practice was the "diplomatic" rejection of an executive's idea that was, in the eyes of the board, offbeat, a bit too wild, or not in keeping with the corporate mission. The reasons given by the board for not being open about the evaluation again reflected adherence to the pyramidal values. For example, a board member would say, "We do not want to embarrass them," or "If you really tell them, you might restrict creativity."

This practice tended to have precisely the impact that the superiors wished to *avoid*. The subordinates reacted by asking, "Why don't they give me an opportunity to really explain it?" or "What do they mean when they suggest that the 'timing is not right' or 'funds are not currently available'?"

Processes Damaged

It is significant that defensive activities like those described are rarely observed during group meetings dealing with minor or relatively routine decisions. These activities become most noticeable when the decision is an important one in terms of

dollars or in terms of the impact on the various departments in the organization. *The forces toward ineffectiveness operate most strongly during the important decision-making meetings.* The group and organizational defenses operate most frequently when they can do the most harm to decision-making effectiveness.

Another interesting finding is that the more effective and more committed executives tend to be upset about these facts, whereas the less effective, less committed people tend simply to lament them. They also tend to take on an "I told them so" attitude—one of resignation and noninvolvement in correcting the situation. In short, it is the better executives who are negatively affected.

WHAT CAN BE DONE?

What can the executive do to change this situation?

I wish that I could answer this question as fully as I should like to. Unfortunately, I cannot. Nevertheless, there are some suggestions I can make.

Blind Alleys

First, let me state what I believe will *not* work.

Learning about these problems by listening to lectures, reading about them, or exploring them through cases is not adequate; an article or book can pose some issues and get thinking started, but—in this area, at least—it cannot change behavior. Thus, in one study with 60 top executives:

Lectures were given and cases discussed on this subject for nearly a week. A test at the end of the week showed that the executives rated the lecturers very high, liked the cases, and accepted the diagnoses. Yet when they attempted to apply their newfound knowledge outside the learning situation, most were unable to do so. The major problem was that they had not learned how to make these new ideas come to life in their behavior.

As one executive stated, pointing to his head: "I know up here what I should do, but when it comes to a real meeting, I behave in the same old way. It sure is frustrating." [1]

Learning about these problems through a detailed diagnosis of executives' behavior is also not enough. For example:

I studied a top management group for nearly four months through interviews and tape recordings of their decision-making meetings. Eventually, I fed back the analysis. The executives agreed with the diagnosis as well as with the statement by one executive that he found it depressing. Another executive, however, said he now felt that he had a clearer and more coherent picture of some of the causes of their problems, and he was going to change his behavior. I predicted that he would probably find that he would be unable to change his behavior—and even if he did change, his subordinates, peers, and superiors might resist dealing with him in the new way.

The executive asked, "How can you be so sure that we can't change?" I responded that I knew of no case where managers were able to alter successfully their behavior, their group dynamics, and so forth by simply realizing intellectually that such a change was necessary. The key to success was for them to be able to show these new strategies in their behavior. To my knowledge, behavior of this type, groups with these dynamics, and organizational cultures endowed with these characteristics were very difficult to change. What kind of thin-skinned individuals would they be, how brittle would their groups and their organizations be if they could be altered that easily?

Three of the executives decided that they were going to prove the prediction to be incorrect. They took my report and studied it carefully. In one case the executive asked his subordinates to do the same. Then they tried to alter their behavior. According to their own accounts, they were unable to do so. The only changes they reported were (1) a softening of the selling activities, (2) a reduction of their aggressive persuasion, and (3) a genuine increase in their asking for the subordinates' views.

My subsequent observations and interviews uncovered the fact that the first two changes were mistrusted by the subordinates, who had by now adapted to the old behavior of their superiors. They tended to play it carefully and to be guarded. This hesitation aggravated the executives, who felt that their subordinates were not responding to their new behavior with the enthusiasm that they (the superiors) had expected.

However, *the executives did not deal with this issue openly.* They kept working at trying to be rational, patient, and rewarding. The more irritated they became and the more they showed this irritation in their behavior, the more the subordinates felt that the superiors' "new" behavior was a gimmick.

Eventually, the process of influencing subordinates slowed down so much that the senior men returned to their more controlling styles. The irony was that in most cases the top executives interpreted the subordinates' behavior as proof that they needed to be needled and pushed, while the subordinates interpreted the top managers' behavior as proof that they did not trust their assistants and would never change.

The reason I doubt that these approaches will provide anything but temporary cures is that they do not go far enough. If changes are going to be made in the behavior of an executive, if trust is to be developed, if risk taking is to flourish, he must be placed in a different situation. He should be helped to (a) expose his leadership style so that he and others can take a look at its true impact; (b) deepen his awareness of himself and the dynamics of effective leadership; and (c) strive for these goals under conditions where he is in control of the amount, pace, and depth of learning.

These conditions for learning are difficult to achieve. Ideally, they require the help of a professional consultant. Also, it would be important to get away from the organization—its interruptions, pressures, and daily administrative tensions.

Value of Questions

The executive can strive to be aware that he is probably programmed with a set of values which cause him to behave in ways that are not always helpful to others and which his subordinates will not discuss frankly even when they believe he is not being helpful. He can also strive to find time to uncover, through careful questioning, his impact on others. Once in a while a session that is focused on the "How am I doing?" question can enlighten the executive and make his colleagues more flexible in dealing with him.

One simple question I have heard several presidents ask their vice presidents with success is: "Tell me what, if anything, I do that tends to prevent (or help) your being the kind of vice president you wish to be?" These presidents are careful to ask these questions during a time when they seem natural (e.g., performance review sessions), or they work hard ahead of time to create a climate so that such a discussion will not take the subordinate by surprise.

Some presidents feel uncomfortable in raising these questions, and others point out that the vice presidents are also uncomfortable. I can see how both would have such feelings. A chief executive officer may feel that he is showing weakness by asking his subordinates about his impact. The subordinate may or may not feel this way, but he may sense that his chief does, and that is enough to make him uncomfortable.

Yet in two companies I have studied where such questions were asked, superiors and subordinates soon learned that authority which gained strength by a lack of openness was weak and brittle, whereas authority resting on open feedback from below was truly strong and viable.

Working With the Group

Another step that an executive can take is to vow not to accept group ineffectiveness as part of life. Often I have heard people say, "Groups are no damned good; strong leadership is what is necessary." I agree that many groups are ineffective. I doubt, however, if either of the two leadership patterns described earlier will help the situation. As we have seen, both patterns tend to make the executive group increasingly less effective.

If my data are valid, the search process in executive decision making has become so complicated that group participation is essential. No one man seems to be able to have all the knowledge necessary to make an effective decision. If individual contributions are necessary in group meetings, it is important that a climate be created that does not discourage innovation, risk taking, and honest leveling between managers in their conversations with one another. The value of a group is to maximize individual contributions.

Interestingly, the chief executive officers in these studies are rarely observed making policy decisions in the classic sense, viz., critical selections from several alternatives and determination of future directions to be taken. This does not mean that they shy away from taking responsibility. Quite the contrary. Many report that they enjoy making decisions by themselves. Their big frustration comes from realizing that most of the major decisions they face are extremely complex and require the coordinated, honest inputs of many different executives. They are impatient at the slowness of meetings, the increasingly quantitative nature of the inputs, and, in many cases,

their ignorance of what the staff groups did to the decision inputs long before they received them.

The more management deals with complexity by the use of computers and quantitative approaches, the more it will be forced to work with inputs of many different people, and the more important will be the group dynamics of decision-making meetings. If anyone doubts this, let him observe the dry runs subordinates go through to get a presentation ready for the top. He will observe, I believe, that much data are included and excluded by subordinates on the basis of what they believe those at the top can hear.

In short, *one of the main tasks of the chief executive is to build and maintain an effective decision-making network.* I doubt that he has much choice *except* to spend time in exploring how well his group functions.

Such explorations could occur during the regular workday. For example:

In one organization the president began by periodically asking members of his top group, immediately after a decision was made, to think back during the meeting and describe when they felt that the group was not being as effective as they wished. How could these conditions be altered?

As trust and openness increased, the members began to level with each other as to when they were inhibited, irritated, suppressed, confused, and withholding information. The president tried to be as encouraging as he could, and he especially rewarded people who truly leveled. Soon the executives began to think of mechanisms they could build into their group functioning so they would be alerted to these group problems and correct them early. As one man said, "We have not eliminated all our problems, but we are building a competence in our group to deal with them effectively if and when they arise."

Utilizing Feedback

Another useful exercise is for the superior and his group members to tape-record a decision-making meeting, especially one which is expected to be difficult. At a later date, the group members can gather and listen to the tape. I believe it is safe to say that simply listening to the tape is an education in itself. If one can draw from skilled company or outside help, then useful analyses can be made of group or individual behavior.

Recently, I experimented with this procedure with an "inside" board of directors of a company. The directors met once a month and listened to tape recordings of their monthly board meetings. With my help they analyzed their behavior, trying to find how they could improve their individual and group effectiveness. Listening to tapes became a very involving experience for them. They spent nearly four hours in the first meeting discussing less than ten minutes of the tape.

"Binds" Created. One of the major gains of these sessions was that the board members became aware of the "binds" they were creating for each other and of the impact they each had on the group's functioning. Thus:

Executive A was frequently heard antagonizing Executive B by saying something that B perceived as "needling." For example, A might seem to be questioning B's competence. "Look here," he would say, "anyone who can do simple arithmetic should realize that. . . ."

Executive B responded by fighting. B's way of fighting back was to utilize his extremely high capacity to verbalize and intellectualize. B's favorite tactic was to show A where he missed five important points and where his logic was faulty.

Executive A became increasingly upset as the "barrage of logic" found its mark. He tended to counteract by (a) remaining silent but manifesting a sense of being flustered and becoming red-faced; and/or (b) insisting that his logic *was* sound even though he did not express it in "highfalutin language" as did B.

Executive B pushed harder (presumably to make A admit he was wrong) by continuing his "barrage of logic" or implying that A could not see his errors because he was upset.

Executive A would respond to this by insisting that he was not upset. "The point you are making is so simple, why, anyone can see it. Why should I be upset?"

Executive B responded by pushing harder and doing more intellectualizing. When Executive A eventually reached his breaking point, he too began to shout and fight.

At this point, Executives C, D, and E could be observed withdrawing until A and B wore each other out.

Progress Achieved. As a result of the meetings, the executives reported in interviews, board members experienced fewer binds, less hostility, less

frustration, and more constructive work. One member wondered if the group had lost some of its "zip," but the others disagreed. Here is an excerpt from the transcript of one discussion on this point:

Executive A: My feeling is, as I have said, that we have just opened this thing up, and I for one feel that we have benefited a great deal from it. I think I have improved; maybe I am merely reflecting the fact that you [Executive B] have improved. But at least I think there has been improvement in our relationship. I also see signs of not as good a relationship in other places as there might be.

I think on the whole we are much better off today than we were a year ago. I think there is a whole lot less friction today than there was a year ago, but there's still enough of it.

Now we have a much clearer organization setup; if we were to sit down here and name the people, we would probably all name exactly the same people. I don't think there is much question about who should be included and who should not be included; we've got a pretty clean organization.

Executive B: You're talking now about asking the consultant about going on with this week's session?

Executive A: It would be very nice to have the consultant if he can do it; then we should see how we can do it without him, but it'd be better with him.

Executive B: But that's the step, as I understand it, that should be taken at this stage. Is that right?

Executive A: Well, I would certainly favor doing something; I don't know what. I'm not making a specific recommendation; I just don't like to let go of it.

Executive C: What do you think?

Executive D: I'm not as optimistic as A. I wonder if anybody here agrees with me that maybe we haven't made as much progress as we think. I've personally enjoyed these experiences, and I'd like to see them continued.

Executive A: Would you like to venture to say why I think we have made progress and why I might be fooled?

Executive D: Well, I think maybe you are in the worst position to evaluate progress because if the worst possible thing that can happen is for people to no longer fight and struggle, but to say, "yes, sir," you might call that progress. That might be the worst thing that could happen, and I sort of sense some degree of resignation—I don't think it's progress. I don't know. I might be all alone in this. What do you think?

Executive C: On one level it is progress. Whether it is institutional progress and whether it produces commensurate institutional benefits is a debatable question. It may in fact do so. I think it's very clear that there is in our meetings and in individual contact less heat, less overt friction, petulance, tension, than certainly was consistently the case. Do you agree?

Executive D: Yes, I think so.

Executive C: It has made us a great deal more aware of the extent and nature of the friction and clearly has made all of us intent on fighting less. There's some benefit to it; but there are some drawbacks.

Executive A: Well, if you and D are right, I would say for that reason we need more of the program.

Laboratory Training

Another possibility is for the executive to attend a program designed to help increase competence in this area, such as laboratory education and its various offshoots ("T-groups," the "managerial grid," "conflict management labs," and so on[2]). These learning experiences are available at various university and National Training Laboratory executive programs. They can also be tailor-made for the individual organization.

I believe outside programs offer the better way of becoming acquainted with this type of learning. Bear in mind, though, that since typically only one or two executives attend from the same organization, the biggest payoff is for the individual. The inside program provides greater possibilities for payoff to the organization.

At the same time, however, it should also be kept in mind that in-house programs *can* be dangerous to the organization. I would recommend that a thorough study be made ahead of time to ascertain whether or not a laboratory educational experience would be helpful to company executives individually and to the organization.

Open Discussion

I have never observed a group whose members wanted it to decay. I have never studied a group or an organization that was decaying where there were not some members who were aware that decay was occurring. Accordingly, one key to group and organizational effectiveness is to get this knowledge out into the open and to discuss it thoroughly. The human "motors" of the group and the organization have to be checked periodically, just as does the motor of an automobile. Without proper maintenance, all will fail.

NOTES

1. See my article, "Explorations in Interpersonal Competence II," *Applied Behavioral Science,* Vol. 1, No. 3, 1965, p. 255.

2. For detailed discussions of such variations see my article, "T-Groups for Organizational Effectiveness," HBR March–April 1964, p. 60; R. R. Blake, J. S. Mouton, L. B. Barnes, and L. E. Greiner, "Breakthrough in Organization Development," HBR November–December 1964, p. 135; and Edgar Schein and Warren Bennis, *Personal and Organizational Change Through Laboratory Methods* (New York, John Wiley & Sons, 1965).

GROUP DIMENSIONS
OF BEHAVIOR

Having examined individual dimensions of behavior in Chapter 1 we are now ready to direct attention to the second major element of the integrative model—the group. In this chapter we examine the major role of group behavior in determining the overall effectiveness of the total organization. A group may be defined as two or more people who interact with one another, are aware of one another, and work toward a common goal. The terms interaction, awareness, and common goal are the key ingredients to understanding group behavior. Articles in this chapter are grouped under two major headings: the nature of groups, and potential problems with groups.

We begin with Dorwin Cartwright's article, "The Nature of Group Cohesiveness." In this article Cartwright maintains that a person's attraction to a particular group is determined by four sets of interacting variables: the individual's motive base for attraction, the incentive properties of the group, the individual's expectancy that membership will be beneficial or detrimental, and the quality of the outcomes the individual believes he or she deserves.

Alan Filley in his article, "Committee Management: Guidelines from Social Science Research," holds that committee effectiveness can be improved by the application of social science research findings. Filley addresses such questions as what functions do committees serve, what size should committees be, and what is the appropriate style of leadership for committee chairmen?

Next some potential problems with groups are discussed. Richard Huseman and Russ Driver in their piece, "Groupthink: Implications for Small-Group Decision Making in Business," examine the phenomenon of "groupthink." The term groupthink describes decisions reached by groups of rational, knowledgeable and experienced individuals—decisions which turn out to be irrational and poorly formulated.

In his article, "Eliminating Intergroup Conflict," Michael Brooker suggests that many organizational conflicts can be reduced through interdepartmental problem solving. In brief, the four articles in this chapter attempt to provide insight into group processes and point out some potential problem areas, as well as provide suggestions for more effective functioning of small groups in the organization.

THE NATURE OF
GROUP COHESIVENESS

DORWIN CARTWRIGHT

The term group cohesiveness has come to have a central place in theories of group dynamics. Although different theorists attribute somewhat different conceptual properties to the term, most agree that group cohesiveness refers to the degree to which the members of a group desire to remain in the group. Thus, the members of a highly cohesive group, in contrast to one with a low level of cohesiveness, are more concerned with their membership and are therefore more strongly motivated to contribute to the group's welfare, to advance its objectives, and to participate in its activities. Cohesiveness contributes to a group's potency and vitality; it increases the significance of membership for those who belong to the group.

Group cohesiveness has been investigated from two points of view—as a dependent variable and as an independent variable. Studies of the first type have undertaken to ascertain the conditions that bring about various levels of cohesiveness, whereas those of the second type have investigated the effects of different levels of cohesiveness upon the group and its members. These two lines of investigation taken together have contributed significantly to our understanding of this basic

"The Nature of Group Cohesiveness" (pp. 91–109) from *Group Dynamics: Research and Theory,* 3rd Edition by Dorwin Cartwright and Alvin Zander. Copyright © 1969 by Dorwin Cartwright and Alvin Zander. By permission of Harper & Row, Publishers, Inc.

aspect of group life, but a theoretical integration of the total body of findings has yet to be achieved.

In this chapter we draw upon this research in an attempt to construct a general formulation of the nature of group cohesiveness, its determinants, and its consequences. Our approach may be described with the help of Figure 1, the details of which will become evident throughout the course of the chapter. We employ the definition advanced by Festinger, who states that group cohesiveness is "the resultant of all forces acting on members to remain in the group." These forces are determined jointly by certain properties of the group and by certain characteristics of the members which, in conjunction, can be conceived as the immediate determinants of cohesiveness. These forces, in turn, have various effects that constitute the consequences of group cohesiveness. Thus, if a study shows that there is a positive correlation between the degree of interpersonal liking among the members of a group and the strength of group norms, we attempt to account for this relationship by showing how interpersonal liking creates forces on members to remain in the group and how these forces contribute to the power of a group over its members.

The resultant force acting on a member to remain in a group has at least two types of components: (*a*) forces that derive fom the group's attractiveness and (*b*) forces whose source is the

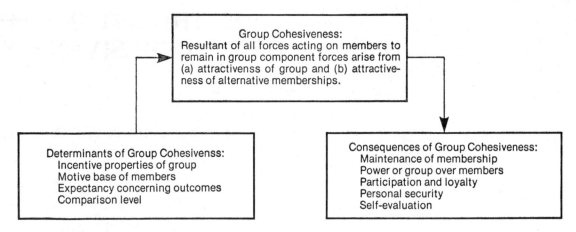

FIGURE 1. A scheme for analyzing group cohesiveness.

attractiveness of alternative memberships.[1] Most investigators have equated the term cohesiveness with "attraction to group," focusing mainly upon the first component of the resultant force acting on members to remain in the group. As a result, the literature on group cohesiveness contains, for the most part, investigations of attraction to, or satisfaction with, group membership. As might be expected in the early stages of research, a great variety of devices have been used to measure attraction and satisfaction. Therefore, before considering further the nature of group cohesiveness, we will review briefly the measuring devices more commonly employed. This should serve also to convey an impression of the meaning of the term group cohesiveness as actually used in research.

APPROACHES TO MEASURING GROUP COHESIVENESS

Five major approaches to the problem of measuring group cohesiveness have established a claim for serious consideration. Each is plausibly related to the definition of cohesiveness, and each has produced meaningful relations between its type of measurement and other properties of groups that might be expected to be associated with cohesiveness.

Interpersonal Attraction Among Members

On the assumption that a group will be more attractive the more its members like one another,

some investigators have constructed indexes designed to measure the extent of interpersonal attraction among members. Thus, for example, Dimock (3, 118) compared the cohesiveness of adolescent clubs by means of a "friendship index," which is the ratio of the number of selections made within a club, when each member is asked to name his ten best friends, to the number that could possibly have been chosen within the club.

A rather similar sociometric index was employed by Festinger, Schachter, and Back in a study of informal groups in a housing project. These investigators asked the residents of each court to name their friends who lived in the entire community and then calculated the proportion that "in-own-court" choices were out of the total number of friends mentioned. They obtained a rank order correlation, across courts, of −.53 between this index and the percentage of the court's residents who deviated from its norms concerning attitudes and behavior. If it is assumed that cohesiveness provides a group with power to influence its members, this correlation suggests that the index is a reasonably good measure of cohesiveness.

It should be noted, however, that this index makes use of the "density" of choices within a group and ignores their patterning. But one might expect different configurations of the same number of choices to result in quite different degrees of group cohesiveness. Thus, for example, mutual choices may reflect attraction to a dyad that contributes little, if at all, to the cohesiveness of the entire group. To explore this possibility, Festinger, Schachter, and Back adjusted their index by counting only half of the reciprocated "in-own-court" choices. With this rather arbitrary adjustment, the correlation with the percentage of deviates in each court changed from −.53 to −.74. This result suggests that measures of cohesiveness based on interpersonal bonds might be improved by a more refined structural analysis.

A slightly different way of assessing interpersonal attraction was employed by Bovard (2) in a study comparing two styles of college teaching, labeled "group centered" and "leader centered." After forty-two hours' experience with a particular style of teaching, each student rated every other student in his class on an eleven-point scale of degree of liking. It was found that those in the group-centered class gave a higher average rating of fellow students than did those in the leader-centered class. Bovard also conducted an experiment designed to measure pressures to uniformity in each class and found that members of the group-centered class were more ready to alter their cognitions in the direction of a common norm.

These results and those of Festinger, Schachter, and Back support the view that cohesiveness gives a group power to influence its members, but they do not provide a basis for determining which method of measuring cohesiveness is superior. For a more detailed discussion of the problems of measuring cohesiveness in terms of interpersonal attraction, the reader is referred to a critical review of the literature by Lott and Lott (22).

Evaluation of a Group as a Whole

A second approach to measuring cohesiveness focuses upon the group as an entity rather than interpersonal relations and develops indexes from members' evaluations of the group. Bovard employed this approach, in addition to the one described above, when he asked each student to rate his liking for the class as a whole. As before, he obtained a higher average rating for the group-centered class than for the leader-centered one,

but the mean rating was more favorable when the object evaluated was the class as a whole than when it was another member. Moreover, the difference between the two types of rating was greater for the group-centered class.

Two different scales to measure each person's attraction to his work group were employed by Jackson (17) in an investigation conducted among staff members of a child welfare agency. One was based upon questions about the amount of benefit the respondent felt he was receiving from membership in the group, and the other was derived from questions about his attraction to the people in the group. The two scales were found to correlate .61 and to relate to other variables in a similar, though not identical, way. This study, along with that of Bovard, suggests that evaluations of group members and of the group as a whole tend to go together but that they are not precisely the same. Systematic research has yet to be done to discover the conditions affecting the association between these two types of evaluation.

The possibility that members of a group may be able to perceive its cohesiveness and to communicate this to others is suggested by research conducted by Mann and Baumgartel (23), who asked employees of a public utility whether or not they endorsed the statement, "Our crew is better than others at sticking together." Among white-collar workers, 62 percent of those with a low rate of absence endorsed the statement, whereas only 21 percent of those with a high rate did so. This result suggests the value of further exploration of the use of group members as informants about the cohesiveness of their groups.

Closeness or Identification with a Group

Questions designed to reveal how strongly members identify with a group or feel personally involved in it have been used by some researchers to measure group cohesiveness. Converse and Campbell report findings illustrative of this approach from a study of the 1956 presidential election. They wished to test the hypothesis that large groups in society, such as Catholics, Jews, Negroes, and trade-union members, display more distinctive voting patterns the more their members identify with them. Toward this end they constructed a scale of member identification based on responses to the following questions: (*a*) Would you say you feel pretty close to (for example, Negroes) in general or that you don't feel much closer to them than you do to other kinds of people? (*b*) How much interest would you say you have in how (for example, Negroes) as a whole are getting along in this country? If it is assumed that this scale measures group cohesiveness and that the distinctiveness of a group's voting pattern arises from the group's ability to influence its members, the results of this study lend additional support to the hypothesis that cohesiveness gives a group power to influence its members.

The question, "How strong a 'sense of belonging' do you feel you have to the people you work with?" was used to construct an index of the cohesiveness of work groups in a study reported by Indik (16). This index correlated $+.41$ with a measure of ease of communication within the group and $-.30$ with the group's absence rate. An eight-item scale of personal involvement in a group was administered to groups of college students by Sagi, Olmstead, and Atelsek (36), who found that those students who voluntarily dropped their group membership over a period of six months had significantly lower values on this scale than those who remained members of the group.

The pattern of findings from studies such as these indicates that measurements of personal involvement, interest, identification, and sense of belonging tap at least one important component of group cohesiveness.

Expressed Desire to Remain in a Group

A fourth approach makes direct use of our conceptual definition of group cohesiveness in that it asks members to indicate the strength of their desire to remain in the group. The following questions, used by Schachter to test the success of experimental manipulations intended to create different degrees of cohesiveness, have been employed also by many other investigators: (*a*) Do you want to remain a member of this group? (*b*) How often do you think this group should meet?

(*c*) If enough members decide not to stay, so that it seems this group might discontinue, would you like the chance to persuade others to stay? Schachter found, as have most others, that an index constructed from these questions distinguishes between groups that on other grounds are presumed to differ in cohesiveness.

Reasoning that members might not always respond candidly to such direct questions, Libo (21) developed a picture-projective test. Libo reasoned that the immediate social environment of an individual influences his feelings and that these, in turn, will be reflected in stories written about the pictures when the test is administered in a meeting of a group. He found that the test distinguishes rather well between subjects who, when subsequently left free to choose, remain in the group and those who leave. The test also correlates highly with the measure of cohesiveness based on Schachter's three direct questions.

Composite Indexes

Research employing the four approaches just described has generated a variety of devices for measuring cohesiveness. Each, taken alone, has been shown to relate to other phenomena in a manner generally consistent with expectations derived from theoretical conceptions of the nature of group cohesiveness. The recognition that cohesiveness may have diverse manifestations has led some investigators to construct composite indexes.

One such index was developed by Seashore (39) from a questionnaire administered to the employees of a large manufacturing firm. Each person was asked the following questions about his work group: (*a*) Do you feel that you are really a part of your work group? (*b*) If you had the chance to do the same kind of work for the same pay in another work group how would you feel about moving? (*c*) How does your work group compare with other work groups at (name of company) on each of the following points? The way the men get along together. The way the men stick together. The way the men help each other on the job. Seashore computed intercorrelations among the answers and found them all to be positively correlated, with values ranging from .15 to .70. He then constructed a single index of cohesiveness which related meaningfully to several indicators of phenomena assumed to be consequences of cohesiveness.

A rather different composite index, based on seven questions concerning feelings of devotion to one's group, was constructed by Scott (38) in a longitudinal study of ten college fraternities and sororities. He found that those who left the organizations during the course of a year had significantly lower mean scores at the beginning of the year than did those who remained. Moreover, pledges as a group scored higher than actives, and younger actives scored higher than seniors, presumably indicating a progressive disenchantment with these organizations. It is important to note, however, that Scott found virtually no correlation between this index of group attraction and the average interpersonal attraction among members. Scott interprets this result to mean that for these organizations group attraction was not based in any significant degree upon interpersonal liking.

A study by Hagstrom and Selvin (12) casts further light upon the problem of constructing composite indexes of group cohesiveness. These investigators gave questionnaires to female college students living in twenty sororities, dormitories, boarding houses, and co-ops. Nineteen items, thought to be relevant to group cohesiveness, were used to construct aggregative measures for each living unit. Intercorrelations among these items across groups were almost entirely positive and rather high. A factor analysis revealed two factors that together account for most of the variation in scores. On the basis of the loadings, the two factors were labeled "social satisfaction" and "sociometric cohesion." Hagstrom and Selvin believe that the first factor measures the instrumental attractiveness of groups—the degree to which they provide opportunities for making friends, having dates, and participating in social life. The second factor, they feel, measures intrinsic attractiveness—the degree to which members are attracted to close personal association with others in the group. They conclude from observations and other measurements on these groups that different combinations of these two types of attrac-

tiveness produce important differences in the nature of group functioning.

The studies reported thus far reveal a general tendency for various indicators to be positively correlated, at least across broad ranges of items. Unfortunately, the research literature is not univocal in this regard. Gross and Martin (11), in an investigation of thirteen residential units for female students, found no substantial positive correlation among three different indicators of cohesiveness. And in a study of eleven student groups, Eisman (6) obtained no significant positive correlations among five different measures. Moreover, a replication of the Eisman study on Dutch female students, conducted by Ramuz-Nienhuis and Van Bergen (31), produced rather similar results.

It is difficult to know how best to interpret these conflicting findings. The bulk of the evidence strongly supports the view that each approach has produced indicators tapping something appropriately identified as group cohesiveness. Moreover, cohesiveness, as measured in these various ways, is meaningfully related to other features of groups. Measuring instruments, when appropriately tailored to fit particular situations, do yield significant results. On the other hand, it is clear that the correlations among various indicators are not consistent across all groups and situations. A standard all-purpose procedure for measuring group cohesiveness does not yet exist. This state of affairs, though disconcerting, is not really unexpected, for the development of measuring instruments cannot proceed much in advance of a basic understanding of the nature of the phenomena to be measured. Theory and measurement must advance together. Toward this end, we next examine more closely the nature of the determinants of attraction to a group.

DETERMINANTS OF ATTRACTION TO A GROUP

What determines how much a person will be attracted to a particular group? We propose that, in most general terms, attraction to group for a given individual will depend upon his assessment of the desirable and undesirable consequences attendant upon membership in the group. Simon,

Smithburg, and Thompson (42) adopt this general view in their theory of organizational survival, one of whose postulates is stated as follows: "Each participant will continue his participation in an organization only so long as the inducements offered him are as great or greater (measured in terms of *his* values and in terms of the alternatives open to him) than the contribution he is asked to make." In a similar way, Thibaut and Kelley (45) analyze attraction to group in terms of the rewards and costs to an individual that are entailed by group membership. Apart from other considerations, an individual will be more attracted to a group the more favorable to him are the outcomes he expects to derive from membership.

Implicit in formulations such as these is the assumption that a person's attraction to a group is determined not simply by the characteristics of the group but also by his view of how these characteristics relate to his needs and values. Thus, for example, a group engaged in a contest with other groups might yield rewards to a self-confident individual with a strong achievement orientation but costs to a timid person with a high fear of failure. A person's actual attraction to the group may be expected to depend upon the magnitude of the rewards or costs afforded by the group but also upon his assessment of the likelihood that he will in fact experience them as a result of membership. Attraction to group depends, then, upon the expected value of the outcomes linked to membership.

One additional determinant of attraction to a group has been emphasized by Thibaut and Kelley (45). They assert that in evaluating the expected outcomes of group membership a person employs a standard, called the comparison level, against which he compares the expected outcomes of membership. This comparison level derives from his previous experience in groups and indicates the level of outcomes he aspires to receive from membership. He will be more attracted to the group the more the level of expected outcomes exceeds his comparison level.

We propose, then, that a person's attraction to a group is determined by four interacting sets of variables: (*a*) his *motive base for attraction,* consisting of his needs for affiliation, recognition, se-

curity, money, or other values that can be mediated by groups; (*b*) the *incentive properties of the group,* consisting of its goals, programs, characteristics of its members, style of operation, prestige, or other properties of significance for his motive base; (*c*) his *expectancy,* the subjective probability, that membership will actually have beneficial or detrimental consequences for him; and (*d*) his *comparison level*—his conception of the level of outcomes that group membership should provide.

With the help of such a formulation several interesting derivations become possible. If, for example, a person joins a group with the expectation of fulfilling certain personal needs but these change while he is a member, the attractiveness of the group will decrease for him unless the group is able to fulfill the new needs equally well or better. It is possible, of course, for an individual's needs to be modified through experience in the group. Indeed, some groups deliberately attempt to change the needs of their members. Sometimes such groups "lure" members into joining, by promising certain inducements, and then work on the member to develop other needs and interests that are considered more important to the group. Just how these conversions of motivation take place, though, is far from clearly understood.

Broad social conditions may modify the needs of large segments of the population more-or-less simultaneously. When such changes take place, we should expect the attractiveness of certain types of groups to be affected accordingly. Thus, it has been suggested that the postwar increase in church membership and attendance resulted from popular anxieties and insecurities brought about by the advent of the atomic age.

In an ingenious program of research, Schachter (37) studied the effects of experimentally induced states of anxiety on the desire to be with other people, which he calls "affiliative tendencies." His results show clearly that a state of anxiety leads to the arousal of affiliative tendencies. In attempting to account for the results of this research, Schachter concludes (37, 132):

It appears theoretically rewarding to formulate this body of findings as a manifestation of needs for anxiety reduction and of needs for self-evaluation; that is, ambiguous situations or feelings lead to a desire to be with others as a means of socially evaluating and determining the "appropriate" and proper reaction.

It would be expected, then, that when the members of a group encounter threatening or ambiguous situations, their attraction to the group will increase unless, perhaps, they believe the group itself to be the source of their disturbance.

Over the course of time the properties of a group may change so as to alter its incentive properties for its members. Thus, for example, a social club may become active in local politics and thereby become less satisfying to those members previously attracted by its friendly social activities. A group riven by a conflict for leadership may become more attractive when one of the contenders withdraws from the group. And a student organization primarily devoted to opposing some policy of the school's administration, if successful in effecting a change, may suddenly lose its attractiveness for those members with a dominant need to rebel against authority.

Even if the incentive properties of a group and the motive bases of its members remain unchanged, the group's attractiveness may be expected to vary with a member's subjective probability that he will actually experience rewards or costs from membership. Consider, for example, an individual who joins a group because he places high value on its purposes—perhaps on such goals as combatting prejudice, getting out the vote, or improving local business practices. If he comes to believe that the chances of achieving this end are slight—perhaps because of inefficiency in the group, poor leadership, friction, lack of money, or any of a number of reasons—he will become less attracted to the group.

The subjective probability of need satisfaction was demonstrated by Ross and Zander (35) to affect the desire of employees to remain in a business organization. These investigators measured the strength of members' needs for autonomy, recognition, fair evaluations, and the like, and obtained the workers' estimates of the probability that these needs would be satisfied by continued employment in the company. After a reasonable number of these employees had resigned, the scores of those who had left were compared with the scores of matched persons who had remained. The strength of the needs was found to be essentially the same for those who resigned and for the continuing workers, but those who stayed in the company had reported a greater likelihood that their needs would be fulfilled than had those who departed.

From the assumption that a person employs his own comparison level in evaluating the expected outcomes of group membership, it follows that determinants of the comparison level are also determinants of the attractiveness of a group. In their discussion of the nature of the comparison level, Thibaut and Kelley (45, 80–99) suggest a variety of such determinants. It will be possible here only to describe their general approach and to indicate some of the ways in which an individual's comparison level affects his attraction to a group.

According to Thibaut and Kelley, a person's comparison level is "some modal or average value of all the outcomes known to him (by virtue of personal or vicarious experience), each outcome weighted by its salience." Thus, if we hold salience constant, a person who has experienced superior outcomes in other groups will have a higher comparison level in the present group than will a person who has experienced generally inferior outcomes. And, the greater number of satisfying memberships a person has, the more he will demand from membership in any particular group.

In support of this conception, Thibaut and Kelley cite data from studies of the American soldier in World War II, reported by Stouffer *et al.* (43). Thus, for example, better-educated soldiers were found to be less satisfied with their status and opportunities for promotion than were less-educated soldiers. Presumably, each soldier was comparing the outcomes to him from army life with those previously enjoyed as a civilian. Noncombat soldiers in rear areas overseas were found, also, to be more satisfied with army life than were noncombat troops in the United States. This surprising finding can be explained if we assume that the salient comparison for the overseas troops was the life of the combat soldier, whereas for those in the United States it was that of the civilian population.

It should be noted that the ability of a group

to meet the desires of an individual may not be totally dependent upon occurrences within the group itself. Group membership may provide access to certain gratifications obtainable outside the group that are not available to the nonmember. Thus, Hagstrom and Selvin (12) found college girls to be attracted to certain social groups because membership made it easier for them to have dates and to engage in campus activities. Similarly, Rose (34) states that the major benefit members say they derive from belonging to a large union local is that it obtains higher wages and job security for them. It should be noted, however, that membership in a group may also have negative effects by limiting the satisfactions a person can receive from activities outside it. A telephone operator on a night shift, for example, cannot participate in normal family life or be available for dates with friends. The extent to which a job interferes with family or community activities may be as important in reducing attraction to the organization as lack of satisfaction on the job (35).

The ways in which changes in an environment may determine the ability of voluntary organizations to meet members' needs have been vividly. described by Eisenstadt (5) in a study in Israel immediately after it became a nation. While the country had been a British mandate, most organizations had had certain typical characteristics: they were closely related to various social movements or political parties; they performed functions of vital importance within the community such as guard duty, defense, medical aid, social welfare, education, and agriculture; they were connected with the social and political centers of the government; and they conceived of themselves as realizing the ideal of national rebirth. Thus, most of the groups enabled their members to participate in the civic life of the country and to feel that they were contributing to its development. Moreover, through participation in these groups the members received recognition and prestige in the community. When Israel became a nation there was rapid centralization of power and services in the hands of the government and an accompanying increase in the value placed upon power. As a result of these changes, voluntary associations lost their former usefulness, and members' interest in active political and social life dwindled. Instead of being concerned with social action, voluntary associations in the new nation became pressure groups, philanthropic societies, and social clubs, all having little connection with the government. The new voluntary groups provided little fulfillment of needs for action and achievement and primarily helped members to understand social or political problems, to promote points of view, and to encourage sociability.

INCENTIVE PROPERTIES OF GROUPS

In our formulation of the determinants of attraction to groups it is assumed that certain properties of a group have potential motivational significance for the people who come in contact with it. But a given property of a group will have incentive value for a particular person only if it is appropriate to his motive base. Thus, if we ask what properties of a group will affect its attractiveness, we must refer, at least implicitly, to the motivational characteristics of the people involved. Unfortunately, these characteristics have not been studied systematically in research on the incentive properties of groups. Great care must be exercised, therefore, in generalizing the results obtained from any particular collection of people. With this caution in mind, we turn now to a summary of findings concerning the properties of groups that influence their attractiveness.

Attractiveness of Members

As noted in our discussion of the problem of measuring group cohesiveness, many investigators have assumed that an individual will be more attracted to membership in a group the more he likes its members. The evidence in support of this assumption is sufficiently convincing to lead Lott and Lott (22) to define cohesiveness as "that group property which is inferred from the number and strength of mutual positive attitudes among the members of a group." But since measures of interpersonal attraction do not always correlate significantly with other indicators of the attraction to group, we prefer to view the attractiveness of members as only one of several possible sources of attraction to group membership. Thus, for example, a man may maintain his membership in a golf club primarily because it affords the best available opportunity to play golf while he may have neutral or even negative feelings about most of the habitués of the place.

A clear specification of the conditions under which interpersonal attraction does have incentive value for group membership is yet to be achieved. It appears, however, that if group membership puts a person in close association and frequent interaction with other members, his evaluation of these members will influence his attraction to membership in the group. Evidence for this proposition is provided by Festinger and Kelley (8) from a study of a housing project in which the residents perceived one another as "low class." In this small community it was extremely difficult to develop a tenants' organization, even with the aid of professional community organizers, since participation in its programs forced people to associate with others they regarded as undesirable.

If conditions are such that the members of a group do engage in frequent interaction, this interaction may affect their evaluations of one another and hence of group membership itself. Homans (15, 112) has proposed the following general hypothesis: "If the frequency of interaction between two or more persons increases, the degree of their liking for one another will increase, and vice versa." Thus, one might expect the attractiveness of a group to increase if the group initiates programs requiring interaction among members, and there is considerable evidence in support of this expectation. It appears, however, from data obtained by Festinger and Kelley that if people who dislike one another are induced to engage in interaction, the result may be an intensification of their antipathies. Further research is clearly required to elucidate the relation between interpersonal attraction and attraction to group membership.

Similarities Among Members

The theory of cognitive balance advanced by Heider (13) and elaborated by Newcomb (26, 27) holds that two people will be more attracted to each other the more similar their evaluations of objects in their common environment. A great deal of evidence in support of this assertion has been accumulated. Thus, for example, Newcomb obtained a wide variety of attitude measurements on a group of college students who were later to live together in a small dormitory. He found that over the course of several weeks high interpersonal attractions tended to develop among those who initially agreed most in their attitudes. He also found a striking correlation between initial similarity in values, as measured by the Allport-Vernon Study of Values, and interpersonal attraction after fourteen weeks of interaction. Results like these suggest that attraction to a group will increase with increasing similarity among members.

A somewhat different line of reasoning leads to the same conclusion. Festinger (7) argues that each individual has a need to evaluate his opinions and abilities, that in making such a self-evaluation he tends to compare himself with others, and that given a range of possible persons for comparison he will tend to choose someone similar to himself. Thus a person will be more attracted to situations in which others are similar to him with respect to abilities and opinions than to ones in which others are divergent. Festinger cites a variety of studies that support this prediction, and additional confirmation has been provided by an experiment conducted by Zander and Havelin (47).

Research has made it clear, however, that similarity does not always generate attraction. Thus, in a study of industrial work groups Seashore (39) found no relation between a group's cohesiveness and its homogeneity with respect to the educational level or age of members. The degree of similarity regarding matters that are irrelevant to the group's functioning appears to have little consequence for interpersonal liking. There is evidence, moreover, that sometimes dissimilarity rather than similarity enhances attraction. A study of informal groups within the Air Force led Gross (10) to distinguish two types of groups: a *symbiotic* group, composed of men with dissimilar characteristics, where attraction is based upon different contributions that one member can make to another, and a *consensual* group made up of men with similar characteristics. He concludes that symbiotic relationships provide a more stable basis for attraction than do consensual ones.

The total body of evidence indicates that similarity with respect to values, interests, attitudes, and beliefs that are important to the members of a group usually heightens attraction but that dissimilarity may sometimes be a source of attraction. Further research is required to clarify the essential differences between these two types of situation.

Group Goals

The goals of a group constitute another possible source of its attractiveness. Different groups may have, of course, widely different goals that may vary considerably in their explicitness and specificity. Having a distinctive goal or purpose serves to attract to the group people with a particular motive base. The members of such a group, being similar to one another with respect to relevant values and interests, may be expected to develop interpersonal bonds and to be attracted to group membership. Scott (38) has provided careful documentation of the ways in which the basic objectives of sororities and fraternities affect the kinds of students who are recruited to membership and who remain members.

Results of a laboratory experiment by Raven and Rietsema (32) indicate that the incentive value of a particular group goal for a particular person will depend not only upon its content but also upon how explicitly the goal is formulated, how clear the paths for goal attainment are, and the likelihood of successful achievement of the goal. When the best procedure for reaching a goal is not clearly evident to all members, disruptive disagreements may reduce the members' attraction to the group. In a study of problem-solving by groups, French (9) found that some members withdrew from participation when disagreements arose among members. He noted that withdrawal was most likely to occur when members were disagreeing over the method they should use in solving the problem.

If a member is highly identified with a group goal, one would expect him to gain satisfaction from group success and dissatisfaction from group failure. On the whole, research findings confirm this expectation, but as noted by Lott and Lott (22) the failure of a group to reach its goal may result, under certain conditions, in an increase in attraction to the group. Such an outcome appears to be most likely where the failure is perceived by the members as arbitrarily imposed by an external source.

Type of Interdependence Among Members

When the members of a group accept a common goal and agree on actions required to reach it, they become cooperatively interdependent. Each member gains satisfaction from contributions made by others toward attainment of their common goal. In a theory of interpersonal cooperation, Deutsch advances the hypothesis that when people are cooperatively interdependent they will develop attraction to one another. He obtained empirical support for this in an experiment comparing cooperative and competitive classroom groups. In the cooperative groups the students were told that all would be given the same grade depending upon the quality of the group's product. The competitive groups were informed that each member would be graded on his merits relative to the others in his own class. The cooperative groups displayed more symptoms of high cohesiveness. Compared to the competitive groups, the members like one another more, made more attempts to influence one another, accepted influence attempts more readily, and were more friendly in their behavior. Other investigations have also produced results supporting the view that group attractiveness is greater when members are cooperatively interdependent than when they are in competition.

In Deutsch's experiment intragroup cooperation was accompanied by intergroup competition. Other studies by Sherif and Sherif (41), Myers (25), and Julian, Bishop, and Fiedler (18) have focused more directly upon the effects of competition between groups and have found that such competition promotes close interpersonal relations within groups. An interpretation of these results, different from that of Deutsch, holds that it is the common threat to the members, posed by a common enemy or opponent, that draws members together. These two interpretations, though different, are not incompatible; both cooperative inter-dependence and common threat may serve to heighten the attractiveness of a group. It should be added, however, that some investigators have found that threat serves to decrease attraction. The conditions producing these different effects of threat have not been thoroughly studied, but a review of the literature by Lott and Lott (22) led them to propose that

attraction among individuals will be found to increase when their common threat stems from an external source (i.e., is not a function of their own lack of skill), when there exists the possibility that coopera-tive behavior may reduce or eliminate the threat, and when single individuals cannot escape from either the group or the threat.

Group Activities

To the extent that membership in a group in-volves a person in certain activities, his evalua-tion of these activities should affect his attraction to the group. Indeed, the attractiveness of some groups, such as social or recreational clubs, de-pends primarily upon the nature of the activities they provide members. Research conducted in business and industrial organizations reveals a general tendency for satisfaction with one's job to be negatively correlated with frequency of ab-sence from work and the probability of voluntar-ily leaving the organization (46). In much of this research "job satisfaction" is loosely defined and represents many factors other than involvement in the task itself. Nevertheless, there is evidence that satisfaction with one's work activities is often a major component of total job satisfaction, and efforts to make work more satisfying through pro-grams of "job enlargement" have generally re-sulted in an increase in total satisfaction (19).

One of the natural resultants of group life is that a member will be asked to assume responsi-bilities. Some of these, perhaps speechmaking, letter-writing, bookkeeping, or leading a discus-sion, are duties for which he feels he is not ade-quately prepared. The attractiveness of the group might well be reduced, then, when it is the source of such embarrassment. Horwitz reports from a laboratory experiment some incidental observa-tions that illustrate this phenomenon. In this ex-

periment the members of each group were girls from the same sorority. A group task was assigned and the girls were highly motivated to do well. In the course of this task it became apparent to some of the girls that their own inability to contribute to the group task might prevent the group from doing well. This realization was quite disturbing and made the whole group activity less attractive. If a group has standards of performance that members cannot meet, the prospect of repeated personal failure should adversely affect the attrac-tiveness of the group. Consistent with this expec-tation are the findings from a study of industrial workers reported by Coch and French. Here it was found that workers whose rate of production fell just below the group standard, so that feel-ings of failure were most intense, had an extremely high rate of leaving the company.

Leadership and Decision-Making

The classical experiments by Lewin, Lippitt, and White on styles of leadership provide several in-dications that children are more attracted to a group with democratic leadership than to one with autocratic or laissez faire leadership. Re-search conducted in quite different settings leads to similar conclusions. A study comparing two styles of leadership, reported by Preston and Heintz (30), showed that members of groups hav-ing participatory leaders, as compared with those having supervisory leaders, expressed more satis-faction with the group's product, felt the group's task to be more interesting, believed the group to be more efficient, and gave more weight to the attitudes of other members in forming their own opinions. And, as noted above, Bovard (2) found that college students rate their class more favor-ably when the teacher is group centered than when he is leader centered.

Further evidence is provided by a field experi-ment, reported by Morse and Reimer (24), con-ducted in a large business organization employing female clerical workers. In two divisions decision-making among rank-and-file workers was increased while in another pair of divisions it was moved to higher levels of management. After one and one-half years, significant changes were found in the employees' satisfaction with the company; an increase in satisfaction occurred among the employees in the divisions affording increased opportunities for decision-making while a decrease occurred among those in the other two divisions. It should be noted, however, that additional analyses undertaken by Tannenbaum and Allport (44) show that people with different personality structures react to these two types of social organization in rather different ways.

These and other studies indicate that a group's attractiveness is influenced by the nature of its leadership. A democratic form of organization that encourages widespread participation in decision-making appears generally to induce more attraction to the group than does one in which decisions are centralized. This conclusion must be tempered, however, by the finding that people with different values and attitudes may react quite differently to the same type of leadership.

Structural Properties

Although the effects of a group's structure upon its attractiveness have not been systematically investigated, there is evidence to suggest that such effects may be substantial. Research initiated by Bavelas shows that the communication structure of a group can affect members' satisfaction with participation in the group. Bavelas created groups in the laboratory that were to work on a problem requiring the exchange of information among members, and he specified for each group the communication network that it could use. He found that the average level of satisfaction was higher among members of groups with a decentralized network than among those with a centralized one. In a review of nineteen subsequent experiments, Shaw (40) reports that the results of seventeen confirm this finding. It would seem likely that research on other structural properties would show similar effects upon the attractiveness of groups.

If a group has a definite structure, a member's location within it may be expected to affect his attraction to the group. Bavelas found that members occupying the most central positions in a communication network were more satisfied with their jobs and with the group's performance than were those in the most peripheral positions. Porter

and Lawler (29) in summarizing research on the effects of a person's position in the supervisory hierarchy of organizations assert "it can be stated with some degree of assurance that the available literature on job satisfaction across different levels of organizations shows increasing job satisfaction at each higher level."

Additional information about the effects of group structure upon attractiveness comes from a laboratory experiment in which Kelley (20) created a prestige hierarchy by giving some members the authority to tell others what to do and how to do it. He informed some of the higher-status persons that they were secure in their jobs and others that they might be changed to a lower status later in the experiment. Similarly, some of the lows were told that they would not be allowed to rise above their low positions, and other lows were informed that they might be promoted. Kelley found that the high-status job with the implied threat of demotion, and the low-status post with the impossibility of promotion, were clearly the most undesirable positions. He also noted that persons who were secure in their high status and those who felt that they might rise in status were most attracted to the rest of the members of the group.

Group Atmosphere

Everyday experience makes it clear that a group often develops a general atmosphere that determines members' reactions to the group as a whole. Some groups are businesslike, impersonal, and efficient. Others are warm, relaxed, and friendly. And still others are full of tension and suspicion. The term "atmosphere," while clearly referring to important features of a group, has remained conceptually unclear. As a result, little research has been directed toward elucidating its effects. Despite the lack of systematic evidence, we would expect a group's atmosphere to have pronounced effects upon its attractiveness.

It seems likely, for instance, that a group whose atmosphere is such that members feel accepted and valued will have attraction for its members. Dittes (4) found in a laboratory experiment that members who were made to feel well-accepted in a group were more attracted to it than were those made to feel poorly accepted. This difference, however, was much larger among persons with lower self-esteem than among those with higher self-esteem, presumably because members with lower self-esteem had a stronger need for acceptance by others. Similar findings have been reported by Jackson (17); in a study of professional workers in a child welfare agency, he obtained a significant correlation between a person's attraction to his work group and the evaluations of him made by the members of the group.

Although it may seem obvious that a warm and friendly atmosphere will contribute to the attractiveness of a group, there is evidence to indicate that under certain conditions such an atmosphere may generate processes leading to dissatisfaction. Riecken (33) has studied a work camp whose prevailing atmosphere placed a high value on friendly and gentle interactions. In the course of performing daily duties, however, minor antagonisms were bound to arise. Since the campers were members of an association that disapproves of both physical and verbal aggression, they found it difficult to raise problems in which some person or a subgroup was at fault. These problems, when discussed in staff meetings, were usually handled in an abstract and intellectual fashion and few of the resulting decisions were carried through. Typically, a member apologized for bringing up the problem and stated that he did not mean to blame anyone for the state of affairs. The resulting condition amounted, consequently, to a failure of communication on important matters, and antagonisms continued, much to the unhappiness of all.

Group Size

The effects of the size of a group upon its attractiveness have interested a number of investigators. Much of the research has focused on units, such as work groups, departments, or factories, within large organizations. The results, as reviewed by Porter and Lawler (29), are remarkably consistent in showing that as the size of these units increases there is a decrease in job satisfaction and a concomitant increase in absence rates, turnover rates, and the incidence of labor disputes.

In an attempt to explain the negative relationship between the size of a group and the satisfac-

tion of its members, Indik (16) made an intensive study of groups in three organizations. He wished to ascertain whether larger groups show the following characteristics, each of which might be expected to reduce member satisfaction: (a) more difficulty in achieving adequate communication among members, (b) a higher degree of task specialization, (c) greater reliance upon impersonal forms of control, and (d) more severe problems of coordination that tend to be handled by inflexible bureaucratic rules and regulations. His results clearly indicate that larger groups do have more difficulties of communication and less satisfaction from work. The findings concerning the effects of size upon forms of control and problems of coordination are not entirely consistent across the three organizations.

It appears, then, that the size of a group affects its attractiveness by means of its effect on other properties of the group. If these properties become less satisfying as size increases, there will be a negative correlation between size and attractiveness. It is conceivable, however, that under certain conditions (for example, where goal achievement requires a large number of people), larger groups will possess more satisfying properties than will smaller ones. As a particular group changes in size, one would expect some of its properties to become less satisfying and some to become more so. The net effect on group attractiveness would then depend upon the balance of these two types of effect.

CONSEQUENCES OF GROUP COHESIVENESS

In the preceding discussion we have implicitly assumed that certain phenomena can be conceived as consequences of group cohesiveness. Thus, for example, we used such criteria as a group's rate of turnover or its ability to influence members in our evaluation of various indexes of cohesiveness and in our search for the determinants of group attractiveness. We turn now to a more systematic consideration of the consequences of cohesiveness. Since most of the relevant findings have already been cited, they will not be repeated here in any detail.

Maintenance of Membership

We asserted at the beginning of the chapter that the resultant force acting on a member to remain in a group is composed of forces arising from two sources: the attractiveness of the group and the attractiveness of alternative memberships. We would expect, then, that if the restraints against leaving are sufficiently weak, the rate of turnover of membership for a group will be negatively correlated with the group's attractiveness and positively correlated with the attractiveness of alternative memberships. As we have seen, there is considerable evidence in support of the first of these predictions—various indicators of group attractiveness correlate negatively with turnover of membership. It seems highly probable that research designed to test the second prediction would support it also.

In their treatment of the factors affecting the maintenance of group membership, Thibaut and Kelley (45) employ different concepts but arrive at conclusions essentially similar to ours. For them, it will be recalled, a person's attraction to a group depends upon how the level of expected outcomes from membership relates to his comparison level. They argue, however, that this attractiveness has no necessary relation to a person's tendency to maintain membership in a group. In order to account for this tendency, they introduce another concept, the *comparison level for alternatives*, which is the level of outcomes the person believes he can receive from the best available alternative membership. A person will remain in a group if and only if his level of outcomes lies above his comparison level for alternatives. According to this formulation, then, given a particular level of outcomes a person's attraction to a group depends upon his comparison level, but his tendency to remain in the group depends upon his comparison level for alternatives. It can be seen, however, that if the comparison levels and the comparison levels for alternatives remain constant for a particular population, then differences among groups in their levels of expected outcomes will result in corresponding differences both in their attractiveness and in their ability to retain members. Under these conditions, we should find a negative correlation between group attractiveness and turnover.

Power of a Group Over Members

The consequence of cohesiveness most thoroughly investigated is the power that cohesiveness gives a group to influence its members. We have reviewed several studies showing that members conform more to the norms of a group the greater the group's cohesiveness. . . . There can be little doubt that members of a more cohesive group more readily exert influence on one another and are more readily influenced by one another. Although the evidence is not so clear, we should also expect the members of a more cohesive group to accept more readily the group's goals, decisions, and assignment to tasks and roles.

Why should cohesiveness contribute to the power of a group over its members? Festinger, who first postulated a relation between cohesiveness and power, asserts that the magnitude of force that a group can set up on a member counter to his own forces cannot exceed the resultant force acting on him to remain in the group, for the member would leave the group rather than submit to such pressure. Thus, the cohesiveness of a group sets an upper limit upon the group's capacity to influence its members. The treatment of this problem by Thibaut and Kelley (45), although essentially similar, takes on a slightly different form. They assert that a person's dependence on a group is greater the more his level of expected outcomes from membership exceeds his comparison level for alternatives and that the power of the group over a member is directly related to his dependence upon the group. Thus, according to Thibaut and Kelley, the power of a group over a member depends upon the level of outcomes he expects to receive from the group in contrast to the level he believes he can receive from his best available alternative membership. Which of these two theories is superior can be determined only by research specifically designed to provide measurements of their respective concepts.

Participation and Loyalty

Since cohesiveness contributes to a group's capacity to retain members and to exert influence over them, we might expect it also to result in a heightening of participation in group activities.

Several studies have shown that as cohesiveness increases there is more frequent communication among members, a greater degree of participation in group activities, and a lower rate of absences. The findings, however, are not always striking nor consistent; factors other than cohesiveness appear to enter into the determinants of participation. And as noted by Hill and Trist (14), the temporary withdrawal from participation, perhaps through absence from work, is not the same as withdrawal from group membership. A member who is highly attracted to the group may nevertheless fail to participate fully because of illness, competing obligations, or the need to avoid tensions arising from participation. Thus, we should expect to find a correlation between cohesiveness and the rate of participation only when these other factors are held constant or when the group exercises its power over members in order to induce participation.

Personal Consequences

There is some evidence concerning the effects of group cohesiveness on the personal adjustment of members. Thus, for example, Seashore (39) obtained a negative correlation between the cohesiveness of industrial work groups and the tendency for members to report that they often felt "jumpy" or nervous on the job. From a program of research on "quasi-therapeutic" effects of intergroup competition, Myers (25) and Julian, Bishop, and Fiedler (18) report results supporting the thesis that intergroup competition produces an increase in group cohesiveness that, in turn, leads to a heightening of self-esteem and a lowering of anxiety among the members of a group. These investigators believe that the improved interpersonal relations involved in an increase in cohesiveness lead to more acceptance, trust, and confidence among members and that each member consequently develops a sense of security and personal worth.

The proposition that group cohesiveness leads to a sense of security among members is supported by the results of an experiment conducted by Pepitone and Reichling (28). In this experiment, two levels of group cohesiveness were created and the reactions of members in each setting were observed following an "insult" delivered to

the group by an outsider. It was found that members of the more cohesive groups freely engaged in hostile remarks against the insulter, whereas those in groups with low cohesiveness sat quietly or spoke of matters unrelated to their embarrassing experiences. This difference in the readiness of members to express hostility presumably resulted, in part at least, from a greater sense of security experienced by members of the cohesive groups.

In summary, we have found evidence for several consequences of group cohesiveness. Other things being equal, as cohesiveness increases there is an increase in a group's capacity to retain members and in the degree of participation by members in group activities. The greater a group's cohesiveness the more power it has to bring about conformity to its norms and to gain acceptance of its goals and assignment to tasks and roles. Finally, highly cohesive groups provide a source of security for members which serves to reduce anxiety and to heighten self-esteem. Further research will undoubtedly discover additional consequences of cohesiveness.

SOME UNSOLVED PROBLEMS

Our definition of group cohesiveness as the resultant of all forces acting on members to remain in the group has helped considerably to bring many discrete research findings into a meaningful conceptual scheme. There remain, however, several ambiguities in this theoretical formulation, which we now consider briefly.

How Various Sources of Attraction Combine

In discussing the determinants of attraction to a group, we observed that a person's motive base may contain several needs and values and that a group may have many incentive properties. Thus, the resultant force acting on a member to remain in the group will usually be made up of component forces having a variety of sources. Little is known about the ways in which these combine into a single resultant force. Can we assume, for example, that forces deriving from different sources combine additively? Does the magnitude of the resultant force equal the sum of the component forces? To put the question in more concrete terms: If the attraction to the group's activities is the same in two groups, will one of them have greater attraction if in addition the members like one another better? We should expect that the addition of attractions from different sources would actually increase the total attractiveness of the group for an individual, but systematic research has yet to establish the fact.

Importance of Source of Attraction

In our theoretical formulation, a variety of factors are conceived as determinants of a single variable, group cohesiveness, which in turn produces certain consequences. If any two of these determinants have equivalent effects on cohesiveness, they should have equivalent effects, mediated by cohesiveness, upon phenomena treated as consequences of cohesiveness. Is there, in fact, some common denominator among the various sources of attraction by which one can obtain consistent relations between a given degree of cohesiveness regardless of its specific source and other properties of a group?

To answer this question with finality, further research is needed. The best evidence bearing directly on this problem is provided by Back (1). In his experiment, three sources of attraction were compared: personal attraction, task attraction, and possible prestige gains from membership. The strength of attraction for each source was varied. It was found that for any two of these sources a similar increase in attraction led to a similar increase in the power of the group to influence its members. With respect to power to influence, then, there is some justification for assuming that different sources of attraction have the same effect. We should add, however, that more recent theorizing by French and Raven suggests that different bases of power affect the nature of power in certain ways. It seems likely, then, that if different sources of attraction serve as different bases of the group's power, the nature of this power will differ depending upon the source of attraction to the group. Further research on this problem would appear to hold considerable promise.

If it turns out that different sources of attrac-

tion do have some common effects, it does not necessarily follow that all of their effects will be the same. Indeed, Back found that differences in the ways in which cohesiveness was produced led to different styles of communication. When cohesiveness was based on personal attractions among members, they made their discussion a long, pleasant conversation in which they expected to be able to persuade one another easily. When cohesiveness was based on effective performance of the task they were given to do, the members wanted to complete the activity quickly and efficiently and discussed only those matters which they thought were relevant to achieving their purposes. And when cohesiveness was based on the prestige obtainable from membership, the members acted cautiously, concentrated on their own actions, and in general were careful not to risk their status.

Combining Several Individual Scores of Attraction to Form a Single Value of Cohesiveness

Even after we achieve a satisfactory method for determining an individual's resultant attraction to the group, there remains the problem of combining individual scores into an index of group cohesiveness. The simplest formulation of group cohesiveness would be that it equals the sum, or average, of the resultant forces on members to remain in the group. Each member would be given equal weight. A formulation essentially of this type has been used in most of the research conducted up to the present, and on the whole it has proved satisfactory. There can hardly be any doubt, however, that the degree to which certain members are attracted to the group makes a critical difference, while the degree of attraction of other members is relatively inconsequential to the group. Only further research can determine the most satisfactory method for relating individual attraction scores to an index of group cohesiveness.

The Special Case of Involuntary Membership

It is not uncommon to find a group where members retain their membership even though the resultant forces acting on them are directed away from the group. In such an instance of "negative cohesiveness," membership is involuntary; members remain in the group simply because the restraints against leaving are too great. What are the consequences of cohesiveness when it takes on a negative value?

Although the literature provides little in the way of a systematic answer to this question, Festinger has made some interesting suggestions concerning the nature of a group's power over its members under such conditions. He argues that a group has power to bring about genuine covert changes in the opinions and attitudes of its members only if its cohesiveness is greater than zero. If, however, a group has negative cohesiveness, it can resort to threats of punishment, whose severity is limited only by the magnitude of the restraining forces on members against leaving the group. Such threats may be successful in bringing about overt compliance to the demands of the group, but it cannot directly produce changes in the private beliefs and attitudes of members. Thus, if we compare groups having positive cohesiveness with ones having negative cohesiveness, we should expect to find in the latter that group-relevant behavior of members is more often governed by the fear of punishment and less often arises from the members' own needs.

For a discussion of other possible consequences of negative cohesiveness, the reader is referred to the stimulating treatment of nonvoluntary relationships given by Thibaut and Kelley (45, 169–187).

Need for a Model of Circular Causation

In our attempt to discover some theoretical order among the many findings related to group cohesiveness, we have identified certain factors as determinants and others as consequences of cohesiveness. Such an approach seems justified as a first step, but there is good reason to believe that some of the consequences serve also as determinants. Thus, a more adequate model is needed to represent circular processes involving group cohesiveness.

These processes may take various forms. In one of these, factors that increase cohesiveness lead to consequences that, in turn, lead to greater cohesiveness. Several examples of such a benign circular system come readily to mind. Similarities of beliefs and values tend to generate interpersonal attractions among members, and the resulting cohesiveness gives the group power to influence members toward greater similarity. As a group becomes more cohesive its ability to satisfy the needs of members increases, thereby raising the incentive value of the group. And cohesiveness tends to generate frequent interaction among members, which, under certain conditions at least, heightens interpersonal attraction and thus cohesiveness. It is apparent that such circular processes cannot go on indefinitely, which raises an interesting question concerning the nature of the limitations on the level of cohesiveness that a group can attain.

Cohesiveness may also be involved in a degenerating circular causal system. Here a reduction in cohesiveness produces consequences that then lead to a further decrease in cohesiveness. Thus, for example, if a group fails to reach an important goal, the members may become less attracted to the group. The resulting decline in cohesiveness may reduce the group's ability to succeed in the future and thereby further diminish its cohesiveness.

It is possible, of course, for circular causal systems to have a more complex form as, for example, when an increase in cohesiveness has consequences that lead to a subsequent decrease in cohesiveness. In this case, cohesiveness will oscillate around a particular level. An instance of this sort may arise when the additional power derived from an increase in group cohesiveness is used to induce members to engage in activities that are frustrating and that then reduce the incentive value of the group.

The development of concepts and related empirical findings appropriate to a model of circular causation should significantly improve our understanding of the nature of group cohesiveness.

SUMMARY

Group cohesiveness is the resultant of two sets of component forces acting on members to remain in the group—those arising from the attractiveness of the group and those deriving from the attractiveness of alternative memberships.

A person's attraction to a group is determined by four interacting sets of variables: (a) his motive base for attraction; (b) the incentive properties of the group; (c) his expectancy that membership will result in beneficial, or detrimental, consequences for him; and (d) his comparison level, or the quality of outcomes he believes he deserves.

Nine properties of groups have been identified which have potential incentive value, depending upon the motive bases of the individuals involved: (a) attractiveness of group members, (b) similarities among members, (c) nature of group goals, (d) type of interdependence among members, (e) activities of the group, (f) style of leadership and opportunity to participate in decisions, (g) various structural properties of the group, (h) the group's atmosphere, and (i) size of the group.

Among the many possible consequences of group cohesiveness, four principal ones have been documented by research: (a) ability of the group to retain its members, (b) power of the group to influence its members, (c) degree of participation and loyalty of members, and (d) feelings of security on the part of members.

Certain problems remain to be solved before a fully satisfactory theory of group cohesiveness can be achieved: (a) How do various sources of attraction combine for a given person? (b) What difference does the source of attraction make? (c) How should separate individuals' scores of attraction to the group be combined to form a single value of cohesiveness? (d) How can the restraining forces against leaving a group be incorporated into a systematic treatment of cohesiveness? (e) Can models of circular causation be developed to give a more adequate account of the development, maintenance, and decline of cohesiveness for a particular group? The solution of these problems will require both theoretical ingenuity and the invention of better methods of measurement.

NOTE

1. The complete set of forces determining whether a member will remain in a group may contain, in addition, forces against leaving the group that result from costs associated with leaving or from other restraints. We do not include these in our conception of cohesiveness, but it is important to recognize that they may influence the findings obtained in research on cohesiveness.

REFERENCES

1. Back, K. Influence through social communication. *Journal of Abnormal and Social Psychology,* 1951, 46, 9–23.

2. Bovard, E. Group structure and perception. *Journal of Abnormal and Social Psychology,* 1951, 46, 389–405.

3. Dimock, H. *Rediscovering the adolescent.* New York: Association Press, 1941.

4. Dittes, J. Attractiveness of group as function of self-esteem and acceptance by group. *Journal of Abnormal and Social Psychology,* 1959, 59, 77–82.

5. Eisenstadt, S. The social conditions of the development of voluntary association. *Scripta Hierasolymitana,* 1955, 3, 104–125.

6. Eisman, B. Some operational measures of cohesiveness and their correlations. *Human Relations,* 1959, 12, 183–189.

7. Festinger, L. A theory of social comparison processes. *Human Relations,* 1954, 7, 117–140.

8. Festinger, L., & Kelley, H. *Changing attitudes through social contact.* Ann Arbor, Mich.: Research Center for Group Dynamics, 1951.

9. French, J. R. P., Jr. The disruption and cohesion of groups. *Journal of Abnormal and Social Psychology,* 1941, 36, 361–377.

10. Gross, E. Symbiosis and consensus in small groups. *American Sociological Review,* 1956, 21, 174–179.

11. Gross, N., & Martin, W. On group cohesiveness. *American Journal of Sociology,* 1952, 57, 533–546.

12. Hagstrom, W. O., & Selvin, H. C. The dimensions of cohesiveness in small groups. *Sociometry,* 1965, 28, 30–43.

13. Heider, F. *The psychology of interpersonal relations.* New York: Wiley, 1958.

14. Hill, J., & Trist, E. Changes in accidents and other absences with length of service. *Human Relations,* 1955, 8, 121–152.

15. Homans, G. *The human group.* New York: Harcourt, Brace, 1950.

16. Indik, B. P. Organization size and member participation. Some empirical tests of alternative explanations. *Human Relations,* 1965, 18, 339–350.

17. Jackson, J. M. Reference group processes in a formal organization. *Sociometry,* 1959, 22, 307–327.

18. Julian, J. W., Bishop, D. W., & Fiedler, F. E. Quasi-therapeutic effects of intergroup competition. *Journal of Personality and Social Psychology,* 1966, 3, 321–327.

19. Katz, D., & Kahn, R. L. *The social psychology of organizations.* New York: Wiley, 1966.

20. Kelley, H. H. Communication in experimentally created hierarchies. *Human Relations,* 1951, 4, 39–56.

21. Libo, L. *Measuring group cohesiveness.* Ann Arbor, Mich.: Institute for Social Research, 1953.

22. Lott, A. J., & Lott, B. E. Group cohesiveness as interpersonal attraction: A review of relationships with antecedent and consequent variables. *Psychological Bulletin,* 1965, 64, 259–309.

23. Mann, F., & Baumgartel, H. *Absences and employee attitudes in an electric power company.* Ann Arbor, Mich.: Institute for Social Research, 1952.

24. Morse, N., & Reimer, E. The experimental change of a major organizational variable. *Journal of Abnormal and Social Psychology,* 1956, 52, 120–129.

25. Myers, A. E. Team competition, success, and adjustment of group members. *Journal of Abnormal and Social Psychology,* 1962, 65, 325–332.

26. Newcomb, T. M. An approach to the study of communicative acts. *Psychological Review,* 1953, 60, 393–404.

27. Newcomb, T. M. Varieties of interpersonal attraction. In D. Cartwright & A. Zander (Eds.), *Group dynamics: Research and theory.* (2nd ed.) Evanston, Ill.: Row, Peterson, 1960. Pp. 104–119.

28. Pepitone, A., & Reichling, G. Group cohesiveness and the expression of hostility. *Human Relations,* 1955, 8, 327–337.

29. Porter, L. W., & Lawler, E. E., III. Properties of organization structure in relation to job attitudes and job behavior. *Psychological Bulletin,* 1965, 64, 23–51.

30. Preston, M. G., & Heintz, R. K. Effects of participatory vs. supervisory leadership on group judgment. *Journal of Abnormal and Social Psychology,* 1949, 44, 345–355.

31. Ramuz-Nienhuis, W., & Van Bergen, A. Relations between some components of attraction-to-group: A replication. *Human Relations,* 1960, 13, 271–277.

32. Raven, B. H., & Rietsema, J. The effect of varied clarity of group goal and group path upon the individual and his relation to his group. *Human Relations,* 1957, 10, 29–44.

33. Riecken, H. Some problems of consensus development. *Rural Sociology,* 1952, 17, 245–252.

34. Rose, A. *Union solidarity.* Minneapolis: Univ. of Minnesota Press, 1952.

35. Ross, I., & Zander, A. Need satisfaction and employee turnover. *Personnel Psychology,* 1957, 10, 327–338.

36. Sagi, P. C., Olmsted, & Atelsek, F. Predicting maintenance of membership in small groups. *Journal of Abnormal and Social Psychology,* 1955, 51, 308–311.

37. Schachter, S. *The psychology of affiliation.* Stanford: Stanford Univ. Press, 1959.

38. Scott, W. A. *Values and organizations.* Chicago: Rand McNally, 1965.

39. Seashore, S. *Group cohesiveness in the industrial work group.* Ann Arbor, Mich.: Institute for Social Research, 1954.

40. Shaw, M. E. Communication networks. In L. Berkowitz (Ed.), *Advances in experimental social psychology.* Vol. 1. New York: Academic Press, 1964. Pp. 111–149.

41. Sherif, M., & Sherif, C. *Groups in harmony and tension.* New York: Harper, 1953.

42. Simon, H. A., Smithburg, D. W., & Thompson, V. A. *Public administration.* New York: Knopf, 1950.

43. Stouffer S. A., *et al. The American soldier.* Vol. I. *Adjustment during army life.* Princeton, N.J.: Princeton Univ. Press, 1949.

44. Tannenbaum, A. S., & Allport, F. H. Personality structure and group structure: An interpretive study of their relationship through an event-structure hypothesis. *Journal of Abnormal and Social Psychology,* 1956, 53, 272–280.

45. Thibaut, J. W., & Kelley, H. H. *The social psychology of groups.* New York: Wiley, 1959.

46. Vroom, V. *Work and motivation.* New York: Wiley, 1964.

47. Zander, A., & Havelin, A. Social comparison and interpersonal attraction. *Human Relations,* 1960, 13, 21–32.

COMMITTEE MANAGEMENT: GUIDELINES FROM SOCIAL SCIENCE RESEARCH

A. C. FILLEY

The committee is one of the most maligned, yet most frequently employed forms of organization structure. Yet despite the criticisms, committees are a fact of organization life. For example, a recent survey of 1,200 respondents revealed that 94 percent of firms with more than 10,000 employees and 64 percent with less than 250 employees reported having formal committees.[1] And, a survey of organization practices in 620 Ohio manufacturing firms showed a similar positive relationship between committee use and plant size.[2] These studies clearly indicate that committees are one of management's important organizational tools.

My thesis is that committee effectiveness can be increased by applying social science findings to answer such questions as:

• What functions do committees serve?

• What size should committees be?

• What is the appropriate style of leadership for committee chairmen?

• What mix of member characteristics makes for effective committee performance?

COMMITTEE PURPOSES AND FUNCTIONS

Committees are set up to pursue economy and efficiency within the enterprise. They do not create direct salable value, nor do they supervise operative employees who create such value.

The functions of the committee have been described by business executives as the exchange of views and information, recommending action, generating ideas, and making major decisions,[3] of which the first may well be the most common. After observing seventy-five conferences (which were also referred to as "committees"), Kriesberg concluded that most were concerned either with communicating information or with aiding an executive's decision process.[4] Executives said they called conferences to "sell" ideas rather than for group decision-making itself. As long as the executive does not manipulate the group covertly, but benefits by its ideas and screening processes, this activity is probably quite legitimate, for members are allowed to influence and to participate, to some extent, in executive decision-making.

Some committees also make specific operating decisions which commit individuals and organization units to prescribed goals and policies. Such is often the province of the general management committee composed of major executive officers. According to one survey, 30.3 percent of the respondents reported that their firms had such a committee and that the committees averaged 8.6 members and met 27 times per year.[5]

Several of the characteristics of committee organization have been the subject of authoritative opinion, or surveys of current practice, and lend themselves to evaluation through inferences from small-group research. Current practice and authoritative opinion are reviewed here, followed by more rigorous studies in which criteria of effectiveness are present. The specific focus is on committee size, membership, and chairmen.

COMMITTEE SIZE

Current Practice and Opinion

The typical committee should be, and is, relatively small. Recommended sizes range from three to nine members, and surveys of actual practice seldom miss these prescriptions by much. Of the 1,658 committees recorded in the Harvard Business Review survey, the average membership was eight. When asked for their preference, the 79 percent who answered suggested an ideal committee size that averaged 4.6 members. Similarly, Kriesberg reported that, for the 75 conferences analyzed, there were typically five or six conferees in the meetings studied.[6]

Committees in the federal government tend to be larger than those in business. In the House of Representatives, Appropriations is the largest standing committee, with fifty members, and the Committee on Un-American Activities is smallest, with nine. Senate committees average thirteen members; the largest, also Appropriations, has twenty-three.[7] The problem of large committee size is overcome by the use of subcommittees and closed executive committee meetings. The larger committees seem to be more collections of subgroups than truly integrated operating units. In such cases, it would be interesting to know the size of the subcommittees.

Inferences from Small-Group Research

The extent to which a number is "ideal" may be measured in part in terms of the effects that size has on socio-emotional relations among group members and thus the extent to which the group operates as an integrated whole, rather than as

fragmented subunits. Another criterion is how size affects the quality of the group's decision and the time required to reach it. Several small experimental group studies have evaluated the effect of size on group process.

Variables related to changes in group size include the individual's capacity to "attend" to differing numbers of objects, the effect of group size on interpersonal relations and communication, its impact on problem-solving functions, and the "feelings" that group members have about proper group size and the nature of group performance. To be sure, the effects of these variables are interrelated.

Attention to the Group. Each member in a committee attends both to the group as a whole and to each individual as a member of the group. There seem to be limits on a person's ability to perform both of these processes—limits which vary with the size of the group and the time available. For example, summarizing a study by Taves,[8] Hare[9] reports that "Experiments on estimating the number of dots in a visual field with very short-time exposures indicate individual subjects can report the exact number up to and including seven with great confidence and practically no error, but above that number confidence and accuracy drop."

Perhaps for similar reasons, when two observers assessed leadership characteristics in problem-solving groups of college students, the raters reached maximum agreement in groups of six, rather than in two, four, eight, or twelve.[10]

The apparent limits on one's ability to attend both to the group and the individuals within it led Hare to conclude:

The coincidence of these findings suggests that the ability of the observing individual to perceive, keep track of, and judge each member separately in a social interaction situation may not extend much beyond the size of six or seven. If this is true, one would expect members of groups larger than that size to tend to think of other members in terms of subgroups, or "classes" of some kind, and to deal with members of subgroups other than their own by more stereotyped methods of response.[11]

Interpersonal Relations and Communication. Given a meeting lasting a fixed length of time, the opportunity for each individual to communicate is reduced, and the type of communication becomes differential among group members. Bales *et al.*[12] have shown that in groups of from three to eight members the proportion of infrequent contributors increases at a greater rate than that theoretically predicted from decreased opportunity to communicate. Similarly, in groups of from four to twelve, as reported by Stephen and Mishler,[13] size was related positively to the difference between participation initiated by the most active and the next most active person.

Increasing the group size seems to limit the extent to which individuals want to communicate, as well. For example, Gibb[14] studied idea productivity in forty-eight groups in eight size categories from 1 to 96. His results indicated that as group size increases a steadily increasing proportion of group members report feelings of threat and less willingness to initiate contributions. Similarly, Slater's[15] study of 24 groups of from two to seven men each working on a human relations problem indicated that members of the larger groups felt them to be disorderly and time-consuming, and complained that other members became too pushy, aggressive, and competitive.

Functions and Conflict. An increase in group size seems to distort the pattern of communication and create stress in some group members, yet a decrease in group size also has dysfunctional effects. In the Slater study check-list responses by members rating smaller groups of 2, 3, or 4 were complimentary, rather than critical, as they had been for larger groups. Yet observer impressions were that small groups engaged in superficial discussion and avoided controversial subjects. Inferences from post hoc analysis suggested that small group members are too tense, passive, tactful, and constrained to work together in a satisfying manner. They are afraid of alienating others. Similar results have been reported in other studies regarding the inhibitions created by small group size, particularly in groups of two.[16]

Groups of three have the problem of an overpowerful majority, since two members can form a coalition against the unsupported third member. Four-member groups provide mutual support when two members oppose the other two, but

such groups have higher rates of disagreement and antagonism than odd-numbered groups.[17]

The data reported above are not altogether consistent regarding the reasons for dysfunctional consequences of small groups. The "trying-too-hard-for-agreement" of the Slater study seems at odds with the conflict situations posed in the groups of three and four, yet both agree that for some reason tension is present.

Groups of Five. While it is always dangerous to generalize about "ideal" numbers (or types, for that matter), there does appear to be logical and empirical support for groups of five members as a suitable size, if the necessary skills are possessed by the five members. In the Slater study, for example, none of the subjects felt that a group of five was too small or too large to carry out the assigned task, though they objected to the other sizes (two, three, four, six, and seven). Slater concluded:

Size five emerged clearly . . . as the size group which from the subjects' viewpoint was most effective in dealing with an intellectual task involving the collection and exchange of information about a situation, the coordination analysis, and evaluation of this information, and a group decision regarding the appropriate administrative action to be taken in the situation. . . .

These findings suggest that maximal group satisfaction is achieved when the group is large enough so that the members feel able to express positive and negative feelings freely, and to make aggressive efforts toward problem solving even at the risk of antagonizing each other, yet small enough so that some regard will be shown for the feelings and needs of others; large enough so that the loss of a member could be tolerated, but small enough so that such a loss could not be altogether ignored.[18]

From this and other studies,[19] it appears that, excluding productivity measures, generally the optimum size of problem-solving groups is five. Considering group performance in terms of quality, speed, efficiency and productivity, the effect of size is less clear. Where problems are complex, relatively larger groups have been shown to produce better quality decisions. For example, in one study, groups of 12 or 13 produced higher quality decisions than groups of 6, 7, or 8.[20] Others have shown no differences among groups in the smaller size categories (2 to 7). Relatively smaller groups are often faster and more productive. For example, Hare found that groups of five take less time to make decisions than groups of 12.[21]

Several studies have also shown that larger groups are able to solve a greater variety of problems because of the variety of skills likely to increase with group size.[22] However, there is a point beyond which committee size should not increase because of diminishing returns. As group size increases coordination of the group tends to become difficult, and thus it becomes harder for members to reach consensus and to develop a spirit of teamwork and cohesiveness.

In general, it would appear that with respect to performance, a task which requires interaction, consensus and modification of opinion requires a relatively small group. On the other hand, where the task is one with clear criteria of correct performance, the addition of more members may increase group performance.

THE CHAIRMAN

Current Practice and Opinion. Most people probably serve on some type of committee in the process of participating in church, school, political, or social organizations and while in that capacity have observed the effect of the chairman on group progress. Where the chairman starts the meeting, for example, by saying, "Well, we all know each other here, so we'll dispense with any formality," the group flounders, until someone else takes a forceful, directive role.

If the committee is to be successful, it must have a chairman who understands group process. He must know the objectives of the committee and understand the problem at hand. He should be able to vary decision strategies according to the nature of the task and the feelings of the group members. He needs the acceptance of the group members and their confidence in his personal integrity. And he needs the skill to resist needless debate and to defer discussion upon issues which are not pertinent or where the committee lacks the facts upon which to act.

Surveys of executive opinion support these impressions of the chairman's role. The Harvard Business Review survey stated that "The great

majority [of the suggestions from survey respondents] lead to this conclusion: the problem is not so much committees in management as it is the management of committees." This comment by a partner in a large management consulting firm was cited as typical:

Properly used, committees can be most helpful to a company. Most of the criticism I have run into, while probably justified, deals with the way in which committees are run (or committee meetings are run) and not with the principle of working with committees.[23]

A chairman too loose in his control of committee processes is by no means the only difficulty encountered. Indeed, the chronic problem in the federal government has been the domination of committee processes by the chairman. This results from the way in which the chairman is typically selected: he is traditionally the member of the majority party having the longest uninterrupted service on the committee. The dangers in such domination have been described as follows:

If there is a piece of legislation that he does not like, he kills it by declining to schedule a hearing on it. He usually appoints no standing subcommittees and he arranges the special subcommittees in such a way that his personal preferences are taken into account. Often there is no regular agenda at the meetings of his committee—when and if it meets . . . they proceed with an atmosphere of apathy, with junior members, especially, feeling frustrated and left out, like first graders at a seventh grade party.[24]

Inferences from Small Group Research. The exact nature of the chairman's role is further clarified when we turn to more rigorous studies on group leadership.

We shall confine our discussion here to leader roles and functions, using three approaches. First, we shall discuss the nature of task leadership in the group and the apparent reasons for this role. Then we shall view more specifically the different roles which the leader or leaders of the group may play. Finally, we shall consider the extent to which these more specific roles may be combined in a single individual.

Leader Control. Studies of leadership in task-oriented, decision-making groups show a functional need for and, indeed, a member preference for directive influence by the chairman. The nature of this direction is illustrated in a study by Schlesinger, Jackson, and Butman.[25] The problem was to examine the influence process among leaders and members of small problem-solving groups when the designated leaders varied on the rated degree of control exerted. One hundred six members of twenty-three management committees participated in the study. As part of an initial investigation, committee members described in a questionnaire the amount of control and regulation which each member exercised when in the role of chairman. Each committee was then given a simulated but realistic problem for 1.5 hours, under controlled conditions and in the presence of three observers.

The questionnaire data showed that individuals seen as high in control were rated as more skillful chairmen and as more valuable contributors to the committee's work.

The study also demonstrated that leadership derives from group acceptance rather than from the unique acts of the chairman. "When the participants do not perceive the designated leader as satisfactorily performing the controlling functions, the participants increase their own attempts to influence their fellow members." [26] The acceptance of the leader was based upon task (good ideas) and chairmanship skills and had little to do with his personal popularity as a group member.

The importance of chairman control in committee action has been similarly demonstrated in several other studies.[27] In his study of 72 management conferences, for example, Berkowitz[28] found that a high degree of "leadership sharing" was related inversely to participant satisfaction and to a measure of output. The norms of these groups sanctioned a "take-charge" chairman. When the chairman failed to meet these expectations, he was rejected and both group satisfaction and group output suffered. These studies do not necessarily suggest that committees less concerned with task goals also prefer a directive chairman. Where the committees are composed of more socially oriented members, the preference for leader control may be less strong.[29]

Leadership Roles. A second approach to understanding the leadership of committees is to investigate leadership roles in small groups. Pervading the research literature is a basic distinction between group activities directed to one or the other of two types of roles performed by leaders. They are defined by Benne and Sheats[30] as task roles, and as group-building and maintenance roles. Task roles are related to the direct accomplishment of group purpose, such as seeking information, initiating, evaluating, and seeking or giving opinion. The latter roles are concerned with group integration and solidarity through encouraging, harmonizing, compromising, and reducing conflict.

Several empirical investigations of leadership have demonstrated that both roles are usually performed within effective groups.[31] However, these roles are not always performed by the same person. Frequently one member is seen as the "task leader" and another as the "social leader" of the group.

Combined Task and Social Roles. Can or should these roles be combined in a single leader? The prototypes of the formal and the informal leader which we inherit from classical management lore tend to lead to the conclusion that such a combination is somehow impossible or perhaps undesirable. The research literature occasionally supports this point of view as well.

There is much to be said for a combination of roles. Several studies have shown that outstanding leaders are those who possess both task and social orientations.[32] The study by Borgotta, Couch, and Bales illustrates the point. These researchers assigned leaders high on both characteristics to problem-solving groups. The eleven leaders whom they called "great men" were selected from 126 in an experiment on the basis of high task ability, individual assertiveness, and social acceptability. These men also retained their ratings as "great men" throughout a series of different problem-solving sessions. When led by "great men" the groups achieved a higher rate of suggestion and agreement, a lower rate of "showing tension," and higher rates of showing solidarity and tension release than comparable groups without "great men."

When viewed collectively two conclusions emerge from the above studies. Consistent with existing opinion, the leader who is somewhat assertive and who takes charge and controls group proceedings is performing a valid and necessary role. However, such task leadership is a necessary but not a sufficient condition for effective committee performance. Someone in the group must perform the role of group-builder and maintainer of social relations among the members. Ideally both roles should probably be performed by the designated chairman. When he does not have the necessary skills to perform both roles, he should be the task leader and someone else should perform the social leadership role. Effective committee performance requires both roles to be performed, by a single person or by complementary performance of two or more members.

Committee Membership

The atmosphere of committee operations described in the classic literature is one where all members seem to be cooperating in the achievement of committee purpose. It is unclear, however, if cooperation is necessarily the best method of solving problems, or if competition among members or groups of members might not achieve more satisfactory results. Cooperation also seems to imply a sharing or homogeneity of values. To answer the question we must consider two related problems: the effects of cooperation or competition on committee effectiveness, and the effects of homogeneous or heterogeneous values on committee effectiveness.

Cooperation or Competition. A number of studies have contrasted the impact of competition and cooperation on group satisfaction and productivity. In some cases the group is given a cooperative or competitive "treatment" through direction or incentive when it is established. In others, competition and cooperation are inferred from measures of groups in which members are operating primarily for personal interest, in contrast with groups in which members are more concerned with group needs. These studies show rather consistently that "group members who have been motivated to cooperate show more positive responses to each other, are more favorable in their perceptions, are more involved in the task, and have greater satisfaction with the task." [33]

The best known study regarding the effects of cooperation and competition was conducted by Deutsch[34] in ten experimental groups of college students, each containing five persons. Each group met for one three-hour period a week for six weeks, working on puzzles and human relations problems. Subjects completed a weekly and postexperimental questionnaire. Observers also recorded interactions and completed over-all rating scales at the end of each problem.

In some groups, a cooperative atmosphere was established by instructing members that the group as a whole would be evaluated in comparison with four similar groups, and that each person's course grade would depend upon the performance of the group itself. In others, a competitive relationship was established by telling the members that each would receive a different grade, depending upon his relative contribution to the group's problem solutions.

The results, as summarized by Hare, show that:

Compared with the competitively organized groups, the cooperative groups had the following characteristics:

1. Stronger individual motivation to complete the group task and stronger feelings of obligation toward other members.
2. Greater division of labor both in content and frequency of interaction among members and greater coordination of effort.
3. More effective inter-member communication. More ideas were verbalized, members were more attentive to one another, and more accepting of and affected by each other's ideas. Members also rated themselves as having fewer difficulties in communicating and understanding others.
4. More friendliness was expressed in the discussion and members rated themselves higher on strength of desire to win the respect of one another. Members were also more satisfied with the group and its products.
5. More group productivity. Puzzles were solved faster and the recommendations produced for the human-relations problems were longer and qualitatively better. However, there were no significant differences in the average individual productivity as a result of the two types of group experience nor were there any clear differences in the amounts of individual learning which occurred during the discussions.[35]

Similar evidence was found in the study of 72 decision-making conferences by Fouriezos, Hutt, and Guetzkow.[36] Based on observer ratings of self-oriented need behavior, correlational evidence showed that such self-centered behavior was positively related to participant ratings of high group conflict and negatively related to participant satisfaction, group solidarity, and task productivity.

In general, the findings of these and other studies suggest that groups in which members share in goal attainment, rather than compete privately or otherwise seek personal needs, will be more satisfied and productive.[37]

Homogeneity or Heterogeneity. The effects of member composition in the committee should also be considered from the standpoint of the homogeneity or heterogeneity of its membership. Homogeneous groups are those in which members are similar in personality, value orientation, attitudes to supervision, or predisposition to accept or reject fellow members. Heterogeneity is induced in the group by creating negative expectations regarding potential contributions by fellow members, by introducing differing personality types into the group, or by creating subgroups which differ in their basis of attraction to the group.

Here the evidence is much less clear. Some homogeneous groups become satisfied and quite unproductive, while others become satisfied and quite productive. Similarly, heterogeneity may be shown to lead to both productive and unproductive conditions. While the answer to this paradox may be related to the different definitions of homogeneity or heterogeneity in the studies, it appears to have greater relevance to the task and interpersonal requirements of the group task.

In some studies, homogeneity clearly leads to more effective group performance. The work of Schutz[38] is illustrative. In his earlier writing, Schutz distinguished between two types of interpersonal relationships: power orientation and personal orientation. The first emphasizes authority symbols. The power-oriented person follows rules and adjusts to external systems of authority. People with personal orientations emphasize interpersonal considerations. They assume that the way a person achieves his goal is by working within a framework of close personal relations, that is, by being a "good guy," by liking others, by getting people to like him. In his later work, Schutz[39] distinguished among three types of needs: *inclusion,* or the need to establish and

maintain a satisfactory relation with people with respect to interaction and association; *control,* or the need to establish and maintain a satisfactory relation with people with respect to control and power; and *affection,* or the need to establish and maintain a satisfactory relation with others with respect to love and affection.

Using attitude scales, Schutz established four groups in which people were compatible with respect to high needs for personal relations with others, four whose members were compatible with respect to low personal orientation, and four which contained subgroups differing in these needs. Each of the twelve groups met twelve times over a period of six weeks and participated in a series of different tasks.

The results showed that groups which are compatible, either on a basis of personalness or counterpersonalness, were significantly more productive than groups which had incompatible subgroups. There was no significant difference between the productivity of the two types of compatible groups. As might be expected, the difference in productivity between compatible and incompatible groups was greatest for tasks which required the most interaction and agreement under conditions of high-time pressure.

A similar positive relationship between homogeneity and productivity is reported for groups in which compatibility is established on the basis of prejudice or degree of conservatism, managerial personality traits, congeniality induced by directions from the researcher, or status congruence.[40] In Adams' study, technical performance first increased, then decreased, as status congruence became greater. Group social performance increased continuously with greater homogeneity, however.

The relationship posited above does not always hold, however. In some studies, heterogeneous groups were more productive than homogeneous. For example, Hoffman[41] constructed heterogeneous and homogeneous groups, based on personality profiles, and had them work on two different types of problems. On the first, which required consideration of a wide range of alternatives of a rather specific nature, heterogeneous groups produced significantly superior solutions. On the second problem, which required primarily group consensus and had no objectively "good" solution, the difference between group types was not significant. Ziller[42] also found heterogeneity to be associated with the ability of Air Force crews to judge the number of dots on a card.

Collins and Guetzkow[43] explain these contradictory findings by suggesting that increasing heterogeneity has at least two effects on group interaction: it increases the difficulty of building interpersonal relations, and it increases the problem-solving potential of the group, since errors are eliminated, more alternatives are generated, and wider criticism is possible. Thus, heterogeneity would seem to be valuable where the needs for task facilitation are greater than the need for strong interpersonal relations.

Considering our original question, it appears that, from the standpoint of cooperation versus competition in committees, the cooperative committee is to be preferred. If we look at the effects of homogeneous or heterogeneous committee membership, the deciding factor seems to be the nature of the task and the degree of interpersonal conflict which the committee can tolerate.

SUMMARY AND CONCLUSIONS

Research findings regarding committee size, leadership, and membership have been reviewed. Evidence has been cited showing that the ideal size is five, when the five members possess the necessary skills to solve the problems facing the committee. Viewed from the standpoint of the committee members' ability to attend to both the group and its members, or from the standpoint of balanced interpersonal needs, it seems safe to suggest that this number has normative value in planning committee operations. For technical problems additional members may be added to ensure the provision of necessary skills.

A second area of investigation concerned the functional separation of the leadership role and the influence of the role on other members. The research reviewed supports the notion that the committee chairman should be directive in his leadership, but a more specific definition of leadership roles makes questionable whether the chairman can or should perform as both the task and the social leader of the group. The evidence regarding the latter indicates that combined task and social leadership is an ideal which is seldom attained, but should be sought.

The final question concerned whether committee membership would be most effective when cooperative or competitive. When evaluated from the standpoint of research on cooperative versus competitive groups, it is clear that cooperative membership is more desirable. Committee operation can probably be enhanced by selecting members whose self-centered needs are of a less intense variety and by directions to the group which strengthen motivations of a cooperative nature. When the proposition is evaluated from the standpoint of heterogeneity or homogeneity of group membership, the conclusion is less clear. Apparently, heterogeneity in a group can produce both ideas and a screening process for evaluating their quality, but the advantage of this process depends upon the negative effects of heterogeneous attitudes upon interpersonal cooperation.

REFERENCES

Based on A. C. Filley and J. Robert House, *Managerial Process and Organizational Behavior* (Glenview, Ill.: Scott-Foresman, 1969).

1. Rollie Tillman, Jr., "Problems in Review: Committees on Trial," *Harvard Business Review,* 38 (May-June 1960), 6–12; 162–172. Firms with 1,001 to 10,000 reported 93 percent use; 250 to 1,000 reported 82 percent use.

2. J. H. Healey, *Executive Coordination and Control,* Monograph No. 78 (Columbus: Bureau of Business Research, The Ohio State University, 1956), p. 185.

3. "Committees," *Management Review,* 46 (October 1957), 4–10; 75–78.

4. M. Kriesberg, "Executives Evaluate Administrative Conferences," *Advanced Management,* 15 (March 1950), 15–17.

5. Tillman, *op. cit.,* p. 12.

6. Kriesberg, *op. cit.,* p. 15.

7. "The Committee System—Congress at Work," *Congressional Digest,* 34 (February 1955), 47–49; 64.

8. E. H. Taves, "Two Mechanisms for the Perception of Visual Numerousness," *Archives of Psychology,* 37 (1941), 265.

9. A. Paul Hare, *Handbook of Small Group Research* (New York: The Free Press of Glencoe, 1962), p. 227.

10. B. M. Bass, and F. M. Norton, "Group Size and Leaderless Discussions," *Journal of Applied Psychology,* 35 (1951), 397–400.

11. Hare, *op. cit.,* p. 228.

12. R. F. Bales, F. L. Strodtbeck, T. M. Mills, and M. E. Roseborough, "Channels of Communication in Small Groups," *American Sociological Review,* 16 (1951), 461–468.

13. F. F. Stephen and E. G. Mishler, "The Distribution of Participation in Small Groups: An Exponential Approximation." *American Sociological Review,* 17 (1952), 598–608.

14. J. R. Gibb, "The Effects of Group Size and of Threat Reduction Upon Creativity in a Problem-Solving Situation," *American Psychologist,* 6 (1951), 324. (Abstract)

15. P. Slater, "Contrasting Correlates of Group Size," *Sociometry,* 21 (1958), 129–139.

16. R. F. Bales, and E. F. Borgotta, "Size of Group as a Factor in the Interaction Profile," in *Small Groups: Studies in Social Interaction,* A. P. Hare, E. F. Borgotta, and R. F. Bales, eds. (New York: Knopf, 1965, rev. ed.), pp. 495–512.

17. *Ibid.,* p. 512.

18. Slater, *op. cit.,* 137–138.

19. R. F. Bales, "In Conference," *Harvard Business Review,* 32 (March-April 1954), 44–50; Also A. P. Hare, "A Study of Interaction and Consensus in Different Sized Groups," *American Sociological Review,* 17 (1952), 261–267.

20. D. Fox, I. Lorge, P. Weltz, and K. Herrold, "Comparison of Decisions Written by Large and Small Groups," *American Psychologist,* 8 (1953), 351. (Abstract)

21. A. Paul Hare, "Interaction and Consensus in Different Sized Groups," *American Sociological Review,* 17 (1952), 261–267.

22. G. B. Watson, "Do Groups Think More Efficiently Than Individuals?" *Journal of Abnormal and Social Psychology,* 23 (1928), 328–336; Also D. J. Taylor and W. L. Faust, "Twenty Questions: Efficiency in Problem Solving as a Function of Size of Group," *Journal of Experimental Psychology,* 44 (1952), 360–368.

23. Tillman, *op. cit.,* p. 168.

24. S. L. Udall, "Defense of the Seniority System," *New York Times Magazine* (January 13, 1957), 17.

25. L. Schlesinger, J. M. Jackson, and J. Butman, "Leader-Member Interaction in Management Committees," *Journal of Abnormal and Social Psychology,* 61, No. 3 (1960), 360–364.

26. *Ibid.,* p. 363.

27. L. Berkowitz, "Sharing Leadership in Small Decision-Making Groups," *Journal of Abnormal and Social Psychology,* 48 (1953), 231–238; Also N. T. Fouriezos, M. L. Hutt, and H. Guetzkow, "Measurement of Self-Oriented Needs in Discussion Groups," *Journal of Abnormal and Social Psychology,* 45 (1950), 682–690; Also H. P. Shelley, "Status Consensus, Leadership, and Satisfaction with the Group," *Journal of Social Psychology,* 51 (1960), 157–164.

28. Berkowitz, *Ibid.,* p. 237.

29. R. C. Anderson, "Learning in Discussions: A Resume of the Authoritarian-Democratic Studies," *Harvard Education Review,* 29 (1959), 201–214.

30. K. D. Benne, and P. Sheats, "Functional Roles of Group Members," *Journal of Social Issues,* 4 (Spring 1948), 41–49.

31. R. F. Bales, *Interaction Process Analysis* (Cambridge: Addison-Wesley, 1951); Also R. M. Stogdill and A. E. Coons (eds.), *Leader Behavior: Its Description and Measurement,* Monograph No. 88 (Columbus: Bureau of Business Research, The Ohio State University, 1957); Also A. W. Halpin, "The Leadership Behavior and Combat Performance of Airplane Commanders," *Journal of Abnormal and Social Psychology,* 49 (1954), 19–22.

32. E. G. Borgotta, A. S. Couch, and R. F. Bales, "Some Findings Relevant to the Great Man Theory of Leadership," *American Sociological Review,* 19 (1954), 755–759; Also E. A. Fleishman, and E. G. Harris, "Patterns of Leadership Behavior Related to Employee Grievances and Turnover," *Personnel Psychology,* 15, No. 1 (1962), 43–56; Also Stogdill and Coons, *Ibid.;* Also H. Oaklander and E. A. Fleishman, "Patterns of Leadership Related to Organizational Stress in Hospital Settings," *Administrative Science Quarterly,* 8 (March 1964), 520–532.

33. Hare, *Handbook of Small Group Research, op. cit.,* p. 254.

34. M. Deutsch, "The Effects of Cooperation and Competition Upon Group Process," in *Group Dynamics, Research and Theory,* D. Cartwright and A. Zander, eds. (New York: Harper and Row, 1953).

35. Hare, *Handbook of Small Group Research, op. cit.,* p. 263.

36. Fouriezos, Hutt, and Guetzkow, *op. cit.*

37. C. Stendler, D. Damrin and A. Haines, "Studies in Cooperation and Competition: I. The Effects of Working for Group and Individual Rewards on the Social Climate of Children's Groups," *Journal of Genetic Psychology,* 79 (1951), 173–197; Also A. Mintz, "Nonadaptive Group Behavior," *Journal of Abnormal and Social Psychology,* 46 (1951), 150–159; Also M. M. Grossack, "Some Effects of Cooperation and Competition Upon Small Group Behavior," *Journal of Abnormal and Social Psychology,* 49 (1954), 341–348; Also E. Gott-

heil, "Changes in Social Perceptions Contingent Upon Competing or Cooperating," *Sociometry,* 18 (1955), 132–137; Also A. Zander and D. Wolfe, "Administrative Rewards and Coordination Among Committee Members," *Administrative Science Quarterly,* 9 (June 1964), 50–69.

38. W. C. Schutz, "What Makes Groups Productive? *Human Relations,* 8 (1955), 429–465.

39. W. C. Schutz, *FIRO: A Three-Dimensional Theory of Interpersonal Behavior* (New York: Holt, Rinehart and Winston, 1958).

40. I. Altman and E. McGinnies, "Interpersonal Perception and Communication in Discussion Groups of Varied Attitudinal Composition," *Journal of Abnormal and Social Psychology,* 60 (May 1960), 390–393; Also W. A. Haythorn, E. H. Couch, D. Haefner, P. Langham and L. Carter, "The Behavior of Authoritarian and Equalitarian Personalities in Groups," *Human Relations,* 9 (1956), 57–74; Also E. E. Ghiselli and T. M. Lodahl,

"Patterns of Managerial Traits and Group Effectiveness," *Journal of Abnormal and Social Psychology,* 57 (1958), 61–66; Also R. V. Exline, "Group Climate as a Factor in the Relevance and Accuracy of Social Perception," *Journal of Abnormal and Social Psychology,* 55 (1957), 382–388; Also S. Adams, "Status Congruency as a Variable in Small Group Performance," *Social Forces,* 32 (1953), 16–22.

41. L. R. Hoffman, "Homogeneity of Member Personality and Its Effect on Group Problem-Solving, *Journal of Abnormal and Social Psychology,* 58 (1959), 27–32.

42. R. C. Ziller, "Scales of Judgment: A Determinant of Accuracy of Group Decisions," *Human Relations,* 8 (1955), 153–164.

43. B. E. Collins and H. Guetzkow, *A Social Psychology of Group Process for Decision-Making* (New York: John Wiley and Sons, 1965), p. 101.

GROUPTHINK: IMPLICATIONS FOR SMALL-GROUP DECISION MAKING IN BUSINESS

RICHARD C. HUSEMAN
RUSSELL W. DRIVER

In modern management there has been an increasing emphasis on the use of small groups to make decisions. The labels for approaches to group management include "participative management," "committee organization," "bottoms-up management," and others. There is little question that small groups have become central to the decision-making process in most modern organizations. Those who write about small-group decision making in organizations frequently stress the idea that groups need the quality of "cohesiveness" in order to function effectively. Most writers stress the positive consequences of cohesiveness in small-group decision making. Indeed, one may easily get the impression by reading much of the available literature dealing with small groups that the more cohesive the group the better. While the advantages of groups and their usually inherent cohesiveness have been supported by many, it is perhaps appropriate now to discuss some of the problems associated with highly cohesive decision-making groups.

There are few Americans now past adolescence who are not familiar with such historical events as crossing the 38th parallel in Korea, the Bay of Pigs, and escalation of the war in Vietnam. Most associate these events with major fiascoes at the

This is an original article prepared especially for this volume.

highest levels of the U.S. government. Irving Janis (1972) in his book *Victims of Groupthink* examines the decision-making process involved in those fiascoes. He points out through the use of vivid detail that faulty decisions can and are reached by highly competent, intelligent people working in a group decision-making context.

That bad decisions can be made by highly competent people is not a revelation to most of us. It is something we have known intuitively all along. Since people normally respond well to things they feel are correct, perhaps explains the intuitive appeal of Janis' book and explains the popularity of his groupthink concept by diverse disciplines. This diversity can be seen in the citation of Janis' groupthink concept in a wide variety of writings.

The purpose of this article is to set forth the concept of groupthink as espoused by Janis, relate the groupthink phenomenon to business organizations, and to provide some suggestions for eliminating or decreasing the effects of groupthink in small-group decision making.

THE GROUPTHINK PHENOMENON

Groupthink is Janis' term to describe decisions reached by a group of rational, knowledgeable, and experienced individuals which turn out to be irrational, and poorly formulated. To phrase it another way, these are decisions the individual members, acting alone, would probably *not* have made. In the words of Janis, groupthink is:

A model of thinking that people engage in when they are deeply involved in a cohesive in-group, when the members' striving for unanimity over-ride their motivation to realistically appraise alternative courses of action.... Groupthink refers to a deterioration of mental efficiency, reality testing, and moral judgment that results from in-group pressures. (Janis, 1972, 9)

Without a thorough understanding of Janis' meaning of groupthink one may get the impression that the members of every cohesive group become victims of groupthink and faulty decisions result, as C. G. Jung might have thought when asserting that "when a hundred clever heads join a group, one big nincompoop is the result" (Illing, 1957, 80). That is not the case. Janis recognizes the many advantages of group decision making and readily agrees with most. More importantly, he does not think that simply because the outcome of a group decision has turned out to be a fiasco that it resulted from groupthink or even that it was the result of defective decision making. Janis does maintain, however, that in-group cohesiveness is the major condition that permits the groupthink phenomenon to occur. With this brief definition of groupthink at hand we are in a position to examine the major condition that promotes groupthink—cohesiveness.

Group cohesiveness may be characterized by friendliness, cooperation, interpersonal attraction, and other variables. Such indications of group cohesiveness exert strong influences upon members who tend to behave in accordance with group expectations. Cohesive group members are thus motivated to respond positively to others in the group (Shaw, 1976). There is other evidence that shows internal cohesion may result from external conflict (Stein, 1976). This in-group/out-group hypothesis is not unfamiliar to students of group dynamics. Viewed in a positive manner those variables that influence cohesiveness can be considered beneficial to sound decision making.

However, under some circumstances other variables may be strong enough to negate the positive effects of cohesiveness. It is the interaction of these other variables that Janis contends can turn the potential for a sound group decision into one that is poorly formulated, irrational, and untenable. The interaction of some of these other variables can be seen in the following:

The prime condition repeatedly encountered in case studies of fiascoes is group cohesiveness. A second major condition suggested by the case studies is insulation of the decision-making group from the judgments of qualified associates who, as outsiders, are not permitted to know about the new policies under discussion until after a final decision has been made. Hence...the more insulated a cohesive group of executives becomes, the greater are the chances that its policy decisions will be products of groupthink. ... The more actively the leader of a cohesive policy-making group promotes his preferred solution, the greater are the chances of consensus based on groupthink, even when the leader does not want the members to be yes-men and the individual members try to resist conforming. (Janis, 1972, 197).

Thus, it is evident that group cohesiveness, usually a much-sought-after goal, can actually result in a boomerang effect. Groupthink resides not in an individual or an organization, but rather in the concurrence-seeking tendency of cohesive groups. The degree of cohesiveness is directly proportional to the degree of concurrence-seeking tendencies that tend to replace independent, critical thinking skills.

At this point an enumeration of what Janis refers to as the symptoms of groupthink will promote an understanding of the syndrome. Janis finds the following as threads of continuity among all the decision-making processes leading to the exemplar fiascoes that he discusses in his book:

1. an illusion of invulnerability, shared by most or all the members, which creates excessive optimism and encourages taking extreme risks;
2. collective efforts to rationalize in order to discount warnings which might lead the members to reconsider their assumptions before they recommit themselves to their past policy decisions;
3. an unquestioned belief in the group's inherent morality, inclining the members to ignore the ethical or moral consequences of their decisions;
4. stereotyped views of enemy [opposition] leaders as too evil to warrant genuine attempts to negotiate, or as too weak and stupid to counter whatever risky attempts are made to defeat their purposes;

5. direct pressure on any member who expresses strong argument against any of the group's stereotypes, illusions, or commitments, making clear that this type of dissent is contrary to what is expected of all loyal members;

6. self-censorship of deviations from the apparent group consensus, reflecting each member's inclination to minimize to himself the importance of his doubts and counter-arguments;

7. a shared illusion of unanimity concerning judgments conforming to the majority view (partly resulting from self-censorship of deviations, augmented by the false assumption that silence means consent);

8. the emergence of self-appointed mindguards—members who protect the group from adverse information that might shatter their shared complacency about the effectiveness and morality of their decisions. (Janis, 1972, 197 and 198).

Our discussion to this point has suggested that a positive relationship can exist among the variables of group cohesiveness, symptoms of groupthink, and defects in decision making. The three variables may be assessed independently, but a causal link can be asserted when discussing them in the context of groupthink as indicated in the groupthink model we offer in Figure 1.

It has also been noted that the insulation of the policy-making group and promotional leadership practices impinge heavily on group cohesiveness to determine whether the cohesiveness will lead to groupthink. Note also that the group is insulated from feedback about the faulty decision once it has been made. The groupthink model is a way of summarizing the groupthink phenomenon. Having discussed the major dimensions of groupthink in general, we are ready to examine the phenomenon in business organizations.

GROUPTHINK IN BUSINESS ORGANIZATIONS

It is hard to imagine that the usually highly competitive atmosphere of the business world permits those with the social and personality attributes necessary for succumbing to groupthink to climb to the top-most corporate positions. However, Janis observes that *none* are immune to groupthink. Even those strong-willed executives with high self-esteem, low dependency on others, and low submissiveness can be carried to faulty decisions through groupthink. In addition, Argyris (1974) notes in his review of Janis' book that in his own experience, groups that have fallen vic-

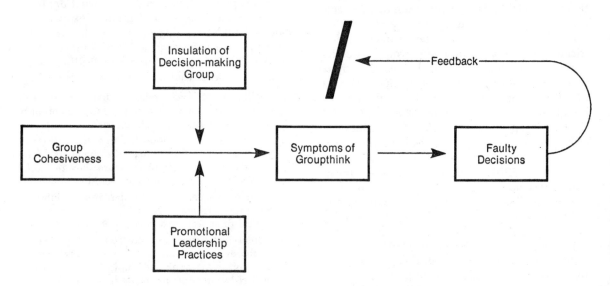

FIGURE 1. Variables and causal inference in a groupthink model.

tim to groupthink would vehemently deny that it exists in their group.

Although Janis is primarily concerned with groupthink in government decision making, he does suggest that by studying unwise and disastrous policy decisions made by industrial firms groupthink may be found in organizations outside the government bureaucracy. As a first step in that direction we propose to examine fiascoes in business where indications are that (1) the decision-making group was cohesive and (2) decision making by that group was extremely defective.

The first case to be discussed involves the groupthink phenomenon in decision making in the U.S. stock market. The other two examples to be briefly discussed here were suggested by Janis: first the planning, producing, and selling of the Edsel automobile, and second, the illegal price-fixing arrangements among electric companies in the 1950s.

The Stock Market

Recently Dreman (1977) has written on the role of psychology in today's stock market activities. He writes from the perspective of one who has had a large amount of experience with brokerage firms and professional investment in general. Dreman's thesis in regard to groupthink is that it may very well be the cause of failure on the part of professional investors (i.e., those that manage large sums of money for bank trust departments, pension funds, mutual funds, investment advisory firms, insurance companies, college endowment funds, and other financial institutions) to make good decisions.

The stock market is now dominated by professional investment organizations as can be seen through a few pertinent facts. The growth of assets under their control was much faster than the rate of growth of the national economy in 1972, and by the end of that year the assets totaled over $900 billion. In 1973 they controlled 70 percent of all the trading and almost 50 percent of the stock holdings on the New York Stock Exchange. Corporate pension funds are the largest category of institutional investors, and by 1975 they owned one-third of all publicly held stock and invested

30 cents of every dollar of pretax corporate profits.

As professional investors have become more prevalent, views of the market as subject to the whims of *individual* investors who can make drastic fluctuations in the market in a less than professional manner have decreased. "The market would be increasingly in the hands of steely-eyed, informed professionals, and price movements would become far more objective and systematic" (Dreman, 1977, 4). Individual investors were concurrently urged to use the professionals, thus exacerbating the current wave of confidence.

The decision-making "group" in the stock-market context may not be quite the same as that envisioned by Janis. The group Dreman asserts is the cohesive group is composed of the professional investment community as a whole. It is this group that suffers from groupthink to the detriment of many who invest in the market. Many of his examples deal with a professional group working for a particular organization, but it is the combined influence of the entire stock market community that leads to the real debacles according to Dreman.

Dreman provides a very convincing argument for the cohesiveness of the professionals. They seem to feel a strength in their ability to prognosticate future market conditions based on their numbers. Once the investment community is swayed in one direction they will stumble onward in the face of overwhelming evidence that they have made a bad decision. Even worse, perhaps, is that once it has been determined that a bad decision has been made, the way in which the attempt to recoup the results of the faulty decision is handled will in itself often turn out to be a knee-jerk reaction with little thought given to the whole picture. In other words, the group attempts to correct a bad decision with one that makes the situation worse. For instance, Dreman points out that a money manager he knew

was convinced, as were many of his colleagues, that Honeywell was headed for extinction [in 1974]. Market conditions, reinforced by his colleagues' views, appeared to be distorting his judgment, and even when he was presented with conclusive statistical refutation, he remained unconvinced and sold the stock heavily. Less than five months later, in a rising market, he forgot his concern for the company's finances and concentrating on other fundamentals, he bought the stock at double the price he had sold it at previously. (Dreman, 1977, 145).

In his examples Dreman points out that the professionals were influenced far more by groupthink than by pressure from their clients. The investment decision makers sincerely believe that if they themselves have reservations the reservations are overstated and that the investment group (or community) is correct. The most convincing argument put forth by Dreman in this light is the fact that the professionals have not outperformed the market over the years regardless of the competitive pressures of the times. The 1973 market collapse is attributed by Dreman in large part to groupthink. Serious and obvious risks were discounted. Investors paid no heed to danger signals such as overconcentration in the same stocks and paying too much for so-called blue-chip stocks. Initially inflation was the reason given for *buying* the top tier stocks and subsequently inflation was given as the reason for *selling* those same top tier stocks. Why the paradox?

If we accept groupthink as even partially responsible for such a deeply felt reversal in the market as that experienced in 1973 and 1974, it is to our benefit to be able to recognize it and do something positive toward reversing the trend. We must keep in mind that "even first rate money managers can succumb to the influence of groupthink and if many do, it can have a disastrous effect on both investors and the economy" (Dreman, 1977, 200). If such highly talented individuals as those involved in money management can inadvertently let groupthink become an albatross around their necks it is certainly a possibility that others in the business world are also subject to its influence.

Earlier it was suggested that the two major prerequisites necessary to demonstrate groupthink in an organization are (1) a cohesive decision-making group and (2) an extremely defective decision by that group. Dreman establishes those two facts in great detail in his book as Janis did in his government case studies. However, these are the only two in-depth case analyses available. In these remaining two case studies of groupthink

it will be suggested that groupthink was a definite possibility in some poor decisions in a business context. It is beyond the scope of this article to conduct an exhaustive study of any of the cases though that would be a rich area for further study of the groupthink/business relationship.

The Edsel

Ford Motor Company produced the Edsel automobile for two and one-half years during 1958, 1959, and 1960. That the Edsel was a monumental failure is common knowledge. There seems hardly a necessity to establish the fact that Ford made a poor decision. The Edsel still has the stigma of being the classic example of a bad decision. As late as 1971 the *New York Times* when headlining a feature about the failure of DuPont to conduct proper market research for its Corfam shoe products heralded "DuPont's $100-Million Edsel: Market Research Doomed Corfam" (Deutsch, 1976, 5).

As a means of establishing Edsel's failure, a few facts are appropriate. The total cost to Ford of research design, tooling, and expansion of production facilities was $250 million over the few years just prior to 1958 (Deutsch, 1976, 43). That was only the cost to get the Edsel to market, however. An additional $200 million was estimated to have been lost during the nearly two and one-half years of production of the car and it was declared one of the most costly mistakes a U.S. corporation has ever made (Deutsch, 1976, 44). It can be said with some conviction that a defective decision was made by Ford in the case of the Edsel. Does that mean groupthink caused the faulty decision? Not necessarily, but a look at the decision-making group to determine the degree of cohesiveness is a logical next step.

Before the restructuring of Ford's top management in 1945 there is a good likelihood that groupthink would not have been a factor in poor decisions because there was a divisiveness at many junctures (Sorensen, 1956), rather than the cohesiveness that developed in the higher echelons in the post–World War II years. Henry Ford II (HF II) became president of Ford in September, 1945, at the age of 28. Realizing his deficiencies, he began to assemble a team of managers and advisors most of whom would be with him for the next fifteen years. Some of those men had a part in initially securing HF II's post as president (Herndon, 1969, 185) and remained close personal advisors until at least late 1959 (Deutsch, 1976, 56).

An examination of Herndon's book *Ford*, Deutsch's book *Selling the People's Cadillac*, and the appropriate newspapers and magazines can readily demonstrate the cohesiveness of the group at Ford that made the Edsel decision. Though HF II seldom saw his executives socially there were strong assertions regarding how highly all members thought of one another. The mutual respect and confidence was evident and strengthened itself through a classic reversal that the group brought about at Ford. In 1945, Ford was losing nearly $9 million a month (Deutsch, 1976, 56), but with the advent of the new management group the rust was shaken out of the mammoth organization and the trend was reversed. By 1955, when the Edsel decisions were being made, that same top Ford group had the company functioning very well indeed. A large degree of cohesiveness was the result of the group's ten years of highly successful association as an entity.

With the above history in mind, it would appear that groupthink could have been a part of the Edsel decision. Further evidence of groupthink is found in what appears to be insulation of the decision-making group. Market research was coming into its own about 1955 and Ford felt that to neglect the information it provided would be violating their responsibility to the public (Deutsch, 1976, 33). However, the group's decision to go with the Edsel seemed to be based on something other than market research for the research indicated that they should *not* have pursued the Edsel line. The closer it came to the show date of the Edsel, the more evidence there was that the public wanted smaller and cheaper autos rather than the Edsel, which was larger and more expensive, being designed to fill the gap between Mercury and Lincoln. But Ford would not reverse its decision even in the face of the most convincing evidence. It has been said that even though huge marketing research efforts took place, the basic mistake was failure to ask questions which elicited meaningful replies (Deutsch, 1976, 41). For example, no one seemed to ask questions about auto prices, maintenance costs, operating costs, rising insurance rates, parking difficulties, cars being too long for garages, etc. The practical questions were foregone for those dealing with owner social status and the like. Lower-level managers were convinced that Edsel was not going to make it even before it came out (Deutsch, 1976, 45). Yet they could not or would not convince the top group.

Later, as the Edsel was being produced and the losses were accumulating the top group at Ford let production continue for *two and one-half years* before entirely accepting the fact that they had made a bad decision. This provides more evidence of the group insulating itself from the realities of the situation.

Referring to Figure 1, notice that there was a cohesive group at Ford with insulation impinging on its decision. Some of the eight symptoms of groupthink can easily be found at Ford during the Edsel years. A degree of self-censoring (symptom 6) is evident in noting that in 1953 Robert McNamara, then an executive at Ford, asked the question about what the new car was supposed to offer the public (Deutsch, 1976, 72). He believed in the car and was not intending to undermine Edsel efforts, but he would not pursue the question, and therefore, it was never discussed at length as it surely should have been.

Shared illusions of unanimity (symptom 7) were obviously present. After the car became a loss a few who had had doubts expressed them haltingly. Herndon (1969) provides evidence that a lot of controversy existed initially but that the group seemed to convince itself of its invulnerability (symptom 1) and thus in turn began to see the arguments *for* the Edsel.

Stereotyped views of the opposition (symptom 4) and an illusion of invulnerability (symptom 1) combined to increase in the top group's minds the original and recent success of the Thunderbird automobile. It was a coup against Chevrolet in particular but all the auto industry, too, and had occurred starting in 1956. As was pointed out in the insulation discussion above there were efforts at rationalization in order to discount warnings that may have led members to reconsider their assumptions before they recommitted themselves to their past policy decisions (symptom 2).

In summary, then, it would seem that Ford and its Edsel decision fit rather well into the groupthink model. While this has necessarily been a somewhat cursory look at the Edsel case it should be sufficient to point out the distinct possibility that groupthink was in effect during the Edsel years.

The Price Conspiracy

Between 1950 and 1960, the greatest antitrust conspiracy in American history (up to that time) had been perpetrated by the multibillion-dollar electrical industry. There is evidence that defective decisions were made in a series of meetings by a few policy makers who constituted a cohesive group during the many years of the conspiracy.

In this example a distinction should be made between micro- and macro-level cohesive decision-making groups. Each of the electrical companies involved had its own micro-level cohesive group that made decisions to conspire with other companies to fix prices. Then there were representatives of each company who made up a macro-level, *inter*organizational group that decided specifics of the price-fixing arrangements. It appears that a high degree of cohesiveness can be attributed to groups at both levels.

Herling in his book *The Great Price Conspiracy* (1962), points out that at the macro level, even with a possibility of antitrust action against them, members of the group (who were not even working for the same organization) would dine at each others' homes, lunch together in public places, play golf and tennis together, and exhibit other such behaviors which are, according to Janis, major indications of cohesiveness.

At both the macro and micro level, codes had been established which only members of the group could properly decipher. Many of the higher-level executives were not a part of the conspiracy and, therefore, could not interpret the signs. This point was made by then president of General Electric, Robert Paxton when he testified before a Senate investigating committee.

He finally decided that these men [members of the group] were using a series of signals—like bridge partners—which they might have assumed that he ... understood, but in fact he would not have the "foggiest" notion of what the others were talking about. (Herling, 1962, 46).

He was referring specifically to a micro-level wink of the eye that would be exchanged when discussing "competitive" bids which were actually prenegotiated (rigged). However, there were other codes such as the attendance list for the macro-level group that was referred to as the "Christmas-card list," and the meetings being referred to as "choir practice" (Smith, 1961a, 170). The listening apparatus of the groups had long since become accustomed to dealing in double entendres. The conspiratorial atmosphere in all the groups added to the cohesiveness over the years.

Besides cohesiveness it can also be shown that this case study meets the other prerequisite of culminating in a faulty decision. In this case, as in most, there was a series of faulty decisions, and their interaction exacerbated the intensity of the results. That the companies involved were knowingly breaking the law would seem to be enough evidence that someone was allowing faulty decisions to be made, assuming that one is of a moral persuasion which finds law-breaking unacceptable, as most of our society does.

The decisions were made to seem worse, though, by the fact that once caught in the act of fixing prices the effects were extremely far reaching. Hundreds of executives and forty corporations admittedly participated. The American people felt betrayed by businessmen.

The conspiracy enmeshed hundreds of communities where electrical industry plants are located. The federal government, with its numerous agencies, was aggressively involved, not only as a bilked customer, but as a guardian of community interest. Regional authorities, state and local bodies, hundreds of electrical cooperatives, privately owned utilities were intimately affected. More than 2,000 damage suits were entered against the electrical manufacturing industry as a result of these conspiracies. (Herling, 1963, viii).

The value of the electrical equipment that was the object of the conspiracies to fix prices, rig bids, and divide markets over the eight year period was estimated at $1,750,000,000. It involved a range of organizations from those the size of General Electric and Westinghouse to those whose shop space was barely larger than the courtroom where proceedings took place. The total of fines levied by the courts was $1,924,500. Additionally, seven jail sentences and twenty-four suspended jail sentences were handed down (Smith, 1961a, 133 and 134). The scope and magnitude of the poor decisions show the conspiracy as deserving of attention in the groupthink context.

Thinking again in terms of the groupthink model, the insulation of the decision-making groups can be gleaned from the fact that on numerous occasions during the years of price fixing (approximately 1950 to 1960) antitrust-law violations were successfully prosecuted. The defendants were in many instances members of the electrical industry, those same organizations caught in the larger proceedings about 1960. As the government began its major investigation, the industry was aware that it was occurring. Yet the companies continued their conspiracy. They clearly refused to accept the realities of their situation: that their long-standing conspiracy was about to become a national scandal. In addition to serving as evidence for insulation, this also demonstrates collective efforts to rationalize in order to discount warnings (symptom 2) and an illusion of invulnerability (symptom 1). The illusion of invulnerability is also apparent when considering that group members *knew* they were breaking the law but continued for years to regard themselves as above or beyond the law. "That one could go to prison for violating the Sherman Act was a possibility that apparently few had considered" (Walton and Cleveland, 1964, 82).

The last symptom of groupthink from the price conspiracy to be cited in this article is the group's unquestioned belief in their inherent morality, inclining members to ignore the ethical or moral consequences of their decisions (symptom 3). We see this symptom plainly in the not-uncommon words espoused by one long-time General Electric executive, "Sure, collusion was illegal, but it wasn't *unethical*" (Smith, 1961a, 135). By their own admission, most of the conspirators knew they were breaking the law. Walton and Cleveland (1964, 82) asserted that "while most of the

men knew that they were breaking a law, the common theme running throughout the testimony was that although violation of the Sherman Act may be a legal offense, it was certainly not a moral one." The groups involved in the conspiracy were convinced of the inherent morality of their acts, regardless of the illegality. In this abbreviated look at the price conspiracy it has been found that cohesive groups, insulation of the groups, illusions of invulnerability, rationalizing to discount warnings, and belief by the group in their inherent morality were all present.

Implications of the Groupthink Phenomenon

It is clear at this point that groupthink can and has occurred in business organizations as it has in government organizations. However, the examples used have dealt with the large-scale, highly publicized fiascoes of huge organizations. It is probably necessary to study the major fiascoes because they are the ones that received sufficient publicity to enable the researcher to find evidence of behavioral trends like groupthink. Additionally, the examples used are of necessity not contemporary because the researcher must wait until enough facts have become available for him to come to reasonable conclusions about the processes and personalities involved in a particular decision.

While it may appear obvious that groupthink was inherent in the highly publicized big decisions cited earlier, it may not be obvious that groupthink takes place in the day-to-day group decisions reached in smaller organizations. Thousands of decisions worth millions of dollars are made in business each day, each with varying degrees of importance. These decisions, made by small groups, are susceptible to the influence of groupthink. Groupthink is not restricted to large organizations and large-scale decisions.

The implication here is that organizations using forms of small-group policy planning and/or decision making should be alert for the possibility of groupthink. By being aware of how detrimental it can be even to relatively minor decisions, organizations can learn to cope with it.

TOWARD OVERCOMING GROUPTHINK

Having discussed the concept of groupthink and related the concept to the decision-making process in the business environment, we are now ready to examine how the groupthink phenomenon can be avoided in small-group decision making. Our discussion will focus on two major areas. First, we will present several suggestions by Janis to help avoid groupthink. Second, we will briefly examine a dialectical approach to decision making which we feel has potential as a means of improving small-group decisions.

Janis' Suggestions for Overcoming Groupthink

Following are some of the suggestions by Janis for overcoming groupthink.

1. *The leader of a decision-making group should assign the role of critical evaluator to each member.* Following this suggestion, doubts and objections are thus more likely to be exposed and discussed rather than suppressed. The group leader must be sure that he sets the example for the other members by accepting criticism of *his* ideas and thoughts on the matter at hand. This critical evaluator suggestion along with others subsequent to it may be difficult to implement. It may be that acceptance of criticism will have to be learned by group members because many of us are naturally averse to it.

2. *The leaders in an organization's hierarchy, when assigning a decision-making mission to a group, should be impartial instead of stating preferences at the outset.* When executives in an organization give guidance to their decision-making groups, many times they have introduced bias unwittingly by being too specific in outlining what they want accomplished and how they want it accomplished. Some guidance is almost always necessary and the extent of it may be a function of the time available for the group to arrive at a decision. If the time is short, more guidance will hasten the decision. However, the less guidance there is the less chance there is that the executive's preconceived notions will unduly influence the decision of the group. Certainly he should not

be so specific as to indicate which of several alternatives he would prefer to have adopted. Admittedly there is a delicate balance between just enough guidance to get the job done and too much, which will cause promotional leadership, but that balance is what a good group leader should strive for.

3. *Members of the decision-making group should frequently seek advice and counsel from trusted associates in their own department within the organization.* Fresh perspectives on the problem can be gained in this manner, and it provides a method for introducing thoughts from those outside the decision-making group. The reactions of these associates should then be taken back and introduced to the group. Discretion must be used in implementing this suggestion when the decision involves highly confidential planning of goals, or policies which need to be kept from public dissemination.

4. *The consensus-seeking tendency could be thwarted effectively by use of a devil's advocate at each meeting of the group that deals with decision making.* The devil's advocate role, to be most effective, should be rotated among the group members and in some cases more than one may be desirable. A real possibility here, which should be avoided, is tokenism on the part of the leader or the group. The devil's advocate(s) should be taken seriously and his criticisms discussed to the satisfaction of all present.

5. *After reading a preliminary consensus about what seems to be the best alternative, the decision-making group should hold a "second chance" meeting at which every member is expected to express as vividly as he can all his residual doubts and to rethink the entire issue before making a definite choice.* The "second chance" meeting allows further discussion of a decision *after* preliminary consensus but *before* the final decision has been delivered from the group. At this meeting all members are asked to rethink their position in regard to the matter at hand and express the residual doubts that result therefrom. A caveat is in order to thwart cognitive dissonance whereby in preparation for these "second chance" meetings the group members may feel too strongly that a wrong decision is made. Thus, support for the

final decision may be less than it otherwise would have been.

Having considered some of the specific suggestions offered by Janis for reducing groupthink, we will complete our discussion with a brief examination of a dialectical approach to decision making as an additional means of reducing the groupthink possibility.

Dialectic Decision Making

While an in-depth consideration of the dialectical approach to decision making is beyond the scope of this article, we do think the approach has real potential for combating groupthink. With that in mind, we are ready to briefly set forth the dialectical approach. A dialectic system examines any situation from at least two different points of view. A minimum of two individuals present opposing interpretations of the data being considered, while a third individual acts as a synthesizer or judge. The opposing interpretations are presented in the format of a structured debate. This parallels Churchman's interpretation of Hegel where a thesis is opposed by an antithesis, both being developed from the same data bank with a third party developing, on the basis of the debate, a new and expanded view or synthesis (Mason, 1969).

Several authors have suggested that a dialectical approach would be useful to the development of effective decisions in many situations (Mason, 1969; Mason and Mitroff, 1973; Mitroff, 1971 and 1974). The application of the dialectical approach to the problem of groupthink seems a logical extension of previous writing. If groupthink is a deterioration of reality testing, then what is needed to overcome its ill effects is a system which forces an examination of a wide range of possible realities. The dialectic's presentation of analysis from opposing world views provides such a range.

For example, envision a manager with a problem. He may use a participative management style whereby a group assists him in making decisions. Upon determination that a decision needs to be made, the manager gathers all pertinent data in reference to that decision. He then presents the identical data to two of his equally capable staff assistants at separate times giving one instructions to determine why the decision should be in the affirmative and instructing the other to determine why the decision should be negative. At the next session of the decision-making group, each of the staff assistants gives a presentation, each presenting opposing interpretations of the data. Each must be allowed to present his case fully and subsequently to defend it. Thus, chances for premature closure and such symptoms as illusions of unanimity are greatly reduced.

In using a dialectical approach, by design, persons from outside the group prevent it from insulating itself against the realities of the situation. Members of the group do not have to endanger cohesiveness by expressing arguments against group commitments; the arguments are made by outsiders. And in a like manner most of the symptoms of groupthink are reduced if not prevented entirely by use of a dialectical approach to decision making.

The dialectical approach is equally well suited for use in organizations of any size. One need only increase the size and/or scope of the parties preparing for and arguing the opposing points of view with increases in the size of the organization.

CONCLUSION

The central purpose of this article has been to bring the groupthink phenomenon to the business world and suggest ways of overcoming it. In an age when business decision making by groups, as opposed to individuals, is increasingly commonplace, groupthink is a greater likelihood than ever before. The three cases (the stock market, the Edsel, and the price conspiracy), confirm the suspicion that decision-making groups in business can produce fiascoes that are equally illuminating in terms of groupthink as those in government.

The large-scale fiascoes were used only to make the point that businesses are indeed susceptible to groupthink. However, the more relevant issue is that smaller organizations are equally susceptible. Susceptibility of the organization to groupthink is not a function of the size of the organization. Rather, it is a function of the variables included in the groupthink model (Figure 1). The magnitude of the results of groupthink is probably a function of the size of the organization, but the consequences of a faulty decision for a smaller firm are just as real and just as detrimental as those of larger firms. Perhaps the consequences are even more severe with smaller organizations because they are generally less able to withstand and absorb large-scale setbacks.

Finally, we have suggested some specific suggestions for overcoming groupthink with an emphasis on a dialectical approach to decision making. It is our contention that in an age when small-group decision making is at the very heart of participative management, a dialectical approach can reduce the possibility of groupthink and improve the environment for small-group decision making.

REFERENCES

Argyris, C. Book reviews. *Sloan Management Review,* Winter 1974, pp. 103–105.

Deutsch, J. G. *Selling the People's Cadillac.* New Haven: Yale University Press, 1976.

Dreman, D. N. *Psychology and the Stock Market.* New York: AMACOM, 1977.

Herling, J. *The Great Price Conspiracy.* Washington: Robert B. Luce, 1962.

Herndon, B. *Ford.* New York: Weybright and Talley, 1969.

Illing, H. A. "C. G. Jung on the Present Trends in Group Psychotherapy." *Human Relations,* 1957, *10,* 77–84.

Janis, I. L. *Victims of Groupthink.* Boston: Houghton Mifflin, 1972.

Mason, R. O. "A Dialectical Approach to Strategic Planning." *Management Science,* 1969, *15,* B403–B414.

Mason, R. O., and Mitroff, I. I. "A Program for Research on Management Information Systems." *Management Science,* 1973, *19,* 475–487.

Mitroff, I. I. "A Communication Model of Dialectic Inquiring Systems—A Strategy for Strategic Planning." *Management Science,* 1971, *17,* B634–B648.

Mitroff, I. I. "A Brunswick Lens Model of Dialectical Inquiring Systems." *Theory and Decision,* 1974, *5,* 45–67.

Shaw, M. E. *Group Dynamics* (2nd ed.). New York: McGraw-Hill, 1976.

Smith, R. A. "The Incredible Electrical Conspiracy, Part I." *Fortune,* April 1961, pp. 132–137; 170, 172; 175–177; 179–180.

Smith, R. A. "The Incredible Electrical Conspiracy, Part II." *Fortune,* May 1961, pp. 161–164; 210; 212; 217–218; 221–223.

Sorensen, C. E. *My Forty Years with Ford.* New York: W. W. Norton, 1956.

Stein, A. A. "Conflict and Cohesion." *Journal of Conflict Resolution,* 1976, *20,* 143–172.

Walton, C. C., and Cleveland, F. W., Jr. *Corporations on Trial: The Electric Cases.* Belmont, California: Wadsworth, 1964.

ELIMINATING INTERGROUP CONFLICTS THROUGH INTERDEPARTMENTAL PROBLEM SOLVING

W. MICHAEL A. BROOKER

When problems arise between persons in a company, the worst thing the personnel consultant (or whoever is in charge of getting people out of the boxing ring and back to work) can do is to try to fix the blame on one person or group of persons. This is a careless and self-defeating means of dealing with a very touchy situation. And it inevitably leads to more—and this time deeper—conflicts.

In most cases, the problem is really due to a breakdown of communication. This is where the blame belongs and where the personnel consultant must focus his efforts. He should assist the persons involved in discovering what went wrong and how best to keep communication problems from happening again.

GETTING TOGETHER

One of the most useful ways of inducing constructive social change in business organizations is the process of "intergroup problem solving." Although this label may sound rather imposing and complex, the process itself is relatively simple. The personnel consultant (or "change agent") persuades the parties involved to sit down together,

Reprinted by permission of the publisher from *S.A.M. Advanced Management Journal,* Spring 1975, © 1975 by S.A.M., a division of American Management Associations.

confront the communication problems they've been having, and work out procedures to avoid future sources of misunderstanding.

The best way to understand just what the "intergroup problem solving" process involves is by examining each of its three distinct organizational phases separately.

The objective of Phase I is two-fold. Members of a group get together and work toward creating a model (i.e., a diagram) that shows (a) the main organizational pressures and influences that devolve upon the group, and (b) the main problems associated with those pressures and influences. The change agent shares these objectives, but also has the further aim of encouraging communication among group members present, perhaps in ways they have not experienced before.

The change agent leads the group discussion and records the proceedings on a large easel pad at the same time. The easel pad serves two purposes: It helps develop a record of the meeting, and it enables those present to approve or modify the record at the time it is being worked up.

BREAKING SOME ICE

To start the discussion it is usually necessary to refer to the circumstances that led up to the meeting. For example, the change agent may address the group in the following manner:

"Gentlemen, as many of you know, I work in this company as an internal consultant. That is, I seek out clients from among our managers and work out assignments with them that meet their needs. Although I work out of the head office, I do not represent head office thinking or policy other than providing the services that I do. One of the clients I have is the ABC department, and the technique I am using with its staff is intergroup problem solving and planning.

"As the name implies, the technique focuses attention on the relationships ABC department has with other departments. One of the important relations ABC has is with you people in XYZ. What I hope to persuade you fellows to do is to meet with ABC to resolve not only what its staff regards as a problem with you, but also what you may regard as a problem with its staff."

Often this initial explanation is greeted with the question, "Does this mean we are the worst department in the company?" This, of course, indicates a serious misunderstanding, which the change agent should correct immediately. He assures the group that meeting to discuss problems is a sign of the department's strength, not a sign of failure.

After a few minutes of explanation and dealing with expressed concerns, the change agent moves directly to the main business of the first meeting—the preparation of a "situation model."

MAKING THINGS "PERFECTLY CLEAR"

The situation model consists of two parts. The first part is what one team member dubbed an "octopus chart" (see the figure on page 113). It shows the participating group in the center (the "head" of the octopus), with its main external relationships radiating out from it like octopus "arms" or the spokes of a wheel. These relationships are indicated on the easel pad by the change agent according to information given by the team members present.

Immediately the question of priorities becomes apparent. Someone may ask whether *all* the spokes in the wheel are to be included. The answer is no; the aim is to focus on only the half-dozen or so most important ones.

A brief description of each external relationship the group has within the company is listed in the column in the lower part of the chart. Relationships usually involve the flow of goods and/or services. For example, a production department receives components or raw materials from one department and passes on processed components or subassemblies to another.

In another column at the bottom of the chart, the team preparing the model lists the problems it has with the team/group/department/section identified. A little more difficulty creeps in here. It is easy for a group to identify a relationship, a little more difficult to define that relationship, and harder still to agree on the wording of a problem. The words on the easel pad often get changed many times before there is general agreement.

When the situation model is complete, the main task of the meeting is finished. There remains only the preparation of a facing sheet. The facing sheet states the name of the group that met and who was present. It states that a situation model was prepared and is attached, and that the group wishes to meet with those "problem" departments it has identified in the situation model.

The objectives of the meeting should now have been achieved. And if the meeting has gone well, hopefully the change agent's objective of encouraging communication has been satisfied as well. In any case, at least there has been a sharing of information. Many groupings in complex organizations exist only on paper, and their members seldom meet as a group. Consequently, individual members often do not really know what others do. A common remark evoked at seeing the top half of the situation model for the first time is, "Heavens! I never realized we had so many contacts."

This sharing of information is also important because it helps increase feelings of cohesiveness in anticipation of meeting with other groups. The meeting format also causes team members to start wondering about their own contributions to a problem situation. Often someone will say, "If that's what we think about them, I sure don't want to know what they think about us," whereupon the group may launch into a revision of the problem statement.

SITUATION MODEL

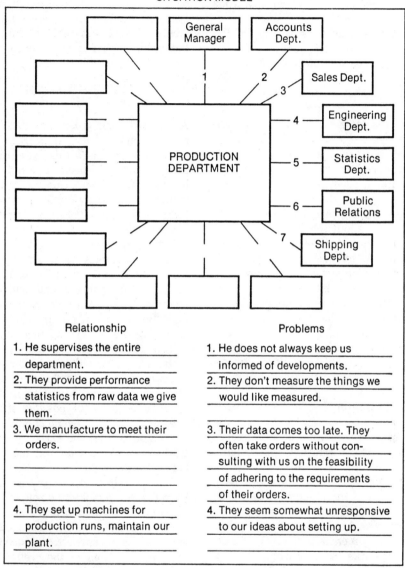

Relationship

1. He supervises the entire department.
2. They provide performance statistics from raw data we give them.
3. We manufacture to meet their orders.

4. They set up machines for production runs, maintain our plant.

Problems

1. He does not always keep us informed of developments.
2. They don't measure the things we would like measured.

3. Their data comes too late. They often take orders without consulting with us on the feasibility of adhering to the requirements of their orders.
4. They seem somewhat unresponsive to our ideas about setting up.

LOOKING INTO INSIGHTS

Thus, insights about objectives other than those on the surface often begin to emerge. Such insights can be further prodded by passing out copies of a "team action sheet" toward the end of the meeting. The team action sheet contains a list of six questions that each member answers on a graded scale of "1" through "5" according to how satisfied or dissatisfied he feels with that part of the meeting. To encourage candor, participants are asked not to sign their names. The list of questions is as follows:

1. How free did you feel to express yourself in the group?
2. How satisfied were you with your group's manner of working?

3. How do you feel about the decisions your group made?
4. How much of the time were you doing the talking? (0–100%)
5. How much influence do you feel you had in your group? (0–100%)
6. Comments, questions, or suggestions.

Once completed, the team action sheets are collected by the change agent, who uses them to encourage one final round of discussion.

The logic of the team action sheet is as follows: If people are inhibited (question no. 1), they will probably feel unhappy about the way the meeting was run (question no. 2); people who are either inhibited or unhappy about the manner of working are likely to be unhappy with the decisions made (question 3). As for questions no. 4 and 5, in any collection of people some talk more than others. One may be quiet either because he is naturally so or because he feels inhibited. As the change agent summarizes the sheet responses on the easel pad, he is able to check to see if low scorers to question no. 4 are also low scorers to question no. 1. If they are, this constitutes a warning signal that some members were inhibited—perhaps dangerously so.

Generally, the totals on the "influence" scale exceed the totals on the "talking" scale, meaning that many group members rate their influence greater than their true contribution. Occasionally the totals of the "talking" scale exceed those of "influence," showing that some members have rated their influence less than their talking. These are the most difficult groups to work with. They tend to be at the lower levels of an organization, and often one or two members exhibit defeatist behavior in the remarks made during the main part of the meeting.

Often the discussion of the results of the completed team action sheets provides significant information on intergroup problems for the group to share. The sheets also tend to make the individual team members more aware of their share of responsibility for the effectiveness of the meeting.

It is important to note that the aim of this discussion is not to identify individual people with their questionnaire responses. If someone is somewhat inhibited, he may become more so if identi-

fied. A technique for avoiding this is to ask questions in a general way, such as, "Some people have indicated they felt less than free to express themselves. What might have caused this?"

A FEW OPTIONS WORTH CONSIDERING

At this point the group may decide that it should resolve some internal difficulties before tackling external ones. To do this the entire first phase of the process would need to be repeated at the next level down. Although this can be time-consuming, it may be necessary for the group to face its own internal problems before trying to work out its external ones.

If the problems identified in Phase I indicate a confusion of roles or a difficulty in clarifying "Who does what?" then Phase II should be completed before going ahead with the intergroup meeting. If no role difficulties have been identified, the group can go straight to the process of arranging the intergroup meetings in Phase III.

The aim of Phase II is to define the role of the group within its wider environment. In the previous model what was shown was the *actual* situation of the group. Attention in Phase II should be given to a set of *possible* situations. In this phase, the change agent should try to open up discussion so that the exchanges really stimulate team members to examine the role alternatives before them.

The overall objective of this discussion is to have the group define the role of its leader—insofar as he is the head of the group—in the form of a "draft position guide." An in Phase I, the results of the discussion are recorded on a large easel pad in front of the group. The avenues of discussion should be as follows:

a. Position title—the precise title of the group's supervisor or manager;
b. Objectives—the supervisor's primary and secondary goals;
c. Control criteria—pre-established measures by which the success of achieving objectives can be gauged;
d. Main activities—the means by which objectives are achieved;

e. Limitations of authority—mandatory limits on the supervisor's ability to achieve objectives;

f. Main relationships—the main reporting relationships of the supervisor, upward and downward.

BRINGING IT ALL TOGETHER

Phase III is where the payoff for the entire exercise should occur. Once the change agent brings the two antagonistic groups together in an "intergroup meeting," success ultimately depends upon the willingness of the two groups to cooperate and change. But this willingness must have been developed by the change agent during previous phases and maintained at the intergroup phase. Most intergroup meetings are problem-solving in nature. The agenda is easily drawn up from the situation models previously completed. The word "problems" should be transcribed on the left side of the easel pad ahead of time, leaving the right side free for agreed-upon corrective action.

The following cycle is used for each problem. First, the problem is read out loud, either by the change agent or by one of the members of the team from which it originated. Second, the change agent asks the responding team whether it needs clarification of the problem as stated. The responding team is asked *not* to rebut the problem or state there is no problem but merely to ask questions. Third, the responding team is asked, having agreed that it understands what the other team is saying, to make suggestions that would reduce or eliminate the problem. This is probably the most difficult moment for the change agent in controlling the group. Attempts by the responding team to rebut the problem must be firmly cut off at this stage because of the danger of counter-rebuttal and uncontrolled, unproductive blame-laying.

SETTING UP GROUND RULES

In explaining the procedure before getting down to the business of the meeting, the change agent stresses the difference between blame-laying behavior and problem-solving behavior and states his intention to cut off any attempt to fix the blame for a problem. The difference between blame-laying and problem-solving behavior, he explains, is the extent to which a *solution* is implied. If one cannot think of a solution for a problem, one might as well say nothing. In the silence that inevitably follows, someone will think to say something that is at least partially constructive. Admittedly, it is not easy to control a group of people who are all too willing to start blaming each other, but it must be done to achieve positive results.

To recapitulate, the first step in the intergroup problem-solving meeting is reading the problem. Second, questions are asked by the responding team of the originating team. Third, the responding team makes proposals for reducing or eliminating the problem. Fourth, the floor is opened for suggestions from the originating team. Actually this fourth step is not clearly demarcated from the previous one, nor does it seem that it should be. Ideas generated by the responding group often include suggestions that involve both teams. The important point here is that the responding team gets the opportunity to respond; even if the response is silence, it can be a thundering silence.

A PLAN FOR THE FUTURE

As a result of suggestions made for reducing or eliminating the problem, a list soon develops from which the groups choose a solution or solutions for action. This constitutes their agreed "corrective action." The names or titles of the people who agree to take action and the dates by which this will be done are included, in order to establish responsibilities and appropriate expectations on the part of all concerned.

This ends the cycle of steps that the intergroup problem-solving meeting goes through with each problem on the agenda. Having done so, a time for a future review of the meeting is set. The review meeting is held between two and six weeks after the original, in order to make sure that the agreed corrective action has, in fact, taken place.

The intergroup problem-solving approach has been used among groups of many different backgrounds: production and engineering, production and personnel, research and development and production. It has been used in many kinds of enterprises: manufacturing plants, head offices, government departments, and others. Its success can be measured by the extent to which agreed corrective action can be made to stick and by the improved communication among the various groups involved.

SOME CONCLUSIONS

Is attitudinal change a prerequisite to behavioral change? I believe it is not. I also believe that attitudes should be regarded primarily as a func-

tion of behavior. If we can change the way people relate to one another, even for a short while, then this change itself becomes a powerful reason for a more appropriate attitude toward other people and other functions. In order to explore the dangers of a "we vs. they" situation, it is not necessary to do so in a laboratory situation; it can be observed quite readily in an actual work situation. And to observe the results of a bad communication problem left unsolved, one has only to look at the failing company, low in managerial morale and productivity, the victim of its own internal fragmentations.

3
ORGANIZATIONAL DIMENSIONS
OF BEHAVIOR

To this point we have examined two important human facets of the integrative model—the individual and the group. We now turn our attention to a close look at organizational dimensions of behavior. These include factors emanating out of the organization itself. It has long been known that characteristics or properties of the formal organization have a powerful impact on the behavior of people within organizations. It thus seems appropriate that we examine more closely the relationship between the properties or dimensions of the formal organization and how they impinge on organizational behavior. Three major concerns are addressed in this chapter: the organization–individual interface, organization design, and technology and organization.

First we look carefully at the specific impact of the organization on the individual. In Chris Argyris' article "Personality vs. Organization," the question is posed "What's wrong with the relationship between the human personality and the formal organization?" Argyris goes on, in what is now a classic article, to discuss how the needs of the two are antithetical, and to suggest the directions in which managers must move to effect a reconciliation.

Next the chapter concerns itself with organization design. Michael McCaskey leads off with a piece entitled "An Introduction to Organization Design." This article can be highlighted well in McCaskey's own words: "Designing a human social organization is extremely complicated. An organization is a system of interrelated parts so that the design of one subsystem or of one procedure has ramifications for other parts of the system." Key concepts introduced and discussed by McCaskey include mechanistic versus organic patterns of organizing, and the important notions of differentiation and integration. The second article concerned with the organization–individual interface is Jay Galbraith's "Matrix Organization Designs." Galbraith posits that matrix organization design attempts to combine the benefits of both functional and project structures. He then illustrates by way of the history of The Standard Products Company how an organization can change from the functional form to a pure matrix form.

Finally, the issue of technology and organization is explored, stressing how technology impacts the structure and, hence, the functioning of the organization in which behavior occurs. In her article, Mariann Jelinek presents a multienvironment, multitechnology model of the firm in "Technology, Organizations, and Contingency." The three concerns of this chapter, taken together, provide a good overview of organizational dimensions of human behavior.

PERSONALITY VS. ORGANIZATION

CHRIS ARGYRIS

Approximately every seven years we develop the itch to review the relevant literature and research in personality and organization theory, to compare our own evolving theory and research with those of our peers—an exercise salutary, we trust, in confirmation and also confrontation. We're particularly concerned to measure our own explicit model of man with the complementary or conflicting models advanced by other thinkers. Without an explicit normative model, personality and organization theory (P. and O. theory) tends to settle for a generalized description of behavior as it is observed in existing institutions—at best, a process that embalms the status quo; at worst, a process that exalts it. Current behavior becomes the prescription for future actions.

By contrast, I contend that behavioral science research should be normative, that it is the mission of the behavioral scientist to intervene selectively in the organization whenever there seems a reasonable chance of improving the quality of life within the organization without imperiling its viability. Before surveying the P. and O. landscape, however, let's review the basic models of man and formal organization.

Reprinted by permission of the publisher from *Organizational Dynamics,* Fall 1974, © 1974 by AMACOM, a division of American Management Associations.

FUNDAMENTALS OF MAN AND ORGANIZATION

The following steps indicate how the worlds of man and formal organization have developed:

1. Organizations emerge when the goals they seek to achieve are too complex for any one man. The actions necessary to achieve the goals are divided into units manageable by individuals—the more complex the goals, other things being equal, the more people are required to meet them.

2. Individuals themselves are complex organizations with diverse needs. They contribute constructively to the organization only if *on balance,* the organization fulfills these needs and their sense of what is just.

3. What are the needs that individuals seek to fulfill? Each expert has his own list and no two lists duplicate priorities. We have tried to bypass this intellectual morass by focussing on some relatively reliable predispositions that remain valid irrespective of the situation. Under any circumstances individuals seek to fulfill these predispositions; at the same time, their exact nature, potency, and the degree to which they must be fulfilled are influenced by the organizational context—for example, the nature of the job. In their attempt to live, to grow in competence, and to achieve self-acceptance, men and women tend to

program themselves along the lines of the continua depicted in Figure 1.

Together, these continua represent a developmental logic that people ignore or suppress with difficulty, the degree of difficulty depending on the culture and the context, as well as the individual's interactions with the key figures in his or her life. The model assumes that the thrust of this developmental program is from left to right, but nothing is assumed about the location of any given individuals along these continua.

A central theme of P. and O. theory has been the range of differences between individuals and how it is both necessary and possible to arrange a match between the particular set of needs an individual brings to the job situation and the requirements—technical and psychological—of the job itself, as well as the overall organizational climate.

We have written four studies that highlighted an individual's interrelationship with the work context. In each study, a separate analysis was made of each participant that included (1) the predispositions that he or she desired to express, (2) the potency of each predisposition, (3) the inferred probability that each would be expressed, and (4) a final score that indicated the degree to which the individual was able to express his or her predispositions.

A personal expression score enabled us to make specific predictions as to how individuals would react to the organization. We had expected individuals with low scores, for example, to state that they were frustrated and to have poorer attendance records and a higher quit rate—expectations that also showed how individual differences in predispositions were differentially rewarded in different types of departments. Bank employees with a need to distrust and control others, for ex-

ample, instinctively opted for positions in the internal audit department of the bank.

So much for the model of man. Now to organizations, which have a life of their own, in the sense that they have goals that unfortunately may be independent of or antagonistic to individual needs. The next step was to determine if there was a genetic logic according to which organizations were programmed.

Observation and reading combined to suggest that most organizations had pyramided structures of different sizes. The logic behind each of these pyramids—great or small—was first, to centralize information and power at the upper levels of the structure; second, to specialize work. According to this logic, enunciated most clearly by Frederick Winslow Taylor and Max Weber, management should be high on the six organizational activities summarized in Figure 2.

This model assumed that the closer an organization approached the right ends of the continua, the closer it approached the ideal of formal organization. The model assumed nothing, however, about where any given organization would be pinpointed along these continua.

PERSONALITY vs. ORGANIZATION

Given the dimensions of the two models, the possibilities of interaction are inevitable and varied; so is the likelihood of conflict between the needs of individuals and the structured configuration of the formal organization. The nature of the interaction between the individual and the organization and the probability of conflict vary according to the conditions depicted in Figure 3.

From this model, we can hypothesize that the more the organization approaches the model of the formal organization, the more individuals will be forced to behave at the infant ends of the con-

FIGURE 1. Developmental continua

Infants begin as

(1) being dependent and submissive to parents (or other significant adult)
(2) having few abilities
(3) having skin-surfaced or shallow abilities
(4) having a short time perspective

Adults strive toward

(1) relative independence, autonomy, relative control over their immediate world
(2) developing many abilities
(3) developing a few abilities in depth
(4) developing a longer time perspective

FIGURE 2. Continua of organizational activities

Designing specialized and fractionalized work

low	high

Designing production rates and controlling speed of work

low	high

Giving orders

low	high

Evaluating performance

low	high

Rewarding and punishing

low	high

Perpetuating membership

low	high

tinua. What if—still operating at the level of an intellectual exercise—the individuals aspired toward the adult end of the continua? What would the consequences be? Wherever there is an incongruence between the needs of individuals and the requirements of a formal organization, individuals will tend to experience frustration, psychological failure, short-time perspective, and conflict.

What factors determine the extent of the incongruence? The chief factors are: first, the lower the employee is positioned in the hierarchy, the less control he has over his working conditions and the less he is able to employ his abilities; second, the more directive the leadership, the more dependent the employee; and last, the more unilateral the managerial controls, the more dependent the employee will feel.

We have said that individuals find these needs difficult to ignore or suppress, and if they are suppressed, frustration and conflict result. These feelings, in turn, are experienced in several ways:

- The employee fights the organization and tries to gain more control—for example, he may join a union.
- The employee leaves the organization, temporarily or permanently.
- The employee leaves it psychologically, becoming a half-worker, uninvolved, apathetic, indifferent.
- The employee downgrades the intrinsic importance of work and substitutes higher pay as the reward for meaningless work. Barnard observed almost 40 years ago that organizations emphasized financial satisfactions because they were the easiest to provide. He had a point—then and now.

FIGURE 3. Condition of interaction

If the individual aspired toward	And the organization (through its jobs, technology, controls, leadership, and so forth) required that the individual aspire toward
(1) adulthood dimensions	(1) infancy dimensions
(2) infancy dimensions	(2) adulthood dimensions
(3) adulthood dimensions	(3) adulthood dimensions
(4) infancy dimensions	(4) infancy dimensions

We want to emphasize several aspects about these propositions. The personality model provides the base for predictions as to the impact of any organizational variable upon the individual, such as organizational structure, job content, leadership style, group norms, and so on. The literature has concentrated on employee frustration expressed in fighting the organization, because it's the commonest form of response, but we shouldn't ignore the other three responses.

In a study of two organizations in which technology, job content, leadership, and managerial controls confined lower-skilled employees to the infancy end of the continua, their response was condition three—no union, almost no turnover or absenteeism, but also apathy and indifference.

Last, we believe that the model holds regardless of differences in culture and political ideology. The fundamental relationships between individuals and organizations are the same in the United States, England, Sweden, Yugoslavia, Russia, or Cuba. A drastic statement but, we think, a true one.

RESEARCH THAT TESTS THE MODEL

Several studies in the past six years designed specifically to test the validity of the model all bore it out, to a greater or lesser extent. One study involved a questionnaire that measured self-expression as defined by our model. In a random sample of 332 U.S. salaried managers, hourly-paid workers, and self-employed businessmen, it was found that the lower the self-actualization, the more likely employees were to exhibit the following behavior: To day-dream, to have aggressive feelings toward their superiors, to have aggressive feelings toward their co-workers, to restrict output or make avoidable errors, to postpone difficult tasks or decisions, to emphasize money as the reward for service, and to be dissatisfied with their current jobs and think about another job.

A study in a different culture—Brazil—dealt with 189 employees in 13 banks. It revealed that 86 percent of the employees registered a discrepancy between their own felt needs and the formal goals of the organization. All agreed that the or-

ganizational goals were important, but only the top managers felt an absence of conflict between their own needs and the goals of the organization.

A second U.S. study involving 329 respondents —104 businessmen, 105 managers, and 120 workers—confirmed the model, but not in most cases to a degree that was statistically significant. On balance, however, the respondents supported the proposition that employees who perceive their work situations as highly bureaucratic feel more isolated, alienated, and powerless.

RESEARCH THAT SUPPORTS THE MODEL

Additional studies with no formal relationship to the model nevertheless tend to underwrite it. A national sample of 1,533 employees in 1972, for example, showed that among all age groups interesting work was more important than money in providing job satisfaction.

Bertil Gardell, a Swedish psychologist, examined four plants in mass production and process industries, seeking to relate production technology to alienation and mental health. Among his findings were these:

• The more skilled the task and the more control the individual feels over how he performs it, the more independence and the less stress he experiences.

• There is a big discrepancy between people as to which jobs they deem interesting; some employees, for example, describe jobs with low discretion as interesting—this is a contradiction of our model, but they account for only 8 percent of the employees surveyed.

• Income is not a factor in determining alienation. A high-income employee with little control over his job feels just as alienated as the man laboring for a pittance.

Gardell concluded:

Severe restrictions in worker freedom and control and in skill level required are found to be related to increased work alienation and lowered level of mental health even after control is made for age, sex, income, type of leadership, and satisfaction with pay. The relation between task organization and mental health is valid, however, only after allowance is made for work alienation. In both industries certain people regard jobs of low discretion and skill level as interesting and free from constraint, but these groups amount to only 8 percent in each industry and are strongly overrepresented as to workers above 50 years of age.

Within the mass-production industry, restrictions in discretion and skill level are found to go together with increased feelings of psychological stress and social isolation. People working under piece rate systems—compared with hourly paid workers—find their work more monotonous, constrained, and socially isolating, as well as having lower social status. . . .

High self-determination and job involvement are found to be related to high demands for increased worker influence on work and company decisions in the process industries, while in the mass production industries demand for increased worker influence is greatest among those who feel their work to be monotonous and constrained. Perceptions of strong worker influence by collective arrangements are accompanied by increased demands for individual decision-power as well as increased job satisfaction and decreased alienation.

A batch of studies reaffirmed the relationship between job specialization and feelings of powerlessness on the job and of frustration and alienation. One that compared craftsmen, monitors, and assemblers found that job satisfaction varied dramatically according to the degree of specialization: Job satisfaction was lowest among the assemblers—14 percent; next were the monitors —52 percent; and last were the craftsmen—87 percent. The same study found a strong relationship between job specialization and powerlessness on the job. Thus, 93 percent of the assemblers and 57 percent of the monitors, but only 19 percent of the craftsmen, experienced a lack of freedom and control.

Still other studies related job levels to the degree of dissatisfaction with the jobs. A comparison of 15 managers with 26 supervisors and 44 workers showed that the degree of satisfaction paralleled their position in the hierarchy, with managers the most satisfied and workers the least satisfied.

Frederick Herzberg reported a study of 2,665 Leningrad workers under 30 that again correlated job level with job satisfaction. Researchers who have concentrated on the higher levels of the organization typically have found a systematic tendency—the higher the positions held by the individuals in the organization, the more positive their attitudes tended to be.

An unusual study by Allan Wicker compared undermanned situations in which participants assumed more responsibility and performed larger tasks with overmanned situations in which the tasks were small and the responsibilities minute. Not surprisingly, in the overmanned situations employees reported less meaningful tasks and less sense of responsibility.

Can we reduce powerlessness at work, a factor closely linked to job alienation? One suggestive article points up three possibilities: Employees should allocate their own tasks; crews should be allowed to select themselves through sociometric procedures; the members of the group should select the group leaders.

Finally, research throws light on the question of whether time is the great reconciler. How long do dissatisfaction and frustration with the job persist? The answer appears to be—indefinitely. An interesting comparison of an old and a new assembly plant found that after 14 years the presumably acclimated employees were more dissatisfied and less involved with the product and the company than the new employees. Familiarity breeds frustration, alienation, and contempt.

RESEARCH RESULTS EXPLAINED BY THE MODEL

If employees are predisposed toward greater autonomy and formal organizations are designed to minimize autonomy, at least at the lower levels, we would expect to find a significant correlation between job status and job satisfaction—the lower the job, the less the job satisfaction. This has been found in a number of studies. Harold Wilensky, for example, reported in one of his studies the proportion of satisfied employees ranged from 90 percent for professors and mathematicians to 16 percent for unskilled auto workers. Furthermore, he found that the percentage of people who would go into similar work if they could start over again varied systematically with the degree of autonomy, control, and the chance to use their abilities that they experienced in their current jobs.

Several studies focused on the relationship between control and job satisfaction. An analysis of 200 geographically separate systems that were parts of larger organizations—for example, automotive dealers, clerical operations, manufacturing plants, and power plants in the same company— revealed that the greatest discrepancy between actual and ideal control occurred at the level of the rank-and-file employee. Ninety-nine percent of the work groups wanted more control over their immediate work area. Still another study found that employees became more dissatisfied after moving to a new, more efficient plant because of the reduction of their control over work. These studies were in the United States. Similar research in Yugoslavia and Norway further buttressed the point that employees want to enlarge the degree of their control over their immediate work world.

What about the impact of control upon turnover? The logic of the model leads us to predict that employees would be more likely to quit an organization when they experienced too much control by the organization or its representatives. Once again, research supports the hypothesis. One study found that the authoritarian foreman was a major factor in labor turnover; a second showed that there was a close relationship between the supervisor's inequitable treatment—he could not be influenced, did not support his subordinates, and did not attempt to redress employee grievances—and the turnover rate. Employees, in short, fled from unfair treatment.

One assemblage of studies would appear at first glance to contradict the model. We refer to those studies that show that lower-skilled workers appear to be more interested in how much money they make than they are in how interesting their jobs are. As John Goldthorpe and others demonstrate, however, they are merely being realists. Goldthorpe, in particular, points out repeatedly and documents in detail the fact that workers do desire intrinsically satisfying jobs, but find such aspirations to be unrealistic. In the long run, however great the reluctance and the pain, they adapt.

His research dealt with British workers but a number of studies in the United States replicate his findings. As you move up the job hierarchy, employees consistently assign a higher value to job characteristics that potentially fulfill growth needs. Medium- and high-status white-collar workers, for example, placed primary emphasis on work-content factors as a source of job satisfaction, while low-status white-collar workers and blue-collar workers tended to play them down. As our model would predict, employees seek out job satisfactions they feel are second rate, because higher-level satisfactions are unattainable—certainly in their current jobs.

In summary, this research demonstrates first, that the overall impact of the formal organization on the individual is to decrease his control over his immediate work area, decrease his chance to use his abilities, and increase his dependence and submissiveness; second, that to the extent to which the individual seeks to be autonomous and function as an adult he adapts by reactions ranging from withdrawal and noninterest, to aggression, or perhaps to the substitution of instrumental money rewards for intrinsic rewards. The weight of the deprivations and the degree of adaptation increase as we descend the hierarchy. Formal organizations, alas, are unintentionally designed to discourage the autonomous and involved worker.

JOB ENLARGEMENT OR ENRICHMENT

Job enlargement in the true sense, not the multiplication of meaningless tasks, but quite literally the enrichment of the job either by adding tasks that provide intrinsic satisfactions or increasing the worker's control over the tasks he already performs, obviously conforms to our models. And we would expect that employees whose jobs were enriched would be more satisfied with their jobs and less likely to manifest their dissatisfaction in ways that undermine the organization. Looking at the other side of the coin, we also would expect that more positive attitudes would be accompanied by increased productivity.

And we would not be disappointed. No fewer than eight studies testify that designing jobs that permit more self-regulation, self-evaluation, self-adjustment, and participation in goal-setting both improved attitudes and increased productivity.

Of particular importance is a study by Hackman and Lawler that correlated the core dimensions of jobs—variety, autonomy, task identity, and feedback—with motivation, satisfaction, performance, and attendance. The principal findings of their study are these:

• The higher the jobs are on core dimensions, the higher the employees are rated by their supervisors as doing better quality work and being more effective performers.

• When jobs rank high on the core dimensions, employees report feeling more intrinsically motivated to perform well.

• Core dimensions are strongly and positively related to job satisfaction and involvement.

• The job satisfaction items that strongly correlate with the job core dimension are related to control over one's own work, feeling of worthwhile accomplishment, and self-esteem.

• The strength of the relationships described above increases with those employees who seek to meet higher-order needs. This finding is significant because research seldom examines individual differences in this way.

Hackman and Lawler differentiate between horizontal enlargement—increasing the number of things an employee does—and vertical enlargement—increasing the degree to which an employee is responsible for making most major decisions about his work. They would argue and we would concur that a combination of both types of enlargement—what we have earlier called role enlargement—is optimal.

What about practice? The concept of job enrichment isn't new. A study of IBM published in 1948 included an assessment of job enrichment and its benefits.

We would expect a concept so fulfilling, so helpful in meeting the goals of both the employee and the organization to be widely adopted. And we would be disappointed. A recent survey of 300 of the top 1,000 *Fortune* industrials showed that only 4 percent had made any formal, systematic attempt to enrich jobs. And even they had enriched only a very small percentage of their total jobs.

What accounts for the lag in adopting job enrichment? Two factors seem to be at work and to reinforce each other. First, most managements are convinced that job enrichment doesn't pay off economically. This belief, in turn, leads them to exhibit signs of the ostrich syndrome—they ignore the accumulating body of evidence as to the substantial psychic dividends that employees derive from job enrichment.

Let me quote from just two of the voluminous research studies that demonstrate the efficiency of job enrichment. The first is the ambitious and significant attempt by the Gaines dog food division of General Foods to design an entire plant using horizontal and vertical enlargement of work. The key features of the design are the following:

1. Autonomous work groups that develop their own production schedules, manage production problems, screen and select new members, maintain self-policing activities, and decide questions such as who gets time off and who fills which work station.
2. Integrated support functions. Each work team performs its own maintenance, quality control, and industrial engineering functions—plus challenging job assignments.
3. Job mobility and rewards for learning. People are paid not on the basis of the job they are doing, but on the basis of the number of jobs that they are prepared to do.
4. Self-government for the plant community.

The transition from a work environment on the infant ends of our continua to the adult ends was not easy for the people involved. Drastic change never is, even when the participants benefit from the change. The results to date, however, are impressive. A similar plant, organized along traditional lines, would require 110 employees; this one was manned by 70. The plant has met or exceeded production goals. Employees reported greater opportunities for learning and self-actualization. And team leaders and plant managers were more involved in community affairs than foremen and managers of comparable plants.

A second significant experiment in job enlargement is taking place at Volvo's new auto assembly plant in Kalmar, Sweden. Volvo faced serious problems—wildcat strikes, absenteeism, and turnover that were getting out of hand. Turnover in the old car assembly plant was over 40 percent annually. Absenteeism was running 20 to 25 percent. Now, assembly has been divided among teams of 15 to 25 workers, who will decide how to distribute the job of car assembly among themselves. Each team determines its own work pace, subject to meeting production standards that are set for them. Each team selects its own boss, and deselects him if it's unhappy with him.

The new plant cost approximately 10 percent more than it would have if it had been constructed along traditional lines. Will the benefits justify the extra expense? Time alone will tell—the plant has been on stream for only a matter of months—but Pehr Gyllenhammar, the managing director of Volvo, hopes that it will realize both his economic and social objectives: "A way must be found to create a workplace that meets the needs of the modern working man for a sense of purpose and satisfaction in his daily work. A way must be found of attaining this goal without an adverse effect on productivity."

THE MODEL OF MAN AND THE DESIGN OF ORGANIZATION

Organizations depend on people. Thus, many organizational variables are designed around an explicit or implicit model of man. Taylor's molecularized jobs, for example, took a one-dimensional view of man and assumed that one could hire a hand; by contrast, the champions of vertical and horizontal job enrichment assume that one hires a whole human being.

Then there are the theorists who take the sociological viewpoint and impoverish their theories by ignoring the psychological element and treating man as a black box.

In each case the complexity of organizational reality leads them into contradictions, the significance of which they either play down or ignore altogether. Crozier, for example, although lacking an explicit model of man, also concluded that his data did not confirm the inhumanity of organizations toward individuals—but how can one define inhumanity without a concept of man? Nevertheless, in the same work he stated that monotonous and repetitive work produces nervous tension in workers, that apathy and social isolation are great, and that work loads produce pressure.

Charles Perrow is a technological determinist

who argues that the structure of organization depends on the requirements of the technology. An electronics plant making components should have a different structure from one making inertial guidance system components because of differences in the kind of research required by their technology, unanalyzable versus analyzable, or the number of exceptions it requires—few or many. Perrow's insight, valid but partial, is an inadequate concept to explain the total relationship between man and organization, an inadequacy that Perrow himself is coming to recognize. He concedes that "personality factors can have a great deal of influence upon the relations between coordination and subordinate power," that Robert McNamara, for example, was the key factor in changes in the Defense Department.

To elevate any one as *the* defining characteristic of organizations as Perrow did with technology and make all other characteristics dependent variables only leads to poor theory and inadequate and incomplete explanations of behavior in organizations. An error of equal magnitude is to ignore either the sociological or the psychological view in studying organizations.

We need a synthesis of the sociological and psychological views in studying man and a recognition that are no fewer than four sets of independent but interacting characteristics that determine the behavior of any organization—structure and technology, leadership and interpersonal relations, administrative controls and regulations, and human controls. The strength of each of the four will vary from organization to organization, vary within different parts of the same organization, and vary over time within the same parts of each organization. However, any major change in an organization's structure is doomed to failure unless major changes take place in all four characteristics.

RATIONAL MAN DECISION THEORISTS

In addition to those with no explicit model of man we have the rational man decision theorists such as Simon, Cyert, and March, whose partial view of man focuses on the concept of man as a finite information processing system striving to be rational and to "satisfice" in his decision making.

What this model neglects are the issues stressed by P. and O. theory, such as dependence, submissiveness, the need for psychological success, confirmation, and feelings of essentiality. As we have written elsewhere, "Simon saw management's task as designing organizational structures and mechanisms of organization influence which ingrained into the nervous system of every member what the organization required him to do. Intendedly, rational man was expected to follow authority, but he was also given appropriate and indirect inducements to produce."

Cyert and March retain the basic perspectives of the pyramidal structure—specialization of tasks and centralization of power and information—but they add elements of reality and sophistication. By cranking into their models the concepts of people as members of coalitions politicking against each other for scarce resources and settling for the quasi-reduction of conflicts between them, they were able to predict more accurately how the organization was going to behave, for example, in setting prices.

That the rational man thinkers have indeed helped managers to make more effective decisions in some situations—those in which the factors involved corresponded to their model—shouldn't lead us to ignore the more frequent situations in which the rational man theories were either a poor predictive tool or acted themselves to exacerbate the situation. Recent research suggests that managers may resist the management information systems designed by the rational man theorists precisely because they work well—for example, accomplish the desired objective of reducing uncertainty. What accounts for the apparent paradox? Man is not primarily rational, or rather he reacts in response to what we like to call the rationality of feelings. He dislikes being dependent and submissive toward others; he recognizes the increased probability that when management information systems work best he will tend to experience psychological failure. The organization's goals are being met at the expense of his own. Management information systems, in consequence, have become to managers at many levels what time-study people were to the rank and file years ago—an object of fear commingled with hatred and aggression.

Another trend that totally escapes the rational man theorists is the increasing hostility of an increasing number of young people toward the idea that organizations should be able to buy off people to be primarily rational, to submit to the mechanisms of organizational influence, and to suppress their feelings.

A third trend flows from the combined impact of the first two. Given the inability to predict the relationship of emotionality versus rationality in any particular context, and the reaction against rational man and organizational mechanisms of influence, add to these elements the largely unintended support of the status quo, and the use of "satisficing" to rationalize incompetence, and we end up with an interaction of forces that makes change in organizations seem almost impossible.

Hard to follow or accept? The line of argument is as follows:

1. To the degree that man accepts inducements to behave rationally, he acts passively in relation to the way power, information, and work are designed in the organization.

2. Over time, such individuals sterilize their self-actualizing tendencies by any one or a combination of approaches: They suppress them, deny them, or distort them. Eventually, they come to see their legitimate role in the organization—at least, as it bears on the design of power, information, and tasks—as pawns rather than as initiators.

3. A little further down the road, individuals come to view being passive and controlled as good, natural, and necessary. Eventually, they may define responsibility and maturity in these terms.

4. Individuals soon create managerial cultures—some have already done so—in which the discussion of self-actualizing possibilities is viewed as inappropriate.

5. The youth who because of the very success of the system are able to focus more on the self-actualizing needs will attempt to change things. They will come up, however, against facts one to four and end up terribly frustrated.

6. The frustration will tend to lead to regression, with two probable polarized consequences—withdrawal into communes or militancy.

7. Because we know very little about how to in-

tegrate self-actualizing activities with rational activities, older people will resent the hostility of youth or look upon their withdrawal as a cop-out.

The last and most important point is that the rational man theory, unlike P. and O. theory, could not predict the single most important trend about public and private organizations—their increasing internal deterioration and lack of effectiveness in producing services or products. As citizen, consumer, and presumably an organization man, you either feel it or you don't. We do feel strongly on this score. And we cite that while 25 years ago 75 percent of the respondents in a national survey felt that public and private organizations performed well, only 25 percent had the same opinion in 1972. How many believe that the percentage would be higher today?

THE CASE FOR NORMATIVE RESEARCH

Most of the research that we have reviewed has been descriptive research that contents itself with describing, understanding, and predicting human behavior within organizations. In our research the emphasis is normative and based upon the potentialities of man. We're interested in studying man in terms of what he is capable of, not merely how he currently behaves within organizations.

Looked at from this normative viewpoint, the most striking fact about most organizations is the limited opportunities they afford most employees to fulfill their potential. We can show empirically that the interpersonal world of most people in ongoing organizations is characterized by much more distrust, conformity, and closedness than trust, individuality, and openness. This world— we call it Pattern A—fits with, if indeed it isn't derived from, the values about effective human behavior endemic in the pyramidal structure or in what Simon calls the mechanisms of organizational influence. Thus, findings based on descriptive research will tend to opt for the status quo.

Moreover, unless we conduct research on new worlds, scholars will tend to use data obtained in the present world as evidence that people do not want to change. Many of them are doing so already. What they forget is how human beings can desire or even contemplate worlds that they have learned from experience to view as unrealistic.

Take a recent publication by Ernest Gross in which he suggests that concepts like individual dignity and self-development probably reflect academic values instead of employee desires, because employees rarely report the need to express such values. The question still remains whether this state of affairs implies that people should accept them and should be trained to adapt to them. Gross appears to think so. He stated that there is little one can do by way of providing opportunities for self-actualization and, if it were possible, providing them would frighten some people. Furthermore, he noted that assembly-line jobs didn't require a worker to demonstrate initiative or to desire variety. "One wants him (the worker) simply to work according to an established pace. Creativity, then, is not always desirable."

Note the logic. Gross starts by asserting that the P. and O. theorists cannot state that one *should* (his italics) provide workers with more challenge or autonomy in accordance with their values because to do so would be to rest their case not on a scientific theory, but on a program for organizations. Then he suggests that no one has proved how harmful dissatisfaction, anxiety, dependency, and conformity are to the individual— which is probably correct. He goes on to argue that these conditions are, to a degree, both unavoidable and helpful, although offering no empirical data to support his assertion. Then he concludes that employees should be educated to live within this world:

Perhaps the most general conclusion we can draw is that since organizations appear to be inevitable . . . a major type of socialization of the young ought to include methods for dealing with the organization. . . . [For example] an important consideration in the preparation of individuals for work should include training for the handling of or adjustment to authority.

At this point Gross has taken a normative position, but one with which I vigorously dissent.

I am very concerned about those who hold that job enrichment may not be necessary because workers in an automobile factory have about the same attitude toward their jobs as do workers in jobs with greater freedom and job variety. But what is the meaning of the response to a question such as "How satisfied would you say you are with your present job?" if the man is working under conditions of relative deprivation? We think that what it means is that workers recognize that they are boxed in, that few opportunities are available to them for better-paid or more interesting work; in consequence, they become satisfied with the jobs they have because the jobs they want are unobtainable. It is frequently observed that the greatest dissatisfaction on a routine job occurs during the first years. After three to five years, the individual adapts to the job and feels satisfied. On the other hand, Neil Herrick in a recent book with the catchy title *Where Have All the Robots Gone?* reported that for the first time, there was a major drop in the number of Americans expressing job satisfaction.

That most jobs as currently designed are routine and provide few opportunities for self-actualization, that the social norms and the political actions that support these norms tend to produce mostly individuals who simultaneously value and fear growth and who strive for security and safety, tell only part of the unfortunate tale of the present industrial conditions. Employees perceive—and the perception is accurate—that few men at the top want to increase their opportunities for self-actualization; even fewer men at the top are competent to do the job.

Make no mistake—employees are conservative on this issue. They have no interest in seeing their physiological and security needs frustrated or denied because their organization collapsed while trying to increase their chances for self-actualization. And the possibility of such a collapse is a real one. Our own experience and the published research combine to suggest that there now does not exist a top-management group so competent in meeting the requirements of the new ethic that they do not lose their competence under stress. With expert help and heavy emphasis on top-management education, one such group was still encountering great difficulties after five years of attempting to raise the quality of life within its organization.

If the ethic, as employees themselves recognize, is so difficult to realize in practice, is the effort worthwhile? Is a game with so many incompetent players worth the playing?

On two counts we feel strongly that it is: First, on normative grounds we feel that social science research has an obligation to help design a better world. Second, we feel that the game is worth the playing because eventually some people and some organizations can be helped to play it effectively. Take the case of job enrichment. Let us assume that all jobs can be enriched. The assumption is probably unrealistic; many jobs in fact, can never be enriched. If we opt for the world that is psychologically richer, however, we will induce employees at every level into developing whatever opportunities for enrichment exist in each job situation.

I believe with Maslow in taking the behavior that characterizes rare peak experiences and making it the behavior toward which all employees should aspire. The skeptic argues that such behavior is so rare that it is useless to try to achieve it. I agree that the behavior is rare, but go on to plead for systematic research that will tell us how the behavior may be made more frequent. Twenty years ago no one had pole-vaulted higher than 16 feet. Yet no one took this as a given. Today the 16-foot mark is broken continually because people refused to view the status quo as the last word and focused on enhancing the potentiality of man. Over time, a similar focus on enhancing the potentiality of man-on-the-job should produce similar breakthroughs.

SELECTED BIBLIOGRAPHY

Chris **Argyris** has been conducting research on understanding organizational illness and health for more than two decades. His major thesis began with *Personality and Organization* (Harper and Row, 1957), and continued with *Integrating the Individual and the Organization* (John Wiley and Sons, 1964), *Organization and Innovation* (Richard D. Irwin, 1965), *Intervention Theory and Method* (Addison Wesley, 1970), culminating in his most recent study of one of our country's leading newspapers entitled *Behind the Front Page* (Jossey-Bass, 1974). With Professor Donald Schon he has also written a book that presents a new theory of action as well as new suggestions on the redesign of professional education (*Theory in Practice*, Jossey-Bass, 1974).

AN INTRODUCTION TO ORGANIZATIONAL DESIGN

MICHAEL B. McCASKEY

How does a manager choose among organizational design alternatives? How does he, for example, decide how precisely to define duties and roles? Should decision-making be centralized or decentralized? What type of people should he recruit to work on a particular task force? Organization design tries to identify the organizational structures and processes that appropriately "fit" the type of people in the organization and the type of task the organization faces.

Organizational design determines what the structures and processes of an organization will be. The features of an organization that can be designed include: division into sections and units, number of levels, location of decision-making authority, distribution of and access to information, physical layout of buildings, types of people recruited, what behaviors are rewarded, and so on. In the process of designing an organization, managers invent, develop, and analyze alternative forms for combining these elements. And the form must reflect the limits and capabilities of humans and the characteristics and nature of the task environment.[1]

Designing a human social organization is extremely complicated. An organization is a system

of interrelated parts so that the design of one subsystem or of one procedure has ramifications for other parts of the system. Furthermore, the criteria by which a system design is to be evaluated (economic performance, survival capability, social responsibility, and the personal growth of organizational members) cannot be maximized simultaneously: the design of a human social organization can never be perfect or final. In short, the design of organizational arrangements is intended to devise a complex set of trade-offs in a field of changing people, environment, and values.

Minor adjustments in organizational design are always being made during the life of an organization, but the times for major concentration on organizational design are:

- early in the life of an organization, most likely after the basic identity and strategy have been largely worked out;
- when significantly expanding or changing the organization's mission; or
- when reorganizing.

Who designs the organization, organizational units, and task forces? Since organizational design concerns the arrangement of people and the division of tasks, a designer or planner has to have some influence or control over these variables. This task is most often handled by middle-level managers and up. However, the charter to design could be broadened to give organizational members at all levels more of a say in organizational design matters.

KEY CONCEPTS AND QUESTIONS

In approaching an organization design problem, some of the important questions to be answered are:

1. How uncertain is the task environment in which the organization operates?
2. In what ways should the organization be mechanistic and in what ways organic?
3. How should the sub-tasks be divided and how should the organization be differentiated? Should subsystems be organized by the *functions* people perform, by the *products* or services the company provides, or should some other form such as a matrix organization be used?
4. What kind of people are (or can be recruited to become) members of the organization? Under what conditions do they work and learn best?
5. How are activities to be coordinated and integrated? What mechanisms will be used, involving what costs?

Research and theory provide some findings that can be used as design guidelines, and we turn to consider them now.

Mechanistic Patterns of Organizing. Tom Burns' and G. M. Stalker's 1961 study[2] of electronics firms and firms contemplating entering the electronics industry in Scotland and England contributed the important design principle of distinguishing between mechanistic and organic patterns of organizing.

Mechanistic organizational units are the traditional pyramidal pattern of organizing. In a mechanistic organizational unit, roles and procedures are precisely defined. Communication is channelized, and time spans and goal orientations are similar within the unit. The objective is to work toward machine-like efficiency. To that end the task is broken into parts that are joined together at the end of the work process. Authority, influence, and information are arranged by levels, each higher level having successively more authority, more influence, and more information. Decision-making is centralized at the top and it is the top levels that make appreciative judgments[3] to determine what is important in the environment. Top levels also determine the channels whereby the lower echelons will gather and process information.

Thus the social organization is designed as a likeness of a machine. People are conceived of as parts performing specific tasks. As employees leave, other parts can be slipped into their places. Someone at the top is the designer, defining what the parts will be and how they will all fit together.

Under what conditions is this pattern of organization appropriate? When the organizational unit is performing a task that is stable, well-defined, and likely to be programmable, or when members of the organization prefer well-defined situations, feel more secure when the day has a routine to it, and tend to want others to supply direction, the mechanistic pattern is applicable. Organization design findings show that, to the extent these conditions hold, a mechanistic form of organizing is more likely to result in high performance.

The mechanistic form is efficient and predictable. For people with a low tolerance for ambiguity it provides a stable and secure work setting. However, the mechanistic form is less flexible: once a direction and procedures have been set, it is hard to change them. Furthermore, mechanistic forms also entail the danger of stultifying their members with jobs that are too simple, with little responsibility, and no sense of worthwhile accomplishment.

Organic Patterns of Organizing. In contrast to mechanistic units, organic organizational units are based on a more biological metaphor for constructing social organizations. The objective in designing an organic unit is to leave the system maximally open to the environment in order to make the most of new opportunities. The demands of the task environment are ambiguously defined and changing, so people have multiple roles which are continually redefined in interaction with others. All levels make appreciations and there are few predetermined information channels. Decision-making is more decentralized, with authority and influence flowing to the person who has the greatest expertise to deal with the problem at hand. An organic organizational unit is relatively heterogeneous, containing a wider variety of time spans, goal orientations, and ways of thinking. The boundaries between the system and the environment are deliberately permeable, and the environment exerts more influence over the activities of the system than is true for the mechanistic unit.

An organic form is useful in the face of an uncertain task or one that is not well enough understood to be programmed. The organic form is also appropriate for people who like the disorder of an ambiguous setting, for people who prefer variety, change, and adventure and who grow restless when they fall into the same routine day after day. The organic form is flexible and responds quickly to unexpected opportunities. However, the organic form is often wasteful of resources. Not having precisely defined authority, control, and information hierarchies, time can be wasted in search activities that duplicate the efforts of other members. Furthermore, the stress of uncertainty and the continual threat of power struggles can be exhausting.

Making the Choice. The choice of the most suitable form of organization is *contingent* upon the task and the people involved. There is no one form of organization that will work best in all situations, in all cultures, with every type of person. Organization design scholars using a contingency theory approach emphasize the need to specify the particular conditions under which a given form is most appropriate.

Note, too, that the same organizational unit can change its position on the organic/mechanistic continuum over time. The unit might start out being very mechanistically organized. But as the environment or staff change, the unit might move toward the organic end of the continuum. In fact, if the unit does not change its structures and processes to meet changed conditions, it is likely to suffer lower performance.

Even more important, one organization is likely to contain both organic units and mechanistic units at the same time. Burns and Stalker[4] characterized whole organizations as mechanistic or organic; but Paul Lawrence and Jay Lorsch[5] found that these descriptions more accurately described units of an organization. They researched and elaborated on a major contribution to organization design in the concepts of differentiation and integration (D&I).

Differentiation

Differentiation, the creation or emergence of differences in the organization, can take place in several ways:

- vertically—into levels;
- horizontally—into sections, department, divisions, and so on;
- division of labor—into occupational roles; and
- patterns of thinking—differences between units in members' goals, time, and interpersonal orientations.

By differentiating, the organization gains the advantages of both economies of scale and people becoming experts in particular areas like production, accounting, contracting, and so on.

Lawrence and Lorsch found horizontal differentiation and the differentiation of patterns of thinking to be the most important types of differentiation for organizational design. The organization segments the environment into parts so that organizational units interact with different subenvironments. While marketing interacts with the media, ad agencies, legal departments, competitors' advertising, and the other elements that make up the marketing subenvironment, production is dealing with the machines, labor market, scheduling, cost consciousness, and safety regulations that pertain to their subenvironment. Furthermore, the structure and setting for each unit must supply the appropriate training and support for different job demands. Scientists, for example, need a milieu that will supply specialized information as well as support in projects that may take years to complete.

An important question in organization design, therefore, is how differentiated should the organization be? How should the environment be segmented and what activities should be grouped together? To what extent should the units differ in structures and procedures, types of people, and patterns of thinking?

Research indicates that business organizations in newer and more uncertain industries, like aerospace and electronics, need to be more highly differentiated because they face a greater range of subenvironments. As James Thompson[6] argues, organizations try to shield their technical core from the uncertainties of the environment. The subenvironment of the core technology unit, then, will be relatively stable and call for more mechanistic patterns of organizing. The units having uncertain subenvironments (often the R&D subenvironment) will need to be more organically organized. Looking at the organization as a whole, the differences between the units will be significant because the range of unit organizational patterns extends from the mechanistic end to the organic end of the continuum.

Conversely, research indicates that organizations in older, more established and more certain industries need to be less differentiated. They face a narrow range of subenvironments near the certainty end of the spectrum, and will probably pursue the efficiency given by more mechanistic patterns of organizing. An organization in a relatively stable and certain environment benefits from having uniform rules and procedures, vocabulary, and patterns of thinking throughout the organization. The problem of integration for these organizations, therefore, is less demanding.

Integration

At the same time the organization is differentiated to work more effectively on tasks, some activities of organizational units must be coordinated and brought together, or integrated. The manager/designer must resist differentiating the organization too radically—the greater the differences between the units, the harder it is for them to coordinate activities with each other. If all the units have similar goals, values, and time horizons, messages and meanings are more likely to be clear. But when an organization is highly differentiated, people have to spend more effort translating and appreciating the frameworks of people in different units. Most people habitually think in their own terms and it takes increased effort to

move into another's frame of reference. The chances for misunderstandings increase in a highly differentiated organization.

The greater the differentiation, the heavier the burden on information processing and upon decision-making in the organization. This shows up in the array of techniques for coordinating the activities of a firm:

1. the use of rules and procedures along with the hierarchy of authority;
2. if two units are crucial and have trouble integrating, the appointment of a liaison;[7]
3. the building of a new unit into the work flow to serve as an integrating department.

This list of coordinating mechanisms shows progressively more elaborate ways to achieve integration. With greater differentiation, an organization has to spend more effort integrating and use the more expensive devices.

So in addition to asking how much the organization should differentiate to meet environment and people requirements, another question must simultaneously be raised. How much differentiation, at that cost, can the organization successfully integrate? How should people be grouped to provide the best working conditions for individuals *and* to secure the most advantageous work flow for the whole organization? A manager/designer works for the best practical answer to these questions. Many times he may decide to stop short of differentiating to perfectly meet task environment demands because his staff would find it too great a strain or because it would be too costly. Research findings show that in uncertain environments, the most successful organizations are the most highly differentiated *and* the most integrated. The difficult design decision of how to differentiate and how to integrate is often framed as the choice between product or functional organization,[8] or some newer form like a matrix organization.[9]

THE RESEARCH STUDIES

Table I summarizes a selection of research findings important for organization design theory. The studies were conducted mainly, although not entirely, with business firms. A wide range of meth-

TABLE I. Empirical research findings on organizational design

Researchers	Types of Organizations Studied	Selected Findings
Burns and Stalker (1961)	20 firms in U.K. including a rayon manufacturer, an engineering firm, several companies in electronics and others contemplating entry into electronics.	"Mechanistic" management system suited to an enterprise operating under relatively stable conditions; "organic" required for conditions of change.
Chandler (1962)	Historical studies of DuPont, General Motors, Standard Oil of New Jersey, and Sears Roebuck, supplemented by brief reviews of over 70 other large American business companies.	By trial and error a new structural form (decentralized, multidivisional form) developed to fit changed environmental conditions.
Woodward (1965)	100 English manufacturing firms.	Patterns in management practice associated with how complex and how predictable production technology is.
Lawrence and Lorsch (1967)	10 U.S. companies in plastics, consumer food, and standardized container industries.	1) High performing organizations are differentiated to meet environmental demands; diverse and uncertain environments require greater differentiation of the organization.
		2) Differentiation and integration are antagonistic states; the more differentiated an organization is, the more elaborate the integrative devices must be.
		3) Additional support for above findings.
Galbraith (1970)	Case study of the Boeing Aircraft Division.	Structural changes to deal with greater task environment uncertainty related to the need to process more information.
Blau and Schoenherr (1971)	The 53 state employment security offices of the U.S. and territories.	1) Increasing size generates structural differentiation in organizations along various dimensions at decelerating rates.
		2) Structural differentiation in organizations raises requirements for managerial manpower.
		3) Horizontal, vertical, and occupational differentiation are positively related to environmental diversity.
Duncan (1971)	22 decision-making units in 3 manufacturing organizations and in 3 R&D organizations.	Structural profile used to make nonroutine decisions differs from that used to make routine decisions; suggests the same unit uses different organizing patterns over time.
Morse and Young (1973)	235 managers from 8 business organizations.	Individuals working on certain tasks preferred controlling authority relations and had a low tolerance for ambiguity; individuals working on uncertain tasks sought independence and autonomy and were high in tolerance for ambiguity.

odologies has been used including historical study methods, an intensive case study of one division, a questionnaire survey of managers in different organizations, surveying and interviewing the top managers of all the business organizations in a given geographical area, and so on. All of the studies support a contingency approach to organizational design. Researchers found that explaining their data required them to specify the conditions upon which the use of a particular organization form was contingent.

In spite of different methods and vocabularies, certain patterns and continuities run through the findings. The design principle of distinguishing between mechanistic and organic forms is supported by the studies. Peter Blau's and Richard Schoenherr's[10] findings based on all instances (53) of one type of government agency lends support to the Lawrence and Lorsch[11] findings based on a selected sample of ten business firms. Both studies found that environmental diversity is related to greater differentiation in the organization. Blau and Schoenherr[12] found that differentiation raises the requirements for managerial manpower, and this is similar to Lawrence and Lorsch's[13] finding that greater differentiation requires more elaborate integrative devices. Furthermore, Jay Galbraith's[14] research provides something of an explanatory picture. His findings suggest that the need for more managerial manpower and more elaborate integrative mechanisms is related to the need for the organization to process more information.

Robert Duncan's[15] findings that an organizational unit appears to change its structure over time simply reinforces managers' feelings that organization charts are often incorrect and out-of-date. This is a promising area of research for developing a more accurate picture of how and when changes in organization structure occur.

As the studies indicate, substantial progress has been made. However, some important questions remain to be answered.

Work Yet to Be Done

Our knowledge of organizational design is still growing. Some of the important subjects which need further research are:

1. We need a better understanding of the *dynamics* of an organization developing a good fit to its environment and its members. The processes that span organization and environment, such as planning and selecting, recruiting and socializing new members, need to be researched. In addition to learning more about the enduring structural patterns, we also need to learn about the ways in which organization and environment adjust to one another.

2. We must consider the assertion of power in the interaction of organizations and their environments. How do organizations seek to make the environment more favorable to their operations? How does the environment coerce or influence the organization to meet its demands? What are the consequences of one element gaining sizeable amounts of control over the other? We need to learn about the processes which mediate this contest for control and influence.

3. Up until now researchers have mainly relied upon the criterion of economic performance to assess good fit. Clearly, using economic criteria alone is too limited. How can we judge goodness of fit in terms of people outcomes? Moreover, what about the people who are content to follow orders from the organization? Some argue that we cannot be normative on this value question. If a person is satisfied to be passive and dependent on the job, who can insist that he take more control over his own work life? My view is that a democracy can hardly afford a work system which mainly trains people to be docile, to follow orders, and above all to be loyal to the organization. But others emphasize that many prefer following orders, and this is where the issue is joined.

4. A related issue is the possible conflict between efficiency and human needs. Some elements of organization design concern social engineering to devise the most efficient organization to accomplish a task. Other elements of organization design are concerned with the full growth and development of individuals. It is too optimistic to assume that efficiently designed organizations will always or even usually be conducive to human intercourse. Mammoth operations built to meet economies of scale considerations teach us that

efficiently engineered operations can be inhumane. If we had better non-economic measures of outcomes, maybe we could more accurately assess the design tradeoffs. As it stands now, much of organization design emphasizes an engineering approach, neglecting human growth aspects. Another challenge: How can we design organizations to meet both people and engineering concerns?

5. We also need to learn more about how facilities design supports or detracts from the intent of an organization design. How does the physical layout influence the pattern of social interaction? How does the visual display of information affect decision-making? At what distance for what types of activities does physical separation of people or units greatly strain the organization's ability to integrate? How can facilities be designed so that physical spaces can be rearranged to fit changes in organizing patterns? Robert Propst,[16] Fritz Steele,[17] and Thomas Allen[18] have begun work on some of these questions.

SUMMARY

A convenient guideline for reviewing what we know about designing organizations is the continuum from mechanistic to organic patterns of organizing. Most suited to stable, certain environments and a staff that prefers stability, the mechanistic form is the traditional hierarchical pyramid that is controlled from the top and programs activities tightly. Most suited to an unstable, uncertain environment and people tolerant of ambiguity, the organic pattern of organizing is more collegial and stresses flexibility in rules, decision-making authority, procedures, and so on. Of course, there are more than these two types of organizing patterns. They should be considered the ends of a continuum of types of organizing patterns.

An organization is likely to contain both organically and mechanistically organized units. How widely the units should range on the mechanistic/organic continuum is part of the question of differentiation. How great should the differences be between units in terms of structures, types of people, and patterns of thinking? Overall, organizations in mature and stable industries con-

tain units that face more or less well-defined and certain subenvironments. Therefore, to meet environmental demands, the units should generally be more mechanistically organized and the organization as a whole will be less differentiated.

On the other hand, organizations in dynamic new industries must have some units organically organized to deal with an uncertain subenvironment. At the same time it should devise more mechanistic units (for example, production and accounting) to face more stable subenvironments. To cover that range of subenvironments, the manager/organization designer creates or allows to develop greater differences between the units. In addition, the organization tends to create more job roles (occupational differentiation) and more levels (vertical differentiation) in response to environmental diversity. The organization, therefore, becomes more highly differentiated.

The opposite tendency from differentiation is the need to integrate, to coordinate the activities of different parts of the organization. The greater the differentiation, the harder it is to integrate. The choice of a particular integrating mechanism, such as a liaison in addition to rules, signals the manager/designer's decision to expend a certain amount of effort to coordinate activities. Concurrent with designing the extent of differentiation in an organization, a manager must consider what effort at what cost will be needed to integrate those differences. The greater the differentiation, the more elaborate and costly are the mechanisms needed for integration.

Organizational design choices are tradeoffs between good fit to the task environment and people characteristics, to monetary and human costs, and to short-term and long-term consequences. Such a design is never perfect or complete. Organizational design seeks to build knowledge about and provide guidelines for designing more efficient and more human organizations.

REFERENCES

1. Herbert A. Simon, *The New Science of Management Decision.* (New York: Harper and Brothers, 1960), pp. 2, 43.
2. Tom Burns and G. M. Stalker, *The Management of Innovation* (London: Tavistock, 1961).

3. Geoffrey Vickers, *The Art of Judgment* (New York: Basic Books, 1965).

4. Burns and Stalker, *loc. cit.*

5. Paul R. Lawrence and Jay W. Lorsch, *Organization and Environment* (Boston: Graduate School of Business Administration, Harvard University, 1967).

6. James D. Thompson, *Organizations in Action* (New York: McGraw-Hill, 1967).

7. Paul R. Lawrence and Jay W. Lorsch, "New Management Job: The Integrator," *Harvard Business Review* (November–December 1967), pp. 142–151.

8. Arthur H. Walker and Jay W. Lorsch, "Organizational Choice: Product Versus Function," *Harvard Business Review* (November–December 1968), pp. 129–138; and Jay R. Galbraith, *Designing Complex Organizations* (Reading, Mass.: Addison-Wesley, 1973).

9. Donald Ralph Kingdon, *Matrix Organization: Managing Information Technologies* (London: Tavistock, 1973).

10. Peter M. Blau and Richard A. Schoenherr, *The Structure of Organizations* (New York: Basic Books, 1971).

11. Jay W. Lorsch and Paul R. Lawrence (eds.), *Studies in Organization Design* (Homewood, Ill.: Irwin-Dorsey, 1970).

12. Blau and Schoenherr, *loc. cit.*

13. Lawrence and Lorsch, *Studies in Organization Design, loc. cit.*

14. Galbraith, *loc. cit.*

15. Robert B. Duncan, *The Effects of Perceived Environmental Uncertainty on Organizational Decision Unit Structure: A Cybernetic Model,* Ph.D. dissertation, Yale University, 1971.

16. Robert Propst, *The Office: A Facility Based on Change* (New York: Taplinger Publishing Co., 1968).

17. Fred I. Steele, "Physical settings and organizational development," in H. Hornstein, *et al.* (eds.), *Social Intervention: A Behavioral Science Approach* (New York: The Free Press, 1971).

18. Thomas J. Allen, "Communication networks in R&D laboratories," *R&D Management, 1,* 1, (1970) Oxford, England, pp. 14–21.

MATRIX ORGANIZATION DESIGNS
How to Combine Functional and Project Forms

Each era of management evolves new forms of organization as new problems are encountered. Earlier generations of managers invented the centralized functional form, the line-staff form, and the decentralized product division structure as a response to increasing size and complexity of tasks. The current generation of management has developed two new forms as a response to high technology. The first is the free-form conglomerate; the other is the matrix organization, which was developed primarily in the aerospace industry.

The matrix organization grows out of the organizational choice between project and functional forms, although it is not limited to those bases of the authority structure.[1] Research in the behavioral sciences now permits a detailing of the choices among the alternate intermediate forms between the project and functional extremes. Detailing such a choice is necessary since many businessmen see their organizations facing situations in the 1970's that are similar to those faced by the aerospace firms in the 1960's. As a result, a great many unanswered questions arise concerning the use of the matrix organization. For example, what are the various kinds of matrix de-

signs, what is the difference between the designs, how do they work, and how do I choose a design that is appropriate for my organization?

The problem of designing organizations arises from the choices available among alternative bases of the authority structure. The most common alternatives are to group together activities which bear on a common product, common customer, common geographic area, common business function (marketing, engineering, manufacturing, and so on), or common process (forging, stamping, machining, and so on). Each of these bases has various costs and economies associated with it. For example, the functional structure facilitates the acquisition of specialized inputs. It permits the hiring of an electromechanical and an electronics engineer rather than two electrical engineers. It minimizes the number necessary by pooling specialized resources and time sharing them across products or projects. It provides career paths for specialists. Therefore, the organization can hire, utilize, and retain specialists.

These capabilities are necessary if the organization is going to develop high technology products. However, the tasks that the organization must perform require varying amounts of the specialized resources applied in varying sequences. The problem of simultaneously completing all tasks on time, with appropriate quality and while fully utilizing all specialist resources, is all but impos-

Copyright, 1971, by the Foundation for the School of Business at Indiana University. Reprinted by permission of *Business Horizons* and Jay R. Galbraith.

sible in the functional structure. It requires either fantastic amounts of information or long lead times for task completion.

The product or project form of organization has exactly the opposite set of benefits and costs. It facilitates coordination among specialties to achieve on-time completion and to meet budget targets. It allows a quick reaction capability to tackle problems that develop in one specialty, thereby reducing the impact on other specialties. However, if the organization has two projects, each requiring one half-time electronics engineer and one half-time electromechanical engineer, the pure project organization must either hire two electrical engineers—and reduce specialization—or hire four engineers (two electronics and two electromechanical)—and incur duplication costs. In addition, no one is responsible for long-run technical development of the specialties. Thus, each form of organization has its own set of advantages and disadvantages. A similar analysis could be applied to geographically or client-based structures.

The problem is that when one basis of organization is chosen, the benefits of the others are surrendered. If the functional structure is adopted, the technologies are developed but the projects fall behind schedule. If the project organization is chosen, there is better cost and schedule performance but the technologies are not developed as well. In the past, managers made a judgment as to whether technical development or schedule

completion was more important and chose the appropriate form.

However, in the 1960's with a space race and missile gap, the aerospace firms were faced with a situation where both technical performance and coordination were important. The result was the matrix design, which attempts to achieve the benefits of both forms. However, the matrix carries some costs of its own. A study of the development of a matrix design is contained in the history of The Standard Products Co., a hypothetical company that has changed its form of organization from a functional structure to a matrix.

A COMPANY CHANGES FORMS

The Standard Products Co. has competed effectively for a number of years by offering a varied line of products that were sold to other organizations. Standard produced and sold its products through a functional organization like the one represented in Figure 1. A moderate number of changes in the product line and production processes were made each year. Therefore, a major management problem was to coordinate the flow of work from engineering through marketing. The coordination was achieved through several integrating mechanisms:

Rules and Procedures. One of the ways to constrain behavior in order to achieve an integrated pattern is to specify rules and procedures. If all

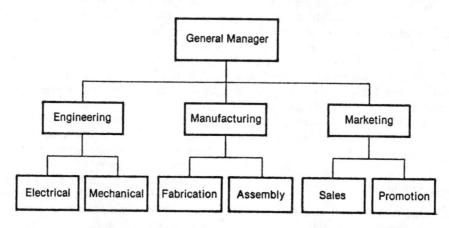

FIGURE 1. Standard's functional organization.

personnel follow the rules, the resultant behavior is integrated without having to maintain on-going communication. Rules are used for the most predictable and repetitive activities.

Planning Processes. For less repetitive activities, Standard does not specify the procedure to be used but specifies a goal or target to be achieved, and lets the individual choose the procedure appropriate to the goal. Therefore, processes are undertaken to elaborate schedules and budgets. The usefulness of plans and rules is that they reduce the need for on-going communication between specialized subunits.

Hierarchical Referral. When situations are encountered for which there are no rules or when problems cause the goals to be exceeded, these situations are referred upward in the hierarchy for resolution. This is the standard management-by-exception principle. This resolves the nonroutine and unpredictable events that all organizations encounter.

Direct Contact. In order to prevent top executives from becoming overloaded with problems, as many problems as possible are resolved by the affected managers at low levels by informal contacts. These remove small problems from the upward referral process.

Liaison Departments. In some cases, where there is a large volume of contacts between two departments, a liaison department evolves to handle the transactions. This typically occurs between engineering and manufacturing in order to handle engineering changes and design problems.[2]

The Standard Products Co. utilized these mechanisms to integrate the functionally organized specialties. They were effective in the sense that Standard could respond to changes in the market with new products on a timely basis, the new products were completed on schedule and within budget, and the executives had sufficient time to devote to long-range planning.

Matrix Begins Evolution

A few years ago, a significant change occurred in the market for one of Standard's major product lines. A competitor came out with a new design utilizing an entirely new raw material. The initial success caused Standard to react by developing one of their own incorporating the new material. They hired some specialists in the area and began their normal new product introduction activities. However, this time the product began to fall behind schedule, and it appeared that the product would arrive on the market at a time later than planned. In response, the general manager called a meeting to analyze the situation.

Task Force. After a briefing, it was obvious to the general manager and the directors of the three functions what was happening. Standard's lack of experience with the new material had caused them to underestimate the number and kinds of problems. The uncertainty led to a deterioration in usefulness of plans and schedules. The problems affected all functions, which meant that informal contacts and liaison processes were cumbersome; therefore, the majority of the problems were referred upward. This led to overloads on the directors of the functions and the general manager, which in turn added to the delays. Thus, the new situation required more decision making and more information processing than the current organization could provide.

The directors of engineering and manufacturing suggested that the cause of the problem was an overly ambitious schedule. More time should have been allowed for the new product; if realistic schedules were set, the current coordination processes would be adequate. They proposed that the schedules be adjusted by adding three to six months to the current due dates, which would allow more time to make the necessary decisions.

The director of marketing objected, reporting that the company would lose a good percentage of the market if the introduction was delayed. A number of big customers were waiting for Standard's version of the new product, and a delay would cost the company some of these customers. The general manager agreed with the marketing director. He proposed that they should not change the schedule to fit their current coordination processes, but that they should introduce some new coordination mechanisms to meet the scheduled due dates.

The group agreed with the general manager's position and began to search for alternative solutions. One of the solution requirements suggested was to reduce the distance between the sources of information and the points of decision. At this point the manufacturing director cautioned them about decentralizing decisions. He reminded them of previous experiences when decisions were made at low levels of the engineering organization. The data the decision makers had were current but they were also local in scope; severe problems in the manufacturing process resulted. When these decisions were centralized, the global perspective prevented these problems from developing. Therefore, they had to increase decision-making power at lower levels without losing the inputs of all affected units. The alternative that met both requirements was a group with representation from all the major departments to enter into joint decisions.

The group was appointed and named the "new product task force." It was to last as long as cross-functional problems occurred on the new product introduction. The group was to meet and solve joint problems within the budget limits set by the general manager and the directors; problems requiring more budget went to the top management group. The purpose was to make as many decisions as possible at low levels with the people most knowledgeable. This should reduce the delays and yet ensure that all the information inputs were considered.

The task force consisted of nine people; three, one from each function, were full-time and the others were part-time. They met at least every other day to discuss and resolve joint problems. Several difficulties caused them to shift membership. First, the engineering representatives were too high in the organization and, therefore, not knowledgeable about the technical alternatives and consequences. They were replaced with lower level people. The opposite occurred with respect to the manufacturing representatives. Quite often they did not have either information or the authority to commit the production organization to joint decisions made by the task force. They were replaced by higher level people. Eventually, the group had both the information and the authority to make good group decisions. The result was ef-

fective coordination: coordination $= f$ (authority $\times$ information).

Creation of the task force was the correct solution. Decision delays were reduced, and collective action was achieved by the joint decisions. The product arrived on time, and the task force members returned to their regular duties.

Teams. No sooner had the product been introduced than salesmen began to bring back stories about new competitors. One was introducing a second-generation design based on improvements in the raw material. Since the customers were excited by its potential and the technical people thought it was feasible, Standard started a second-generation redesign across all its product lines. This time, they set up the task force structure in advance and committed themselves to an ambitious schedule.

Again the general manager became concerned. This time the product was not falling behind schedule, but in order to meet target dates the top management was drawn into day-to-day decisions on a continual basis. This was leaving very little time to think about the third-generation product line. Already Standard had to respond twice to changes initiated by others. It was time for a thorough strategy formulation. Indeed, the more rapid the change in technology and markets, the greater the amount of strategic decision making that is necessary. However, these are the same changes that pull top management into day-to-day decisions. The general manager again called a meeting to discuss and resolve the problem.

The solution requirements to the problem were the same as before. They had to find a way to push a greater number of decisions down to lower levels. At the same time, they had to guarantee that all interdependent subunits would be considered in the decision so that coordination would be maintained. The result was a more extensive use of joint decision making and shared responsibility.

The joint decision making was to take place through a team structure. The teams consisted of representatives of all functions and were formed around major product lines. There were two levels of teams, one at lower levels and another at the middle-management level. Each level had defined discretionary limits; problems that the lower level could not solve were referred to the middle-level team. If the middle level could not solve the problem, it went to top management. A greater number of day-to-day operating problems were thereby solved at lower levels of the hierarchy, freeing top management for long-range decisions.

The teams, unlike the task force, were permanent. New products were regarded as a fact of life, and the teams met on a continual basis to solve recurring interfunctional problems. Task forces were still used to solve temporary problems. In fact, all the coordination mechanisms of rules, plans, upward referral, direct contact, liaison men, and task forces were used, in addition to the teams.

Product Managers. The team structure achieved interfunctional coordination and permitted top management to step out of day-to-day decision making. However, the teams were not uniformly effective. Standard's strategy required the addition of highly skilled, highly educated technical people to continue to innovate and compete in the high technology industry. Sometimes these specialists would dominate a team because of their superior technical knowledge. That is, the team could not distinguish between providing technical information and supplying managerial judgment after all the facts were identified. In addition, the specialists' personalities were different from the personalities of the other team members, which made the problem of conflict resolution much more difficult.[3]

Reports of these problems began to reach the general manager, who realized that a great number of decisions of consequence were being made at lower and middle levels of management. He also knew that they should be made with a general manager's perspective. This depends on having the necessary information and a reasonable balance of power among the joint decision makers. Now the technical people were upsetting the power balance because others could not challenge them on technical matters. As a result, the general manager chose three technically qualified men and made them product managers in charge of the three major product lines.[4] They were to act as chairmen of the product team meetings and generally facilitate the interfunctional decision making.

Since these men had no formal authority, they had to resort to their technical competence and their interpersonal skills in order to be effective. The fact that they reported to the general manager gave them some additional power. These men were successful in bringing the global, general manager perspective lower in the organization to improve the joint decision-making process.

The need for this role was necessitated by the increasing differences in attitudes and goals among the technical, production, and marketing team participants. These differences are necessary for successful subtask performance but interfere with team collaboration. The product manager allows collaboration without reducing these necessary differences. The cost is the additional overhead for the product management salaries.

Product Management Departments. Standard Products was now successfully following a strategy of new product innovation and introduction. It was leading the industry in changes in technology and products. As the number of new products increased, so did the amount of decision making around product considerations. The frequent needs for trade-offs across engineering, production, and marketing lines increased the influence of the product managers. It was not that the functional managers lost influence; rather, it was the increase in decisions relating to products.

The increase in the influence of the product managers was revealed in several ways. First, their salaries became substantial. Second, they began to have a greater voice in the budgeting process, starting with approval of functional budgets relating to their products. The next change was an accumulation of staff around the products, which became product departments with considerable influence.

At Standard this came about with the increase in new product introductions. A lack of information developed concerning product costs and revenues for addition, deletion, modification, and pricing decisions. The general manager instituted a new information system that reported costs and revenues by product as well as by function. This gave product managers the need for a staff and a basis for more effective interfunctional collaboration.

In establishing the product departments, the

general manager resisted requests from the product managers to reorganize around product divisions. While he agreed with their analysis that better coordination was needed across functions and for more effective product decision making, he was unwilling to take the chance that this move might reduce specialization in the technical areas or perhaps lose the economies of scale in production. He felt that a modification of the information system to report on a product and a functional basis along with a product staff group would provide the means for more coordination. He still needed the effective technical group to drive the innovative process. The general manager also maintained a climate where collaboration across product lines and functions was encouraged and rewarded.

The Matrix Completed

By now Standard Products was a high technology company; its products were undergoing constant change. The uncertainty brought about by the new technology and the new products required an enormous amount of decision making to plan-replan all the schedules, budgets, designs, and so on. As a result, the number of decisions and the number of consequential decisions made at low levels increased considerably. This brought on two concerns for the general manager and top management.

The first was the old concern for the quality of decisions made at low levels of the organization. The product managers helped solve this at middle and top levels, but their influence did not reach low into the organization where a considerable number of decisions were made jointly. They were not always made in the best interest of the firm as a whole. The product managers again recommended a move to product divisions to give these low-level decisions the proper product orientation.

The director of engineering objected, using the second problem to back up his objection. He said the move to product divisions would reduce the influence of the technical people at a time when they were having morale and turnover problems with these employees. The increase in joint decisions at low levels meant that these technical people were spending a lot of time in meetings.

Their technical input was not always needed, and they preferred to work on technical problems, not product problems. Their dissatisfaction would only be aggravated by a change to product divisions.

The top management group recognized both of these problems. They needed more product orientation at low levels, and they needed to improve the morale of the technical people whose inputs were needed for product innovations. Their solution involved the creation of a new role—that of subproduct manager.[5] The subproduct manager would be chosen from the functional organization and would represent the product line within the function. He would report to both the functional manager and the product manager, thereby creating a dual authority structure. The addition of a reporting relation on the product side increases the amount of product influence at lower levels.

The addition of the subproduct manager was intended to solve the morale problem also. Because he would participate in the product team meetings, the technical people did not need to be present. The subproduct manager would participate on the teams but would call on the technical experts within his department as they were needed. This permitted the functional department to be represented by the subproduct manager, and the technical people to concentrate on strictly technical matters.

Standard Products has now moved to a pure matrix organization as indicated in Figure 2. The pure matrix organization is distinguished from the previous cross-functional forms by two features. *First,* the pure matrix has a dual authority relationship somewhere in the organization. *Second,* there is a power balance between the product management and functional sides. While equal power is an unachievable razor's edge, a reasonable balance can be obtained through enforced collaboration on budgets, salaries, dual information and reporting systems, and dual authority relations. Such a balance is required because the problems that the organization faces are uncertain and must be solved on their own merits—not on any predetermined power structure.

Thus over a period of time, the Standard Products Co. has changed from a functional organization to a pure matrix organization using dual

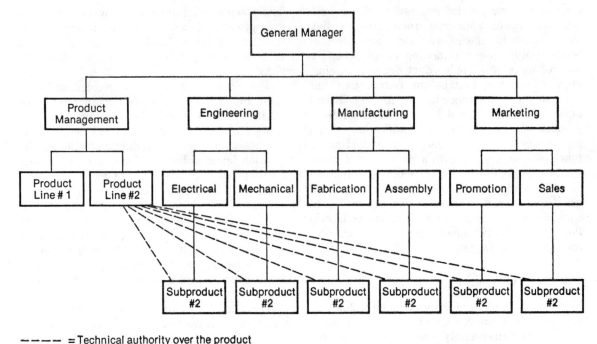

FIGURE 2. Standard's pure matrix organization.

authority relationships, product management departments, product teams at several levels, and temporary task forces. These additional decision-making mechanisms were added to cope with the change in products and technologies. The changes caused a good deal of uncertainty concerning resource allocations, budgets, and schedules. In the process of task execution, more was learned about the problem causing a need for rescheduling and rebudgeting. This required the processing of information and the making of decisions.

In order to increase its capacity to make product relevant decisions, Standard lowered the level at which decisions were made. Coordination was achieved by making joint decisions across functions. Product managers and subproduct managers were added to bring a general manager's perspective to bear on the joint decision-making processes. In addition, the information and reporting system was changed in order to provide reports by function and by product. Combined, these measures allowed Standard to achieve the

high levels of technical sophistication necessary to innovate products and simultaneously to get these products to the market quickly to maintain competitive position.

HOW DO I CHOOSE A DESIGN?

Not all organizations need a pure matrix organization with a dual authority relationship. Many, however, can benefit from some cross-functional forms to relieve top decision makers from day-to-day operations. If this is so, how does one choose the degree to which his organization should pursue these lateral forms? To begin to answer this question, let us first lay out the alternatives, then list the choice determining factors.

The choice, shown in Figure 3, is indicated by the wide range of alternatives between a pure functional organization and a pure product organization with the matrix being half-way be-

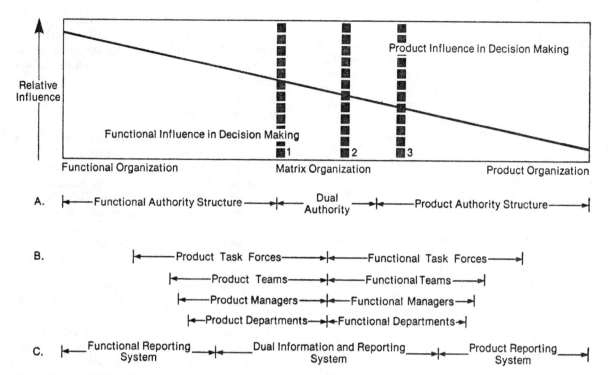

FIGURE 3. The range of alternatives.

tween. The Standard Products Co. could have evolved into a matrix from a product organization by adding functional teams and managers. Thus there is a continuum of organization designs between the functional and product forms. The design is specified by the choice among the authority structure; integrating mechanisms such as task forces, teams and so on; and by the formal information system. The way these are combined is illustrated in Figure 3. These design variables help regulate the relative distribution of influence between the product and functional considerations in the firm's operations.

The remaining factors determining influence are such things as roles in budget approvals, design changes, location and size of offices, salary, and so on. Thus there is a choice of integrating devices, authority structure, information system, and influence distribution. The factors that determine choice are diversity of the product line, the rate of change of the product line, interdependencies among subunits, level of technology, presence of economies of scale, and organization size.

Product Lines

The greater the diversity among product lines and the greater the rate of change of products in the line the greater the pressure to move toward product structures.[6] When product lines become diverse, it becomes difficult for general managers and functional managers to maintain knowledge in all areas; the amount of information they must handle exceeds their capacity to absorb it. Similarly, the faster the rate of new product introduction, the more unfamiliar are the tasks being performed.

Managers are, therefore, less able to make precise estimates concerning resource allocations, schedules, and priorities. During the process of new product introduction, these same decisions are made repeatedly. The decisions concern trade-offs among engineering, manufacturing, and marketing. This means there must be greater product influence in the decision process. The effect of diversity and change is to create a force to locate the organization farther to the right in Figure 3.

Interdependence

The functional division of labor in organizations creates interdependencies among the specialized subunits. That is, a problem of action in one unit has a direct impact on the goal accomplishment of the other units. Organizations usually devise mechanisms that uncouple the subunits, such as in-process-inventory and order backlogs. The degree to which inventories and backlogs develop is a function of how tight the schedule is. If there is a little slack in the schedule, then the functional departments can resolve their own problems. However, if rapid response to market changes is a basis of competition, then schedules are squeezed and activities run in parallel rather than series.[7] This means that problems in one unit directly affect another. The effect is a greater number of joint decisions involving engineering, manufacturing, and production. A greater need for product influence in these decisions arises due to the tight schedule. Thus the tighter the schedule, the greater the force to move to the right in Figure 3.

Although the tightness of the schedule is the most obvious source of interdependence, tight couplings can arise from reliability requirements and other design specifications. If the specifications require a more precise fit and operation of parts, then the groups designing and manufacturing the parts must also "fit and operate" more closely. This requires more coordination in the form of communication and decision making.

Level of Technology

If tight schedules and new products were the only forces operating, every organization would be organized around product lines. The level of technology or degree to which new technology is being used is a counteracting force. The use of new technologies requires expertise in the technical specialties in engineering, in production engineering, in manufacturing, and market research in marketing. Some of the expertise may be purchased outside the organization.

However, if the expertise is critical to competitive effectiveness, the organization must acquire it internally. If the organization is to make effective use of the expertise, the functional form of organization is superior, as described earlier in the article. Therefore the greater the need for expertise, the greater the force to move to the left in Figure 3.

Economies of Scale and Size

The other factor favoring a functional form is the degree to which expensive equipment in manufacturing, test facilities in engineering, and warehousing facilities in marketing are used in producing and selling the product. (Warehousing introduces another dimension of organization structure, for example, geographical divisions. For our purposes, we will be concerned only with product and function dimensions.) It is usually more expensive to buy small facilities for product divisions than a few large ones for functional departments. The greater the economies of scale, the greater the force to move to the left in Figure 3. Mixed structures are always possible. That is, the capital intensive fabrication operation can organize along functional process lines, and the labor intensive assembly operation can organize along product lines.

The size of the organization is important in that it modifies the effect of expertise and economies of scale. That is, the greater the size of the organization the smaller the costs of lost specialization and lost economies of scale when the product form is adopted. Thus while size by itself has little effect on organization structure, it does moderate the effects of the previously mentioned factors.

The Choice

While research on organizations has not achieved a sophistication that would allow us to compute the results of the above factors and locate a point in Figure 3, we can still make our subjective weightings. In addition, we can locate our present position and make changes in the appropriate directions as product lines, schedules, technologies, and size change during the normal course of business. The framework provides some basis for planning the organization along with planning the strategy and resource allocations.

If the organization's present structure is on the left side of the figure, many of the symptoms occurring in the Standard Products example signal a need for change. To what degree are communication overloads occurring? Are top executives being drawn into day-to-day decisions to the detriment of strategy development? How long does it take to get top level decisions made in order to continue work on new products? If the answers to these questions indicate an overload, then some movement toward a matrix is appropriate. Probably a sequence of moves until the bottlenecks disappear is the best strategy; this will allow for the proper attitudinal and behavioral changes to keep pace.

If the organization is product organized, then movements to the left toward a matrix are more subtle. They must be triggered by monitoring the respective technological environments.

An example from the aerospace industry may help. In the late fifties and early sixties the environment was characterized by the space race and missile gap. In this environment, technical performance and technology development were primary, and most firms adopted organizations characterized by the dotted line at "1" in Figure 3. The functional departments had the greatest influence on the decision-making process. During the McNamara era, they moved to point "2." The environment shifted to incentive contracts, PERT-cost systems, and increased importance of cost and schedule considerations.

Currently, the shift has continued toward point "3." Now the environment is characterized by tight budgets, a cost overrun on the C-5 project, and Proxmire hearings in the Senate. The result is greater influence by the project managers. All these have taken place in response to the changing character of the market. A few firms recently moved back toward point "2" in response to the decreasing size of some firms. The reduction in defense spending has resulted in cutbacks in projects and employment. In order to maintain technical capabilities with reduced size, these firms

have formed functional departments under functional managers with line responsibility. These changes show how changes in need for expertise, goals, and size affect the organization design choice.

Many organizations are experiencing pressures that force them to consider various forms of matrix designs. The most common pressure is increased volume of new products. Organizations facing this situation must either adopt some form of matrix organization, change to product forms of organization, or increase the time between start and introduction of the new product process.

For most organizations, the matrix design is the most effective alternative. Managers must be aware of the different kinds of matrix designs and develop some basis for choosing among them.

NOTES

1. See John F. Mee, "Matrix Organization," *Business Horizons* (Summer, 1964), p. 70.

2. For a more detailed explanation, see Jay R. Galbraith, *Organization Design* (Reading, Mass.: Addison-Wesley Publishing Co., Inc., 1971).

3. See Paul R. Lawrence and Jay Lorsch, "Differentiation and Integration in Complex Organizations," *Administrative Science Quarterly* (June, 1967).

4. Paul R. Lawrence and Jay Lorsch, "New Management Job: the Integration," *Harvard Business Review* (November–December, 1967).

5. Jay Lorsch, "Matrix Organization and Technical Innovations" in Jay Galbraith, ed., *Matrix Organizations: Organization Design for High Technology* (Cambridge, Mass.: The M.I.T. Press, 1971).

6. For product line diversity, see Alfred Chandler, *Strategy and Structure* (Cambridge, Mass.: The M.I.T. Press, 1962); for product change rate, see Tom Burns and G. M. Stalker, *Management and Innovation* (London: Tavistock Publications, 1958).

7. For a case study of this effect, see Jay Galbraith, "Environmental and Technological Determinants of Organization Design" in Jay Lorsch and Paul R. Lawrence, eds., *Studies in Organization Design* (Homewood, Ill.: Richard D. Irwin, Inc., 1970).

TECHNOLOGY, ORGANIZATIONS, AND CONTINGENCY

MARIANN JELINEK

Technology has been recognized as a crucially important variable from the very beginnings of formal organization theory. It was quickly realized that, however important technology might be, it was neither the single determinant of organizational structure, nor a simple determinant. Organization theory itself has become more sophisticated in modelling complex organizations: contingency approaches now include both technology and environment as interactive variables affecting organization structure. Recent developments in contingency theory, combined with newly elaborated views of technology and of environment, suggest a multiple-environment, multiple-technology view of complex organizations. Earlier studies provide support both for this elaborated view of organization structure, and for the notion of intervening technologies, mediating the fit between the organization and its environment, and among organization parts. This article surveys relevant studies of technology, environment, and organizational contingency to construct a synthesis of theory and suggests directions for further research.

THEORETICAL BEGINNINGS

Contingency theory essentially began with socio-technical theory, which combined the technolog-

Reprinted with the permission of the Academy of Management Review.

ical emphasis of earlier classical theory with the later human relations school's attention to people (30, 31, 35, 36, 45, 49). Socio-technical theory goes beyond either of its predecessor schools in a systems-based, wholistic approach to the organization of work. The Tavistock group in England, chief proponents of the approach, see both organizational effectiveness and member satisfaction as dependent upon how well suited structure is to the accomplishment of task. Walker and Guest (60) came to similar conclusions in this country. For socio-technical theorists, the primary task and its "prevalent cleavages" along lines of technology, time, and territory will determine an appropriate organization structure, consisting of autonomous work groups, each responsible for a complete task (37, 38, 53, 54).

"Prevalent cleavages" give little specific guidance for structure. It is difficult to see from the theory just how structure and technology interact, or how to define primary tasks. Further attention to the specifics of the interaction was needed, and that meant defining what technological characteristics affected what structural characteristics.

Characteristics of Technology

Woodward (63) was the first to isolate technical variables on which organization depended. She defined three levels of increasing technological complexity: unit and small batch production, large batch and mass production, and process production. These distinctions uncovered clear patterns among sample firms, as organizational characteristics like levels of hierarchy and span of control did not. She saw increasing technical complexity as increasing control over the production process, its physical limitations and results. Trends in organizational structure appeared to be associated with increasing ability to predict and control production. Some characteristics showed a curvilinear relation to increasing technical complexity, notably organizational form (which was seen as typically organic at the extremes of high and low technical complexity). Technical complexity of the production process describes the firm as a whole in this study.

Bright (5) had earlier defined 17 progressive levels of automation in terms of sources of power, control, and response. His investigations revealed that the degree of mechanization in an enterprise varied, with greatest advances typically in the central production process, and along the main flow in and out of the conversion process. Elsewhere, mechanization was usually much less advanced. Although this was a key finding for a theory of complex organizations, Bright did not investigate the implications of these findings for structure.

Harvey (22) used the works of Bright, Woodward, and others, to propose a scale of increasing technological specificity according to the number of major product changes his sample firms had experienced in the ten years prior to the study. Technically *diffuse* enterprises (akin to Woodward's job shops) could turn their technology to a variety of products; technically *intermediate* shops (Woodward's large batch and mass production categories) had less possible variation; while technically *specific* operations (Woodward's process production) had least variation. Harvey found that structure—defined in terms of organizational mechanisms like sub-unit specialization, levels of authority, and program specification—increased with increasing technological specificity. Highly specific technologies are accompanied by highly structured organizations, and are thus to be classified as mechanistic organizations, in the terminology of Burns and Stalker (7), a finding at variance with Woodward.

In a more broadly based study (using data from Bright and Woodward and others), Burack (6) argued that in advanced production systems there is an increasing tendency toward managerial innovations, rather than technological innovation. As technical complexity increases, the complexity of the organization intended to control it also increases, with elaboration of job descriptions, control technologies, support functions, and so on. Moreover, the nature of the production process changes job requirements: worker intervention is typically indirect, concerned with adjusting the process rather than affecting the product itself.

Harvey's scale of increasing technical specificity is much like that of Thompson and Bates (52), who use the degree to which machines, skills, materials, and knowledge can be used for purposes other than those initially intended. They hypothesize that "the type of technology available sets limits on the types of structure appropriate for organizations" (52, p. 325). Automation (increasing technical complexity and specificity) increases the speed and precision of tasks at the cost of increased rigidity. Processes which are automated have less tolerance for disturbance (6, 15, 52), and input-output functions are also less tolerant of variance (5). Udy (57) suggested a general proposition to describe this relationship between tolerance for variation and structural constraint: "The more flexible the technology, the less salient it will be" in determining structure (57, p. 690). Further, technological complexity seems to require a more elaborate administrative structure, because the complex technology is likely to involve the organization in more contact with its setting (50, 51, 52, 55, 57); because complex technology elaborates and subdivides formerly simple tasks (5, 15, 52); or because larger amounts of differentiation associated with increasing complexity demand an increasingly larger administrative capability to reintegrate the task (1, 6, 30, 31, 49, 58, 59).

Differentiation and Integration

Lawrence and Lorsch (29) address sub-unit differentiation from a different point of view than Bright's. They hypothesize the need for fit between the organization and its several external environments. This shift in focus is a major change from earlier "contingent" socio-technical theory, which looks exclusively to internal contingencies governed by the task or the interpersonal relations of organization members. They look instead to perceived environmental uncertainties and responses to them as critical determinants of structural differences (differentiation) and of the resulting coordinative interactions (integration) thereby implied. They document varieties of differentiated response to perceived uncertainty along dimensions like clarity of goals, interpersonal or task orientation, locus of decision-making power in related sub-units, and timing of environmental feedback. Balance of differentiation with environmental uncertainty, and of integration with differentiation is required for success. Since the emphasis is upon function, there is no universally applicable organization structure. Instead, varied responses to environmental factors—including such "internal" environmental factors as related sub-units' structure and orientation along relevant dimensions—determine the structure of the organization as a whole.

This is essentially a systems approach, with "system" defined classically as an integrated assembly of specialized parts acting together toward a common end. The individual sub-units of the organization can be seen as specialized entities, and also as parts of the whole. Implicit in this multiple focus, on the organization as a whole, its sub-units, and their sub-units, are notions of both internal and external environmental fit.

ENVIRONMENTS AND COMPLEXITIES

Multiple Environments, Multiple Technologies

The Lawrence and Lorsch usage of environmental uncertainty as a prime determinant of structure brings a number of theoretical issues forward. In contrast with earlier work, their model hypothesizes multiple task environments (both internal and external) with differing degrees of uncertainty. While this may seem obvious from the concept of task specialization, they are the first

to take this critical possibility into account. The dual fit—internal and external—makes coherent both the interconnectedness and the discreteness of organizational parts. It now becomes possible to speak meaningfully of multiple environments and multiple technolog*ies* of an organization. The magnitude of this departure from the work of earlier theorists is not to be understated: Woodward (63), the Aston group (23, 24, 25, 43), and most other thinkers take the workflow or production technology as indicative of the entire organization. Although the Aston group does mention both "materials technology" and "knowledge technology" as categories, only production technology is explored (24). While this viewpoint addresses the dominance of production technology, it ignores the internal variance and fit issues upon which Lawrence and Lorsch insist. Thus earlier schemes, because they are limited to the central transformation technology, fail to account for systematic, organization-wide, and inter-organizational phenomena.

Uncertainty. Perrow's (41) typologies allow further precision in the description of multiple environments. Although Perrow's intention is to compare organizations, rather than organizational parts, some empirical investigation supports this usage (33). Perrow's variables, the nature and frequency of problems encountered, the nature of the raw materials, and the type of search process required, hold implications for such structural and managerial characteristics as discretion and degree of centralization (3, 4, 41, 47). These details give more shape to normative statements about organization structure—particularly when combined with the idea of internal fit.

Perrow's concepts can be seen as an "uncertainty processing" view of the organization and its parts, with structure related to the degree of freedom (discretion) implied by a given amount of uncertainty. Similar approaches by Galbraith (17, 18) and postulates by Rushing (47), as well as suggestive developments by Hage and Aiken (20, 21), Lynch (33), and Van de Ven and Delbecq (58) all lend weight to Perrow's interpretation. His typology and these supporting studies go beyond manufacturing enterprises to health, education, and other service organizations, thus confirming the more general applicability of uncertainty concepts.

Dependency. A number of environmental typologies carry Perrow's look at the environment into other dimensions. Although they ultimately limit their attention to task environment, excluding even technology, Osburn and Hunt (40) note a wide range of environmental factors affecting service agencies. They limit the task environment to organizations with which the focal agency interacts, as separate from macro socio-cultural factors. Economic and market factors are also absent in the Osburn and Hunt study. Conceptually, they do not prohibit a multiple-environment viewpoint, although they treat their agencies as entities interacting with a spectrum of relevant external organizations. They differentiate *dependency* from risk, identifying dependency as the explanatory variable for their sample.

Duncan goes even farther in defining the environment as "the totality of physical and social factors that are taken directly into consideration in the decision-making" (13, p. 314) of the organization. He delineates both internal and external environments with considerable finesse, including, for instance, technological background and skills of personnel and technological characteristics of organizational units as internal factors. He considers the impact of new technology on existing products both in terms of production improvements and in terms of new products or services arising from the new technology. (Burack's framework would include specifically managerial "technology" as well (6).) Duncan's typology focuses on *perceived* environmental uncertainty—as do those of Lawrence and Lorsch (29), Lynch (33), Perrow (41), Van de Ven and Delbecq (58)—seeking to explore the factors that lead to perceptual differences. Duncan takes varying individual tolerances for uncertainty into account as well. His model is an individual-level model (as are those of Perrow, and Hage and Aiken), where the model of Lawrence and Lorsch looks to the sub-unit or departmental level. The Woodward (63) and the Aston group (23, 24, 25, 43) models are organizational-system models, on yet a higher level of abstraction.

Thompson's typology of technologies (51) is also on the organizational level, but he suggests that different types of internal interdependencies (departmental and individual levels) are associated with each technological type—elaborating somewhat on his earlier article with Bates (52). Long-linked technology (type: automobile assembly line) involves *sequential* interdependence; mediating technology (types: bank or telephone company) invloves *pooled* interdependence: and intensive technology (type: medical treatment of a patient) involves *reciprocal* interdependence. Thompson's focus is internal, where that of Osburn and Hunt is external; the dimension of dependency is similar.

Thompson's three types of technology, and thus the interdependencies involved, are increasingly contingent. They are also increasingly difficult to coordinate, because they respond increasingly to uncertainty. Thus they are increasingly costly. Varied types of coordinating mechanisms of increasing complexity—plans, standardization, mutual adjustment—are suitable to each technology type and the associated mode of interdependence. These suitabilities constrain the organization for Thompson—rather more specifically than in the Lawrence and Lorsch model. Thompson, like Perrow, suggests that structural limitations are implied by technological characteristics.

Kynaston Reeves and Turner (28) propose the addition of large batch technology to Thompson's three types, with the associated interdependence being somewhat like overall pooled interdependence with sequential and reciprocal elements due to sequential and overlapping use of facilities. Batch production is substantially more contingent, in that coordination by plan is impossible. Here, mutual adjustment is a direct response to environmental uncertainty. The form it takes is iterative revision of schedules.

TECHNOLOGIES, ENVIRONMENTS, AND STRUCTURE

An Attempt at Synthesis

As the environment becomes more complex, an organization must adjust both internal structure and process to maintain effectiveness. Environmental uncertainty (lack of specificity) has a major impact upon core technology, with the impact of uncertainty inversely proportional to technological specificity (5, 6, 15, 22, 52, 57). This impact is buffered by various structural and administrative devices (5, 6, 22, 51). The more specific the technology, the greater the need for protection; the more uncertain the environment, the greater the need for protection. Thus under conditions of great uncertainty or great technological specificity, we may expect elaboration of structure and devices to protect the technology. While some evidence has been cited in support of this assertion, there is clearly a need for further investigation in a variety of technological settings. (See Gillespie and Mileti (19) present a rather different view of technologies as a variable in the study of organizations.)

This elaborated contingency model joins multiple environments and multiple technologies. The basic configuration sees environments, technology, and infrastructure—various organizational buffers —interacting with one another and with organizational structure. The core technology is a major shaping factor among others. Infrastructure, the organization as apart or distinct from its core technology and associated core structure, takes its shape from the necessity of providing a dual fit, both with the core technology it buffers and with the external environment. But this infrastructure —classically purchasing departments, personnel, shipping, and the like—also has technologies and environments. These technologies and their implied interdependencies must be chosen for this dual fit. As Lawrence and Lorsch (29) have it, differentiation requires reintegration. The lesson is also to be read in the attention paid to coordination by the early Systematic Management school (30, 31).

Thus we might expect these intervening technologies to fall somewhere between the core and the environment in tolerance for uncertainty or adaptability to it: this hypothesis is clearly testable. The choice of intervening technology implies choices in structure and management devices (6, 15, 16, 42, 47, 48, 51), constrained by the core technology and its interdependencies. The basic configuration (environment-infrastructure-technology) provides a frame or skeleton of increasing specificity and control, to be fleshed out with mul-

tiple intervening technologies meeting various aspects of the core technology's buffering needs.

A further step must take into account the varying importance of these internal technologies and the environments they produce. The potency of their effects might be related to their proximity to the main throughput flow, as with automation (5). Or relative potency might depend on pervasiveness of effect (throughout the organization, or localized). A rigorous test of the model would seek to quantify such a prioritizing or weighting, and to predict the relative impact of multiple technologies and environments, and of changes in them. In a related fashion, the impact of these internal technologies on one another might be assessed in terms of internal fit or constraining factors (2, pp. 23ff). The difficulties of changing pervasive internal technologies (like installing centralized "word processing centers" in place of private secretaries, or of putting in a new computer system) provide cases in point.

Kynaston Reeves and Turner call attention to a dimension of complexity similar to that used by Harvey to define technology, namely specificity (26). The close relationship between specificity and structure emerges when specificity is applied to internal fit characteristics like responses and roles. Thus specialization, an important measure of organizational complexity indicating how finely subdivided responsibilities for the task are, is a specificity measure describing the closeness of internal fit. Very specialized organizations imply "many little steps" rather than fewer larger steps to achieve fit. Specificity in procedures or responses is an administrative device; the highly specific organization may be said to have gone far in structuring the activities of its employees (3, 4, 43, 47) and thus in controlling internal fit among them. Those activities *not* well specified in advance are progressively more contingent and responsive to environmental change, whether internal to the organization or not. Specification of activity is clearly an administrative attempt to control output ("Scientific Management" and Taylor's time-motion studies provide a classic example (49)), ultimately to increase predictability in the performance of tasks. The cost is a more elaborate administrative structure. Roles and rule specifications—much akin in development to the

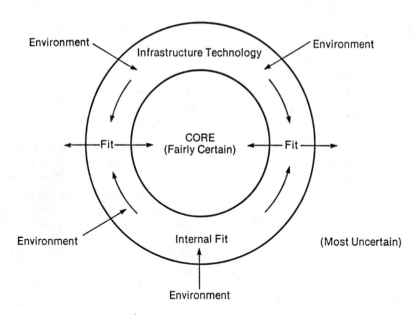

FIGURE 1. A Multiple-environment, multiple-technology model of the firm.

increasing technical complexity which addresses the physical production processes—are administrative technologies (6, 32).

These parallel developments make sense in the framework of Thompson's propositions of organizational rationality (51). Under norms of rationality, an organization seeks to protect its technological core from environmental disturbances. These disturbances may easily come from the *internal* environment, which presumably is more subject to organizational control. But increasing technical complexity increases the urgency of such protection by making the core more sensitive to disturbance and, frequently, by making the results of the disturbance more severe (5, 15). Bright's findings of diminishing automation (for which we may read diminishing technical specificity or complexity), moving away from the central throughput process or technical core, corroborate Thompson's propositions. The technological core, the main conversion process, is sealed off and buffered via the elaboration of non-production functions and their coordination into an administrative structure less sensitive to disturbance. Non-throughput tasks—maintenance and regulation

functions, as distinguished from transformation, in Litterer's terminology (30)—do indeed absorb environmental shocks and buffer the core; but they can be the source of internal uncertainty as well, and must be chosen and managed with this possibility in mind, if the internal fit is to be managed.

Multiple environments engendered by multiple technologies fit together by means of internal structuring and buffering. These require interdependencies which, together with the need to buffer, jointly constrain the choice of structure. Thus the core technology and its delineation of primary task environment and characteristics impose an initial configuration, relating this technology to an uncertain external environment. The core is buffered by the articulation of input-output, regulation, and maintenance functions. However, all of these functions are dependent upon their own technologies and environments, as well as upon the central conversion process. These buffering elements themselves are contingent for structure upon their own technologies; upon the "external" interface between themselves and their environments; upon the "internal" interface between themselves and the core; and upon the "internal" interfaces among one another. This suggests a structure dependent upon multiple technologies and multiple environments and their uncertainties, with effects weighted differentially, according to salience.

The organizational sub-units, the infrastructure accreted around the technological core, are attempts to control the internal environment in response to external uncertainties. "Environment" and "environmental uncertainty" must include both internal and external factors. But the distinction is of some use, since presumably internal factors are far more controllable, via rewards and punishments, recruitment, communication, role programs, decision-making locus, information flow, and the like, than external factors, which must nevertheless be taken into account. Further, structural mechanisms such as the division of labor assign responsibility for monitoring the environmental uncertainty, while programs determine which factors shall be monitored and how, and evaluation systems affect the actions that are taken upon uncertainties by rewarding only *some* responses. Thus organizations' internal and external environments are interdependent. Organizations "see" to a large extent what they program employees to perceive. They thus "create" the environment around them by controlling the means and modes of perception—to a degree.

Under these circumstances, more complex and inclusive descriptions of the environments of organizations are needed, along with clearer measures of uncertainty in these environments. Both objective and subjective measures might be useful. At the same time, the principle of equifinality asserts that assessments of uncertainty will merely indicate the kinds of differentiation required, and the nature of the fit. Assessment of technological tolerance for variance or of required interdependence will narrow the choice of structural means, but will not necessarily determine the form of buffering, of maintenance, or of regulation.

Directions for Further Research

While some evidence from earlier work supports the contentions of this article for a multi-variate contingency model, a number of propositions

could use further research. A specific test of the hypothesis of increasing structural elaboration of infrastructure to buffer increasingly sensitive core technologies would be especially helpful in non-manufacturing organizations. The postulate of increasing tolerance for disturbance with increasing distance from the technical core of the main conversion process is also testable. Similarly, the differential impact of internal technologies on the core, and of a complex internal environment is susceptible to test. Finally, Osburn and Hunt (40) pose an important challenge to the concept of external fit, in redefining dependency rather than risk as the key characteristic—albeit in a "protected" environment, where "short-run survival is assured and market contingencies are not important" (40, p. 241).

REFERENCES

1. Anderson, T. R., and S. Warkov. "Organizational Size and Functional Complexity," *American Sociological Review*, Vol. 26 (1961), 23–38.
2. Barnard, Chester. *The Functions of the Executive* (Cambridge, Mass.: Harvard University Press, 1938 and 1968).
3. Bell, Gerald D. "The Influence of Technological Components of Work Upon Management Control." *Academy of Management Journal*, Vol. 8, No. 2 (1965), 127–132.
4. Bell, Gerald D. "Predictability of Work Demands and Professionalization as Determinants of Workers' Discretion," *Academy of Management Journal*, Vol. 9, No. 1 (1966), 20–28.
5. Bright, James R. *Automation and Management* (Boston: Harvard University Press, 1958).
6. Burack, Elmer H. "Industrial Management in Advanced Production Systems: Some Theoretical Concepts and Preliminary Findings," *Administrative Science Quarterly*, Vol. 12 (1967), 479–500.
7. Burns, T., and G. M. Stalker. *The Management of Innovation* (London: Tavistock, 1961).
8. Child, John. "Predicting and Understanding Organizational Structure," *Administrative Science Quarterly*, Vol. 18 (1973), 168–185.
9. Cooper, Robert. "Man, Task and Technology: Three Variables in Search of a Future," *Human Relations*, Vol. 25, No. 2 (1972), 131–157.
10. Dill, William. "Environment as an Influence on Managerial Autonomy," *Administrative Science Quarterly*, Vol. 2 (1958), 409–443.

11. Dubin, Robert. *The World of Work* (Englewood Cliffs, N.J.: Prentice-Hall, 1958).

12. Dubin, Robert. "Stability of Human Organizations," in Mason Haire (Ed.), *Modern Organization Theory* (New York: Wiley, 1959).

13. Duncan, Robert B. "Characteristics of Organizational Environments and Perceived Environmental Uncertainty," *Administrative Science Quarterly,* Vol. 17, No. 3 (1972), 313–327.

14. Eisenstadt, S. N. "Bureaucracy, Bureaucratization, and Debureaucratization," *Administrative Science Quarterly,* Vol. 4 (1959), 302–20.

15. Emery, F. E., and J. Marek. "Socio-technical Aspects of Automation," *Human Relations,* Vol. 15 (1962), 17–25.

16. Emery, F. E., and E. L. Trist. "The Causal Texture of Organizational Environments," *Human Relations,* Vol. 18 (1963), 20–26.

17. Galbraith, Jay R. "Organizational Design: An Information Processing View," in Jay W. Lorsch and Paul R. Lawrence (Eds.), *Organization Planning: Cases and Concepts* (Homewood, Ill.: Irwin, 1972).

18. Galbraith, Jay R. *Designing Complex Organizations* (Reading, Mass.: Addison-Wesley, 1973).

19. Gillespie, David F., and Dennis S. Mileti. "Technology and the Study of Organizations: An Overview and Appraisal," *Academy of Management Review,* Vol. 2, No. 1 (January 1977), 7–16.

20. Hage, Jerald, and Michael Aiken. "Relationship of Centralization to Other Structural Properties," *Administrative Science Quarterly,* Vol. 12, No. 1 (June 1967), 72–92.

21. Hage, Jerald, and Michael Aiken. "Routine Technology, Social Structure, and Organization Goals," *Administrative Science Quarterly,* Vol. 14, No. 3 (September 1969), 366–376.

22. Harvey, Edward. "Technology and the Structure of Organizations" *American Sociological Review,* Vol. 33 (April 1968), 247–259.

23. Hickson, D. J. "A Convergence in Organization Theory," *Administrative Science Quarterly,* Vol. 11, No. 2 (1966), 224–237.

24. Hickson, David, Derek Pugh, and Diana Pheysey, "Operations, Technology, and Organizational Structure," *Administrative Science Quarterly,* Vol. 14 (September 1969), 378–398.

25. Inkson, J. H., Derek Pugh, and David Hickson. "Organizational Context and Structure: An Abbreviated Replication," *Administrative Science Quarterly,* Vol. 15 (September 1970), 318–329.

26. Jurkovich, Ray. "A Core Typology of Organizational Environments," *Administrative Science Quarterly,* Vol. 19, No. 3 (September 1974), 380–394.

27. Katz, Daniel, and Robert L. Kahn. *The Social Psychology of Organizations* (New York: Wiley, 1966).

28. Kynaston Reeves, Tom, and Barry A. Turner. "A Theory of Organization and Behavior in Batch Production Factories," *Administrative Science Quarterly,* Vol. 17, No. 1 (1972), 81–98.

29. Lawrence, Paul R., and Jay W. Lorsch. *Organization and Environment* (Homewood, Ill.: Irwin, 1969).

30. Litterer, Joseph A. "Systematic Management, The Search for Order and Integration," *Business History Review,* Vol. 35 (1961), 461–76.

31. Litterer, Joseph A. "Systematic Management, Design for Organizational Recoupling in American Manufacturing Firms," *Business History Review,* Vol. 37 (1963), 369–91.

32. Litterer, Joseph A. *The Analysis of Organizations,* 2d ed. (New York: Wiley, 1973).

33. Lynch, Beverly P. "An Empirical Assessment of Perrow's Technology Construct," *Administrative Science Quarterly,* Vol. 19, No. 3 (1974), 338–356.

34. Mann, F. C., and L. R. Hoffman. *Automation and the Worker* (New York: Holt, 1960).

35. Massie, Joseph L. "Management Theory," in James G. March (Ed.), *Handbook of Organizations* (Chicago: Rand McNally, 1965).

36. Mayo, Elton. *The Human Problems of an Industrial Civilization* (New York: Macmillan, 1933).

37. Miller, E. "Technology, Territory and Time: The Internal Differentiation of Complex Production Systems," *Human Relations,* Vol. 12 (1959), 243–72.

38. Miller, E. J., and A. K. Rice. *Systems of Organization* (London: Tavistock, 1967).

39. Negandhi, Anant R., and Bernard C. Reimann. "Task Environment, Decentralization and Organizational Effectiveness," *Human Relations,* Vol. 26, No. 2 (1973), 203–214.

40. Osburn, Richard N., and James G. Hunt. "Environment and Organizational Effectiveness." *Administrative Science Quarterly,* Vol. 19, No. 3 (June 1974), 231–246.

41. Perrow, Charles. "A Framework for the Comparative Analysis of Organizations," *American Sociological Review,* Vol. 32 (1967), 194–208.

42. Perrow, Charles. *Organizational Analysis: A Sociological View* (Belmont, Calif.: Wadsworth, 1970).

43. Pugh, D. S., D. J. Hickson, C. R. Hinings, and C. Turner. "Dimensions of Organization Structure," *Administrative Science Quarterly,* Vol. 13, No. 2 (June 1968), 65–105.

44. Rice, A. K. *The Enterprise and Its Environment* (London: Tavistock, 1963).

45. Roethlisberger, F., and W. Dickson. *Management and the Worker* (Boston: Harvard University Press, 1939).

46. Rushing, William A. "Hardness of Material as Related to Division of Labor in Manufacturing Industries," *Administrative Science Quarterly*, Vol. 13 (1968), 229–245.

47. Rushing, William A. "Organizational Rules and Surveillance: Propositions in Comparative Organizational Analysis," *Administrative Science Quarterly*, Vol. 10, No. 4 (March 1966), 423–443.

48. Sutherland, John W. "Toward an Array of Organizational Control Modalities," *Human Relations*, Vol. 27 (1974), 149–168.

49. Taylor, Frederick W. *The Principles of Scientific Management* (New York: Norton, 1967; first published in 1911).

50. Terreberry, Shirley. "The Evolution of Organizational Environments," *Administrative Science Quarterly*, Vol. 12 (1968), 590–613.

51. Thompson, James D. *Organizations in Action* (New York: McGraw-Hill, 1967).

52. Thompson, James D., and F. L. Bates. "Technology, Organization, and Administration," *Administrative Science Quarterly*, Vol. 2 (1957), 325–343.

53. Trist, E. L., and K. W. Bamforth. "Social and Psychological Consequences of the Longwall Method of Coal-Getting," *Human Relations*, Vol. 4 (1951), 6–38.

54. Trist, E. L., G. W. Higgin, H. Murray, and A. B. Pollock. *Organizational Choice* (London: Tavistock, 1963).

55. Udy, S. H., Jr. *Organization of Work* (New Haven: Hraf, 1959).

56. Udy, S. H., Jr. "Administrative Rationality, Social Setting, and Organizational Development," *American Journal of Sociology*, Vol. 68 (1962), 299–308.

57. Udy, S. H., Jr. "The Comparative Analysis of Organizations," in James G. March (Ed.), *Handbook of Organizations* (Chicago: Rand McNally, 1965).

58. Van de Ven, Andrew H., and André L. Delbecq. "A Task Contingent Model of Work-Unit Structure," *Administrative Science Quarterly*, Vol. 19 (1974), 183–197.

59. Walker, C. R. (Ed.). *Modern Technology and Civilization* (New York: McGraw-Hill, 1962).

60. Walker, Charles R., and Robert Guest. *Man on the Assembly Line* (Cambridge, Mass.: Harvard University Press, 1952).

61. Weber, Max. *From Max Weber: Essays in Sociology*, Ed. and Trans. by H. H. Gerth and C. Wright Mills (New York: Oxford, 1958).

62. Whyte, W. F. "An Interaction Approach to the Theory of Organizations," in Mason Haire (Ed.), *Modern Organization Theory* (New York: Wiley, 1959).

63. Woodward, Joan. *Industrial Organizations* (London: Oxford, 1965).

64. Zwerman, William L. *New Perspectives on Organization Theory* (Westport, Conn.: Greenwood, 1970).

4
ENVIRONMENTAL DIMENSIONS
OF BEHAVIOR

Just as the organization has its impact on human behavior, the environment also assumes an important role. Only recently has the environment been considered a significant determinant of behavior. However, it deserves special attention because of the research that has surfaced suggesting an environment–behavior linkage, and the turbulence and change that has manifested itself in recent times. The environment, here, is construed as the sum total of all that exists or is taking place outside the boundaries of the formal organization. To deal with such an amorphous aggregate, however, is practically impossible. Thus, we conceptualize the environment as having a number of facets (for example)—economic, social, technological, political, competitive—with various characteristics—homogeneity, heterogeneity, turbulence, and placidity. In this chapter we look at selected aspects of the environment–behavior relationship: the organization–environment interface, and social environmental change and behavior. Such an examination will give us an appreciation of the crucial contingency known as environment.

Under the organization–environment interface, we open with an article by Don Hellriegel and John Slocum. Though their article covers organizational design concepts and, therefore, might have been placed in the previous chapter, its special emphasis is on organizational adaptation to the environment. Using the notions presented earlier of differentiation and integration, they develop a model for linking organizational design with environmental conditions, and illustrate their model with nationally known companies as examples.

In the second article on this aspect, Dennis Organ discusses "Linking Pins Between Organizations and Environment." Organ suggests that adaptation to the environment is achieved only through the behavior of individuals acting as boundary agents. He then goes on to discuss in detail the nature and characteristics of the boundary-agent role.

Next we focus on one important segment of the organization's environment—the social environment. The social environment, perhaps more than any other component of modern organizations' environments, accounts for a turbulence heretofore unwitnessed by managers. The many dimensions of this environment cannot be treated in a volume of this size; hence we have chosen to limit our examination to the changing work ethic, worker attitudes, and the connection between management ethics and organizational behavior.

In "Toward Understanding the Changing Work Ethic," M. Scott Myers and Susan S. Myers document how concepts of work influence employees' behavior and attitudes regarding their roles in organizations. Robert Gatewood and Archie Carroll pick up with this same concern for people's attitudes about work, but concentrate on youth's attitudes toward the work ethic. This careful look is especially important given the surge of youth into work today and the somewhat different values they hold vis-à-vis earlier generations.

Archie Carroll closes out this section with a piece addressing the connection between ethics and organizational behavior. The social environment has taken on a new importance in recent years, and one significant aspect of this is the concern with ethical behavior. Watergate, the political slush funds, overseas bribery, and a multitude of other revelations have brought concern for ethical behavior in the workplace into a prominent position. Carroll suggests that, in addition to the broad social milieu, workers' values and ethics, and hence their behavior, are being shaped by management actions that are conducive to unethical behavior. It is then suggested that steps can be taken to manage ethical organizational behavior. Though the readings in this chapter do not touch upon all facets of the environment, segments that are of special importance in modern times are emphasized.

ORGANIZATIONAL DESIGN:
A CONTINGENCY APPROACH
A MODEL FOR
ORGANIC MANAGEMENT DESIGN

DON HELLRIEGEL

JOHN W. SLOCUM, JR.

During the past several years, many approaches incorporating open systems concepts have been advanced in organizational design. Underlying these new approaches is the idea that the internal functioning of an organization must be consistent with the demands of the organization's tasks, market environment, and technological capabilities and with the needs of its members if the organization is to be effective. Rather than searching for the one best way to organize, these approaches seem to be leading to the development of a situational theory of organizational design. Different environmental conditions external to the firm necessitate different organizational relationships within it.

This approach raises several questions. Is the organizational structure necessary to operate successfully in the automobile industry different from that needed in the fast-food-service industry? Is there one best way to structure and administer organizations by which the major economic criteria (return on investment, profit or loss, and net worth) can be reasonably satisfied? Given the task of organizing a functional unit—such as a research and development laboratory—how can we motivate its personnel to work effectively?

What system of management should be adopted?

The need for answering these questions is imperative if an effective understanding of complex organizations is to be achieved. One of management's major concerns is that the market environments facing their organizations are becoming more diverse and are constantly changing. Also, the technology of production is becoming more complex. Organizations are increasingly multinational, operating over wider geographical areas and under more diverse economic and cultural conditions.

ORGANIZATION-ENVIRONMENT MODEL

This article cannot address itself to all the issues raised in the preceding paragraphs. It will, however, present a model relating types of management systems and structures to particular market and technological conditions. The model will offer a way of understanding the complexities of any organization and provide a basis for managerial decisions about matters of organizational design.

Organizations cope with their external environment by creating organizational units or functions specifically to handle uncertainty arising from two sources. The first source of uncertainty is the number of changes in product lines and the length of production runs. For example, a job shop usually handles numerous jobs which require different machine feeds and speeds, realignment of men, and reorganization of other resources. However, in an oil refinery, once the operation has been established and is functioning, the number of product line changes is substantially less than those in a job shop. Uncertainty arises because the exact nature of the relationships between men and machine has not been worked through and because production standards have not been finalized.

The second source of uncertainty is the structure of the marketplace. The number of competitive products, manufacturers, and price ranges can lead to market uncertainty. Volkswagen, for example, operated in a market with few competitors until recently. Practices adopted in the 1950s and early 1960s are no longer effective in keeping Volkswagen a leader in its market. The quality and quantity of its competition have created market uncertainty and have reduced Volkswagen's foremost position in the marketplace.

To deal with these variations in the external environment, an organization becomes segmented into different units. Accordingly, each unit has as its major concern the problem of dealing with the uncertainty in its specific market environment. For example, the vice-president of broadcasting, learning and leisure at Westinghouse faces different problems and sources of market uncertainty than the vice-president in charge of power generation. The units must be linked together for the successful accomplishment of the organization's goals. This need for a division of labor and the simultaneous need for unified effort have led to studies of two fundamental activities of organizations—differentiation of activities and their integration.

DIFFERENTIATION AND INTEGRATION

Complex organizations are often characterized by a high degree of task specialization. For example, NASA headquarters is organized so that particular departments are responsible for the performance of specialized activities. The Office of Manned Space Flight is concerned with the Apollo program, while the Office of Space Science

and Applications is concerned with propulsion and bioscience activities. Each of these departments is internally divided to meet its various demands.

As organizations specialize in order to cope more effectively with their environment, they become more differentiated or segmented: "Differentiation is defined as the state of segmentation of the organizational system into subsystems, each of which tends to develop particular attributes in relation to the requirements posed by the relevant external environment." [1] Organizations and their subunits are categorized as more or less differentiated according to their emphases on certain concepts. Four of the specific dimensions which comprise the differentiation concept are illustrated in Figure 1. One can map out the differentiation of the organization and any of its subunits along this continuum.

One might propose, for example, that the corporate structure of Westinghouse Electric Corporation matches several of these dimensions quite well and should be placed toward the differentiated end of the continuum. That is, it is concerned with long-range planning, consumer products, and relationships among its employees, and it has many departments. On the other hand, the power generation product division of Westinghouse might be placed far on the right side, as it has relatively little need for differentiation because of the relatively homogeneous structure of the market environment, the few changes in technology, and its limited product lines.

Thus, each subsystem of the entire organization may be placed at any one point along this continuum. In successful firms, the formal organizational structure and these dimensions tend to be consistent with the demands from the corresponding parts of their environment. Since it is beyond the scope of this article to describe complex organizations on all these dimensions in detail, we will use the corporate level to show how organizations can be categorized using the concept of differentiation.

The second important consideration in the design of organization structures is integration. "Integration is defined as the process of achieving unity of effort among the various subsystems in the accomplishment of the organization's task." [2]

Dimensions of Differentiation
1. Time orientation: long- or short-range planning
2. Goal orientation: market or scientifically oriented
3. Interpersonal orientation: concern for getting work done
   or concern for relationships with others
4. Formal hierarchical structure: many parts or few parts

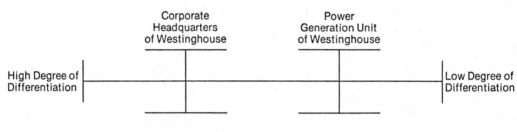

FIGURE 1. Dimensions of differentiation.

Differentiation specifies that the activities required for organizational performance be separated. However, in most organizations, activities must also be coordinated or brought together again so that the organization acts as a consistent whole.

Organizations such as NASA, which require a high state of differentiation and a high degree of integration to operate in their unstable environments, have a different structure than organizations not requiring a high degree of integration. For example, large department store chains, such as the May Company or Sears, have different structures and simpler means for achieving integration. The meshing of diverse activities may be accomplished by executive committees, task teams, project managers, and project offices.

The problems of integration for organizations operating in relatively stable environments, characterized by a constant technology and a homogeneous market structure, are substantially different from those problems of organizations operating with changing technologies in heterogeneous markets. The organization operating in a stable environment can rely upon the hierarchical structure and established procedures to ensure coordination, whereas elaborate integrating mechanisms may be needed for those firms in an unstable environment.

The varying degree of uncertainty, differentiation, and integration across organizations has

been incorporated in Figure 2. This figure suggests a contingency approach to organizational design, emphasizing the relationship between the internal mechanisms of an organization and its external environment. Each unit must fit the demands of the environment. For example, in highly heterogeneous markets and changing technologies, successful organizations tend to become more differentiated than organizations in more homogeneous and stable technological environments.

Problems of integrating diverse activities in complex organizations can also vary from high to low, depending upon the degree of coordination needed to achieve the organization's objectives. By dichotomizing and cross-classifying differentiation and examining the possible modes of integration required by the organization's environment, we can see the possible ways in which organizations can vary in terms of these two variables. To better understand the relationship between differentiation and integration, we shall explore each of the quadrants in terms of these two dimensions.

THE FOUR QUADRANTS

High Uncertainty/Low Integration

Successful firms operating under these conditions tend to be highly differentiated into units or

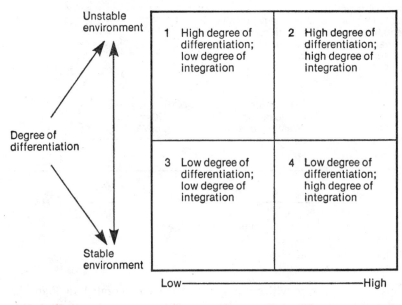

FIGURE 2. Differentiation-integration grid.

functions. The uncertainty of the environment necessitates that the firm be adaptive and flexible. Firms operating in this quadrant have been described along the following dimensions: wide span of control, few levels of authority; low number of rules and regulations; advisory and informational communications content; knowledge-based authority; high ratio of administrative personnel to production personnel; and decentralized decision-making.

At the corporate level, General Motors is an example of a large corporation with a high degree of differentiation and low need for integration. GM is decentralized along product lines; this structure permits quick and effective response to changes in each product's environment. Each of GM's product departments—Pontiac, Oldsmobile, and so on—is a profit center responsible for its own sales, marketing research, and manufacturing processes. Since each of the product lines is a profit center, and thus semiautonomous from other product lines, a low degree of integration is needed at the corporate level.

Within each product line, however, the degree of integration will vary depending upon the de-

mands of the environment. For example, the Vega plant in Lordstown, Ohio, within the Chevrolet division, requires a high degree of integration because of the requirements of assembly-line technology.

The integration of these diverse product lines is accomplished at GM through top management committees, which provide policy guidelines for decisions that are made by executives of each product line. The policy-making responsibilities of top management are divided into two areas: financial and administrative. The financial committee provides guidelines for capital expenditures, methods of accounting to be followed by the product line managers, rate of return on investment, and other financial matters. The administrative committee is concerned with issues like long-range planning activities, production and sales policies, and purchase commitments.

Thus, the day-to-day operating decisions are handled at the product manager level, while long-term decisions requiring coordination among the various product lines are the concern of top management committees. The multidivisional structure of General Motors provides for adaptability

Characteristics of organic and mechanistic management systems

	Type of Organization System	
Organizational Characteristics Index	*Organic*	*Mechanistic*
Number of hierarchical levels	Few	Many
Degree of centralization of decision making	Low	High
Quantity of formal rules	Low	High
Specificity of goals	Low	High
Span of control	Wide	Narrow
Content and direction of communications	Advice and information; lateral	Instructions and decisions; vertical
Role relations	Consultation; interdependence	Rules and regulations; independence
Specificity of required activities	Low	High
Knowledge-based authority	High	Low
Position-based authority	Low	High

SOURCE: Adapted from Ralph M. Hower and Jay Lorsch, "Organizational Inputs," in John Seiler, *Systems Analysis in Organizational Behavior* (Homewood, Ill.: Dorsey Press, 1967), p. 168.

to unstable market conditions. With its increasing trend toward differentiation and its lessening need for integration, this firm has fostered a managerial and structural system which can respond effectively to changes in its environment.

In a study of some twenty industrial firms in the United Kingdom, researchers have found that an "organic" management system is appropriate for firms that operate in changing market environments, while mechanistic systems are more appropriate for firms operating in a relatively stable environment.[3] The accompanying table summarizes the characteristics of the organic and the mechanistic systems.

In general, the organic system provides for more frequent changes of positions and roles, less hierarchical structure, and more dynamic interplay among the various functions of an organization. Continual readjustment and redefinition of individual tasks are necessary when the firm is adjusting to a changing market situation. The unstructured and dynamic marketplace often creates demands upon the organization that can best be handled through technical expertise and influence rather than bureaucratic rules.

Obviously, all firms cannot be classified as either totally organic or totally mechanistic. In many firms, it will be necessary to operate such functions as research and development with a more organic approach and other sections, such as an assembly line, with a more mechanistic system. The major finding of the British study was that, for firms operating in a changing environment, those with a characteristically organic management system were more successful than firms with a mechanistic one. Instead of providing for permanent, highly structured relations among functions, the organic system has less structure, and relies more on the ability of the different functions to cope with the uncertainties of their particular environments. Integration is achieved through the hierarchical structure and through committees.

High Uncertainty/High Integration

Effective means for dealing with problems of uncertainty in complex organizations can also be accomplished with a high degree of integration (quadrant 2, Figure 2). The greater the differentiation between any two highly interdependent units, the more difficult it becomes to achieve a high degree of integration. For example, Hughes Aircraft Company is organized into seven product lines—space and communications, systems, aerospace, industrial electronics, Hughes International, Santa Barbara Research Center, and research laboratories. When Hughes Aircraft is awarded a contract, the work is subcontracted to the appropriate divisions. If the contract is awarded to the systems division, the manager of that division determines the extent to which other divisions will be utilized in completing the contract.

The horizontal communication requirements in this kind of organization are more complex compared to those of Westinghouse, General Motors, or other organizations with less need for integration. The impact of a newly awarded contract requires that a large number of people in various divisions work closely together to successfully complete the contract. The continuous influx of new contracts, with their subsequent allocation of products or tasks to other divisions, places constant burdens on the organization. This procedure not only requires changes in the number and orientation of people, but also in the mix of managerial, professional, and technical personnel required to complete any project.

The pressures from new technologies and short lead times have made it necessary to establish some formalized managerial agency to provide overall coordination of these activities. One of the most frequently used management integrative mechanisms is that of project management.

Project management provides a means of integrating diverse functions of an organization and controlling all related activities involved in the project from start to finish. This approach requires organizational modification, emphasizing

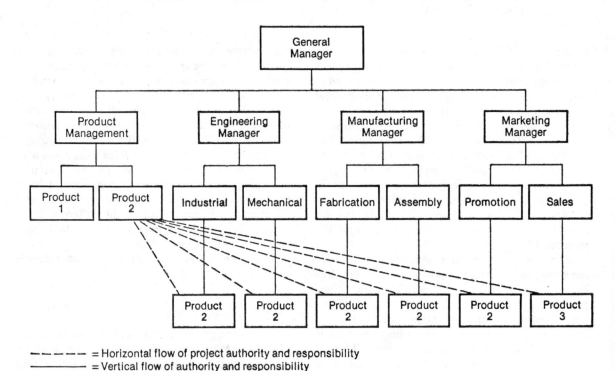

------ = Horizontal flow of project authority and responsibility
———— = Vertical flow of authority and responsibility

FIGURE 3. Functional organization with project management.

SOURCE: Adapted from David I. Cleland and William R. King, *Systems Analysis and Project Management* (New York: McGraw-Hill, 1968), p. 177, and Jay Galbraith, "Matrix Organization Design: How to Combine Functional and Project Forms," *Business Horizons*, XIV (February 1971), p. 36.

the development of horizontal communications, diagonal information-decisions networks, and authority systems not found in more conventional forms of organizations.

The project form of management is illustrated in Figure 3. The functional managers—manufacturing, engineering, and marketing—are responsible to the general manager for their special activities. The project manager reports to the general manager. He has personnel from the other divisions (for example, manufacturing, engineering, and marketing) assigned to him as required on a temporary basis until the project has been completed. Thus, there are two flows of authority in this kind of organization—the vertical flow of functional authority from the various functional managers and the horizontal flow of project authority of the project manager.

Problems associated with dual authority relationships have been discussed at length by many researchers.[4] The project manager's authority and influence flow in different directions than those described by some classical management theorists. A project manager's authority flows horizontally across the superior-subordinate relationships existing within the functional activities of an organization. Throughout the life span of a given project, personnel at various levels and with varying skills must contribute their efforts to allow for the sequential development of the project. For each new project awarded to the firm, new lateral information and decision-making networks must be worked out, which might differ significantly from those followed in the functional scheme.

In essence, the project manager has no clear-cut communication channels; he is faced with a web of communications that frequently crosses vertical lines of authority and involves outside subcontractors. His authority is *de facto* and stems from his charge from top management to get the project done within time and cost constraints. In practice, the project manager must rely heavily upon the alliances he builds with his peers through negotiations, knowledge, and resolution of conflict. These relationships replace the lack of formal authority over all the resources needed to complete the project.

Thus, a project manager's success will partly depend upon his ability to influence other organizational members through information and communication inputs rather than just upon his formal authority in the organization.[5] Authority cannot be dictated in advance because of the changing nature of project work and the dynamics of the many competing projects which vie for the firm's scarce resources.

The emphasis upon flexibility rather than permanency of job assignments strongly affects the employees who work for organizations using project management. Subordinates in project organizations have been reported to be significantly more insecure concerning possible employment, career retardation, and personal development than subordinates in a functional organization.[6]

As a consequence, project employees may feel less loyal to the organization and are more likely to report that they are frustrated on the job. As the project begins to phase out, members attempt to latch on to new projects for fear of being laid off upon completion of their project. However, the organization cannot always absorb these employees in other projects, either because of the cycle stage of the project or because of the lack of contract awards. This fear of possible unemployment is confirmed in project organizations by such examples as the layoff of aerospace engineers in the Boeing Corporation in 1971 when the SST contract was not funded.

High Certainty/Low Integration

Firms operating in quadrant 1 were in unstable environments because of continually emerging scientific knowledge, the impact on markets of this new scientific and technological knowledge, and the uncertainty that the firm will be able to maintain its competitive advantage in the marketplace. In a stable environment, is the same organization structure and management system effective? The model suggests that firms operating in relatively stable market structures (homogeneous) with little need for integration are more effective if they adopt a different organization structure and management system.

Continental Can Corporation might be one example of a firm operating in quadrant 3 (see Figure 2). The container industry's technology and market are relatively stable, emphasizing delivery and quality control. The remarks of one marketing executive in the container industry illustrate this point:

> We and our competitors all use the same machines produced by the same company. The product has got to be virtually the same as your competitor's unless your process is off, as you produce to the same specifications. Nor is there any process competition in this industry. So all we have to know is: How many cases does the customer want, and when.[7]

The most important part of this statement is the relative certainty of the container market. This certainty has led several researchers to suggest that, in industries such as this, effective firms would not be as differentiated as they would be in uncertain environments.[8]

In the container industry, it has been found that the most effective firms had the lowest need for integration.[9] Integration in the high-performing firms was accomplished through the managerial hierarchy. No special departments, teams, or roles (other than the scheduling clerk) had been established to facilitate the integrative function. Decision-making prerogatives were maintained at the top of the organization within the hands of managers who had the requisite knowledge to make decisions. This was especially true for technical and quality-control problems.

In less effective firms operating in this quadrant, efforts to decentralize decision making did not fit the environmental demands; moreover, lower-level managers were not able to resolve interdepartmental conflict because they did not possess the knowledge and influence to do so. This might suggest that, in a stable environment, high-performing organizations more closely fit the classical closed-system organizational model.

High Certainty/High Integration

The major characterteristics of the managerial system of this quadrant have been summarized in the table. Successful firms in a stable industry tend to adopt a management system referred to as "mechanistic." There is more reliance on prescriptive rules, operating regulations, and formal procedures. Decisions are reached at higher levels of the organization and communicated down the scalar chain of authority. The spans of supervision tend to be narrow.

A typical franchise arrangement, such as McDonald's, Kentucky Fried Chicken, Pancake House, and Dunkin' Donuts, are examples of firms operating in this quadrant. The market environment is homogeneous. Promotional strategies and production technology are similar among competitors. The managers of the franchise have market-oriented goals and short-time horizons in terms of service and future markets; they have been described as more likely to be preoccupied with getting the job done (high production-oriented) than with maintaining good interpersonal relations (low people-oriented).

The integrative mechanisms employed by McDonald's, for example, not only include a detailed organizational structure but also continual service, through bookkeeping systems, company trouble-shooters, and advertising, to ensure that the franchise manager conforms to McDonald's rules and regulations. The company's operations manual consists of 385 pages of details covering the most minute facet of operating an outlet. It spells out, for example, what equipment (such as cigarette, gum, candy, and pinball machines) is not permitted on store premises.

The franchise manager is visited monthly by one of thirty field service managers. The franchise sends weekly financial reports to the company, and the manager must attend a three-week intensive training at the so-called "Hamburger U." in Elk Grove, Illinois. While attending Hamburger U., the new manager is exposed to such techniques as how to regulate production in order to meet the service standard of "No customer has to wait for more than 50 seconds." He also learns how to organize the grill man, "shake" man, and countermen into an effective team.

These managers also learn the strict standards for personal grooming, the few variations allowed in types of food because of regional tastes, and how to deal with college students as customers and employees. The company also provides the franchise manager with a different maintenance reminder for each day of the year, such as, "Lubricate and adjust potato-peeler belt" or "Contact snow removal company." Because each member of the McDonald's organization has a specified role, it is not difficult to get integrated programs of action.

The quality of collaboration that exists among department at headquarters to achieve unity in the franchises is great. The design department at the parent organization, for example, works closely with the site and location department to ensure that the franchise meets the standards set by the organization and blends with the general architectural style of the community. Once these departments have reached an agreement, the franchise operator must erect the structure according to the plans set for that location. Fred Turner, McDonald's president since 1968, says: "In an age when so many Americans are on the move, one of our main assets is our consistency and uniformity. It's very important that a man who's used to eating at a McDonald's in Hempstead, Long Island, knows he can get the same food and service when he walks into one in Albuquerque or Omaha." [10]

The companies we have used to analyze how organizations vary in their internal structure to handle different environmental circumstances (market and technology) and needed levels of integration were only illustrative. The environment is a major determinant of an organization's internal structure.

In the differentiation-integration model we saw that, as each part of the organization strives to cope with a different part of its external environment, it demands a different mode of integration. Effective organizations operating in unstable environments develop organic management systems, while effective organizations in stable environments tended to have mechanistic management systems.

NOTES

1. Paul Lawrence and Jay Lorsch, *Studies in Organizational Design* (Homewood, Ill.: Richard D. Irwin, Inc., 1970), p. 6, and also "Differentiation and Integration in Complex Organizations," *Administrative Science Quarterly*, XII (June 1967), p. 3.

2. Lawrence and Lorsch, "Differentiation and Integration," p. 4.

3. L. Burns and G. M. Stalker, *The Management of Innovation* (London: Tavistock Publications, 1964).

4. George A. Steiner and William G. Ryan, *Industrial Project Management* (New York: Macmillan Co., 1968); Jay R. Galbraith, "Matrix Organizational Design: How to Combine Functional and Project Forms," *Business Horizons*, XIV (February, 1971), pp. 29–40; Arlyn Melcher and Thomas Kayser, "Leadership Without Formal Authority: The Project Department," *California Management Review*, XIII (Winter 1970), pp. 57–64; and David Wilemon and John Cicero, "The Project Manager—Anomalies and Ambiguities," *Academy of Management Journal*, XIII (September 1970), pp. 269–82.

5. Gary Gemmill and David Wilemon, "The Project Manager as an Influence Agent," *Journal of Marketing*, XXXVI (January 1972), pp. 26–31; John M. Stewart, "Making Project Management Work," *Business Horizons*, VIII (Fall 1965), pp. 54–71; and Richard D. Hodgetts, "Leadership Techniques in the Project Organization," *Academy of Management Journal*, XI (June 1968), pp. 211–19.

6. Clayton Resser, "Some Potential Human Problems of the Project Form of Organization," *Academy of Management Journal*, XII (December 1969), pp. 459–67.

7. Paul Lawrence and Jay Lorsch, *Organization and Environment* (Homewood, Ill.: Richard D. Irwin, Inc., 1969), p. 92.

8. Lawrence and Lorsch, *Organization and Environment*, p. 103. See also Burns and Salker, *Management of Innovation* and Charles Perrow, *Organizational Analysis: A Sociological View* (Belmont, Calif.: Wadsworth Publishing Co., 1970).

9. Lawrence and Lorsch, *Organization and Environment*, p. 103.

10. Anthony Lukas, "As American as McDonald's Hamburger on the Fourth of July," *New York Times Magazine* July 4, 1971, p. 5–29.

LINKING PINS
BETWEEN ORGANIZATIONS
AND ENVIRONMENT
Individuals Do the Interacting

DENNIS W. ORGAN

Management circles in recent years have returned again and again to the environment theme with the regularity of a Greek chorus. The term is used to mean different things by different people, and sometimes it is not clear if it really means anything at all. Nevertheless, it is perhaps reasonable to assume that most people who use the word with reference to organizations have in mind something like the definition suggested by Churchman: the environment of an organization is composed of those agencies or forces that affect the performance of the organization, but over which the organization has little or no direct control.[1]

The development and popularization of open systems theory and its application to organization and management have undoubtedly contributed greatly to the environmental theme, at least in academic writings. The recent attention given to ecology in the mass media has perhaps generalized the popular concern over environment beyond that of physical environment to broad classes of external constraints and forces. However, underlying the pervasive emphasis of management practitioners on organizations' environments is, most likely, simply a heightened awareness of the complex interdependence among elements of modern society.

Thus, more than ever before, leaders of organizations realize their dependence upon other organizations and other parts of society for the recruitment of new members; acquisition of raw materials, technology, knowledge, and money; the disposal of finished products (whether they be goods and services, or, in the case of universities, trained and educated personnel); and, perhaps most important, the legitimacy and social support attached to the organization's existence and objectives.

Furthermore, it is acknowledged that the environments of many organizations are maelstroms of accelerating change, or, in the apt words of Emery and Trist, "turbulent fields." [2] Consequently, there is a growing suspicion that the more relevant criterion of organizational effectiveness is not, as it used to be, that of efficiency, but rather that of adaptability to changes in the environment.

ROLE OF THE "BOUNDARY AGENT"

This increased awareness of organizational dependency on other elements of the social matrix has, in turn, suggested the strategic importance of interaction with the environment. To the extent that organizations depend on other organizations for survival and growth, they must establish linkages, or mechanisms of some kind, with those organizations in order to reduce the threats of uncertainty posed by dependence. Ultimately, of course, such linkages take the form of organizational roles, acted out by "boundary agents" who fill these roles. It is not really organizations that interact—it is people. It is such roles as those of salesman, purchasing agent, labor negotiator, credit manager, liaison personnel, lobbyist, and so forth that constitute the interorganizational linkages.

More important, it is through the behavior of these boundary agents that the organization adapts (or fails to adapt) to changes in the environment. It is through the reports of boundary agents that other organization members acquire their knowledge, perceptions, and evaluations of organization environments. It is through the vigilance of boundary agents that the organization is able to monitor and screen important happenings in the environment. To use a very strained analogy, it is the organization's boundary agents that function as sensory organs for the organization.

Given the strategic importance of the functions performed by these linkages (roles), one must presume that leaders of organizations would have considerable interest in the type of person who is best suited for these roles. The question is no idle one, because, as will be shown, there is evidence that these roles are qualitatively different from those that are largely internal to the organization.

The evidence suggests that the positions considered here are best manned by persons with rather distinctive profiles of abilities, traits, and values. Kahn and his associates, who have made significant contributions to the study of these positions, have called them boundary positions.[3] Obviously, specific kinds of boundary positions (such as purchasing agent or industrial relations spokesman) require job-specific knowledge and skills. However, to the extent that they share the feature of important transactions with outsiders, they seem to share also the need for certain personal attributes of individuals in those positions.

NATURE OF BOUNDARY POSITIONS

Role Conflict

Kahn and his associates have gathered evidence that documents the distinctive nature of boundary positions. First of all, people in such positions are susceptible to a high degree of role conflict—that is, they frequently get caught in the cross fire between people who expect different things of them.

This is not too surprising, since the boundary agent has to maintain interaction with, and owes allegiance to, two different kinds of people: those constituents in his own organization plus those agents representing other constituencies on whom his organization depends. The management spokesman in collective bargaining must contend not only with the expectations and pressures of his management colleagues, but also with those of the union spokesmen. The manager of the foreign subsidiary must take into account both the directives issuing from U.S. headquarters and those from the government and pressure groups in the host country. The industrial salesman must balance customer demands for quality, price, and custom-made features against his constituents' needs for unit profit, balanced production lines, low set-up cost, and so forth.

In short, the boundary agent has to grapple with at least two different—sometimes contradictory—sets of goals, values, and beliefs. Therefore, the performance of the boundary agent is likely to be a key variable in the prevention, mitigation, and resolution of interorganizational conflict. If he is skillful in the judicious bending to pressures, compromising between conflicting demands, and balancing off some issues against others, he may be able to ward off serious conflict between organizations. On the other hand, if he is impulsive, rigid, or insensitive to others' beliefs and values, he may engender conflict even where it is not inherent in relationships between organizations.

Perhaps less obvious is the finding that the boundary agent frequently gets caught in cross fires even among his own constituents. He is likely to find that his constituents have varying, biased conceptions of his role. The credit officer's role may be viewed by financial people as that of minimizing losses due to bad debts (calling for a stringent credit policy), while marketing managers conceive his task to be that of facilitating the growth of sales and new customers (using flexible, lenient credit procedures). Strauss conducted a study of purchasing agents and found that different departments (such as engineering, production scheduling, and manufacturing) tried to impose their own goals on the purchasing agent's office.[4]

The point is that large organizations seldom have explicit, concrete over-all goals; rather, each specialized department has its own goal because different functional divisions or sections are evaluated by different criteria. Therefore, any important transaction between the boundary agent and the environment will have differential effects on the "track records" of various departments. Thus, the boundary agent will often find himself caught in the middle between conflicting expectations of his own organizational kinsmen.

Lack of Authority

Second, the boundary agent, by virtue of the fact that he has to interact with outsiders, must operate in situations where he does not have formal authority. He cannot solve his problems by "pulling rank" on persons who owe no allegiance to his organization. He must, therefore, use other and more subtle means of influence. He may be able to use expertise as power, as in the case of industrial salesmen who have encyclopedic technical knowledge about customers' products and the constraints imposed by their production methods.

In many cases, however, he must use the power of friendship or even the tactic of ingratiation. In short, he must be able to increase his attractiveness as a person to outsiders, even if it involves such acts as gently deriding his own organization, projecting an image of himself as an understanding ally of outsiders, making concessions to their beliefs and values, compromising on "principles," and "talking their language."

Unfortunately, it is precisely these tactics that his constituents may frown upon, if they are aware of them, even though they are of strategic value to the boundary agent for securing more substantive benefits for his organization. Such tactics may be interpreted by his constituents as reflecting disloyalty.

It should also be pointed out that the boundary agent often has to use these same informal methods of influence (such as friendship power or ingratiation) with his constituents. For example,

the field salesman is adversely affected by low product quality, but he probably has no direct authority over quality control personnel.

Of course, informal modes of influence are often used also by persons in internal organization positions. Few organization officials use formal authority exclusively; certainly most officers would at least prefer to avoid the explicit invocation of the authority of their office, and much important communication is lateral rather than vertical. Still, a common ingredient of all intraorganizational interactions is the implicit obligation of all participants to follow standard procedures, policies, and traditions. This backdrop is lacking in typical interchanges between boundary agents and the environment.

The boundary agent's job is made doubly difficult simply because of his greater exposure to the organization's environment. Because of his frequent interaction with outsiders and his susceptibility to being influenced by them, his constituents may withhold their trust and support, granting him only a narrow range of discretion and decision making.

Agent of Change

Because the boundary agent has to listen to outsiders' criticisms and attempt to view his own organization through outsiders' eyes, he is apt to feel more keenly than his constituents the defects in his organization and the need for change. The advocacy of change then initiates protracted struggles with organization officials who simply do not see the organization from the vantage point of the boundary agent and defend the status quo.

These struggles may generate further suspicions about the boundary agent's commitment to the organization's values and objectives. The boundary agent in a sense becomes an activist broker between the viewpoints, criticisms, values, and information of outsiders, on the one hand, and the values, objectives, policies, and attitudes of his constituents. Not only must he represent the organization to its environment, but he must also represent the environment to his constituents.

The preceding considerations produce an over-all picture of the nature of boundary agents' jobs. These persons are often caught between conflicting pressures, both between constituents and outsiders and even among constituents. They often have to become agents of organizational change by modifying the beliefs and attitudes of constituents. They have to represent the organization—with all of its faults—to outsiders, and they have to negotiate the resolution of conflicts of interest. Their jobs are further complicated by their lack of authority over important persons, an inevitable violation of the classic principle that authority must be sufficient to carry out responsibility.[5]

The need to modify constituents' attitudes, to enhance and maintain their support and trust so as to preserve ample discretion for his own decision making, coupled with the need to make himself attractive to outsiders, puts the boundary agent in the position of having to be two-faced and to lead something of a double life.

THE BOUNDARY AGENT'S PROFILE

Given a description of the nature of boundary positions, can we draw any tentative conclusions about the kind of persons who should fill such positions? That is, what type of person—in terms of his abilities, traits, and values—would probably be most effective in this role for attaining substantive benefits for his organization and avoiding needless conflicts with important other parties? What type of person would experience greater job satisfaction and less strain in these positions?

General Abilities and Intelligence

Probably more important than any measure of over-all intelligence are the verbal and memory skills of the boundary agent. The boundary agent must represent the norms and values of his organization to outsiders in a way that does not offend or alienate them. Therefore, he must "watch his language." He must avoid the use of words that have unpleasant emotional connotations for other parties. The manager of the overseas subsidiary is perhaps well-advised not to use the word "capitalism" indiscriminately in certain underdeveloped nations because of the term's historic con-

notations. The bargaining spokesman for management, in negotiation with union officials, uses such terms as "management prerogatives" with some risk.

Legislative lobbyists probably do not get very far if their active vocabulary is confined to such emotional symbols as "free enterprise," "corporate sovereignty," or "bureaucratic flunkies." The choice of relatively sterile, even awkward, terminology is less likely to conjure up specters of demons and ideological straw men that only impede the process of communication and negotiation.

The boundary agent must also be sensitive to the values of the parties with whom he deals, and those values are probably manifested in their selective use of certain words and phrases. He must be careful that semantics does not inflate the true differences of interests. He must be able to decode the positions taken by other parties and then encode them into the customary verbal repertoire of his own constituents; in a sense, he must be bilingual, at least with regard to the connotative dimensions of words.

Especially important, he can ingratiate himself with outsiders if he is sensitive to the symbols and words they use, and judiciously uses these words in his dealings with outside parties. Walton and McKersie tell of a labor official who was able to win the favor of high-ranking management people with the use of such business-like language as "the policy of our organization" and "the decisions of our executive board."[6] This technique can also act as a cue to outsiders that the boundary agent understands, and appreciates the reasons for, their positions.

The above requirements place a premium on facility in manipulating words and symbols. Note that it is not vocabulary size that is important, although that may help, but a type of verbal skill represented by sensitivity to the connotations of words and the subtleties of semantics.

Good memory is important because it increases the potential of the boundary agent for ingratiating. A mind that holds onto otherwise trivial facts, dates, names, and so on about people can be used to project the impression that he is really interested in those people. We assume that people with average memories remember only those things they understand, like, or are interested in. Thus, the boundary agent who readily recalls isolated details about an outsider's place of birth, accomplishments, previous occupations, public statements, and so on has an advantage in establishing a viable relationship with that outsider. The outsider, for his part, feels subtle obligations to reciprocate in some way that may be of importance to the boundary agent's task.

Personality Traits

It would seem that the boundary agent must be, above all, a person of flexibility, as opposed to rigidity. The rigid person strives for consistency in thought and behavior, has a distaste for ambiguity, commits himself strongly to beliefs and values, and tends to structure his behavior according to internally programmed rules rather than external situational factors.

These characteristics might be desirable for organizational members in many internal positions, but they would probably be dysfunctional for boundary role performance. The rigid person might easily allow his internally programmed rules to warp his perception of trends in the organization's environment, imputing structure to those trends where structure or certainty do not exist. He might forego long-run organizational benefits for the sake of abstract principles.

The flexible person would find it easier to vary his behavior according to the audience, the situation, or the issues. He would likely concede minor principles if the substantive outcomes were worth it. His thinking would be guided more by the criteria of feasibility and opportunity than by the norms and traditions of his constituency.

Unfortunately, these same characteristics may cause his constituents to view him as "wishy-washy" and deficient in his commitment to the organization. They may, therefore, deny him the support and discretion he needs for transactions with outsiders. This dilemma almost inevitably leads the effective boundary agent to be a little two-faced; he must be flexible when carrying out his job at the boundary (when interacting with outsiders and assessing environmental trends), yet he must project an image of staunch commitment and steadfastness before his constituents in

order to preserve the flexibility of action which he needs.

The boundary agent is also likely to be more effective if he is more of an extrovert than an introvert. The extrovert, according to Kahn and his associates, is "extremely responsive to changes in external stimuli" and enjoys the company of other people. For this reason, the extrovert would probably be more skillful at establishing and using friendship power with outsiders, and he would probably be more sensitive to outsiders' norms and values. The introvert, on the other hand, has difficulty maintaining interpersonal relationships under conditions of stress and tends to be unrealistic in his assessments of external constraints on his behavior.

Values

Here the Allport-Vernon-Lindzey framework of six basic value categories—theoretical, economic, aesthetic, social, political, and religious—will serve as a basis for discussion. (The social and theoretical values will not be included because they yield less obvious predictions than the other four.) Economic and political values would seem to be desirable for the boundary agent. Economic values reflect a pragmatic style of thought and behavior, and a preference for solutions that work, even if they are not logical, elegant, internally consistent, or even unqualifiedly ethical if considered out of context. The person with strong political values would have the habit of forecasting the effects of his statements and behavior on the attitudes of outsiders, as well as his own constituents. He would appreciate the importance of personal and group persuasion as substitutes for formal authority and rigidly specified rules and obligations.

Macauley, in his study of noncontractual relationships between business organizations, found that such officials as financial officers and controllers desired written contracts with buyers and vendors, while industrial salesmen and purchasing agents preferred the flexible give-and-take of informal understanding.[7]

On the other hand, a person with strong aesthetic or religious values might balk at using ingratiation as an influence tactic or shrink from the concession of principles that might be necessary in order to effect substantive benefits for the organization. Such a person might also be repelled by the "hypocrisy" required of the boundary agent as he moves from one audience to another.

It may seem to the reader that an unnecessarily dark portrait has been drawn of the "ideal" boundary agent—that what is called for is a person without convictions, courage, or principles. But that is not the case. It is simply suggested here that the boundary agent, because of his concern for the organization's dependence on other agencies and the larger set of forces and constraints within which the organization exists, must necessarily evaluate his behavior within a larger framework than is true of internal organization members. Organizational morality, if that term must be used, must have a much more relativistic dimension, as Machiavellian as that may sound.

The reader may also respond with the query, "Are not the personal attributes suggested here simply desirable qualities for *any* organizational member? Wouldn't these traits be able to predict superior individual performance in any position?"

To some extent, the answer to the above question is "yes." For example, a number of studies have demonstrated a positive correlation between various measures of verbal ability and managerial performance.[8] However, it is difficult to imagine how extroversion or political values would be essential for the job effectiveness of a cost accountant or production engineer. Furthermore, the position taken in this article is that the attributes discussed—even though some of them are perhaps desirable for people in a variety of organizational offices—are of greater importance for the performance of the boundary agent.

A SOCIAL ROLE ORIENTATION IN SELECTION AND PLACEMENT

Essentially, what is at issue here is the need for a social role orientation for the analysis of organizational positions and the placement of persons in those positions. Boundary positions constitute only one class of organization offices along the social-psychological role dimension, and even this one class could perhaps be further divided. Divi-

sion might be based, for example, on the importance of the interaction with outsiders, the degree of conflict with outsiders, whether the outside party is dealt with in a one-shot episode or in a continuing relationship, the degree of status or authority the boundary agent has among his own constituents by virtue of his position, or by the percentage of working time that must be allocated to dealing with outside parties.

For the most part, the development and use of selection and placement techniques have ignored the implications of social role dynamics for individual attributes. Yet, if a unifying framework for the prediction of managerial performance is to emerge, there must be more emphasis on the social roles inherent in various kinds of organizational positions. For the manager's role is largely defined by the different groups of persons he must interact with, the congruence and/or conflict among those persons' expectations of him, and the need for "shifting gears" in his behavioral style as he confronts different social situations. The variations in managerial social roles, it would seem, call for corresponding variations in the abilities, personality traits, and values among the people needed to carry out those roles.

Furthermore, if the role analysis of an organizational position seems to call for certain individual attributes, one can specify how those attributes would be reflected in biographical data. If, as has been argued, boundary agents should have above-average memory and verbal skills, political and economic values, and a personality profile marked by extroversion and flexibility, then one can go a bit further and suggest how these would be manifested in a person's previous life experience. One would, for example, look for numerous college courses and good marks in the humanities, social sciences, or other disciplines rich in verbal content. Such a finding would probably reflect a sensitivity to semantics, a good memory for the trivia that help make impressive essay exam answers, and an ability and willingness to use "buzz" words for ingratiation purposes.

Another relevant biographical item would be membership in numerous social organizations of a nonideological character, reflecting extroversion, political values, the use of friendship power, and practice in ingratiation. On the other hand, one would hope to find that the person is not a member of organizations demanding ideological purity. Membership in these groups might indicate rigidity in thought and behavior. In fact, the use of biographical items such as these could lead to an operational program to test the validity of the arguments put forth here.

We have heard much about the importance of organizational environments and related issues of how different departments and divisions should be structured to match the demands of their particular environments. We should not forget that organizations, as such, do not interact with the environment.

Individuals do the interacting, and they do it within a greater or less detailed framework of role demands, role expectations, role conflicts, and resultant role stress. What is needed now is a program for identifying persons with the requisite skills and attributes which enable them to cope with the problems confronting the organization boundary agent.

NOTES

1. C. W. Churchman, *The Systems Approach* (New York: Dell Publishing Co., 1968), p. 36.

2. F. E. Emery and E. L. Trist, "The Causal Texture of Organizational Environments," *Human Relations,* XVIII (August, 1968), pp. 20–26.

3. R. L. Kahn, D. Wolfe, R. Quinn, J. D. Snoek, and R. Rosenthal, "System Boundaries," in *Organizational Stress* (New York: John Wiley & Sons, Inc., 1964), pp. 99–124.

4. G. Strauss, "Tactics of Lateral Relationship: the Purchasing Agent," *Administrative Science Quarterly* (No. 7, 1962), pp. 161–86.

5. Kahn and others, *Organizational Stress*, p. 106.

6. R. E. Walton and R. B. McKersie, *A Behavioral Theory of Labor Negotiations* (New York: McGraw-Hill Book Company, 1965), pp. 226–27.

7. S. Macauley, "Non-contractual Relations in Business: a Preliminary Study," *American Sociological Review*, XXVIII, pp. 55–67.

8. See, for example, J. P. Campbell, M. D. Dunnette, E. E. Lawler, III, and K. E. Weick, Jr., *Managerial Behavior, Performance, and Effectiveness* (New York: McGraw-Hill Book Company, 1970), p. 130, 181–88.

TOWARD UNDERSTANDING
THE CHANGING
WORK ETHIC

M. SCOTT MYERS

SUSAN S. MYERS

The work that a person does for his living is important to him in many ways. He may approach it in any one of the following ways:

a. I prefer work of my own choosing that offers continuing challenge, and requires imagination and initiative, even if the pay is low.
b. I am responsible for my own success, and I am always on the lookout for new opportunities which will lead to a more responsible position and a greater financial reward.
c. I don't like any kind of work that ties me down, but I'll do it if I have to in order to get some money; then I'll quit and do what I want until I have to get another job.
d. I have worked hard for what I have, and think I deserve some good breaks. I think others should realize it is their *duty* to be loyal to the organization if they want to get ahead.
e. The kind of work I usually do is o.k., as long as it's a steady job and I have a good boss.
f. I believe that doing what I like to do, such as working with people toward a common goal, is more important than getting caught up in a materialistic rat race.

© 1974 by the Regents of the University of California. Reprinted from *California Management Review,* volume XVI, number 3, pp. 7 to 20 by permission of the Regents.

Each of the above six responses represents a legitimate point of view about work, but each response reflects a different system of values held by members of most organizations. Your opinion about work may be significantly different than both your supervisor's and your subordinate's, and either your or their effectiveness may be influenced by these disparate values.

As organizational psychologists, we are finding supervisory problems to be symptoms of clashing or poorly understood value systems. A supervisor in a production department expressed it this way:

People here aren't what they used to be. Several years ago most of our employees had WASP (White, Anglo-Saxon, Protestant) values. They were ambitious, conscientious, hard-working and honest, and you could count on them to get the job done. It was relatively easy to supervise this kind of person.

We still have some of these, but now we're getting some different types who are difficult to supervise. Some are hippies who are bright enough, but their ideas are far-out, and they don't seem to care about pay, job security or recognition from their supervisor.

At the other extreme is a trouble-maker or free-loader type who isn't interested in the quantity or quality of work and is frequently absent or tardy. Some of them seem to look for opportunities to break the rules and will lie, cheat and steal. Many of these come from the ghetto.

This supervisor's lament is echoed by those who apply traditional supervisory methods to people of the new work ethic. The problem is not restricted to business organizations, but is encountered in all walks of life. Parents and teachers are sometimes distressed by the appearance and behavior of young people. Clergymen are finding more concern with the here-and-now than in the hereafter, and government officials are encountering increasing rebellion against bureaucratic constraints. Union leaders are losing control of their members, and athletic coaches are learning that Lombardi-like charisma and domination no longer assure obedience and commitment among athletes. Some managers see these problems as symptoms of illness in society. A board chairman of a billion-dollar corporation cited as a sign of deteriorating values the inability of small local art shop managers to hire and retain young people. Noting that the pay was adequate and the work not uninteresting, he suggested that perhaps exposure to a severe economic depression might help realign their values.

This paper provides a framework for understanding this problem, and defines some practical guidelines for organizational behavior, climate, and systems appropriate for people of today's values.

VALUES—OLD AND NEW

Based on sixteen years of observation and research, Professor Clare Graves[1] of Union College found that people seem to evolve through consecutive levels of "psychological existence" that are descriptive of personal values and life styles. Relatively independent of intelligence, a person's level of psychological existence can become arrested at a given level or it can move upward or downward depending on that person's cultural conditioning and his perception of the opportunities and constraints in his environment.

A diagrammatic version of Graves' framework is presented in Exhibit I. The single-term label used at each stage of existence inadequately describes the syndrome it represents, but is used for convenience of discussion.

Level 1. The *reactive* level of existence is most commonly observed in newborn babies or in people psychologically arrested in, or regressed to, infancy. They are unaware of themselves or others as human beings, and simply react to hunger, thirst, urination, defecation, sex, and other periodic physiological stimuli. Few people remain at this stage as they move toward adulthood; however, those at the threshold of subsistence in some of the larger cities of the Middle East seem to be little beyond this stage of existence. People at this level are generally not found on payrolls of organizations.

Level 2. Most people, as a matter of course, move out of the reactive existence to a *tribalistic* stage. Tribalism is characterized by concern with feelings of pain, temperature control, safety, and by tacit submission to an authority figure, whether he be a supervisor, policeman, government official, teacher, priest, parent, big brother or gang leader. Tribalism is commonly observed in primitive cultures where magic, witchcraft, ritual, and superstition prevail. For example, the Bantu who work in the coal, gold and diamond mines of South Africa are largely tribalistic. Man at this level is locked into the rigid traditions of his tribe, and he is dominated by the tribal chieftain or his substitute.

Level 3. Egocentrism is an overly assertive form of rugged individualism. This person's behavior reflects a philosophy which seems to say, "to hell with the rest of the world, I'm for myself." He, or she, is typically pre-moral—thus unscrupulous, selfish, aggressive, restless, impulsive and, in general, not psychologically inclined to live within the constraints imposed by society's moral precepts. To this person, might is right, and authoritarian management, preferably benevolent, seems necessary to keep him in line. Typical group techniques are not usually successful for this type of person, but structured participative management, properly administered, promises to be an effective strategy for getting him out of this egocentric mode.

Both egocentrism and tribalism are found in U.S. ghettos—not as a function of ethnic determinants, but rather as a result of cultural disad-

EXHIBIT I. Levels of psychological existence.

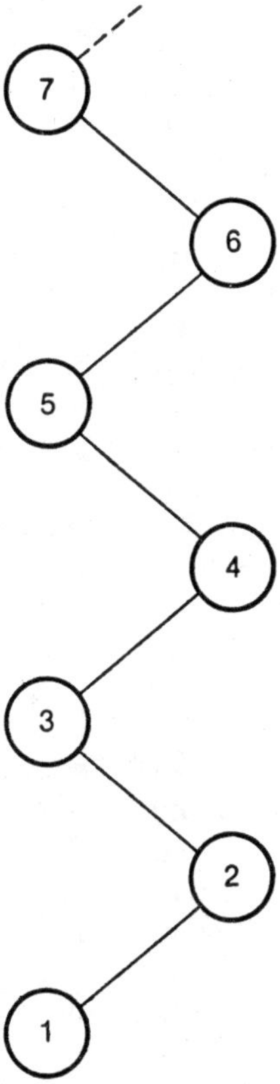

EXISTENTIAL
High tolerance for ambiguity and people with differing values. Likes to do jobs in his own way without constraints of authority or bureaucracy. Goal oriented but toward a broader arena and longer time perspective.

MANIPULATIVE
Ambitious to achieve higher status and recognition. Strives to manipulate people and things. May achieve goals through gamesmanship, persuasion, bribery or official authority.

EGOCENTRIC
Rugged individualism. Selfish, thoughtless, unscrupulous, dishonest. Has not learned to function within the constraints imposed by society. Responds primarily to power.

REACTIVE
Not aware of self or others as individuals or human beings. Reacts to basic physiological needs. Mostly restricted to infants.

SOCIOCENTRIC
High affiliation needs. Dislikes violence, conformity, materialism and manipulative management. Concerned with social issues and the dignity of man.

CONFORMIST
Low tolerance for ambiguity and for people whose values differ from his own. Attracted to rigidly defined roles in accounting, engineering, military, and tends to perpetuate the status quo. Motivated by a cause, philosophy, or religion.

TRIBALISTIC
Found mostly in primitive societies and ghettos. Lives in a world af magic, witchcraft and superstition. Strongly influenced by tradition and the power exerted by the boss, tribal chieftain, policeman, schoolteacher, politician, and other authority figures.

vantage. Now that equal opportunity laws are accelerating the employment of minority people, egocentric and tribalistic behavior is more prevalent in organizations.

Level 4. Persons at the *conformity* level of existence have low tolerance for ambiguity, have difficulty in accepting people whose values differ from their own, and have a need to get others to accept their values. They usually subordinate themselves to a philosophy, cause, or religion, and tend to be attracted to vocations circumscribed by dogma or clearly defined rules. Though often perceived as docile, the conformist will assert or sacrifice him-

self in violence if his values are threatened. For example, in 1954, the normally law-abiding conformists of Little Rock, Arkansas, erupted in violence against equal opportunity measures which violated the predominant value system of that region. Conformists prefer authoritarianism to autonomy, but will respond to participation if it is prescribed by an acceptable authority, and if it does not violate deep-seated values. They like specific job descriptions and procedures, and have little tolerance for supervisory indecision or weakness. People at this level have been the mainstay of the hourly work force since the beginning of the Industrial Revolution.

Level 5. The fifth level of psychological existence is characterized by *manipulative* or materialistic behavior. Persons at this level are typically products of the Horatio Alger, rags-to-riches philosophy—striving to achieve their goals by manipulating things and people within their environment. They thrive on gamesmanship, politics, competition, and entrepreneurial effort, measure their success in terms of materialistic gain and power, and are inclined to flaunt self-earned (as against hereditary) status symbols. Typical of level 5 persons are business managers who define their goals and strategies in terms such as cash flow, return on investment, profits, share of the market and net sales billed, and their focus is generally on short-term targets such as the quarterly review or annual plan. They tend to perceive people as expense items rather than assets, to be manipulated as supplies and equipment.

Level 6. People at the sixth, or *sociocentric,* level of existence have high affiliation needs. Getting along is more important than getting ahead, and the approval of people they respect is valued over individual fame. At this level he may return to religiousness, not for its ritual or dogma, but rather for its spiritual attitude and concern with social issues. Many members of the original "hippie" cult were sociocentrics—their hirsute and dungareed appearance being a symbolic put-down of the organization-man appearance approved by the establishment. On the job the sociocentric responds well to participative management, but only on the condition that he and the others he values believe in his product or service. He tends to articulate his protests openly, but characteristically dislikes violence and would counter authoritarianism with passive resistance. Sociocentrics are frequently perceived as "cop-outs" by 4s and 5s, and their behavior is not generally rewarded in business organizations. As a result, persons at this level who do not ultimately capitulate by regressing to the organizationally accepted modes of manipulation and conformity, or adapt by evolving to the seventh level of psychological existence, may become organizational problems because of alcoholism, drug abuse, or other self-punitive behavior.

Level 7. The individual at the *existential* level of existence has high tolerance for ambiguity, and for persons whose values differ from his own. On the job his behavior might say, "O.K., I understand the job to be done—now leave me alone and let me do it my way." In some respects he is a blend of levels 5 and 6 in that he is goal-oriented toward organizational success (level 5) and concerned with the dignity of his fellowman (level 6). Like the level 5, he is concerned with organizational profits, the quarterly review, and the annual plan, but he is also concerned with the ten-year or fifty-year plan and the impact of the organization on its members, the community and the environment. Like the level 6, he is repelled by the use of violence. However, his outspoken intolerance of inflexible systems, restrictive policy, status symbols, and the arbitrary use of authority is threatening to most level 4 and 5 managers, and he may be expelled from the organization for reasons of nonconformity or insubordination.

Most people in today's organizations can be described in terms of levels 2 through 7. Though level 7 is not the ultimate level of development, models for higher levels are sufficiently scarce to make their definition difficult and, for the purpose of this paper, unnecessary.

MEASURING VALUES IN THE BUSINESS ORGANIZATION

Seeing in Graves' theory a possible explanation for many organizational problems, we chose this framework for analyzing the problem of disparate values in organizations. The first step was to develop and standardize a questionnaire[2] for measuring levels of psychological existence and for determining the extent to which the various levels are represented in the business organization. Twenty-seven job and employment-oriented types of items, such as systems and procedures, job descriptions, benefits, career development, and supervision were written in the context of the theory, administered experimentally, and refined to eighteen items on the basis of internal consistency. For example, in the following item about Boss, these relationships are expressed as correlation coefficients:

The kind of boss I like is one who	Correlation Coefficients					
	T	E	C	M	S	X
a. calls the shots and isn't always changing his mind, and sees to it that everyone follows the rules.	20	00	44	01	−17	−28
b. gives me access to the information I need and lets me do my job in my own way.	−28	−33	−27	−29	11	46
c. tells me exactly what to do and how to do it, and encourages me by doing it with me.	26	11	19	04	06	−12
d. doesn't ask questions as long as I get the job done.	13	15	01	28	−12	−24
e. gets us working together in close harmony by being more a friendly person than a boss.	01	12	−15	00	32	−13
f. is tough but allows me to be tough too.	06	33	17	19	−26	−13

IMPLICATIONS FOR MANAGEMENT

Data collected from salaried exempt persons in three manufacturing organizations comprise norms for making subgroup comparisons. Sources of potential conflict are revealed in Exhibit II which shows actual value profiles (not necessarily typical) of individuals in various levels and functions in industry.

For example, Profile A represents a conservative president (solid line) in a large electrical equipment manufacturing organization and one of his vice presidents (broken line), who left the company to become president of a smaller organization in the same industry. The vice president, with his greater need for independence, higher tolerance for people of differing values, and lower conformity needs, clashed with the more egocentric and highly conforming president who had little tolerance for people whose views differed from his own.

The profile of the new president offers better potential for the development of free thinking and inner-directed vice presidents than that of his former boss. The senior president's role, in practice, is similar to that of an overprotecting parent who has high expectations of his children, arbitrarily dispensing rewards and punishments, and developing dependency relationships. But the president is only perpetuating values that he was rewarded for possessing by his dynamic board chairman boss.

Knowing that the chairman dislikes yes-men, these high level yes-men have learned how to protest in an acceptable fashion. For example, on one occasion the president pounded the table during a board meeting in exaggerated protest to the chairman's perceptive allegation that managerial dereliction was a cause of the unionization of a plant and that other union penetrations were imminent. The president asserted loudly that unionization of the one plant was caused by forces beyond the control of the company and that until the other plants were, in fact, unionized, such an accusation was only speculation. However, the board chairman's concern with unionization touched off a manipulative anti-union strategy far more costly than preventive measures would have been. But the table-pounding in the board room probably served to show the chairman that he was not surrounded by docile conformists.

In a young organization, independent, entrepreneurial types come to the top. But, as success is achieved, these early risk-takers become more conservative and intolerant of the very type of behavior that enabled them to succeed. Ambitious managers on the way up have a choice of leaving the organization, asserting their initiative under a facade of conformity, or acquiescing to puppetry. Under this style of leadership, conformity-oriented managers are promoted.

Profile B in Exhibit II is a vice president from the same organization, and illustrates the type of behavior that is often rewarded in organizations that are beginning to experience hardening

EXHIBIT II. Value profiles.

(a) Two Company Presidents

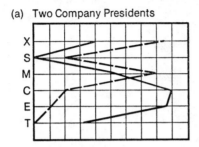

(d) Hourly-Traditional

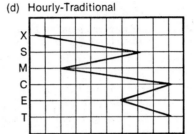

(b) Vice President

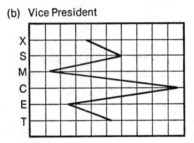

(e) Hourly-Enlightened

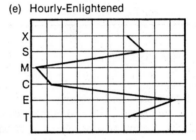

(c) Foreman

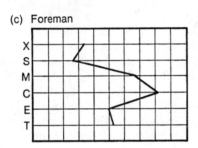

(f) Hourly-Ghetto

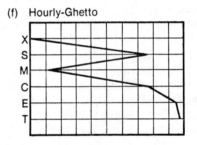

(g) Hourly-Women

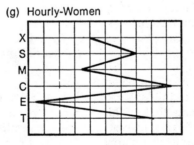

of the arteries. His higher conformity, sociocentric and tribalistic profile and lower manipulative, egocentric and existential scores are descriptive of a person who seeks to please the boss, perpetuate tradition and avoid rocking the boat. Frequently prefacing his directives to subordinates with "Now

what I believe Max (president) wants is . . ." or "Max is quite concerned (for example) with blocked growth opportunities in the company, therefore, we should be collecting data to shed light on this problem—just in case he asks for it," he is more concerned with anticipating the boss's whims than he is with the real problem facing the organization. Sometimes a simple and innocent observation or question by the president is transformed and amplified by this conformist zealot into a high priority and arbitrary edict. Though it is the vice president's interpretations that are in error, it is the president's fault for having nurtured conformity behavior.

The foreman's high conformity and manipulative profile (C) is typical of the person who has been promoted from the ranks, and is ideal for evoking and perpetuating conformity behavior among the traditional hourly ranks (D). Though the high egocentric score of the traditional hourly reflects self-centered opportunism, it is strongly counterbalanced by high tribalistic, conformity and sociocentric scores. In other words, this person needs to protect his self-esteem by following a strong and respected leader, clearly defined rules, and group acceptance, rather than take the risk of striking out on his own.

The "enlightened hourly" employee (E) tends to be younger, better informed, concerned with social issues, idealistic, and somewhat anti-establishment in his views. Potentially, this more enlightened person would not have the high egocentric score shown here. This regression to lower level values typically occurs when this type of person finds himself boxed in by inappropriate management, as would come from foreman C. Often restless and unwilling to adjust to automaton conformity, he has the ability to view life in perspective, and recoils at the thought of thirty years of monotony climaxed by retirement with a gold watch. Though their educational backgrounds range from college dropouts to little formal education, most enlightened hourlies have acquired much information (selectively assimilated) from television, travel, and social interaction. They respond best to a supervisor who respects them, asks for and uses their ideas, and gives them freedom to socialize and manage a job.

The foreman also encounters problems in dealing with the culturally disadvantaged from the ghetto (F), whose high egocentrism-tribalism combination often focuses their conforming and socializing activities toward peer group rebellion against the organization. Egocentrics are against the world in general, and, if he's black, against "whitey" in particular. Hence, the white supervisor, regardless of his qualifications, has little opportunity to succeed with black egocentrics. The black supervisor, on the other hand, can impose supervisory constraints in the language of the ghetto, avoiding allegations of racial discrimination. However, experience in both private and municipal organizations is showing that one level of black supervision is not enough—it is often perceived as tokenism or "Uncle Tomism." But if at least two levels of black supervision exist in the organization (for example, foreman and superintendent), a new message comes through to the black egocentric that "this is my organization too, and I and my people can succeed here." If two or more levels of black supervision exist in the organization, the white supervisor can successfully supervise blacks as long as blacks are also supervising whites. This principle is not restricted to black-white relationships, but applies wherever occupational discrimination occurs, as was once the case, for example, between the English- and French-speaking Canadians in the Province of Quebec.

Profile G is derived from hourly-paid women in an oil company. High in 2, 4 and 6, and low in 3, 5 and 7, it reflects women's cultural conditioning to be friendly, loyal and obedient followers. Reinforced by tradition, women have been rewarded for performing support roles, both in the home and at the work place. Thus, they can be found in large numbers on assembly lines, behind typewriters, in libraries, at telephone switchboards and at keypunch machines—but not in board rooms or offices—unless they are serving the coffee. It is interesting to note, however, the similarity between their profile (G) and that of the vice president in profile B.

LEVEL 4 AND 5 PROTOTYPES

Conservative or manipulative managers, who tend to dominate most organizations, typically engage in defensive strategies ranging from pretending a problem doesn't exist, through adopting more restrictive personnel selection criteria, to attempting to reshape the values of the "misfits" now on the work force. For example, in reviewing organization development strategies designed around the Exhibit I frame of reference, the officers of one corporation objected to the implied superiority of the 6s and 7s on the chart. Sensing new manipulative insights, they felt what was needed was a revised framework showing the 5s on top!

A manager from another organization deplored the disappearance of what he referred to as the "old style, dynamic leaders—like Vince Lombardi." "What we need in our organization," he said, "is a lot of Vince Lombardis—leaders who will drive through and achieve organizational objectives"—not realizing that Lombardi's leadership, effective for coaching a football team in the '60s, may be inappropriate for today's business organization. In the first place, his style leadership tends to overshadow the talent in the organization, creating little opportunity for the development of subordinates. For instance, none of the coaches that served under Lombardi succeeded in emulating his success as a result of his tutelage. Furthermore, there is room for only one Lombardi in an organization, as he calls all the shots; but a business organization has many interdependent functions to be managed through the cooperation of many able leaders. When the Lombardi-type person leaves, the organization tends to lose its effectiveness because of the dependency relationship fostered by his personality.

By and large, Lombardi's life style fit the pattern of a level 4. For example, he was a faithful churchgoer, he dictated the life styles of his players, and reinforced his values by replaying a recording of an evangelistic West Point speech about love, honor and duty by Douglas Mac-Arthur, one of his heroes. Most level 4 people need heroes, just as they, in turn, need to be heroes and need to dominate people in their organization. This is not a criticism of Lombardi; his success as a football coach speaks for itself. But it is a criticism of this style of leadership for organizations in which increasing numbers are above the 2, 3, and 4 levels of psychological existence.

Some managers, if they thought they could, would sustain people at stages of psychological existence where they could be more easily controlled. One national government that seems to be engaged in such a strategy is that of South Africa. The Bantu of that country are sustained in tribalism by management policies established by the conservative Afrikans government. The Bantu, who comprise more than 90 percent of the labor force in the coal, gold and diamond mines, are conscripted from their tribes for work periods not to exceed eighteen months. During this work period in the mines (which appears to be accepted by the Bantu as part of their tribal life ritual), the Bantu are fed, cared for, and disciplined by managers who serve as substitute tribal leaders during their stay in the mine. Though tribes may intermingle beneath the ground, on Sundays they reinforce their identities as well as provide entertainment by elaborate and unique tribal dances performed in arenas before large audiences of segregated blacks and whites. Television, which might lead to self-awareness, understanding and dissatisfaction with tribalism, is absent in what is perceived by many as a deliberate strategy to perpetuate the status quo. Certainly egocentrism, the next stage of psychological existence, if unbridled, would pose serious problems to the governing whites who are outnumbered by the Bantu four to one.

Managers are not only culturally conditioned by the tradition of 4 and 5 style management, but they are also influenced by persons outside the organization whose values can affect the organization's status. Market analysts, for example, will respond positively to a layoff that will improve the cost earnings ratio in a way that increases stock prices. Hence, short-range 4 and 5 thinking by analysts inspires and perpetuates 4 and 5 management strategies in organizations.

Of course, some of the level 4 and 5 influence may come more directly from the manager's wife and other members of his family. Women, long conditioned to conservative support roles or defensively skilled in manipulation, often exert subtle but significant influences on the life style of the manager. However, increasing numbers of wives and children are beginning to serve as bridges between industry and society, providing a counterbalancing influence to the organization by sensitizing managers to sociocentric and existential concepts.

GUIDELINES FOR COMPATIBILITY

In spite of their conditioned high regard for Lombardi-like leadership, managers are, with increasing frequency, finding themselves out of step with the people they supervise. Conformity behavior, once taken for granted, can no longer be expected. Not only are the managers out of step, but so are many of the systems which they use to achieve organizational goals. Since systems reflect the values of their designers and administrators, it is only natural to find people responding to systems as they do to the managers who created and administer them. Exhibit III presents capsule descriptions of supervisory values, systems characteristics, and subordinate or systems user values. These capsule descriptions are derived from items in the refined *Values for Working* questionnaire and their extrapolations to the specific systems listed in the exhibit.

The three left columns of Exhibit III show characteristic supervisory (S) attitudes toward subordinates at levels 2 through 7 as they relate to the supervisory functions of performance review, communication and career planning. Immediately beneath the supervisor's value statement at each level is shown a characteristic value statement for supervised employees (E) at that level.

The right side of Exhibit III contains descriptors and values relating to three personnel management systems—compensation, attitude survey, and job posting. At each level is a capsule descriptor of the system (S) as it might characteristically be conceived by a system designer at that level of psychological existence. Immediately beneath each descriptor is summarized an expectation of the system as it might characteristically be expressed by an employee (E) at that level.

This table identified conditions of compatibility and conflict within the organization. For example, in considering the "communication" relationships, the level 7 supervisor's view (We discuss things informally, and I give them access to any information they want) is compatible with the needs of the 7s, 6s, and 5s he supervises:

7: I like to feel free to talk to anyone, to get the information I want.

6: He's easy to talk to, and is interested in us personally.

5: If I'm to do a good job, I need to know everything my boss knows.

However, in reading further down the column it becomes apparent that the needs of the 4s, 3s and 2s are less compatible:

4: He should tell us what we're supposed to know to do our job properly.

3: The less I hear from my boss, the better.

2: He tells us what to do in a friendly way and lets us know he'll help us.

The 4s and 2s want more structure, and the 3s need more structure than the 7 would naturally provide.

However, the actual situation in organizations is more serious than the partial incompatibility reflected in the above example. Managers are typically more 5 or 4 than 7 in their orientation and, consequently, encounter more conflict. For example, the level 5 supervisor's communication philosophy (I give them the information I think they need to get the job done), is not easily compatible with any level except 4 (He should tell us what we're supposed to know to do our job properly). This means that level 5, the most common type of leadership style, has little opportunity to succeed unless he surrounds himself with conformists. In the long run, he and the organization would, of course, be defeated by excessive conformity.

The same phenonmenon exists regarding the compatibility of people and management systems. Compensation, attitude surveys, and job posting systems designed in terms of level 7 concepts are compatible with 7, 6 and 5 values, but not with 4, 3 and 2 values. Since most systems are designed in terms of level 4 and 5 concepts, they tend to satisfy the 2, 3 and 4 levels and frustrate people at the 5, 6 and 7 levels. In other words, systems in most organizations are designed more for people at the conformist, egocentric and tribalistic level than they are for the entrepreneurial self-starters in 5, 6 and 7. This stems in part from the fact that the job of systems and procedures writer

EXHIBIT III. Expectations and needs by value level.

Level	S/E	Performance Review	Communication	Career Planning	Compensation	Attitude Survey	Job Posting
		(Supervision)				*(Systems)*	
7	S	We work together in setting goals and reviewing progress.	We discuss things informally, and I give them access to any information they want.	Self-development is the key; people should have the opportunity to plan their own careers.	A smorgasbord approach which rewards merit and adapts to individual needs.	A democratic process involving all people in analyzing problems and suggesting improvements.	A system for maximizing organizational effectiveness by encouraging the natural flow of talent.
	E	I like to have a major role in defining my goals and methods for achieving them.	I like to feel free to talk to anyone, and to get the information I want.	I am responsible for my own career, and require the opportunity to develop my capabilities.	A good system rewards merit and doesn't tie you to the organization.	Greater commitment and solidarity are achieved when people have a hand in solving problems.	Now that I know what the openings and requirements are, I can run my own maze.
6	S	I try to review their performance without hurting their feelings.	I want to be on good terms with them so they will feel they can discuss anything with me.	Every career should include the ingredients of social and civic responsibility.	Pay and benefits tailored to the needs of the people and their circumstances.	A vehicle for diagnosing and solving human problems.	A system providing opportunity for employees to find compatible work groups and supervisors.
	E	He should use this occasion to get better acquainted with us.	He's easy to talk to and is interested in us personally.	Our careers should be oriented toward bettering relationships among all people.	Money should serve all people, and be more equitably distributed.	Working with others in analyzing survey results is a good way to improve human relations.	I like being able to find a job where the people and work don't clash with my values.
5	S	I find that the carrot and stick works best.	I give them the information I think they need to get the job done.	I keep track of their progress and specify developmental programs and assignments.	Distribution of money according to amount of responsibility and level of performance.	A management tool for taking the pulse of an organization.	A controlled, competitive system to upgrade the best employees into company job openings.
	E	I like to set my own goals and get recognition for achieving them.	If I'm to do a good job, I need to know everything my boss knows.	My career depends on my taking the initiative in finding opportunity for advancement.	Money is a measure of my success.	If what we learn from an attitude survey can make our employees more productive, I'm all for it.	It's one way to find advancement opportunities, but it helps to know the right people.
4	S	I define the goals and standards I expect them to follow.	I give them the information they should have, and keep our relations businesslike.	I define their career paths and promotional opportunities and give them continuous guidance.	Compensation programs based on community and industry surveys and standard practice.	The systematic measurement of attitudes toward company goals, policies and practices.	The orderly, systematic and fair implementation of a promotion-from-within policy.
	E	We need to know the company goals and how we can support them.	He should tell us what we're supposed to know to do our job properly.	I will be promoted when I earn it through productiveness and loyalty.	Money is a reward for loyalty and hard work, and should not be subject to favoritism.	Management is asking for our help, and it is our duty to answer all questions as honestly as possible.	I will be given the job I bid on if I deserve it.
3	S	I make clear what he has to do if he wants to keep his job.	I tell them whatever I feel like telling them.	It's every man for himself—don't look to me for your breaks.	Manipulative, arbitrary and secretive use of money.	Rigged questions and whitewashed reports.	Posting of jobs that can't be filled more economically from the outside.
	E	I don't like anyone finding fault with me and telling me how to act.	The less I hear from my boss, the better.	I don't want anyone planning my life—I'll look after No. 1 myself.	I'll work for the highest bidder.	I don't want any part of a stool pigeon system that can be used against me.	It's no use trying—the cards are stacked against you.
2	S	I tell them how I think they did and how they can improve.	I explain company rules to them and talk with them about their problems.	They expect me to tell them what to do and to take care of them.	A fair and uniform system administered by the boss.	A way of letting employees know the company is interested in their ideas.	A way of increasing job security by filling job openings from within.
	E	I want him to tell me if I've done what he wanted me to do, and if I've let him down.	He tells us what to do in a friendly way and lets us know he'll help us.	What's more important is that I'll always have a steady job and a good boss.	I need steady pay to make ends meet.	My boss should know how we feel so he can help us.	I'll bid on a job if my supervisor tells me to.

S   (Supervisor System)   E   (Employee)

is more likely to attract level 4 conformists than any other level. Hence, as a counterbalancing influence, level 7 criteria must be applied to remove the unnecessary and inflexible constraints typically reflected in policy and procedure statements.

Generally speaking, supervisory style or system characteristics at any psychological level is best suited for the level below it, and except for level 7, is not usually satisfactory for people at the same level. Exhibit IV postulates the relationship between supervisors and supervised by terms of three levels of compatibility—compatible, difficult, and incompatible.

This chart does not imply that the relationships depicted as + assure compatibility. Some 7 supervisors will, for example, clash with some 5 subordinates, some 5 supervisors with some 4 subordinates, and so on. Nor does it mean that a 4 can never supervise a 5. It happens all the time in real life, and both individuals may have made what each considers to be a satisfactory adaptation to each other. However, understanding your boss or subordinate is more important, though more difficult, when the two exist in one of the naturally incompatible relationships (−) shown on the chart.

This information contradicts the view sometimes expressed that people are best supervised by one of their own kind. (In correspondence with the authors, Professor Graves[3] indicates that people whose psychological growth is arrested should be managed by people at the same psychological level. However, for most persons who have open or growing personalities, the relationships portrayed in Exhibit IV are valid.) It probably seems to work as well as it does because the individual elevated to supervision from a peer group consisting largely of 4s, for example, was selected because he displayed level 5 characteristics. Moreover, most individuals are not restricted to a single value level but, rather, are more accurately described in terms of several levels as shown in the profiles of Exhibit II. It appears that only at level 7 does homogeneity of values between the supervisor and supervised provide a natural basis for compatibility.

These realms of natural incompatibility can be overcome through understanding and deliberate adaptation. It was pointed out earlier in the paper

EXHIBIT IV. Supervisory compatibility.

		SUPERVISORS					
		7	6	5	4	3	2
SUPERVISED	7	+	0	−	−	−	−
	6	+	0	−	−	−	−
	5	+	+	0	−	−	−
	4	0	0	+	0	−	−
	3	0	−	0	+	0	−
	2	0	−	0	0	+	−

+	Compatible
0	Difficult
−	Incompatible

that psychological level is not correlated strongly with intelligence. Hence, it is possible through training programs for supervisors and non-supervisors at any level to understand the problem of potential incompatibility and to learn how to adapt to each other.

Fred Fiedler,[4] in reviewing processes for improving leadership, concludes that new training strategies are needed. He suggests that training efforts might focus on helping the supervisor modify his interpersonal relationships, the structure of tasks to be performed and his subordinates' perception of his position power. This position is consistent with the viewpoint of the authors and the insights summarized in Exhibit III and discussed throughout this paper offer a framework for such a training strategy.

CONCLUSIONS

The new work ethic is not a new set of values; rather, it represents a shift in the source of influence. The seven levels of psychological existence described in this paper have long existed, but people in the middle ranges of manipulation and conformity have, until recently, been the unchallenged source of influence in business organizations and in most realms of society for at least the past 600 years.

Now, thought leaders are beginning to come from the existential and sociocentric levels. Though they still represent a minority, their values are permeating our culture at an accelerating rate through mass media. In business organizations, for example, pressures are being felt on many fronts. Corporate managers are beginning to forego promotional transfers to stay in the community of their choice. Some employees are refusing to work on implements of war. Others pressure their management to cease trade with South Africa. Union members are more interested in meaningful work than fatter benefits. Thus, neither management nor labor is immune to the influence of 6 and 7 thinking.

New thought leaders are also surfacing issues which precipitate social, civic and legislative action. It was largely level 5 interests that planned to host the 1976 Winter Olympics in Colorado, but it was apparently level 7 and 6 leadership (concerned with ecology and commercialism), coupled with level 4 conservatism, that defeated the effort at the polls. The 4s were probably always against exploitation of their area, but heretofore were not psychologically predisposed toward organizing opposition.

Women's liberation groups have initiated a number of reforms under level 7 leadership, such as that of Aileen Hernandez. Their influence has reduced employment discrimination against women, changed abortion laws, opened vocational opportunities in restricted fields such as business, law, and medicine, and promises to secure legal implementation of the Equal Rights Amendment to the Constitution.

Though conformists still conform, they are beginning to emulate new models. For example, the mod look of the level 6 has become the conformity model of the level 4 in American society. People of other values adopt the new look, but for different reasons. Level 5s wear sideburns and variegated apparel when it is advantageous to do so, and level 7s may wear the new look simply because it suits their fancy. Level 3s wear anything that symbolizes independence, and 2s wear what their "tribal chieftains" expect them to wear.

Value conflicts that exist today are not resolved, of course, by simply adopting the mod clothing and language. They can be ameliorated only by learning to operate from a new source of influence. The level 4 or 5 manager tends to operate from influence derived from official authority and tradition. To succeed with the new work ethic, he must operate from a base of influence stemming from the competence of people at all levels of the organization. That is, he will be skilled in organizing manpower and material in such a way that human talent can find expression in solving problems and setting goals. He will know he is succeeding when the people stop fighting him, and show commitment in achieving job goals. Incidentally, when he reaches this level of competence, he will find that the person who has changed the most is himself—and he and the level 7s are now talking the same language.

REFERENCES

1. Clare W. Graves, "Levels of Existence: An Open System Theory of Values," *Journal of Humanistic Psychology,* Fall, 1970, Vol. 10, No. 2, pp. 131–155.
2. M. Scott Myers and Susan S. Myers, *Values for Working,* Form A, cpyrt. 1973, Dallas, Texas.
3. Graves, *op. cit.*
4. Fred E. Fiedler, "Effects of Leadership Training and Experience: A Contingency Model Interpretation," *Administrative Science Quarterly,* Vol. 17, No. 4, December 12, 1972, pp. 453–470.

THE INTERACTION OF THE SOCIAL ENVIRONMENT AND TASK SPECIALIZATION ON WORKER ATTITUDES

ROBERT D. GATEWOOD

ARCHIE B. CARROLL

In recent years many management practitioners and writers have become concerned by an apparent shift in the work attitudes of large segments of the labor force. Much less interest and importance currently seems to be placed on job tasks and accomplishment than in the past. The effects are noticeable in increased labor costs, higher absenteeism and turnover and, in some cases, open hostility. Sorcher and Meyer write:

> Surveys show that hourly-paid workers...frequently report that their work has little or no meaning and just seems to go on endlessly and monotonously. This kind of work not only leads to boredom, apathy, fatigue, and dissatisfaction, but leads to resentment and active resistance...[1]

Gyllenhammar discusses the same phenomena:

> We begin to find today the symptoms of a new industrial illness. We invent machines to eliminate some of the physical stresses of work, and then we find that psychological tensions cause even more health and behavior problems. People don't want to be subservient to machines and systems. They react to inhuman conditions in very human ways: by job-hopping, absenteeism, apathetic attitudes, antagonism and even malicious mischief.[2]

Several writers, Rosow,[3] and Jenkins,[4] have explained this phenomenon in terms of a shift in

This is an original article prepared especially for this volume.

fundamental values of today's workers resulting from a deterioration of the traditional work ethic.

According to this view the central values of industrialized Western societies have clustered around the belief that hard, steady work is necessary for both the individual and society. During the Protestant Reformation hard work took on moral connotations as being necessary for heavenly reward. Occupational and material success were interpreted as indications of one's state of grace. Conversely, unwillingness to work hard was judged to be indicative of moral decline and the absence of grace.

This work ethic was perpetuated in America by the Puritans who were followers of Calvin. The Puritans abhorred "idleness" to the extent that they punished their followers for engaging in it. In addition, they preached to their youth that "the devil finds uses for idle hands," and that "God helps those who help themselves."[5] Numerous corollaries with religious overtones emerged to support the basic work ethic. For example, "waste of time was the deadliest of sins since every hour wasted was negating the opportunity to labor for the glory of God," and that consumption beyond basic needs was wasteful and therefore sinful—"Waste not, want not." This dedication to work and the pursuit of economic gain was also characteristic of the steady stream of immigrants that came to America throughout

187

the 1800s. The result was, of course, continued economic growth.[6]

The work ethic continued during the Great Depression because workers were forced to labor to survive and flourished during World War II under the rationalization of patriotism and dedication to country.

In the 1970s, however, there are fewer and fewer workers that have experienced the rigors of the 1930s and 1940s and more and more that have experienced only the fruits of that hard work that have been reaped during the 1950s and 1960s. The argument is that these workers, having grown up in a period of relatively stable affluence, have no perspective about the necessity or value of hard work and its intrinsic link to success. In the absence of such a perspective, traditional values of work have apparently been replaced by condemnation of continual labor, competition, and work achievement.

Quite naturally, singular interest has been focused on young workers, especially those that in the late 1960s and early 1970s have completed their education and have entered the work force. This group seems to embody most clearly the change in work attitudes and also seems to stand in contrast to the older workers' attitudes and values. They are of special interest also in that if they are the first of many similar generations of workers, then fundamental changes may be necessary in at least supervisory and motivational techniques, if not the methods of doing work in general.

COMPARISON OF ATTITUDES OF YOUNGER AND OLDER WORKERS

Recently there have been several empirical studies that have reported data of pertinence to the question of changes in work values, especially of young workers. Their combined results question this argument of deterioration of traditional work values.

Yankelovich[7] reports the findings of two national surveys taken in 1968 and 1971 concerning the attitudes of college students toward work. The main findings were:

1. 79% believe that commitment to a meaningful career is a very important part of a person's life.
2. 85% believe that business is entitled to make a profit.
3. 75% believe that it is morally wrong to collect welfare when you can work.
4. only 30% would welcome less emphasis on working hard.

In general, it appears from this survey that youth have a much higher regard for work than is frequently attributed to them. However, the Yankelovich research group did find that youth's values with regard to authority were changing at a rapid rate. Over one-half (56%) of the students in 1968 indicated that they did not mind the future prospect of being "bossed around" on the job. In 1971, however, only about one-third (36%) perceived themselves willing to submit to such authority. In addition, although 86% of these youths still believe that society needs some legally based authority to prevent chaos, they see a distinction between this necessity and an authoritarian work environment.

The 1969–1970 Survey of Working Conditions reported by the Survey Research Center[8] compared work-related attitudes of various age groups. Young workers valued relationships with coworkers more than did older workers, but placed less emphasis on physical comfort. No significant differences were found on the issues of importance of financial rewards, availability of resources for effective work, job challenge, or various aspects of the work itself. However, on five of the seven factors of job satisfaction, younger workers scored significantly lower.

Taylor and Thompson[9] also compared reported work values of people of various ages. They concluded that the results did *not* support the presence of a generation gap in work values. On the factors *ecosystem distrust* (which measured distrust of people, things, and institutions in one's environment), and *pride of work,* there were no significant differences among the age groups. However, younger workers were found to value *self-expression* in work (which measured the opportunity to learn), and both *intrinsic rewards,* and *extrinsic rewards* more highly than did older workers.

Taken together, the results of these studies do not seem indicative of a major restructuring of work-ethic values by younger workers. A large majority still seem to endorse the necessity and importance of work and the realization of rewards based on that work. However, some differences are apparent. Intrinsic job factors such as individual discretion, variety and interest of job task, and skill development seem to have acquired added importance. The absence of these job characteristics seems to result in the job dissatisfaction, apathy, and counter-organizational behavior previously cited. These results become clear when one views the historical development of both the nature of work in Western industrialized society, and the present societal attitudes and values that characterize today's workers, especially the younger ones.

AN INEVITABLE CONFLICT?

Early writers such as Smith and Babbage stressed the importance of *work specialization* and *division of labor* in expanding manufacturing capability and profitability of organizations.[10] These two principles lead to: (a) efficiency in the rapid development of work skills owing to the limited number of tasks to be learned and (b) savings in labor and materials because of less wasted material, a lessening of start-up and change-over time, and the possibility of purchasing only the exact skill level of labor needed.

Weber and Fayol extended these principles of specialization and division of labor to managerial components of organizations.[11] Weber outlined the characteristics of rational bureaucracies, organizations in which accurate information flowed both up and down with utmost efficiency. Fayol described the common management functions of organizations, specifying characteristics of effective organizations. Both emphasized the necessity of specification of job duties and responsibilities, narrow prescription of assignments, and complete adherence to both company rules and orders of higher authority.

It was left for men such as Taylor, Gilbreth, and Ford to operationalize the principles into tangible, organizational divisions of work. Through the work of these men, job duties were described in the smallest feasible units, and optimum procedures for these units were developed and assigned to workers. Many times a worker had not more than the repetition of one or two of these elementary work units as the composite of his entire job.

These job-design principles still characterize the nature of work and work flow in many present-day organizations. Even many service-delivery agencies have copied the principles of this industrial-manufacturing model and utilize them in their structure. The result, in a majority of cases, are very restricted, repetitive jobs with few job activities and little direct interface with other jobs in the organization. This is especially characteristic of entry-level jobs. While such jobs are theoretically, at least, economically advantageous for the organization, it must be remembered that they were designed for workers sixty or more years ago.

Individual attitudes are to a large extent products of the society in which the individuals find themselves. It is an understatement to say that both the current society and the characteristics of individual members are radically different from those of the work force that corresponded to the development of the early work on organization and work design. For one thing, the continued economic growth of America has provided a high standard of living for the majority of workers. The ability of hard work to dramatically upgrade life-style is somewhat diminished. Also, the nature of the relationship between worker and employer has also been altered. Through governmental regulations, labor unions, and competition for labor the dependency of employees on employers is no longer characteristic of today's work force. In light of these and other differences between today's workers and those of previous periods, there is an alternative explanation to the seemingly changed attitudes toward work. The same basic attitudes about work exist, but the nature of the work as designed by traditional methods is incompatible with the expectations about work held by a more sophisticated society. The result of this incompatibility is apathy, frustration, or hostility.

These feelings should be more characteristic of younger workers because they, to a larger extent than any other age group, reflect the changes in societal values and attitudes. There are a number of explanations for this. As a result of the constantly increasing educational attainments of today's young people, coupled with the generally affluent times in which they have been brought up, it is not too surprising that they are optimistic and idealistic about what they expect out of life in general, and their work in particular. In addition, they are members of an age which has been vastly influenced by the mass media, particularly television. They have been constantly barraged by the "good life" as portrayed in a materialistic vein on television.

If it were only the highly educated individuals who were continuously exposed to the good life on television that would be one thing. But the materialistic good life that is available is watched by all. Most members of society have access to television, even the lower economic classes. Those who presumably have the mental equipment, skills, and training to achieve high levels of economic success at least have some capability to acquire the good life, but that is not necessarily so with some of the lower economic classes. Nevertheless, they are exposed to the good life and thus develop high aspirations and rising expectations regarding it. As a consequence, these workers become frustrated and stymied when they take monotonous and boring jobs that do not even offer a challenge or provoke interest, much less opportunities for material affluence.

Rising expectations have to some extent affected many of today's workers, and are causing them to anticipate a great deal from the work environment. Without a doubt, many workers are expecting meaningful experiences that carry with them large amounts of intrinsic rewards and "psychic income." This psychic income, however, is not to supplant monetary income, but to supplement financial remuneration. Such expectations as "job challenge," "self actualization," and "involvement" are considered perquisites of modern work rather than illustrations of idealism.

This expectations gap is one of the consequences of employers demanding higher qualifications for a job than the performance of it requires. Most students have been told that a bachelor's degree is a prerequisite for access to the job market ... As a result of the increasing educational attainments of young executives, it is not surprising that they are optimistic and idealistic about what they expect from life and their work.[12]

One can also view this situation in reference to Maslow's Theory of Needs. Most organizations, either because of union contracts, governmental pressures, social responsibility, competition for labor, or some combination of these variables have placed themselves in positions of meeting Maslow's three basic need categories as a condition of employment. Motivation and behavior should therefore be prompted by the attempt to fulfill higher-order needs. Given the nature of many entry-level positions such attempts will frequently be frustrated, leading to nonproductive behaviors.

IMPLICATIONS FOR ORGANIZATIONS

It does seem apparent that some fundamental problems exist in the work place which, if not resolved, could have serious consequences on the American economy and standard of living. Those problems may be viewed as the logical consequence of the continued development and sophistication of our society and the lack of corresponding development in the institutions that employ societal members. Many organizations are still operated according to traditional economic principles. Such principles have ignored the variable and multi-need nature of employees. What we may be experiencing now is evidence of the necessity to alter a number of organizational procedures to accommodate the changes of people working in them.

On the positive side is the apparent fact that for large segments of our young workers the traditional work ethic seems to be at least recognizable if not exactly unchanged. Most seem to be taking the work ethic quite literally. Work is not only to be undertaken, but it is also to be utilized as an important aspect of life, hence the emphasis on self-expression and individual development. The challenge to provide such characteristics in work is indeed formidable to most organizations; however, if successful, the benefits could be correspondingly great.

The answer logically lies in the reformulation of the nature of work and jobs within organizations. While difficult, such changes would seem easier than resocializing the working population. Headed by Herzberg's work on job redesign, the recent management literature has been replete with recommendations such as job enrichment, management by objectives, participative decision making, team building, organizational development, etc. All share the central feature of concentrating on redefining the nature of the work contract between employee and organization. All expand the workers' traditional task boundaries.

It would be naïve to believe that such principles are a panacea for work attitude and performance problems. There have been sufficient studies to indicate that not all workers desire enrichment features in their work and subsequently do not react positively to job redesign principles. One of the few universal truths is that nothing is universally true. Such it is with this problem. However, it seems that this is a crucial period for many organizations; the conflict between traditional work theory and the expectations of workers will most probably become greater if left unattended. The momentum of societal change does not seem to be reversing. For many workers, therefore, these modern approaches to job redesign seem to represent the appropriate avenue of modification and change.

REFERENCES

1. Sorcher, M. and Meyer, H. "Motivating Factory Employees," *Personnel,* January–February, 1968, pp. 22–28.
2. Gyllenhammar, P. G. "How Volvo Adapts Work to People." *Harvard Business Review,* July–August, 1977, pp. 102–113.
3. Rosow, J. M. *The Worker and the Job: Coping with Change.* Englewood Cliffs, N.J.: Prentice-Hall, 1974.
4. Jenkins, D. *Job Power.* Baltimore, Md.: Penguin Books, 1973.
5. "Is the Work Ethic Going Out of Style?" *Time,* October 30, 1972, p. 96.
6. Wren, D. A. *The Evolution of Management Thought.* New York: The Ronald Press Company, 1972.
7. Yankelovich, D. "The Changing Values on Campus, 1972," In *Work in America.* Cambridge, Mass.: MIT Press, 1973.
8. Survey Research Center. *The 1969–1970 Survey of Working Conditions: Chronicles of an Unfinished Enterprise.* Ann Arbor, Mich.: Survey Research Center, The University of Michigan, 1973.
9. Taylor, R. and Thompson, M. "Work Value Systems of Young Workers," *Academy of Management Journal,* 19, *4,* 1976, pp. 522–535.
10. Merrill, H. F. (ed.) *Classics in Management.* New York: American Management Association, 1960.
11. Matteson, M. and Ivancevich, J. (eds.) *Management Classics.* Santa Monica, California: Goodyear Publishing Company, Inc., 1977.
12. Bowman, J. S. "The Meaning of Work and the Middle Manager," *California Management Review,* 21, *3,* 1977, pp. 63–71.

MANAGERIAL ETHICS AND ORGANIZATIONAL BEHAVIOR: A FIRST LOOK

ARCHIE B. CARROLL

The current state of business ethics cannot be characterized as a static phenomenon. Each day seems to bring forth an outpouring of new revelations further substantiating the ethical dilemmas managers face. And, unfortunately, these revelations frequently paint a dismal picture of the state of business morality in America and abroad.

It is difficult to pinpoint whether the state of business ethics has indeed deteriorated over the past several years, or that simply renewed interest in ethics has been stimulated by such dramatic events as Watergate and related incidents. In any event, news accounts of the last several years have been documenting corporate wrongdoing at an unprecedented pace. Beginning with revelations of illegal corporate giving traceable to the 1972 presidential election, news accounts have surfaced identifying questionable business practices ranging from kickbacks and fraud schemes to paying bribes to foreign officials in order to gain business abroad.

Our purpose here, however, is not to further document the state of ethics in American business. That has been effectively done elsewhere.[1] Rather, it is to raise the question of the relationship between *managerial ethics and organizational behavior*. The concern for business ethics that has been manifested for the past five or six years is

This is an original article prepared especially for this volume.

but one facet of the broader concern for social trends that is occurring and affecting business practices and organizational behavior. By raising the question of the relationship between ethics and behavior we are, in effect, examining just a special case of the impact of the social environment on the behavior of managers and workers in organizations.

This article has "A First Look" appended to its title because very little has been written about the connection between the newly emergent interest in ethics and the behavior of people in organizations. In fact, more has been written to suggest that ethics are individual and thus cannot be managed than has been written about how ethics can be managed; that is, how ethical behavior can be shaped or controlled. This, however, is a first look, and by its nature, therefore, is suggestive of a relationship that it is hoped will receive increased attention and research in the future.

The purposes of this article, therefore, beyond calling attention to the general relationship between ethics and behavior, are two-fold: (1) To examine the extent to which management acts and hierarchy are related to ethical behavior, and (2) to suggest, at least at a rudimentary level, some of the actions that managers can take to improve the quality of ethical behavior in their organizations. By doing this it is hoped that further research and thought will be stimulated in this crucial relationship that evidence seems to indicate will be a problem of managerial concern for years to come.

MANAGEMENT AND UNETHICAL BEHAVIOR

In the past, many have felt that ethics were something determined and shaped by the broad social values and attitudes in existence at a given point in time. Granted, these broad social forces do impinge on behavior in such a way as to cause behavior to be more or less "ethical" as the social climate changes. But could not there be more proximate causes affecting the ethics of one's behavior in a social or organizational setting? Recent research suggests that this is indeed the case. In fact, recent research has demonstrated that these proximate causes of behavior are found in the characteristics of modern organizations, or more specifically, in the characteristics of modern management practices. If this is the case, this ought to provide special impetus for us to examine management's practices and their relationship to organizational behavior.

Three studies in particular suggest that it is the behavior of managers—the expectations they place on subordinates—that leads to pressures toward unethical behavior. In a survey of business ethics conducted by Carroll, for example, interesting findings emerged. When asked to respond to the proposition "Managers today feel under pressure to compromise personal standards to achieve company goals," 65 percent of the managers surveyed agreed with the statement. A close examination of the data also disclosed that this feeling is much more widely felt at the middle- and lower-management levels.[2]

The managers were also asked to respond to the proposition: "I can conceive of a situation where you have sound ethics running from top to bottom, but because of pressures from the top to achieve results, the person down the line compromises." Seventy-eight percent of the respondents agreed with this statement. In a final research question, the managers were asked to respond to the proposition: "The junior members of Nixon's reelection committee who confessed that they went along with their bosses to show their loyalty is just what young managers would have done in

business." In a pattern similar to the first findings presented above, 37 percent of the top managers agreed with this proposition, 61 percent of the middle managers agreed with it, and 85 percent of the lower managers surveyed agreed with it. Coupled with the earlier findings, these data not only indicate that subordinate managers are under pressure to behave unethically but that the pressure seems to be felt the most as one descends the managerial hierarchy.

Another recent study also suggests that the pressure to behave unethically stems in significant part from the managerial hierarchy. In a wide-ranging survey of managers, Brenner and Molander conclude that "Relations with superiors are the primary category of ethical conflict." They found that respondents to their study "frequently complained of superiors' pressure to support incorrect viewpoints, sign false documents, overlook supervisors' wrongdoing, and do business with superiors' friends."[3] These two studies, then, lend additional credence to the view that managers' expectations of subordinates are a proximate determinant of unethical behavior.

Sims and Hegarty, in one final study meriting mention here, conclude from their research that "it is clear that ethical behavior can be influenced by both contingent rewards and clearly stated organizational policies."[4]

These studies, collectively, suggest that superior–subordinate relationships are the source of much pressure to engage in unethical behavior, and therefore forms the justification for a close look at how managers deal with subordinate managers and other employees.

MANAGING ETHICAL BEHAVIOR

Though much could be written about directions that could be taken in society to bring about more ethical behavior, our attention here is directed to suggesting specific actions that could be taken by managers in an organizational context.

The popular view for many years has been that ethics are "personal," that ethics cannot be legislated, and, by inference, that ethics cannot be managed. Perhaps, in the final analysis these statements are true. But short of arriving at the final analysis, could it not be that managers could engage in some activities or practices, that might have some effect on channeling organizational behavior into ethical directions? This section of the article hopes to explore that question and to suggest that "yes" is the answer.

In fact, a number of different actions that management can take to improve ethical behavior in the organization can be set forth. Some are more specific or tangible than others, but taken together they suggest some general directions in which management might move to bring about a more positive ethical climate than has previously existed in many organizations.

Personal Leadership from Top Management

Though one might think that this should go without specific mention, it has been held by numerous practicing managers to be an extremely important factor in creating an ethical climate in the organization. The moral tone of the organization is set by top management. In this connection, the Fifty-second American Assembly which met to consider the topic "The Ethics of Corporate Conduct" concluded that:

The corporation itself is a moral community; therefore all measures such as compensation, working conditions, and pension programs which contribute to the dignity of work and respect for the individual must be fostered.[5]

The view espoused above clearly suggests that many operational matters affected by top management constitute contributing forces toward improving the organization's ethical behavior. Carrying this point further, L. W. Foy, Chairman of Bethlehem Steel Corporation has asserted that:

It is a primary responsibility of business management to instruct, motivate, and inspire their employees to conduct themselves with honesty, probity, and fairness. Starting at the top, management has to set an example for all the others to follow.[6]

Foy elaborates: "... management has to make company policy absolutely clear to all employees. People have to be told and re-told in unmistakable terms that the company is firmly committed to integrity in all its activities."[7] Fred T. Allen, Chairman and President of Pitney-Bowes, Inc., summarizes this point well. "It is up to the leader

to make sure that ethical behavior permeates the entire company."[8]

Establishment of Realistic Goals

One area that management has direct control over is the establishment of sales, cost, and profit goals. Assuring that these goals are realistically set can have a definite bearing on the creation of a situation conducive to ethical behavior. Fred Allen remarks on this point:

Top management must establish sales and profit goals that are realistic—goals that can be achieved with current business practices. Under the pressure of unrealistic goals, otherwise responsible subordinates will often take the attitude that "anything goes" in order to comply with the chief executive's targets.[9]

Managers frequently do not think about the effect that unrealistically high goals might have on the ethical behavior of subordinates. Our argument here is that if goals are unrealistically high then employees might be inclined to do whatever is necessary (including unethical acts) to achieve them. The temptation is strong for managers to set goals high, but consideration needs to be given to the problem suggested here lest managers create conditions that may unintentionally be conducive to unethical behavior.

Create a Mechanism for "Whistle Blowing"

One of the problems that frequently leads to the cover up of unethical acts by persons in the organization is that they do not know how to respond, behaviorally, when they observe questionable practices taking place. An effective ethical climate is contingent upon employees having a mechanism for and top management support of blowing the whistle on violators. Allen has summarized this point well: "Employees must know exactly what is expected of them in the moral arena and how to respond to warped ethics."[10]

It frequently occurs that unethical practices or crimes come to the attention of organizational members several layers down in the organization's structure. John J. McCloy, who served as chairman of the Special Review Committee to study the use of corporate funds by Gulf Oil Corporation, suggests that some boards of directors of companies have "adopted and disseminated throughout their companies a policy which encourages any employee who observes a criminal practice to report the incident to his or her superior. If the superior is not responsive, the employee then has direct access to the board, usually through its audit committee." [11] This would be an illustration of how a whistle-blowing mechanism might work. Care should be exercised, however, in use of the whistle-blowing approach as there is evidence of whistle-blowing blackfiring.[12]

Employing Codes of Ethics

Though the concept of codes of ethics has been around for some time and has been abused by many organizations, there is still merit in a thoughtfully designed and carefully articulated code of ethics. Baumhart, in his studies conducted during the early 1960s, concluded that managers favored the establishment of professional codes of ethics. There has been much reported success and failure with organizational codes of ethics, but the key seems to be to make them "living documents" not just platitudinous public relations statements that find the bottom of a file drawer upon dissemination. As Purcell has noted, "ethical codes are no panacea . . . but they can help to clarify ethical thinking and to encourage ethical behavior." [13] Most importantly, codes of ethics should embody the thinking and policy beliefs that management and employees alike feel should prevail in the organization and, as such, they should represent communication efforts that guide employee acts and behavior in questionable situations.

Disciplining Violators at All Levels

Essential to bringing about an ethical climate that all organizational personnel will come to believe in is the necessity for management to come down hard on violators of generally accepted ethical norms. One of the reasons the general public and employees in many organizations have questioned businesses' sincerity in desiring a more ethical environment in recent years has been businesses' unwillingness to discipline violators. There are numerous cases of top management personnel who have been found to have been behaving unethically who have been retained in their positions by the organization's board of directors. At a lower level there have been cases of top management overlooking or failing to discipline unethical behavior of managers or employees in their organizations. This evidence of inaction on the part of management or the board constitutes in the minds of many implicit approval of the individual's acts or behavior.

Allen asserts that the organization should respond forcefully to the individual who is guilty of deliberately or flagrantly violating its code of ethics:

From the pinnacle of the corporate pyramid to its base there can only be one course of action: dismissal. And should actual criminality be involved, there should be total cooperation with law enforcement authorities.[14]

Blumberg agrees with this general line of reasoning with his statement that "There should be effective sanctions for violations so that there is no doubt that the code really represents corporate policy and that the effort is more than a public relations charade." [15]

The effort has to be complete, then, in communicating to all by way of disciplining offenders that unethical behavior will not be tolerated in the organization. It is the implied approval that has been suggested by management's "turning its head" on violators that has seriously undermined efforts to bring about a more ethical climate in many organizations.

Employ an "Ethical Advocate"

A creative concept proposed by Theodore Purcell is that each organization appoint or hire an ethical "devil's advocate"—a top-level corporate manager whose responsibility it is to serve as an ethical catalyst for management by constantly asking probing questions regarding the organization's actions. For example, whereas now a strategic planner might ask with respect to a certain decision "What would our market share be?" or "What would our discounted cash flow be?" the ethical advocate might ask: "How will a given decision affect the rights of our employees versus the rights of the corporation?" [16]

One potentially serious problem with this approach is that managers might feel they can "delegate" ethical concerns to the advocate and not worry about the ethical dimension of behavior or decision making themselves. This must be carefully guarded against. Very little experience exists on how the ethical-advocate concept might work in practice; however, it does represent innovative thinking as to how management might take actions to improve, or manage, the ethical climate in their organizations.

Management Training in Ethics

Some debate has taken place in recent years as to whether managerial ethics can and should be taught. One school of thought argues that ethics are personal, already embedded within the manager, and hence not alterable or teachable. A growing school of thought, however, argues that classes and instruction in business ethics should be made a part of management training and development programs and seminars.

Indeed, the latter course of action is taking place in a number of organizations in the U.S. today. What might be the purposes or objectives of such ethics training? A number or purposes have been suggested: (1) to increase the manager's sensitivity to ethical problems, (2) to encourage critical evaluation of value priorities, (3) to increase awareness toward organizational realities, (4) to increase awareness toward societal realities, and (5) to improve understanding of the importance of public image and public/society relations.[17] To this list might be added the desirability of: (1) examining the ethical facets of business decision making, (2) bringing about a greater degree of fairness and honesty in the workplace, and (3) more completely responding to the organization's social responsibilities.

Without question there will be difficulties in training or teaching managers in an amorphous subject like ethics. However, difficulties should not preclude serious consideration and experimentation with case studies, incidents, role playing, and discussion of crucial ethical issues. With respect to the teaching of ethics, John Adair has asserted: "a good teacher can help managers to become generally aware of their values and to

compare them with the consensus of value judgments in a particular company, industry, or profession."[18] It is concluded, therefore, that there is merit in considering management training and development in ethics as a viable alternative for bringing about more ethical organizational behavior.

SUMMARY AND CONCLUSION

We suggested at the outset that this was to be a "first look" at the relationship between one aspect of the social environment—ethics—and the behavior of individuals within organizations. First, we demonstrated the interconnection between management actions and unethical behavior, suggesting that a significant reason for unethical behavior may be found in the superior–subordinate relationship in many organizations. More specifically, management has been shown to create environments conducive to unethical behavior.

Second, we discussed a number of ways in which management can take specific actions to bring about a more ethical organizational milieu. Specifically, we suggested that management might (1) provide personal leadership from the top, (2) assure the establishment of realistic goals, (3) create a mechanism for whistle blowing, (4) employ codes of ethics, (5) discipline violators at all levels, (6) employ an "ethical advocate," and (7) provide management training and development in principles and concepts of ethics.

Our attempt in the second part of the article was to be illustrative rather than exhaustive of the strategies available to management to bring about a more ethical behavioral climate. In effect, we are discounting the many statements that have been made about ethics not being subject to management. We are arguing that ethics can be managed, that ethics can be shaped by efforts taken by management, and that management does not have to consider ethical values and actions as a dimension of human behavior that is totally out of their realm of control. As a first look then, we conclude that there is a relationship between ethics—representing a facet of the social environment—and organizational behavior, and suggest that additional research, thinking, and speculation be addressed to this crucial contingency.

NOTES

1. See, for example, James S. Bowman, "Managerial Ethics in Business and Government," *Business Horizons* (October, 1976), pp. 48–54; Steven N. Brenner and Earl A. Molander, "Is the Ethics of Business Changing?" *Harvard Business Review* (January–February, 1977), pp. 57–71; "The Pressure to Compromise Personal Ethics," *Business Week,* January 31, 1977, p. 107.

2. Archie B. Carroll, "Managerial Ethics: A Post-Watergate View," *Business Horizons,* April, 1975, pp. 75–80.

3. Brenner and Molander, p. 60.

4. Henry P. Sims and W. Harvey Hegarty, "Policies, Objectives, and Ethical Decision Behavior: An Experiment" paper presented at the Academy of Management meeting, 1977, p. 15.

5. "The Ethics of Corporate Conduct," Report of the Fifty-second American Assembly, April 14–17, 1977, Arden House, Harriman, New York, p. 5.

6. L. W. Foy, "Business Ethics: A Reappraisal," Distinguished Leaders Lecture Series, Columbia University Graduate School of Business, January 30, 1975, p. 2.

7. *Ibid.*

8. Fred T. Allen, "Corporate Morality: Is the Price Too High?" *Wall Street Journal,* October 17, 1975, p. 16.

9. *Ibid.*

10. *Ibid.*

11. Myles L. Mace, "John J. McCloy on Corporate Payoffs," *Harvard Business Review,* July–August, 1976, p. 28.

12. For example, see the accounts cited in "Disclosing Misdeeds of Corporations Can Backfire on Tattlers," *Wall Street Journal,* May 5, 1976, p. 1.

13. Theodore V. Purcell, "A Practical Guide to Ethics in Business," *Business and Society Review,* Spring, 1975, pp. 43–50.

14. Allen, p. 16.

15. Phillip I. Blumberg, "Corporate Morality and the Crisis of Confidence in American Business," Beta Gamma Sigma Invited Essay (St. Louis: Beta Gamma Sigma, January, 1977), p. 7.

16. Purcell, p. 47.

17. Ron Zemke, "Ethics Training: Can We Really Teach People Right From Wrong?" *Training HRD,* May, 1977, p. 39.

18. John E. Adair, *Management and Morality: The Problems and Opportunities of Social Capitalism.* London: David & Charles, 1974, p. 143.

PART II

MANAGEMENT-INITIATED ACTIONS

5
MOTIVATION

In this chapter we begin our consideration of actions initiated by managers. The first topic, motivation, has received more attention in the literature than any of the other management-initiated actions. No doubt much of this attention stems from the view that most managers see motivation as the major ingredient in improving organizational effectiveness. Five major areas are explored in this chapter in an effort to provide a fair coverage of this significant topic: basic issues in motivation theory, job enrichment and design, expectancy approach to motivation, behavior modification, and power and motivation.

We first present two articles that address rather basic issues in motivation—the satisfaction–performance controversy, and the intrinsic–extrinsic distinction. Charles Greene provides an excellent discussion of the "satisfaction causes performance" view and the "performance causes satisfaction" proposition. He then discusses the implications of these two positions for management. Laurie Broedling then gives an overview of "The Uses of the Intrinsic–Extrinsic Distinction in Explaining Motivation and Organizational Behavior."

Under job enrichment and design, Kae Chung and Monica Ross discuss "Differences in Motivational Properties between Job Enlargement and Job Enrichment." They conclude that both job enlargement and job enrichment as alternatives to job design may be appropriate under certain conditions. They then proceed to spell out the motivational properties of each approach. In the next article, Hackman, Oldham, Janson, and Purdy present "A New Strategy for Job Enrichment."

Norman Oglesby, in a specially prepared article for this volume, presents "Expectancy Theory: Overview and Management Perspectives." Oglesby's piece provides an easy-to-understand treatment, along with examples, of what has typically been a rather complexly presented topic. Of particular importance are his implications for management practice.

To open the section on behavior modification, Clay Hamner and Ellen

Hamner present "Behavior Modification on the Bottom Line." This excellent treatment of a difficult topic addresses the question "Does positive reinforcement improve employee performance?" After surveying ten companies, the authors conclude that if properly applied, positive reinforcement offers substantial payoffs. In the second piece in this section, Fred Luthans and Robert Kreitner examine O.B. Mod. (Organizational Behavior Modification) further by discussing "The Management of Behavioral Contingencies."

The discussion of motivation closes out with a frequently neglected subject—power. In "Power Is the Great Motivator," David McClelland and David Burnham assert that "Good managers are not motivated by a need for personal aggrandizement, or by a need to get along with subordinates, but rather by a need to influence others' behavior for the good of the whole organization." In other words, managers want power.

Taken together, the five sections of this chapter provide a representative coverage of the major issues in contemporary managerial motivation. Each of these approaches to motivation has practical as well as theoretical implications for motivating effective performance.

THE SATISFACTION-PERFORMANCE CONTROVERSY
New Developments and Their Implications

CHARLES N. GREENE

As Ben walked by smiling on the way to his office, Ben's boss remarked to a friend: "Ben really enjoys his job and that's why he's the best damn worker I ever had. And that's reason enough for me to keep Ben happy." The friend replied: "No, you're wrong! Ben likes his job because he does it so well. If you want to make Ben happy, you ought to do whatever you can to help him further improve his performance."

Four decades after the initial published investigation on the satisfaction-performance relationship, these two opposing views are still the subject of controversy on the part of both practitioners and researchers. Several researchers have concluded, in fact, that "there is no present technique for determining the cause-and-effect of satisfaction and performance." Current speculations, reviewed by Schwab and Cummings, however, still imply at least in theory that satisfaction and performance are causally related although, in some cases, the assumed cause has become the effect, and, in others, the relationship between these two variables is considered to be a function of a third or even additional variables.[1]

THEORY AND EVIDENCE

"Satisfaction Causes Performance"

At least three fundamental theoretical propositions underlie the research and writing in this area. The first and most pervasive stems from the human relations movement with its emphasis on the well-being of the individual at work. In the years following the investigations at Western Electric, a number of studies were conducted to identify correlates of high and low job satisfaction. The interest in satisfaction, however, came about not so much as a result of concern for the individual as concern with the presumed linkage of satisfaction with performance.

According to this proposition (simply stated and still frequently accepted), the degree of job satisfaction felt by an employee determines his performance, that is, satisfaction causes performance. This proposition has theoretical roots, but it also reflects the popular belief that "a happy worker is a productive worker" and the notion that "all good things go together." It is far more pleasant to increase an employee's happiness than to deal directly with his performance whenever a performance problem exists. Therefore, acceptance of the satisfaction-causes-performance proposition as a solution makes good sense, particularly for the manager because it represents the path of least resistance. Furthermore, high job satisfaction and high performance are both good, and, therefore, they ought to be related to one another.

At the theoretical level, Vroom's valence-force model is a prime example of theory-based support of the satisfaction-causes-performance case.[2] In Vroom's model, job satisfaction reflects the valence (attractiveness) of the job. It follows from his theory that the force exerted on an employee to remain on the job is an increasing function of the valence of the job. Thus, satisfaction should be negatively related to absenteeism and turnover, and, at the empirical level, it is.

Whether or not this valence also leads to higher performance, however, is open to considerable doubt. Vroom's review of twenty-three field studies, which investigated the relationship between satisfaction and performance, revealed an insignificant median static correlation of 0.14, that is, satisfaction explained less than 2 percent of the variance in performance. Thus, the insignificant results and absence of tests of the causality question fail to provide support for this proposition.

"Performance Causes Satisfaction"

More recently, a second theoretical proposition has been advanced. According to this view, best represented by the work of Porter and Lawler, satisfaction is considered not as a cause but as an effect of performance, that is, performance causes satisfaction.[3] Differential performance determines rewards which, in turn, produce variance in satisfaction. In other words, rewards constitute a necessary intervening variable and, thus, satisfaction is considered to be a function of performance-related rewards.

At the empirical level, two recent studies, each utilizing time-lag correlations, lend considerable support to elements of this proposition. Bowen and Siegel, and Greene reported finding relatively strong correlations between performance and satisfaction expressed later (the performance-causes-satisfaction condition), which were significantly higher than the low correlations between satisfaction and performance which occurred during the subsequent period (the "satisfaction-causes-performance" condition).[4]

In the Greene study, significant correlations were obtained between performance and rewards granted subsequently and between rewards and subsequent satisfaction. Thus, Porter and Lawler's predictions that differential performance determines rewards and that rewards produce variance in satisfaction were upheld.

"Rewards" as a Causal Factor

Closely related to Porter and Lawler's predictions is a still more recent theoretical position, which considers both satisfaction and performance to be functions of rewards. In this view, rewards cause satisfaction, and rewards that are based on current performance cause affect subsequent performance.

According to this proposition, formulated by Cherrington, Reitz, and Scott from the contributions of reinforcement theorists, there is no inherent relationship between satisfaction and performance.[5] The results of their experimental investigation strongly support their predictions. The rewarded subjects reported significantly greater satisfaction than did the unrewarded subjects. Furthermore, when rewards (monetary bonuses, in this case) were granted on the basis of performance, the subjects' performance was significantly higher than that of subjects whose rewards were unrelated to their performance. For example, they found that when a low performer was not rewarded, he expressed dissatisfaction but that his later performance improved. On the other hand, when a low performer was in fact rewarded for his low performance, he expressed high satisfaction but continued to perform at a low level.

The same pattern of findings was revealed in the case of the high performing subjects with one exception; the high performer who was not rewarded expressed dissatisfaction, as expected, and his performance on the next trial declined significantly. The correlation between satisfaction and subsequent performance, excluding the effects of rewards, was 0.00, that is, satisfaction does *not* cause improved performance.

A recent field study, which investigated the source and direction of causal influence in satisfaction-performance relationships, supports the Cherrington-Reitz-Scott findings.[6] Merit pay was identified as a cause of satisfaction and, contrary to some current beliefs, was found to be a significantly more frequent source of satisfaction than dissatisfaction. The results of this study further revealed equally significant relationships between (1) merit pay and subsequent performance and (2) current performance and subsequent merit pay. Given the Cherrington-Reitz-Scott findings that rewards based on current performance cause improved subsequent performance, these results do suggest the possibility of reciprocal causation.

In other words, merit pay based on current performance probably caused variations in subsequent performance, and the company in this field study evidently was relatively successful in implementing its policy of granting salary increases to an employee on the basis of his performance (as evidenced by the significant relationship found between current performance and subsequent merit pay). The company's use of a fixed (annual) merit increase schedule probably obscured some of the stronger reinforcing effects of merit pay on performance.

Unlike the Cherrington-Reitz-Scott controlled experiment, the fixed merit increase schedule precluded (as it does in most organizations) giving an employee a monetary reward immediately after he successfully performed a major task. This constraint undoubtedly reduced the magnitude of the relationship between merit pay and subsequent performance.

IMPLICATIONS FOR MANAGEMENT

These findings have several apparent but nonetheless important implications. For the manager who desires to enhance the satisfaction of his subordinates (perhaps for the purpose of reducing turnover), the implication of the finding that "rewards cause satisfaction" is self-evident. If, on the other hand, the manager's interest in his subordinates' satisfaction arises from his desire to increase their performance, the consistent rejection of the satisfaction-causes-performance proposition has an equally clear implication: increasing subordinates' satisfaction will have no effect on their performance.

The finding that rewards based on current performance affect subsequent performance does, however, offer a strategy for increasing subordinates' performance. Unfortunately, it is not the path of least resistance for the manager. Granting differential rewards on the basis of differences in his subordinates' performance will cause his subordinates to express varying degrees of satisfaction or dissatisfaction. The manager, as a result, will soon find himself in the uncomfortable position of having to successfully defend his basis for evaluation or having to put up with dissatisfied subordinates until their performance improves or they leave the organization.

The benefits of this strategy, however, far outweigh its liabilities. In addition to its positive effects on performance, this strategy provides equity since the most satisfied employees are the rewarded high performers and, for the same reason, it also facilitates the organization's efforts to retain its most productive employees.

If these implications are to be considered as prescriptions for managerial behavior, one is tempted at this point to conclude that all a manager need do in order to increase his subordinates' performance is to accurately appraise their work and then reward them accordingly. However, given limited resources for rewards and knowledge of appraisal techniques, it is all too apparent that the manager's task here is not easy.

Moreover, the relationship between rewards and performance is often not as simple or direct as one would think, for at least two reasons. First, there are other causes of performance that may have a more direct bearing on a particular problem. Second is the question of the appropriateness of the reward itself, that is, what is rewarding for one person may not be for another. In short, a manager also needs to consider other potential causes of performance and a range of rewards in coping with any given performance problem.

Nonmotivational Factors

The element of performance that relates most directly to the discussion thus far is effort, that element which links rewards to performance. The employee who works hard usually does so because of the rewards or avoidance of punishment that he associates with good work. He believes that the magnitude of the reward he will receive is contingent on his performance and, further, that his performance is a function of how hard he works. Thus, effort reflects the motivational aspect of performance. There are, however, other nonmotivational considerations that can best be considered prior to examining ways by which a manager can deal with the motivational problem."

Direction. Suppose, for example, that an employee works hard at his job, yet his performance is inadequate. What can his manager do to alleviate the problem? The manager's first action should be to identify the cause. One likely possibility is what can be referred to as a "direction problem."

Several years ago, the Minnesota Vikings' defensive end, Jim Marshall, very alertly gathered up the opponent's fumble and then, with obvious effort and delight, proceeded to carry the ball some fifty yards into the wrong end zone. This is a direction problem in its purest sense. For the employee working under more usual circumstances, a direction problem generally stems from his lack of understanding of what is expected of him or what a job well done looks like. The action indicated to alleviate this problem is to clarify or define in detail for the employee the requirements of his job. The manager's own leadership style may also be a factor. In dealing with an employee with a direction problem, the manager needs to exercise closer supervision and to initiate structure or focus on the task, as opposed to emphasizing consideration or his relations with the employee.[7]

In cases where this style of behavior is repugnant or inconsistent with the manager's own leadership inclinations, an alternative approach is to engage in mutual goal setting or management-by-objectives techniques with the employee. Here, the necessary structure can be established, but at the subordinate's own initiative, thus creating a more participative atmosphere. This approach, however, is not free of potential problems. The employee is more likely to make additional undetected errors before his performance improves, and the approach is more time consuming than the more direct route.

Ability. What can the manager do if the actions he has taken to resolve the direction problem fail to result in significant improvements in performance? His subordinate still exerts a high level of effort and understands what is expected of him —yet he continues to perform poorly. At this point, the manager may begin, justifiably so, to doubt his subordinate's ability to perform the job. When this doubt does arise, there are three useful questions, suggested by Mager and Pipe, to which the manager should find answers before he treats the problem as an ability deficiency: Could the subordinate do it if he really had to? Could he do it if his life depended on it? Are his present abilities adequate for the desired performance? [8]

If the answers to the first two questions are negative, then the answer to the last question also will be negative, and the obvious conclusion is that an ability deficiency does, in fact, exist. Most managers, upon reaching this conclusion, begin to develop some type of formal training experience for the subordinate. This is unfortunate and frequently wasteful. There is probably a simpler, less expensive solution. Formal training is usually required only when the individual has never done the particular job in question or when there is no way in which the ability requirement in question can be eliminated from his job.

If the individual formerly used the skill but now uses it only rarely, systematic practice will usually overcome the deficiency without formal training. Alternatively, the job can be changed or simplified so that the impaired ability is no longer crucial to successful performance. If, on the other hand, the individual once had the skill and still rather frequently is able to practice it, the manager should consider providing him greater feedback concerning the outcome of his efforts. The subordinate may not be aware of the deficiency and its effect on his performance, or he may no longer know how to perform the job. For example, elements of his job or the relationship between his job and other jobs may have changed, and he simply is not aware of the change.

Where formal training efforts are indicated, systematic analysis of the job is useful for identifying the specific behaviors and skills that are closely related with successful task performance and that, therefore, need to be learned. Alternatively, if the time and expense associated with job analysis are considered excessive, the critical incidents approach can be employed toward the same end.[9] Once training needs have been identified and the appropriate training technique employed, the manager can profit by asking himself one last question: "Why did the ability deficiency develop in the first place?"

Ultimately, the answer rests with the selection and placement process. Had a congruent man-job match been attained at the outset, the ability deficiency would have never presented itself as a performance problem.[10]

Performance Obstacles. When inadequate performance is not the result of a lack of effort, direction, or ability, there is still another potential cause that needs attention. There may be obstacles beyond the subordinate's control that interfere with his performance. "I can't do it" is not always an alibi; it may be a real description of the problem. Performance obstacles can take many forms to the extent that their number, independent of a given situation, is almost unlimited.

However, the manager might look initially for some of the more common potential obstacles, such as a lack of time or conflicting demands on the subordinate's time, inadequate work facilities, restrictive policies or "right ways of doing it" that inhibit performance, lack of authority, insufficient information about other activities that affect the job, and lack of cooperation from others with whom he must work.

An additional obstacle, often not apparent to the manager from his face-to-face interaction with a subordinate, is the operation of group goals and norms that run counter to organizational objectives. Where the work group adheres to norms of restricting productivity, for example, the subordinate will similarly restrict his own performance to the extent that he identifies more closely with the group than with management.

Most performance obstacles can be overcome either by removing the obstacle or by changing the subordinate's job so that the obstacle no longer impinges on his performance. When the obstacle stems from group norms, however, a very different set of actions is required. Here, the actions that should be taken are the same as those that will be considered shortly in coping with lack of effort on the part of the individual. In other words, the potential causes of the group's lack of effort are identical to those that apply to the individual.

The Motivational Problem

Thus far, performance problems have been considered in which effort was not the source of the performance discrepancy. While reward practices constitute the most frequent and direct cause of effort, there are, however, other less direct causes. Direction, ability, and performance obstacles may indirectly affect effort through their direct effects on performance. For example, an individual may perform poorly because of an ability deficiency and, as a result, exert little effort on the job. Here, the ability deficiency produced low performance, and the lack of effort on the individual's part resulted from his expectations of failure. Thus, actions taken to alleviate the ability deficiency

Rewards and effort.

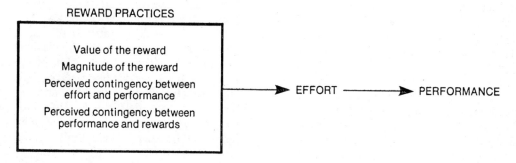

should result in improved performance and, subsequently, in higher effort.

Effort is that element of performance which links rewards to performance. The relationship between rewards and effort is, unfortunately, not a simple one. As indicated in the figure, effort is considered not only as a function of the (1) value and (2) magnitude of reward, but also as a function of the (3) individual's perceptions of the extent to which greater effort on his part will lead to higher performance, and (4) that his high performance, in turn, will lead to rewards. Therefore, a manager who is confronted with a subordinate who exerts little effort must consider these four attributes of reward practices in addition to the more indirect, potential causes of the lack of effort. The key issues in coping with a subordinate's lack of effort—the motivation problem—or in preventing such a problem from arising involve all four of the attributes of rewards just identified.[11]

Appropriateness of the Reward. Regardless of the extent to which the individual believes that hard work determines his performance and subsequent rewards, he will obviously put forth little effort unless he *values* those rewards—that is, the rewards must have value in terms of his own need state. An accountant, for example, may value recognition from his boss, an opportunity to increase the scope of his job, or a salary increase; however, it is unlikely that he will place the same value on a ten-year supply of budget forms.

In other words, there must be consistency between the reward and what the individual needs or wants and recognition that there are often significant differences among individuals in what they consider rewarding. Similarly, individuals differ in terms of the *magnitude* of that valued reward they consider to be positively reinforcing. A 7 or 8 percent salary increase may motivate one person but have little or no positive effect on another person at the same salary level. Furthermore, a sizable reward in one situation might be considered small by the same individual in a different set of circumstances.

These individual differences, particularly those concerning what rewards are valued, raise considerable question about the adequacy of current organization reward systems, virtually none of which make any formal recognition of individual differences. Lawler, for example, has suggested that organizations could profit greatly by introducing "cafeteria-style" wage plans.[12] These plans allow an employee to select any combination of cash and fringe benefits he desires. An employee would be assigned "X" amount in compensation, which he may then divide up among a number of fringe benefits and cash. This practice would ensure that employees receive only those fringe benefits they value; from the organization's point of view, it would reduce the waste in funds allocated by the organization to fringe benefits not valued by its members. As a personal strategy, however, the manager could profit even more by extending Lawler's plan to include the entire range of nonmonetary rewards.

Rewards can be classified into two broad categories, extrinsic and intrinsic. Extrinsic rewards are those external to the job or in the context of the job, such as job security, improved working facilities, praise from one's boss, status symbols, and, of course, pay, including fringe benefits. Intrinsic rewards, on the other hand, are rewards that can be associated directly with the "doing of the job," such as a sense of accomplishment after successful performance, opportunities for advancement, increased responsibility, and work itself.

Thus, intrinsic rewards flow immediately and directly from the individual's performance of the job and, as such, may be considered as a form of self-reward. For example, one essentially must decide for himself whether his level of performance is worthy of a feeling of personal achievement. Extrinsic rewards, to the contrary, are administered by the organization; the organization first must identify good performance and then provide the appropriate reward.

Generally speaking, extrinsic rewards have their greatest value when the individual is most strongly motivated to satisfy what Maslow has referred to as lower level needs, basic physiological needs and needs for safety or security, and those higher level ego needs that can be linked directly to status. Pay, for example, may be valued by an individual because he believes it is a determinant of his social position within the community or because it constitutes a means for acquiring status symbols.

Intrinsic rewards are likely to be valued more by the individual after his lower level needs have been largely satisfied. In other words, there must be an adequate level of satisfaction with the extrinsic rewards before intrinsic rewards can be utilized effectively. In order to make the subordinate's job more intrinsically rewarding, the manager may want to consider several actions.

Perhaps most important, the manager needs to provide meaningful work assignments, that is, work with which the subordinate can identify and become personally involved. He should establish challenging yet attainable goals or, in some cases, it may be more advantageous for him to create conditions that greatly enhance the likelihood that his subordinate will succeed, thus increasing the potential for attaining feelings of achievement, advancement, and recognition. The manager may also consider such means as increased delegation and job enlargement for extending the scope and depth of the subordinate's job and thereby increasing the subordinate's sense of responsibility and providing greater opportunity to make the job into something more compatible with his own interests.

In short, the manager should as best he can match the rewards at his disposal, both extrinsic and intrinsic rewards, with what the subordinate indicates he needs or wants. Second, he should, by varying the magnitude and timing of the rewards granted, establish clearly in the subordinate's mind the desired effort-performance-reward contingencies.

Establishing the Contingencies. The contingency between effort and performance (that is, the extent to which the individual believes that by working harder, he will improve his performance) is largely a function of his confidence in his own abilities and his perceptions of the difficulty of the task and absence of obstacles standing in the way of successful task performance. When the effort-performance contingency is not clear for these reasons, the manager should consider several actions. He can reassign work or modify the task to be more consistent with the individual's perceptions of his own abilities; treat the problem as a "real" ability deficiency; remove the apparent performance obstacles; or simply reassure the individual.

The second contingency, the individual's belief that the rewards he receives reflect his accomplishments, is usually more difficult to establish. Here, two rather vexing predicaments are frequently encountered, both of which stem primarily from administration of extrinsic rewards. First, the instrument (usually a merit evaluation or performance appraisal device) may inaccurately measure the individual's contribution and thus his performance is rewarded in error. Reward schedules constitute the source of the second problem. Given fixed reward schedules (that is, the ubiquitous annual salary increase) adopted by the great majority of organizations, there is more frequently than not a considerable delay between task accomplishment and bestowal of the reward. As a result, the individual may not only fail to perceive the intended contingency but may incorrectly associate the reward with his behavior just prior to being rewarded. In other words, he may perceive a nonexistent contingency, and his subsequent behavior will reflect that contingency and, this time, go unrewarded.

Reward Schedules. The manner in which a given reward, or reinforcer, is scheduled is as strong a determinant of the effectiveness of that reward as is the value of the reward itself, or, for that matter, any other attribute of the reward. In organizations, the only plausible forms of reward schedules are intermittent as opposed to the continuous reward schedule in which the reward or punishment is administered after every behavioral sequence to be conditioned. In the case of the intermittent schedules, the behavior to be conditioned is reinforced only occasionally. There are four schedules of interest to the manager, each with varying effects on performance as a number of investigations in the field of experimental psychology have revealed.

1. *Fixed-interval schedule*—Rewards are bestowed after a fixed period, usually since the last reward was granted. This schedule is equivalent

to the annual salary increase schedule in organizations, and its effects on performance are well-known. Typically, the individual "saves up," that is, he exerts a high level of effort just prior to the time of the reinforcement, usually his annual performance review. His performance more than likely will then taper off until the time just prior to his next annual review.

2. *Variable-interval schedule*—Rewards are administered at designated time periods, but the intervals between the periods vary. For example, a reward may be given one day after the last rewarded behavior sequence, then three days later, then one week later, and so on, but only if the behavior to be conditioned actually occurs. This schedule results in fairly consistent rates of performance over long periods of time. Praise or other forms of social reinforcement from one's peers and superior, as an example, usually occur according to a variable-interval schedule, not by intention but simply because they are too involved with their own affairs to provide systematic reinforcement.

3. *Fixed-ratio schedule*—Reinforcement is provided after a fixed number of responses or performances by the individual. Incentive wage plans so frequently utilized in organizations constitute the prime example of this type of schedule. It is characterized by higher rates of effort than the interval schedules unless the ratio is large. When significant delays do occur between rewards, performance, much like in the fixed schedule, declines immediately after the reward is bestowed and improves again as the time for the next reward approaches.

4. *Variable-ratio schedule*—The reward is administered after a series of responses or performances, the number of which varies from the granting of one reward to the next.

For example, an individual on a 15:1 variable-interval schedule might be reinforced after ten responses, then fifteen responses, then twenty responses, then ten responses, and so on, an average of one reinforcement for every fifteen responses. This schedule tends to result in performance that is higher than that of a comparable fixed ratio schedule, and the variation in performance both before and after the occurrence of the reward or reinforcement is considerably less.

Virtually all managers must function within the constraints imposed by a fixed-interval schedule (annual salary schedule) or fixed ratio schedule (wage incentives). However, this fact should not preclude consideration of the variable schedules, even within the framework of fixed schedules. Given their more positive effects on performance, such consideration is indeed highly desirable. It is conceivable, at least in a sales organization, for example, that monetary rewards (bonuses in this case) could be administered according to a variable-ratio schedule. From a more practical point of view, the entire range of nonmonetary rewards could be more profitably scheduled on a variable-interval basis, assuming that such scheduling was done in a systematic fashion.

CONCLUSIONS

This article has reviewed recent research concerning the relationship between satisfaction and performance and discussed the implications of the results of this research for the practicing manager. As noted at the outset, current speculation on the part of most practitioners and researchers continues to imply that satisfaction and performance are causally related, although confusion exists concerning the exact nature of the relationship. While the performance-causes-satisfaction proposition is a more recent development, the contention that satisfaction causes performance, nonetheless, remains the more widely held of the two beliefs, particularly among practitioners.

The recent research findings, however, offer only moderate support of the former view and conclusively reject the latter. Instead, the evidence provides rather strong indications that the relationship is more complex: (1) rewards constitute a more direct cause of satisfaction than does performance and (2) rewards based on current performance (and not satisfaction) cause subsequent performance.

For the manager who is concerned about the well-being of his subordinates, the implication of the finding that rewards cause satisfaction is self-evident. In order to achieve this end, the manager must provide rewards that have value or utility in terms of the subordinate's own need state and provide them in sufficient magnitude to be perceived as positively reinforcing. The manager whose goal is to increase a subordinate's performance, on the other hand, is faced with a more difficult task for two reasons. First, the relationship between rewards and performance is not a simple one. Second, there are other causes of performance—direction, the subordinate's ability, and existence of performance obstacles standing in the way of successful task performance—which the manager must deal also with.

The relationship between rewards and performance is complex because in reality there is at least one intervening variable and more than one contingency that needs to be established. An employee exerts high level effort usually because of the valued rewards he associates with high performance. Effort, the intervening variable, may be considered a function of the value and magnitude of the reward and the extent to which the individual believes that high effort on his part will lead to high performance and that his high performance, in turn, will lead to rewards.

Therefore, the manager in addition to providing appropriate rewards, must establish contingencies between effort and performance and between performance and rewards. The first contingency, the extent to which the individual believes that "how hard he works" determines his performance, is perhaps the more readily established. This contingency is a function, at least in part, of the individual's confidence in his own abilities, his perceptions of the difficulty of the task, and the presence of performance obstacles. When a problem does arise here, the manager can take those actions indicated earlier in this article to overcome an apparent ability deficiency or performance obstacle. The performance-reward contingency requires the manager, by means of accurate performance appraisals and appropriate reward practices, to clearly establish in the subordinate's mind the belief that his own performance determines the magnitude of the rewards he will receive.

The establishment of this particular contingency, unfortunately, is becoming increasingly difficult as organizations continue to rely more heavily on fixed salary schedules and nonperformance-related factors (for example, seniority) as determinants of salary progression. However, the manager can, as a supplement to organizationally determined rewards, place more emphasis on nonmonetary rewards and both the cafeteria-style reward plans and variable-interval schedules for their administration.

It is apparent that the manager whose objective is to significantly improve his subordinates' performance has assumed a difficult but by no means impossible task. The path of least resistance—that is, increasing subordinates' satisfaction—simply will not work.

However, the actions suggested concerning reward practices and, particularly, establishment of appropriate performance-reward contingencies will result in improved performance, assuming that such improvement is not restricted by ability or direction problems or by performance obstacles. The use of differential rewards may require courage on the part of the manager, but failure to use them will have far more negative consequences. A subordinate will repeat that behavior which was rewarded, regardless of whether it resulted in high or low performance. A rewarded low performer, for example, will continue to perform poorly. With knowledge of this inequity, the high performer, in turn, will eventually reduce his own level of performance or seek employment elsewhere.

NOTES

1. Initial investigation by A. A. Kornhauser and A. W. Sharp, "Employee Attitudes: Suggestions from a Study in a Factory," *Personnel Journal*, X (May, 1932), pp. 393–401.

First quotation from Robert A. Sutermeister, "Employee Performance and Employee Need Satisfaction —Which Comes First?" *California Management Review*, XIII (Summer, 1971), p. 43.

Second quotation from Donald P. Schwab and Larry L. Cummings, "Theories of Performance and Satisfaction: a Review," *Industrial Relations*, IX (October, 1970), pp. 408–30.

2. Victor H. Vroom, *Work and Motivation* (New York: John Wiley & Sons, Inc., 1964).

3. Lyman W. Porter and Edward E. Lawler, III, *Managerial Attitudes and Performance* (Homewood, Ill.: Richard D. Irwin, Inc., 1968).

4. Donald Bowen and Jacob P. Siegel, "The Relationship Between Satisfaction and Performance: the Question of Causality," paper presented at the annual meeting of the American Psychological Association, Miami Beach, September, 1970.

Charles N. Greene, "A Causal Interpretation of Relationship Among Pay, Performance, and Satisfaction," paper presented at the annual meeting of the Midwest Psychological Association, Cleveland, Ohio, May, 1972.

5. David J. Cherrington, H. Joseph Reitz, and William E. Scott, Jr., "Effects of Contingent and Noncontingent Reward on the Relationship Between Satisfaction and Task Performance," *Journal of Applied Psychology,* LV (December, 1971), pp. 531–36.

6. Charles N. Greene, "Source and Direction of Causal Influence in Satisfaction-Performance Relationships," paper presented at the annual meetings of the Eastern Academy of Management, Boston, May, 1972. Also reported in Greene, "Causal Connections Among Managers' Merit Pay, Satisfaction, and Performance," *Journal of Applied Psychology,* 1972 (in press).

7. For example, a recent study reported finding that relationships between the leader's initiating structure and both subordinate satisfaction and performance were moderated by such variables as role ambiguity, job scope, and task autonomy perceived by the subordinate. See Robert J. House, "A Path Goal Theory of Leader Effectiveness," *Administrative Science Quarterly,* XVI (September, 1971), pp. 321–39.

8. Robert F. Mager and Peter Pipe, *Analyzing Performance Problems* (Belmont, Calif.: Lear Siegler, Inc., 1970), p. 21.

9. See, for example, J. D. Folley, Jr., "Determining Training Needs of Department Store Personnel," *Training Development Journal,* XXIII (January, 1969), pp. 24–27, for a discussion of how the critical incidents approach can be employed to identify job skills to be learned in a formal training situation.

10. For a useful discussion of how ability levels can be upgraded by means of training and selection procedures, the reader can refer to Larry L. Cummings and Donald P. Schwab, *Performance in Organizations: Determinants and Appraisal* (Glenview, Ill.: Scott, Foresman & Co., 1972; in press).

11. The discussion in this section is based in part on Cummings and Schwab, *Performance in Organizations,* and Lyman W. Porter and Edward E. Lawler, III, "What Job Attitudes Tell About Motivation," *Harvard Business Review,* LXVI (January–February, 1968), pp. 118–26.

12. Edward E. Lawler, III, *Pay and Organizational Effectiveness: a Psychological View* (New York: McGraw-Hill Book Company, 1971).

THE USES OF THE INTRINSIC-EXTRINSIC MOTIVATION AND ORGANIZATIONAL BEHAVIOR[1]

LAURIE A. BROEDLING

The terms *intrinsic* and *extrinsic* have received increasingly frequent use in the field of organizational behavior (OB), but the distinction between them remains unclear. The use of different definitions of this distinction, both theoretical and operational, has resulted in conceptual ambiguity. The existence of confusion has empirical support from Dyer and Parker's (18) sample survey of American Psychological Association members of the Division of Industrial and Organizational Psychology. By asking the respondents to define the terms intrinsic and extrinsic, as well as to classify 21 job outcomes into categories of intrinsic, extrinsic, or both, they found considerable support for the confusion hypothesis. This conceptual ambiguity leads to difficulty in comparing empirical results from different studies and also in deciding whether the intrinsic-extrinsic distinction is really theoretically useful. The purpose of this article is to describe, categorize and compare various uses of the intrinsic-extrinsic distinction and to evaluate its usefulness.

An even more pressing reason to reduce the ambiguity of the distinction is the recent flurry of interest in how intrinsic and extrinsic motivation combine to affect total motivation. Previously the assumption had been that the two are additive,

Reprinted with the permission of the *Academy of Management Review* and Laurie A. Broedling.

but there have been recent findings indicating they may be subtractive or interactive (14, 40). While the latter findings have gained considerable attention, they have also been criticized (8, 17, 22, 49). Critics argue that it is premature to draw conclusions regarding how intrinsic and extrinsic motivation combine when different definitions and measures of the concepts are used.

The intrinsic-extrinsic distinction has been used to describe several factors and hypothetical constructs in OB, including motivation, needs, outcomes, satisfaction, rewards, and values. This article describes the use of the distinction with relation to a number of these constructs, with the emphasis on motivation since the distinction has been most commonly applied to this construct. But if interpretation is to be possible, the nature of the distinction should remain fundamentally similar no matter which construct is being described.

HISTORICAL DEVELOPMENT OF THE INTRINSIC-EXTRINSIC DISTINCTION

The roots of the intrinsic-extrinsic distinction can be traced back to the work of the first contemporary cognitive theorists, Lewin (33) and Tolman (50). Their work directed psychology away from an exclusively behaviorist, stimulus-response outlook, which considered all motivation to be extrinsic. Throughout the 1940s and 1950s the intrinsic concept was developed by need theorists who emphasized the importance of higher-order needs and cognitions. These included the needs for autonomy (2), self-esteem and self-actualization (34), mastery (24), achievement (35), and competence (54). Additional fuel was added to the fire by neo-behaviorists, working with non-human organisms, who named experimentally-observed phenomena not easily explained within behaviorist theory, e.g., exploratory drive (39), curiosity drive (4), and manipulative drive (23). Ironically, the last publication was among the first to use the term intrinsic motivation. The real popularization of the distinction occurred when Herzberg introduced his distinction between motivators and hygiene factors (25).

The intrinsic-extrinsic distinction grew out of a need to explain behaviors not easily accounted for within the extrinsic, behaviorist framework. The immense current popularity of the intrinsic concept attests to the fact that many aspects of human behavior are not extrinsic. But unfortunately the term "intrinsic" has often simply been applied to those aspects of behavior which cannot be explained as extrinsic; it has been applied as a catchall explanation whenever behaviors occur which cannot be clearly linked to external outcomes.

CURRENT USES OF THE DISTINCTION

The intrinsic-extrinsic distinction has been employed in a variety of ways. Usages can be descriptively categorized into two major types: as an individual characteristic or fairly stable personality *trait* on which people differ, and as a fairly changeable psychological *state*. Table 1 summarizes this categorization.

As a Trait

When used to characterize individual differences, the intrinsic-extrinsic distinction is most often used in OB to describe a person's orientation toward his or her work. There are three common measures of work orientation, each incorporating a somewhat different conception of the intrinsic-extrinsic distinction.

The first is the Job Attitude Scale (JAS), comprised of six intrinsic and ten extrinsic job-related statements, presented in forced-choice pairs (46, 47). Although job orientation here is distinct from job motivation (considered to be a process) or job satisfaction (considered a state), this intrinsic-extrinsic distinction is derived from the distinction made for motivation:

...a person is intrinsically motivated to perform some task if there is no apparent reward for the performance except the activity itself and the feeling of satisfaction or enjoyment which is derived from doing the activity. Alternatively, one is extrinsically motivated to perform the task if he does it primarily for some external reward (46, p. 1).

Job orientation is based on one's personal value system, with intrinsically-oriented people being more interested in job content and extrinsically-oriented people being more interested in job context (48). It is postulated that intrinsically-oriented people tend to reject stability and routine, to have more initiative, and to be approach oriented. Saleh (46) related this conception of the distinction to Maslow's need hierarchy and to Herzberg's two-factor theory. Growth needs are seen as underlying intrinsic factors and deficiency needs as underlying extrinsic factors. If Herzberg's theory is valid, it could also be expected that intrinsic factors are the main source of satisfaction and motivation, while extrinsic factors are the main source of dissatisfaction.

A second measure of intrinsic-extrinsic job orientation is the Survey of Work Values (SWV) (55), based on the presumption that people who value the Protestant Work Ethic are primarily intrinsically-oriented. Some of the factors are intrinsic (e.g., pride in work); some are extrinsic (e.g., social status of the job); and one factor is viewed as mixed—upward striving.

A third measure is the Job Orientation Inventory (JOI) (5). Organizational rewards are classified into ten categories, some intrinsic and some extrinsic. The format is forced-choice, with the intent to measure an individual's preference for the various types of potential rewards.

While there is a fundamental similarity in pur-

TABLE 1. Summary of material pertaining to the intrinsic-extrinsic distinction

Category of Use	Relevant Material in Literature

Trait	Measures of work orientation
	   Job Attitude Scale (46, 47, 48)
	   Survey of Work Values (55)
	   Job Orientation Inventory (5)
	Related trait concepts
	   Internal-external Control (45)
	   Origin/Pawn (12)
	   Inner-directed/Other-directed (43)
	   Achievement motivation (3)
	   Level of need satisfaction (34)

State—as a Function of Situation	Independent variables
	   Type of rewards (41)
	   Work content (42)
	   Control of work (16)
	   Leadership style (36)
	   Reward contingencies (15, 16)
	Theoretical concepts/models
	   Expectancy theory (38)
	   Internal task goals (10)
	   Intrinsic Activity Value (7, 51)
	   Attribution theory (9, 28, 29, 30)
	   Information-processing theory (19)

State—as a Function of Interaction between Situation and Trait	Independent variables
	   Task design and work values (26)
	   Content of tasks and work values (44)
	   Job rewards and work orientation (11)
	   Perceptions of job content and desired level of
	     need satisfaction (20, 21, 31)
	Theoretical models
	   Cognitive evaluation theory (16)

pose of these three scales, there are differences in their conceptions of the intrinsic-extrinsic distinction, and the three scales have been shown not to have convergent validity (1). The first two scales measure work values, while the JOI measures preference for type of organizational rewards. On the intrinsic dimension, the SWV includes the work groups as a vehicle while the JAS does not (11).

The JAS and JOI are both ipsative, forced-choice scales which means that scoring high on intrinsic orientation necessarily means scoring low on extrinsic orientation and vice versa. This approach makes sense in an individual trait framework, since intrinsic-extrinsic is seen as a continuum on which individuals are located in only one spot. The ipsative model implies that people do not respond to both intrinsic and extrinsic motivators; therefore it does not represent a combinatorial model of intrinsic and extrinsic motivation (either additive or subtractive). Persons who are intrinsically motivated presumably will be relatively unaffected by the presence of extrinsic rewards, and vice versa.

When the intrinsic-extrinsic distinction is employed as a characteristic of individuals, it is similar to several other personality trait distinctions and is often used to describe them. One is Rotter's Internal-External (I-E) Locus of Control (45), which refers to the extent to which one person perceives events as under one's control (internal) or as a result of forces beyond one's control (external). A similar distinction is de Charms' Origin/Pawn (12, 13), which describes the perception of controlling one's own behavior versus having it controlled by outside agents. It is essentially the difference betwen perceiving oneself as free versus forced, a feeling of personal causation versus a feeling of powerlessness or ineffectiveness. According to de Charms, Origins are intrinsically motivated, while Pawns are extrinsically motivated.

Riesman's inner-directed/other-directed distinction (43) pertains to whether one acts in accordance with one's own beliefs or the expectations of those around one. A fourth related distinction is that of high versus low achievement motivation. Deci maintains that achievement motivation is a special case of intrinsic motivation (16). In Atkinson's model (3), achievement motivation is conceived as a relatively stable personality trait because it is a function of two other stable traits—tendency to approach success and tendency to avoid failure. The fifth distinction is that of higher-order versus lower-order need satisfaction, designating where the individual is situated on Maslow's need hierarchy.

The commonality between the intrinsic-extrinsic distinction and the five distinctions described here is that all are used to explain why some people in a given situation engage in certain classes of behaviors, loosely categorized as growth or self-actualizing behaviors, more than do other people in the same situation. The other common thread is that all these distinctions relate directly or indirectly to a person's feelings of control of both self and environment.

As a State

The intrinsic-extrinsic distinction also has been used to describe states of the individual—a person's motivation or satisfaction at a given time, subject to change depending on circumstances. Within this broad category are two subcategories: (a) the state is primarily a function of the characteristics of the immediate situation; (b) the state is a function of an interaction between the situational characteristics and the individual personal traits.

One major situational characteristic considered to be a determining factor in employees' intrinsic-extrinsic states is the type of rewards available. Porter and Lawler (41) distinguished between extrinsic rewards, which are collected and awarded by the organization, and intrinsic rewards, which are awarded to the employee by himself or herself.

A second important situational characteristic is job content, that is, how much of the job is intrinsically interesting. Based on the Porter and Lawler distinction between intrinsic and extrinsic rewards, Pritchard and Peters (42) hypothesized that intrinsic job satisfaction should be more closely related to the actual work content than extrinsic satisfaction. They measured intrinsic and extrinsic satisfaction using the Minnesota Satisfaction Questionnaire (MSQ) (53), which has intrinsic and extrinsic subscales. Not only was their hypothesis supported, but it also was found that intrinsic satisfaction was predicted better by the actual job duties than by the employees' interest in performing their job duties.

A third situational characteristic is job autonomy. To the extent that employees do not perceive themselves controlling their own work, they will be in no position to receive intrinsic rewards, develop intrinsic satisfaction, etc. (16). A fourth characteristic is leadership style—the extent to which supervisors employ participative practices allowing employees to exercise control over their work (36).

A fifth characteristic in the work environment is the reward contingencies—whether or not job outcomes are contingent upon performance and perceived as such. Deci (15) found that when extrinsic rewards were contingent upon performance, there was a detrimental effect on intrinsic motivation, but no such detriment appeared when rewards were not contingent upon performance. In this experiment, as in most experimental work on the relationship of extrinsic and intrinsic motivation, the operational definition of an intrinsically motivated activity is one which is done in the absence of any apparent external reward (16). Therefore, the measure of intrinsic motivation was the number of seconds of free choice time which the subjects spent engaged in the experimental task.

In the OB field, the effects of perceived contingencies have been stressed within the rubric of expectancy theory. Expectancy theory explains motivation as a function of how much an employee values the various potential outcomes of the job (valence), whether one sees those outcomes as contingent upon job performance (instrumentality), and whether one sees oneself as able and willing to perform sufficiently well to obtain (or avoid) the relevant outcomes (expectancy). Although expectancy theory does not discount the influences of personality traits, it emphasizes the immediate influences of the situation. For instance, an employee's perception of instrumentality is more dependent upon the factors present in the immediate work situation than on his or her generalized perceptions of internal-external control. Expectancy theory is ahistorical in that it does not dwell on the formative processes resulting in employees' perceptions. In this respect it can be contrasted to trait theories, such as Atkinson's which emphasizes how the personality traits underlying achievement motivation are formed.

Because expectancy theory explains behavior in terms of perceptions regarding job outcomes, it is primarily a theory of extrinsic motivation (16). This is particularly true of the original Vroom model (52), which focuses on first level outcomes (e.g., money, recognition) and second level outcomes which can be obtained with first level outcomes (e.g., food, status). The fact that expectancy theory does not lend itself directly to explaining intrinsically motivated behavior has resulted in many extensions and modifications to the model. One approach has been to partition job outcomes into intrinsic and extrinsic categories (38). But this strategy does not resolve the basic difficulty that the concept of an "intrinsic outcome" is inherently contradictory, because the concept of outcome is basically extrinsic. Moreover, there is no clearcut theoretical basis for deciding which outcomes are intrinsic and which are extrinsic, so the decision is subjective to the investigator. The Dyer and Parker (18) survey demonstrates that it is unreasonable to expect consensus across investigators in this regard. One way of coping with this problem was used by Meir (37) in developing a list of intrinsic and extrinsic needs. Only those need items were included on which a board of five to ten psychologists could reach an 80 percent consensus.

Campbell, Dunnette, Lawler, and Weick (10) modified the basic expectancy model specifically to better account for certain aspects of behavior which are not clearly extrinsic. In this model, two facets of motivation are included, one based on external task goals and one on internal task goals. External task goals are specified by someone else, while internal task goals are specified by the individual based on his or her value system. Motivation as affected by external task goals is a function of: valences of the goals, first and second level outcomes, perceived probabilities of goal accomplishment, and perceived probabilities of obtaining first and second level outcomes. Motivation as affected by internal task goals is a function of valence of the goals and of perceived probability of goal accomplishment. Therefore, for internal task goals, task accomplishment is an outcome in itself. This approach follows the tradition of dividing outcomes into two types, but it is superior to other attempts in that a qualitative distinction is made between the two in terms of what factors affect the two types of resulting motivation.

In a related line of thinking, Turney developed the concept of Intrinsic Activity Value (IAV), the value which employees place on their job duties, irrespective of external outcomes associated with performance (51). IAV is the intrinsic analog of valence. But there is a fundamental difference between IAV and internal task goal. The former pertains to values placed on actually engaging in job activities, while the latter pertains to values placed on task accomplishment. Thus the concept of IAV obviates the need for using the somewhat self-contradictory concept of intrinsic outcome.

Extending Turney's work, Broedling (7) measured extrinsic motivation in a standard, expectancy theory manner, as the mean sum of the products of the valences and instrumentalities of the individual job outcomes (e.g., getting a promotion) times the expectancy of being able to perform well. Intrinsic motivation was defined as a function of employees' feelings about their job activities apart from job outcomes. The two variables which determine intrinsic motivation were taken to be: (a) Intrinsic Activity Value—measured as the perceived pleasantness or unpleasantness of engaging in each particular job activity (e.g., evaluating your employees); (b) self-expectancy—the employees' perception that they can perform each job activity well if they try hard. Intrinsic motivation was the mean sum of the products of the IAVs and self-expectancies for each activity. Intrinsic motivation was found to be a much better predictor of job performance (measured by self, peer, and supervisor ratings) than extrinsic motivation.

A large body of pertinent current research in social psychology derives from attribution theory, the study of how people assign motives to themselves and to others. This work is similar to expectancy theory in that, while it does not discount historical influences and individual differences, its primary purpose is to explain a person's intrinsic-extrinsic state at a given time. Calder and Staw (9) argued that the usual use of intrinsic to apply to behaviors which are self-sustained and valued for their own sake only serves as a descriptive label, not as an explanation. Instead, they advocate use of intrinsic-extrinsic as a perception on the part of individuals to explain their own behavior to themselves.

Kruglanski (28, 29) rejected the distinction of extrinsic pertaining to causes of behavior which are external to the person and intrinsic pertaining to causes internal to the person. His distinction is that extrinsically motivated behavior is exogenously-attributed, that is, behavior which the person sees as a means to an end; intrinsically motivated behavior is endogenously-attributed, that is, seen as an end in itself. Kruglanski maintains that this distinction can better predict the effects of extrinsic rewards on intrinsic motivation. For example, one experimental study found that money depressed intrinsic motivation only when money was not inherent to the task (a model construction game which is not typically played for money). Money enhanced intrinsic motivation for a task where money was inherent to it (a coin toss game typically played for money) (30).

Greene and Lepper (19) also utilize this means-end distinction in their information-processing approach to intrinsic and extrinsic motivation. Their goal is to account for the adverse effects of extrinsic rewards on intrinsic motivation, both in the immediate and in the longer term. They distinguish between extrinsic incentives, which are not only means to ends but also

situation-specific, and intrinsic incentives, which are more general and are associated with task content and internal states. A person's choice of behavior at any given moment is a result of the sum of extrinsic and intrinsic incentives.

The other sub-category of uses are those which explain individual states as resulting from an interaction between situational characteristics and personal traits. There is a growing tendency within OB toward explaining work behavior as an interaction, rather than strictly in terms of either personal traits or situational characteristics. Hulin and Blood (26) indicate that job performance and satisfaction are affected by the interaction of task design (situational) and work values (personal). Robey (44) found an interaction between intrinsic-extrinsic work values and the content of tasks, in terms of the subjects' satisfaction and partially in terms of their performance. Cascio (11) hypothesized that job satisfaction would be highest for employees whose intrinsic-extrinsic value orientation (as measured by the SWV) matched the intrinsic-extrinsic nature of the rewards present in the work situation. As expected, for the extrinsic employees, satisfaction with work environment factors was the most significant determinant of overall satisfaction, but satisfaction with the work itself was not found to be the most important determinant of overall satisfaction for intrinsic employees.

The work of Lawler, Hackman and Oldham (20, 21, 31) is another example of a conceptual model which postulates that motivation is the result of a situational-personal interaction. In their framework, internal motivation (that which is mediated by the person and tied directly to job content) is a function of the interaction between an employee's desire for higher-order need satisfaction (trait) and the job itself (situation). The job content is considered in terms of four core dimensions—variety, autonomy, task identity, feedback—and the Job Diagnostic Survey has been developed to measure these dimensions. While there is empirical support for this conceptual model, the role of the higher-order need strength trait may be more complex than originally thought (6).

The concept of intrinsic and extrinsic feedback might be one way of explaining the variety of results in job enrichment studies. Intrinsic feedback is internally-sent, and extrinsic feedback is externally-sent. To the extent that the situation gives an employee the leeway to call upon skills and abilities which he or she values, and thus to rely primarily on intrinsic feedback, the employee will be intrinsically motivated.

Another major theoretical development which might be classified as interactive is Deci's (16) cognitive evaluation theory. This was developed to account for findings that intrinsic and extrinsic motivation are not additive. Deci's work draws heavily on that of de Charms (12) and therefore can be considered to include both the effect of traits (Origin/Pawn) and situational characteristics. Deci's theoretical definition of intrinsic motivation is that which is "based in the human need to be competent and self-determining in relation to the environment" (16, p. 65). According to cognitive evaluation theory, there are two processes through which extrinsic rewards affect intrinsic motivation. One is if the reward changes the person's perception of locuses of causality of his or her own behavior, from internally controlled to externally controlled. The other is if the reward changes the person's feelings about his or her own competence and self-determination.

DISCUSSION AND CONCLUSIONS

As shown in this review, the intrinsic-extrinsic distinction has been applied in a variety of ways. In addition to describing individual traits and states, it has been used to characterize the working environment (e.g., an assembly-line is not intrinsically motivating). While most commonly used to explain the behavior of others, Calder and Staw (9) advocate its use as a description of one's own behavior. Some uses emphasize specific perceptions of individuals regarding their control of distinct environmental events, while others emphasize the individual's global feelings of competence and locus of control. While there is variation in usages, the common thread is the individual's perception of control, of both environmental events and his or her own behavior. There is also extensive variety in operational definitions, ranging from self-report questionnaire measures to actual behavior in a free-choice situation.

Is the intrinsic-extrinsic distinction useful in explaining organizational behavior, or is it simply a superfluous label for phenomena that have already been described in other terms? Although similar to other distinctions, there is empirical evidence that it accounts for a unique dimension (32). Moreover, its frequent use is a strong argument that there is need for a distinction of this sort. A potential problem is that it may be an over-simplification, that there may be more than two categories of motivation (27). Future research on the nature of the distinction would best be directed toward investigating whether more categories of motivation could better account for organizational behavior.

While the intrinsic-extrinsic distinction is basically useful, the OB field would benefit if the distinction were more uniformly applied. Specifically, it is confusing to use the distinction to describe both traits and states. Since the latter usage is more frequent, it might be helpful not to label people as intrinsic or extrinsic types, but rather as those high in feelings of control (of both their behavior and the environment) and those low in feelings of control. It also seems inappropriate to label environment characteristics as intrinsic or extrinsic since those labels are tied to perceptions, not to physical reality. If the intrinsic-extrinsic distinction is applied in a more uniform manner, and if investigators clearly define their use of the term, it will become easier to compare results and draw conclusions regarding the explanation of work behavior.

NOTE

1. The views expressed in this article are those of the author and do not necessarily represent those of the Department of the Navy.

REFERENCES

1. Alexander, R. A., L. L. Balascoe, G. V. Barrett, E. J. O'Connor, and J. B. Forbes. *The Relationships among Measures of Work Orientation, Attribute Preferences and Ability, Technical Report No. 7,* (Akron, Ohio: Department of Psychology, University of Akron, 1975).
2. Angyal, A. *Foundations for a Science of Personality* (New York: Commonwealth Fund, 1941).

3. Atkinson, J. W. *An Introduction to Motivation* (Princeton, N.J.: van Nostrand, 1964).

4. Berlyne, D. E. *Conflict, Arousal, and Curiosity* (New York: McGraw-Hill, 1960).

5. Blood, M. R. "Intergroup Comparisons of Intraperson Differences: Rewards from the Job," *Personnel Psychology,* Vol. 26, No. 1 (1973), 1–9.

6. Brief, A. B., and R. G. Aldag. "Employee Reactions to Job Characteristics: A Constructive Replication," *Journal of Applied Psychology,* Vol. 60, No. 2 (1975), 182–186.

7. Broedling, L. A. "The Use of an Intrinsic Index of Motivation in an Expectancy Theory Framework." Paper presented at the Western Division of the Academy of Management, 1975.

8. Calder, B. J., and B. M. Staw. "Interaction of Intrinsic and Extrinsic Motivation: Some Methodological Notes," *Journal of Personality and Social Psychology,* Vol. 31, No. 1 (1975), 76–80.

9. Calder, B. J., and B. M. Staw. "Self-perception of Intrinsic and Extrinsic Motivation," *Journal of Personality and Social Psychology,* Vol. 31, No. 4 (1975), 599–605.

10. Campbell, J. P., M D. Dunnette, E. E. Lawler, and K. E. Weick. *Managerial Behavior, Performance and Effectiveness* (New York: McGraw-Hill, 1970).

11. Cascio, W. F. *Value Orientation, Organizational Rewards, and Job Satisfaction, Technical Report 82* (Rochester, N.Y.: Graduate School of Management, University of Rochester, 1973).

12. deCharms, R. *Personal Causation* (New York: Academic Press, 1968).

13. deCharms, R. "Personal Causation Training in the Schools," *Journal of Applied Social Psychology,* Vol. 2, No. 2 (1972), 95–113.

14. Deci, E. L. "Effects of Externally Mediated Rewards on Intrinsic Motivation," *Journal of Personality and Social Psychology,* Vol. 18, No. 1 (1971), 105–115.

15. Deci, E. L. "The Effects of Contingent and Noncontingent Rewards and Controls on Intrinsic Motivation," *Organizational Behavior and Human Performance,* Vol. 8, No. 2 (1972), 217–229.

16. Deci, E. L. *Intrinsic Motivation* (New York: Plenum Press, 1975).

17. Dermer, J. "The Interrelationship of Intrinsic and Extrinsic Motivation," *Academy of Management Journal,* Vol. 18, No. 1 (1975), 125–128.

18. Dyer, L., and D. F. Parker. "Classifying Outcomes in Work Motivation Research: An Examination of the Intrinsic-extrinsic Dichotomy," *Journal of Applied Psychology,* Vol. 60, No. 4 (1975), 455–458.

19. Greene, D., and M. R. Lepper. "An Information-processing Approach to Intrinsic and Extrinsic Motivation." Paper presented at the American Psychological Association Convention, 1975.

20. Hackman, J. R., and E. E. Lawler. "Employee Reactions to Job Characteristics," *Journal of Applied Psychology Monograph,* Vol. 55 (1971), 259–286.

21. Hackman, J. R., and G. R. Oldham. "Development of the Job Diagnostic Survey," *Journal of Applied Psychology,* Vol. 60, No. 2 (1975), 159–170.

22. Hamner, W. C., and L. W. Foster. "Are Intrinsic and Extrinsic Rewards Additive: A Test of Deci's Cognitive Evaluation Theory," *Organizational Behavior and Human Performance,* Vol. 14 (1975), 398–415.

23. Harlow, H. F., M. K. Harlow, and D. R. Meyer. "Learning Motivated by a Manipulation Drive," *Journal of Experimental Psychology,* Vol. 40, No. 2 (1950), 228–234.

24. Hendrik, I. "The Discussion of the 'Instinct to Master'," *Psychoanalytic Quarterly,* Vol. 12 (1943), 561–565.

25. Herzberg, F., B. Mausner, and B. Snyderman. *The Motivation to Work* (New York: Wiley, 1959).

26. Hulin, C. L., and M. R. Blood. "Job Enlargement, Individual Differences, and Worker Responses," *Psychological Bulletin,* Vol. 69, No. 1 (1968), 41–55.

27. Korman, A. K., B. E. Goodstadt, A. S. Glickman, and A. P. Romanczuk. *An Exploratory Study of Enlistment Incentives among Junior College Students* (Washington, D.C.: American Institutes for Research, 1973).

28. Kruglanski, A. "An Endogenous Attribution Theory of Intrinsic Motivation." Paper presented at the American Psychological Association Convention, 1975.

29. Kruglanski, A. "The Endogenous-exogenous Partition in Attribution Theory," *Psychological Review,* Vol. 82 (1975), 387–406.

30. Kruglanski, A., A. Riter, A. Amitai, B. Margolin, L. Shabtai, and D. Zaksh. "Can Money Enhance Intrinsic Motivation? A Test of the Content-consequence Hypothesis," *Journal of Personality and Social Psychology,* Vol. 31 (1975), 744–750.

31. Lawler, E. E. "Job Design and Employee Motivation," *Personnel Psychology,* Vol. 22, No. 4 (1969), 426–435.

32. Lawler, E. E., and D. T. Hall. "The Relationship of Job Characteristics to Job Involvement, Satisfaction and Intrinsic Motivation," *Journal of Applied Psychology,* Vol. 54, No. 4 (1970), 305–312.

33. Lewin, K. *A Dynamic Theory of Personality* (New York: McGraw-Hill, 1935).

34. Maslow, A. H. "A Theory of Human Motivation," *Psychological Review*, Vol. 50 (1943), 370–396.

35. McClelland, D., J. W. Atkinson, R. A. Clark, and E. L. Lowell. *The Achievement Motive* (New York: Appleton-Century-Crofts, 1953).

36. McGregor, D. *The Human Side of Enterprise* (New York: McGraw-Hill, 1960).

37. Meir, E. I. "Relationship between Intrinsic Needs and Women's Persistence at Work," *Journal of Applied Psychology*, Vol. 56, No. 4 (1972), 293–296.

38. Mitchell, T. R., and D. W. Albright. "Expectancy Theory Predictions of the Satisfaction, Effort, Performance, and Retention of Naval Aviation Officers," *Organizational Behavior and Human Performance*, Vol. 8, No. 1 (1972), 1–20.

39. Montgomery, K. C. "The Role of Exploratory Drive in Learning," *Journal of Comparative Physiological Psychology*, Vol. 47 (1954), 60–64.

40. Notz, W. W. "Work Motivation and the Negative Effects of Extrinsic Rewards: A Review with Implications for Theory and Practice," *American Psychologist*, Vol. 30, No. 9 (1975), 884–891.

41. Porter, L. W., and E. E. Lawler. "The Effect of Performance on Job Satisfaction," *Industrial Relations*, Vol. 7 (1967), 20–28.

42. Pritchard, R. D., and L. H. Peters. "Job Duties and Job Interests as Predictors of Intrinsic and Extrinsic Satisfaction," *Organizational Behavior and Human Performance*, Vol. 12, No. 3 (1974), 315–330.

43. Riesman, D. *The Lonely Crowd* (New Haven, Conn.: Yale University Press, 1950).

44. Robey, D. "Task Design, Work Values, and Worker Response: An Experimental Test," *Organizational Behavior and Human Performance*, Vol. 12, No. 2 (1974), 264–273.

45. Rotter, J. B. "Generalized Expectancies for Internal versus External Control of Reinforcement," *Psychological Monographs*, Vol. 80 (1966), No. 1 (Whole No. 609).

46. Saleh, S. D. *Development of the Job Attitude Scale (JAS)* (University of Waterloo: Department of Management Sciences, 1971).

47. Saleh, S. D., and T. G. Grygier. "Psychodynamics of Intrinsic and Extrinsic Job Orientation," *Journal of Applied Psychology*, Vol. 53, No. 6 (1969), 446–450.

48. Saleh, S. D., and V. Pasricha. "Job Orientation and Work Behavior," *Academy of Management Journal*, Vol. 18, No. 3 (1975), 638–645.

49. Scott, W. E., Jr. "The Effects of Extrinsic Rewards on 'Intrinsic Motivation.' A Critique," *Organizational Behavior and Human Performance*, Vol. 15, No. 1 (1976), 117–129.

50. Tolman, E. C. *Purposive Behavior in Animals and Man* (New York: Century, 1932).

51. Turney, J. R. "Expectancy × Valence and Intrinsic Activity Value as Predictors of Motivation in a Technical-Professional Organization," *Proceedings of the 80th Annual Convention of the American Psychological Association*, 1972, 453–454.

52. Vroom, V. H. *Work and Motivation* (New York: Wiley, 1964).

53. Weiss, D., R. Dawis, G. England, and L. Lofquist. "Manual for the Minnesota Satisfaction Questionnaire," *Minnesota Studies in Vocational Rehabilitation*, Vol. 12, Bulletin 45 (1967).

54. White, R. W. "Motivation Reconsidered: The Concept of Competence," *Psychological Review*, Vol. 66, No. 5 (1959), 297–334.

55. Wollack, S., J. G. Goodale, J. P. Wijting, and P. C. Smith. "Development of the Survey of Work Values," *Journal of Applied Psychology*, Vol. 55, No. 4 (1971), 331–338.

DIFFERENCES IN MOTIVATIONAL PROPERTIES BETWEEN JOB ENLARGEMENT AND JOB ENRICHMENT

KAE H. CHUNG

MONICA F. ROSS

Though often viewed as inseparable or interchangeable concepts, job enlargement and job enrichment are best implemented as two distinct managerial strategies. Job enlargement requires changes in the technical aspects of a job, while job enrichment requires changes in behavioral systems in an organization. Although enriching a job is said to have a stronger motivational impact on employees than job enlargement, it is extremely complex and time-consuming to implement because it involves changes in attitudes and values of organizational as well as societal members. Behavioral changes tend to arouse resistance from organizational members. But job enlargement involves technical changes, which can be adopted more expediently than behavioral changes, and is therefore less likely to cause organizational resistance. Contrary to Herzberg's (1) argument that job enlargement is a futile exercise in expanding the meaninglessness of a job, an optimally enlarged job possesses a number of properties that can have a motivational impact on some workers. Workers with low need for self-control and growth may be perfectly happy with enlarged jobs without job enrichment.

This article: (a) investigates the differences in motivational properties (task attributes, motiva-

Reprinted by permission of the Academy of Management Review and Kae H. Chung.

tional effects, and managerial implications of job enlargement and job enrichment and (b) suggests a set of managerial strategies to accommodate the differences in employees' motivation in job design.

MOTIVATIONAL PROPERTIES OF JOB ENLARGEMENT

Job enlargement is often called "horizontal job loading," simply adding more task elements to an existing job. When a job is enlarged, the worker performs a large work unit involving a variety of task elements rather than a fragmented job. An enlarged job can elicit intrinsic motivation for a number of reasons, as explained by the following task attributes.

Task Attributes of Enlarged Jobs

Task Variety. A fragmented job requiring a limited number of unchanging responses can lead to boredom. Introduction of task variety causes a series of mental activations requiring a variety of responses and thus reducing monotony. According to neuropsychological activation theory, the level of activation (the extent of an organism's energy release) is affected by stimulus intensity and variation; the greater the intensity and variation of stimuli, the higher the level of activation

(8, 41). But there is an inverted-V relationship between activation level and performance. At low activation levels, performance is depressed due to lack of alertness, decrease in sensory sensitivity, and lack of muscular coordination. At intermediate levels, performance is optimal; at high levels, performance is again depressed due to hypertension and loss of control. Job enlargement is supported by activation theory because task variation increases the level of activation; an intermediate level of task variety should sustain an optimal level of activation as well as performance.

Meaningful Work Module. By combining related task elements, the job becomes larger and closer to a whole work unit. The worker who performs a whole work unit, or at least a major portion of a product or project, begins to appreciate his or her contribution to the completion of the product or project. The worker who completes a work module within a time unit that is psychologically and technically meaningful (20) will find the job interesting and worthwhile. The time unit can range from one-half hour to days, depending on the nature of the job and individual differences in attention level. Key points for designing meaningful work modules are: a worker who completes a work module should feel a sense of accomplishment; and each undertaking of a new module should rejuvenate the level of activation. Homans (16) suggested that tasks be designed so that repeated activities lead up to the accomplishment of some final result. When this happens, the enlarged job will have high motivation value.

Performance Feedback. A worker performing a fractionated job with short performance cycles repeats the same set of motions endlessly without obtaining a meaningful finishing point. It is difficult to count the number of finished performance cycles, and even if counted, the feedback is meaningless. Knowledge of results (KR) on enlarged jobs measures the worker's level of accomplishment, which can be evaluated for organizational rewards. KR serves two motivational functions. First, KR is an external stimulus if added to a repetitive and dull task; because activation level increases, the performance level can be sustained or even improved at least temporarily (41). Second, KR can have a greater motivational value if

it is internally generated from task performance than if it is externally introduced (10). The worker is more likely to utilize internally generated KR in setting performance goals or standards in evaluating progress toward these goals (6, 28, 29, 40).

Ability Utilization. People derive satisfaction from jobs that permit utilization of skills and abilities, and enlarged jobs usually require more mental and physical abilities. Vroom (44) reported a positive correlation between opportunity for self-expression in the job (ability utilization) and job satisfaction for blue-collar workers. Kornhauser (21) also reported a significant relationship between ability utilization and mental health for young and middle-aged workers across various occupational levels. According to expectancy theorists (e.g., 2, 3, 26, 45), a task should be designed so that exertion of effort or energy results in task accomplishment. Simplified jobs are less motivating because they require low levels of ability and effort utilization. Since mechanized job productivity depends primarily on machines, workers' skills and abilities are not perceived to be principal determinants of task accomplishment. Overly enlarged jobs are not motivating because they require more skills and abilities than workers possess, creating frustration and obstacles to task accomplishment. Enlarged jobs with optimum levels of complexity allow effort to be closely related to task accomplishment, creating a task situation that is challenging but attainable.

Worker-Paced Control. Job enlargment makes it difficult to place workers on a machine-paced production line. Since work modules are completed by workers with different temperaments, work habits, and skill and ability levels, production speeds and work methods cannot be completely standardized. The worker-paced production line is motivational because it satisfies the worker's desire to control the work environment. Workers can develop their own work methods and habits, suitable to their personalities, and reflecting their own work rhythms. Enlarged jobs organized around the worker-paced production line may help to reduce employee turnover and absenteeism.

Motivational Effects of Job Enlargement

Although a number of studies have attempted to measure the effects of new work systems on employee job satisfaction and performance, relatively few have used only one type of work system based on either horizontal or vertical job loading. Thus it is difficult to test any performance prediction that one work system is superior to another in arousing employee motivation. But the following studies help in predicting motivational effects of job enlargement.

Conant and Kilbridge (17), Guest (11), Lawler (25), Walker (46), and Walker and Guest (47) studied the effects of job enlargement (primarily horizontal job loading) on employee motivation. They concluded that job enlargement is more likely to improve employee satisfaction and product quality and, to a certain extent, to reduce costs and increase productivity. But a situation may be created in which workers have to exert more energy and effort to produce the same rate of production as before the jobs were enlarged. Enlarged jobs usually involve worker-paced production methods that may reduce production speed and prevent optimal human movements. Workers may draw more job satisfaction from producing quality products than from producing a large quantity of low quality products. Thus, job enlargement is most likely to (a) have a positive effect on employee satisfaction, (b) have a positive influence on the quality of product, and (c) have an effect on productivity.

Costs for Enlarging Jobs

Although job enlargement is much simpler to implement than job enrichment, potential users should be aware of its costs. In many instances, the existing assembly production lines need to be broken up and restructured into work modules that can be considered as natural and psychologically meaningful work units. Redesigning and balancing production lines is costly. Volvo estimated that a new work system would cost about 10 percent more than a comparable conventional auto plant (1). Workers and supervisors need to be retrained to adjust to new work systems. Outside consultants are usually invited to monitor the im-

plementation process. Many companies experience drops in productivity during the initial stage of new work system implementation. Finally, under job enlargement workers perform more complicated jobs and may demand higher wages.

In summary, a properly enlarged job possesses motivational characteristics which may arouse job satisfaction of rank-and-file employees who are not interested in performing overly demanding jobs. Furthermore, job enlargement is a prerequisite for job enrichment. Although job enlargement incurs some costs, it can be recommended to employers on the basis of humanistic considerations and cost savings attributable to reduced absenteeism, lower turnover, and decreased product rejects.

MOTIVATIONAL PROPERTIES OF JOB ENRICHMENT

Job enrichment, often called "vertical job loading," allows workers to perform managerial functions previously restricted to managerial and supervisory personnel. If founded on enlarged jobs, it allows workers to perform more task components, and also to have more control over the tasks they perform. Motivating characteristics of job enrichment—including participation, autonomy, and responsibility—appeal to employees who strive for the satisfaction of higher-order needs such as self-control, self-respect, and self-actualization.

Task Attributes of Job Enrichment

Employee Participation. Employee participation in managerial decisions can influence employee job performance, as well as satisfaction. Employees who participate in the decision-making process tend to internalize organizational decisions and feel personally responsible for carrying them out. Thus, the success or failure of a decision and subsequent action becomes their success or failure (45). But the quality of decisions seems to depend on other factors, such as quality and quantity of participants' information and the type of decisions to be made. Decision quality is enhanced when participants have the necessary information (43) and when participants' goals are congruent with organizational goals. When their goals are not congruent with organizational goals, workers may not find any reason to set high standards and increase productivity.

Goal Internalization. Motivation is goal-oriented behavior. If a job enrichment program is to be successful, workers should be involved in the goal-setting process for their work group. According to Likert (27) and Odiorne (35), participation itself does not guarantee high productivity unless it results in the workers' establishment of high performance goals for themselves.

A supportive supervisory climate must also be present if an organization is to achieve high productivity. According to Locke (28), empirical studies showing a positive relationship between participation and high performance have involved the establishment of high performance goals by participants. Bryan and Locke (5), Latham and Baldes (22), Latham and Kinne (23), Latham and Yukl (24), and Ronan, Latham, and Kinne (40) generally support Locke's theory of goal-setting in producing high performance.

Proponents of job enrichment suggest that the goal-setting technique be applied to all levels of employees in order to achieve maximum effect on employee motivation (e.g., 15, 34, 37). But implementation of participatory goal-setting systems at lower levels of organizational hierarchy may not be practical because workers at these levels may not be technically and psychologically prepared to perform highly demanding managerial jobs. Thus it seems necessary to reexamine the simplistic notion of goal-setting systems applied to all levels of employees.

Autonomy. Job enrichment programs should go beyond employee participation in operational decisions. Employees should be given autonomy and control over the means of achieving organizational goals. They should be allowed to evaluate their own performance, take risks, and learn from their mistakes. When workers are given authority to manage their own jobs, it should be unnecessary for managers to exercise close supervision; supervisors can then be available to employees for consultation, advice, guidance, and training. When autonomy is working, managers can spend their time planning, trouble-shooting, and helping their

supervisors. Even the number of supervisory personnel can be reduced somewhat. But employee autonomy is frequently in conflict with management's desire to have control over, or be informed of, subordinates' activities. Managers may delegate authority to workers, but they are still responsible for their subordinates' actions. Even if a manager does not mean to interfere with workers, his or her concern for production may lead to frequent review of subordinates' progress. This behavior may make workers feel that they do not really have autonomy in managing their jobs.

Group Management. Autonomy can be granted to employees collectively or individually. Most proponents of job enrichment programs prefer group action over the individualized approach (e.g., 1, 17, 48). The work group defines its task-goals, undertakes its tasks jointly, appraises its accomplishments and individual members' contributions to the group effort, and distributes the outcomes among its members. For example, self-managed work teams at the General Foods plant are given collective responsibility for managing day-to-day production problems. Assignments of individual tasks are subject to team consensus, and tasks can be reassigned by the team to accommodate individual differences in skills, capacities, and interests (48).

The group management approach is desirable for most jobs that require a high degree of interaction among work group members. Managers and workers must coordinate their efforts to achieve organizational or group goals. When employee job performances are mutually interdependent, it is difficult to identify individualized performance standards and accomplishments. An individualized performance system can be detrimental to such job situations, leading the employee to pursue personal goals while ignoring joint organizational responsibilities.

Motivational Effects of Job Enrichment

Vroom (45) and Maier (32) indicated that participation in decision making leads to greater acceptance of decisions by workers and thus increases employee motivation. But other studies indicate that participation does not necessarily lead to high motivation and productivity unless it results in high performance goals set by the participants themselves (5, 24, 27, 28, 35). Individual and organizational constraints may prevent effective utilization of goal-setting systems, including workers' technical and psychological readiness to perform demanding jobs, pay, job security, and organizational climate. Further, employees will not set high performance goals unless their jobs have been horizontally enlarged to make their tasks psychologically meaningful. Thus, it is doubtful whether job enrichment alone can have a strong motivational impact on employee behavior. When these two types of work systems are jointly applied under favorable circumstances, job enrichment can exert more influence on employee motivation than can job enlargement because it gives workers more opportunities to utilize their abilities and exert control over their work environment.

Combined Approach to Job Design

Job enrichment seems to gain motivational power when combined with job enlargement. It is predicted that job satisfaction and productivity will be highest when both job enlargement and job enrichment are jointly applied to redesigning work systems. HEW's report *Work in America* (14) advocated that the work system should include both horizontal and vertical job loadings if it is to have a strong impact on employee satisfaction and job performance. Such a complete work system resulted in a productivity increase from five percent to 40 percent. A number of industrial experiences with the combined approach to job design support such a prediction.

AT&T reported that after it had introduced the new work system into a service representatives' office at Southwestern Bell, the absenteeism rate in the experimental unit was 0.6 percent, compared with 2.5 percent in other groups. The errors per 100 orders were 2.9 as compared with 4.6 in the control group. The nine typists in the group were producing service order pages at a rate one-third higher than the 51 service order typists in the control group (9). At the General Foods plant, people involved in the new work system reported high job satisfaction, reductions in manufacturing costs through fewer quality rejects, a lower absenteeism rate, and an increase in productivity. On the average, 77 people achieved the production level which was estimated to require 110 employees if conventional engineering principles were adopted (48). Roche and MacKinnon (39) and Paul, Robertson, and Herzberg (36) also reported positive results in job satisfaction and performance at Texas Instruments and Imperial Chemical (England), respectively.

The editor of *Organizational Dynamics* (1) reported that at Philips (Netherlands), job redesign improved employee morale, reduced production costs by 10 percent, and increased product quality. Saab-Scania (Sweden) reported that after job redesign there were some improvements in employee attitudes, absenteeism, and product quality (1), but no proof of increased productivity as a result of job redesign. Volvo (Sweden) also reported some improvements in absenteeism, turnover, and product quality, but no measurable improvement in production. The general feeling among all these companies is that improved product quality and reduced labor problems (such as absenteeism and turnover) could cover the costs of redesigning the work systems.

Implementation Constraints

Despite considerable enthusiasm generated by job enrichment, many employers find it difficult to implement this concept in their organizations. Luthans and Reif (30) found that out of 125 industrial firms surveyed, only five had made any formal efforts to enrich jobs. Even in these firms only a small portion of employees were affected by the job enrichment programs. For example, the job enrichment program at Texas Instruments, which is considered a pioneer in this field, has involved only about 10 percent of its total work force. Another 25 percent of the surveyed firms have applied these programs to a small portion of their employees on an informal basis.

There are a number of reasons why job enrichment is not used as widely as many industrial psychologists would like and why it fails to produce positive results in some companies. First, job enlargement should precede job enrichment to make the job interesting before managerial autonomy is given. Second, employees will not positively respond to new work systems unless they are reasonably satisfied with lower-order needs, such as economic well-being and affiliation. When these needs are not satisfied, employees become preoccupied with satisfying them, and higher-order needs do not emerge as motivators. Third, job enrichment tends to sensitize workers to expect satisfaction of higher-order needs because they are usually told that the work systems are being redesigned to fulfill these needs. While raising the level of expectation is relatively simple, meeting the raised expectation is more complex, since it involves a time-consuming effort of orchestrating the divergent goals of individuals, groups, and the organization into workable terms. Finally, there are significant differences in workers' responses to job enrichment. In particular, higher-order needs and urban-rural backgrounds of employees moderate the effectiveness of job enrichment (4, 12, 19). Workers who are motivated by lower-order needs and urban backgrounds tend to respond poorly to job enrichment.

JOB DESIGN STRATEGIES

Job design, especially in its combined approach, can have a significant influence on employee motivation because it contains the major motivational components as suggested in instrumental/expectancy theory of motivation. Job design affects the employee's expectancy (a) that effort leads to task performance (E-P); (b) that task performance leads to intrinsic as well as extrinsic incentive rewards (P-I); and (c) that these incentive rewards have the power of satisfying the person's needs (I-N).

Workers respond to job design differently, reflecting individual differences in perceiving these motivational components, and these differences often determine the effectiveness of new work systems. For example, not all workers are interested in performing demanding jobs, nor are they all motivated by higher-order need satisfaction. Also, not all organizations are able to supply adequate hygiene factors, such as pay and job security, and have a supportive climate for managerial innovation. Thus, these individual and organizational characteristics should be reflected in job design.

Individual Differences and Task Difficulty

Job design affects workers' expectancy that effort leads to task performance (E-P). It is necessary to design a job to contain an optimal level of task performance difficulty in order to elicit work motivation.

The optimal level of task design or difficulty varies for different individuals. Some can handle demanding jobs effectively and thus are reinforced by successful accomplishment, while others are not able to perform and become discouraged. Hulin (18) and Hulin and Blood (19) indicated an inverted-V relationship between task difficulty and job satisfaction, with the optimal level of job satisfaction varying for different workers. Contrary to the view that routinized and repetitive jobs lead to boredom and job dissatisfaction, some workers find them suitable or even desirable. Hackman and Lawler (12), Hackman and Oldham (13), and Brief and Aldag (4) also reported that individuals with higher-order need strength generally display stronger relationships between core task attributes (e.g., task variety, task identity, autonomy, and feedback) and job satisfaction than do individuals who are lower in higher-order need strength.

The relationship between task attributes and individual differences is shown in Figure 1. Employees with strong desire for and ability to perform demanding jobs (professional and managerial personnel) will find the highest level of job satisfaction and performance when their jobs are heavily enriched and complex, whereas workers with lower desire for and limited ability to perform demanding jobs (unskilled and semi-skilled) will find their optimal levels of job satisfaction and productivity when their jobs are relatively simple. Most skilled workers then will find their optimal levels of job satisfaction and productivity when their jobs are moderately enlarged and enriched.

The task difficulty index (TDI), shown in Figure 1, can be derived from the task attributes (task variety, meaningful work module, performance feedback, ability utilization, worker-paced

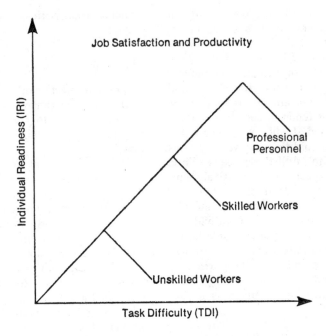

FIGURE 1. Task difficulty and individual difference.

control, group interaction, responsibility, and autonomy). The individual readiness index (IRI) is then derived from workers' skill levels and their psychological states. The skill levels measure workers' technical readiness for performing given tasks, while the psychological need states measure their psychological readiness for undertaking the tasks. The inverted-V chart indicated that job satisfaction and performance increase when both TDI and IRI increase, but they decrease as the gap between TDI and IRI widens. The figure also implies that a worker's readiness (IRI) should be matched with the task difficulty (TDI) to maximize job satisfaction and productivity. Motivational problems arise when the worker is either over-qualified or under-qualified for the job.

Effects on Performance-Reward Tie

Job design influences workers' perception of the performance-incentive reward tie (P-I) in several ways. First, workers performing enriched jobs can see a direct relationship between task accomplish-ment and feelings of achievement, recognition, and growth. If they perform successfully, they will be immediately reinforced by task accomplishment without going through supervisory evaluation. However, less productive workers will merely be frustrated when they cannot accomplish their assigned demanding jobs. Thus, job enrichment is highly motivational for productive work groups but it can be a liability for unskilled workers.

The E-P tie is closely related to workers' perceptions of the P-I tie. When task difficulty is low and every employee can perform the job, all will be rewarded for its completion regardless of effort level. If the task difficulty is too high, an average employee is not able to accomplish the task and will not be rewarded for effort no matter how hard he or she may try. In either case, workers will perceive that their efforts are not related to performance (E-P) and are not rewarded (P-I). This will discourage employees from exerting efforts to accomplish their tasks. But workers will be motivated to perform their tasks when these tasks possess an intermediate degree of performance difficulty because their perceptions of the E-P and P-I ties at this task difficulty level will be highly motivational.

Matching Incentives with Needs

A critical task in developing an effective incentive-reward system is to match organizational incentives with individual needs (I-N). Workers who strive for satisfaction of existence needs will be motivated by such extrinsic incentives as pay, job security, and working conditions (34), and may easily tolerate or even prefer simplified and routinized jobs. Some workers are primarily motivated by socializing opportunities on their jobs. Reif and Luthans (38) found that unskilled workers prefer routinized tasks because these jobs provide them with opportunities to socialize or daydream without undue mental exhaustion and responsibility. Employees with higher-order needs are motivated by such incentives as achievement, recognition, responsibility, and growth opportunity. Thus, job enrichment is recommended to motivate employees with higher-order needs, while establishing an effective reward system and building a sociable organizational climate are suggested for workers with such maintenance needs as socialization and existence. But a minimum to moderate level of job enlargement can be motivational even for maintenance seekers because such an enlarged job can be less boring and requires a minimum level of skill and responsibility.

CONCLUSION

Several implications can be drawn from this discussion for designing work systems. First, job enrichment (vertical job loading) may not be applicable to all employees in an organization. It can have a strong motivational value for employees who prefer challenge in performing demanding jobs, have abilities to perform, and are motivated to satisfy higher-order needs. It may have little or even a negative effect on workers who prefer lower task difficulty, are unskilled, and are primarily motivated by lower-order needs. Second, job enlargement (horizontal job loading) with a limited degree of job enrichment is recommended for most skilled workers who are reasonably satisfied with lower-order needs and yet who

are not ready to undertake highly demanding jobs. Finally, job enlargement is more suitable to workers at lower levels of organizational echelons who are primarily motivated by lower-order needs. Enlarged jobs with opportunities for socialization may better satisfy their needs. Since no one particular job design is a cure-all managerial remedy, management should carefully study the differences in employees' technical and psychological readiness before any specific job design is implemented.

REFERENCES

1. AMACOM'S Editor. "Job Redesign on the Assembly Line: Farewell to Blue-Collar Blues?" *Organizational Dynamics*, Vol. 2 (1973), 51–67.

2. Atkinson, J. W. *An Introduction to Motivation* (Princeton, N.J.: D. Van Nostrand, 1964).

3. Atkinson, J. W., and N. T. Feather. *A Theory of Achievement Motivation* (New York: Wiley, 1966).

4. Brief, A. P., and R. J. Aldag. "Employee Reactions to Job Characteristics: A Constructive Replication," *Journal of Applied Psychology*, Vol. 60 (1975), 182–186.

5. Bryan, J. F., and E. A. Locke. "Goal Setting as a Means of Increasing Motivation," *Journal of Applied Psychology*, Vol. 51 (1967), 274–277.

6. Chung, K. H., and W. D. Vickery. "Relative Effectiveness and Joint Effects of Three Selected Reinforcements in a Repetitive Task Situation." *Organizational Behavior and Human Performance*, Vol. 16 (1976), 114–142.

7. Conant, E. H., and M. D. Kilbridge. "An Interdisciplinary Analysis of Job Enlargement: Technology, Costs, and Behavioral Implications," *Industrial and Labor Relations Review*, Vol. 18 (1975), 377–395.

8. Duffy, Elizabeth. *Activation and Behavior* (New York: Wiley, 1962).

9. Ford, R. N. "Job Enrichment Lessons From AT&T," *Harvard Business Review*, Vol. 51 (1973), 96–106.

10. Greller, M. M., and D. M. Herold. "Sources of Feedback: A Preliminary Investigation," *Organizational Behavior and Human Performance*, Vol. 13 (1975), 244–256.

11. Guest, R. H. "Job Enlargement: A Revolution in Job Design," *Personnel Administration*, Vol. 20 (1967), 9–16.

12. Hackman, J. R., and E. E. Lawler. "Employee Reactions to Job Characteristics," *Journal of Applied Psychology*, Vol. 55 (1971), 259–286.

13. Hackman, J. R., and G. R. Oldham. "Development of the Job Diagnostic Survey," *Journal of Applied Psychology,* Vol. 60 (1975), 159–170.

14. H. E. W. *Work in America* (Cambridge, Mass.: MIT Press, 1973).

15. Herzberg, Frederick. "One More Time: How Do You Motivate Employees?" *Harvard Business Review,* Vol. 46 (1968), 53–62.

16. Homans, G. C. *Social Behavior: Its Elementary Forms* (New York: Harcourt, Brace, and World, 1961).

17. Howell, R. A. "A Fresh Look at Management By Objectives," *Business Horizons,* Vol. 11 (1967), 51–58.

18. Hulin, C. L. "Individual Differences and Job Enrichment—The Case Against General Treatments," in J. R. Maher (Ed.), *New Perspectives in Job Enrichment* (New York: Van Nostrand, 1971), 162–191.

19. Hulin, C. L., and M. R. Blood. "Job Enlargement, Individual Differences and Worker Responses," *Psychological Bulletin,* Vol. 69 (1968), 41–55.

20. Kahn, R. L. "The Work Module-A Tonic for Lunchpail Lassitude," *Psychology Today,* Vol. 6 (1973), 35–39, 94–95.

21. Kornhauser, A. W. *Mental Health of the Industrial Worker: A Detroit Study* (New York: Wiley, 1962).

22. Latham, G. P., and J. J. Baldes. "The 'Practical Significance' of Locke's Theory of Goal Setting," *Journal of Applied Psychology,* Vol. 60 (1975), 122–124.

23. Latham, G. P., and S. B. Kinne. "Improving Job Performance Through Training in Goal Setting," *Journal of Applied Psychology,* Vol. 59 (1974), 187–191.

24. Latham, G. P., and G. A. Yukl. "Assigned Versus Participative Goal Setting with Educated and Uneducated Wood Workers," *Journal of Applied Psychology,* Vol. 60 (1975), 299–302.

25. Lawler, E. E. "Job Design and Employee Motivation," *Personnel Psychology,* Vol. 22 (1969), 526–435.

26. Lawler, E. E. *Motivation in Work Organizations* (Monterey, Calif.: Brooks/Cole, 1973).

27. Likert, Rensis. *New Patterns of Management* (New York: McGraw-Hill, 1967).

28. Locke, E. A. "Toward a Theory of Task Motivation and Incentives," *Organizational Behavior and Human Performance,* Vol. 3 (1968), 157–189.

29. Locke, E. A., N. Cartledge, and J. Koeppel. "Motivational Effects of Knowledge of Results: A Goal-Setting Phenomenon?" *Psychological Bulletin,* Vol. 70 (1968), 474–485.

30. Luthans, F., and W. E. Reif. "Job Enrichment: Long on Theory, Short on Practice," *Organizational Dynamics,* Vol. 2 (1974), 30–43.

31. Mahone, C. H. "Fear of Failure and Unrealistic Vocational Aspiration," *Journal of Abnormal Social Psychology,* Vol. 60 (1960), 253–261.

32. Maier, N. R. F. *Problem-Solving Discussions and Conferences: Leadership Methods and Skills* (New York: McGraw-Hill, 1963).

33. Morris, J. L. "Propensity for Risk Taking as Determinant of Vocational Choice: An Extension of the Theory of Achievement Motivation," *Journal of Personality and Social Psychology,* Vol. 3 (1967), 328–335.

34. Myers, M. S. *Every Employee A Manager* (New York: McGraw-Hill, 1970).

35. Odiorne, G. S. *Management-By-Objectives* (New York: Pitman, 1970).

36. Paul, W. J., K. B. Robertson, and F. Herzberg. "Job Enrichment Pays Off," *Harvard Business Review,* Vol. 47 (1964), 61–78.

37. Raia, A. P. *Management By Objectives* (Glenview, Ill.: Scott, Foresman, 1974).

38. Reif, W. E., and F. Luthans. "Does Job Enrichment Really Pay Off?" *California Management Review,* Vol. 14 (1972), 30–37.

39. Roche, W. J., and N. L. MacKinnon. "Motivating People With Meaningful Work," *Harvard Business Review,* Vol. 48 (1970), 97–110.

40. Ronan, W. W., G. P. Latham, and S. B. Kinne. "The Effects of Goal Setting and Supervision on Worker Behavior in an Industrial Situation," *Journal of Applied Psychology,* Vol. 57 (1973), 302–307.

41. Scott, W. E. "Activation Theory and Task Design," *Organizational Behavior and Human Performance,* Vol. 1 (1966), 3–30.

42. Sirota, D., and A. D. Wolfson. "Pragmatic Approach to People Problems," *Harvard Business Review,* Vol. 51 (1973), 120–128.

43. Swinth, R. L. "Organizational Joint Problem-Solving," *Management Science,* Vol. 18 (1971), B68–B79.

44. Vroom, V. H. "Ego-involvement, Job Satisfaction, and Job Performance," *Personnel Psychology,* Vol. 15 (1962), 159–177.

45. Vroom, V. H. *Work and Motivation* (New York: Wiley, 1964).

46. Walker, C. R. "The Problem of the Repetitive Job," *Harvard Business Review,* Vol. 28 (1950), 54–59.

47. Walker, C. R., and R. H. Guest. *The Man on the Assembly Line* (Cambridge, Mass.: Harvard University Press, 1952).

48. Walton, R. E. "How to Counter Alienation in the Plant," *Harvard Business Review,* Vol. 50 (1972), 70–81.

A NEW STRATEGY FOR JOB ENRICHMENT

J. RICHARD HACKMAN, GREG OLDHAM,
ROBERT JANSON, KENNETH PURDY

Practitioners of job enrichment have been living through a time of excitement, even euphoria. Their craft has moved from the psychology and management journals to the front page and the Sunday supplement. Job enrichment, which began with the pioneering work of Herzberg and his associates, originally was intended as a means to increase the motivation and satisfaction of people at work—and to improve productivity in the bargain.[1-5] Now it is being acclaimed in the popular press as a cure for problems ranging from inflation to drug abuse.

Much current writing about job enrichment is enthusiastic, sometimes even messianic, about what it can accomplish. But the hard questions of exactly what should be done to improve jobs, and how, tend to be glossed over. Lately, because the harder questions have not been dealt with adequately, critical winds have begun to blow. Job enrichment has been described as yet another "management fad," as "nothing new," even as a fraud. And reports of job-enrichment failures are beginning to appear in management and psychology journals.

This article attempts to redress the excesses that have characterized some of the recent writ-

© by the Regents of the University of California. Reprinted from the *California Management Review,* volume XVII, number 4, pp. 57 to 72 by permission of the Regents.

ings about job enrichment. As the technique increases in popularity as a management tool, top managers inevitably will find themselves making decisions about its use. The intent of this paper is to help both managers and behavioral scientists become better able to make those decisions on a solid basis of fact and data.

Succinctly stated, we present here a new strategy for going about the redesign of work. The strategy is based on three years of collaborative work and cross-fertilization among the authors—two of whom are academic researchers and two of whom are active practitioners in job enrichment. Our approach is new, but it has been tested in many organizations. It draws on the contributions of both management practice and psychological theory, but it is firmly in the middle ground between them. It builds on and complements previous work by Herzberg and others, but provides for the first time a set of tools for *diagnosing* existing jobs—and a map for translating the diagnostic results into specific action steps for change.

What we have, then, is the following:

1. A theory that specifies when people will get personally "turned on" to their work. The theory shows what kinds of jobs are most likely to generate excitement and commitment about work, and what kinds of employees it works best for.

2. A set of action steps for job enrichment based on the theory, which prescribe in concrete terms what to do to make jobs more motivating for the people who do them.

3. Evidence that the theory holds water and that it can be used to bring about measurable —and sometimes dramatic—improvements in employee work behavior, in job satisfaction, and in the financial performance of the organizational unit involved.

The Theory Behind the Strategy

What Makes People Get Turned on to Their Work? For workers who are really prospering in their jobs, work is likely to be a lot like play. Consider, for example, a golfer at a driving range, practicing to get rid of a hook. His activity is *meaningful* to him; he has chosen to do it because he gets a "kick" from testing his skills by playing the game. He knows that he alone is *responsible* for what happens when he hits the ball. And he has *knowledge of the results* within a few seconds.

Behavioral scientists have found that the three "psychological states" experienced by the golfer in the above example also are critical in determining a person's motivation and satisfaction on the job.

• Experienced meaningfulness: The individual must perceive his work as worthwhile or important by some system of values he accepts.

• Experienced responsibility: He must believe that he personally is accountable for the outcomes of his efforts.

• Knowledge of results: He must be able to determine, on some fairly regular basis, whether or not the outcomes of his work are satisfactory.

When these three conditions are present, a person tends to feel very good about himself when he performs well. And those good feelings will prompt him to try to continue to do well—so he can continue to earn the positive feelings in the future. That is what is meant by "internal motivation"—being turned on to one's work because of the positive internal feelings that are generated by doing well, rather than being dependent on external factors (such as incentive pay or com-

pliments from the boss) for the motivation to work effectively.

What if one of the three psychological states is missing? Motivation drops markedly. Suppose, for example, that our golfer has settled in at the driving range to practice for a couple of hours. Suddenly a fog drifts in over the range. He can no longer see if the ball starts to tail off to the left a hundred yards out. The satisfaction he got from hitting straight down the middle—and the motivation to try to correct something whenever he didn't—are both gone. If the fog stays, it's likely that he soon will be packing up his clubs.

The relationship between the three psychological states and on-the-job outcomes is illustrated in Figure 1. When all three are high, then internal work motivation, job satisfaction, and work quality are high, and absenteeism and turnover are low.

What Job Characteristics Make It Happen? Recent research has identified five "core" characteristics of jobs that elicit the psychological states described above.[6-8] These five core job dimensions provide the key to objectively measuring jobs and to changing them so that they have high potential for motivating people who do them.

• Toward meaningful work. Three of the five core dimensions contribute to a job's meaningfulness for the worker:

1. Skill Variety—the degree to which a job requires the worker to perform activities that challenge his skills and abilities. When even a single skill is involved, there is at least a seed of potential meaningfulness. When several are involved, the job has the potential of appealing to more of the whole person, and also of avoiding the monotony of performing the same task repeatedly, no matter how much skill it may require.

2. Task Identity—the degree to which the job requires completion of a "whole" and identifiable piece of work—doing a job from beginning to end with a visible outcome. For example, it is clearly more meaningful to an employee to build complete toasters than to attach electrical cord after electrical cord, especially if he never sees a completed toaster. (Note that the whole job, in this example,

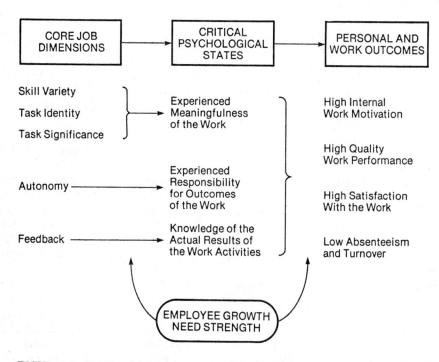

FIGURE 1. Relationships among core job dimensions, critical psychological states, and on-the-job outcomes.

probably would involve greater skill variety as well as task identity.)

3. Task Significance—the degree to which the job has a substantial and perceivable impact on the lives of other people, whether in the immediate organization or the world at large. The worker who tightens nuts on aircraft brake assemblies is more likely to perceive his work as significant than the worker who fills small boxes with paper clips—even though the skill levels involved may be comparable.

Each of these three job dimensions represents an important route to experienced meaningfulness. If the job is high in all three, the worker is quite likely to experience his job as very meaningful. It is not necessary, however, for a job to be very high in all three dimensions. If the job is low in any one of them, there will be a drop in overall experienced meaningfulness. But even when two dimensions are low the worker may

find the job meaningful if the third is high enough.

• Toward personal responsibility. A fourth core dimension leads a worker to experience increased responsibility in his job. This is *autonomy,* the degree to which the job gives the worker freedom, independence, and discretion in scheduling work and determining how he will carry it out. People in highly autonomous jobs know that they are personally responsible for successes and failures. To the extent that their autonomy is high, then, how the work goes will be felt to depend more on the individual's own efforts and initiatives—rather than on detailed instructions from the boss or from a manual of job procedures.

• Toward knowledge of results. The fifth and last core dimension is *feedback.* This is the degree to which a worker, in carrying out the work activities required by the job, gets information about the effectiveness of his efforts. Feedback is most powerful when it comes directly from the work itself—for example, when a worker has the responsibility for gauging and otherwise checking a component he has just finished, and learns in the process that he has lowered his reject rate by meeting specifications more consistently.

• The overall "motivating potential" of a job. Figure 1 shows how the five core dimensions combine to affect the psychological states that are critical in determining whether or not an employee will be internally motivated to work effectively. Indeed, when using an instrument to be described later, it is possible to compute a "motivating potential score" (MPS) for any job. The MPS provides a single summary index of the degree to which the objective characteristics of the job will prompt high internal work motivation. Following the theory outlined above, a job high in motivating potential must be high in at least one (and hopefully more) of the three dimensions that lead to experienced meaningfulness and high in both autonomy and feedback as well. The MPS provides a quantitative index of the degree to which this is in fact the case (see Appendix for detailed formula). As will be seen later, the MPS can be very useful in diagnosing jobs and in assessing the effectiveness of job-enrichment activities.

Does the Theory Work for Everybody? Unfortunately not. Not everyone is able to become internally motivated in his work, even when the motivating potential of a job is very high indeed.

Research has shown that the *psychological needs* of people are very important in determining who can (and who cannot) become internally motivated at work. Some people have strong needs for personal accomplishment, for learning and developing themselves beyond where they are now, for being stimulated and challenged, and so on. These people are high in "growth-need strength."

Figure 2 shows diagrammatically the proposition that individual growth needs have the power to moderate the relationship between the characteristics of jobs and work outcomes. Many workers with high growth needs will turn on eagerly when they have jobs that are high in the core dimensions. Workers whose growth needs are not so strong may respond less eagerly—or, at first, even balk at being "pushed" or "stretched" too far.

Psychologists who emphasize human potential argue that everyone has within him at least a spark of the need to grow and develop personally. Steadily accumulating evidence shows, however, that unless that spark is pretty strong, chances are it will get snuffed out by one's experiences in typical organizations. So, a person who has worked for twenty years in stultifying jobs may find it difficult or impossible to become internally motivated overnight when given the opportunity.

We should be cautious, however, about creating rigid categories of people based on their measured growth-need strength at any particular time. It is true that we can predict from these measures who is likely to become internally motivated on a job and who will be less willing or

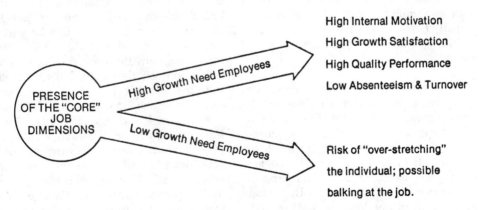

FIGURE 2. The moderating effect of employee growth-need strength.

able to do so. But what we do not know yet is whether or not the growth-need "spark" can be rekindled for those individuals who have had their growth needs dampened by years of growth-depressing experience in their organizations.

Since it is often the organization that is responsible for currently low levels of growth desires, we believe that the organization also should provide the individual with the chance to reverse that trend whenever possible, even if that means putting a person in a job where he may be "stretched" more than he wants to be. He can always move back later to the old job—and in the meantime the embers of his growth needs just might burst back into flame, to his surprise and pleasure, and for the good of the organization.

FROM THEORY TO PRACTICE: A TECHNOLOGY FOR JOB ENRICHMENT

When job enrichment fails, it often fails because of inadequate *diagnosis* of the target job and employees' reactions to it. Often, for example, job enrichment is assumed by management to be a solution to "people problems" on the job and is implemented even though there has been no diagnostic activity to indicate that the root of the problem is in fact how the work is designed. At other times, some diagnosis is made—but it provides no concrete guidance about what specific aspects of the job require change. In either case, the success of job enrichment may wind up depending more on the quality of the intuition of the change agent—or his luck—than on a solid base of data about the people and the work.

In the paragraphs to follow, we outline a new technology for use in job enrichment which explicitly addresses the diagnostic as well as the action components of the change process. The technology has two parts: (1) a set of diagnostic tools that are useful in evaluating jobs and people's reactions to them prior to change—and in pinpointing exactly what aspects of specific jobs are most critical to a successful change attempt; and (2) a set of "implementing concepts" that provide concrete guidance for action steps in job enrichment. The implementing concepts are tied directly to the diagnostic tools; the output of the

diagnostic activity specifies which action steps are likely to have the most impact in a particular situation.

The Diagnostic Tools. Central to the diagnostic procedure we propose is a package of instruments to be used by employees, supervisors, and outside observers in assessing the target job and employees' reactions to it.[9] These instruments gauge the following:

1. The objective characteristics of the jobs themselves, including both an overall indication of the "motivating potential" of the job as it exists (that is, the MPS score) and the score of the job on each of the five core dimensions described previously. Because knowing the strengths and weaknesses of the job is critical to any work-redesign effort, assessments of the job are made by supervisors and outside observers as well as the employees themselves—and the final assessment of a job uses data from all three sources.

2. The current levels of motivation, satisfaction, and work performance of employees on the job. In addition to satisfaction with the work itself, measures are taken of how people feel about other aspects of the work setting, such as pay, supervision, and relationships with co-workers.

3. The level of growth-need strength of the employees. As indicated earlier, employees who have strong growth needs are more likely to be more responsive to job enrichment than employees with weak growth needs. Therefore, it is important to know at the outset just what kinds of satisfactions the people who do the job are (and are not) motivated to obtain from their work. This will make it possible to identify which persons are best to start changes with, and which may need help in adapting to the newly enriched job.

What, then, might be the actual steps one would take in carrying out a job diagnosis using these tools? Although the approach to any particular diagnosis depends upon the specifics of the particular work situation involved, the sequence of questions listed below is fairly typical.

Step 1. Are Motivation and Satisfaction Central to the Problem? (Sometimes organizations undertake job enrichment to improve the work motivation and satisfaction of employees when in fact the real problem with work performance lies elsewhere—for example, in a poorly designed production system, in an error-prone computer, and so on. The first step is to examine the scores of employees on the motivation and satisfaction portions of the diagnostic instrument. (The questionnaire taken by employees is called the Job Diagnostic Survey and will be referred to hereafter as the JDS). If motivation and satisfaction are problematic, the change agent would continue to Step 2; if not, he would look to other aspects of the work situation to identify the real problem.

Step 2. Is the Job Low in Motivational Potential? To answer this question, one would examine the motivating potential score of the target job and compare it to the MPS's of other jobs to determine whether or not *the job itself* is a probable cause of the motivational problems documented in Step 1. If the job turns out to be low on the MPS, one would continue to Step 3; if it scores high, attention should be given to other possible reasons for the motivational difficulties (such as the pay system, the nature of supervision, and so on).

Step 3. What Specific Aspects of the Job Are Causing the Difficulty? This step involves examining the job on each of the five core dimensions to pinpoint the specific strengths and weaknesses of the job as it is currently structured. It is useful at this stage to construct a "profile" of the target job, to make visually apparent where improvements need to be made. An illustrative profile for two jobs (one "good" job and one job needing improvement) is shown in Figure 3.

Job A is an engineering maintenance job and is high on all of the core dimensions; the MPS of this job is a very high 260. MPS scores can range from 1 to about 350; an "average" score would be about 125.) Job enrichment would not be recommended for this job; if employees work-

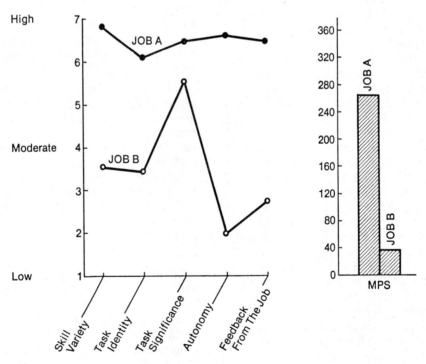

FIGURE 3. The JDS diagnostic profile for a "good" and a "bad" job.

ing on the job were unproductive and unhappy, the reasons are likely to have little to do with the nature or design of the work itself.

Job B, on the other hand, has many problems. This job involves the routine and repetitive processing of checks in the "back room" of a bank. The MPS is 30, which is quite low—and indeed, would be even lower if it were not for the moderately high task significance of the job. (Task significance is moderately high because the people are handling large amounts of other people's money, and therefore the quality of their efforts potentially has important consequences for their unseen clients.) The job provides the individuals with very little direct feedback about how effectively they are doing it; the employees have little autonomy in how they go about doing the job; and the job is moderately low in both skill variety and task identity.

For Job B, then, there is plenty of room for improvement—and many avenues to examine in planning job changes. For still other jobs, the avenues for change often turn out to be considerably more specific: for example, feedback and autonomy may be reasonably high, but one or more of the core dimensions that contribute to the experienced meaningfulness of the job (skill variety, task identity, and task significance) may be low. In such a case, attention would turn to ways to increase the standing of the job on these latter three dimensions.

Step 4. How "Ready" Are the Employees for Change? Once it has been documented that there is need for improvement in the job—and the particularly troublesome aspects of the job have been identified—then it is time to begin to think about the specific action steps which will be taken to enrich the job. An important factor in such planning is the level of growth needs of the employees, since employees high on growth needs usually respond more readily to job enrichment than do employees with little need for growth. The JDS provides a direct measure of the growth-need strength of the employees. This measure can be very helpful in planning how to introduce the changes to the people (for instance, cautiously versus dramatically), and in deciding who should

be among the first group of employees to have their jobs changed.

In actual use of the diagnostic package, additional information is generated which supplements and expands the basic diagnostic questions outlined above. The point of the above discussion is merely to indicate the kinds of questions which we believe to be most important in diagnosing a job prior to changing it. We now turn to how the diagnostic conclusions are translated into specific job changes.

The Implementing Concepts. Five "implementing concepts" for job enrichment are identified and discussed below.[10] Each one is a specific action step aimed at improving both the quality of the working experience for the individual and his work productivity. They are: (1) forming natural work units; (2) combining tasks; (3) establishing client relationships; (4) vertical loading; (5) opening feedback channels.

The links between the implementing concepts and the core dimensions are shown in Figure 4—which illustrates our theory of job enrichment, ranging from the concrete action steps through the core dimensions and the psychological states to the actual personal and work outcomes.

After completing the diagnosis of a job, a change agent would know which of the core dimensions were most in need of remedial attention. He could then turn to Figure 4 and select those implementing concepts that specifically deal with the most troublesome parts of the existing job. How this would take place in practice will be seen below.

• Forming natural work units. The notion of distributing work in some logical way may seem to be an obvious part of the design of any job. In many cases, however, the logic is one imposed by just about any consideration except jobholder satisfaction and motivation. Such considerations include technological dictates, level of worker training or experience, "efficiency" as defined by industrial engineering, and current workload. In many cases the cluster of tasks a worker faces during a typical day or week is natural to anyone *but* the worker.

For example, suppose that a typing pool (con-

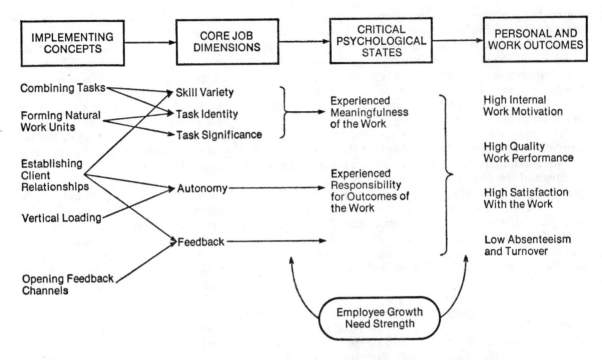

FIGURE 4. The full model: how use of the implementing concepts can lead to positive outcomes.

sisting of one supervisor and ten typists) handles all work for one division of a company. Jobs are delivered in rough draft or dictated form to the supervisor, who distributes them as evenly as possible among the typists. In such circumstances the individual letters, reports, and other tasks performed by a given typist in one day or week are randomly assigned. There is no basis for identifying with the work or the person or department for whom it is performed, or for placing any personal value upon it.

The principle underlying natural units of work, by contrast, is "ownership"—a worker's sense of continuing responsibility for an identifiable body of work. Two steps are involved in creating natural work units. The first is to identify the basic work items. In the typing pool, for example, the items might be "pages to be typed." The second step is to group the items in natural categories. For example, each typist might be assigned continuing responsibility for all jobs requested by one or several specific departments. The assignments should be made, of course, in such a way that workloads are about equal in the long run.

(For example, one typist might end up with all the work from one busy department, while another handles jobs from several smaller units.)

At this point we can begin to see specifically how the job-design principles relate to the core dimensions (cf. Figure 4). The ownership fostered by natural units of work can make the difference between a feeling that work is meaningful and rewarding and the feeling that it is irrelevant and boring. As the diagram shows, natural units of work are directly related to two of the core dimensions: task identity and task significance.

A typist whose work is assigned naturally rather than randomly—say, by departments—has a much greater chance of performing a whole job to completion. Instead of typing one section of a large report, the individual is likely to type the whole thing, with knowledge of exactly what the product of the work is (task identity). Furthermore, over time the typist will develop a growing sense of how the work affects co-workers in the department serviced (task significance).

• Combining tasks. The very existence of a

pool made up entirely of persons whose sole function is typing reflects a fractionalization of jobs that has been a base precept of "scientific management." Most obvious in assembly-line work, fractionalization has been applied to nonmanufacturing jobs as well. It is typically justified by efficiency, which is usually defined in terms of either low costs or some time-and-motion type of criteria.

It is hard to find fault with measuring efficiency ultimately in terms of cost-effectiveness. In doing so, however, a manager should be sure to consider *all* the costs involved. It is possible, for example, for highly fractionalized jobs to meet all the time-and-motion criteria of efficiency, but if the resulting job is so unrewarding that performing it day after day leads to high turnover, absenteeism, drugs and alcohol, and strikes, then productivity is really lower (and costs higher) than data on efficiency might indicate.

The principle of combining tasks, then, suggests that whenever possible existing and fractionalized tasks should be put together to form new and larger modules of work. At the Medfield, Massachusetts plant of Corning Glass Works the assembly of a laboratory hot plate has been redesigned along the lines suggested here. Each hot plate now is assembled from start to finish by one operator, instead of going through several separate operations that are performed by different people.

Some tasks, if combined into a meaningfully large module of work, would be more than an individual could do by himself. In such cases, it is often useful to consider assigning the new, larger task to a small *team* of workers—who are given great autonomy for its completion. At the Racine, Wisconsin plant of Emerson Electric, the assembly process for trash disposal appliances was restructured this way. Instead of a sequence of moving the appliance from station to station, the assembly now is done from start to finish by one team. Such teams include both men and women to permit switching off the heavier and more delicate aspects of the work. The team responsible is identified on the appliance. In case of customer complaints, the team often drafts the reply.

As a job-design principle, task combination,

like natural units of work, expands the task identity of the job. For example, the hot-plate assembler can see and identify with a finished product ready for shipment, rather than a nearly invisible junction of solder. Moreover, the more tasks that are combined into a single worker's job, the greater the variety of skills he must call on in performing the job. So task combination also leads directly to greater skill variety—the third core dimension that contributes to the overall experienced meaningfulness of the work.

• Establishing client relationships. One consequence of fractionalization is that the typical worker has little or no contact with (or even awareness of) the ultimate user of his product or service. By encouraging and enabling employees to establish direct relationships with the clients of their work, improvements often can be realized simultaneously on three of the core dimensions. Feedback increases, because of additional opportunities for the individual to receive praise or criticism of his work outputs directly. Skill variety often increases, because of the necessity to develop and exercise one's interpersonal skills in maintaining the client relationship. And autonomy can increase because the individual often is given personal responsibility for deciding how to manage his relationships with the clients of his work.

Creating client relationships is a three-step process. First, the client must be identified. Second, the most direct contact possible between the worker and the client must be established. Third, criteria must be set up by which the client can judge the quality of the product or service he receives. And whenever possible, the client should have a means of relaying his judgments directly back to the worker.

The contact between worker and client should be as great as possible and as frequent as necessary. Face-to-face contact is highly desirable, at least occasionally. Where that is impossible or impractical, telephone and mail can suffice. In any case, it is important that the performance criteria by which the worker will be rated by the client must be mutually understood and agreed upon.

• Vertical loading. Typically the split between the "doing" of a job and the "planning" and "controlling" of the work has evolved along with horizontal fractionalization. Its rationale, once again, has been "efficiency through specialization." And once again, the excess of specialization that has emerged has resulted in unexpected but significant costs in motivation, morale, and work quality. In vertical loading, the intent is to partially close the gap between the doing and the controlling parts of the job—and thereby reap some important motivational advantages.

Of all the job-design principles, vertical loading may be the single most crucial one. In some cases, where it has been impossible to implement any other changes, vertical loading alone has had significant motivational effects.

When a job is vertically loaded, responsibilities and controls that formerly were reserved for higher levels of management are added to the job. There are many ways to accomplish this:

• Return to the job holder greater discretion in setting schedules, deciding on work methods, checking on quality, and advising or helping to train less experienced workers.

• Grant additional authority. The objective should be to advance workers from a position of no authority or highly restricted authority to positions of reviewed, and eventually, near-total authority for his own work.

• Time management. The job holder should have the greatest possible freedom to decide when to start and stop work, when to break, and how to assign priorities.

• Troubleshooting and crisis decisions. Workers should be encouraged to seek problem solutions on their own, rather than calling immediately for the supervisor.

• Financial controls. Some degree of knowledge and control over budgets and other financial aspects of a job can often be highly motivating. However, access to this information frequently tends to be restricted. Workers can benefit from knowing something about the costs of their jobs, the potential effect upon profit, and various financial and budgetary alternatives.

When a job is vertically loaded it will inevitably increase in *autonomy*. And as shown in Figure 4, this increase in objective personal con-

trol over the work will also lead to an increased feeling of personal responsibility for the work, and ultimately to higher internal work motivation.

• Opening feedback channels. In virtually all jobs there are ways to open channels of feedback to individuals or teams to help them learn whether their performance is improving, deteriorating, or remaining at a constant level. While there are numerous channels through which information about performance can be provided, it generally is better for a worker to learn about his performance *directly as he does his job*—rather than from management on an occasional basis.

Job-provided feedback usually is more immediate and private than supervisor-supplied feedback, and it increases the worker's feelings of personal control over his work in the bargain. Moreover, it avoids many of the potentially disruptive interpersonal problems that can develop when the only way a worker has to find out how he is doing is through direct messages or subtle cues from the boss.

Exactly what should be done to open channels for job-provided feedback will vary from job to job and organization to organization. Yet in many cases the changes involve simply removing existing blocks that isolate the worker from naturally occurring data about performance—rather than generating entirely new feedback mechanisms. For example:

• Establishing direct client relationships often removes blocks between the worker and natural external sources of data about his work.

• Quality-control efforts in many organizations often eliminate a natural source of feedback. The quality check on a product or service is done by persons other than those responsible for the work. Feedback to the workers—if there is any—is belated and diluted. It often fosters a tendency to think of quality as "someone else's concern." By placing quality control close to the worker (perhaps even in his own hands), the quantity and quality of data about performance available to him can dramatically increase.

• Tradition and established procedure in many organizations dictate that records about performance be kept by a supervisor and transmitted up (not down) in the organizational hierarchy.

Sometimes supervisors even check the work and correct any errors themselves. The worker who made the error never knows it occurred—and is denied the very information that could enhance both his internal work motivation and the technical adequacy of his performance. In many cases it is possible to provide standard summaries of performance records directly to the worker (as well as to his superior), thereby giving him personally and regularly the data he needs to improve his performance.

• Computers and other automated operations sometimes can be used to provide the individual with data now blocked from him. Many clerical operations, for example, are now performed on computer consoles. These consoles often can be programmed to provide the clerk with immediate feedback in the form of a CRT display or a print-out indicating that an error has been made. Some systems even have been programmed to provide the operator with a positive feedback message when a period of error-free performance has been sustained.

Many organizations simply have not recognized the importance of feedback as a motivator. Data on quality and other aspects of performance are viewed as being of interest only to management. Worse still, the *standards* for acceptable performance often are kept from the workers as well. As a result, workers who would be interested in following the daily or weekly ups and downs of their performance, and in trying accordingly to improve, are deprived of the very guidelines they need to do so. They are like the golfer we mentioned earlier, whose efforts to correct his hook are stopped dead by fog over the driving range.

THE STRATEGY IN ACTION: HOW WELL DOES IT WORK?

So far we have examined a basic theory of how people get turned on to their work; a set of core dimensions of jobs that create the conditions for such internal work motivation to develop on the job; and a set of five implementing concepts that are the action steps recommended to boost a job on the core dimensions and thereby increase employee motivation, satisfaction, and productivity.

The remaining question is straightforward and important: *Does it work?* In reality, that question is twofold. First, does the theory itself hold water, or are we barking up the wrong conceptual tree? And second, does the change strategy really lead to measurable differences when it is applied in an actual organizational setting?

This section summarizes the findings we have generated to date on these questions.

Is the Job-Enrichment Theory Correct? In general, the answer seems to be yes. The JDS instrument has been taken by more than 1,000 employees working on about 100 diverse jobs in more than a dozen organizations over the last two years. These data have been analyzed to test the basic motivational theory—and especially the impact of the core job dimensions on worker motivation, satisfaction, and behavior on the job. An illustrative overview of some of the findings is given below.[8]

1. People who work on jobs high on the core dimensions are more motivated and satisfied than are people who work on jobs that score low on the dimensions. Employees with jobs high on the core dimensions (MPS scores greater than 240) were compared to those who held unmotivating jobs (MPS scores less than 40). As shown in Figure 5 employees with high MPS jobs were higher on (a) the three psychological states, (b) internal work motivation, (c) general satisfaction, and (d) "growth" satisfaction.

2. Figure 6 shows that the same is true for measures of actual behavior at work—absenteeism and performance effectiveness—although less strongly so for the performance measure.

3. Responses to jobs high in motivating potential are more positive for people who have strong growth needs than for people with weak needs for growth. In Figure 7 the linear relationship between the motivating potential of a job and employees' level of internal work motivation is shown, separately for people with high versus low growth needs as measured by the JDS. While both groups of employees show increases in internal motivation as MPS increases, the *rate* of increase is significantly greater for the group of employees who have strong needs for growth.

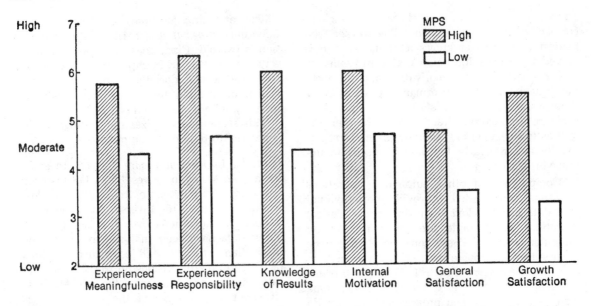

FIGURE 5. Employee reactions to jobs high and low in motivating potential for two banks and a steel firm.

How Does the Change Strategy Work in Practice? The results summarized above suggest that both the theory and the diagnostic instrument work when used with real people in real organizations. In this section, we summarize a job-enrichment project conducted at The Travelers Insurance Companies, which illustrates how the change procedures themselves work in practice.

The Travelers project was designed with two purposes in mind. One was to achieve improve-

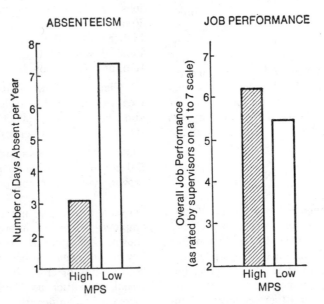

FIGURE 6. Absenteeism and job performance for employees with jobs high and low in motivating potential.

ments in morale, productivity, and other indicators of employee well-being. The other was to test the general effectiveness of the strategy for job enrichment we have summarized in this article.

The work group chosen was a keypunching operation. The group's function was to transfer information from printed or written documents onto punched cards for computer input. The work group consisted of ninety-eight keypunch operators and verifiers (both in the same job classification), plus seven assignment clerks. All reported to a supervisor who, in turn, reported to the assistant manager and manager of the data-input division.

The size of individual punching orders varied considerably, from a few cards to as many as 2,500. Some work came to the work group with a specified delivery date, while other orders were to be given routine service on a predetermined schedule.

Assignment clerks received the jobs from the user departments. After reviewing the work for obvious errors, omissions, and legibility problems, the assignment clerk parceled out the work in batches expected to take about one hour. If the clerk found the work not suitable for punching it went to the supervisor, who either returned the work to the user department or cleared up problems by phone. When work went to operators for punching, it was with the instruction, "Punch only what you see. Don't correct errors, no matter how obvious they look."

Because of the high cost of computer time, keypunched work was 100 percent verified—a task that consumed nearly as many man-hours as the punching itself. Then the cards went to the supervisor, who screened the jobs for due dates before sending them to the computer. Errors detected in verification were assigned to various operators at random to be corrected.

The computer output from the cards was sent to the originating department, accompanied by a printout of errors. Eventually the printout went back to the supervisor for final correction.

A great many phenomena indicated that the problems being experienced in the work group might be the result of poor motivation. As the only person performing supervisory functions of

FIGURE 7. Relationship between the motivating potential of a job and the internal work motivation of employees. (Shown separately for employees with strong versus weak growth-need strength.)

any kind, the supervisor spent most of his time responding to crisis situations, which recurred continually. He also had to deal almost daily with employees' salary grievances or other complaints. Employees frequently showed apathy or outright hostility toward their jobs.

Rates of work output, by accepted work-measurement standards, were inadequate. Error rates were high. Due dates and schedules frequently were missed. Absenteeism was higher than average, especially before and after weekends and holidays.

The single, rather unusual exception was turnover. It was lower than the companywide average for similar jobs. The company has attributed this fact to a poor job market in the base period just before the project began, and to an older, relatively more settled work force—made up, incidentally, entirely of women.

The Diagnosis. Using some of the tools and techniques we have outlined, a consulting team from the Management Services Department and from

Roy W. Walters & Associates concluded that the keypunch-operator's job exhibited the following serious weaknesses in terms of the core dimensions.

- Skill variety: there was none. Only a single skill was involved—the ability to punch adequately the data on the batch of documents.
- Task identity: virtually nonexistent. Batches were assembled to provide an even workload, but not whole identifiable jobs.
- Task significance: not apparent. The keypunching operation was a necessary step in providing service to the company's customers. The individual operator was isolated by an assignment clerk and a supervisor from any knowledge of what the operation meant to the using department, let alone its meaning to the ultimate customer.
- Autonomy: none. The operators had no freedom to arrange their daily tasks to meet schedules, to resolve problems with the using department, or even to correct, in punching, information that was obviously wrong.
- Feedback: none. Once a batch was out of the operator's hands, she had no assured chance of seeing evidence of its quality or inadequacy.

Design of the Experimental Trial. Since the diagnosis indicated that the motivating potential of the job was extremely low, it was decided to attempt to improve the motivation and productivity of the work group through job enrichment. Moreover, it was possible to design an experimental test of the effects of the changes to be introduced: the results of changes made in the target work group were to be compared with trends in a control work group of similar size and demographic make-up. Since the control group was located more than a mile away, there appeared to be little risk of communication between members of the two groups.

A base period was defined before the start of the experimental trial period, and appropriate data were gathered on the productivity, absenteeism, and work attitudes of members of both groups. Data also were available on turnover; but since turnover was already below average in the

target group, prospective changes in this measure were deemed insignificant.

An educational session was conducted with supervisors, at which they were given the theory and implementing concepts and actually helped to design the job changes themselves. Out of this session came an active plan consisting of about twenty-five change items that would significantly affect the design of the target jobs.

The Implementing Concepts and the Changes. Because the job as it existed was rather uniformly low on the core job dimensions, all five of the implementing concepts were used in enriching it.

- Natural units of work. The random batch assignment of work was replaced by assigning to each operator continuing responsibility for certain accounts—either particular departments or particular recurring jobs. Any work for those accounts now always goes to the same operator.
- Task combination. Some planning and controlling functions were combined with the central task of keypunching. In this case, however, these additions can be more suitably discussed under the remaining three implementing concepts.
- Client relationships. Each operator was given several channels of direct contact with clients. The operators, not their assignment clerks, now inspect their documents for correctness and legibility. When problems arise, the operator, not the supervisor, takes them up with the client.
- Feedback. In addition to feedback from client contact, the operators were provided with a number of additional sources of data about their performance. The computer department now returns incorrect cards to the operators who punched them, and operators correct their own errors. Each operator also keeps her own file of copies of her errors. These can be reviewed to determine trends in error frequency and types of errors. Each operator receives weekly a computer printout of her errors and productivity, which is sent to her directly, rather than given to her by the supervisor.
- Vertical loading. Besides consulting directly with clients about work questions, operators now have the authority to correct obvious coding errors on their own. Operators may set their own

schedules and plan their daily work, as long as they meet schedules. Some competent operators have been given the option of not verifying their work and making their own program changes.

Results of the Trial. The results were dramatic. The number of operators declined from ninety-eight to sixty. This occurred partly through attrition and partly through transfer to other departments. Some of the operators were promoted to higher-paying jobs in departments whose cards they had been handling—something that had never occurred before. Some details of the results are given below.

- Quantity of work. The control group, with no job changes made, showed an increase in productivity of 8.1 percent during the trial period. The experimental group showed an increase of 39.6 percent.

- Error rates. To assess work quality, error rates were recorded for about forty operators in the experimental group. All were experienced, and all had been in their jobs before the job-enrichment program began. For two months before the study, these operators had a collective error rate of 1.53 percent. For two months toward the end of the study, the collective error rate was 0.99 percent. By the end of the study the number of operators with poor performance had dropped from 11.1 percent to 5.5 percent.

- Absenteeism. The experimental group registered a 24.1 percent decline in absences. The control group, by contrast, showed a 29 percent *increase*.

- Attitudes toward the job. An attitude survey given at the start of the project showed that the two groups scored about average, and nearly identically, in nine different areas of work satisfaction. At the end of the project the survey was repeated. The control group showed an insignificant 0.5 percent improvement, while the experimental group's overall satisfaction score rose 16.5 percent.

- Selective elimination of controls. Demonstrated improvements in operator proficiency permitted them to work with fewer controls. Travelers estimates that the reduction of controls had the same effect as adding seven operators—a sav-

ing even beyond the effects of improved productivity and lowered absenteeism.

- Role of the supervisor. One of the most significant findings in the Travelers experiment was the effect of the changes on the supervisor's job, and thus on the rest of the organization. The operators took on many responsibilities that had been reserved at least to the unit leaders and sometimes to the supervisor. The unit leaders, in turn, assumed some of the day-to-day supervisory functions that had plagued the supervisor. Instead of spending his days supervising the behavior of subordinates and dealing with crises, he was able to devote time to developing feedback systems, setting up work modules and spearheading the enrichment effort—in other words, managing. It should be noted, however, that helping supervisors change their own work activities when their subordinates' jobs have been enriched is itself a challenging task. And if appropriate attention and help are not given to supervisors in such cases, they rapidly can become disaffected—and a job-enrichment "backlash" can result.[11]

Summary. By applying work-measurement standards to the changes wrought by job enrichment—attitude and quality, absenteeism, and selective administration of controls—Travelers was able to estimate the total dollar impact of the project. Actual savings in salaries and machine rental charges during the first year totaled $64,305. Potential savings by further application of the changes were put at $91,937 annually. Thus, by almost any measure used—from the work attitudes of individual employees to dollar savings for the company as a whole—The Travelers test of the job-enrichment strategy proved a success.

CONCLUSIONS

In this article we have presented a new strategy for the redesign of work in general and for job enrichment in particular. The approach has four main characteristics:

1. It is grounded in a basic psychological theory of what motivates people in their work.
2. It emphasizes that planning for job changes

should be done on the basis of *data* about the jobs and the people who do them—and a set of diagnostic instruments is provided to collect such data.

3. It provides a set of specific implementing concepts to guide actual job changes, as well as a set of theory-based rules for selecting *which* action steps are likely to be most beneficial in a given situation.

4. The strategy is buttressed by a set of findings showing that the theory holds water, that the diagnostic procedures are practical and informative, and that the implementing concepts can lead to changes that are beneficial both to organizations and to the people who work in them.

We believe that job enrichment is moving beyond the stage where it can be considered "yet another management fad." Instead, it represents a potentially powerful strategy for change that can help organizations achieve their goals for higher quality work—and at the same time further the equally legitimate needs of contemporary employees for a more meaningful work experience. Yet there are pressing questions about job enrichment and its use that remain to be answered.

Prominent among these is the question of employee participation in planning and implementing work redesign. The diagnostic tools and implementing concepts we have presented are neither designed nor intended for use only by management. Rather, our belief is that the effectiveness of job enrichment is likely to be enhanced when the tasks of diagnosing and changing jobs are undertaken *collaboratively* by management and by the employees whose work will be affected.

Moreover, the effects of work redesign on the broader organization remain generally uncharted. Evidence now is accumulating that when jobs are changed, turbulence can appear in the surrounding organization—for example, in supervisory-subordinate relationships, in pay and benefit plans, and so on. Such turbulence can be viewed by management either as a problem with job enrichment, or as an opportunity for further and broader organizational development by teams of managers and employees. To the degree that management takes the latter view, we believe, the oft-espoused goal of achieving basic organizational change through the redesign of work may come increasingly within reach.

The diagnostic tools and implementing concepts we have presented are useful in deciding on and designing basic changes in the jobs themselves. They do not address the broader issues of who plans the changes, how they are carried out, and how they are followed up. The way these broader questions are dealt with, we believe, may determine whether job enrichment will grow up—or whether it will die an early and unfortunate death, like so many other fledgling behavioral-science approaches to organizational change.

Appendix

For the algebraically inclined, the Motivating Potential Score is computed as follows

$$MPS = \left[\frac{\text{Skill Variety} + \text{Task Identity} + \text{Task Significance}}{3} \right] \times \text{Autonomy} \times \text{Feedback}$$

It should be noted that in some cases the MPS score can be *too* high for positive job satisfaction and effective performance—in effect overstimulating the person who holds the job. This paper focuses on jobs which are toward the low end of the scale—and which potentially can be improved through job enrichment.

Acknowledgments:
The authors acknowledge with great appreciation the editorial assistance of John Hickey in the preparation of this paper, and the help of Kenneth Brousseau, Daniel Feldman, and Linda Frank in collecting the data that are summarized here. The research activities reported were supported in part by the Organizational Effectiveness Research Program of the Office of Naval Research, and the Manpower Administration of the U.S. Department of Labor, both through contracts to Yale University.

REFERENCES

1. F. Herzberg, B. Mausner and B. Snyderman, *The Motivation to Work* (New York: John Wiley & Sons, 1959).

2. F. Herzberg, *Work and the Nature of Man* (Cleveland: World, 1966).

3. F. Herzberg, "One More Time: How Do you Motivate Employees?" *Harvard Business Review* (1968), pp. 53–62.

4. W. J. Paul, Jr.; K. B. Robertson and F. Herzberg, "Job Enrichment Pays Off," *Harvard Business Review* (1969), pp. 61–78.

5. R. N. Ford, *Motivation Through the Work Itself* (New York: American Management Association, 1969).

6. A. N. Turner and P. R. Lawrence, *Industrial Jobs and the Worker* (Cambridge, Mass.: Harvard Graduate School of Business Administration, 1965).

7. J. R. Hackman and E. E. Lawler, "Employee Reactions to Job Characteristics," *Journal of Applied Psychology Monograph* (1971), pp. 259–286.

8. J. R. Hackman and G. R. Oldham, *Motivation Through the Design of Work: Test of a Theory,* Technical Report No. 6, Department of Administrative Sciences, Yale University, 1974.

9. J. R. Hackman and G. R. Oldham, "Development of the Job Diagnostic Survey," *Journal of Applied Psychology* (1975), pp. 159–170.

10. R. W. Walters and Associates, *Job Enrichment for Results* (Cambridge, Mass.: Addison-Wesley, 1975).

11. E. E. Lawler III; J. R. Hackman, and S. Kaufman, "Effects of Job Redesign: A Field Experiment," *Journal of Applied Social Psychology* (1973), pp. 49–62.

EXPECTANCY THEORY: OVERVIEW AND MANAGEMENT PERSPECTIVES

NORMAN G. OGLESBY

INTRODUCTION

Managers and scholars have long been interested in work motivation. To the scholar, knowledge of the variables and processes involved in motivation is basic to the development of a comprehensive theory of organizational behavior. To the manager, a good working knowledge of the motivation process is an essential part of leadership, since effective leadership obviously must be based on some reasonable assumptions about the processes involved in work motivation. In expectancy theory, both manager and scholar find an explicit statement of the process by which work motivation occurs and through which performance choices are made. Of the many possible levels of work performance, which one is most likely to be exhibited by a worker in a particular situation? And *why*? These are the salient questions expectancy theory seeks to answer.

As might be expected of a new, relatively robust theory of work motivation, expectancy theory has generated a vast amount of research. Considerable debate and controversy have been generated as to the validity of the theory and how it should be made operational.[1] That debate is continuing; but it is too lengthy to be treated in detail here.

This is an original paper prepared especially for this volume.

This paper is a summative description of expectancy theory, designed to provide a working acquaintance with the theory and its implications for management. Scholars seeking more definitive analysis of expectancy theory will, of course, wish to consult further sources.

ROOTS OF THE THEORY

The first unified statement of expectancy theory is generally attributed to Victor Vroom.[2] In his landmark book, *Work and Motivation*, Vroom developed the proposition that work performance is a function of the interaction between the force to perform and the ability to perform. That is:

$$\text{Performance} = f \text{ (force} \times \text{ability)}$$

In *Work and Motivation*, Vroom dealt at length with the notion of "force," or, more simply, *motivation*. He was the first to suggest that the process leading to work motivation could be represented by an expectancy-theory model. Later, Porter and Lawler[3] adapted Vroom's expectancy model to deal specifically with the process leading to managerial motivation. It is fair to say that the work of these three theorists is the standard of reference for practically all work in expectancy theory today. Their work is also the basic source for this paper.

Underlying all expectancy theory is the assumption that man is *hedonistic*—that workers prefer pleasure to pain, reward to punishment, and more reward to less. Hence, if other things are equal, the expectancy theory assumes that a worker will choose the behavioral alternative that offers the highest reward payoff. Or, if no rewards are possible for any behavioral alternative, the theory assumes that a worker will choose that alternative which offers the *least* amount of *non-reward* (i.e., the least amount of displeasure). Clearly, the theory has epistemological roots not only in hedonism, but also in the work of psychologists such as Thorndike, Tolman, Lewin, and Skinner, all of whom have explored the proposition that the propensity to engage in a particular type of behavior is related to the consequences of doing so.

BASIC ELEMENTS OF THE THEORY

Expectancy theory is built on the assumption that workers calculate their chances of being able to perform in a certain way, and the consequences of doing so, *before* overt work performance is manifested. Specifically, the expectancy theory assumes that before an individual chooses to *try* to perform at a given level, the individual first makes a subjective estimate of the value of three variables, called *expectancy, instrumentality,* and *valence,* as they pertain to that performance level. These three variables form the bone and sinew of expectancy theory.[4] When combined in the multiplicative expectancy theory model, they yield an estimate of individual motivation to exert any particular level of effort.

Expectancy refers to the perceived likelihood of being able to perform at a particular performance level, *j,* given that a certain level of effort, *i,* is exerted. That is, expectancy is a *subjective* probability estimate that can take on values from zero to one in the expectancy theory model, depending on individual perception of the situation. In essence, expectancy is concerned with this question: If an individual exerts the *i*th level of effort, what is the (subjective) probability that the *j*th level of performance will result?

Instrumentality is concerned with the individual's perception of the consequences associated with the *j*th level of performance. Suppose we

assume that an individual is contemplating a level of work performance called "selling 100 products today." The expectancy theory posits that the individual first mentally identifies the *n* personal *consequences* that may result if 100 products are sold. The individual then estimates the *subjective probability* that each of these consequences will, in fact, occur. It is these subjective probabilities that constitute the instrumentality variable in expectancy theory.[5] Hence, the instrumentality aspect of expectancy theory asks this question: Given the possible consequences of performance at a certain level, how probable is each consequence?

Valence, in the expectancy theory, means *desirability* to the individual of the possible consequences of performing at a particular level. That is, an individual contemplating a certain level of performance not only evaluates the possible consequences of performing at that level, but also evaluates the personal desirability of *each* consequence. The theory is often operationalized such that valence is scaled from -1 (very undesirable) to $+1$ (very desirable).

Suppose a certain salesperson perceives three consequences to be associated with an assigned performance goal called "sell 100 products today":

1. Receiving a bonus.
2. Becoming fatigued.
3. Being promoted.

Expectancy theory posits that in considering how hard to try to meet this goal, the salesperson will first evaluate the consequences of doing so, and the desirability of those consequences. The result of this process might be as follows:

Consequence	Subjective Probability of Occurrence (Instrumentality)	Desirability to the Individual (Valence)
1. Receive a bonus	0.90	+1
2. Become fatigued	0.50	−1
3. Be promoted	0.10	+0.5

In this hypothetical case, consequence 1 is thought to be very likely (0.90), and it is apparently the most desirable consequence anticipated if 100 products are sold. Fatigue is perceived as a very undesirable consequence (-1), but less likely to occur (0.50). Consequence 3 (being promoted) is moderately desirable $(+0.5)$, but not very likely to occur (0.10).

Combining the Variables: The Expectancy Theory Model

Given values for expectancy, instrumentality, and valence,[6] expectancy theory combines them into a multiplicative model such that the motivation to exert any level of effort, i, can be predicted. This makes it possible to *compare* the motivational force behind any level of effort. Hence, given that several alternative work behaviors could occur, the expectancy model provides a prediction as to which alternative an individual will be most strongly motivated to choose. The basic expectancy model may be formulated as follows:[7]

$$M(i) = \sum_{j=1}^{n} [\text{Expectancy}_{ij} \cdot (\sum_{k=1}^{n} \text{Instrumentality}_k \cdot \text{Valence}_k)]$$

Where:

$M(i)$	= The motivation to exert the ith level of effort.
Expectancy_{ij}	= The subjective probability that the ith amount of effort will lead to some performance result, j.
Instrumentality_k	= The subjective probability of each of the n consequences of performance result j.
Valence_k	= The desirability to the individual of each of the n consequences of performance result j.

This rather formidable-looking expression is really not as complex to use as it appears. A brief

example should clarify the mechanics of the model.

Assume that management has set a new goal for its sales force of selling 100 products each day. If the goal is achieved, management rewards this "superior performance" with a $50 bonus plus "early promotion consideration." But sales, after all, is a probabilistic process; and there will be times when 100 products cannot be sold. Let us assume that, recognizing this, management has set a quota of 75 sales per day as the minimum amount required for "acceptable" performance. Management's interest, then, is: What is the relative motivational force tending to encourage "superior" performance versus "acceptable" performance?

Suppose one salesperson sees the chances of meeting the new goal (and achieving "superior" performance) as follows:

Effort Level (i)	E_{ij}: The subjective probability that the ith level of effort will lead to the jth performance result (here, $j = i =$ selling 100 products)
$i = 1$, maximum effort $i = 2$, usual amount of effort	$E_{11} = 0.75$ $E_{21} = 0.00$

Apparently, this salesperson believes that only maximum effort can achieve the new sales goal, since $E1_j = 0.75$, and $E2_j = 0$.

Now, the expectancy model tells us, we must look to the *consequences* of performance result j (selling 100 products), and to how this salesperson *feels* about those consequences. Let us assume the following perceived values for *instrumentality* and *valence:*

Consequence Number (k)	Consequence	Subjective Probability of Occurrence (Instrumentality)	Desirability of This Consequence (Valence)
$k = 1$	$50 bonus	0.90	$+1$
$k = 2$	Become fatigued	0.50	-1
$k = 3$	Get promoted	0.10	$+0.5$
$k = 4$	Peer-group pressure	0.10	-1

Recall that our simplified expectancy model stated:

$$M(i) = \sum_{j=1}^{n} [\text{Expectancy}_{ij} \cdot (\sum_{k=1}^{n} \text{Instrumentality}_{k} \cdot \text{Valence}_{k})]$$

Hence, based on the preceding data, we might estimate the motivation to exert effort level 1 (maximum effort) as:

$$M(1) = 0.75 \times [0.90 \ (+1) + 0.50(-1) + 0.10 \ (+.5) + 0.10(-1)] = 0.26$$

and, apparently:

$$M(2) = 0 \ (\text{Since } E_{21} = 0)$$

But notice that while effort level 2 ("effort as usual") probably will not sell 100 products (result 1), it can lead to *other* performance results. One of these may be "acceptable performance." The expectancy model requires that we evaluate *all n* performance results associated with a particular level of effort, and sum them, in order to estimate the net motivational force behind that effort. Suppose our hypothetical salesperson sees the situation this way:

Effort level (i)	E_{ij}: The subjective probability that effort level 2 will lead to performance result 2 ("acceptable performance")
$i = 2$, effort as usual	$E_{22} = 1.0$

Suppose that the consequences of "acceptable performance" are perceived as in the table below.

Again computing the strength of motivation to exert effort level 2 ($M(2)$), this time considering *both* performance results (i.e., "outstanding" and "acceptable") as they relate to "effort as usual," we find:

$$M(2) = \sum_{j=1}^{2} [\text{Expectancy}_{ij} \cdot (\sum_{k=1}^{n} \text{Instrumentality}_{k} \cdot \text{Valence}_{k})]$$

$$= E_{21} \cdot (\sum_{k=1}^{n} I_k \cdot V_k) + E_{22} \cdot (\sum_{k=1}^{n} I_k \cdot V_k)$$

$$= 0 + E_{22} \cdot (\sum_{k=1}^{5} I_k \cdot V_k) \qquad (\text{Since } E_{21} = 0)$$

$$= 1[0.50(1) + (0.75)(-0.5) + 1(-1) + 1(1) + 1(1)] = 1.13$$

which is *greater than* 0.26, the value of $M(1)$.

Since $M(2)$ is greater than $M(1)$, our expectancy model tells us that *this salesperson should be more motivated to exert "effort as usual" than to exert maximum effort!* Obviously, this is not what management intended. What can be done to generate higher motivation toward "superior" performance? As a process model of work motivation, expectancy theory offers an approach to such questions that is based on management's ability to influence the perceived value of the expectancy theory variables.

Implications: Expectancy Theory and Management Practice

Expectancy theory is rich in working hypotheses for management. Its tenets provide an excellent point of departure for devising—and revising—motivational strategy. Perhaps the best way to highlight the managerial implications of the theory is to make explicit two of the premises on which it rests.

Consequence Number (k)	Consequence	Subjective Probability of Occurrence	Valence
$k = 1$	Avoid fatigue	0.50	+1
$k = 2$	Lose promotion	0.75	−0.5
$k = 3$	Lose bonus	1.0	−1
$k = 4$	Avoid peer-group pressure	1.0	+1
$k = 5$	Receive routine salary increase	1.0	+1

Premise 1

The motivation to perform is a function, in part, of an individual's expectation that he or she *can* perform.

Empirical findings by Korman[8] and Locke[9] tend to support the proposition that there is indeed power in positive thinking about one's ability to perform. If the expectancy model is a reasonable characterization of the motivation process —and there is some evidence to this effect[10]— then it behooves management to consider means of *increasing workers' performance expectancies* as they pertain to organizational objectives.

Why would a worker have a low expectation of being able to accomplish assigned work? While there are many possible answers, it is reasonable to hypothesize that performance expectations may be relatively low if:

1. The worker is not properly trained for the job.
2. The worker does not have the resources required to do the job.
3. The job is perceived as being quite difficult.
4. The job is ambiguous and not clearly defined.

With testable working hypotheses such as these, the manager can evaluate and increase performance expectations through such means as training, counseling, and setting clearer performance objectives. Even so, the greatest value of expectancy theory does not lie in suggesting definitive "motivational therapy," but in limiting the search for underlying pathology. In this way, the theory provides a more rational and efficient basis for leadership.

Premise 2

The motivation to perform is a function, in part, of the anticipated consequences of performance.

What expectancy theory is saying to management is that, before motivation and performance are manifested, workers inevitably ask—and *answer*—one simple question about performance contemplated: *"What's in it for me?"* Expectancy theorists believe that workers answer this question through *experience* and *learning*.[11] By influencing this learning process, the manager can strengthen and guide motivation.

Expectancy theory recognizes that a worker's perception of the consequences of performance are, in part, a result of past action—outcome (or performance—result) learning experiences. That is, the motivation to work is, in part, a function of *learned associations* between past performance and the results of that performance. What a manager wants the work force to "learn," of course, is that desired performance can be achieved; that high performance yields high reward or reinforcement; and that low performance does not. Learning theory[12] suggests several elements which may be critical in this process. I have chosen to call them:

1. Timing of reinforcement,
2. Definitive reinforcement, and
3. Relevant reinforcement.

Timing is critical because, given a considerable time between performance and reinforcement, there may be little or no perceived connection between desired performance and the reward for it. Or, even worse, there may be a misconception such that a worker believes he or she has been rewarded for behavior which management does *not* desire. While the performance-reward sequence does not have to be immediate, it should be sufficiently short to facilitate learning of *desired* cause-effect relationships.

Definitive reinforcement means specific reinforcement for specific performance. For the manager, this necessitates distinguishing between observed levels of performance and dispensing organizationally mediated rewards in proportion to achievement. No experienced manager need be told that performance appraisal and reward is a difficult process that is far easier said than done. But done it must be, the expectancy theory tell us, because superior performance will not be forthcoming unless—in the eyes of the performer —there is a premium for it. Furthermore, if management refuses to distinguish mediocrity from magnificence, there is the risk that eventually no one will know the difference.

By *relevant reinforcement*, I mean that the definition of a "desirable" reward must not be made *a priori* by management, without reference to the individuals at hand. Valence is value in the eye of the beholder, and it is to the beholder that management must look for guidance in designing a performance reinforcement system. Otherwise, what the workers may learn in the course of performing is that good performance generates meaningless, or possibly *undesirable* consequences. The implications of such a "lesson" for motivation and productivity should be obvious.

CONCLUSIONS AND CAVEATS

Expectancy theory is a very promising system of thought. It has great potential for improving the theory and practice of management, particularly as related to work motivation and managerial leadership. Recent developments in path-goal theory[13] attest to this observation. The vast amount of management research now being devoted to the theory promises exciting new insights into the motivation process. But expectancy theory has not yet solidified enough to permit the conclusion that it represents unequivocal consensus about work motivation. There are numerous criticisms and qualifications that remain to be resolved. Management theory and practice are sure to benefit in the process.

NOTES

1. See, for example, H. P. Dachler and W. H. Mobley, "Construct Validation of an Instrumentality–Expectancy–Task-Goal Model of Work Motivation," *Journal of Applied Psychology Monograph*, December, 1973, pp. 397–418; and T. R. Mitchell, *Instrumentality Theories: Conceptual And Methodological Problems* (Washington, D.C.: Journal Supplement Abstract Service, American Psychological Association, 1972).

2. Victor H. Vroom, *Work and Motivation* (New York: John Wiley and Sons, 1964).

3. Lyman W. Porter and E. E. Lawler III, *Managerial Attitudes and Performance* (Homewood, IL: R. D. Irwin, 1968).

4. There are terminological differences between the Vroom, Porter and Lawler, ar d other versions of the theory. These have been ignored for the sake of brevity.

5. There is disagreement as to whether the instrumentality variable should be a subjective *probability* or a *correlation coefficient*. Vroom advocated the latter, but later investigations have preferred the former. See Dachler and Mobley, note 1 *supra*, pp. 402–403.

6. The reader should recognize that this is a very big "given," as the measurement of the expectancy theory variables is one of the more troublesome aspects of the theory.

7. I have modified Vroom's original model here for expository purposes. The changes are not substantive, however.

8. A. K. Korman, "Expectancies As Determinants of Performance," *Journal of Applied Psychology*, 1971, *55*, pp. 218–222.

9. Edwin A. Locke, "Toward a Theory of Task Motivation and Incentives," *Organizational Behavior And Human Performance*, 1968, *3*, pp. 157–189.

10. H. G. Heneman III and D. P. Schwab, "Evaluation of Research on Expectancy Theory Predictors of Employee Performance," *Psychological Bulletin*, 1972, *78*, pp. 1–9; R. J. House, H. J. Shapiro, and M. A. Wabba, "Expectancy Theory As A Predictor of Work Behavior And Attitude: A Re-evaluation of Empirical Evidence," *Decision Sciences*, 1974, *5*, pp. 481–506; T. R. Mitchell, "Expectancy Models of Job Satisfaction, Occupational Preference, and Effort: A Theoretical, Methodological, and Empirical Appraisal," *Psychological Bulletin*, 1974, *81*, pp. 1053–1077.

11. E. E. Lawler III, *Motivation In Work Organizations* (Belmont, California: Wadsworth Publishing Co., 1973).

12. See S. H. Hulse, James Deese, and Howard Egeth, *The Psychology of Learning* (New York: McGraw-Hill, 1975).

13. For an excellent summary of path-goal theory and its relationship to both expectancy theory and management practices, see R. J. House and T. R. Mitchell, "Path-Goal Theory of Leadership," *Journal of Contemporary Business*, Autumn, 1974, pp. 81–97.

BEHAVIOR MODIFICATION
ON THE
BOTTOM LINE

W. CLAY HAMNER
ELLEN P. HAMNER

It may be easy to say *what* a manager does. Telling *how* he influences the behavior of the employee in the direction of task accomplishment is far more difficult to comprehend and describe. The purpose of this article is to describe and spell out the determinants of employee productivity or performance from a reinforcement theory point of view, and to show how managing the contingencies of positive reinforcement in organizational settings leads to successful management. We hope these descriptions will enable the manager to understand how his or her behavior affects the behavior of subordinates and to see that, in many cases, a worker's failure to perform a task properly is a direct outcome of the manager's own behavior. The employee has failed to perform because the manager has failed to motivate.

MANAGING THE CONTINGENCIES
OF REINFORCEMENT

The interrelationship among three components—work environment, task performance, and consequences of reinforcements—are known as the contingencies of reinforcement. The reward that is

Reprinted by permission of the publisher from *Organizational Dynamics,* Vol. 4, No. 4, Spring 1976. © 1976 by AMACOM, a division of American Management Associations.

contingent upon good performance in a given work situation (environment) acts as a motivator for future performance. The manager controls the *work environment* (Where am I going? What are the goals? Is the leader supportive? Is this a pleasant place to work?), the *task assignment* (How will I get there? What behavior is desired? What is considered appropriate performance?), and the *consequences* of job performance (How will I know when I've reached the desired goal? Is the feedback relevant and timely? Is my pay based upon my performance?). By shaping these three components of behavior so that all are positive, the manager can go a long way toward creating a work climate that supports high productivity.

ARRANGING THE CONTINGENCIES
OF REINFORCEMENT

Someone who expects to influence behavior must be able to manipulate the consequences of behavior. Whether managers realize it or not, they constantly shape the behavior of their subordinates by the way they utilize the rewards at their disposal. Employers intuitively use rewards all the time—but their efforts often produce limited results because the methods are used improperly, inconsistently, or inefficiently. In many instances employees are given rewards that are not conditional or contingent on the behavior the manager wishes to promote. Even when they are, long delays often intervene between the occurrence of the desired behavior and its intended consequences. Special privileges, activities, and rewards are often furnished according to length of service rather than performance requirements. In many cases, positive reinforcers are inadvertently made contingent upon the wrong kind of behavior. In short, intuition provides a poor guide to motivation.

A primary reason managers fail to "motivate" workers to perform in the desired manner is their failure to understand the power of the contingencies of reinforcement over the employee. The laws or principles for arranging the contingencies to condition behavior are not hard to understand; if properly applied, they constitute powerful managerial tools that can be used for increasing supervisory effectiveness.

Conditioning is the process by which behavior is modified through manipulation of the contingencies of behavior. To understand how this works, we will first look at various kinds of arrangements of the contingencies: *positive reinforcement* conditioning, *escape* conditioning, *extinction* conditioning, and *punishment* conditioning. The differences among these kinds of contingencies depend on the consequences that result from the behavioral act. Positive reinforcement and avoidance learning are methods of strengthening desired behavior, while extinction and punishment are methods of weakening undesired behavior.

Positive Reinforcement. According to B. F. Skinner, a positive reinforcer or reward is a stimulus that, when added to a situation, strengthens the probability of the response in that situation. Behavior that appears to lead to a positive consequence tends to be repeated, while behavior that appears to lead to a negative consequence tends not to be repeated.

Once it has been determined that a specific consequence has reward value to a work group, we can use it to increase that group's performance. Thus the first step in the successful application of reinforcement procedures is to select reinforcers that are sufficiently powerful and durable to establish and strengthen desired behavior.

These could include such things as an interesting work assignment, the chance to use one's mind, seeing the results of one's work, good pay, recognition for a job well done, promotion, freedom to decide how to do a job, and so on.

The second step is to design the contingencies in such a way that the reinforcing events are made contingent on the desired level of performance. This is the rule of reinforcement most often violated. Rewards *must* result from performance—and the better an employee's performance is, the greater his or her rewards should be.

Unless a manager is willing to discriminate among employees on the basis of their performance levels, the effectiveness of his or her power over the employee is nil. For example, Edward E. Lawler III, a leading researcher on pay and performance, has noted that one of the major reasons managers are unhappy with their salary system is that they do not perceive the relationship between how hard they work (productivity) and how much they earn. In a survey of 600 managers, Lawler found virtually no relationship between their pay and their rated level of performance.

The third step is to design the contingencies in such a way that a reliable procedure for eliciting or inducing the desired response patterns is established; when desired responses rarely occur, there are few opportunities to influence behavior through contingency management. Training programs, goal-setting programs and similar efforts should be undertaken to let workers know what is expected of them. If the criterion for reinforcement is unclear, unspecified or set too high, most —if not all—of the worker's responses go unrewarded; eventually his or her efforts will be extinguished.

Escape Conditioning. The second kind of contingency arrangement available to the manager is called escape or avoidance conditioning. Just as with positive reinforcement, this is a method of strengthening desired behavior. A contingency arrangement in which an individual's performance can terminate a noxious environment is called escape learning. When behavior can prevent the onset of a noxious stimulus, the procedure is called avoidance learning.

An employee is given an unpleasant task assignment, for example, with the promise that when he completes it, he can move on (escape) to a more pleasant job. Or a manager is such an unpleasant person to be around that the employees work when he is present in order to "avoid" him.

Let's note the distinction between strengthening behavior through positive reinforcement techniques and doing so through avoidance learning techniques. In one case, the individual works hard to gain the consequences from the environment (provided by the manager in most cases) that result from good work, and in the second case, the individual works hard to avoid the negative aspects of the environment itself (again, the manager is the source). In both cases the same behavior is strengthened over the short run. In escape learning, however, the manager is more process-oriented; he or she must be present in order to elicit the desired level of performance. Under positive reinforcement, however, the manager is outcome-oriented and does not have to be physically present at all times in order to maintain the desired level of performance.

Extinction. When positive reinforcement for a learned or previously conditioned response is withheld, individuals will still continue to exhibit that behavior for an extended period of time. With repeated nonreinforcement, however, the behavior decreases and eventually disappears. This decline in response rate as a result of non-rewarded repetition of a task is defined as *extinction.*

This method, when combined with a positive reinforcement method, is the procedure of behavior modification recommended by Skinner. It leads to the fewest negative side effects. Using the two methods together allows employees to get the rewards they desire and allows the organization to eliminate the undesired behavior.

Punishment. Punishment is the most controversial method of behavior modification. Punishment is defined as presenting an aversive or noxious consequence contingent upon a response, or removing a positive consequence contingent upon a response. The Law of Effect operates here, too: As rewards strengthen behavior, punishment weakens it. Notice carefully the difference between withholding rewards in the punishment process and withholding rewards in the extinction process. In the extinction process, we withhold rewards for behavior that has previously been rewarded because the behavior was previously desired. In punishment, we withhold a reward because the behavior is undesired, has never been associated with the reward before, and is plainly an undesirable consequence.

RULES FOR USING OPERANT CONDITIONING TECHNIQUES

Rule 1. Don't give the same level of reward to all. Differentiate rewards based on performance in relation to defined objectives or standards. We know that people compare their performance with the performance of their peers to determine how well they are doing and that they compare their rewards with peer rewards to determine how to evaluate theirs. Some managers may think that the fairest compensation system is one in which everyone in the same job classification gets the same pay, but employees want differentiation as evidence of how important their services are to the organization. Managers who reward all people at the same level are simply encouraging, at most, only average performance. Behavior leading to high performance is being extinguished (ignored), while average and poor performance are being strengthened by means of positive reinforcement.

Rule 2. Failure to respond to behavior has reinforcing consequences. Managers who find the job of differentiating between workers so unpleasant or so difficult that they fail to respond to their behavior must recognize that failure to respond is itself a form of response that, in turn, modifies behavior. Superiors are bound to shape the behavior of their subordinates by the way in which they utilize the rewards at their disposal. Therefore, managers must be careful that they examine the consequences on performance of their non-actions as well as their actions.

Rule 3. Tell a person what behavior gets reinforced. By making clear to a worker the contingencies of reinforcement, a manager may actually be increasing his individual freedom. The employee who has a standard against which to measure his job will have a built-in feedback system that allows him or her to make judgments about his or her own level of performance. The awarding of reinforcements in an organization where workers' goals are specified will be associated with worker performance, not supervisory bias. The assumption is, of course, that the supervisor rates the employee accurately and then reinforces the employee according to his ratings. If the supervisor fails to rate accurately or administer rewards based on performance, then the worker will be forced to search for the "true" contingencies—that is, what behavior he or she should display in order to get rewarded (ingratiation? loyalty? positive attitude?).

Rule 4. Tell a person what he or she is doing wrong. As a general rule, very few people find failure rewarding. One assumption of behavior conditioning therefore is that a worker wants to be rewarded for positive accomplishments. A supervisor should never use extinction or punishment as the sole method for modifying behavior—but if one of these is used judiciously in conjunction with positive reinforcement techniques, such combined procedures can hasten the change process. If the supervisor fails to specify why a reward is being withheld, the employee may associate the withholding of the reward with past desired behavior instead of the behavior that the supervisor is trying to extinguish. Thus the supervisor extinguishes good performance while having no effect on the undesired behavior.

Rule 5. Don't punish in front of others. The reason for this rule is quite simple. The punishment (for example, a reprimand) should be enough to extinguish the undesired behavior. By administering the punishment in front of the work group, the worker is doubly punished; he also "loses face." This additional punishment may lead to negative side-effects in three ways. First, the worker whose self-image is damaged may feel that he must retaliate in order to protect himself. Therefore, the supervisor has actually increased undesired responses. Second, the work group may associate the punishment with another behavior of the worker and, through "avoidance learning" techniques, may modify their own behavior in ways not intended by the

supervisor. Third, the work group is also being punished—in the sense that observing a member of their team being reprimanded is unpleasant to most people. This may result in lowered performance of the total work group.

Rule 6. Make the consequences equal to the behavior. In other words, don't cheat the worker out of his just rewards. If he is a good worker, tell him. Many supervisors find it very difficult to praise an employee. Others find it very difficult to counsel an employee about what he is doing wrong. When a manager fails to use these reinforcement tools, he is actually reducing his effectiveness. Over-rewarding a worker may make him feel guilty and certainly reinforces his current performance level. If the performance level is lower than that of others who get the same reward, he has no reason to increase his output. When a worker is underrewarded, he becomes angry with the system. His behavior is being extinguished and the company may be forcing the good employee (underrewarded) to seek employment elsewhere while encouraging the poor employee (overrewarded) to stay on.

SETTING UP A POSITIVE REINFORCEMENT PROGRAM IN INDUSTRY

Many organizations are setting up formal motivational programs in an attempt to use the principles of positive reinforcement to increase employee productivity.

A positive reinforcement approach to management differs from traditional motivational theories in two basic ways. First, as noted above, a positive reinforcement program calls for the maximum use of reinforcement and the minimum use of punishment. Punishment tends to leave the individual feeling controlled and coerced. Second, a positive reinforcement program avoids psychological probing into the worker's attitudes as a possible cause of behavior. Instead, the work situation itself is analyzed, with the focus on the reward contingencies that cause a worker to act the way in which he does.

A positive reinforcement program, therefore, is results-oriented rather than process-oriented. Geary A. Rummler, president of Praxis Corporation, a management consultant firm, claims that the motivational theories of such behavioral scientists as Herzberg and Maslow, which stress workers' psychological needs, are impractical. "They can't be made operative. While they help classify a problem, a positive reinforcement program leads to solutions."

Stages in Program Development. Positive reinforcement programs currently used in industry generally involve at least four stages. The *first stage,* according to Edward J. Feeney, formerly vice-president, systems, of Emery Air Freight Corporation, is to define the behavioral aspects of performance and do a performance audit. This step is potentially one of the most difficult, since some companies do not have a formal performance evaluation program, especially for nonmanagerial employees, and those that do have a program often rate the employee's behavior on nonjob related measures (such as friendliness, loyalty, cooperation, overall attitude, and so on). But once these behavioral aspects are defined, the task of convincing managers that improvement is needed and of persuading them to cooperate with such a program is simplified. Feeney asserts, "Most managers genuinely think that operations in their bailiwick are doing well; a performance audit that proves they're not comes as a real and unpleasant surprise."

The *second stage* in developing a working positive reinforcement program is to develop and set specific goals for each worker. Failure to specify concrete behavioral goals is a major reason many programs do not work. Goals should be expressed in such terms as "decreased employee turnover" or "schedules met" rather than only in terms of "better identification with the company" or "increased job satisfaction." The goals set, therefore, should be in the same terms as those defined in the performance audit, goals that specifically relate to the task at hand. Goals should be reasonable—that is, set somewhere between "where you are" (as spelled out in the performance audit) and some ideal.

While it is important for the manager to set goals, it is also important for the employee to accept them. An approach that tends to build in goal acceptance is to allow employees to work with management in setting work goals. According to John C. Emery, president of Emery Air Freight Corporation, the use of a participatory management technique to enlist the ideas of those performing the job not only results in their acceptance of goals, but also stimulates them to come up with goals.

The *third stage* in a positive reinforcement program is to allow the employee to keep a record of his or her own work. This process of self-feedback maintains a continuous schedule of reinforcement for the worker and helps him obtain intrinsic reinforcement from the task itself. Where employees can total their own results, they can see whether they are meeting their goals and whether they are improving over their previous performance level (as measured in the performance audit stage). In other words, the worker has two chances of being successful—either by beating his previous record or by beating both his previous record and his established goal. E. D. Grady, general manager—operator services for Michigan Bell, maintains that the manager should set up the work environment in such a way that people have a chance to succeed. One way to do this, he says, is to "shorten the success interval." Grady says, "If you're looking for success, keep shortening the interval of measurement so you can get a greater chance of success which you can latch on to for positive reinforcements." Instead of setting monthly or quarterly goals, for example, set weekly or daily goals.

The *fourth stage*—the most important step in a positive reinforcement program—is one that separates it from all other motivation plans. The supervisor looks at the self-feedback report of the employee and/or other indications of performance (sales records, for example) and then praises the positive aspects of the employee's performance (as determined by the performance audit and subsequent goal setting). This extrinsic reinforcement should strengthen the desired performance, while the withholding of praise for substandard performance should give the employee incentive to improve that performance level. Since the worker already knows the areas of his or her deficiencies, there is no reason for the supervisor to criticize the employee. In other words, negative feedback is self-induced, whereas positive feedback comes from both internal and external sources.

As noted previously, this approach to feedback follows the teachings of B. F. Skinner, who believes that use of positive reinforcement leads to a greater feeling of self-control, while the avoidance of negative reinforcement keeps the individual from feeling controlled or coerced. Skinner says, "You can get the same effect if the supervisor simply discovers things being done right and says something like 'Good, I see you're doing it the way that works best.' "

While the feedback initially used in step four of the positive reinforcement program is praise, it is important to note that other forms of reinforcement can have the same effect. M. W. Warren, the director of organization and management development at the Questor Corporation, says that the five "reinforcers" he finds most effective are (1) money (but only when it is a consequence of a specific performance and when the relation to the performance is known); (2) praise or recognition; (3) freedom to choose one's own activity; (4) opportunity to see oneself become better, more important, or more useful; and (5) power to influence both co-workers and management. Warren states, "By building these reinforcers into programs at various facilities, Questor is getting results." The need for using more than praise after the positive reinforcement program has proved effective is discussed by Skinner.

It does not cost the company anything to use praise rather than blame, but if the company then makes a great deal more money that way, the worker may seem to be getting gypped. However, the welfare of the worker depends on the welfare of the company, and if the company is smart enough to distribute some of the fruits of positive reinforcement in the form of higher wages and better fringe benefits, everybody gains from the supervisor's use of positive reinforcements. (*Organizational Dynamics,* Winter, 1973, p. 35.)

EARLY RESULTS OF POSITIVE REINFORCEMENT PROGRAMS IN ORGANIZATIONS, 1960–1973

Companies that claimed to be implementing and using positive reinforcement programs such as the one described above include Emery Air Freight,

Michigan Bell Telephone, Questor Corporation, Cole National Company in Cleveland, Ford Motor Company, American Can, Upjohn, United Air Lines, Warner-Lambert, Addressograph-Multigraph, Allis-Chalmers, Bethlehem Steel, Chase Manhattan Banks, IBM, IT&T, Procter and Gamble, PPG Industries, Standard Oil of Ohio, Westinghouse, and Wheeling-Pittsburgh Steel Corporation (see *Business Week,* December 18, 1971 and December 2, 1972). Because such programs are relatively new in industrial settings (most have begun since 1968), few statements of their relative effectiveness have been reported. In the Winter 1973 issue of *Organizational Dynamics* (p. 49), it was stated that "there's little objective evidence available, and what evidence there is abounds in caveats—the technique will work under the proper circumstances, the parameters of which are usually not easily apparent."

In the area of employee training, Northern Systems Company, General Electric Corporation, and Emery Air Freight claim that positive reinforcement has improved the speed and efficiency of their training program. In their programmed learning program, the Northern Systems Company structures the feedback system in such a way that the trainee receives positive feedback only when he demonstrates correct performance at the tool station. The absence of feedback is experienced by the trainee when he fails to perform correctly. Therefore, through positive reinforcements, he quickly perceives that correct behaviors obtain for him the satisfaction of his needs, and that incorrect behaviors do not. Emery has designed a similar program for sales trainees. *Business Week* reported the success of the program by saying:

It is a carefully engineered, step-by-step program, with frequent feedback questions and answers to let the salesman know how he is doing. The course contrasts with movies and lectures in which, Feeney says, the salesman is unable to gauge what he has learned. The aim is to get the customer on each sales call to take some kind of action indicating that he will use Emery services. Significantly, in 1968, the first full year after the new course was launched, sales jumped from $62.4 million to $79.8 million, a gain of 27.8 percent compared with an 11.3 percent rise the year before.

Since 1969, Emery has instituted a positive reinforcement program for all of its employees and credits the program with direct savings to the company of over $3 million in the first three years and indirectly with pushing 1973 sales over the $160 million mark. While Emery Air Freight is and remains the biggest success story for a positive reinforcement program to date, other companies also claim improvements as a result of initiating similar programs. At Michigan Bell's Detroit office, 2,000 employees in 1973 participated in a positive reinforcement program. Michigan Bell credits the program with reducing absenteeism from 11 percent to 6.5 percent in one group, from 7.5 percent to 4.5 percent in another group, and from 3.3 percent to 2.6 percent for all employees. In addition, the program has resulted in the correct completion of reports on time 90 percent of the time as compared with 20 percent of the time before the program's implementation. The Wheeling-Pittsburgh Steel Corporation credits its feedback program with saving $200,000 a month in scrap costs.

In an attempt to reduce the number of employees who constantly violated plant rules, General Motors implemented a plan in one plant that gave employees opportunities to improve or clear their records by going through varying periods of time without committing further shop violations. They credit this positive reinforcement plan with reducing the number of punitive actions for shop-rule infractions by two-thirds from 1969 to 1972 and the number of production-standard grievances by 70 percent during the same period.

While there was a great deal of interest in applying behavior modification in industrial settings after the successes of Emery Air Freight and others who followed suit were made known in 1971, the critics of this approach to worker motivation predicted that it would be short-lived. Any success would owe more to a "Hawthorne Effect" (the positive consequences of paying special attention to employees) than to any real long-term increase in productivity and/or worker satisfaction. The critics pointed out—quite legitimately, we might add—that most of the claims were testimonial in nature and that the length of experience between 1969–1973 was too short to allow enough data to accumulate to determine the true

successes of positive reinforcement in improving morale and productivity. With this in mind, we surveyed ten organizations, all of which currently use a behavior modification approach, to see if the "fad" created by Emery Air Freight had died or had persisted and extended its gains.

Specifically, we were interested in knowing (1) how many employees were covered; (2) the kinds of employees covered; (3) specific goals (stages 1 & 2); (4) frequency of self-feedback (stage 3); (5) the kinds of reinforcers used (stage 4); and (6) results of the program. A summary of companies surveyed and the information gained are shown in Figure 1.

CURRENT RESULTS OF POSITIVE REINFORCEMENT PROGRAMS IN ORGANIZATIONS

The ten organizations surveyed included Emery Air Freight, Michigan Bell—Operator Services, Michigan Bell—Maintenance Services, Connecticut General Life Insurance Company, General Electric, Standard Oil of Ohio, Weyerhaeuser, City of Detroit, B. F. Goodrich Chemical Company, and ACDC Electronics. In our interviews with each of the managers, we tried to determine both the successes and the failures they attributed to the use of behavior modification or positive reinforcement techniques. We were also interested in whether the managers saw this as a fad or as a legitimate management technique for improving the productivity and quality of work life among employees.

Emery Air Freight. Figure 1 shows Emery Air Freight still using positive reinforcement as a motivational tool. John C. Emery commented: "Positive reinforcement, always linked to feedback systems, plays a central role in performance improvement at Emery Air Freight. *All* managers and supervisors are being trained via self-instructional, programmed instruction texts—one on reinforcement and one on feedback. No formal off-the-job training is needed. Once he has studied the texts, the supervisor is encouraged immediately to apply the learning to the performance area for which he is responsible."

Paul F. Hammond, Emery's manager of system

performance and the person currently in charge of the positive reinforcement program, said that there are a considerable number of company areas in which quantifiable success has been attained over the last six or seven years. Apart from the well-publicized container savings illustration (results of which stood at $600,000 gross savings in 1970 and over $2,000,000 in 1975), several other recent success stories were noted by Emery and Hammond. They include:

• Standards for customer service on the telephone had been set up and service was running 60 to 70 percent of standard. A program very heavily involved with feedback and reinforcement was introduced a few years ago and increased performance to 90 percent of objectives within three months—a level that has been maintained ever since.

• Several offices have installed a program in which specified planned reinforcements are provided when targeted levels of shipment volume are requested by Emery customers. All offices have increased revenue substantially; one office doubled the number of export shipments handled, and another averages an additional $60,000 of revenue per month.

• A program of measuring dimensions of certain lightweight shipments to rate them by volume rather than weight uses reinforcement and feedback extensively. All measures have increased dramatically since its inception five years ago, not the least of which is an increase in revenue from $400,000 per year to well over $2,000,000 per year.

While this latest information indicates that positive reinforcement is more than a fad at Emery Air Freight, Emery pointed out that a major flaw in the program had to be overcome. He said, "Inasmuch as praise is the most readily available no-cost reinforcer, it tends to be the reinforcer used most frequently. However, the result has been to *dull* its effect as a reinforcer through its sheer repetition, even to risk making praise an *irritant* to the receiver." To counter this potential difficulty, Emery managers and supervisors have been taught and encouraged to expand their reinforcers beyond praise. Among the recommended reinforc-

ers have been formal recognition such as a public letter or a letter home, being given a more enjoyable task after completing a less enjoyable one, invitations to business luncheons or meetings, delegating responsibility and decision making, and tying such requests as special time off or any other deviation from normal procedure to performance. Thus it seems that Skinner's prediction made in 1973 about the need for using more than praise after the reinforcement program has been around for a while has been vindicated at Emery Air Freight.

Michigan Bell—Operator Service. The operator services division is still actively using positive reinforcement feedback as a motivational tool. E. D. Grady, general manager for Operator Services said, "We have found through experience that when standards and feedback are not provided, workers generally feel their performance is at about the 95 percent level. When the performance is then compared with clearly defined standards, it is usually found to meet only the 50th percentile in performance. It has been our experience, over the past ten years, that when standards are set and feedback provided in a positive manner, performance will reach very high levels —perhaps in the upper 90th percentile in a very short period of time.... We have also found that when positive reinforcement is discontinued, performance returns to levels that existed prior to the establishment of feedback." Grady said that while he was not able at this time to put a specific dollar appraisal on the cost savings from using a positive reinforcement program, the savings were continuing to increase and the program was being expanded.

In one recent experiment, Michigan Bell found that when goal setting and positive reinforcement were used in a low-productivity inner-city operator group, service promptness (time to answer call) went from 94 to 99 percent of standard, average work time per call (time taken to give information) decreased from 60 units of work time to 43 units of work time, the percentage of work time completed within ideal limits went from 50 to 93 percent of ideal time (standard was 80 percent of ideal), and the percentage of time operators made proper use of references went

FIGURE 1. Results of positive reinforcement and Similar behavior modification programs in organizations in 1976

Organization & Person Surveyed	Length of Program	Number of Employees Covered/Total Employees	Type of Employees	Specific Goals	Frequency of Feedback	Reinforcers Used	Results
EMERY AIR FREIGHT John C. Emery, Jr., *President* Paul F. Hammond, *Manager—Systems Performance*	1969–1976	500/2800	Entire workforce	(a) Increase productivity (b) Improve quality of service	Immediate to monthly, depending on task	Previously only praise and recognition; others now being introduced	Cost savings can be directly attributed to the program
MICHIGAN BELL—OPERATOR SERVICES E. D. Grady, *General Manager—Operator Services*	1972–1976	2000/5500	Employees at all levels in operator services	(a) Decrease turnover & absenteeism (b) Increase productivity (c) Improve union-management relations	(a) Lower level—weekly & daily (b) Higher level—monthly & quarterly	(a) Praise & recognition (b) Opportunity to see oneself become better	(a) Attendance performance has improved by 50% (b) Productivity and efficiency has continued to be above standard in areas where positive reinforcement (PR) is used
MICHIGAN BELL—MAINTENANCE SERVICES Donald E. Burwell, *Division Superintendent, Maintenance & Services* Dr. W. Clay Hamner, *Consultant*	1974–1976	220/5500	Maintenance workers, mechanics, & first- & second-level supervisors	Improve (a) productivity (b) quality (c) safety (d) customer-employee relations	Daily, weekly, and quarterly	(a) Self-feedback (b) Supervisory feedback	(a) Cost efficiency increase (b) Safety improved (c) Service improved (d) No change in absenteeism (e) Satisfaction with superior & co-workers improved (f) Satisfaction with pay decreased
CONNECTICUT GENERAL LIFE INSURANCE CO. Donald D. Illig, *Director of Personnel Administration*	1941–1976	3000/13,500	Clerical employees & first-line supervisors	(a) Decrease absenteeism (b) Decrease lateness	Immediate	(a) Self-feedback (b) System-feedback (c) Earned time off	(a) Chronic absenteeism & lateness has been drastically reduced (b) Some divisions refuse to use PR because it is "outdated"
GENERAL ELECTRIC[1] Melvin Sorcher, *Ph.D., formerly Director of Personnel Research Now Director of Management Development, Richardson-Merrell, Inc.*	1973–1976	1000	Employees at all levels	(a) Meet EEO objectives (b) Decrease absenteeism & turnover (c) Improve training (d) Increase productivity	Immediate—uses modeling & role playing as training tools to teach interpersonal exchanges & behavior requirements	Social reinforcers (praise, rewards, & constructive feedback)	(a) Cost savings can be directly attributed to the program (b) Productivity has increased (c) Worked extremely well in training minority groups and raising their self-esteem (d) Direct labor cost decreased
STANDARD OIL OF OHIO T. E. Standings, *Ph.D., Manager of Psychological Services*	1974	28	Supervisors	Increase supervisor competence	Weekly over 5 weeks (25-hour) training period	Feedback	(a) Improved supervisory ability to give feedback judiciously (b) Discontinued because of lack of overall success

Organization	Years	Ratio	Target group	Specific goals	Frequency	Reinforcers	Results
WEYERHAEUSER COMPANY Gary P. Latham, *Ph.D., Manager of Human Resource Research*	1974–1976	500/40,000	Clerical, production (tree planters) & middle-level management & scientists	(a) To teach managers to minimize criticism & to maximize praise (b) To teach managers to make rewards contingent on specified performance levels & (c) To use optimal schedule to increase productivity	Immediate—daily & quarterly	(a) Pay (b) Praise & recognition	(a) Using money obtained 33% increase in productivity with one group of workers, an 18% increase with a second group, an 8% decrease in a third group (b) Currently experimenting with goal setting & praise and/or money at various levels in organization (c) With a lottery-type bonus, the cultural & religious values of workers must be taken into account
CITY OF DETROIT GARBAGE COLLECTORS[2]	1973–1975	1122/1930	Garbage collectors	(a) Reduction in paid man-hour per ton (b) Reduction on overtime (c) 90% of routes completed by standard (d) Effectiveness (quality)	Daily & quarterly based on formula negotiated by city & sanitation union	Bonus (profit sharing) & praise	(a) Citizen complaints declined significantly (b) City saved $1,654,000 first year after bonus paid (c) Worker bonus = $307,000 first year or $350 annually per man (d) Union somewhat dissatisfied with productivity measure and is pushing for more bonus to employee (e) 1975 results not yet available
B. F. GOODRICH CHEMICAL Co. Donald J. Barnicki, *Production Manager*	1972–1976	100/420	Manufacturing employees at all levels	(a) Better meeting of schedules (b) Increase productivity	Weekly	Praise & recognition; freedom to choose one's own activity	Production has increased over 300%
ACDC ELECTRONICS DIVISION OF EMERSON ELECTRONICS Edward J. Feeney, *Consultant*	1974–1976	350/350	All levels	(a) 96% attendance (b) 90% engineering specifications met (c) Daily production objectives met 95% of time (d) Cost reduced by 10%	Daily & weekly feedback from foreman to company president	Positive feedback	(a) Profit up 25% over forecast (b) $550,000 cost reduction on $10 M sales (c) Return of 1900% on investment including consultant fees (d) Turnaround time on repairs went from 30 to 10 days (e) Attendance is now 98.2% (from 93.5%)

[1] Similar programs are now being implemented at Richardson-Merrell under the direction of Dr. Sorcher and at AT&T under the direction of Douglas W. Bray, Ph.D., director of management selection and development, along with several other smaller organizations (see A. P. Goldstein, Ph.D. & Melvin Sorcher, Ph.D., *Changing Supervisor Behavior*, Pergamon Press, 1974).

[2] From *Improving Municipal Productivity: The Detroit Refuse Incentive Plan*, The National Commission on Productivity, April, 1974.

from 80 to 94 percent. This led to an overall productivity index score for these operators that was significantly higher than that found in the control group where positive reinforcement was not being used, even though the control group of operators had previously (six months earlier) been one of the highest producing units.

Michigan Bell—Maintenance Services. Donald E. Burwell, Division Superintendent of Maintenance and Services at Michigan Bell established a goal-setting and positive reinforcement program in early 1974. He said, "After assignment to my present area of responsibility in January, I found that my new department of 220 employees (maintenance, mechanics, and janitorial services), including managers, possessed generally good morale. However, I soon became aware that 1973 performances were generally lower than the 1973 objectives. In some cases objectives were either ambiguous or nonexistent."

With the help of a consultant, Burwell overcame the problem by establishing a four-step positive reinforcement program similar to the one described earlier in this article. As a result, the 1974 year-end results showed significant improvements over the 1973 base-year averages in all areas, including safety (from 75.6 to 89.0), service (from 76.4 to 83.0), cost performance/hour (from 27.9 to 21.2, indexed), attendance (from 4.7 to 4.0) and worker satisfaction and cooperation (3.01 to 3.51 on a scale of 5), and worker satisfaction with the supervisors (2.88 to 3.70, also on a scale of five). 1975 figures reflect continuing success.

While Burwell is extremely pleased with the results of this program to date, he adds a word of caution to other managers thinking of implementing such a program: "I would advise against accepting any one method, including positive reinforcement, as a panacea for all the negative performance trends that confront managers. On the other hand, positive reinforcement has aided substantially in performance improvement for marketing, production, and service operators. Nevertheless, the manager needs to know when the positive effects of the reinforcement program have begun to plateau and what steps he should consider taking to maintain his positive performance trends."

Connecticut General Life Insurance Company. The Director of Personnel Administration at Connecticut General Life Insurance Company, Donald D. Illig, stated that Connecticut General has been using positive reinforcement in the form of an attendance bonus system for 25 years with over 3,200 clerical employees. Employees receive one extra day off for each ten weeks of perfect attendance. The results have been outstanding. Chronic absenteeism and lateness have been drastically reduced, and the employees are very happy with the system. Illig noted, however, that, "Our property and casualty company, with less than half the number of clerical employees countrywide, has not had an attendance-bonus system ... and wants no part of it. At the crux of the problem is an anti-Skinnerian feeling, which looks at positive reinforcement—and thus an attendance-bonus system—as being overly manipulative and old-fashioned in light of current theories of motivation."

General Electric. A unique program of behavior modification has been introduced quite successfully at General Electric as well as several other organizations by Melvin Sorcher, formerly director of personnel research at G.E. The behavior modification program used at G.E. involves using positive reinforcement and feedback in training employees. While the first program centered primarily on teaching male supervisors how to interact and communicate with minority and female employees and on teaching minority and female employees how to become successful by improving their self-images, subsequent programs focused on the relationship between supervisors and employees in general. By using a reinforcement technique known as behavior modeling, Sorcher goes beyond the traditional positive reinforcement ("PR") program. The employee is shown a videotape of a model (someone with his own characteristics—that is, male or female, black or white, subordinate or superior) who is performing in a correct or desired manner. Then, through the process of role playing, the employee is encouraged to act in the successful or desired manner shown on the film (that is, he is asked to model the behavior). Positive reinforcement is given when the goal of successful display of this behavior is made in the role-playing session.

Sorcher notes that this method has been successfully used with over 1,000 G.E. supervisors. As a result, productivity has increased, the self-esteem of hard-core employees has increased, and EEO objectives are being met. He says, "The positive results have been the gratifying changes or improvements that have occurred, especially improvements that increase over time as opposed to the usual erosion of effort after most training programs have passed their peak.... On the negative side, some people and organizations are calling their training 'behavior modeling' when it does not fit the criteria originally defined for such a program. For example, some programs not only neglect self-esteem as a component, but show little evidence of how to shape new behaviors.... Regarding the more general area of behavior modification and positive reinforcement, there is still a need for better research. There's not a lot taking place at present, which is unfortunate because on the surface these processes seem to have a lot of validity."

Standard Oil of Ohio. T. E. Standings, manager of psychological services at SOHIO, tried a training program similar to the one used by Sorcher at General Electric. After 28 supervisors had completed five weeks of training, Standings disbanded the program even though there were some short-term successes. He said, "My feelings at this point are that reinforcement cannot be taught at a conceptual level in a brief period of time. (Of course, the same comments can no doubt be made about Theory Y, MBO, and TA.) I see two alternatives: (1) Identify common problem situations, structure an appropriate reinforcement response for the supervisor, and teach the response through the behavioral model, or (2) alter reinforcement contingencies affecting defined behaviors through direct alternatives in procedural and/or informational systems without going through the supervisor directly."

Weyerhaeuser Company. Whereas Emery Air Freight has the longest history with applied re-inforcement theory, Weyerhaeuser probably has the most experience with controlled experiments using goal setting and PR techniques. The Human Resource Research Center at Weyerhaeuser, under the direction of G. P. Latham, is actively seeking ways to improve the productivity of all levels of employees using the goal-setting, PR feedback technique.

According to Dr. Latham, "The purpose of our positive reinforcement program is threefold: (1) To teach managers to embrace the philosophy that 'the glass is half-full rather than half-empty.' In other words, our objective is to teach managers to minimize criticism (which is often self-defeating since it can fixate the employee's attention on ineffective job behavior and thus reinforce it) and to maximize praise and hence fixate both their and the employee's attention on effective job behavior. (2) To teach managers that praise by itself may increase job satisfaction, but that it will have little or no effect on productivity unless it is made contingent upon specified job behaviors. Telling an employee that he is doing a good job in no way conveys to him what he is doing correctly. Such blanket praise can inadvertently reinforce the very things that the employee is doing in a mediocre way. (3) To teach managers to determine the optimum schedule for administering a reinforcer—be it praise, a smile, or money in the employee's pocket."

Weyerhaeuser has found that by using money as a reinforcer (that is, as a bonus over and above the worker's hourly rate), they obtained a 33 percent increase in productivity with one group of workers, an 18 percent increase in productivity with a second group of workers, and an 8 percent decrease in productivity with a third group of workers. Latham says, "These findings point out the need to measure and document the effectiveness of any human resource program. The results obtained in one industrial setting cannot necessarily be expected in another setting."

Latham notes that because of its current success with PR, Weyerhaeuser is currently applying reinforcement principles with tree planters in the rural South as well as with engineers and scientists at their corporate headquarters. In the latter case, they are comparing different forms of goal setting (assigned, participative, and a generalized goal of "do your best") with three different forms of reinforcement (praise or private recognition from a supervisor, public recognition in terms of a citation for excellence, and a monetary reward). Latham adds, "The purpose of the program is to motivate scientists to attain excellence. Excellence is defined in terms of the frequency with which an individual displays specific behaviors that have been identified by the engineers/scientists themselves as making the difference between success and failure in fulfilling the requirements of their job."

City of Detroit, Garbage Collectors. In December 1972, the City of Detroit instituted a unique productivity bonus system for sanitation workers engaged in refuse collection. The plan, which provides for sharing the savings for productivity improvement efforts, was designed to save money for the city while rewarding workers for increased efficiency. The city's Labor Relations Bureau negotiated the productivity contract with the two unions concerned with refuse collection: The American Federation of State, County and Municipal Employees (AFSCME), representing sanitation laborers (loaders), and the Teamsters Union, representing drivers. The two agreements took effect on July 1, 1973.

The bonus system was based on savings gained in productivity (reductions in paid man-hours per ton of refuse collected, reduction in the total hours of overtime, percentage of routes completed on schedule, and effectiveness or cleanliness). A bonus pool was established and the sanitation laborers share 50-50 in the pool with the city—each worker's portion being determined by the number of hours worked under the productivity bonus pool, exclusive of overtime.

By any measure, this program was a success. Citizen complaints decreased dramatically. During 1964, the city saved $1,654,000 after the bonus of $307,000 ($350 per man) was paid. The bonus system is still in effect, but the unions are currently disputing with the city the question of what constitutes a fair day's work. Both unions involved have expressed doubts about the accuracy of the data used to compute the productivity

index or, to be more precise, how the data are gathered and the index and bonus computed. Given this expected prenegotiation tactic by the unions, the city and the customers both agree that the plan has worked.

B. F. Goodrich Chemical Company. In 1972, one of the production sections in the B. F. Goodrich Chemical plant in Avon Lake, Ohio, as measured by standard accounting procedures, was failing. At that time, Donald J. Barnicki, the production manager, introduced a positive reinforcement program that included goal setting and feedback about scheduling, targets, costs, and problem areas. This program gave the information directly to the foreman on a once-a-week basis. In addition, daily meetings were held to discuss problems and describe how each group was doing. For the first time the foreman and their employees were told about costs that were incurred by their group. Charts were published that showed area achievements in terms of sales, cost, and productivity as compared with targets. Films were made that showed top management what the employees were doing, and these films were shown to the workers so they would know what management was being told.

According to Barnicki, this program of positive reinforcement turned the plant around. "Our productivity has increased 300 percent over the past five years. Costs are down. We had our best startup time in 1976 and passed our daily production level from last year the second day after we returned from the holidays."

ACDC Electronics. Edward J. Feeney, of Emery Air Freight fame, now heads a consulting firm that works with such firms as General Electric, Xerox, Braniff Airways, and General Atomic in the area of positive reinforcement programs. One of Mr. Feeney's current clients is the ACDC Electronics Company (a division of Emerson Electronics). After establishing a program that incorporated the four-step approach outlined earlier in this article, the ACDC Company experienced a profit increase of 25 percent over the forecast; a $550,000 cost reduction on $10 million in sales; a return of 1,900 percent on investment, including consultant fees; a reduction in turnaround time on repairs from 30 to 10 days; and a significant increase in attendance.

According to Ken Kilpatrick, ACDC President, "The results were as dramatic as those that Feeney had described. We found our output increased 30–40 percent almost immediately and has stayed at that high level for well over a year." The results were not accomplished, however, without initial problems, according to Feeney. "With some managers there were problems of inertia, disbelief, lack of time to implement, interest, difficulty in defining output for hard-to-measure areas, setting standards, measuring past performance, estimating economic payoffs, and failure to apply all feedback or reinforcement principles." Nevertheless, after positive results began to surface and initial problems were overcome, the ACDC management became enthused about the program.

CONCLUSION

This article has attempted to explain how reinforcement theory can be applied in organizational settings. We have argued that the arrangement of the contingencies of reinforcement is crucial in influencing behavior. Different ways of arranging these contingencies were explained, followed by a recommendation that the use of positive reinforcement combined with oral explanations of incorrect behaviors, when applied correctly, is an underestimated and powerful tool of management. The correct application includes three conditions: *First*, reinforcers must be selected that are sufficiently powerful and durable to establish and strengthen behavior; *second*, the manager must design the contingencies in such a way that the reinforcing events are made contingent on the desired level of performance; *third*, the program must be designed in such a way that it is possible to establish a reliable training procedure for inducing the desired response patterns.

To meet these three conditions for effective contingency management, many firms have set up a formal positive reinforcement motivational program. These include firms such as Emery Air Freight, Michigan Bell, Standard Oil of Ohio,

General Electric, and B. F. Goodrich, among others. Typically, these firms employ a four-stage approach in designing their programs: (1) A performance audit is conducted in order to determine what performance patterns are desired and to measure the current levels of that performance; (2) specific and reasonable goals are set for each worker; (3) each employee is generally instructed to keep a record of his or her own work; and (4) positive aspects of the employee's performance are positively reinforced by the supervisor. Under this four-stage program, the employee has two chances of being successful—he can beat his previous level of performance or he can beat that plus his own goal. Also under this system, negative feedback routinely comes only from the employee (since he knows when he failed to meet the objective), whereas positive feedback comes from both the employee and his supervisor.

While we noted that many firms have credited this approach with improving morale and increasing profits, several points of concern and potential shortcomings of this approach should also be cited. Many people claim that you cannot teach reinforcement principles to lower-level managers very easily and unless you get managers to understand the principles, you certainly risk misusing these tools. Poorly designed reward systems can interfere with the development of spontaneity and creativity. Reinforcement systems that are deceptive and manipulative are an insult to employees.

One way in which a positive reinforcement program based solely on praise can be deceptive and manipulative occurs when productivity continues to increase month after month and year after year, and the company's profits increase as well, but employee salaries do not reflect their contributions. This seems obviously unethical and contradictory. It is unethical because the workers are being exploited and praise by itself will not have any long-term effect on performance. Emery Air Freight, for example, has begun to experience this backlash effect. It is contradictory because the manager is saying he believes in the principle of making intangible rewards contingent on performance but at the same time refuses to make the tangible monetary reward contingent on performance. Often the excuse given is that "our employees are unionized." Well, this is not always the case. Many firms that are without unions, such as Emery, refuse to pay on performance. Many other firms with unions have a contingent bonus plan. Skinner in 1969 warned managers that a poorly designed monetary reward system may actually reduce performance. The employee should be a willing party to the influence attempt, with both parties benefitting from the relationship.

Peter Drucker's concern is different. He worries that perhaps positive reinforcers may be misused by management to the detriment of the economy. He says, "The carrot of material rewards has not, like the stick of fear, lost its potency. On the contrary, it has become so potent that it threatens to destroy the earth's finite resources if it does not first destroy more economies through inflation that reflects rising expectations." In other words, positive reinforcement can be too effective as used by firms concerned solely with their own personal gains.

Skinner in an interview in *Organizational Dynamics* stated that a feedback system alone may not be enough. He recommended that the organization should design feedback and incentive systems in such a way that the dual objective of getting things done and making work enjoyable is met. He says what must be accomplished, and what he believes is currently lacking, is an effective training program for managers. "In the not-too-distant future, however, a new breed of industrial managers may be able to apply the principles of operant conditioning effectively."

We have evidence in at least a few organizational settings that Skinner's hopes are on the way to realization, that a new breed of industrial managers are indeed applying the principles of operant conditioning effectively.

SELECTED BIBLIOGRAPHY

For an understandable view of Skinner's basic ideas in his own words, see B. F. Skinner's *Contingencies of Reinforcement* (Appleton-Century-Crofts, 1969) and Carl R. Rogers and B. F. Skinner's "Some Issues Concerning the Control of Human Behavior" (*Science*, 1965, Vol. 24, pp. 1057–1066). For Skinner's views on the applications of his ideas in industry see "An Interview with B. F. Skinner (*Organizational Dynamics*, Winter 1973, pp. 31–40).

For an account of Skinner's ideas in action, see the same issue of *Organizational Dynamics* (pp. 41–50) and "Where Skinner's Theories Work" (*Business Week*, December 2, 1972, pp. 64–69).

An article highly critical of the application of Skinner's ideas in industry is W. F. Whyte's "Pigeons, Persons, and Piece Rates" (*Psychology Today*, April 1972, pp. 67–68). For a more sympathetic and more systematic treatment see W. R. Nord's "Beyond the Teaching Machine: The Negative Area of Operant Conditioning" in *The Theory and Practice of Management, Organizational Behavior and Human Performance* (1969, No. 4, pp. 375–401).

For previous comments on behavior modification by the author, see W. Clay Hamner's "Reinforcement Theory and Contingency Management" in L. Tosi and W. Clay Hamner, eds., *Organizational Behavior and Management: A Contingency Approach* (St. Clair Press, 1974, pp. 188–204) and W. Clay Hamner's "Worker Motivation Programs: Importance of Climate Structure and Performance Consequences" in W. Clay Hamner and Frank L. Schmidt's *Contemporary Problems in Personnel* (St. Clair Press, 1974, pp. 280–308).

Last, the best discussion of the general subject of pay and performance is Edward E. Lawler III's *Pay and Organizational Effectiveness* (McGraw-Hill, 1971).

THE MANAGEMENT OF
BEHAVIORAL CONTINGENCIES

FRED LUTHANS
ROBERT KREITNER

It looks as if the path leading out of the jungle of management theory may follow the guideposts of contingency theory—linking quantitative, behavioral, and systems concepts and techniques with economic, technological, environmental, and social variables affecting the organization and its people.

To date, there are only two well known contingency approaches to management. The first, dealing with organizational design, resulted from the work in the 1950s of Joan Woodward, who discovered the impact that technology had on the British manufacturing firms she studied. Later, Paul Lawrence and Jay Lorsch found an environmental impact on the internal structures of the organizations they studied, and today, this contingency approach to organization design is widely accepted in theory and practice. Second, Fred Fiedler developed a contingency model of leadership effectiveness, which he found to be a function of the style—human relations-oriented or task-directed—and the situation—favorable or unfavorable. Fiedler objectively and systematically assessed the dimensions of particular situations according to position power, acceptance by subordinates, and task definition and concluded that

in very favorable and very unfavorable situations the task-directed leader was most effective, whereas in moderately favorable and moderately unfavorable situations a human relations-oriented leader was most effective.

Here, we propose a third contingency approach, identified as organizational behavior modification, or O.B. Mod. Based on operant learning theory and the principles of behavior modification, this approach assumes that organizational behavior depends on its consequences, that organizational behavior with reinforcing consequences tends to increase in frequency, whereas organizational behavior with punishing consequences tends to diminish in frequency. To be sustained, specific responses must be reinforced or strengthened by immediate environmental contingencies. The important point is that the relationship between behavioral responses and their environmental consequences involves the concept of contingency, which this article discusses in terms of how it can be applied to the management of human resources.

THE BEHAVIORAL
CONTINGENCY CONCEPT

Contingency denotes a relationship in which something is dependent on chance or on the fulfillment of a condition. Behaviorists such as B. F. Skinner borrowed the word contingency for scientific behavioral analysis, and even in that context contingency denotes a dependent relationship, between observable behavioral events and certain environmental conditions. According to Skinner: "An adequate formulation of the interaction between an organism and its environment must always specify three things: (1) the occasion upon which a response occurs, (2) the response itself, and (3) the ... consequences." The interrelationships among the three elements (occasion, response, and consequence) form a behavioral contingency. The process of breaking complex behavior down into the identifiable contingencies is called functional analysis.

The concept of behavioral contingency can be clarified by a simple example in a company. An employee's specific behavior of standing at the pay window will lead to the consequence of being paid only if it is payday. Hence, payday sets the occasion for the behavioral response of standing in front of the pay window and that, in turn, leads to the consequence of being paid. Tracing the dependent relationships backward, being paid is contingent (dependent) upon standing at the pay window, which is contingent upon its being payday. The three elements necessary for the existence of a behavioral contingency are present: occasion, response, and consequence. According to the premises of operant learning theory, behavior changes as a result of such a contingency. In other words, the employee learns to associate certain consequences with a specific behavioral response and a particular setting or occasion. He learns to stand in front of the pay window on payday, because that specific behavior in that

particular setting consistently leads to the reinforcing consequence of being paid.

The three elements that collectively form a behavioral contingency and lead to its behavioral outcome are illustrated in Figure 1, in a schematic called the A→B→C functional analysis (antecedent—a, behavior—b, and consequence—c). It depicts the functional and empirically validated interface between a specific behavior and its immediate antecedent and consequent environment. (In this context, environment includes the total human and nonhuman surroundings.)

Through past experience, organizational participants learn to associate specific consequences with various environmental settings. As a result, environmental cues are generated, which tell a person when certain behaviors have a good chance of leading to specific consequences. For example, the supervisor's office is often associated with punishing consequences. Thus, isolating the contingencies through functional analysis may help explain why otherwise creative, active, and outgoing work group members frequently become sullen upon entering their supervisor's office. The office cues, or signals, a high probability of forthcoming punishing consequences, because it has been the scene of punishing consequences in the past.

As has been shown, contingent consequences may be reinforcing, punishing, or nonexistent. Reinforcing consequences, as the term implies, strengthen replications of the preceding behaviors upon which they are contingent. Punishing and nonexistent consequences weaken preceding behaviors. (The word nonexistent may be mislead-

FIGURE 1. Behavioral contingency A → B → C functional analysis

Antecedent ———→ A	Behavior ———→ B	Consequence C	Behavioral Outcome
The previous occasion upon which a particular emitted behavior led to a specific type of consequence.	Specific and observable, quantifiable in terms of frequency of occurrence.	Reinforcing, punishing, or nonexistent.	An increase or decrease in the frequency of the behavior or its extinction.

ing. What is meant is that, as a general rule, behavior with no contingent consequences tends to be repeated with decreasing frequency and eventually will disappear—that is, the nonreinforced behavior is extinguished.) In all cases, the consequence must be contingent upon a particular behavior if it is to alter the frequency of that behavior in the future.

The key to functionally defining the three general types of behavioral contingencies lies in measuring the frequency of the behavioral outcomes. For example, as a result of certain contingencies, does an employee punch in on time more or less often? If the frequency of the behavior increases, the contingency can be properly called reinforcing. A punishing or nonexistent contingency is responsible for a drop in frequency of behavior.

INDIVIDUALITY OF BEHAVIORAL CONTINGENCIES

Whether reinforcing or punishing, contingencies are idiosyncratic; one employee's reinforcer may be another's punisher. A manager who assumes that specific consequences will affect all employees' behavior in the same way falls into a commonly unheeded trap. A contingent manager must learn what turns individual subordinates on and what turns them off. Again, the common denominator in this determination is frequency of specific behavior outcomes, so a manager using the contingency approach must discerningly monitor the frequency of job-related behaviors that are to be changed.

There can be no rigid definitions of reinforcers and punishers. Only after observing behavior and charting its frequency can a contingency manager know whether a particular consequence was reinforcing or punishing. And managers cannot assume their subordinates will be reinforced or punished by the same consequences that they personally find reinforcing or punishing. To repeat, one employee's reinforcer may be another's punisher. The contingency manager must examine an employee's *reinforcement history*. What contingent consequences have reinforced or punished an employee's particular job-related behav-

iors in the past? If a particular behavior increased in frequency, then the contingent consequence was reinforcing. Conversely, if a specific behavior that led to a particular contingent consequence decreased in frequency, the consequence must have been punishing. Behavior that had no contingent consequence diminished in frequency from lack of reinforcement. By carefully examining reinforcement histories a contingency manager can use the past to predict the utility of future behavioral strategies.

Managers who absolutely accept or reject money as a motivator do not understand the contingency concept. Money *may* be reinforcing, but many modern compensation methods, especially those based on time, such as the hourly wage or fixed salary, are noncontingent. This means they do not tie specific pay to specific work.

If money is not seen as a motivator, careful functional analysis of present work behavior may turn up alternative reinforcers on the job. For example, if the task variables permit, contingent time off can be an excellent alternative reinforcer. A contingent time off plan makes early time off contingent upon satisfactory, stable performance. Task standardization is a necessary element of such a plan. In a routine task situation the employee sees a direct connection between each piece or unit of work and getting off early.

There are many indicators on the current scene of the need for an alternative to more, more, and more money. For one, in the recent Chrysler settlement the major issue was mandatory overtime, not more money. While doing preliminary field research on contingent time off, the authors came across an interesting illustration of the desire for time off in lieu of more money. A manufacturing firm instituted a yearly plan whereby each of more than 85 production department employees doing routine tasks was given the option of taking 40 hours whenever he wished or selling back the unused time for money at the end of the year. (It should be noted that this plan supplemented a generous sick leave program.) To date, 73 percent of the maximum allowable time off has been taken; only three employees have not taken any of their 40-hour allotment. The contingency manager would take advantage of such a powerful reinforcer by making it contingent upon performance.

BEHAVIORAL CONTINGENCY MANAGEMENT BY O. B. MOD.

There are several steps in the process of becoming a contingent manager. The O.B. Mod. model shown in Figure 2 contains five essential steps: (1) identify, (2) measure, (3) analyze, (4) intervene, and (5) evaluate. The first step involves the identification of behavior problems. Inferred internal states and processes such as attitudes, needs, and drives have little utility in this approach. The behavior problems must be reduced to observable behavioral events that are measurable in terms of frequency. With behavior frequency as the basic datum, the contingency manager is prepared to measure the target behavior, shown in Step 2. The frequency of the problem behavior can be graphed as a function of occurrence and time; subsequent assessment of the ef-

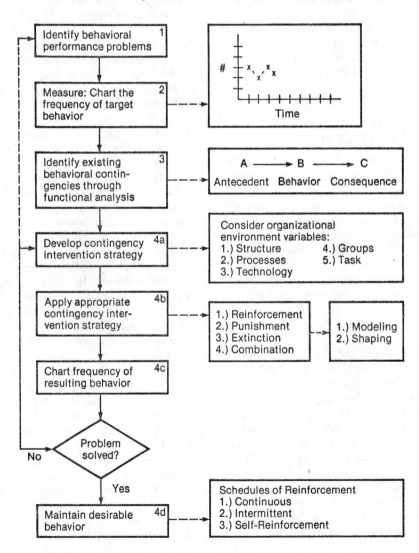

FIGURE 2. Steps in organizational behavior modification (O. B. Mod.)

fectiveness of various intervention strategies is possible only with an adequate baseline measure.

The functional analysis in Step 3 indicates what antecedent and consequent events are presently paired with the target behavior. Before any intervention is attempted, it must be ascertained what is maintaining the present behavior—a difficult but critical step. After consideration of relevant organizational environment variables, a contingency management intervention strategy is developed (Step 4a) and applied (Step 4b). When the intervention strategy is implemented, the frequency of the target behavior is again monitored by measuring (Step 4c). Random time samples may be utilized here to cut down the time-consuming work of charting relatively high-frequency behaviors.

Next, the question of whether or not the targeted behavioral problem has been solved is answered. If the problem behavior maintains its baseline frequency or even accelerates, then another strategy (recycle to Step 4a) must be developed or the entire process, starting with Step 1, must begin again. If the targeted behavior diminishes in frequency, then attention must be turned to maintaining its low frequency (Step 4d).

Often, especially when a combination of strategies (such as reinforcement plus extinction) is used, alternative desirable behaviors must be shaped and reinforced as the problem behavior diminishes. The maintenance of alternative desirable behavior starts on a continuous schedule and gradually moves to an intermittent schedule; self-reinforcement is the ultimate maintenance goal.

In the last step (5), an evaluation is made of the overall effectiveness of the particular contingency intervention strategy. Each contingency manager must build his own empirical data base to help determine the efficiency of various intervention strategies. What works for a manager in one situation may not work in another because of numerous complex human and organizational variables. And strategies that work for one manager may not work for another. As the manager's O.B. Mod. contingency skills develop, however, he will find that more and more behavioral performance problems are adaptable to the logic of the sequential steps shown in the model.

WHAT O. B. MOD. IS AND IS NOT

As the direct or indirect controller of much of a subordinate's work environment, the practicing manager is in a position to use O.B. Mod. in predicting and changing behavior by managing environmental contingencies. It is important to note that the contingency manager manipulates the environment, not the person; the employee self-adjusts to his environment. Since a fundamental aspect of O.B. Mod. is the systematic management of contingencies, haphazard and intuitive managerial techniques not only are of little utility but actually may interfere with the process. Implicit in the systematic management of subordinates' work contingencies is self-control. The manager himself is a significant part of an employee's immediate work environment, so in a sense environmental control by the manager is often tantamount to self-control. Noncontingent reinforcement and/or arbitrary and capricious reinforcement are the antithesis of sound contingency management.

It is very essential to distinguish systematically managed contingencies from accidental contingencies, which are a way of life in the typical work situation. Suppose a foreman in an exceptionally good mood bursts into the shop and socially reinforces several machine operators with solicitous conversation, jokes, and laughter. Suppose, too, that one of the operators was taking advantage of unsupervised time to work on a personal project and that in the past, the foreman has come down hard on those who used company time and tools for personal work. With the boss laughing and joking right in front of the illegal work, the worker might assume the foreman was aware of it but no longer cared. If the frequency of the operator's personal work on shop time increases, because the exuberant but thoughtless foreman had created an accidental reinforcing contingency, an already mistaken situation worsens a week or two later when the foreman severely reprimands the operator for misusing company time and property. The net result is a frustrated, confused employee who is completely out of tune with his work environment.

With systematically managed contingencies, on the other hand, the manager puts the worker in tune with his work environment. At the outset, care must be taken to structure the employee's expectations appropriately through relevant skill development, work environment orientation (an explanation of contingencies), and understandable instructions. Then the manager should systematically reinforce all desirable behavior and ignore or, as a last resort, systematically penalize undesirable behavior. As was said earlier, new behaviors have to be shaped by reinforcing successively closer approximations to the target behavior. Once the behavior is established, continuous reinforcement is called for and later, intermittent reinforcement at frequencies that will lead to improved performance and organizational goal achievement.

An O.B. Mod. approach is not the easy way to manage human resources—in fact, it may turn out to be the most difficult. However, preliminary research findings by the authors and their associates are very encouraging. A pilot program in a manufacturing firm was able to significantly increase the performance of every supervisor trained in O.B. Mod. Follow-up research in a number of organizations is currently in progress.

In contemporary management, human problems override technological ones. Chronic absenteeism, turnover, and quality control flaws on the operative level and diminished commitment, innovation, and leadership in the managerial ranks collectively constitute a major human resource challenge to management. For over two decades various behavioral approaches have been explored and used, with spotty results. Yet, realistic analysis shows that virtually all of today's human resource problems are behavior/performance problems. A systematic and reliable process that modifies behavior through control of environmental contingencies presents itself as a promising way to go.

With operant learning theory and the principles of behavior modification serving as the base, O.B. Mod. allows the practicing manager to get back to basics. Empirically validated and consistent man-environment contingencies enable this move to be disciplined, in contrast to the traditional bits-and-pieces approach. The impetus for O.B. Mod. contingency-based management of human resources must come from the practicing managers themselves, but the promise of potential payoffs in improved job performance should be a strong incentive for them to tackle it.

POWER IS THE
GREAT MOTIVATOR

DAVID C. McCLELLAND
DAVID H. BURNHAM

What makes or motivates a good manager? The question is so enormous in scope that anyone trying to answer it has difficulty knowing where to begin. Some people might say that a good manager is one who is successful; and by now most business researchers and businessmen themselves know what motivates people who successfully run their own small businesses. The key to their success has turned out to be what psychologists call "the need for achievement," the desire to do something better or more efficiently than it has been done before. Any number of books and articles summarize research studies explaining how the achievement motive is necessary for a person to attain success on his own.[1]

But what has achievement motivation got to do with good management? There is no reason on theoretical grounds why a person who has a strong need to be more efficient should make a good manager. While it sounds as if everyone ought to have the need to achieve, in fact, as psychologists define and measure achievement motivation, it leads people to behave in very special ways that do not necessarily lead to good management.

For one thing, because they focus on personal improvement, on doing things better by themselves, achievement-motivated people want to do things themselves. For another, they want concrete short-term feedback on their performance so that they can tell how well they are doing. Yet a manager, particularly one of or in a large complex organization, cannot perform all the tasks necessary for success by himself or herself. He must manage others so that they will do things for the organization. Also, feedback on his subordinate's performance may be a lot vaguer and more delayed than it would be if he were doing everything himself.

The manager's job seems to call more for someone who can influence people than for someone who does things better on his own. In motivational terms, then, we might expect the successful manager to have a greater "need for power" than need to achieve. But there must be other qualities beside the need for power that go into the makeup of a good manager. Just what these qualities are and how they interrelate is the subject of this article.

To measure the motivations of managers, good and bad, we studied a number of individual managers from different large U.S. corporations who were participating in management workshops designed to improve their managerial effectiveness. (The workshop techniques and research methods and terms used are described in the ruled insert on pages 282–283.)

The general conclusion of these studies is that the top manager of a company must possess a high need for power, that is, a concern for influencing people. However, this need must be disciplined and controlled so that it is directed toward the benefit of the institution as a whole and not toward the manager's personal aggrandizement. Moreover, the top manager's need for power ought to be greater than his need for being liked by people.

Now let us look at what these ideas mean in the context of real individuals in real situations and see what comprises the profile of the good manager. Finally, we will look at the workshops themselves to determine how they go about changing behavior.

MEASURING MANAGERIAL EFFECTIVENESS

First off, what does it mean when we say that a good manager has a greater need for "power" than for "achievement"? To get a more concrete idea, let us consider the case of Ken Briggs, a sales manager in a large U.S. corporation who joined one of our managerial workshops (see the ruled insert). Some six or seven years ago, Ken Briggs was promoted to a managerial position at corporate headquarters, where he had responsibility for salesmen who service his company's largest accounts.

In filling out his questionnaire at the workshop, Ken showed that he correctly perceived what his job required of him, namely, that he should influence others' success more than achieve new goals himself or socialize with his subordinates. However, when asked with other members of the workshop to write a story depicting a managerial situation, Ken unwittingly revealed through his fiction that he did not share those concerns. Indeed, he discovered that his need for achievement was very high—in fact over the 90th percentile—and his need for power was very low, in about the 15th percentile. Ken's high need to achieve was no surprise—after all, he had been a very successful salesman—but obviously his motiva-

tion to influence others was much less than his job required. Ken was a little disturbed but thought that perhaps the measuring instruments were not too accurate and that the gap between the ideal and his score was not as great as it seemed.

Then came the real shocker. Ken's subordinates confirmed what his stories revealed: he was a poor manager, having little positive impact on those who worked for him. Ken's subordinates felt that they had little responsibility delegated to them, that he never rewarded but only criticized them, and that the office was not well organized, but confused and chaotic. On all three of these scales, his office rated in the 10th to 15th percentile relative to national norms.

As Ken talked the results over privately with a workshop leader, he became more and more upset. He finally agreed, however, that the results of the survey confirmed feelings he had been afraid to admit to himself or others. For years, he had been miserable in his managerial role. He now knew the reason: he simply did not want to nor had he been able to influence or manage others. As he thought back, he realized that he had failed every time he had tried to influence his staff, and he felt worse than ever.

Ken had responded to failure by setting very high standards—his office scored in the 98th percentile on this scale—and by trying to do most things himself, which was close to impossible; his own activity and lack of delegation consequently left his staff demoralized. Ken's experience is typical of those who have a strong need to achieve but low power motivation. They may become very successful salesmen and, as a consequence, may be promoted into managerial jobs for which they, ironically, are unsuited. If achievement motivation does not make a good manager, what motive does? It is not enough to suspect that power motivation may be important; one needs hard evidence that people who are better managers than Ken Briggs do in fact possess stronger power motivation and perhaps score higher in other characteristics as well. But how does one decide who is the better manager?

Real-world performance measures are hard to come by if one is trying to rate managerial effectiveness in production, marketing, finance, or research and development. In trying to determine who the better managers were in Ken Briggs's company, we did not want to rely only on the opinions of their superiors. For a variety of reasons, superiors' judgments of their subordinates' real-world performance may be inaccurate. In the absence of some standard measure of performance, we decided that the next best index of a manager's effectiveness would be the climate he or she creates in the office, reflected in the morale of subordinates.

Almost by definition, a good manager is one who, among other things, helps subordinates feel strong and responsible, who rewards them properly for good performance, and who sees that things are organized in such a way that subordinates feel they know what they should be doing. Above all, managers should foster among subordinates a strong sense of team spirit, of pride in working as part of a particular team. If a manager creates and encourages this spirit, his subordinates certainly should perform better.

In the company Ken Briggs works for, we have direct evidence of a connection between morale and performance in the one area where performance measures are easy to come by—namely, sales. In April 1973, at least three employees from this company's 16 sales districts filled out questionnaires that rated their office for organizational clarity and team spirit (see the ruled insert). Their scores were averaged and totaled to give an overall morale score for each office. The percentage gains or losses in sales for each district in 1973 were compared with those for 1972. The difference in sales figures by district ranged from a gain of nearly 30% to a loss of 8%, with a median gain of around 14%. Exhibit I shows the average gain in sales performance plotted against the increasing averages in morale scores.

In Exhibit I we can see that the relationship between sales and morale is surprisingly close. The six districts with the lowest morale early in the year showed an average sales gain of only around 7% by years' end (although there was wide variation within this group), whereas the two districts with the highest morale showed an

EXHIBIT I. Correlation between morale score and sales performance for a large U.S. corporation

Average percent gain in sales by district from 1972 to 1973

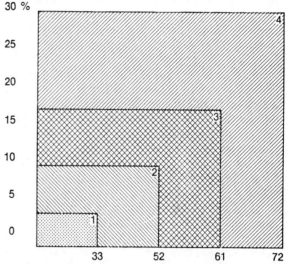

Morale score (perceived organizational clarity plus team spirit)

1 = 6 districts   2 = 4 districts   3 = 4 districts   4 = 2 districts

average gain of 28%. When morale scores rise above the 50th percentile in terms of national norms, they seem to lead to better sales performance. In Ken Briggs's company, at least, high morale at the beginning is a good index of how well the sales division actually performed in the coming year.

And it seems very likely that the manager who can create high morale among salesmen can also do the same for employees in other areas (production, design, and so on), leading to better performance. Given that high morale in an office indicates that there is a good manager present, what general characteristics does he possess?

A Need for Power

In examining the motive scores of over 50 managers of both high and low morale units in all sections of the same large company, we found that most of the managers—over 70%—were high in power motivation compared with men in general. This finding confirms the fact that power motivation is important for management. (Remember that as we use the term "power motivation," it refers not to dictatorial behavior, but to a desire to have impact, to be strong and influential.) The better managers, as judged by the morale of those working for them, tended to score even higher in power motivation. But the most important determining factor of high morale turned out not to be how their power motivation compared to their need to achieve but whether it was higher than their need to be liked. This relationship existed for 80% of the better sales managers as compared with only 10% of the poorer managers. And the same held true for other managers in nearly all parts of the company.

In the research, product development, and operations divisions, 73% of the better managers had a stronger need for power than a need to be liked (or what we term "affiliation motive") as compared with only 22% of the poorer managers. Why should this be so? Sociologists have long argued that, for a bureaucracy to function effectively, those who manage it must be universalistic in applying rules. That is, if they make exceptions for the particular needs of individuals, the whole system will break down.

The manager with a high need for being liked is precisely the one who wants to stay on good terms with everybody, and, therefore, is the one most likely to make exceptions in terms of particular needs. If a male employee asks for time off to stay home with his sick wife to help look after her and the kids, the affiliative manager agrees almost without thinking, because he feels sorry for the man and agrees that his family needs him.

When President Ford remarked in pardoning ex-President Nixon that he had "suffered enough," he was responding as an affiliative manager would, because he was empathizing primarily with Nixon's needs and feelings. Sociological theory and our data both argue, however, that the person whose need for affiliation is high does not make a good manager. This kind of person creates poor morale because he or she does not understand that other people in the office will tend to regard exceptions to the rules as unfair to

themselves, just as many U.S. citizens felt it was unfair to let Richard Nixon off and punish others less involved than he was in the Watergate scandal.

Socialized Power

But so far our findings are a little alarming. Do they suggest that the good manager is one who cares for power and is not at all concerned about the needs of other people? Not quite, for the good manager has other characteristics which must still be taken into account.

Above all, the good manager's power motivation is not oriented toward personal aggrandizement but toward the institution which he or she serves. In another major research study, we found that the signs of controlled action or inhibition that appear when a person exercises his or her imagination in writing stories tell a great deal about the kind of power that person needs.[2] We discovered that, if a high power motive score is balanced by high inhibition, stories about power tend to be altruistic. That is, the heroes in the story exercise power on behalf of someone else. This is the "socialized" face of power as distinguished from the concern for personal power, which is characteristic of individuals whose stories are loaded with power imagery but which show no sign of inhibition or self-control. In our earlier study, we found ample evidence that these latter individuals exercise their power impulsively. They are more rude to other people, they drink too much, they try to exploit others sexually, and they collect symbols of personal prestige such as fancy cars or big offices.

Individuals high in power and in control, on the other hand, are more institution minded; they tend to get elected to more offices, to control their drinking, and to want to serve others. Not surprisingly, we found in the workshops that the better managers in the corporation also tend to score high on both power and inhibition.

PROFILE OF A GOOD MANAGER

Let us recapitulate what we have discussed so far and have illustrated with data from one company. The better managers we studied are high in power motivation, low in affiliation motivation, and high in inhibition. They care about institutional power and use it to stimulate their employees to be more productive. Now let us compare them with affiliative managers—those in whom the need for affiliation is higher than the need for power—and with the personal power managers—those in whom the need for power is higher than for affiliation but whose inhibition score is low.

In the sales division of our illustrative company, there were managers who matched the three types fairly closely. Exhibit II shows how their subordinates rated the offices they worked in on responsibility, organizational clarity, and team spirit. There are scores from at least three subordinates for each manager, and several managers are represented for each type, so that the averages shown in the exhibit are quite stable. Note that the manager who is concerned about being liked by people tends to have subordinates who feel that they have very little personal responsibility, that organizational procedures are not clear, and that they have little pride in their work group.

In short, as we expected, affiliative managers make so many ad hominem and ad hoc decisions that they almost totally abandon orderly procedures. Their disregard for procedure leaves employees feeling weak, irresponsible, and without a sense of what might happen next, of where they stand in relation to their manager, or even of what they ought to be doing. In this company, the group of affiliative managers portrayed in Exhibit II were below the 30th percentile in morale scores.

The managers who are motivated by a need for personal power are somewhat more effective. They are able to create a greater sense of responsibility in their divisions and, above all, a greater team spirit. They can be thought of as managerial equivalents of successful tank commanders such as General Patton, whose own daring inspired admiration in his troops. But notice how in Exhibit II these men are still only in the 40th percentile in the amount of organizational clarity they create, as compared to the high power, low affiliation, high inhibition managers, whom we shall term "institutional."

EXHIBIT II. Average scores on selected climate dimensions by subordinates of managers with different motive profiles

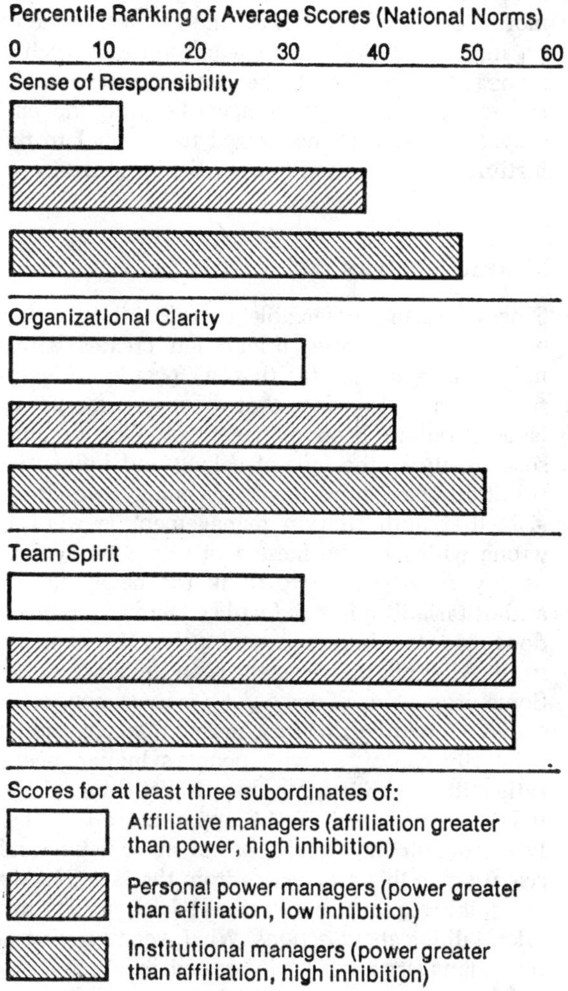

Percentile Ranking of Average Scores (National Norms)

Scores for at least three subordinates of:
- Affiliative managers (affiliation greater than power, high inhibition)
- Personal power managers (power greater than affiliation, low inhibition)
- Institutional managers (power greater than affiliation, high inhibition)

Managers motivated by personal power are not disciplined enough to be good institution builders, and often their subordinates are loyal to them as individuals rather than to the institution they both serve. When a personal power manager leaves, disorganization often follows. His subordinates' strong group spirit, which the manager has personally inspired, deflates. The subordinates do not know what to do for themselves.

Of the managerial types, the "institutional"

manager is the most successful in creating an effective work climate. Exhibit II shows that his subordinates feel that they have more responsibility. Also, this kind of manager creates high morale because he produces the greatest sense of organizational clarity and team spirit. If such a manager leaves, he or she can be more readily replaced by another manager, because the employees have been encouraged to be loyal to the institution rather than to a particular person.

Managerial Styles

Since it seems undeniable from Exhibit II that either kind of power orientation creates better morale in subordinates than a "people" orientation, we must consider that a concern for power is essential to good management. Our findings seem to fly in the face of a long and influential tradition of organizational psychology, which insists that authoritarian management is what is wrong with most businesses in this country. Let us say frankly that we think the bogeyman of authoritarianism has in fact been wrongly used to downplay the importance of power in management. After all, management is an influence game. Some proponents of democratic management seem to have forgotten this fact, urging managers to be primarily concerned with people's human needs rather than with helping them to get things done.

But a good deal of the apparent conflict between our findings and those of other behavioral scientists in this area arises from the fact that we are talking about *motives,* and behaviorists are often talking about *actions.* What we are saying is that managers must be interested in playing the influence game in a controlled way. That does not necessarily mean that they are or should be authoritarian in action. On the contrary, it appears that power motivated managers make their subordinates feel strong rather than weak. The true authoritarian in action would have the reverse effect, making people feel weak and powerless.

Thus another important ingredient in the profile of a manager is his or her managerial style. In the illustrative company, 63% of the better

managers (those whose subordinates had higher morale) scored higher on the democratic or coaching styles of management as compared with only 22% of the poorer managers, a statistically significant difference. By contrast, the latter scored higher on authoritarian or coercive management styles. Since the better managers were also higher in power motivation, it seems that, in action, they express their power motivation in a democratic way, which is more likely to be effective.

To see how motivation and style interact, let us consider the case of George Prentice, a manager in the sales division of another company. George had exactly the right motive combination to be an institutional manager. He was high in the need for power, low in the need for affiliation, and high in inhibition. He exercised his power in a controlled, organized way. His stories reflected this fact. In one, for instance, he wrote, "The men sitting around the table were feeling pretty good; they had just finished plans for reorganizing the company; the company has been beset with a number of organizational problems. This group, headed by a hard-driving, brilliant young executive, has completely reorganized the company structurally with new jobs and responsibilities. . . ."

This described how George himself was perceived by the company, and shortly after the workshop he was promoted to vice president in charge of all sales. But George was also known to his colleagues as a monster, a tough guy who would "walk over his grandmother" if she stood in the way of his advancement. He had the right motive combination and, in fact, was more interested in institutional growth than in personal power, but his managerial style was all wrong. Taking his cue from some of the top executives in the corporation, he told people what they had to do and threatened them with dire consequences if they didn't do it.

When George was confronted with his authoritarianism in a workshop, he recognized that this style was counterproductive—in fact, in another part of the study we found that it was associated with low morale—and he subsequently changed to acting more like a coach, which was the scale on which he scored the lowest initially. George saw more clearly that his job was not to force other people to do things but to help them to figure out ways of getting their job done better for the company.

The Institutional Manager

One reason it was easy for George Prentice to change his managerial style was that in his imaginative stories he was already having thoughts about helping others, characteristic of men with the institution-building motivational pattern. In further examining institution builders' thoughts and actions, we found they have four major characteristics:

1

They are more organization-minded; that is, they tend to join more organizations and to feel responsible for building up these organizations. Furthermore, they believe strongly in the importance of centralized authority.

2

They report that they like to work. This finding is particularly interesting, because our research on achievement motivation has led many commentators to argue that achievement motivation promotes the "Protestant work ethic." Almost the precise opposite is true. People who have a high need to achieve like to get out of work by becoming more efficient. They would like to see the same result obtained in less time or with less effort. But managers who have a need for institutional power actually seem to like the discipline of work. It satisfies their need for getting things done in an orderly way.

3

They seem quite willing to sacrifice some of their own self-interest for the welfare of the organization they serve. For example, they are more willing to make contributions to charities.

4

They have a keen sense of justice. It is almost as if they feel that if a person works hard and sacri-

fices for the good of the organization, he should and will get a just reward for his effort.

It is easy to see how each of these four concerns helps a person become a good manager, concerned about what the institution can achieve.

Maturity

Before we go on to look at how the workshops can help managers to improve their managerial style and recognize their own motivations, let us consider one more fact we discovered in studying the better managers at George Prentice's company. They were more mature (see ruled insert, pp. 282–283). Mature people can be most simply described as less egotistic. Somehow their positive self-image is not at stake in what they are doing. They are less defensive, more willing to seek advice from experts, and have a longer range view. They accumulate fewer personal possessions and seem older and wiser. It is as if they have awakened to the fact that they are not going to live forever and have lost some of the feeling that their own personal future is all that important.

Many U.S. businessmen fear this kind of maturity. They suspect that it will make them less hard driving, less expansion-minded, and less committed to organizational effectiveness. Our data do not support their fears. These fears are exactly the ones George Prentice had before he went to the workshop. Afterward he was a more effective manager, not despite his loss of some of the sense of his own importance, but because of it. The reason is simple: his subordinates believed afterward that he genuinely was more concerned about the company than about himself. Where once they respected his confidence but feared him, they now trust him. Once he supported their image of him as a "big man" by talking about the new Porsche and the new Honda he had bought; when we saw him recently he said, almost as an aside, "I don't buy things anymore."

CHANGING MANAGERIAL STYLE

George Prentice was able to change his managerial style after learning more about himself in a

EXHIBIT III. Average scores on selected climate dimensions by over 50 salesmen before and after their managers were trained

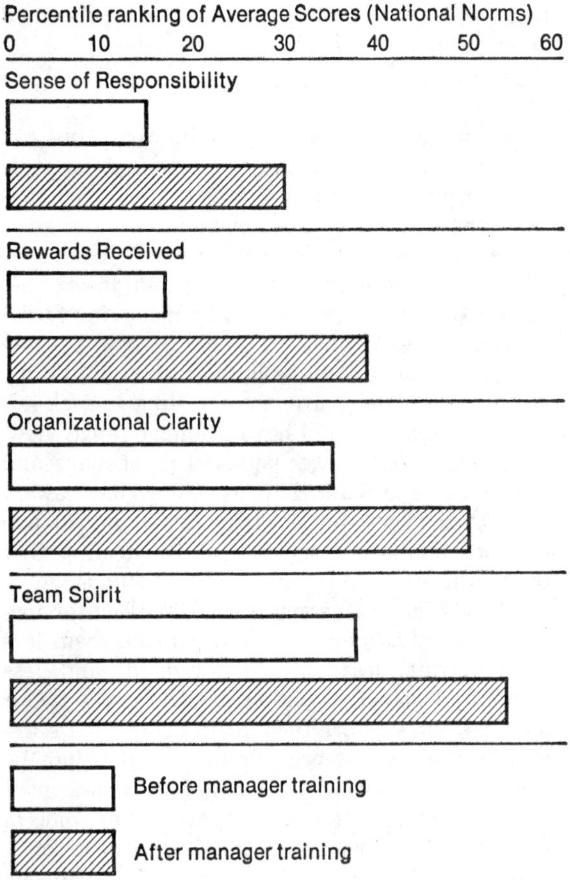

Percentile ranking of Average Scores (National Norms)

```
0        10       20       30       40       50       60
```

Sense of Responsibility

Rewards Received

Organizational Clarity

Team Spirit

☐ Before manager training

▨ After manager training

workshop. But does self-knowledge generally improve managerial behavior?

Some people might ask, "What good does it do to know, if I am a manager, that I should have a strong power motive, not too great a concern about being liked, a sense of discipline, a high level of maturity, and a coaching managerial style? What can I do about it?" The answer is that workshops for managers that give information to them in a supportive setting enable them to change.

Consider the results shown in Exhibit III, where "before" and "after" scores are compared. Once again we use the responses of subordinates

to give some measure of the effectiveness of managers. To judge by their subordinates' responses, the managers were clearly more effective afterward. The subordinates felt that they were given more responsibility, that they received more rewards, that the organizational procedures were clearer, and that morale was higher. These differences are all statistically significant.

But what do these differences mean in human terms? How did the managers change? Sometimes they decided they should get into another line of work. This happened to Ken Briggs, for example, who found that the reason he was doing so poorly as a manager was because he had almost no interest in influencing others. He understood how he would have to change if he were to do well in his present job, but in the end decided, with the help of management, that he would prefer to work back into his first love, sales.

Ken Briggs moved into "remaindering," to help retail outlets for his company's products get rid of last year's stock so that they could take on each year's new styles. He is very successful in this new role; he has cut costs, increased dollar volume, and in time has worked himself into an independent role selling some of the old stock on his own in a way that is quite satisfactory to the business. And he does not have to manage anybody anymore.

In George Prentice's case, less change was needed. He was obviously a very competent person with the right motive profile for a top managerial position. When he was promoted, he performed even more successfully than before because he realized the need to become more positive in his approach and less coercive in his managerial style.

But what about a person who does not want to change his job and discovers that he does not have the right motive profile to be a manager?

The case of Charlie Blake is instructive. Charlie was as low in power motivation as Ken Briggs, his need to achieve was about average, and his affiliation motivation was above average. Thus he had the affiliative manager profile, and, as expected, the morale among his subordinates was very low. When Charlie learned that his subordinates' sense of responsibility and perception of a reward system were in the 10th percentile and that team spirit was in the 30th, he was shocked. When shown a film depicting three managerial climates, Charlie said he preferred what turned out to be the authoritarian climate. He became angry when the workshop trainer and other members in the group pointed out the limitations of this managerial style. He became obstructive in the group process and objected strenuously to what was being taught.

In an interview conducted much later, Charlie said, "I blew my cool. When I started yelling at you for being all wrong, I got even madder when you pointed out that, according to my style questionnaire, you bet that that was just what I did to my salesmen. Down underneath I knew something must be wrong. The sales performance for my division wasn't so good. Most of it was due to me anyway and not to my salesmen. Obviously their reports that they felt very little responsibility was delegated to them and that I didn't reward them at all had to mean something. So I finally decided to sit down and try to figure what I could do about it. I knew I had to start being a manager instead of trying to do everything myself and blowing my cool at others because they didn't do what I thought they should. In the end, after I calmed down on the way back from the workshop, I realized that it is not so bad to make a mistake; it's bad not to learn from it."

After the course, Charlie put his plans into effect. Six months later, his subordinates were asked to rate him again. He attended a second workshop to study these results and reported, "On the way home I was very nervous. I knew I had been working with those guys and not selling so much myself, but I was very much afraid of what they were going to say about how things were going in the office. When I found out that the team spirit and some of those other low scores had jumped from around 30th to the 55th percentile, I was so delighted and relieved that I couldn't say anything all day long."

When he was asked how he acted differently from before, he said, "In previous years when the corporate headquarters said we had to make 110% of our original goal, I had called the salesmen in and said, in effect, 'This is ridiculous; we are not going to make it, but you know perfectly well

what will happen if we don't. So get out there and work your tail off.' The result was that I worked 20 hours a day and they did nothing.

"This time I approached it differently. I told them three things. First, they were going to have to do some sacrificing for the company. Second, working harder is not going to do much good because we are already working about as hard as we can. What will be required are special deals and promotions. You are going to have to figure out some new angles if we are to make it. Third, I'm going to back you up. I'm going to set a realistic goal with each of you. If you make that goal but don't make the company goal, I'll see to it that you are not punished. But if you do make the company goal, I'll see to it that you will get some kind of special rewards."

When the salesmen challenged Charlie saying he did not have enough influence to give them rewards, rather than becoming angry Charlie promised rewards that were in his power to give —such as longer vacations.

Note that Charlie has now begun to behave in a number of ways that we found to be characteristic of the good institutional manager. He is, above all, higher in power motivation, the desire to influence his salesmen, and lower in his tendency to try to do everything himself. He asks the men to sacrifice for the company. He does not defensively chew them out when they challenge him but tries to figure out what their needs are so that he can influence them. He realizes that his job is more one of strengthening and supporting his subordinates than of criticizing them. And he is keenly interested in giving them just rewards for their efforts.

The changes in his approach to his job have certainly paid off. The sales figures for his office in 1973 were up more than 16% over 1972 and up still further in 1974 over 1973. In 1973 his gain over the previous year ranked seventh in the nation; in 1974 it ranked third. And he wasn't the only one in his company to change managerial styles. Overall sales at his company were up substantially in 1973 as compared with 1972, an increase which played a large part in turning the overall company performance around from a $15 million loss in 1972 to a $3 million profit in 1973. The company continued to improve its performance in 1974 with an 11% further gain in sales and a 38% increase in profits.

Of course not everyone can be reached by a workshop. Henry Carter managed a sales office for a company which had very low morale (around the 20th percentile) before he went for training. When morale was checked some six months later, it had not improved. Overall sales gain subsequently reflected this fact since it was only 2% above the previous year's figures.

Oddly enough, Henry's problem was that he was so well liked by everybody that he felt little pressure to change. Always the life of the party, he is particularly popular because he supplies other managers with special hard-to-get brands of cigars and wines at a discount. He uses his close ties with everyone to bolster his position in the company, even though it is known that his office does not perform well compared with others.

His great interpersonal skills became evident at the workshop when he did very poorly at one of the business games. When the discussion turned to why he had done so badly and whether he acted that way on the job, two prestigious participants immediately sprang to his defense, explaining away Henry's failure by arguing that the way he did things was often a real help to others and the company. As a result, Henry did not have to cope with such questions at all. He had so successfully developed his role as a likeable, helpful friend to everyone in management that, even though his salesmen performed badly, he did not feel under any pressure to change.

CHECKS AND BALANCES

What have we learned from Ken Briggs, George Prentice, Charlie Blake, and Henry Carter? Principally, we have discovered what motive combina-

---

WORKSHOP TECHNIQUES

The case studies and data on companies used in this article were derived from a number of workshops we conducted where executives came to learn about their managerial styles and abilities as well as how to change them. The workshops had a dual purpose, however. They provided an opportunity for us to study which motivation pattern, whether it be a concern for achievement, power, people, or a combination thereof, makes the best managers.

When the managers first arrived at the workshops, they were asked to fill out a questionnaire about their job. Each participant analyzed his job, explaining what he or she thought it required of him. The managers were asked to write a number of stories to pictures of various work situations. The stories were coded for the extent to which an individual was concerned about achievement, affiliation, or power, as well as for the amount of inhibition or self-control they revealed. The results were then matched against national norms. The differences between a person's job requirements and his or her motivational patterns can often help assess whether the person is in the right job, whether he is a candidate for promotion to another job, or whether he is likely to be able to adjust to fit his present position.

At the workshops and in this article, we use the technical terms "need for achievement," "need for power," and "need for affiliation" as defined in the books *The Achieving Society* and *Power: The Inner Experience*. The terms refer to measurable factors in groups and individuals. Briefly, these characteristics are measured by coding an individual's spontaneous thoughts for the frequency with which he thinks about doing something better or more efficiently than before (need for achievement), about establishing or maintaining friendly relations with others (need for affiliation), or about having impact on others (need for power). (When we talk about power, we are not talking about dictatorial power, but about the need to be strong and influential.) As used here, therefore, the motive labels are precise terms, referring to a particular method of defining and measuring, much as "gravity" is used in physics, or "gross national product" is used in economics.

To find out what kind of managerial style the participants had, we gave them a questionnaire in which they had to choose how they would handle various realistic work situations in office settings. Their answers were coded for six different management styles or ways of dealing with work situations. The styles depicted were democratic, af-tion makes an effective manager. We have also seen that change is possible if a person has the right combination of qualities.

Oddly enough, the good manager in a large company does not have a high need for achievement, as we define and measure that motive, although there must be plenty of that motive somewhere in his organization. The top managers shown here have a high need for power and an interest in influencing others, both greater than their interest in being liked by people. The manager's concern for power should be socialized—controlled so that the institution as a whole, not only the individual, benefits. Men and nations with this motive profile are empire builders; they tend to create high morale and to expand the organizations they head.

But there is also danger in this motive profile; empire building can lead to imperialism and authoritarianism in companies and in countries.

The same motive pattern which produces good power management can also lead a company or a country to try to dominate others, ostensibly in the interests of organizational expansion. Thus it is not surprising that big business has had to be regulated from time to time by federal agencies. And it is most likely that international agencies will perform the same regulative function for empire-building countries.

For an individual, the regulative function is performed by two characteristics that are part of the profile of the very best managers—a greater emotional maturity, where there is little egotism, and a democratic, coaching managerial style. If an institutional power motivation is checked by maturity, it does not lead to an aggressive, egotistic expansiveness.

For countries, this checking means that they can control their destinies beyond their borders without being aggressive and hostile. For individ-

---

filiative, pace-setting, coaching, coercive, and authoritarian. The managers were asked to comment on the effectiveness of each style and to name the style that they prefer.

One way to determine how effective managers are is to ask the people who work for them. Thus, to isolate the characteristics that good managers have, we surveyed at least three subordinates of each manager at the workshop to see how they answered questions about their work situations that revealed characteristics of their supervisors along several dimensions, namely: (1) the amount of conformity to rules required, (2) the responsibility they feel they are given, (3) the emphasis the department places on standards of performance, (4) the degree to which they feel rewards are given for good work as opposed to punishment for something that goes wrong, (5) the degree of organizational clarity in the office, and (6) its team spirit.[1] The managers who received the highest morale scores (organizational clarity plus team spirit) from their subordinates were determined to be the best managers, possessing the most desirable motive patterns.

The subordinates were also surveyed six months after the managers returned to their offices to see if the morale scores rose after the workshop.

One other measure was obtained from the participants to find out which managers had another characteristic deemed important for good management: maturity. Scores were obtained for four stages in the progress toward maturity by coding the stories which the managers wrote for such matters as their attitudes toward authority and the kinds of emotions displayed over specific issues.

People in Stage I are dependent on others for guidance and strength. Those in Stage II are interested primarily in autonomy, in controlling themselves. In Stage III, people want to manipulate others; in Stage IV, they lose their egotistic desires and wish to selflessly serve others.[2]

The conclusions presented in this article are based on workshops attended by over 500 managers from over 25 different U.S. corporations. However, the data in the exhibits are drawn from just one of these companies for illustrative purposes.

1. Based on G. H. Litwin and R. A. Stringer's *Motivation and Organizational Climate* (Boston: Division of Research, Harvard Business School, 1966).
2. Based on work by Abigail Stewart reported in David C. McClelland's *Power: The Inner Experience* (New York: Irvington Publishers, 1975).

uals, it means they can control their subordinates and influence others around them without resorting to coercion or to an authoritarian management style. Real disinterested statesmanship has a vital role to play at the top of both countries and companies.

Summarized in this way, what we have found out through empirical and statistical investigations may just sound like good common sense. But the improvement over common sense is that now the characteristics of the good manager are objectively known. Managers of corporations can select those who are likely to be good managers and train those already in managerial positions to be more effective with more confidence.

Whatever else organizations may be (problem-solving instruments, sociotechnical systems, reward systems, and so on), they are political structures. This means that organizations operate by distributing authority and setting a stage for the exercise of power. It is no wonder, therefore, that individuals who are highly motivated to secure and use power find a familiar and hospitable environment in business. (From: "Power and Politics in Organizational Life," by Abraham Zaleznik, HBR May-June 1970, p. 47.)

NOTES

Author's note: All the case material in this article is disguised.

1. For instance, see my books *The Achieving Society* (New York: Van Nostrand, 1961) and (with David Winter) *Motivating Economic Achievement* (New York: Free Press, 1969).

2. David C. McClelland, William N. Davis, Rudolf Kalin, and Eric Warner, *The Drinking Man* (New York: The Free Press, 1972).

6
LEADERSHIP

The subject of leadership follows logically from a consideration of motivation. In fact, they are two sides of the same coin. Whereas with motivation we consider what induces human performance, in leadership we concentrate on the total configuration of management style in the superior-subordinate relationship. Leadership focuses on the dynamic process of influencing organizational members toward the achievement of the organization's goals, with full consideration given to the stylistic aspects of the managers' interpersonal relationship with his subordinates.

In this chapter we examine both fundamental concepts of leadership, and participative management as a leadership approach.

In the first part of this chapter we present three distinct views of leadership fundamentals. In "The Uses of Leadership Theory," James Owens presents a descriptive account of various leadership styles along with a summary of managers' views as to how and when these styles might be used, along with anticipated advantages and disadvantages. Owens concludes that leadership is still an art despite attempts to make it more of a science.

Robert House and Terence Mitchell in "Path-Goal Theory of Leadership" present a different perspective on what constitutes leadership. They refer to their approach as path-goal because it "suggests that a leader's behavior is motivating or satisfying to the degree that the behavior increases subordinate goal attainment and clarifies the paths to these goals."

In the third article on this topic, Fred Fiedler presents a case for his now famous theory of leadership in "The Leadership Game: Matching the Man to the Situation." Fiedler argues that "in leadership, the situation is the thing. There are . . . no born leaders—merely people with the potential to be successful leaders under certain conditions or resounding failures under other conditions."

On the subject of participative management as a leadership dimension, Arlyn Melcher in "Participation: A Critical Review of Research Findings," "critically reviews several classical research studies that have contributed largely to the view that a participation leadership style is necessary for effective leadership regardless of the circumstances." Collectively, the articles on leadership in this chapter constitute a representative view of the state of contemporary leadership theory and practice.

THE USES OF
LEADERSHIP THEORY

JAMES OWENS

Carl L. was facing a crisis. A technician by background and now in his late thirties, he had recently become manager of a group of technicians and found himself in the midst of almost open rebellion. He knew the job well and was outstanding in his abilities to organize, handle detail, plan and control. His technicians were competent. But the group's morale had fallen to a point where all spirit and will seemed suctioned out of the group; the talent was there in abundance but simply not operating. What had gone wrong? And what should he do about it? His career depended on the answers.

Carl's managerial failure and variations of it are, unfortunately, commonplace incidents within organizations, despite the personal tragedy and organizational nightmares involved.

What had gone wrong in Carl's group? Probably leadership, that still mysterious and only vaguely understood ingredient which must be created and sustained daily by a manager; with it, other managerial skills and resources come to life and work; without it, managerial skills and group talents become paralyzed—and work results grind to a halt.

This article aims (1) to present a practical

Reprinted by permission from the January, 1973 issue of the *Michigan Business Review,* published by the Graduate School of Business Administration, The University of Michigan.

framework, consisting of essential leadership theory, which can serve to facilitate a manager's understanding, analysis and evaluation of his personal leadership skills; and (2) to report on a composite managerial opinion about leadership practices, drawn from the author's work with many practicing managers over the past seven years, summarizing the insights of these managers themselves based on their years of practical experience.

Thus, my intent is to present a blend of research theory and practical *managerial experience* as, hopefully, a rich information-base for any manager seriously intent on improving his own managerial performance and career growth.

TRAIT THEORY VERSUS
BEHAVIOR THEORY

The earliest studies of leadership hypothesized that what makes a leader (manager) effective is his personality, what he is as a person. Proponents of this "trait theory" searched for some set of built-in traits which successful leaders possess and ineffective leaders lack, such as "aggressiveness," "self-control," "independence," "friendliness," "religious orientation," "optimism," and many others. Decades of social science research, when finally tallied, added up disappointingly to very ambiguous results: effective leaders were found to be sometimes aggressive, self-disciplined,

289

independent, friendly, religious, and optimistic—but often none or few of these things.

The mystery of leadership was not so easily or simplistically to be revealed and entered, definitively, into neat columns. Such research proved what most managers know intuitively, sometimes from bitter experience—such as Carl's—that effective leadership is one of the most complex phenomena in human relations and an ever-elusive riddle to those who must master it. (The obvious irony here is that the successful manager must master this phenomenon in practice, if not in theory and understanding, because—unlike social scientists—his very survival, as a career manager, depends on it!)

A "behavior theory" of leadership then came upon the scene: what makes a leader effective is (quite independently of his personality) simply what he does. Much less ambitious than trait theory, behavior theory tried to search out the right things that effective leaders do: such as how they communicate, give directions, motivate, delegate, plan, handle meetings, and so on. The value of the theory, to the extent it was valid, was its implication that "leaders need not be born to it but could be trained to do the right things," independently of their inner personality traits. Unfortunately, this approach, too, missed the essence of leadership and proved to be not only unambitious but too often degenerated into mechanical "techniques" and other superficial "gimmicks," which, on the job, emerged as robot-like counterfeits of genuine leadership—and thus failed.

The decades of work by both camps, however, were not wasted. It seems clear, today, that, on balance, there is truth—and valuable knowledge—to be gained from each theory.

The Uses of Trait Theory

Although trait theory advocates failed to build a comprehensive model of leadership, their work articulated and forced into sharp focus a practical truth: one's personality, what he fundamentally is as a person, is an everpresent and massive influence on how, and with what success, he functions as a manager.

The personality of a man is his inner life, in-

cluding such inner elements as background, life history, beliefs, life experiences, attitudes, prejudices, self-image, fears, loves, hates, hopes and philosophy of life. In this sense, a man is like an iceberg: only a small fraction of what he is appears above the surface (his observable behavior, what he does); the rest is his inner life, the 7/8ths of the iceberg that lie, unobservable, below the surface.

However, the manager's inner personality causes—or "spills over" into—his behavior which, in turn, affects others with whom he works, eliciting from them either cooperative or resistance reactions. And, therein lies the manager's fate: cooperative reactions from his people spell success; resistance reactions, however irrational from the manager's viewpoint, usually assure his failure (as, probably, in the case of Carl above).

Any attempt to "formulize" this cause-effect process in the form of simple one-to-one correlations, such as trait "Z_1" causing invariably behavior "Z_2" causing invariably effect "Z_3", is doomed to failure as the efforts of the trait-theorists proved. However, it is clear that there is an influential relationship between a manager's total personality and his success, as a manager, on the job. I have submitted this precise concept to several thousand practicing managers over the years and, based on their experience, virtually all acknowledge its validity. For example, most of these managers concluded that a manager who is naturally low in his ability to trust others, has little chance to succeed; despite his best efforts, he will be unable to delegate properly and thus becomes a "bottle-neck," as work piles up on his desk, and a source of frustration to people who want a chance to get involved and grow. Or, a manager whose personality requires a high degree of security in his life, is unable to take any risks, and thus fails because he decides and does nothing! Or, a manager who struggles within himself with a poor self-image and an inherent low level of self-confidence, avoids decisions and radiates, as a kind of "self-fulfilling prophesy," certain failure. Other examples include the effect on managerial success of personality characteristics like racial prejudice, intolerance for unfamiliar ideas, dislike or distrust of the young, respect for (or general cynicism about) other people because of their background, sex, intelligence, experience, or appearance, and so on.

The virtually unanimous opinion of these thousands of practical managers has been that any manager, who genuinely has ambitions for managerial growth and advancement, can achieve it only if he adds to his efforts a periodic evaluation of his total personality, especially his attitudes, and their effect on his people as well as the success (or failure) they produce for him. Such a manager, who is capable even of managing his own career, will find that most of his personality characteristics are assets; but, if he pursues the search objectively, he will find, too, that some are liabilities. These he must begin to change, if he can or wishes; and, if he can not, then he must, as a mature person with mature judgment, assess himself carefully and find the kind of job that fits his personality.

In short, these managers believe—and I do too—that a manager can grow in his managerial career only if he grows as a total personality, which he is long before he begins to function as a manager. What a man is and brings to the office in the form of a total personality largely determines what and how he does and with what degree of success. What this means is that personal growth as a human being underlies and becomes, to a great extent, the real foundation upon which managerial and career growth can develop. Managerial success is not a peripheral set of "techniques"; it is a working-out of one's essential being in the form of action.

The Uses of Behavior Theory

What "behavior theory" has taught us, over the years, is that, within certain limits imposed by the inner personality of the individual, each person has the capability of cultivating habits of behavior (by act of will) which optimize his effects upon people. Many of us feel moody, but, by act of will, virtually never act moody. Constructive habits of courtesy, self-control, two-way communication, delegation and interest in the problems of others can be learned and practiced, by act of will.

The most important contribution of "behavior theory," however, is the development of a classification of leadership behaviors (styles) which provides a manager an analytical tool with which he can consciously and intelligently build a personally successful leadership style.

A MATRIX OF LEADERSHIP STYLES

Probably the most practical contribution of research to the day-to-day life of the manager is the analytic model of leadership styles—their description and properties. Virtually all of the managers to whom I have presented this classic model agree that it clarifies their options and serves well as a means for productive analysis and evaluation of their personal leadership styles as well as their relative success.

The exact form of the leadership matrix varies as do its details but the following version is standard. The brief descriptions of each style are, of course, stereotyped and over-simplified for purposes of clear identification and analysis. Also, they are defined in neutral language, avoiding, as much as possible, either favoring or disparaging overtones at this point. The five leadership styles, which comprise the matrix, are as follows:

1. The Autocratic Leader: The autocrat has authority, from some source such as his position, knowledge, strength, or power to reward and punish, and he uses this authority as his principal, or only, method of getting things done. He is frankly authoritarian, knows what he wants done, and how, "tells" people what their work-assignments are, and demands unquestioning obedience. The autocrat ranges from "tough" to "paternalistic" depending on how much he stresses, as motivation, threat and punishment in the former case or rewards in the latter. The "tough" autocrat demands and gets compliance, "or else." The "paternalistic" autocrat demands and expects compliance but mainly on a "father-knows-best" —and often very personal—relationship, implying personal dependence, rewards, and security. The autocrat permits people little or no freedom.

2. The Bureaucratic Leader: Like the autocrat, the bureaucrat "tells" people what to do, and how, but the basis for his orders is almost exclusively the organization's policies, procedures, and rules.

For the bureaucrat, these rules are absolute. He manages entirely "by the book," and no exceptions are permitted. He treats rules and administers their force upon people as a judge might treat —and permit no departure or exception from— laws, including their every technicality. Like the autocrat, the bureaucrat permits people little or no freedom.

3. The Diplomatic Leader: The diplomat is an artist who, like the salesman, lives by the arts of personal persuasion. Although he has the same clear authority as the autocrat, the diplomat prefers to "sell" people and operate, as much as possible, by persuasion and broadscale individual motivation of people. He will "revert," if necessary, to the autocratic style, but prefers to avoid this. Some term him a "sell-type" leader who uses a large variety and degree of persuasion-tactics, ranging from simple explanation of the reasons for an order to fullscale bargaining with people. He will usually relate his organizational goals to the personal individual needs and aspirations of his people. Such a leader retains his authority in that he knows and will insist on a particular course of action; but, he provides some—limited— freedom to his people in that he permits them to react, question, raise objections, discuss, and even argue their side of the issue.

4. The Participative Leader: The participative leader openly invites his people to participate or share, to a greater or lesser extent, in decisions, policy-making and operation methods. He is either a "democratic" or a "consultative" leader.

The "democratice" leader "joins" his group and makes it clear, in advance, that he will abide by the group's decision whether arrived at by consensus or majority vote. (This style is sometimes seen in the operations of research and developments groups.)

The "consultative" leader consults his people and invites frank involvement, discussion, pro and con argument, and recommendations from the group, but makes it clear that he alone is accountable and reserves the final decision to himself.

In both forms of the participative style of leadership, people are given a high degree of freedom—as they are, too, in the Free-Rein style.

5. The Free-Rein Leader: The "free-rein" leader (the analogy, of course, is to a horseman who has left the reins free) does not literally abandon all control. He sets a goal for his subordinate as well as clear parameters such as policies, deadlines, and budget and then drops the "reins" and sets his subordinate free to operate without further direction or control, unless the subordinate himself requests it.

The "Best" Leadership Style

Despite certain implications in the literature that there is a "best" and ideal leadership style, the managers I surveyed categorically reject this simple solution suggested by some social scientists. Their virtually unanimous view was that the "best" leadership style DEPENDS ON:

(a) the individual personality of the manager himself ("Trait theory" revisited);
(b) the individual followers, the kind of people they are and the kind of work they do;
(c) and, the particular situation and circumstances on any given day or hour.

In short, no "cook-book" or formulized recipe for effective leadership "rang true" as realistic with these managers. The complexity and mystery of leadership does not permit simplistic approaches.

Only a manager, himself, examining, and exploring the varieties of leadership styles, their advantages and weaknesses, as well as the people and the situation with which he is dealing, can decide what is the "best" leadership style for him, and with them, and in this particular situation. It must be an act of individual judgment. A theoretical framework can assist, as can the opinions of thousands of managers, but the choice and practice of leadership style must always remain the act of judgment of the individual manager.

Some authors have coined the expression "toolbox approach" for this necessity that faces managers of choosing the "right style" at the "right time" in the "right situation" (as opposed to the easy and utopian formula of a single, predominant leadership style for all people and all situations).

A SUMMARY
OF MANAGERS' VIEWS

Working closely over the years with many practicing managers, I have had the opportunity to learn much of what they learned about leadership—based, not on textbook abstractions, but realistically on years of hard experience. The essential results of this seven-year informal survey of these managers are organized below as telegraphic propositions expressed as either advantages or weaknesses of each classic leadership style. Each proposition is a kind of composite view representing a virtual consensus of the opinions of these managers. Naturally, they are general statements and, as such, allow for exceptions in individual cases. Even so, these propositions are experience-based insights of managers themselves and should be helpful to any manager seriously intent on evaluating and improving his own leadership.

1. The Autocratic Leadership Style:
(a) Advantages:
   When appropriate, can increase efficiency, save time and get quick results, especially in a crisis or emergency situation.
   The paternalistic form of this style of leadership works well with employees who have a low tolerance for ambiguity, feel insecure with freedom and even minor decision-making requirements, and thrive under clear, detailed, and achievable directives.
   Chain of command and division of work (who is supposed to do what) are clear and fully understood by all.
(b) Weaknesses:
   The apparent efficiency of one-way communication often becomes a false efficiency since one-way communication, without "feedback," typically leads to misunderstandings, communication breakdowns and costly errors.
   The autocratic manager must really be an expert, not just think he is, because he receives little, if any, information and ideas from his people as inputs into his decision-making. He is really alone in his decision-making and this is generally dangerous in today's environment of technological and organizational complexity.
   The critical weakness, however, of the autocratic style is its effect on people. Many managers pine for the good old days when the boss gave orders and people obeyed meekly and without question. These managers, however, agree that—like it or not—those days are gone forever. Today, most people resent authoritarian rule which excludes them from involvement and reduces them to machine-like cogs without human dignity or importance. They express their resentment in the form of massive resistance, low morale and low productivity (if not downright work stoppage or sabotage). This is especially true, today, with technical or educated people, youths entering the job market, and members of most minority groups.

2. The Bureaucratic Leadership Style:
(a) Advantages:
   Insures consistency of policy and operations which can be critical in industries where legal parameters are common (banking, sales, etc.). Every manager must be a bureaucrat to some reasonable extent.
   Consistent application of personnel-related rules, for one and for all, contributes a sense of fairness and impartiality in the manager's many and complex dealings with people.
   People know where they stand. Most decisions concerning them are by known—and accepted—rule, predictable, objective (rather than by the whim or mood of a manager)—and there is security and a sense of fairness.
(b) Weaknesses:
   Inflexibility in situations where exceptions to rules should be made or requested.
   Paralysis in situations not covered by rules or where rules are ambiguous (as is often the case: policies and rules represent legislation for the majority of situations but can never substitute for individual human judgment in a particular specific situation.)
   The reaction of people working under a strongly bureaucratic manager is essentially the same as described above in the case of the autocratic manager: again, resentment, resistance, and low morale.

3. The Diplomatic Leadership Style:

(a) Advantages:

People cooperate and work more enthusiastically if managers take even a few minutes —and respect people enough—to give them the simple reasons and explanations of the reasons that make a particular task important —rather than just a blind chore.

A manager's personal effort to explain to or persuade a subordinate is usually received as an important compliment and show of respect —and usually appreciated and responded to with a high degree of cooperation and effort. This style of leadership is indispensable for the legions of so-called "staff" people (and even "line" people who realize the inadequacy of their real authority). They must achieve the results, for which they are accountable, "unfairly" deprived of the clear-cut authority required and, therefore, are utterly dependent on the skills of persuasion to get the help and cooperation needed.

(b) Weaknesses:

Some people interpret efforts to persuade them, rather than order them, as a sign of weakness and, thus, lose respect for a manager.

The basic weakness, however, of the diplomatic style is the same as the pit-fall always facing those who use consistently the "tool-box" approach to leadership; namely, hypocrisy. Unless handled with judgment, skill and sincerity, the diplomatic style—as well as any "tool-box" approach with people— quickly degenerates and "comes through" to people as insincerity, frank manipulation and exploitation—and is, thus, deeply resented and resisted. And, naturally, a complete failure.

Anyone employing the diplomatic style must be a skilled and competent salesman, who usually "wins" the "sale." A salesman routinely expects and invites objections—a manager who operates this way must be able to convince and "sell" people, or he will be forced to "revert" (hypocritically) to a frank autocratic order. The effect of this on people is both obvious and disastrous.

4. The Participative Leadership Style:

(a) Advantages:

When people participate in and help formulate a decision, they support it (instead of fighting or ignoring it) and work hard to make it work, because it's their idea and, now, part of their life and their "ego."

The manager consistently receives the benefit of the best information, ideas, suggestions, and talent—and operating experience—of his people. The rich information-source which they represent becomes his and a key input into his decision-making.

Group discussion, even though time-consuming, before a decision is made, can force critical information to the surface which, when considered, improves decision-making—or, in some cases, actually averts a disaster which would have occurred if key operating-level information were not made available.

This style of leadership permits and encourages people to develop, grow and rise in the organization (both in terms of responsibility they can assume and service they can contribute).

Most people work better, more enthusiastically and at a high level of motivation when they are given a reasonable degree of freedom to act and contribute. Because, thus, they enjoy a sense of personal importance, value and achievement. (Unlike human cogs in machine-like organizational systems.)

Most importantly, as already implied above, the participative manager establishes a work-climate which easily unleashes the enormous power of people who are motivated by—and will strive hard for—goals which they help create and in the accomplishment of which they gain deep personal satisfaction in the form of recognition, sense of accomplishment, sense of importance and personal value. In short, the participative manager has the critical factor of built-in personal motivation working for him.

(b) Weaknesses:

The participative style can take enormous amounts of time and, when used inappropriately, be simply inefficient.

Some managers "use" the democratic style as a way of avoiding (or abdicating) responsibility.

People resent the invitation to offer recommendations when such recommendations are consistently ignored and rejected. It follows that any manager, who must reject a recommendation, should quickly explain why such recommendations had to be rejected.

Use of the participative styles can easily, if not handled well, degenerate into a complete loss of managerial control.

5. The Free-Rein Leadership Style:

(a) Advantages:

This style comprises the essence of full managerial delegation with its benefits of optimum utilization of time and resources.

Many people are motivated to full effort only if given this kind of free-rein.

(b) Weaknesses:

Very little managerial control and a high degree of risk.

This style can be a disaster if the manager does not know well the competence and integrity of his people and their ability to handle this kind of freedom.

CONCLUSION

Leadership is still an art despite the efforts of social science researchers to make it a science. The summaries, here, of essential leadership theory and managerial opinion (based on experience) are presented only as a help to (not a substitute for) the final individual judgment of the manager as he lives with his particular people in his particular situation.

Every such manager, however, must operate by some leadership style or styles and it is hoped that the ideas presented above will aid the manager in his analysis, evaluation and development of his own personal leadership style.

PATH-GOAL THEORY
OF LEADERSHIP

ROBERT J. HOUSE
TERENCE R. MITCHELL

An integrated body of conjecture by students of leadership, referred to as the "Path-Goal Theory of Leadership," is currently emerging. According to this theory, leaders are effective because of their impact on subordinates' motivation, ability to perform effectively and satisfactions. The theory is called Path-Goal because its major concern is how the leader influences the subordinates' perceptions of their work goals, personal goals and paths to goal attainment. The theory suggests that a leader's behavior is motivating or satisfying to the degree that the behavior increases subordinate goal attainment and clarifies the paths to these goals.

HISTORICAL FOUNDATIONS

The path-goal approach has its roots in a more general motivational theory called expectancy theory.[1] Briefly, expectancy theory states that an individual's attitudes (e.g., satisfaction with supervision or job satisfaction) or behavior (e.g., leader behavior or job effort) can be predicted from: (1) the degree to which the job, or behavior, is seen as leading to various outcomes (expectancy) and (2) the evaluation of these outcomes (valences). Thus, people are satisfied with their job if they think it leads to things that are highly valued, and they work hard if they believe that effort leads to things that are highly valued. This type of theoretical rationale can be used to predict a variety of phenomena related to leadership, such as why leaders behave the way they do, or how leader behavior influences subordinate motivation.[2]

This latter approach is the primary concern of this article. The implication for leadership is that subordinates are motivated by leader behavior to the extent that this behavior influences expectancies, e.g., goal paths and valences, e.g., goal attractiveness.

Several writers have advanced specific hypotheses concerning how the leader affects the paths and the goals of subordinates.[3] These writers focused on two issues: (1) how the leader affects subordinates' expectations that effort will lead to effective performance and valued rewards, and (2) how this expectation affects motivation to work hard and perform well.

While the state of theorizing about leadership in terms of subordinates' paths and goals is in its infancy, we believe it is promising for two reasons. First, it suggests effects of leader behavior that have not yet been investigated but which appear to be fruitful areas of inquiry. And, second, it suggests with some precision the situational factors on which the effects of leader behavior are contingent.

Reprinted with permission of the *Journal of Contemporary Business,* Autumn, 1974.

The initial theoretical work by Evans asserts that leaders will be effective by making rewards available to subordinates and by making these rewards contingent on the subordinate's accomplishment of specific goals.[4] Evans argued that one of the strategic functions of the leader is to clarify for subordinates the kind of behavior that leads to goal accomplishment and valued rewards. This function might be referred to as path clarification. Evans also argued that the leader increases the rewards available to subordinates by being supportive toward subordinates, i.e., by being concerned about their status, welfare and comfort. Leader supportiveness is in itself a reward that the leader has at his or her disposal, and the judicious use of this reward increases the motivation of subordinates.

Evans studied the relationship between the behavior of leaders and the subordinates' expectations that effort leads to rewards and also studied the resulting impact on ratings of the subordinates' performance. He found that when subordinates viewed leaders as being supportive (considerate of their needs) and when these superiors provided directions and guidance to the subordinates, there was a positive relationship between leader behavior and subordinates' performance ratings.

However, leader behavior was only related to subordinates' performance when the leader's behavior also was related to the subordinates' expectations that their effort would result in desired rewards. Thus, Evans' findings suggest that the major impact of a leader on the performance of subordinates is clarifying the path to desired rewards and making such rewards contingent on effective performance.

Stimulated by this line of reasoning, House, and House and Dessler advanced a more complex theory of the effects of leader behavior on the motivation of subordinates.[5] The theory intends to explain the effects of four specific kinds of leader behavior on the following three subordinate attitudes or expectations: (1) the satisfaction of subordinates, (2) the subordinates' acceptance of the leader and (3) the expectations of subordinates that effort will result in effective performance and that effective performance is the path to rewards. The four kinds of leader behavior included in the theory are: (1) directive leadership, (2) supportive leadership, (3) participative leadership and (4) achievement-oriented leadership. Directive leadership is characterized by a leader who lets subordinates know what is expected of them, gives specific guidance as to what should be done and how it should be done, makes his or her part in the group understood, schedules work to be done, maintains definite standards of performance and asks that group members follow standard rules and regulations. Supportive leadership is characterized by a friendly and approachable leader who shows concern for the status, well-being and needs of subordinates. Such a leader does little things to make the work more pleasant, treats members as equals and is friendly and approachable. Participative leadership is characterized by a leader who consults with subordinates, solicits their suggestions and takes these suggestions seriously into consideration before making a decision. An achievement-oriented leader sets challenging goals, expects subordinates to perform at their highest level, continuously seeks improvement in performance *and* shows a high degree of confidence that the subordinates will assume responsibility, put forth effort and accomplish challenging goals. This kind of leader constantly emphasizes excellence in performance and simultaneously displays confidence that subordinates will meet high standards of excellence.

A number of studies suggest that these different leadership styles can be shown by the same leader in various situations.[6] For example, a leader may show directiveness toward subordinates in some instances and be participative or supportive in other instances.[7] Thus, the traditional method of characterizing a leader as either highly participative and supportive *or* highly directive is invalid; rather, it can be concluded that leaders vary in the particular fashion employed for supervising their subordinates. Also, the theory, in its present stage, is a tentative explanation of the effects of leader behavior—it is incomplete because it does not explain other kinds of leader behavior and does not explain the effects of the leader on factors other than subordinate acceptance, satisfaction and expectations. However, the theory is stated so that additional variables may be included in it as new knowledge is made available.

PATH-GOAL THEORY

General Propositions

The first proposition of path-goal theory is that leader behavior is acceptable and satisfying to subordinates to the extent that the subordinates see such behavior as either an immediate source of satisfaction or as instrumental to future satisfaction.

The second proposition of this theory is that the leader's behavior will be motivational, i.e., increase effort, to the extent that (1) such behavior makes satisfaction of subordinate's needs contingent on effective performance and (2) such behavior complements the environment of subordinates by providing the coaching, guidance, support and rewards necessary for effective performance.

These two propositions suggest that the leader's strategic functions are to enhance subordinates' motivation to perform, satisfaction with the job and acceptance of the leader. From previous research on expectancy theory of motivation, it can be inferred that the strategic functions of the leader consist of: (1) recognizing and/or arousing subordinates' needs for outcomes over which the leader has some control, (2) increasing personal payoffs to subordinates for work-goal attainment,

(3) making the path to those payoffs easier to travel by coaching and direction, (4) helping subordinates clarify expectancies, (5) reducing frustrating barriers and (6) increasing the opportunities for personal satisfaction contingent on effective performance.

Stated less formally, the motivational functions of the leader consist of increasing the number and kinds of personal payoffs to subordinates for work-goal attainment and making paths to these payoffs easier to travel by clarifying the paths, reducing road blocks and pitfalls and increasing the opportunities for personal satisfaction en route.

Contingency Factors

Two classes of situational variables are asserted to be contingency factors. A contingency factor is a variable which moderates the relationship between two other variables such as leader behavior and subordinate satisfaction. For example, we might suggest that the degree of structure in the task moderates the relationship between leaders' directive behavior and subordinates' job satisfaction. Figure I shows how such a relationship might look. Thus, subordinates are satisfied with directive behavior in an unstructured task and are satisfied with nondirective behavior in a structured task. Therefore, we say that the relationship between leader directiveness and subordinate satisfaction is contingent upon the structure of the task.

The two contingency variables are (a) personal characteristics of the subordinates and (b) the environmental pressures and demands with which subordinates must cope in order to accomplish the work goals and to satisfy their needs. While other situational factors also may operate to determine the effects of leader behavior, they are not presently known.

With respect to the first class of contingency factors, the characteristics of subordinates, path-goal theory asserts that leader behavior will be acceptable to subordinates to the extent that the subordinates see such behavior as either an immediate source of satisfaction or as instrumental to future satisfaction. Subordinates' characteristics are hypothesized to partially determine this perception. For example, Runyon[8] and Mitchell[9]

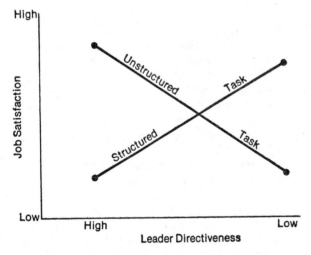

FIGURE I. Hypothetical relationship between directive leadership and subordinate satisfaction with task structure as a contingency factor

show that the subordinate's score on a measure called Locus of Control moderates the relationship between participative leadership style and subordinate satisfaction. The Locus-of-Control measure reflects the degree to which an individual sees the environment as systematically responding to his or her behavior. People who believe that what happens to them occurs because of their behavior are called internals; people who believe that what happens to them occurs because of luck or chance are called externals. Mitchell's findings suggest that internals are more satisfied with a participative leadership style and externals are more satisfied with a directive style.

A second characteristic of subordinates on which the effects of leader behavior are contingent is subordinates' perception of their own ability with respect to their assigned tasks. The higher the degree of perceived ability relative to task demands, the less the subordinate will view leader directiveness and coaching behavior as acceptable. Where the subordinate's perceived ability is high, such behavior is likely to have little positive effect on the motivation of the subordinate and to be perceived as excessively close control. Thus, the acceptability of the leader's behavior is determined in part by the characteristics of the subordinates.

The second aspect of the situation, the environment of the subordinate, consists of those factors that are not within the control of the subordinate but which are important to need satisfaction or to ability to perform effectively. The theory asserts that effects of the leader's behavior on the psychological states of subordinates are contingent on other parts of the subordinates' environment that are relevant to subordinate motivation. Three broad classifications of contingency factors in the environment are:

- The subordinates' tasks
- The formal authority system of the organization
- The primary work group.

Assessment of the environmental conditions makes it possible to predict the kind and amount of influence that specific leader behaviors will have on the motivation of subordinates. Any of the three environmental factors could act upon the subordinate in any of three ways: first, to serve as stimuli that motivate and direct the subordinate to perform necessary task operations; second, to constrain variability in behavior. Constraints may help the subordinate by clarifying expectancies that effort leads to rewards or by preventing the subordinate from experiencing conflict and confusion. Constraints also may be counterproductive to the extent that they restrict initiative or prevent increases in effort from being associated positively with rewards. Third, environmental factors may serve as rewards for achieving desired performance, e.g., it is possible for the subordinate to receive the necessary cues to do the job and the needed rewards for satisfaction from sources other than the leader, e.g., coworkers in the primary work group. Thus, the effect of the leader on subordinates' motivation will be a function of how deficient the environment is with respect to motivational stimuli, constraints or rewards.

With respect to the environment, path-goal theory asserts that when goals and paths to desired goals are apparent because of the routine nature of the task, clear group norms or objective controls of the formal authority systems, attempts by the leader to clarify paths and goals will be both redundant and seen by subordinates as imposing unnecessary, close control. Although such control may increase performance by preventing soldiering or malingering, it also will result in decreased satisfaction (see Figure I). Also with respect to the work environment, the theory asserts that the more dissatisfying the task, the more the subordinates will resent leader behavior directed at increasing productivity or enforcing compliance to organizational rules and procedures.

Finally, with respect to environmental variables the theory states that leader behavior will be motivational to the extent that it helps subordinates cope with environmental uncertainties, threats from others or sources of frustration. Such leader behavior is predicted to increase subordinates' satisfaction with the job context and to be motivational to the extent that it increases the subordinates' expectations that their effort will lead to valued rewards.

These propositions and specification of situational contingencies provide a heuristic framework on which to base future research. Hopefully, this will lead to a more fully developed, explicitly formal theory of leadership.

Figure II presents a summary of the theory. It is hoped that these propositions, while admittedly tentative, will provide managers with some insights concerning the effects of their own leader behavior and that of others.

EMPIRICAL SUPPORT

The theory has been tested in a limited number of studies which have generated considerable empirical support for our ideas and also suggest areas in which the theory requires revision. A brief review of these studies follows.

Leader Directiveness

Leader directiveness has a positive correlation with satisfaction and expectancies of subordinates who are engaged in ambiguous tasks and has a negative correlation with satisfaction and expectancies of subordinates engaged in clear tasks. These findings were predicted by the theory and have been replicated in seven organizations. They suggest that when task demands are ambiguous or when the organization procedures, rules and policies are not clear, a leader behaving in a directive manner complements the tasks and the orga-

nization by providing the necessary guidance and psychological structure for subordinates.[10] However, when task demands are clear to subordinates, leader directiveness is seen more as a hindrance.

However, other studies have failed to confirm these findings.[11] A study by Dessler[12] suggests a resolution to these conflicting findings—he found that for subordinates at the lower organizational levels of a manufacturing firm who were doing routine, repetitive, unambiguous tasks, directive leadership was preferred by closed-minded, dogmatic, authoritarian subordinates and nondirective leadership was preferred by nonauthoritarian, open-minded subordinates. However, for subordinates at higher organizational levels doing nonroutine, ambiguous tasks, directive leadership was preferred for both authoritarian and nonauthoritarian subordinates. Thus, Dessler found that two contingency factors appear to operate simultaneously: subordinate task ambiguity and degree of subordinate authoritarianism. When measured in combination, the findings are as predicted by the theory; however, when the subordinate's personality is not taken into account, task ambiguity does not always operate as a contingency variable as predicted by the theory. House, Burill and Dessler recently found a similar interaction between subordinate authoritarianism and task ambiguity in a second manufacturing firm, thus adding confidence in Dessler's original findings.[13]

Leader Behavior and Contingency Factors		cause	Subordinate Attitudes and Behavior
1 Directive	1 Subordinate Characteristics Authoritarianism Locus of Control Ability	Influence⟩ Personal Perceptions	1 Job Satisfaction Job → Rewards
2 Supportive			2 Acceptance of Leader Leader → Rewards
3 Achievement-Oriented	2 Environmental factors The Task Formal Authority System Primary Work Group	Influence⟩ Motivational Stimuli Constraints Rewards	3 Motivational Behavior Effort → Performance Performance → Rewards
4 Participative			

FIGURE II. Summary of path-goal relationships

Supportive Leadership

The theory hypothesizes that supportive leadership will have its most positive effect on subordinate satisfaction for subordinates who work on stressful, frustrating or dissatisfying tasks. This hypothesis has been tested in 10 samples of employees,[14] and in only one of these studies was the hypothesis disconfirmed.[15] Despite some inconsistency in research on supportive leadership, the evidence is sufficiently positive to suggest that managers should be alert to the critical need for supportive leadership under conditions where tasks are dissatisfying, frustrating or stressful to subordinates.

Achievement-Oriented Leadership

The theory hypothesizes that achievement-oriented leadership will cause subordinates to strive for higher standards of performance and to have more confidence in the ability to meet challenging goals. A recent study by House, Valency and Van der Krabben provides a partial test of this hypothesis among white collar employees in service organizations.[16] For subordinates performing ambiguous, nonrepetitive tasks, they found a positive relationship between the amount of achievement orientation of the leader and subordinates' expectancy that their effort would result in effective performance. Stated less technically, for subordinates performing ambiguous, nonrepetitive tasks, the higher the achievement orientation of the leader, the more the subordinates were confident that their efforts would pay off in effective performance. For subordinates performing moderately unambiguous, repetitive tasks, there was no significant relationship between achievement-oriented leadership and subordinate expectancies that their effort would lead to effective performance. This finding held in four separate organizations.

Two plausible interpretations may be used to explain these data. First, people who select ambiguous, nonrepetitive tasks may be different in personality from those who select a repetitive job and may, therefore, be more responsive to an achievement-oriented leader. A second explanation is that achievement orientation only affects expectancies in ambiguous situations because there is more flexibility and autonomy in such tasks. Therefore, subordinates in such tasks are more likely to be able to change in response to such leadership style. Neither of the above interpretations have been tested to date; however, additional research is currently under way to investigate these relationships.

Participative Leadership

In theorizing about the effects of participative leadership it is necessary to ask about the specific characteristics of both the subordinates and their situation that would cause participative leadership to be viewed as satisfying and instrumental to effective performance.

Mitchell recently described at least four ways in which a participative leadership style would impact on subordinate attitudes and behavior as predicted by expectancy theory.[17] First, a participative climate should increase the clarity of organizational contingencies. Through participation in decision making, subordinates should learn what leads to what. From a path-goal viewpoint participation would lead to greater clarity of the paths to various goals. A second impact of participation would be that subordinates, hopefully, should select goals they highly value. If one participates in decisions about various goals, it makes sense that this individual would select goals he or she wants. Thus, participation would increase the correspondence between organization and subordinate goals. Third, we can see how participation would increase the control the individual has over what happens on the job. If our motivation is higher (based on the preceding two points), then having greater autonomy and ability to carry out our intentions should lead to increased effort and performance. Finally, under a participative system, pressure towards high performance should come from sources other than the leader or the organization. More specifically, when people participate in the decision process they become more ego-involved; the decisions made are in some part their own. Also, their peers know what is expected and the social pressure has a greater impact. Thus, motivation to perform well stems from internal and social factors as well as formal external ones.

A number of investigations prior to the above formulation supported the idea that participation appears to be helpful,[18] and Mitchell presents a number of recent studies that support the above four points.[19] However, it is also true that we would expect the relationship between a participative style and subordinate behavior to be moderated by both the personality characteristics of the subordinate and the situational demands. Studies by Tannenbaum and Alport and Vroom have shown that subordinates who prefer autonomy and self-control respond more positively to participative leadership in terms of both satisfaction and performance than subordinates who do not have such preferences.[20] Also, the studies mentioned by Runyon[21] and Mitchell[22] showed that subordinates who were external in orientation were less satisfied with a participative style of leadership than were internal subordinates.

House also has reviewed these studies in an attempt to explain the ways in which the situation or environment moderates the relationship between participation and subordinate attitudes and behavior.[23] His analysis suggests that where participative leadership is positively related to satisfaction, regardless of the predispositions of subordinates, the tasks of the subjects appear to be ambiguous and ego-involving. In the studies in which the subjects' personalities or predispositions moderate the effect of participative leadership, the tasks of the subjects are inferred to be highly routine and/or nonego-involving.

House reasoned from this analysis that the task may have an overriding effect on the relationship between leader participation and subordinate responses, and that individual predispositions or personality characteristics of subordinates may have an effect only under some tasks. It was assumed that when task demands are ambiguous, subordinates will have a need to reduce the ambiguity. Further, it was assumed that when task demands are ambiguous, participative problem solving between the leader and the subordinate will result in more effective decisions than when the task demands are unambiguous. Finally, it was assumed that when the subordinates are ego-involved in their tasks they are more likely to

want to have a say in the decisions that affect them. Given these assumptions, the following hypotheses were formulated to account for the conflicting findings reviewed above:

• When subjects are highly ego-involved in a decision or a task and the decision or task demands are ambiguous, participative leadership will have a positive effect on the satisfaction and motivation of the subordinate, *regardless* of the subordinate's predisposition toward self-control, authoritarianism or need for independence.

• When subordinates are not ego-involved in their tasks and when task demands are clear, subordinates who are not authoritarian and who have high needs for independence and self-control will respond favorably to leader participation and their opposite personality types will respond less favorably.

These hypotheses were derived on the basis of path-goal theorizing; i.e., the rationale guiding the analysis of prior studies was that both task characteristics and characteristics of subordinates interact to determine the effect of a specific kind of leader behavior on the satisfaction, expectancies and performance of subordinates. To date, one major investigation has supported some of these predictions[24] in which personality variables, amount of participative leadership, task ambiguity and job satisfaction were assessed for 324 employees of an industrial manufacturing organization. As expected, in nonrepetitive, ego-involving tasks, employees (regardless of their personality) were more satisfied under a participative style than a nonparticipative style. However, in repetitive tasks which were less ego-involving the amount of authoritarianism of subordinates moderated the relationship between leadership style and satisfaction. Specifically, low authoritarian subordinates were *more satisfied* under a participative style. These findings are exactly as the theory would predict, thus, it has promise in reconciling a set of confusing and contradictory findings with respect to participative leadership.

SUMMARY AND CONCLUSIONS

We have attempted to describe what we believe is a useful theoretical framework for understanding the effect of leadership behavior on subordinate satisfaction and motivation. Most theorists today have moved away from the simplistic notions that all effective leaders have a certain set of personality traits or that the situation completely determines performance. Some researchers have presented rather complex attempts at matching certain types of leaders with certain types of situations, e.g., the articles written by Vroom and Fiedler in this issue. But, we believe that a path-goal approach goes one step further. It not only suggests what type of style may be most effective in a given situation—it also attempts to explain *why* it is most effective.

We are optimistic about the future outlook of leadership research. With the guidance of path-goal theorizing, future research is expected to unravel many confusing puzzles about the reasons for and effects of leader behavior that have, heretofore, not been solved. However, we add a word of caution: the theory, and the research on it, are relatively new to the literature of organizational behavior. Consequently, path-goal theory is offered more as a tool for directing research and stimulating insight than as a proven guide for managerial action.

NOTES

* This article is also to be reprinted in *Readings in Organizational and Industrial Psychology* by G. A. Yukl and K. N. Wexley, 2nd edition (1975). The research by House and his associates was partially supported by a grant from the Shell Oil Company of Canada. The research by Mitchell and his associates was partially supported by the Office of Naval Research Contract NR 170-761, N00014-67-A-0103-0032 (Terence R. Mitchell, Principal Investigator).

1. T. R. Mitchell, "Expectancy Model of Job Satisfaction, Occupational Preference and Effort: A Theoretical, Methodological and Empirical Appraisal," *Psychological Bulletin* (1974, in press).

2. D. M. Nebeker and T. R. Mitchell, "Leader Behavior: An Expectancy Theory Approach," *Organization Behavior and Human Performance,* 11 (1974), pp. 355–367.

3. M. G. Evans, "The Effects of Supervisory Behavior on the Path-Goal Relationship," *Organization Behavior and Human Performance,* 55 (1970), pp. 277–298; T. H. Hammer and H. T. Dachler, "The Process of Supervision in the Context of Motivation

Theory," Research Report No. 3 (University of Maryland, 1973); F. Dansereau, Jr., J. Cashman and G. Graen, "Instrumentality Theory and Equity Theory As Complementary Approaches in Predicting the Relationship of Leadership and Turnover Among Managers," *Organization Behavior and Human Performance,* 10 (1973), pp. 184–200; R. J. House, "A Path-Goal Theory of Leader Effectiveness, *Administrative Science Quarterly,* 16, 3 (September 1971), pp. 321–338; T. R. Mitchell, "Motivation and Participation: An Integration," *Academy of Management Journal,* 16, 4 (1973), pp. 160–179; G. Graen, F. Dansereau, Jr. and T. Minami, "Dysfunctional Leadership Styles," *Organization Behavior and Human Performance,* 7 (1972), pp. 216–236; _____, "An Empirical Test of the Man-in-the-Middle Hypothesis Among Executives in a Hierarchical Organization Employing a Unit Analysis," *Organization Behavior and Human Performance,* 8 (1972), pp. 262–285; R. J. House and G. Dessler, "The Path-Goal Theory of Leadership: Some Post Hoc and A Priori Tests," to appear in J. G. Hunt, ed., *Contingency Approaches to Leadership* (Carbondale, Ill.: Southern Illinois University Press, 1974).

4. M. G. Evans, "Effects of Supervisory Behavior"; _____, "Extensions of a Path-Goal Theory of Motivation," *Journal of Applied Psychology,* 59 (1974), pp. 172–178.

5. R. J. House, "A Path-Goal Theory"; R. J. House and G. Dessler, "Path-Goal Theory of Leadership."

6. R. J. House and G. Dessler, "Path-Goal Theory of Leadership"; R. M. Stogdill, *Managers, Employees, Organization* (Ohio State University, Bureau of Business Research, 1965); R. J. House, A. Valency and R. Van der Krabben, "Some Tests and Extensions of the Path-Goal Theory of Leadership" (in preparation).

7. W. A. Hill and D. Hughes, "Variations in Leader Behavior As a Function of Task Type," *Organization Behavior and Human Performance* (1974, in press).

8. K. E. Runyon, "Some Interactions Between Personality Variables and Management Styles," *Journal of Applied Psychology,* 57, 3 (1973), pp. 288–294; T. R. Mitchell, C. R. Smyser and S. E. Weed, "Locus of Control: Supervision and Work Satisfaction," *Academy of Management Journal* (in press).

9. T. R. Mitchell, "Locus of Control."

10. R. J. House, "A Path-Goal Theory"; _____ and G. Dessler, "Path-Goal Theory of Leadership"; A. D. Szalagyi and H. P. Sims, "An Exploration of the Path-Goal Theory of Leadership in a Health Care Environment," *Academy of Management Journal* (in press); J. D. Dermer, "Supervisory Behavior and Budget Motivation" (Cambridge, Mass.: unpublished, MIT, Sloan School of Management, 1974); R. W. Smetana, "The Relationship Between Managerial Behavior and Subordinate Attitudes and Motivation: A Contribution to a Behavioral Theory of

Leadership" (Ph.D. diss, Wayne State University, 1974).

11. S. E. Weed, T. R. Mitchell and C. R. Smyser, "A Test of House's Path-Goal Theory of Leadership in an Organizational Setting" (paper presented at Western Psychological Assoc., 1974); J. D. Dermer and J. P. Siegel, "A Test of Path-Goal Theory: Disconfirming Evidence and a Critique" (unpublished, University of Toronto, Faculty of Management Studies, 1973); R. S. Schuler, "A Path-Goal Theory of Leadership: An Empirical Investigation" (Ph.D. diss, Michigan State University, 1973); H. K. Downey, J. E. Sheridan and J. W. Slocum, Jr., "Analysis of Relationships Among Leader Behavior, Subordinate Job Performance and Satisfaction: A Path-Goal Approach" (unpublished mimeograph, 1974); J. E. Stinson and T. W. Johnson, "The Path-Goal Theory of Leadership: A Partial Test and Suggested Refinement," *Proceedings* (Kent, Ohio: 7th Annual Conference of the Midwest Academy of Management, April 1974), pp. 18–36.

12. G. Dessler, "An Investigation of the Path-Goal Theory of Leadership" (Ph.D. diss, City University of New York, Bernard M. Baruch College, 1973).

13. R. J. House, D. Burrill and G. Dessler, "Tests and Extensions of Path-Goal Theory of Leadership, I" (unpublished, in process).

14. R. J. House, "A Path-Goal Theory"; ———— and G. Dessler, "Path-Goal Theory of Leadership"; A. D. Szalagyi and H. P. Sims, "Exploration of Path-Goal"; J. E. Stinson and T. W. Johnson, *Proceedings*; R. S. Schuler, "Path-Goal: Investigation"; H. K. Downey, J. E. Sheridan and J. W. Slocum, Jr., "Analysis of Relationships"; S. E. Weed, T. R. Mitchell and C. R. Smyser, "Test of House's Path-Goal."

15. A. D. Szalagyi and H. P. Sims, "Exploration of Path-Goal."

16. R. J. House, A. Valency and R. Van der Krabben, "Tests and Extensions of Path-Goal Theory of Leadership, II" (unpublished, in process).

17. T. R. Mitchell, "Motivation and Participation."

18. H. Tosi, "A Reexamination of Personality As a Determinant of the Effects of Participation," *Personnel Psychology*, 23 (1970), pp. 91–99; J. Sadler "Leadership Style, Confidence in Management and Job Satisfaction," *Journal of Applied Behavioral Sciences*, 6 (1970), pp. 3–19; K. N. Wexley, J. P. Singh and J. A. Yukl, "Subordinate Personality As a Moderator of the Effects of Participation in Three Types of Appraisal Interviews," *Journal of Applied Psychology*, 83, 1 (1973), pp. 54–59.

19. T. R. Mitchell, "Motivation and Participation."

20. A. S. Tannenbaum and F. H. Allport, "Personality Structure and Group Structure: An Interpretive Study of Their Relationship Through an Event-Structure Hypothesis," *Journal of Abnormal and Social Psychology*, 53 (1956), pp. 272–280; V. H. Vroom, "Some Personality Determinants of the Effects of Participation," *Journal of Abnormal and Social Psychology*, 59 (1959), pp. 322–327.

21. K. E. Runyon, "Some Interactions Between Personality Variables and Management Styles," *Journal of Applied Psychology*, 57, 3 (1973), pp. 288–294.

22. T. R. Mitchell, C. R. Smyser and S. E. Weed, "Locus of Control."

23. R. J. House, "Notes on the Path-Goal Theory of Leadership" (University of Toronto, Faculty of Management Studies, May 1974).

24. R. S. Schuler, "Leader Participation, Task Structure and Subordinate Authoritarianism (unpublished mimeograph, Cleveland State University, 1974).

THE LEADERSHIP GAME: MATCHING THE MAN TO THE SITUATION

Most people in management would agree that leadership training accomplishes something. Whether it always does what it is intended to do is another question. Most of us know someone whose behavior changed or whose performance improved after he went through a leadership training program. Unfortunately, most of us also know about as many people who have gone through one training program after another and still perform as poorly as ever. Even more intriguing are the many outstanding leaders who have had little or no leadership training at all—Joan of Arc being a stellar example.

Empirical studies of leadership training generally reveal the same disappointing results. On the average, people with much training perform about as well as people with little or no training, and reviews by Stogdill; Campbell, Dunnette, Lawler, and Weick; and others present no evidence that any particular leadership training method consistently improves organizational performance.

Research by my associates and me has revealed the same disappointing results. When we compared a group of Belgian navy recruits and a well-trained and experienced group of petty offi-

cers, for example, we found no overall differences in leadership performance. In a follow-up study in Canada, basic trainees performed their leadership tasks as well as captains and majors who had graduated from military college. These experimental studies are supported by results from field research. Nealey and I found no relationship between amount of training and performance of post office managers as rated by their immediate superiors. In addition, I found zero correlations between amount of training and performance of police patrol sergeants. Recent studies show similar findings for officers and noncommissioned officers of an American infantry division.

This does not necessarily mean that leadership training need be ineffective. Quite the contrary. Our data suggest that leadership training, under certain conditions, systematically improves the performance of some leaders while it decreases the performance of others. Obviously, we have to understand the conditions under which leadership training is effective if we are to make much progress in this area.

While recognizing the legitimacy of leadership training designed to improve job satisfaction and to enhance personal growth, I want to confine my remarks here to training that aims to improve task performance as it is defined by an organization.

First, let me briefly comment on present training approaches. Then I will propose a prelimi-

Reprinted by permission of the publisher from *Organizational Dynamics*, Vol. 5, No. 2, Fall, 1976, © 1976 by AMACOM, a division of American Management Associations.

nary theory of leadership training as well as present some data that support this formulation. Last, I will describe the training program that we have developed on the basis of this theory and that we are currently validating.

CURRENT PRACTICES BASED ON QUESTIONABLE ASSUMPTIONS

Let us first look at present practices and, in particular, their underlying assumptions. One assumption that guides many training programs is the notion that there is one ideal kind of leadership behavior or attitude that is related to good performance under all conditions and that every trainee therefore needs to adopt. For example, several prominent authorities contend that a good leader has to be permissive, participative, or human-relations-oriented.

If we take a close look at the empirical results, however, it is obvious that neither the permissive, considerate leaders nor the autocratic, directive leaders obtain optimum performance under all conditions. Yet any training program that seeks to develop the same kind of leadership behavior or attitude implicitly assumes that there is one best leadership style.

A second major assumption in many programs is that leadership behavior is under voluntary control, that a few weeks of telling a leader how to behave or convincing him that a certain kind of behavior is best will result in the appropriate behavior changes.

This ignores the fact that leadership situations are highly emotion-changed, interpersonal relationships that mean a great deal to the subordinate as well as to his boss. We probably expect more change in interpersonal behavior than a routine training program can hope to deliver. The manner in which we relate to authority figures and subordinates is for most of us a very important interaction that we learn over many years. And it is very difficult indeed to change such significant emotional relationships. It is essential, therefore, that we ask just how much control the typical leader actually has over his own behavior. Our studies suggest that a leader can voluntarily change his leadership behavior only in situations in which he has a great deal of control.

In situations in which a leader is under pressure, in which there is considerable uncertainty and insecurity, leadership behavior seems to depend on the way the individual's personality interacts with his leadership situation. A didactic approach —telling a leader to be more considerate, permissive, or decisive—is about as effective as telling someone that he should be more lovable or less anxious.

A third assumption is that the more powerful and influential leader will be more effective because he will be able to make his group work harder on the organization's tasks. On the basis of this assumption, many training programs try to increase a leader's control and influence in various ways. They give him human-relations training so that he can make himself more acceptable to his subordinates. This supposedly will enable him to motivate his subordinates to work harder. These programs may give a leader technical training so that he can increase his expertise. They teach him the intricacies of an organization so that he can make full use of his legitimate power, knowing where power lies within the organization as well as knowing what rewards and punishments the organization has to offer.

This approach ignores the fact that the leadership situation is an arena in which a leader must satisfy his own needs as well as the needs of his organization. Where a leader's and an organization's needs are incompatible, the leader's needs are apt to take precedence. At the very least, they are likely to interfere with satisfying the needs of the organization.

An equally questionable assumption is at the basis of participative management training, which holds that a leader who shares his decision-making functions with his subordinates will therefore be more effective. As Jon Blades has recently shown, the effectiveness of participative management depends in large part on the intelligence and ability of the group members. The leader who listens to the advice of unintelligent people can hardly expect brilliant answers.

Let me stress again, however, that training in participative management or in any other kind of leadership approach is not necessarily bad practice, nor will it be ineffective for all trainees. Rather, we need to be more discriminating about whom we train and the situation for which we attempt to train a particular leader. Most leadership training programs fail to do this because they give all trainees the same training despite the fact that practically all of the empirical evidence tells us that the performance of a group depends in part on the kind of task and the situation in which the leader has to operate.

Where do we go from here?

THE CONTINGENCY APPROACH TO LEADERSHIP TRAINING

My position on training, not surprisingly, is based on the contingency model of leadership effectiveness. In essence, this theory holds that the effectiveness of a group or an organization depends on the interaction between the leader's personality and the situation. Specifically, we have to match the leader's motivational structure (that is, the goals to which he gives the highest priority) with the degree to which the situation gives the leader control and influence over the outcomes of his decisions.

We measure the leader's motivation by the *Least Preferred Co-worker Scale* (LPC). This scale asks the individual first to think of everyone with whom he has ever worked, and then to describe the one person with whom he could work *least* well. This can be someone with whom he worked years ago or someone with whom he works at the moment. (See Figure 1 for the scale

FIGURE 1. Least preferred co-worker scale

Think of the person with whom you can work least well. He may be someone you work with now, or someone you knew in the past. He does not have to be the person you like least well, but should be the person with whom you had the most difficulty in getting a job done. Describe this person as he appears to you.

	8	7	6	5	4	3	2	1	
Pleasant									Unpleasant
Friendly	8	7	6	5	4	3	2	1	Unfriendly
Rejecting	1	2	3	4	5	6	7	8	Accepting
Helpful	8	7	6	5	4	3	2	1	Frustrating
Unenthusiastic	1	2	3	4	5	6	7	8	Enthusiastic
Tense	1	2	3	4	5	6	7	8	Relaxed
Distant	1	2	3	4	5	6	7	8	Close
Cold	1	2	3	4	5	6	7	8	Warm
Cooperative	8	7	6	5	4	3	2	1	Uncooperative
Supportive	8	7	6	5	4	3	2	1	Hostile
Boring	1	2	3	4	5	6	7	8	Interesting
Quarrelsome	1	2	3	4	5	6	7	8	Harmonious
Self-assured	8	7	6	5	4	3	2	1	Hesitant
Efficient	8	7	6	5	4	3	2	1	Inefficient
Gloomy	1	2	3	4	5	6	7	8	Cheerful
Open	8	7	6	5	4	3	2	1	Guarded

of opposing attributes used to describe the least preferred co-worker.)

An individual who describes his or her least preferred co-worker in very negative and rejecting terms (a low LPC) in effect shows a strong emotional reaction to people with whom he or she cannot work—in effect, *"If I can't work with you, you are no damn good!"* This is the typical pattern of a person who, when forced to make the choice, opts first for getting on with the task and worries about his interpersonal relations later.

Someone who describes even his least preferred co-worker in relatively more positive terms in effect looks at the individual not only as a co-worker but also as a person who might otherwise have some acceptable, if not admirable, traits. The "high LPC" leader sees close interpersonal relations as a requirement for task accomplishment.

Let me, however, strongly emphasize that we are here talking about different priorities of goals. We are not speaking about leader behaviors. The accomplishment of the task might well call for very considerate and pleasant interpersonal behaviors, while the maintenance of close interpersonal relations might be possible only by driving the group to success. In this latter case the relationship-motivated, high LPC leader might be quite single-minded about accomplishing the task. In general we find that uncertain and anxiety-arousing conditions tend to make the low LPC leaders concentrate on the task, while the high LPC leaders concentrate on their relations with their subordinates. The opposite is the case in situations in which the leader is secure and in control.

The other major factor in this theory is defined by the "situational favorableness" that basically indicates the degree to which the leader has control and influence and, therefore, feels that he can determine the outcomes of the group interaction. We generally measure situational favorableness on the basis of three subscales: leader-member relations, task structure, and position power. The leader has more control and influence if (1) his members support him, (2) he knows exactly what to do and how to do it, and (3) the organization gives him the means to reward and punish his subordinates.

The crucial question then is to determine the specific situations under which various types of leaders perform best. The contingency model has consistently shown that the task-motivated (low LPC) leaders tend to perform most effectively in situations in which their control and influence are very high and in situations in which it is relatively low. By contrast, relationship-motivated (high LPC) leaders tend to perform best in situations in which their control and influence is moderate.

Validating the Model

This relationship has now been found in well over 50 different studies; in fact, a carefully controlled experiment by Chemers and Skrzypek showed that the contingency model accounted for 28 percent of the variance in task performance. The model is most easily described by the schematic drawing in Figure 2. The vertical axis shows the group's or the organization's performance. The horizontal axis indicates "situational favorableness"—that is, the degree to which the situation provides the leader with control and influence. The solid line shows the performance of high LPC leaders, and the broken line the performance of low LPC leaders. As can be seen, the high LPC, or relationship-motivated, leaders generally perform best in situations in which their relations with subordinates are good but task structure and position power are low. They also perform well when their relations with subordinates are poor but task structure and position power are high (both situations of moderate favorableness as defined in Figure 2). Task-motivated leaders perform best when all three factors that define their control and influence are either high or low.

It should be clear from Figure 2 that we can improve group performance either by changing the leader's motivational structure—that is, the basic goals he pursues in life—or else by modifying his leadership situation. While it is possible, of course, to change personality and the motivational structure that is a part of personality, this is clearly a difficult and uncertain process. It is, however, relatively easy to modify the leadership situation. We can select a person for certain

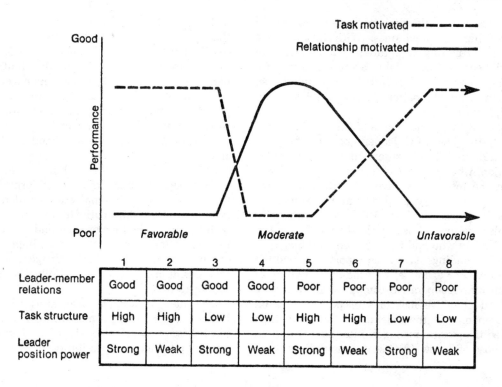

FIGURE 2. Schematic representation of the performance of relationship- and task-motivated leaders in different situational favorableness conditions

kinds of jobs and not others, we can assign him certain tasks, give him more or less responsibility, or we can give him leadership training in order to increase his power and influence.

As we said before, most leadership training seeks to increase the favorableness of a situation —that is, it increases the leader's control and influence. It follows that leaders who, for example, start off in an unfavorable situation will gradually move into a zone of moderate situational favorableness. Such a change in control and influence would also change leadership performance: The task-motivated leader who performs well in the unfavorable zone will perform less well with training, while the relationship-motivated leader should improve with training as he moves from the unfavorable to the moderately favorable zone, toward the left of the graph. Training should, therefore, decrease performance of some leaders but increase it for others.

This was recently demonstrated by a labora-

tory experiment conducted by Chemers, Rice, Sundstrom, and Butler at the University of Utah. These researchers assembled four-man groups composed of ROTC and psychology students, with an ROTC cadet as the leader. Half the leaders were high and half were low LPC persons. Half were assigned at random to receive training, while the others were given an assignment unrelated to the task.

The group task consisted of deciphering a series of cryptograms. Training consisted of teaching leaders such rules as counting all the alphabet letters and then assuming that the most frequent letter would be an *e*. A three-letter word with an *e* at the end would be *the*. The only one-letter words in English are *a* and *I*, and so on. As it happened in that particular study, the groups had very poor leader-member relations, low position power, and an unstructured task if the leaders were untrained—thus an unfavorable situation.

We would therefore expect that the task-motivated leaders would perform better than would relationship-motivated ones. With training, the task would become structured and the situation would become moderately favorable. The relationship-motivated, high LPC leaders should then perform relatively better than would task-motivated, low LPC leaders.

Figure 3 shows the results of this study. As expected, the low LPC leaders performed better than did high LPC leaders in the unfavorable situation, while high LPC leaders performed better in the moderately favorable situation. However, as the theory predicts but we would not normally expect, the low LPC leaders with training also performed less well than did the low LPC leaders who had not received training.

Similar findings have been reported in real-life situations. For example, we conducted a study of 32 consumer cooperative companies in which we obtained objective measures of performance on all companies in the federation. When we then divided the general managers into those with high and those with low LPC scores, as well as those with relatively little experience and training and those with relatively high experience and concomitant training, we obtained Figure 4. Evaluations from several judges indicated that the experienced and trained general manager had a favorable leadership situation. A relatively inexperienced and untrained manager would have correspondingly less control and influence, hence a situation that would be only moderately favorable.

As Figure 4 shows, the task-motivated leaders with experience and training performed better than did relationship-motivated leaders. However, the relationship-motivated general managers with relatively less experience and training performed better than did the more highly experienced and trained general managers who were relationship-motivated. Several other studies give similar results.

The question usually arises as to whether the leader could change his motivational structure or his behavior to suit the situation. I would not want to preclude this possibility, but I also really

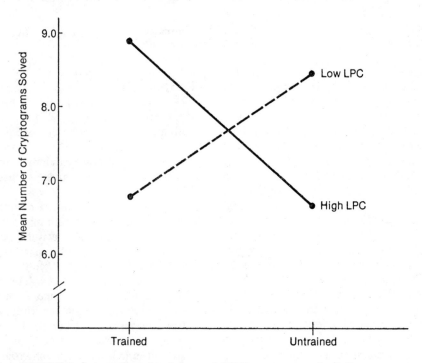

FIGURE 3. Interaction of training and LPC on group productivity

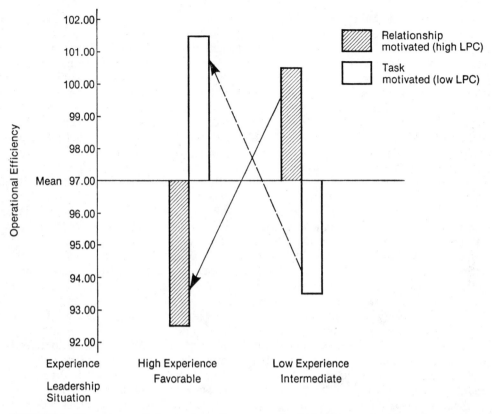

FIGURE 4. The presumed change in performance of relationship- and task-motivated company managers as a function of increased experience

do not think that this is done very easily. As we said before, leadership is a very ego-involving relationship, and in such relationships it is very difficult to control our behavior. It is certainly much more emotionally charged than, say, the interaction between a salesman and a customer or a lawyer and his client. We are talking about patterns of interaction that are fairly central to our personality. The degree to which a person is affected by his relations with others, or the degree to which he is driven to get a job done, is not very easily changed from one day to the next. I don't really think that you can make someone who is cold and businesslike into a warm, cuddly leader in the course of a few hours or even days. Chris Argyris's account of these difficulties documents this point all too well.

A NEW APPROACH TO TRAINING

Let me now get to the point of this symposium. What kind of training would the contingency model call for? We have tended to look at people as infinitely malleable, as infinitely capable of changing their behavior and of being changed by just a few hours of training even though the behavior we are trying to change may have been acquired over a whole lifetime. In contrast, we have tended to look at the organization as relatively inflexible and rigid. Most people see themselves as having very little control over their work situation. This is clearly not true. We have to teach people that they have much more control over the relevant aspects of their own leadership jobs than they generally realize. We have to teach them, therefore, that they can change the situation so that it will better match their personality.

The research on the contingency model shows that effective leadership depends on maintaining the right match of personality and of situation. We can certainly teach people how to recognize the particular situations in which they are likely to succeed and those in which they are likely to be less effective. And we can tell them, "If you avoid jobs in which you are likely to fail, you are bound to be a success."

We now have reason to believe that we can teach people with reasonable accuracy to assess the degree to which their subordinates and their superiors are supportive, the degree to which a task is structured, and the degree to which they have position power.

The next step is to give trainees guidance in seeking or developing leadership situations in which they are most likely to be successful, or to modify their situations to match their personalities. We can also train them in ways to provide their subordinate leaders with conditions that match their motivational patterns.

Successful leaders do this intuitively. They may say about a person that "you have to give him a lot of backing if you want him to be effective." For one person, they may spell out in detail what to do and how to do it; for another, they may just explain what the problem is and then let him run with the ball.

We may not be able to change the warmth and emotional closeness of our relations with others. However, we can frequently modify our accessibility to subordinates, the degree to which we share information, and the extent to which contacts with subordinates are formal and businesslike or informal, social, and relaxed. We can give detailed, step-by-step task instructions or general policies and guidelines. We can use our position power under some conditions and share decision making under others.

Martin Chemers, Linda Mahar, and I have developed a self-administered programmed manual for leadership training called *Leader Match* that attempts to teach managers how to diagnose their leadership situation, how to determine the kind

of situation that best matches their personality or motivational pattern, and how to modify the situation so that it does match their leadership style. One validation study has now been successfully completed, using second-level leaders of a volunteer public health organization that operates in Latin America. Another one involves middle managers of a government agency. In these studies the leaders who were trained with *Leader Match* performed significantly better than did leaders in a comparable, randomly selected control group. At the time of this writing, a third validation study also seems to be producing significant results. These early results are highly encouraging, and we hope to obtain further evidence during this coming year.

In summary, my own position is that we must train people differentially—not everyone should be trained to behave in the same way or to adopt the same attitudes. In fact, we will be better served by training our leaders in how to change their leadership situations than in how to change their personalities. Leadership effectiveness requires a proper match of person and situation, and trying to change personality is the hard way of achieving this balance. It is an effort with uncertain success that requires years, not weeks. Our recent studies of contingency model training show that leaders can recognize the situations in which they tend to be most successful, and they can modify their situations so that they perform more effectively. We have reason to believe that this approach holds considerable promise for the future of leadership training.

SELECTED BIBLIOGRAPHY

The most extensive description of the contingency model can be found in Fred Fiedler's *A Theory of Leadership Effectiveness* (McGraw-Hill, 1967). In it, he reviews some of the validation studies in detail and provides technical information about the various scales. A subsequent volume co-authored by Martin M. Chemers, *Leadership and Effective Management* (Scott, Foresman and Company, 1975), provides a less technical summary and presents some of the more recent work on validation as well as on training, selection, and experience.

The leader who is interested in a complete bibliography of the current literature should read Ralph Stogdill's *Handbook of Leadership* (The Free Press, 1974). Another excellent reference is Campbell, Dunnette, Lawler, and Weick's *Managerial Behavior, Performance, and Effectiveness* (McGraw-Hill, 1970).

The reader who would like a more popular descrip-

tion of recent work on leadership training should read Fred Fiedler's article in *Psychology Today* (February 1973). A clear, but somewhat less popular, description, "How Do You Make Leaders More Effective?" appears in *Organizational Dynamics* (Autumn 1972).

PARTICIPATION:
A CRITICAL REVIEW
OF RESEARCH FINDINGS

In management literature, more attention has been given to participation as a leadership dimension than nearly any other element of leadership style. This essay critically reviews several classic research studies that have contributed largely to the view that a participation leadership style is necessary for effective leadership regardless of the circumstances.

PARTICIPATION DEFINED

A number of conceptual problems have confounded the interpretation of research results. First, this discussion of "participation" will be limited to cases where the decisions that are reached affect an entire group rather than only the individual(s) making the decision. Second, the distinction between "delegation of authority" and "participation" must be clarified. Little authority or considerable authority may be delegated in an organization in the sense that decisions are centralized or decentralized; independent of the degree of delegation is the degree to which a leader uses participation in making decisions which have been allocated to his level. For in-

stance, in a university, where decisions may be centralized at the higher levels (with relatively little decentralization down to the college or department level), there is little potential for meaningful participation at lower levels; however, either broad or limited participation may be used at the central level. Our concern here is with the effects of participation rather than delegation.

Third, the term *"participation"* is often used diffusely, or equated with "democratic" approaches to leadership. "Participation" is only one of the building blocks that make up a democratic leadership style; the term should be defined as the extent to which subordinates, or other groups who are affected by decisions, are consulted with, and involved in the making of decisions. This may vary from extensive involvement to restrictive involvement.

POPULAR CONCEPTIONS OF THE EFFECTS OF PARTICIPATION

George Strauss raises the question of when participation is most effective, and to what extent involvement in some decisions carries over into a more positive attitude and orientation generally.[1]

It is often said that, if a worker is permitted to participate in making decisions, he will work harder. But work harder at what? At making the decision? At

Reprinted by permission from Arlyn Melcher and *Human Resource Management*, Volume 15, No. 2, Summer, 1976, pp. 12–21, Graduate School of Business Administration, University of Michigan, Ann Arbor, Michigan 48109.

implementing the decision? Or at implementing *other* decisions? Suppose, for example, workers are permitted to decide for themselves *when* coffee breaks should be taken (though management still determines how long they should be). The discussion itself may well be quite lively. But will the mere fact of participation lead to workers taking their breaks only at the times agreed upon? Will they be less likely to take breaks which are excessively long? And will they also produce more on the job? And, to consider a related question: when will decision-making within the small group lead to greater support of the goals of the entire organization? Many managers assume that participation in regard to a relatively trivial problem will lead to higher productivity generally. Perhaps this will occur at times. But when? Why?

Strauss comments that there is no research directed to answering these questions and we can only speculate on the probable relationships. This skepticism is, however, not broadly shared by other writers.

One of the most broadly accepted ideas in organizational practice is that there *should* be participation. Even where a supervisor makes little use of it, he is unlikely to defend his practice, and will rather point to areas where he uses it to some degree. McGregor, for instance, develops the thesis that broad use of participation incorporates the values of Theory Y: [2]

The effective use of participation is a consequence of a managerial point of view which includes confidence in the potentialities of subordinates, awareness of management's dependency downwards, and a desire to avoid some of the negative consequences of emphasis on personal authority. It is consistent with Theory Y—with management by integration and self-control.

McGregor feels that participation encourages subordinates' growth and ability to accept responsibility, and, by assisting their integration into the organization, it provides them an opportunity to increase their satisfaction and their motivation to achieve organizational objectives. He further sees this as contributing to greater independence (a sense of controlling one's destiny) and the ability to gain recognition from peers and superiors—these results presumably help to satisfy personal needs which are consistent with working toward organizational objectives.

Many other books with the "human relations viewpoint" present similar lists of advantages

without mentioning any apparent appreciable risks. We need to examine more closely the studies on which these generalizations have been built, and to critically assess whether this degree of optimism is justified.

FIELD STUDIES OF PARTICIPATION

Consultation at the Top Levels

A classic study in the uses and limitations of participation was done by Nyman and Smith, who investigated the Pequot Mills, a textile firm, for a period of over four years in the early 1930's.[3] The Mills employed approximately 1200 employees located in five departments. The company's deteriorating position pressured it to introduce labor-saving technological changes, and to resist the demands of a strong, well-organized union for improvements in wages and other protections. In the face of the company's resistance, the union began having internal problems: factional groups formed and dissatisfaction with the union leadership developed. However, the business agent was a man of considerable imagination and foresight. He foresaw that a union-management cooperation plan for joint adjustments to the competitive conditions facing the company would both strengthen the position of the union and improve the relationship with the company. He proposed the plan and management accepted it. Under the plan, management agreed to meet regularly with the union officials to discuss labor relations problems; this enabled the union to participate in conferences where it could exert influence on company policies—an objective which it had previously sought to reach through collective bargaining.

At first, fairly large-scale monthly conferences were held with about thirty-five representatives for company and union; later, they were held less regularly with fewer officials. In effect, a system was established that permitted close consultation between top union officials and top management officials in the plant; lower echelon management and employees were not involved.

In the next couple of years, the company competed in a continually depressed market; it reduced costs by introducing labor-saving machinery, changes in work flow arrangements, and other technical approaches. Then, as these became inadequate to meet competition, the company initiated a series of wage reductions. The participation was effective in that the union leadership developed an understanding of the problems facing the company and accepted the fact that the union and the workers had to make adjustments; the union leadership supported management efforts in these directions.

However, this understanding was not achieved by lower-level supervision or operative employees. Lower-level management regarded participation as a device to gain acceptance of changes they wanted to implement, rather than as a joint sharing of decision process or a joint consultation on decisions. Workers regarded it as a device for speed-up. Before long, a division developed between the local union membership and its leadership.

As management increasingly used consultation with top union leadership, participation became less acceptable to the workers. Relations deteriorated until a strike was called under highly adverse economic circumstances—despite the strong opposition of the union leadership. Internal union factionalism made it difficult to settle the strike and, ultimately, an independent union was formed with new leadership.

The study illustrates some of the advantages of participation but it also suggests that the value is limited to those who are actively involved in the consultative process.

The Ahmedabad Studies: Consultation at the Bottom Levels

Rice, representing the Tavistock Institute (a research group in England), studied the introduction of technical changes and reorganization in a small textile plant, part of a larger company, in Ahmedabad, India.[4] The reorganization, in effect, permitted the establishment of small integrated work groups. The elements of the idea were proposed to lower-level supervision who, in turn, proposed them to the workers. The workers accepted the idea and immediately proceeded to implement it along the lines they saw as most

useful. They made decisions about the organization of the experimental groups including the size of the groups and who would be members. The move was successful in that productivity moderately increased and, especially, in that a basic change in traditional working relationships was immediately accepted.

Rice later replicated the experiment in a somewhat different setting in the same company:[5] an experimental group of seven workers was formed (later enlarged to eleven workers) and Rice planned out the form of structure and task arrangement. Neither the operating managers nor the workers were initially consulted in the planning of the system; when problems developed, though, Rice discussed the difficulties with the workers and out of the discussions came modifications in the plan. These meetings operated on an open-ended basis where expression of viewpoints spontaneously developed. This resulted in broad participation and involvement on the part of supervision and the workers. A cohesive group developed with considerable enthusiasm for the new arrangements.

The acceptance of the changes was remarkable in many respects: the changes occurred during a period when there was broad resistance to *rationalization* in India (i.e., introduction of labor-saving methods); permission to introduce the change had to be obtained from union officials and workers; and many people from the city and region opposed to both the introduction of automatic machinery and increased productivity of individual workers made the experiment the center of their agitation. Still, the change was maintained in spite of the hostile environment.

Yet, however impressive Rice's study-findings may appear, they were affected by a number of factors: 1) the workers had volunteered to participate in the experiment; 2) the experimental shed was located on a main thoroughfare through the mill, where anyone could observe what was happening; 3) extensive attention was given to the unit by trade union officials, top management, and others who visited the operation, and 4) therefore, the "Hawthorne Effect" was partially relevant. Even so, technical changes are often vigorously resisted and in this case they were actively supported.

The Haywood Studies: Is This a Study of Participation?

The Haywood Manufacturing Company was a small family-owned manufacturer of textiles, located in the small town of Marion, Virginia. The plant employed mostly women who were recruited from the rural mountainous areas surrounding the town and who normally did not have previous industrial experience. The average age and education was twenty-three with eight years of grammar school. The firm became a center of behavioral research when Kurt Lewin began working with the plant management in 1939, bringing in co-workers such as Alex Bavelas and John R. P. French, Jr., to carry out a number of projects. These studies purportedly demonstrate the values of participation in changing basic beliefs, making individuals more responsive to technical change, increasing productivity, and simply contributing to more positive employee attitudes.

One of these famous studies investigated the value of participation in changing a stereotype widely believed in the plant—that women over thirty were slow in developing speed in production, were frequently absent, had a shorter working life, and were difficult to teach.[6] French, who was employed as a psychologist in the plant, attempted, but failed, to convince management that their conclusions about older women were not true; so he devised a simple study for management to carry out to determine the relationship between women's ages, productivity, and other relevant factors. The idea was that if management participated in the study, they would accept the conclusions more readily. When the top management did find that, in fact, the older women were highly desirable employees, they changed their opinion and were ready to change hiring policy. Those, however, who did not participate in the study were not persuaded by the opinions of top management; so a series of meetings was established to discuss the evidence, their reservations, and the general nature of stereotypes. Out of these meetings came wide acceptance of the new policy and group decisions recommending that the experiment be made in training older workers.

Because the Haywood studies have been broadly quoted, the study design merits a closer look.

There is always a problem, in field studies, separating the effects of the variable under study from other possible causal factors: in the case of the Haywood studies, management had been actively committed to support the intensive study of their organization over a period of thirty years and were committed to an intellectual position that participation is a pervasive force in affecting behavior.

In the last reported study of the Haywood organization, a great number of changes in technology, formal structure, and control systems occurred when the firm took over another plant. Yet, the sharp changes in behavior in productivity have been attributed to "participation."[7] One has to view the findings with some skepticism. Three other studies by these researchers reveal consistent problems in interpreting results.

To determine whether participation influenced acceptance of technical change, Coch and French studied a company whose experience with technical change had been poor:[8] employees had a high quit rate or were slow in achieving previous levels of productivity when technical changes were implemented. The research approach was to contrast three groups: "no-participation," "participation through representatives" and "total participation."

No Participation Group

The production department modified the job, and the new piece rate was set. A group meeting was held in which the group was told that the change was necessary because of competitive conditions, and that a new piece rate had been set. The new piece rate was thoroughly explained by the time-study man, questions were answered, and the meeting dismissed.

Participation Through Representatives

The new plan (and the reasons for it) was explained to the entire work group; the workers then were asked to select a small number of operators who would serve in four functions: 1) as the basis for a study to determine how the job was presently done, and what steps could be eliminated; 2) as the basis for time studies to set the new piece rate; 3) as the initial group of trainees for the new rate; and (4) after they had had a chance to discuss these changes, as instructors to train the remaining operators on the new job.

Total Participation

This group followed the same steps as the preceding, with only two variations: the group was smaller and all the operators were given the special training. In both groups, suggestions were solicited and recorded by a stenographer.

The results were that the "no participation" group had lower productivity, higher conflict with supervisory and staff personnel, and a greater rate of turnover as compared with the other two groups. There was little difference between the "total participation" group and the "participation through representation" group.

Ten years later, a replication in the same plant of the experiment showed most of the same characteristics and results.[9] Yet, the difference between the groups was caused not so much by "participation" but, first, by variations in training to adjust to the change, and second, by an unspecified degree of methods change. "Participation" was the opportunity for employees to present suggestions; but management made the *decisions* about what was going to be done and how it was to be done, and trained the employees to do it.

Another replication of the Haywood study was done in a Norwegian manufacturing plant to determine how participation in planning technical changes affected employee productivity and behavior.[10] The study involved 9 four-member groups: participation was practically unchanged in two groups, only moderately changed in three groups, and the remaining four groups were set up as test-groups. The authors hypothesized that:

Increased participation (and the opportunity to participate) would affect production, labor-management relations, and job satisfaction only to the extent that four conditioning variables were present: 1) the decisions were important, 2) the content of the decisions was relevant to the dependent variable, production, labor relations, or job satisfaction, 3) the participation was considered legitimate, and 4) there was no resistance to change, i.e., no negative reaction to the methods of managing the change.

The experimental design only partially provided evidence related to these premises. Taking nine groups (36 employees) out of a larger group of nearly 400 employees and in only a minor way increasing their participation limits the potential influence on behavior and productivity. The effects of participation on behavior could not be reliably determined from their data; and there was no effect at all on their productivity. In effect, the group norms defined the level of production and participation didn't touch these norms.

Another study, by Bavelas, sought to determine how participation in goal setting influenced production.[11] Bavelas met with one group of workers to discuss the establishment of goals. These goals were set at a high level and were subsequently reached. Another group also met with Bavelas for interviews: "They received the same attention and friendly encouragement, but no production goal was decided upon." In this group, there was no change in production. This study was replicated in another midwestern garment manufacturing plant and while the results were not as clean-cut as Bavelas had achieved, the results (as interpreted by the authors) supported the conclusion that participation in goal setting improved subsequent productivity.[12]

While these results indicate that participation was the relevant factor, a closer look suggests that goal setting, not participation, was the key variable. In effect, we have a research design where cells a and b are explored rather than a and a, or b and b.

TABLE ONE

		Some Participation	No Participation
Goals	Set	a_1	a_2
	Not Set	b_1	b_2

It is apparent that other variables may confound the results in a field study. "Participation," as we have defined it and as it usually is used, is being changed only in a mild degree; other factors are changing sharply. Employees under "participation" conditions receive training; those under "no participation" conditions don't. Goals are set for a "participating" group but not for a nonparticipating group. The authors consistently ignore other variables that also affect behavior and productivity. Numerous studies suggest that participation importantly affects behavior; but we shall want to check whether these generalizations are borne out by somewhat narrower but better controlled studies.

Interaction of Participation and Personality

Victor Vroom explored the extent to which personality mediates the influence of participation on behavior.[13] In a field study of two branches of a parcel post firm located in New York and Chicago, Vroom sampled 108 supervisors from five levels in the firm. His concern was with how participation interacted with personality to affect job attitudes of subordinates and job performance. His measure of participation included two questions directed at how much influence the subordinate had over the supervisor, and two questions which measured the extent the supervisor consulted with the subordinate and was responsive to the subordinate's suggestions.

The index of participation was derived from the following questions: (a) In general, how much say or influence do you have on what goes on in your station? (b) Do you feel you can influence the decisions of your immediate superior regarding things about which you are concerned? (c) Does your immediate superior ask your opinion when a problem comes up which involves your work? (d) If you have a suggestion improving the job or changing the setup in some way, how easy is it for you to get your ideas across to your immediate superior? These questions were scored from one to five with one representing low participation and five high participation.

Two measures of personality—a measure of the need for independence and a measure of authoritarian qualities—were used. Table Two, summarizing the material on attitude toward the job and how it is related to participation level and personality measures, reveals that neither the dimension of personality nor participation alone had much influence over attitudes toward the job; there is, though, some interaction between participation and the two measures of personality. High participation combined with high need for independence results in the most favorable job atti-

TABLE TWO Mean scores on attitude toward the job for persons with different personalities under three participation conditions

Personality Variables	Participation		
	High	Moderate	Low
Total group	13.4 *	12.5	12.2
Need for independence			
High	14.0	12.1	11.9
Moderate	13.7	12.3	12.3
Low	12.7	13.1	12.5
Authoritarian measures			
Low	13.4	12.9	11.7
	13.7	12.3	12.6
High	12.7	12.7	12.4

* Theoretical range for attitude toward the job was 3–15 with low values indicating poor attitudes.

tude; low participation and high need for independence is associated with the least job satisfaction. Low participation in combination with low need for independence provide more favorable results than low participation and high need for independence. The same relations hold with interaction of authoritarian qualities and participation except the influences are smaller. A correlation analysis of the data suggests the interaction is even more pronounced.

Authoritarian persons or those with low independence needs don't have either a more favorable or unfavorable attitude under different degrees of participation, i.e., there is little relationship. Those, however, who have high need for independence, or are low on authoritarian qualities are affected to some degree by the level of participation. Lower level participation adversely affects their attitudes.

We find, therefore, that one of the better-regarded studies indicates that participation alone has little effect on behavior. There is some interaction with personality when those high on independence and low on authoritarian qualities react slightly more positively with greater participation. This study, however, does not support the more optimistic statements of the effects of participation. If participation is effective, a supervisory force should be particularly responsive toward different levels of participation; we don't find the sharp differences in behavior in this study.

TABLE THREE Correlation between participation and attitude toward the job for persons with different personalities (age, education, and occupational level are held constant)

Total group	.27
Need for independence	
High	.51
Moderate	.25
Low	.04
Authoritarian qualities	
Low	.50
Moderate	.35
High	.09

Participation in Goal Setting

Another field study by French and his colleagues focused on management in a division at General Electric.[14] G.E. had an appraisal system where individual performance levels were periodically evaluated in terms of pre-established standards. One part of this appraisal interview was the establishment of goals for the next period. The researchers were concerned with the question of whether different degrees of participation in establishing goals affected achievement in the next period. They also explored how participation affected various aspects of superior-subordinate relations and job satisfaction. The measurement of the variables was in part a modification and extension of Vroom's work.

The experimental design varied the degree of participation the subordinate had in setting his performance goals and planning of how to achieve these goals. One half the subjects participated to a high degree and the other half very little. In the high participation group, the manager asked each individual to write out a set of goals for improving his future performance, methods for achieving goals, and appropriate measures of progress toward them. Following this, a meeting was held where the subordinate presented his goals; through discussion with the manager he modified or added to these goals if necessary. The manager tried to elicit additional goals from the subordinate.

In the low participation group, the manager presented the goals to the subordinate, the means for achieving them and the ways to measure his progress. He then secured the subject's agree-

TABLE FOUR Effects of participation on acceptance of goals, confidence in the supervisor, and knowledge of supervisor's expectation[15]

	Participation					
	High			Low		
	Time Periods*					
	t_1	t_2	t_3	t_1	t_2	t_3
Acceptance of job goals**	4.2	5.2	4.9	3.9	4.4	4.3
Acceptance of the manager as an expert planner†	3.2	3.5	3.2	2.9	3.2	3.1
Knowledge of supervisor's goal expectations‡	3.5	3.6	3.4	3.4	3.7	3.4

*t_1—Before goal planning session.
t_2—Immediately after goal planning session.
t_3—10–12 weeks after goal planning session.
**—Varied on a six point scale from "High acceptance" to "Low acceptance."
†—Varied on a four point scale of "Well" to "Poorly."
‡—Varied on a four point scale from "Very sure" to "Not sure at all."

ment; he allowed modification of key goals only if necessary, and accepted goals suggested by the subordinate with a minimum of discussion and emphasis.

Several things are noticeable about the data. Consistent differences existed between the high and low participation groups *before* goal planning sessions were set up. If this is taken into account, participation in goal setting had little effect on behavior either immediately after the goal planning session or ten to twelve weeks later. The only exception was somewhat greater acceptance of job goals under higher participation.

In contrast, the establishment of goals improved behavior in all the groups. The improvement occurred immediately after the goal planning session, and deteriorated somewhat after ten or twelve weeks; but some degree of positive attitudes was retained ten to twelve weeks later. We thus have to attribute differences to goal setting —not participation.

One finding of this research is the interaction

TABLE FIVE Percentage achievement of performance goals as affected by threat in first appraisal, participation and employees' perceived influence

		Low Threat in First Appraisal *		High Threat in First Appraisal *	
		Low Assigned Participation	High Assigned Participation	Low Assigned Participation	High Assigned Participation
Employees' perceived influence	High	68	83	46	75
	Low	67	71	72	49

* French did not indicate how he measured the degree of threat in the first appraisal interview and we are operating on the assumption that the measurement is accurate.

between degree of threat, participation, and degree of influence. One of the factors that was included in the design was "the usual level of participation." This was operationalized by the following question:

"In general, how much say or influence do you feel you have on what goes on in your manager's work component?" (This varied on a six point scale from "very much" to "no influence at all.") Table Five provides the results of the interaction of the factors. Participation in goal setting improved achievement of performance goals for all groups with one exception. Where high threat in the first appraisal interview was coupled with the subordinate's judgment that he had *low influence*, goal achievement deteriorated from 72% to 49% *when participation increased*. This contrasts with where an individual feels he has high influence. Under the high threat condition, if participation increased, goal achievement increased from 46% to 75%. The high threat condition created anxiety that those with low influence were unable to handle. An increased opportunity to participate only increased their anxiety further as they felt they had little influence over the goals that were set.

In summary, our analysis of French's data indicates that participation in establishing goals has little effect on the three dimensions of behavior. The establishment of goals, in contrast, generally improved behavior immediately, but there was some deterioration after twelve weeks. When two other dimensions are introduced, we find the results are somewhat modified. Where the degree of threat in the first appraisal interview and the de-

gree of influence are held constant, then higher level participation improves performance attainment of performance goals. We find, however, a high degree of interaction between these three dimensions. If high threat exists in the interview along with low participation in goal setting, we have a degree of performance attainment; but when participation is increased under this circumstance, goal attainment is reduced sharply.*

SUMMARY

These studies suggest four conclusions:

1. Participation in decisions sharply increases the acceptance of decisions. This is most dramatic where changes from traditional beliefs or habits are involved as in the classic study of Pequot Mills where the union leadership accepted cost cutting steps, the Haywood Factory studies where a stereotype about older woman workers was changed, and the acceptance of sharply different work arrangements in the India textile mills case.

2. The process of participation affects the attitudes only of those actually consulted; those who stand outside the process apparently aren't influenced.

3. Participation in inconsequential decisions doesn't affect general attitudes. This is suggested by the study in the Norwegian manufacturing plant.

* This analysis departs fairly sharply from that provided in the article. We have partially excerpted material that seemed to be relevant and arrived at different conclusions than the authors.

4. The effects of participation may be mediated by personality. Those with an authoritarian orientation and low need for independence react positively where little participation is used.

Directions for Continued Study

Other factors that may mediate the effects of participation haven't been explored. For instance, Wilensky suggested that low participation (or what he called authoritarian leadership) might be acceptable and effective when the following conditions are met:[16]

1. Clearly defined goals exist,
2. There is clear-cut division of labor,
3. The group has developed necessary skills,
4. Outside pressures threaten the group,
5. The members perceive that speedy action is necessary, and
6. Individuals have previous group experience such as in the family that has been authoritarian in nature.

Presumably, when the opposite conditions prevail, broad participation elicits more favorable results. To put this more generally, low participation is expected and more effective in a complex organization context; while high participation is expected, and more effective, in a simpler context. Complexity of organization can be described in terms of size of group, degree of specialization, the extent to which spatial-physical barriers exist among personnel and between employees and superiors, the extent to which problems are structured and predictable solutions obtainable, and the level of work demands.[17] Table Six indicates this.

TABLE SIX Factors determining complexity of organizations

| | Complexity of Organizations | |
	Simple	Complex
Size of group	Small	Large
Degree of specialization	Low	High
Spatial-physical barriers	Few	Many
Nature of problems	Structured	Unstructured
Work demands	Low	High

TABLE SEVEN Complexity of organization context, nature of personalities and implications for leadership style

| | Complexity of Organization | |
Nature of Personalities	Simple	Complex
Nonauthoritarian	High participation	Moderate participation
Authoritarian	Moderate participation	Low participation

The complexity of organizations and the personality orientation probably determine the degree that a participative approach is functional. Table Seven suggests that to the extent that a simple organization and nonauthoritarian personality exists, a high participation approach would be most effective. When opposite conditions prevail, a nonparticipative approach would be acceptable and contribute to positive behavioral responses. Limited evidence is available that supports this thesis.

High participation is feasible in small groups, but in large groups broad involvement is time consuming and it is difficult to achieve consensus in issues.[18]

Similarly, under low specialization, decisions are simpler and consensus is easier to achieve; where high specialization exists, the narrow perspective of specialists and interdependence of positions contribute to greater problems while at the same time creating conditions of stress that impede achieving consensus.[19] This latter should result in greater acceptance of a directive, low participative approach. Spatial-physical barriers among personnel or between a leader and followers exerts pressure that sharply reduces both interaction and participation levels.[20] It is thus reasonable that a directive, low participative orientation would be acceptable to the extent these barriers exist.

As work demands and accompanying standards increase, greater attention is given to simply getting the job done. Decisions are accepted under high stress that wouldn't be accepted when stress is sharply reduced. Similarly, when measures and ends are ambiguous and confused, the group is more eager for a decision.[21] Broad participation is likely to be rejected since it tends to be associated with confusion, frustration and endless discussion as members present proposals and their criticisms with implicit assumptions on ends and means.

As mentioned above, the nature of personalities also mediates the influence of participation with authoritarian-oriented individuals and those with a low need for independence reacting positively to being told rather than sharing in decision process. When these factors are combined, the analysis suggests that in a simple organization context with nonauthoritarian type personalities, broad use of participation would be most effective. Contrarily, in a complex organization context and authoritarian personalities, low participative approach is likely to be most functional. Under the other combinations, a moderate level of participation would contribute to the desirable individual, intragroup, and intergroup behavioral patterns and unit effectiveness.

As further work is done, it is likely to be increasingly clear that under varying conditions, broad use of participation has different effects. A participative approach to leadership is unlikely to prove to be the magic elixer that can be successfully applied to all situations.

NOTES

1. George Strauss, "Some Notes on Power-Equalization," in Harold J. Leavitt (ed.), *The Social Science of Organizations* (Englewood Cliffs, N.J.: Prentice-Hall & Co., 1963), pp. 68–70.

2. Douglas McGregor, *The Human Side of Enterprise*, McGraw-Hill, 1960, pp. 125–126.

3. C. Nyman and Elliott D. Smith, *Union-Management Cooperation in the "Stretch Out": Labor Extension at the Pequot Mills*. New Haven: Yale University Press, 1934.

4. A. K. Rice, "Productivity and Social Organization in an Indian Weaving Shed," *Human Relations*, VI, November, 1953, pp. 297–330.

5. A. K. Rice, "The Experimental Reorganization of Non-Automatic Weaving in an Indian Mill," *Human Relations*, VIII, August, 1955, pp. 199–250.

6. Alfred J. Marrow and John R. P. French, Jr., "Changing a Stereotype in Industry," *Journal of Social Issues*, I, No. 3 (1945), pp. 33–37.

7. Al Coch and J. R. P. French, Jr., "Overcoming Resistance to Change," *Human Relations*, I (1948),

pp. 512–532; J. R. P. French, I. C. Ross, S. Kirby, J. R. Nelson, P. Smyth, "Employee Participation in a Program of Industrial Change," *Personnel*, XXXV, No. 3 (November–December, 1958), pp. 16–29; Norman Maier, *Psychology in Industry*, New York, Houghton-Mifflin, 1965; Alfred J. Marrow, David G. Bowers, and Stanley B. Seashore, *Management by Participation*. New York: Harper & Row, 1967.

8. Lester Coch and John R. P. French, Jr., "Overcoming Resistance to Change," *Human Relations*, I (1948), pp. 512–532, 257–279.

9. J. R. P. French, Jr., I. C. Ross, S. Kirby, J. R. Nelson, and P. Smyth, "Employee Participation in a Program of Industrial Change," *Personnel*, XXXV, No. 3 (1958), pp. 16–29.

10. John R. P. French, Jr., Joachim Israel, and Dagfinn As, "An Experiment on Participation in a Norwegian Factory," *Human Relations*, XIII (1960), 3–19.

11. Maier, *Psychology in Industry*, pp. 160–162.

12. John R. P. French, Jr., Emanual Kay, and Herbert H. Meyer, *Human Relations*, Vol. 19, 1966, pp. 3–19.

13. Victor H. Vroom, *Some Personality Determinants of the Effects of Participation*, Englewood Cliffs, New Jersey, Prentice-Hall, 1960. The study is also briefly reported in Victor H. Vroom, "Some Personality Determinants of the Effects of Participation," *Journal of Abnormal and Social Psychology*, LIX (1959), pp. 322–327.

14. John R. P. French, Jr., Emanuel J. Kay, and Herbert H. Meyer, "Participation and the Appraisal System," *Human Relations*, XIX (1966), pp. 3–20.

15. Constructed from French, Kay, and Meyer, *Human Relations*, XIX, Table 3, p. 13.

16. Harold L. Wilensky, "Human Relations in the Workplace: An Appraisal of Some Recent Research," in *Research in Industrial Human Relations*, edited by Conrad Arensberg, *et al.* New York: Harper, 1957, footnote, p. 34–35.

17. See Arlyn J. Melcher, "A Systems Model," in Anant Neghandi and Joseph Schwitter (ed.), *Organizational Behavioral Models*, Kent, Ohio, Comparative Administration Research Institute, 1970, pp. 109–131.

18. A. Paul Hare, "A Study of Interaction and Consensus in Different Sized Groups," *American Sociological Review*, Vol. 17 (June, 1952), pp. 261–267; Robert F. Bales and Edgar F. Borgotta, "Size of Group as a Factor in the Interaction Profile," in Paul Hare, Edward Borgotta, and Robert Bales, *Small Groups*, Knopf, 1960, pp. 495–512; Philip E. Slater, "Contrasting Correlates of Group Size," *Sociometry*, Vol. 2 (1958), pp. 129–139.

19. Elliot Chapple and Leonard Sayles, *The Measure of Management*, New York, The Macmillan Co.,

pp. 18–45; James C. Worthy, "Some Aspects of Organizational Structure in Relation to Pressures on Company Decision Making," in L. Reed Tripp (ed.), *Industrial Relations Research Proceedings,* New York, Harper and Brothers, 1953.

20. Robert Sommer, "Small Group Ecology," *Psychological Bulletin,* Vol. 67 (1967), pp. 145–152. Miles Patterson, "Spatial Factors in Social Interactions," *Human Relations,* Vol. 21 (1968), pp. 351–361.

21. E. Paul Torrence, "A Theory of Leadership and Interpersonal Behavior Under Stress," in Luigi Petrullo and Bernard Bass (ed.), *Leadership and Interpersonal Behavior* (New York: Holt, Rinehart & Winston, 1961).

7

COMMUNICATION

Early writers on organizational theory placed little emphasis on communication. However, beginning with Chester Barnard in the late 1930s there has been an increasing emphasis on the vital role that communication plays in theory and practice. Message transmission, feedback control, and interpersonal relations are topics that provide some idea of the broad range of communication concerns in the modern organization. The topic of communication is addressed under two broad headings in this chapter: the nature of management communication, and communication barriers. The articles in this chapter provide an overview of communication in organizations as well as some specific suggestions for improving communication.

Under the nature of management communication, Richard Huseman and Elmore Alexander III provide an overview of organizational communication in their article, "Organizational Communication: A Contingency Approach." The authors examine contingency views of organizational design as they relate to the manager's communication role and then present a contingency model for managerial communication. The second reading in this section is "Communication Revisited," by Jay Hall. Of particular interest in Hall's article in his discussion of interpersonal communication styles and managerial impact.

Next we examine several communication barriers. In David Brown's two-part article, "Barriers to Successful Communication," he examines macrobarriers and microbarriers to communication in organizations. The macrobarriers include the larger world in which communication takes place, and the microbarriers include those in the immediate communication situation. Brown maintains that with all the new knowledge, techniques, and tools available to us our ability to communicate is not keeping pace with the demands we face.

COMMUNICATION AND THE MANAGERIAL FUNCTION: A CONTINGENCY APPROACH

RICHARD C. HUSEMAN
ELMORE R. ALEXANDER, III

The importance of communication to organizational theory has long been recognized. As early as 1938 Chester Barnard (in *The Functions of the Executive*) stated that:

... in an exhaustive theory of organization, communication would occupy a central place, because the structure, extensiveness, and scope of organizations are almost entirely determined by communication. (p. 9)

Barnard specifically related communication to the managerial function when he noted that the first function of the executive is to "establish and maintain a system of communication." (p. 221)

More recently, Connolly has suggested that an appropriate conception of organizations is "in terms of complex, decision related communication networks." (1977, p. 205) In addition, Farace, Monge, and Russell maintain that "the managerial dyad, linking hierarchical levels in an organization, has long been recognized as the basic unit of instruction, report, and performance appraisal." (1977, p. 8) Inherent in the managerial dyad is communication between the manager and the managed.

The central role of face-to-face communication in the managerial function is also supported by numerous empirical studies of manager time allo-

cation. For example, a study by Burns (1954) found that communication activity accounted for 80 percent of the middle manager's time. A later study of managers in a manufacturing company stated that 89 percent of the manager's time was spent in face-to-face communication (Lawler, Porter, and Tennenbaum, 1968). More recently in a detailed analysis of how managers spend their time, Mintzberg (1973) revealed that 78 percent of a manager's time is spent in face-to-face communication. When one adds to that percentage the element of written communication, the conclusion reached is that for all practical purposes communication is the managerial function.

Having established the importance of communication to the managerial function, what can be said in terms of how the manager can communicate more effectively and thereby increase his managerial effectiveness? Traditionally, approaches for improving communication effectiveness have not been tailored to specific organizational variables such as particular people, tasks, or uncertainty. Approaches to improving communication effectiveness have frequently been tied to "fixed" models of communication. There has, however, been an increasing tendency for those who study organizational behavior to support the view that effective managerial behavior is situation specific. It is this approach, contingency theory, that enables one to deal more comfortably

This is an original article prepared especially for this volume.

with a basic fact of life in large organizations: different units of the organization may operate best under different philosophies and different managerial approaches. It would also seem reasonable that contingency theory would promote the best configuration of communication strategies and procedures for specific situations in organizational life.

If contingency theory holds promise for managerial communication in organizations, important questions emerge. Namely, how and on what variables is communication behavior contingent? The purpose of the remainder of this article is (1) to examine contingency views of organizational design as they relate to the manager's communication roles, and (2) to develop a contingency model for managerial communication.

CONTINGENCY VIEWS OF ORGANIZATIONS AND THE MANAGER'S COMMUNICATION ROLES

As a communicator within his organization, the manager is primarily engaged in the activity of coordinating the work of his subordinates. Of the seven internal managerial roles suggested by Mintzberg (1973), for example, six involve communication for the purpose of coordination—monitor, disseminator, spokesman, disturbance handler, resource allocator, and negotiator. Several alternatives for handling these responsibilities are available. March and Simon (1958) made the classic distinction between coordination techniques when they suggested that organizations could be coordinated in two basic ways: by feedback and by plan. Coordination by plan is achieved by preestablished procedures and schedules, while coordination by feedback entails the interchange of information between superior and subordinate with a corresponding adjustment of either subordinate activity or superior expectations. We would suggest, however, that this dichotomous classification is not entirely sufficient for the modern organization. Rather there is a need to add a third category of coordination—coordination by lateral interaction. The distinction suggested here is that organizations not only utilize coordination by vertical interchange as is implied by March and Simon's concept of feedback but also establish coordination via lateral interaction (i.e., direct contact between individuals in different departments). As will be seen in subsequent sections, this distinction is becoming increasingly important for the modern manager.

The purpose of this section is to look at the writings of several organizational researchers to ascertain the implications of their positions as they relate to the nature of the manager's communicative roles. More specifically, we will be examining several contingency views of organizational design, seeking to understand how the demands on the manager as a communicator vary across different organizational environments. This analysis will center around the work of Galbraith and Perrow. In some respects the selection of any one or two writers from the wide range of articulations of contingency theory could be considered arbitrary. However, both of these writers present analyses based on attempts to integrate the work of numerous other theorists, and thus a reasonable claim for their appropriateness for our purposes (developing a contingency model of managerial communication) can be made. This is not to say that our analysis does not exclude many aspects of contingency theory as it is currently developed. However, the limits of space and time dictate these exclusions. Specifically, our analysis will attempt to highlight factors that effect the degree to which the three identified coordination techniques—plan, feedback, and lateral interaction—are appropriate in various organizational settings.[1]

PERROW: TECHNOLOGY AS A BASIS FOR COMPARING ORGANIZATIONS

Perrow (1967) views technology as the defining characteristic of organizations. In this sense technology is considered to be the "actions that an individual performs upon an object . . . in order to make some change in the object." (Perrow, 1967, p. 195) Perrow operationalizes technology as a function of two factors—the number of exceptional cases encountered in the work and the search process that is undertaken by the individual when exceptions occur. Dichotomizing, he in-

	Few	Many
Unanalyzable Problems	electronics manufacturing **CRAFT** graduate education	research & development organization **NONROUTINE** organizational consulting firm
Analyzable Problems	assembly line operations **ROUTINE** personnel placement	machine operation **ENGINEERED** data processing center

SEARCH (vertical axis label); EXCEPTIONS (horizontal axis label)

(Adapted from Perrow, 1967, pp. 196 & 198.)

FIGURE 1. Perrow's concept of technology

dicates that organizations may encounter few or many exceptions in accomplishing their work and that the search process when exceptions are encountered can treat either analyzable or unanalyzable problems. He labels the four combinations of these conditions of technology routine, engineered, craft, and nonroutine. Figure 1 summarizes his typology providing examples of both service and industrial organizations exhibiting the particular technologies.

Before proceeding further into a discussion of the implications of Perrow's typology for communication, it will be useful to note a similar typology developed by Shull (see Shull, Delbecq and Cummings, 1970; or Shull and Judd, 1971). Whereas Perrow's typology applies to interorganizational variations in technology, Shull's views intraorganizational variations. Shull considers technology to be a function of two factors similar to those of Perrow—task characteristics (repetitive vs. nonrepetitive) and personal characteristics (technical vs. professional). With the exception of the replacement of the label "nonroutine" with "heuristic," their labels for the four dichotomized conditions of technology are the same. The

importance of Shull's typology to our discussion is that his attention to intraorganizational variation allows us to extend any conclusions concerning interorganizational variation to differences within organizations as well.

Perrow views task-related interaction patterns or what we have referred to previously as the internal communication or coordination function as concerning two distinct areas: (1) technical control and support, and (2) supervision.[2] Technical control and support involves such areas as accounting, quality control, and scheduling, normally considered to be staff activities or coordination. Supervision, on the other hand, relates to typical line supervision. Perrow notes that within routine technologies both types of coordination should utilize coordination by plan. Engineered technologies utilize supervision coordination by plan, but technical coordination should be by feedback. Craft technologies, on the other hand, should exhibit the exact reverse of engineered technologies—technical coordination by plan and supervisory coordination by feedback. In nonroutine technologies, both types of coordination should be of the feedback type.

Perrow notes further that while the routine technology resembles the "mechanistic" organization of the Burns and Stalker (1961) dichotomy the nonroutine technology resembles the "organic" organization. This is quite useful because Burns and Stalker were specific in outlining the types of communication that would be effective in the two types of organizations. With respect to the effective "mechanistic" organization, they indicated that interaction between incumbents tends to be vertical (between superiors and subordinates) and that this interaction contains primarily instructions and decisions issued by the superior. (Burns and Stalker, 1961, p. 75) In effective "organic" organizations, communication tends to be lateral rather than vertical and resembles consultation as opposed to command. (Burns and Stalker, 1961, p. 76) From the standpoint of our terminology, the "mechanistic" organization utilizes coordination by plan whereas the "organic" organization utilizes coordination by lateral interaction. Thus, we can more precisely define the nature of communication in the nonroutine technology as resembling what we have called lateral interaction. Figure 2 summarizes this relationship.

GALBRAITH: AN INFORMATION PROCESSING VIEW OF ORGANIZATIONAL DESIGN

Galbraith (1971, 1973, 1974) views the question of the appropriateness of various organizational designs from an information-processing point of view. From his perspective, the task of organizational design is to coordinate across the various subtasks of the organization. However, since no manager can communicate with *all* subgroups (managers who try suffer from what is referred to as "information overload"), it is necessary to design mechanisms or communication patterns that will allow for the accomplishment of the necessary coordination. The appropriateness of various mechanisms depends on the degree of task uncertainty. As he puts it, "the greater the task uncertainty, the greater the amount of information that must be processed among decision makers during task execution in order to achieve a given level of performance." (1974, p. 28) Thus, as task uncertainty increases, the manager must develop mechanisms to facilitate the processing of greater amounts of information without resulting in information overload.

It is useful at this point to consider what constitutes a certain or an uncertain task environment. In this respect Galbraith depends on the work of Lawrence and Lorsch (1967). Lawrence and Lorsch measured task uncertainty by the rate of new product introduction. Thus, an industry such as the container industry in which no new products have been introduced in the past ten years exhibits a high degree of task certainty, whereas an industry such as the plastics industry in which thirty-five percent of its products have been introduced in the last ten years exhibits a high degree of task uncertainty. Uncertainty can

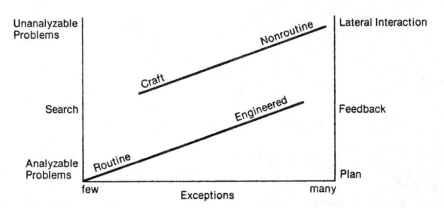

FIGURE 2. The relationship of technology and coordination technique

thus be viewed as the degree to which organizational tasks are made unsure due to the changefulness of production activities. Although this is primarily related to industrial production, it seems certain that a similar dimension operates in service organizations.

Having indicated that information-processing demands vary as a function of task uncertainty and having defined task uncertainty, it is now appropriate to describe the hierarchy of communication patterns or design mechanisms that allow for the accomplishment of necessary coordination.

At the low end of the hierarchy where task uncertainty is low, coordination can be achieved through rules, organizational hierarchy, or goals. This is comparable to what we identified earlier as coordination by plan. In such a situation, organizational tasks are broken into various subtasks and the precise functioning and interrelationship of each is defined by rules, procedures, hierarchy, or goals. As one encounters increased levels of uncertainty, the demands on information processing increase correspondingly. Galbraith indicates that the organization faced with such increased demands has two options. The organization may either attempt to reduce the need for information processing or it must increase its capacity to process information. Since the former entails no new coordination or communication mechanisms, we will not concern ourselves with it. We will examine the two mechanisms that Galbraith indicates can be used to increase information processing capacity.

The appropriate response to intermediate demands on information processing is to create vertical information systems. Computerization and formalization of communication channels are two examples of vertical information systems. The concept at this point is to create mechanisms that will allow more information to be processed vertically (as is the case with feedback coordination) without encountering information overload. Such mechanisms will work to a point. However, as uncertainty increases, information demand eventually outstrips the vertical system's capacity. At this point, Galbraith suggests the creation of lateral relationships. This is effective in increasing information-processing capacity in that it moves decision making down in the organization to a point where the information needed for decision making is already present. This reduces the need for the formal organization to process as much information.

The following figure represents a summarization of Galbraith's position. As uncertainty increases, demands on organization information processing increase and the organization must move from coordination by plan to coordination by feedback and finally to coordination by lateral interaction.

TOWARD A CONTINGENCY MODEL OF MANAGERIAL COMMUNICATION

What we have attempted up to this point is to indicate the implications of two contingency mod-

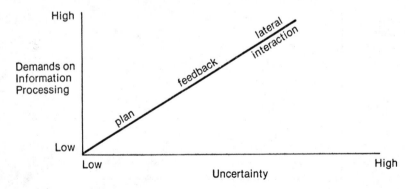

FIGURE 3. The relationship of uncertainty, information processing demands, and coordination technique

els for the manager's role as a communicator. This role is seen as being primarily concerned with coordination of subordinate tasks. Three distinct mechanisms or communication patterns are available—plan, feedback, and lateral interaction. Two tasks remain in the development of a useful contingency model of managerial communication. First, we must attempt to integrate the position articulated by Galbraith with that articulated by Perrow; and second, we must attempt to integrate this model with our knowledge from organizational communication research. The first task will be attempted in this section along with laying the groundwork for attempting the second in the following section.

It seems to these authors that Galbraith and Perrow are not talking about terribly dissimilar aspects of the organizational environment. What Galbraith views as uncertainty, Perrow seems to call technology and proceeds to divide up into notions of exceptions and search processes. In this respect, Perrow adds precision to the distinction articulated by Galbraith; however, Galbraith adds to our understanding by identifying the intervening variable of concern to this discussion—demands on information processing. Thus, it seems reasonable to suggest by way of synthesis that the appropriateness of particular communication patterns is a function of organizational technology. Additionally, through the link provided by Shull, we can state further that intraorganizational variations in the appropriateness of particular communication patterns are a function of subunit technology. By way of Galbraith's analysis, we expect that this relationship operates through technology's impact on demands on information technology. Thus, as technology moves from routine to nonroutine, the demands on information processing increase; and to remain effective, coordination must move from a dependence on plans to feedback and finally to lateral interaction.

The question of how this relates to what we know from traditional organizational research remains to be answered. Although this question will be addressed in the main in the next section, a brief discussion is appropriate at this point. The link to be made is between coordination by plan, feedback, and lateral interaction and more traditional concepts of organizational communication. The claim to be made here is that coordination by plan is downward communication; feedback implies upward communication; and lateral communication implies horizontal and diagonal communication. If the reader recalls our initial distinctions of the three coordination mechanisms, the link to the three communication patterns above should be evident. Coordination by plan involves sending information (rules, regulations, schedules) down through the organizational hierarchy. Coordination by feedback, on the other hand, adds the solicitation of information from lower levels by higher levels within the hierarchy. Finally, lateral interaction engages individuals at varying organizational levels in the exchange of task-related information. Figure 4 integrates these traditional concepts of organizational communication into our previous model.

IMPLEMENTING A CONTINGENCY MODEL OF MANAGERIAL COMMUNICATION

At this juncture we will attempt to examine the implications of the contingency model of communication. Special attention will be given to attempting to integrate those implications with previous organizational communication research.

As is suggested in Figure 4, the manager's attention should move from one type of communication mode to another as the organizational environment (technology) changes. For example, the manager whose organization (or department) faces few exceptions in its work and whose problems are highly analyzable (e.g., routine assembly-line operations) should concentrate on facilitating the downward flow of information. On the other hand, if the technology is nonroutine, the manager should focus his attention on horizontal and diagonal communication. This is not to argue that one type of communication should be the manager's sole concern, but rather that the particular type suggested represents the area where the manager can most profitably concentrate his attention. All three types of communication occur and deserve each manager's attention. However, the effectiveness of coordination will primarily depend on one type and that type

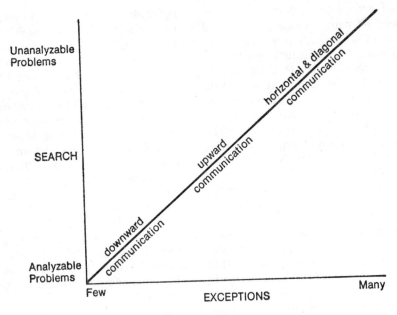

FIGURE 4. A contingency model of managerial communication

should correspondingly receive more attention from the manager.

The remainder of this article will highlight how the manager can facilitate various types of communication within his organization or department. A section will be devoted to each of the three basic types of organizational communication. Problems associated with each type of communication will be identified and an attempt will be made to suggest strategies for dealing with the problems.

Downward Communication

Problems. The most persistent problem with downward communication that has been identified in the literature concerns the accuracy and adequacy of information reaching lower organizational levels. The magnitude of this problem was highlighted by an Opinion Research Corporation study which found in examining a large metal-producing firm that whereas ninety-one percent of top management was aware of profit information only five percent of the first-line supervisors had such knowledge. (Smith, Richetto, and Zima, 1972) This problem is magnified by management's

failure to recognize its existence. For example, Odiorne (1954) found that management perceptions of the amount of information communicated downward were significantly higher than was actually the case.

What would appear to be happening in many cases with downward communication is that messages are being filtered and distorted as they are passed from one individual to another through the organizational hierarchy. The situation resembles the familiar party game "pass the message." The game involves whispering a message from one person to another forming a chain of communication. It is unusual if the original message is recognizable after it has passed through five or six links in the chain. Likewise, messages communicated downward in organizations are often unrecognizable by the time that they reach lower level employees.

Strategies. Two suggestions are offered as a means of mitigating the problems of inadequate downward communication. The first would be to emphasize the importance of two-way communication. In a classic experiment, Haney (1964) illustrated that information distorted in a one-way communication situation was accurately communicated when feedback between the communicator and the communicatee was allowed. Thus, a manager concerned with the accuracy of downward communication should develop methods of seeking feedback from subordinates to determine their understanding of his messages. Furthermore, he should attempt to ensure that his subordinates adopt a similar communication style in transmitting the messages on down through the hierarchy.

A second suggestion would be to note the importance of using multiple and coordinated communication media. At a minimum, the manager has both written and oral communication media at his disposal. Written media include not only memos and letters but also the in-house newspaper and the bulletin board. Several studies indicate that the most effective means of communicating information downward in organizations involves a combination of the various media in a coordinated fashion. This position has been confirmed experimentally by Dahle (1953) and from survey data by Level (1972). Additionally, Davis' research on "grapevine" communication (e.g., see Davis, 1973) would suggest that even the corporate grapevine can be managed to serve as an effective communicative instrument of the manager. The important factor to keep in mind is that multiple and coordinated media approaches to downward communication will increase the likelihood that intended messages are received and understood by the maximum number of lower-level employees.

Upward Communication

Problems. The problems of distortion and filtering identified as problems of downward communication are also present in upward communication. Additionally, these problems are exacerbated by status differences. The fact that superiors possess greater power and authority than their subordinates results in unique pressures that add further distortion to the serial transmission of information.

Huseman, Lahiff, and Wells (1974) identified several bases of distortion in and the lack of adequate upward communication. They suggest, for example, that since individuals often feel that the

relinquishment of sole possession of information decreases their power, there is a pressure to hoard information. The psychological costs of sharing information add to these pressures. Additionally, information-sharing norms within many organizations forestall adequate upward communication. Good examples of this are the manager who uses his higher status to communicate his separateness from his workers and the manager who listens to subordinate suggestions but never follows through on them. Rosen and Tesser (1970) have empirically tested the operation of one of these bases for problems with upward communication which they call the MUM effect. The MUM effect implies that, in an attempt to create as favorable an impression on their superiors as possible, subordinates filter out unpleasant messages so that only pleasant information passes upward through the organization. All of these factors create distortions in the upward flow of information within organizations, which may have dangerous implications in terms of decisions made at higher levels in the organization.

Solutions. With slight alterations, the solutions suggested in the preceding section with regard to downward communication are applicable to problems of upward communication. While the manager cannot necessarily tap multiple media in obtaining messages from the lower levels of the organization, he can tap multiple information sources. That is, the effective manager will not rely on a single source of information but will seek out confirmation of important facts from several sources. Two-way communication is also useful in developing the type of climate that results in less filtering and distortion of upward-communicated messages. There is nothing that will be more effective in acquiring accurate and complete information than rewarding subordinates for such behavior. Two-way communication serves that end in that attention given through feedback communicates to the employee that he has been heard and appreciated. The manager must make sure, however, that organizational rewards reflect a recognition of the importance of communicating completely and accurately.

Several group techniques exist to facilitate the securing of information from lower levels of the organization. One of the most effective of these is the nominal group process. This process combines individual listing of suggestions in a group atmosphere in a manner designed to maximize creativity and to forestall closure. Subordinates are asked first to list their suggestions silently on a sheet of paper. After a period of time (approximately 15 minutes), individual suggestions are listed on flip charts or a blackboard in a round-robin fashion (first listing everyone's first suggestion, then everyone's second, and so on). Comments are not allowed during either of these first two steps. After everyone's suggestions have been listed, each person ranks the total list of ideas on the basis of quality. Low ranking ideas are eliminated and the group begins discussion on the remaining ideas. If it is difficult to bring subordinates together, the delphi method can be used. The basic steps of the nominal group process are maintained; however, suggestions are exchanged through the mail. The delphi method can be especially useful to the large geographically diversified organization. Several recent publications explain the use of these two techniques in detail (Delbecq and Van de Ven, 1975; Huseman et al., 1974).

Horizontal and Diagonal Communication

Problems. Managing horizontal and diagonal communication entails very different and perhaps more difficult problems than does either upward or downward communication. Classical theories of organization recognized neither the existence nor the importance of horizontal or diagonal communication, and it is only recently that much has been written about how they function within the organization. This lack of recognition has had a definite impact on the quality of nonvertical organizational communication. For example, Walton (1962) found that communicating horizontally is not rewarded within the typical organization. That this lack of rewards would decrease the amount of horizontal communication should be obvious, and Wickesberg (1968) goes further to suggest, as a result of a study he conducted, that the lack of official organizational sanction of nonvertical communications results in a decrease in the quality of the nonvertical communication that

does exist. Thus, a prime problem of horizontal and diagonal communication is its quantity and quality.

A second problem is that of conflict. Any time that individuals from different departments within an organization interact there is a great potential for conflict. Such conflict may be perceptually based (caused by the development of different perceptions of relevant factors within the various departments) or goal based (caused by the differing importance of various organizational goals within the various departments). Whatever its cause, conflict is an inevitable result of interdepartmental (nonvertical) interaction.

Strategies. An obvious solution to the problem of quality and quantity, although certainly not an easy one, is a restructuring of the organizational reward structure so that nonvertical communication is both sanctioned and rewarded. This may mean as little as managers becoming involved in establishing and promoting relationships between their subordinates and members of other departments. It may entail the allocation of additional organizational resources in the form of the establishment of interdepartmental committees and the hiring of liaison personnel. For the organization whose environment demands nonvertical interaction, however, such investments are essential to effective coordination.

Effective management of conflict is an extremely difficult task. Although we will not attempt to review the entirety of the conflict resolution research, two approaches deserve mention at this point. First, Lawrence and Lorsch (1967) suggest that managers who effectively manage interdepartmental conflict of the sort implied in the previous section exhibit use of a problem orientation. This implies that such managers avoid smoothing over differences or resolving the differences through the imposition of power, but rather confront the issues at hand and seek integrative solutions that attempt to meet both departments' needs. Second, in situations where perceptual differences are the prime source of disagreement, perception expansion training may improve the quality of interdepartmental interaction significantly. Huseman (1973) has described the format of such a training program.

The program involves nominal grouping to identify departmental perceptions and then structured and controlled discussions between the two departments concerning the identified conflicting perceptions.

CONCLUSION

Our purpose in this article has been to examine communication and the managerial function. In brief, we have attempted to address the broad question of how the manager can communicate effectively and improve his managerial effectiveness. Our basic approach has been to suggest that contingency theory holds promise for managerial communication. Specifically, we have suggested a contingency model of managerial communication that identifies the major variables on which communication is contingent.

While we have identified major communication problem areas, and suggested strategies for coping with these problems, our major thrust has been to draw attention to the fact that managerial communication in organizations is situation specific. Or, to put it more simply: communication strategies that are appropriate for one situation may be inappropriate for the next. It is our conviction that a contingency approach to organizational communication enables the modern manager to identify communication strategies that will maximize managerial effectiveness.

REFERENCES

Barnard, C. *The Functions of the Executive.* Cambridge, Mass.: Harvard University Press, 1938.

Burns, T. "The Directions of Activity and Communication in a Departmental Executive Group." *Human Relations,* 1954, *7,* 73–97.

Burns, T. and Stalker, G. *The Management of Innovation.* London: Tavistock, 1961.

Connolly, T. "Information Processing and Decision Making in Organizations." In Staw, B. and Salancik, G. (eds.) *New Directions in Organizational Behavior.* Chicago: St. Clair, 1977, pp. 205–234.

Dahle, T. "An Objective and Comparative Study of Five Methods of Transmitting Information to Business and Industrial Employees." Unpublished Ph.D. Dissertation, Purdue University, 1953.

Davis, K. "The Care and Cultivation of the Corporate Grapevine." *Dun's Review,* July, 1973, *101,* 44–47.

Delbecq, A. and Van de Ven, A. *A Guide to Nominal Group and Delphi Processes.* Glenview, Illinois: Scott Foresman, 1974.

Galbraith, J. "Designing Matrix Organizations." *Business Horizons,* 1971, *14,* 29–40.

Galbraith, J. *Organization Design.* Reading, Mass.: Addison-Wesley, 1973.

Galbraith, J. "Organization Design: An Information Processing View." *Interfaces,* 1974, *4,* 28–36.

Hage, J., Aiken, M., and Marrett, C. "Organizational Structure and Communications." *American Sociological Review,* 1971, *36,* 860–871.

Haney, W. "A Comparative Study of Unilateral and Bilateral Communication." *Academy of Management Journal,* 1964, *7,* 128–136.

Huseman, R. "Perception Expansion Training: An Approach to Conflict Reduction." Presented to the International Communication Association Convention, Montreal, Canada, April 25–28, 1973.

Huseman, R., Lahiff, J., and Wells, R. "Communication Thermoclines: Toward a Process of Identification." *Personnel Journal,* 1974, *53,* 124–135.

Lawler, E., Porter, L., and Tennenbaum, A. "Managers' Attitudes Toward Interaction Episodes." *Journal of Applied Psychology,* 1968, *52,* 432–439.

Lawrence, P. and Lorsch, J. *Organization and Environment.* Boston: Division of Research, Harvard Business School, 1967.

Level, D. "Communication Effectiveness: Method and Situation." *The Journal of Business Communication,* 1972, *10,* 19–25.

March, J. and Simon, H. *Organizations.* New York: Wiley, 1958.

Mintzberg, H. *The Nature of Managerial Work.* New York: Harper & Row, 1973.

Odiorne, G. "An Application of the Communication Audit." *Personnel Psychology,* 1954, *7,* 235–243.

Perrow, C. "A Framework for the Comparative Analysis of Organizations." *American Sociological Review,* 1967, *32,* 194–208.

Rosen, S. and Tesser, A. "On Reluctance to Communicate Undesirable Information: The MUM Effect." *Sociometry,* 1970, *33,* 253–263.

Shull, F., Delbecq, A., and Cummings, L. *Organizational Decision Making.* New York: McGraw-Hill, 1970.

Shull, F. and Judd, R. "Matrix Organization and Control Systems." *Management International Review,* 1971, *6,* 65–87.

Smith, R., Richetto, G., and Zima, J. "Organizational Behavior: An Approach to Human Communication." In Huseman, R., Logue, C., and Freshley, D. (eds.) *Readings in Interpersonal and Organizational Communication.* Boston: Holbrook, 1977, pp. 3–24.

COMMUNICATION REVISITED

JAY HALL

High on the diagnostic checklist of corporate health is communication; and the prognosis is less than encouraging. In a recent cross-cultural study,[1] roughly 74 percent of the managers sampled from companies in Japan, Great Britain, and the United States cited communication breakdown as the single greatest barrier to corporate excellence.

Just what constitutes a problem of communication is not easily agreed upon. Some theorists approach the issue from the vantage point of information bits comprising a message; others speak in terms of organizational roles and positions of centrality or peripherality; still others emphasize the directional flows of corporate data. The result is that more and more people are communicating about communication, while the achievement of clarity, understanding, commitment, and creativity—the goals of communication—becomes more and more limited.

More often than not, the communication dilemmas cited by people are not communication problems at all. They are instead *symptoms* of difficulties at more basic and fundamental levels of corporate life. From a dynamic standpoint, problems of communication in organizations frequently reflect dysfunctions at the level of *corpo-*

rate climate. The feelings people have about where or with whom they work—feelings of impotence, distrust, resentment, insecurity, social inconsequence, and all the other very human emotions—not only define the climate which prevails but the manner in which communications will be managed. R. R. Blake and Jane S. Mouton[2] have commented upon an oddity of organizational life: when management is effective and relationships are sound, problems of communication tend not to occur. It is only when relationships among members of the organization are unsound and fraught with unarticulated tensions that one hears complaints of communication breakdown. Thus, the quality of relationships in an organization may dictate to a great extent the level of communication effectiveness achieved.

INTERPERSONAL STYLES AND THE QUALITY OF RELATIONSHIPS

The critical factor underlying relationship quality in organizations is in need of review. Reduced to its lowest common denominator, the most significant determinant of the quality of relationships is the interpersonal style of the parties to a relationship. The learned, characteristic, and apparently preferred manner in which individuals relate to others in the building of relationships—the manner in which they monitor, control, filter, divert, give and seek the information germane to a given relationship—will dictate over time the quality of relationships which exist among people, the emotional climate which will characterize their interactions, and whether or not there will be problems of communication. In the final analysis, individuals are the human links in the corporate network, and the styles they employ interpersonally are the ultimate determinants of what information goes where and whether it will be distortion-free or masked by interpersonal constraints.

The concept of interpersonal style is not an easy one to define; yet, if it is to serve as the central mechanism underlying the quality of relationships, the nature of corporate climate, managerial effectiveness, and the level of corporate excellence attainable, it is worthy of analysis. Fortunately, Joseph Luft[3] and Harry Ingham—two behavioral scientists with special interests in interpersonal and group processes—have developed a model of social interaction which affords a way of thinking about interpersonal functioning, while handling much of the data encountered in everyday living. The Johari Window, as their model is called, identifies several interpersonal styles, their salient features and consequences, and suggests a basis for interpreting the significance of style for the quality of relationships. An overview of the Johari model should help to sharpen the perception of interpersonal practices among managers and lend credence to the contention of Blake and Mouton that there are few communication problems as such, only unsound relationships. At the same time, a normative statement regarding effective interpersonal functioning and, by extension, the foundations of corporate excellence may be found in the model as well. Finally, the major tenets of the model are testable under practical conditions, and the latter portion of this discussion will be devoted to research on the managerial profile in interpersonal encounters. The author has taken a number of interpretive liberties with the basic provisions of the Johari Awareness model. While it is anticipated that none of these violate the integrity of the model as originally described by Luft, it should be emphasized that many of the inferences and conclusions discussed are those of the au-

thor, and Dr. Luft should not be held accountable for any lapses of logic or misapplications of the model in this paper.

THE JOHARI WINDOW: A GRAPHIC MODEL OF INTERPERSONAL PROCESSES

As treated here, the Johari Window is essentially an information processing model; interpersonal style and individual effectiveness are assessed in terms of information processing tendencies and the performance consequences thought to be associated with such practices. The model employs a four celled figure as its format and reflects the interaction of two interpersonal sources of information—Self and Others—and the behavioral processes required for utilizing that information. The model, depicted in Figure 1, may be thought of as representing the various kinds of data available for use in the establishment of interpersonal relationships. The squared field, in effect, represents a personal space. This in turn is partitioned into four regions, with each representing a particular combination or mix of relevant information and having special significance for the quality of relationships. To fully appreciate the implications that each informational region has for interpersonal effectiveness, one must consider not only the size and shape of each region but also the reasons for its presence in the interpersonal space. In an attempt to "personalize" the model, it is helpful to think of oneself as the *Self* in the relationship for, as will be seen presently, it is what the Self does interpersonally that has the most direct impact on the quality of resulting relationships. In organizational terms, it is how the management-Self behaves that is critical to the quality of corporate relationships.

Figure 1 reveals that the two informational sources, Self and Others, have information which is pertinent to the relationship and, at the same time, each lacks information that is equally germane. Thus, there is relevant and necessary information which is *Known by the Self, Unknown by the Self, Known by Others* and *Unknown by Others*. The Self/Other combinations of known and unknown information make up the four regions within the interpersonal space and, again,

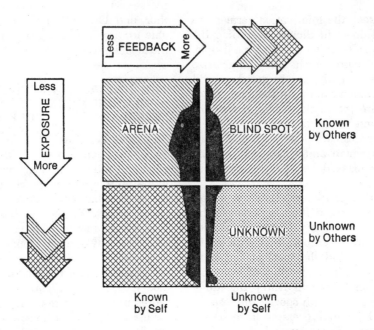

FIGURE 1. The Johari window: a model of interpersonal processes.

characterize the various types and qualities of relationships possible within the Johari framework.

Region I, for example, constitutes that portion of the total interpersonal space which is devoted to mutually held information. This Known by Self-Known by Others facet of the interpersonal space is thought to be the part of the relationship which, because of its shared data characteristics and implied likelihood of mutual understanding, controls interpersonal productivity. That is, the working assumption is that productivity and interpersonal effectiveness are directly related to the amount of mutually held information in a relationship. Therefore, the larger Region I becomes, the more rewarding, effective, and productive the relationship. As the informational context for interpersonal functioning, Region I is called the "Arena."

Region II, using the double classification approach just described, is that portion of the interpersonal space which holds information Known by Others but Unknown by the Self. Thus, this array of data constitutes an interpersonal handicap for the Self, since one can hardly understand the behaviors, decisions, or potentials of others if he doesn't have the data upon which these are based. Others have the advantage of knowing their own reactions, feelings, perceptions, and the like while the Self is unaware of these. Region II, an area of hidden unperceived information, is called the "Blindspot." The Blindspot is, of course, a limiting factor with respect to the size of Region I and may be thought of, therefore, as inhibiting interpersonal effectiveness.

Region III may also be considered to inhibit interpersonal effectiveness, but it is due to an imbalance of information which would seem to favor the Self; as the portion of the relationship which is characterized by information Known by the Self but Unknown by Others, Region III constitutes a protective feature of the relationship for the Self. Data which one perceives as potentially prejudicial to a relationship or which he keeps to himself out of fear, desire for power, or whatever, make up the "Facade." This protective front, in turn, serves a defensive function for the Self. The question is not one of whether a Facade is necessary but rather how much Facade is required realistically; this raises the question of how much conscious defensiveness can be tolerated before the Arena becomes too inhibited and interpersonal effectiveness begins to diminish.

Finally, Region IV constitutes that portion of the relationship which is devoted to material neither known by the self nor by other parties to the relationship. The information in this Unknown by Self-Unknown by Others area is thought to reflect psychodynamic data, hidden potential, unconscious idiosyncrasies, and the data-base of creativity. Thus, Region IV is the "Unknown" area which may become known as interpersonal effectiveness increases.

Summarily, it should be said that the information within all regions can be of any type—feeling data, factual information, assumptions, task skill data, and prejudices—which are relevant to the relationship at hand. Irrelevant data are not the focus of the Johari Window concept: just those pieces of information which have a bearing on the quality and productivity of the relationship should be considered as appropriate targets for the information processing practices prescribed by the model. At the same time, it should be borne in mind that the individuals involved in a relationship, particularly the Self, control what and how information will be processed. Because of this implicit personal control aspect, the model should be viewed as an open system which is *dynamic* and amenable to change as personal decisions regarding interpersonal functioning change.

Basic Interpersonal Processes: Exposure and Feedback

The dynamic character of the model is critical; for it is the movement capability of the horizontal and vertical lines which partition the interpersonal space into regions which gives individuals control over what their relationships will become. The Self can significantly influence the size of his Arena in relating to others by the behavioral processes he employs in establishing relationships. To the extent that one takes the steps necessary to apprise others of relevant information which he has and they do not, he is enlarging his Arena in a downward direction. Within the framework of the model, this enlargement occurs in concert with a reduction of one's Facade. Thus,

if one behaves in a non-defensive, trusting, and possibly risk taking manner with others, he may be thought of as contributing to increased mutual awareness and sharing of data. The process one employs toward this end has been called the "Exposure" process. It entails the open and candid disclosure of one's feelings, factual knowledge, wild guesses, and the like in a conscious attempt to share. Frothy, intentionally untrue, diversionary sharing does not constitute exposure; and, as personal experience will attest, it does nothing to help understanding. The Exposure process is under the direct control of the Self and may be used as a mechanism for building trust and for legitimizing mutual exposures.

The need for mutual exposures becomes apparent when one considers the behavioral process required for enlarging the Arena laterally. As a behavior designed to gain reduction in one's Blindspot, the Feedback process entails an active solicitation by the Self of the information he feels others might have which he does not. The active, initiative-taking aspect of this solicitation behavior should be stressed, for again the Self takes the primary role in setting interpersonal norms and in legitimizing certain acts within the relationship. Since the extent to which the Self will actually receive the Feedback he solicits is contingent upon the willingness of others to expose their data, the need for a climate of mutual exposures becomes apparent. Control by the Self of the success of his Feedback-seeking behaviors is less direct therefore than in the case of self-exposure. He will achieve a reduction of his Blindspot only with the cooperation of others; and his own prior willingness to deal openly and candidly may well dictate what level of cooperative and trusting behavior will prevail on the part of other parties to the relationship.

Thus, one can theoretically establish interpersonal relationships characterized by mutual understanding and increased effectiveness (by a dominant Arena) if he will engage in exposing and feedback soliciting behaviors to an optimal degree. This places the determination of productivity and amount of interpersonal reward—and the quality of relationships—directly in the hands of the Self. In theory, this amounts to an issue of interpersonal competence; in practice, it amounts to the conscious and sensitive management of interpersonal processes.

Interpersonal Styles and Managerial Impacts

While one can theoretically employ Exposure and Feedback processes not only to a great but to a similar degree as well, individuals typically fail to achieve such an optimal practice. Indeed, they usually display a significant preference for one or the other of the two processes and tend to overuse one while neglecting the other. This tendency promotes a state of imbalance in interpersonal relationships which, in turn, creates disruptive tensions capable of retarding productivity. Figure 2 presents several commonly used approaches to the employment of Exposure and Feedback processes. Each of these may be thought of as reflecting a basic interpersonal style—that is, fairly consistent and preferred ways of behaving interpersonally. As might be expected, each style has associated with it some fairly predictable consequences.

Type A. This interpersonal style reflects a minimal use of both Exposure and Feedback processes; it is a fairly impersonal approach to in-

terpersonal relationships. The Unknown region dominates under this style; and unrealized potential, untapped creativity, and personal psychodynamics prevail as the salient influences. Such a style would seem to indicate withdrawal and an aversion to risk-taking on the part of its user; interpersonal anxiety and safety-seeking are likely to be prime sources of personal motivation. Persons who characteristically use this style appear to be detached, mechanical, and uncommunicative. They may often be found in bureaucratic highly structured organizations of some type where it is possible, and perhaps profitable, to avoid personal disclosure or involvement. People using this style are likely to be reacted to with more than average hostility, since other parties to the relationship will tend to interpret the lack of Exposure and Feedback solicitation largely according to their own needs and how this interpersonal lack affects need fulfillment.

Subordinates whose manager employs such a style, for example, will often feel that his behavior is consciously aimed at frustrating them in their work. The person in need of support and encouragement will often view a Type A manager as aloof, cold, and indifferent. Another individual in need of firm directions and plenty of order in his work may view the same manager as indecisive and administratively impotent. Yet another person requiring freedom and opportunities to be innovative may see the Type A interpersonal style as hopelessly tradition-bound and as symptomatic of fear and an overriding need for security. The use of Type A behaviors on a large scale in an organization reveals something about the climate and fundamental health of that organization. In many respects, interpersonal relationships founded on Type A uses of exposure and feedback constitute the kind of organizational ennui about which Chris Argyris[4] has written so eloquently. Such practices are, in his opinion, likely to be learned ways of behaving under oppressive policies of the sort which encourage people to act in a submissive and dependent fashion. Organizationally, of course, the result is lack of communication and a loss of human potentials; the Unknown becomes the dominant feature of corporate relationships, and the implications for organizational creativity and growth are obvious.

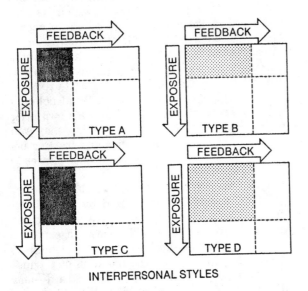

INTERPERSONAL STYLES

FIGURE 2. Interpersonal styles as functions of exposure use and feedback solicitation

Type B. Under this approach, there is also an aversion to Exposure, but aversion is coupled with a desire for relationships not found in Type A. Thus, Feedback is the only process left in promoting relationships and it is much overused. An aversion to the use of Exposure may typically be interpreted as a sign of basic mistrust of self and others, and it is therefore not surprising that the Facade is the dominant feature of relationships resulting from neglected Exposure coupled with overused Feedback. The style appears to be a probing supportive interpersonal ploy and, once the Facade becomes apparent, it is likely to result in a reciprocal withdrawal of trust by other parties. This may promote feelings of suspicion on the part of others; such feelings may lead to the manager being treated as a rather superficial person without real substance or as a devious sort with many hidden agenda.

Preference for this interpersonal style among managers seems to be of two types. Some managers committed to a quasi-permissive management may employ Type B behaviors in an attempt to avoid appearing directive. Such an approach results in the manager's personal resources never being fully revealed or his opinions being expressed. In contrast—but subject to many of the same inadequacies—is the use of Type B behaviors in an attempt to gain or maintain one's personal power in relationships. Many managers build a facade to maintain personal control and an outward appearance of confidence. As the Johari model would suggest, however, persons who employ such practices tend to become isolated from their subordinates and colleagues alike. Lack of trust predominates and consolidation of power and promotion of an image of confidence may be the least likely results of Type B use in organizations. Very likely, the seeds of distrust and conditions for covert competitiveness—with all the implications for organizational teamwork—will follow from widespread use of Type B interpersonal practices.

Type C. Based on an over-use of Exposure to the neglect of Feedback, this interpersonal style may reflect ego-striving and/or distrust of others' competence. The person who uses this style usually feels quite confident of his own opinions and is likely to value compliance from others. The fact that he is often unaware of his impact or of the potential of others' contributions is reflected in the dominant Blindspot which results from this style. Others are likely to feel disenfranchised by one who uses this style; they often feel that he has little use for their contributions or concern for their feelings. As a result, this style often triggers feelings of hostility, insecurity, and resentment on the part of others. Frequently, others who learn to perpetuate the manager's Blindspot by withholding important information or giving only selected feedback; as such, this is a reflection of the passive-aggressiveness and unarticulated hostility which this style can cause. Labor-management relations frequently reflect such Blindspot dynamics.

The Type C interpersonal style is probably what has prompted so much interest in "listening" programs around the country. As the Johari model makes apparent, however, the Type C over-use of Exposure and neglect of Feedback is just one of several interpersonal tendencies that may disrupt communications. While hierarchical organizational structure or centrality in communication nets and the like may certainly facilitate the use of individual Type C behaviors, so can fear of failure, authoritarianism, need for control, and over-confidence in one's own opinions; such traits vary from person to person and limit the utility of communication panaceas. Managers who rely on this style often do so to demonstrate competence; many corporate cultures require that the manager be *the* planner, director, and controller and many managers behave accordingly to protect their corporate images. Many others are simply trying to be helpful in a paternalistic kind of way; others are, of course, purely dictatorial. Whatever the reason, those who employ the Type C style have one thing in common: their relationships will be dominated by Blindspots and they are destined for surprise whenever people get enough and decide to force feedback on them, solicited or not.

Type D. Balanced Exposure and Feedback processes are used to a great extent in this style; candor, openness, and a sensitivity to others' needs to participate are the salient features of the style. The Arena is the dominant characteristic, and productivity increases. In initial stages, this style may promote some defensiveness on the part of others who are not familiar with honest and trusting relationships; but perseverance will tend to promote a norm of reciprocal candor over time in which creative potential can be realized.

Among managers, Type D practices constitute an ideal state from the standpoint of organizational effectiveness. Healthy and creative climates result from its widespread use, and the conditions for growth and corporate excellence may be created through the use of constructive Exposure and Feedback exchanges. Type D practices do not give license to "clobber," as some detractors might claim; and, for optimal results, the data explored should be germane to the relationships and problems at hand, rather than random intimacies designed to overcome self-consciousness. Trust is slowly built, and managers who experiment with Type D processes should be prepared to be patient and flexible in their relationships. Some managers, as they tentatively try out Type D strategies, encounter reluctance and distrust on the part of others, with the result that they frequently give up too soon, assuming that the style doesn't work. The reluctance of others should be assessed against the backdrop of previous management practices and the level of prior trust which characterizes the culture. Other managers may try candor only to discover that they have opened a Pandora's box from which a barrage of hostility and complaints emerges. The temptation of the naive manager is to put the lid back on quickly; but the more enlightened manager knows that when communications are opened up after having been closed for a long time, the most emotionally laden issues—ones which have been the greatest source of frustration, anger, or fear—will be the first to be discussed. If management can resist cutting the dialogue short, the diatribe will run its course as the emotion underlying it is drained off, and exchanges will become more problem centered and future oriented. Management intent will have been tested and found worthy of trust, and creative unrestrained interchanges will occur. Organizations built on such practices are those headed for corporate climates and resource utilization of the type necessary for true corporate excellence. The manager's interpersonal style may well be the catalyst for this reaction to occur.

Summarily, the Johari Window model of interpersonal processes suggests that much more is needed to understand communication in an organization than information about its structure or one's position in a network. People make very critical decisions about what information will be processed, irrespective of structural and network considerations. People bring with them to organizational settings propensities for behaving in certain ways interpersonally. They prefer certain interpersonal styles, sharpened and honed by corporate cultures, which significantly influence—if not dictate entirely—the flow of information in organizations. As such, individuals and their preferred styles of relating one to another amount to the synapses in the corporate network which control and coordinate the human system. Central to an understanding of communication in organizations, therefore, is an appreciation of the complexities of those human interfaces which comprise organizations. The work of Luft and Ingham, when brought to bear on management practices and corporate cultures, may lend much needed insight into the constraints unique to organizational life which either hinder or facilitate the processing of corporate data.

Research on the Managerial Profile: The Personnel Relations Survey

As treated here, one of the major tenets of the Johari Window model is that one's use of Exposure and Feedback soliciting processes is a matter of personal decision. Whether consciously or unconsciously, when one employs either process or fails to do so he has decided that such practices somehow serve the goals he has set for himself. Rationales for particular behavior are likely to be as varied as the goals people seek; they may be in the best sense of honest intent or they may simply represent evasive logic or systems of self-deception. The *purposeful* nature of interpersonal styles remains nevertheless. A manager's style of relating to other members of the organization is never simply a collection of random, unconsidered acts. Whether he realizes it or not, or admits it or denies it, his interpersonal style *has purpose* and is thought to serve either a personal or interpersonal goal in his relationships.

Because of the element of decision and purposeful intent inherent in one's interpersonal style, the individual's inclination to employ Exposure and Feedback processes may be assessed. That is, his decisions to engage in open and candid behaviors or to actively seek out the information that others are thought to have may be sampled, and his Exposure and Feedback tendencies thus measured. Measurements obtained may be used in determining the manager's or the organization's Johari Window configuration and the particular array of interpersonal predilections which underlie it. Thus, the Luft-Ingham model not only provides a way of conceptualizing what is going on interpersonally, but it affords a rationale for actually assessing practices which may, in turn, be coordinated to practical climate and cultural issues.

Hall and Williams have designed a paper-and-pencil instrument for use with managers which reveals their preferences for Exposure and Feedback in their relationships with subordinates, colleagues, and superiors. The *Personnel Relations Survey*,[5] as the instrument is entitled, has been used extensively by industry as a training aid for providing personal feedback of a type which "personalizes" otherwise didactic theory sessions on the Johari, on one hand, and as a catalyst to evaluation and critique of ongoing relationships, on the other hand. In addition to its essentially training oriented use, however, the *Personnel Relations Survey* has been a basic research tool for assessing current practices among managers. The results obtained from two pieces of research are of particular interest from the standpoint of their implications for corporate climates and managerial styles.

Authority Relationships and Interpersonal Style Preferences. Using the *Personnel Relations Survey*, data were collected from 1000 managers. These managers represent a cross-section of those found in organizations today; levels of management ranging from company president to just above first-line supervisor were sampled from all over the United States. Major manufacturers and petroleum and food producers contributed to the research, as well as a major airline, state and federal governmental agencies, and nonprofit service organizations.

Since the *Personnel Relations Survey* addresses the manner in which Exposure and Feedback processes are employed in one's relationships with his subordinates, colleagues, and superiors, the data from the 1000 managers sampled reveal some patterns which prevail in organizations in terms of downward, horizontal, and upward communications. In addition, the shifting and changing of interpersonal tactics as one moves from one authority relationship to another is noteworthy from the standpoint of power dynamics underlying organizational life. A summary of the average tendencies obtained from managers is presented graphically in Figure 3.

Of perhaps the greatest significance for organizational climates is the finding regarding the typical manager's use of Exposure. As Figure 3 indicates, one's tendency to deal openly and candidly with others is directly influenced by the amount of power he possesses relative to other parties to the relationship. Moving from relationships with subordinates in which the manager obviously enjoys greater formal authority, through colleague relationships characterized by equal authority positions, to relationships with superiors in which the manager is least powerful, the plots of Exposure use steadily decline. Indeed, a straight linear relationship is suggested between amount of authority possessed by the average manager and his use of candor in relationships.

While there are obvious exceptions to this depiction, the average managerial profile on Exposure reveals the most commonly found practices in organizations which, when taken diagnostically, suggest that the average manager in today's organizations has a number of "hang-ups" around authority issues which seriously curtail his interpersonal effectiveness. Consistent with other findings from communication research, these data point to power differences among parties to relationships as a major disruptive influence on the flow of information in organizations. A more accurate interpretation, however, seems to be that it is not power differences as such which impede communication, but the way people *feel* about

344   *Communication*

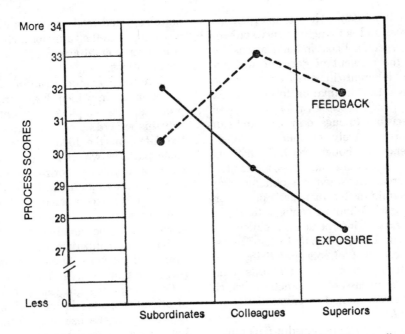

FIGURE 3. Score plots on exposure and feedback for the "average" manager from a sample of 1000 managers in the United States

these differences and begin to monitor, filter, and control their contributions in response to their own feelings and apprehensions.

Implications for overall corporate climate may become more obvious when the data from the Exposure process are considered with those reflecting the average manager's reliance on Feedback acquisition. As Figure 3 reveals, Feedback solicitation proceeds differently. As might be expected, there is less use of the Feedback process in relationships with subordinates than there is of the Exposure process. This variation on the Type C interpersonal style, reflecting an overuse of Exposure to some neglect of Feedback, very likely contributes to subordinate feelings of resentment, lack of social worth, and frustration. These feelings—which are certain to manifest themselves in the *quality* of subordinate performance if not in production quantity—will likely remain as hidden facets of corporate climate, for a major feature of downward communication revealed in Figure 3 is that of managerial Blindspot.

Relationships at the colleague level appear to be of a different sort with a set of dynamics all

their own. As reference to the score plots in Figure 3 will show, the typical manager reports a significant preference for Feedback seeking behaviors over Exposure in his relationships with his fellow managers. A quick interpretation of the data obtained would be that, at the colleague level, everyone is seeking information but very few are willing to expose any. These findings may bear on a unique feature of organizational life—one which has serious implications for climate among corporate peers. Most research on power and authority relationships suggests that there is the greatest openness and trust among people under conditions of equal power. Since colleague relationships might best be considered to reflect equal if not shared distributions of power, maximum openness coupled with maximum solicitation of others' information might be expected to characterize relationships among management co-workers. The fact that a fairly pure Type B interpersonal style prevails suggests noise in the system. The dominant Facade which results from reported practices with colleagues signifies a lack of trust of the sort which could seriously limit the success of collaborative or co-operative ventures among colleagues. The climate implications of mistrust are obvious, and the present data may shed some light on teamwork difficulties as well as problems of horizontal communication so often encountered during inter-departmental or inter-group contacts.

Interviews with a number of managers revealed that their tendencies to become closed in encounters with colleagues could be traced to a competitive ethic which prevailed in their organizations. The fact was a simple one: "You don't confide in your 'buddies' because they are bucking for the same job you are! Any worthwhile information you've got, you keep to yourself until a time when it might come in handy." To the extent that this climate prevails in organizations, it is to be expected that more effort goes into facade building and maintenance than is expended on the projects at hand where colleague relationships are concerned.

Superiors are the targets of practices yielding the smallest, and therefore least productive, Arena of the three relationships assessed in the survey. The average manager reports a significant reluctance to deal openly and candidly with his superior while favoring the Feedback process as his major interpersonal gambit; even the use of Feedback, however, is subdued relative to that employed with colleagues. The view from on high in organizations is very likely colored by the interpersonal styles addressed to them; and, based on the data obtained, it would not be surprising if many members of top management felt that lower level management was submissive, in need of direction, and had few creative suggestions of their own. Quite aside from the obvious effect such as expectation might have on performance reviews, a characteristic reaction to the essentially Type B style directed at superiors is, on their part, to invoke Type C behaviors. Thus, the data obtained call attention to what may be the seeds of a self-reinforcing cycle of authority-obedience-authority. The long-range consequences of such a cycle, in terms of relationship quality and interpersonal style, has been found to be corporate-wide adoption of Type A behaviors which serve to depersonalize work and diminish an organization's human resources.

Thus, based on the present research at least, a number of interpersonal practices seem to characterize organizational life which limit not only the effectiveness of communication within, but the attainment of realistic levels of corporate excellence without. As we will see, which style will prevail very much depends upon the individual manager.

Interpersonal Practices and Managerial Styles. In commenting upon the first of their two major concerns in programs of organization development, Blake and Mouton[6] have stated: "The underlying causes of communication difficulties are to be found in the character of supervision.... The solution to the problem of communication is for men to manage by achieving production and excellence through sound utilization of people." To the extent that management style is an important ingredient in the communication process, a second piece of research employing the Johari Window and Managerial Grid models in tandem may be of some interest to those concerned with corporate excellence.

Of the 1000 managers sampled in the *Personnel Relations Survey*, 384 also completed a second instrument, the *Styles of Management Inventory*,[7] based on the Managerial Grid (a two-dimensional model of management styles).[8] Five "anchor" styles are identified relative to one's concern for production vis-a-vis people, and these are expressed in grid notation as follows: 9,9 reflects a high production concern coupled with high people concern; 5,5 reflects a moderate concern for each; 9,1 denotes high production coupled with low people concerns, while 1,9 denotes the opposite orientation; 1,1 reflects a minimal concern for both dimensions. In an attempt to discover the significance of one's interpersonal practices for his overall approach to management, the forty individuals scoring highest on each style of management were selected for an analysis of their interpersonal styles. Thus, 200 managers—forty each who were identified as having dominant managerial styles of either 9,9; 5,5; 9,1; 1,9; or 1,1—were studied relative to their tendencies to employ Exposure and Feedback processes in relationships with their subordinates. The research question addressed was: How do individuals who prefer a given managerial style differ in terms of their interpersonal orientations from other individuals preferring other managerial approaches?

The data were subjected to a discriminant function analysis and statistically significant differences were revealed in terms of the manner in which managers employing a given dominant managerial style also employed the Exposure and Feedback processes. The results of the research findings are presented graphically in Figure 4. As the bar graph of Exposure and Feedback scores reveals, those managers identified by a dominant management style of 9,9 displayed the strongest tendencies to employ both Exposure and Feedback in their relationships with subordinates. In addition, the Arena which would result from a Johari plotting of their scores would be in a fairly good state of balance, reflecting about as much use of one process as of the other. The data suggest that the 9,9 style of management—typically described as one which achieves effective production through the sound utilization of people—also entails the sound utilization of personal resources in establishing relationships. The Type D interpersonal style which seems to be associated with the 9,9 management style is fully consistent with the open and unobstructed communication which Blake and Mouton view as essential

to the creative resolution of differences and sound relationships.

The 5,5 style of management appears, from the standpoint of Exposure and Feedback employment, to be a truncated version of the 9,9 approach. While the reported scores for both processes hover around the fiftieth percentile, there is a noteworthy preference for Exposure over Feedback. Although a Johari plotting of these scores might also approach a Type D profile, the Arena is less balanced and accounts for only 25 percent of the data available for use in a relationship. Again, such an interpersonal style seems consistent with a managerial approach based on expediency and a search for the middle ground.

As might be expected, the 9,1 managers in the study displayed a marked preference for Exposure over Feedback in their relationships with subordinates. This suggests that managers who are maximally concerned with production issues also are given to an overuse of Exposure—albeit not maximum Exposure—and this is very likely to maintain personal control. In general, a Type C interpersonal style seems to underlie the 9,1 approach to management; and it is important that such managerial practices may be sustained by enlarged Blindspots.

Considering the opposing dominant concerns of the 1,9 manager as compared to the 9,1, it is not too surprising to find that the major interpersonal process of these managers is Feedback solicitation. As with the 9,1 style, the resulting Arena for 1,9 managers is not balanced; but the resulting tension likely stems from less than desired Exposure, leading to relationships in which the managerial Facade is the dominant feature. The Type B interpersonal style may be said to characterize the 1,9 approach to management, with its attendant effects on corporate climate.

Finally, the use of Exposure and Feedback processes reported by those managers identified as dominantly 1,1 is minimal. A mechanical impersonal approach to interpersonal relationships which is consistent with the low profile approach to management depicted under 1,1 is suggested. The Unknown region apparently dominates relationships, and hidden potential and untapped resources prevail. The consequences of such practices for the quality of relationships, climates,

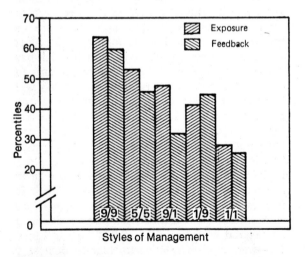

FIGURE 4. A comparison of exposure and feedback use among managers with different dominant managerial styles

and communication effectiveness have already been described in the discussion of Type A interpersonal behaviors.

In summary, it appears that one's interpersonal style is a critical ingredient in his approach to management. While the uses of Exposure and Feedback reported by managers identified according to management style seem to be quite consistent with what one might expect, it is worthy to mention that the test items comprising the *Personnel Relations Survey* have very little, if anything, to do with production versus people concerns. Rather, one's willingness to engage in risk-taking disclosures of feelings, impressions, and observations coupled with his sensitivity to others' participative needs and a felt responsibility to help them become involved via Feedback solicitation were assessed. The fact that such purposive behaviors coincide with one's treatment of more specific context-bound issues like production and people would seem to raise the question: Which comes first, interpersonal or managerial style? The question is researchable, and management practices and information flow might both be enhanced by the results obtained.

CORPORATE CLIMATE AND PERSONAL DECISION

The major thesis of this article has been that interpersonal styles are at the core of a number of corporate dilemmas: communication breakdowns, emotional climates, the quality of relationships, and even managerial practices have been linked to some fairly simple dynamics between people. The fact that the dynamics are simple should not be taken to mean that their management is easy—far from it. But, at the same time, the fact that individuals can and do change their interpersonal style—and thereby set in motion a whole chain of events with corporate significance—should be emphasized. A mere description of one's interpersonal practices has only limited utility, if that is as far as it goes. The value of the Johari Window model lies not so much with its utility for assessing what is but, rather, in its inherent statement of what might be.

Although most people select their interpersonal styles as a *reaction* to what they anticipate from other parties, the key to effective relationships lies in "pro-action"; each manager can be a norm setter in his relationships if he will but honestly review his own interpersonal goals and undertake the risks necessary to their attainment. Organizations can criticize their policies—both formal and unwritten—in search for provisions which serve to punish candor and reward evasiveness while equating solicitation of data from others with personal weakness. In short, the culture of an organization and the personal and corporate philosophies which underlie it may be thought of as little more than a *decision product* of the human system. The quality of this decision will directly reflect the quality of the relationships existing among those who fashion it.

If the model and its derivations make sense, then corporate relationships and managerial practices based on candor and trust, openness and spontaneity, and optimal utilization of interpersonal resources are available options to every member of an organizational family. As we have seen, power distributions among people may adversely influence their interpersonal choices. Management styles apparently constrain individuals, but the choice is still there. Type A practices require breaking away from the corporate womb into which one has retreated; personal experiments with greater Exposure and Feedback, however anxiety producing, may be found in the long-run to be their own greatest reward. For the manager locked into Type B behaviors, the task is more simple; he already solicits Feedback to an excellent degree. Needed is enough additional trust in others—whether genuine or forced—to allow a few experiences with Exposure. Others may be found to be less fragile or reactionary than one imagined. Learning to listen is but part of the task confronting managers inclined toward Type C styles; they must learn to seek out and encourage the exposures of others. This new attention to the Feedback process should not be at the expense of Exposure, however. Revamping Type C does not mean adopting Type B. These are all forms of low-risk high-potential-yield personal experiments. Whether they will ever be undertaken and their effects on corporate excellence determined depends upon the individual; the matter is one of personal decision.

REFERENCES

1. R. R. Blake and Jane S. Mouton, *Corporate Excellence Through Grid Organization Development* (Houston, Texas: Gulf Publishing Co., 1968), p. 4.

2. *Ibid.*, pp. 3–5.

3. Joseph Luft, *Of Human Interaction* (Palo Alto, California: National Press Books, 1969), *passim.*

4. C. Argyris, *Interpersonal Competence and Organizational Effectiveness* (Homewood, Illinois: Dorsey, 1962), *passim.*

5. J. Hall and Martha S. Williams, *Personnel Relations Survey* (Conroe, Texas: Teleometrics International, 1967).

6. R. R. Blake and Jane S. Mouton, *op. cit.,* p. 5.

7. J. Hall, J. B. Harvey, and Martha S. Williams, *Styles of Management Inventory* (Conroe, Texas: Teleometrics International 1963).

8. R. R. Blake and Jane S. Mouton, *The Managerial Grid* (Houston, Texas: Gulf Publishing Co., 1964), *passim.*

BARRIERS TO SUCCESSFUL COMMUNICATION: PART I MACROBARRIERS

DAVID S. BROWN

Communication is a part of all human endeavor. It is always with us, always related to whatever we do. An improvement in communication, while not the universal cure-all many seem to expect from it, will usually help with the problems we face. Certainly poor communication distorts and aggravates them.

We have learned much about the communication process, but most of us continue to be frustrated by it. We communicate easily, enthusiastically, and copiously—but often mechanically and negligently as well. Most of us are rich in communicative experience but poor in performance. We do not use what we know. Despite all the new knowledge, techniques, and tools available to us, our ability to communicate is not even keeping pace with the demands we face.

Understandably, we are eager for help. Understandably, also, we are ready to try any new nostrum—from TA to TV—that is available to us. Alas, poor communication, like the common cold, seems to be impervious to all our efforts to remedy it, and the situation will undoubtedly get worse.

Communication does not occur unless a message is received and understood in basically the form the sender intended—and acknowledged. A person who speaks to another in language unknown to him is, of course, not communicating with him. And even if the words are understood, if the concepts are beyond the receiver's grasp, communication has not occurred. So, the sender must have evidence that the message has gotten through; thus the importance of feedback.

The reasons why messages are not received, not understood, and not acknowledged involve macro- and microbarriers. Macrobarriers concern the environment, the larger world in which communication takes place. Microbarriers are those of the immediate situation, Mr. A talking to Mr. B. Each enormously affects the communication process.

There are more macrobarriers than most of us realize, and, unfortunately, they seem to be increasing. They affect not only what we communicate but how, when, how much, and why. The most important include:

- The role of information as a "currency."
- The increasing need for more information.
- The escalating number of messages.
- The increasing complexity of the subject matter.
- The imprecision of the communication process.
- The variety of languages.
- The variety of media.

- The amount and nature of interference.
- The problem of the generalized message.
- The pressure of time.
- Self-defense systems.

INFORMATION AS A "CURRENCY"

Information has great value. Those who possess it have something others do not have and, presumably, need or want. And whether a person possesses information or not also indicates his status and role.

When something has high value, people try to acquire it. Many of them use extraordinary means to do so. Once acquired, it is used to influence others. It may even be hoarded. Those with access to inside information have both prestige and power. They know what others do not. When we whisper, it is not so much to convey information as to insure that the "wrong" persons do not gain it without our permission. People who are not in the know are nonequals. Small wonder that we get so uptight about communications. Small wonder that we give our own needs high priority and so often neglect the needs of others.

THE INCREASING NEED FOR
MORE INFORMATION

The amount of information a peasant might require in the Middle Ages was limited, but the information needed today is boundless. Our time is one in which, willy-nilly, we must have information, vast amounts of it. Our jobs change, our needs change, our lifestyles change rapidly and greatly. No sooner have we accommodated to one situation than we are faced with another. Each of us learns new things daily. In fact, we must learn if we are to survive. We are trained to search for more and better information, and so we place new and greater burdens on our already overloaded communication systems.

THE ESCALATING NUMBER
OF MESSAGES

Such needs and desires lead inescapably to an increasing number of communications. We are bombarded with messages from morning until night. And we bombard others. This results in a frightful cacophony. That the Adam-and-Eve model of the human receiving set—which is all we are—may not be equal to the new demands should surprise no one. In fact, the majority of the messages beamed at us—the specific as well as the general—pass by us. There are just too many of them for us to handle, despite the selective listening all of us practice.

THE INCREASING COMPLEXITY
OF THE SUBJECT MATTER

English has become the language of science, commerce, diplomacy, and profanity largely because of its flexibility. But the demands placed upon it have in fact outstripped even its great capabilities.

We devise more than we can describe—and often more than we can name. This applies not only to physical things but to ideas as well. While many of us are still wrestling with such basic concepts as gravity and space, others are already into curved light, magnetic pull, and black-holes. We are involved with abstractions, contractions, and distractions. "What with the tendency of one thing to lead to another," E. B. White has noted, "I predict a bright future for complexity." His future has already arrived, but most of us are still not prepared to cope with it.

THE IMPRECISION OF THE
COMMUNICATION PROCESS

Communication as a process is not precise. Neither is language. One does not need to be a lawyer to note the extent to which the Supreme Court labors to discover the intent of those who have put the law into words. "Yes" has many meanings, depending upon the tone or emphasis one gives it, including "no." The word "difficulty," used earlier in this piece, has 107 synonyms—including scrape, stew, and pickle, which have other more specific meanings—in my thesaurus. ("Thesaurus" has 25 synonyms itself.) The task of both sender and receiver is to agree on common meanings, not an easy assignment when they are often not on speaking—to say nothing of listening—terms.

THE VARIETY OF LANGUAGES

The world has thousands of languages—tongues, dialects, and patois—of which English is only the second most popular. But these are dwarfed by the vocabularies of subjects and professions that one must know to understand what is being communicated. We learn also, thanks to the study of chimpanzees, dolphins, and dogs, that other creatures have their own communication systems, some of which man may be able to master. All of us speak several languages and some of us speak many, but we need to understand that the language must be a shared one if we are to communicate fully. We must, in short, get on the same wave length.

THE VARIETY OF MEDIA

So far we have been concerned with the spoken or written language. There are also sign languages, as deaf-mutes remind us; the language of gestures and inflections, which all of us use without ever having taken a course in it; the so-called "body language"—what we use besides our lips and hands; and, most recently, "skin talk," which is what our skin says by way of heat or conductivity. McLuhan has reminded us that "the medium is the message." Said another way, what is conveyed is greatly influenced by the medium or conveyance. Our choices are many. We can rent a billboard to tell our enamored what we think of him/her; we can convey the same idea in a letter; or we may say it by telephone, by our looks, or, more feelingly, by touch. (The pun is intentional.) This, of course, does not exhaust the possibilities. "The media" is the name given to newspapers, magazines, TV, and radio, but it is really a broader term that can and should be applied to *all* means of communicating. The receiver as well as the sender must have at least a working familiarity with most of these.

THE AMOUNT AND NATURE OF INTERFERENCE

To be successful, a communication must overcome —or at least escape—many kinds of interference. Some of this is within the sender, some within the receiver, some in the process itself, and some is from the outside. Outside interference is easiest to identify: It is, as with your radio, the background noise that keeps you from getting the signal as clearly as it was sent. It may derive from other (and competing) messages, such as tuning in Baltimore and getting San Juan; or it may be sun spots, a passing thunderstorm, or the like. Interference may be due to a defective tube in the sending or receiving apparatus or someone standing too near or too far from the transmitter. Or—insidious thought—it may also be because you have a number of messages to send and get them mixed up. We will say more about this kind of interference later.

THE GENERALIZED MESSAGE

To compensate for some of the problems we know we face, we try to make one message serve a number of purposes. We send "to whom it may concern" and "box holder" messages because we do not know who all our targets are, or we may not be able to address each of them individually. This, of course, takes something from the message. Good sense suggests that we should not address an adult as we would a child, and yet because we often have no really good alternative, we do this a great deal of the time. Nor should we address a Spanish-speaking audience in English or advertise women's clothing in a publication aimed at men—not until recently, at least. We face additional problems when, to avoid naming the addressee, we use the imperative verb form. To generalize is often to overgeneralize, yet this is what we consistently do. And so our messages go undelivered.

THE PRESSURE OF TIME

All of us feel the pressure of time. We may live longer than our forebears, but we seem to have much less time than they had to do the things we like. Our communications must fit time demands, and even when time pressure is not rigorous, we find we have developed a habit about it and make it so anyway. We cram our communications with information, whether needed or not. We compete with each other to talk. We set arbitrary deadlines and unneeded requirements. Talk is cheap, so we spend it recklessly, overloading our message systems and thereby depreciating their contents. With so much garbage in the system, much of it will inevitably be sent out.

SELF-DEFENSE SYSTEMS

Ultimately the germ becomes impervious to the drug, and so also do we become impervious to the battering we get from the innumerable communicative thrusts addressed to us. It is not enough to say "No Smoking"; we must now say "POSITIVELY No Smoking" to get the message through—and then we must be prepared to police it as well. We build barriers to protect ourselves against radiation, and also against communication. These take a variety of forms. The individual *assumes* what others are intending to say and then turns off his hearing aid. He *hurdles* to get

to the ending ahead of the communicator. He *interprets*, he *interpolates*, he *fills in*, he *selects out* as he thinks—at the moment—is appropriate. And he *prejudges*. *Pre*-judicial, incidentally, is the root of the word "prejudice."

The mind is a restless receiver. We talk at the rate of two- or three-hundred words a minute, but our mind is capable of thinking in the thousands. In fact, we think in terms of scenarios—to use a popular word—rather than dialogue. We use the time we "save" to think of other things: whether what is being said is true or not; whether we agree with it; what effect it will have on us; how we should respond to it. We appear to listen, and sometimes we do, but we become preoccupied with other, if not unrelated, matters. And in doing so, we receive less than we might of what is being sent us.

These are some of the macrobarriers to communication.

BARRIERS TO SUCCESSFUL COMMUNICATION: PART 2 MICROBARRIERS

DAVID S. BROWN

The microbarriers are those that the message Mr. A intends to send to Mr. B must avoid or surmount if the message is to get through as he intends it. In many respects they are similar to the macrobarriers, but they differ in that they have to do with the specific message, its transmission and receipt.

There is nothing theoretical about microbarriers. They are there and they must be overcome. This is a critical point. For an individual message to make it, it must escape whatever traps or hazards lie in its way. Any one of these can warp or waylay it. This is, of course, why we so often send a number of messages, hoping that if one is held up, another will make it. It also explains why we often dress the message in different ways, depending on the disguise to help its progress, but knowing at the same time that it increases the likelihood of its being misunderstood.

The microbarriers are more insidious than the macrobarriers. After all, the receiver *is* there: We can identify him, what we are saying is in his interest to hear, and he *should* be listening. (Or so we fancy, applying different rules to him than to ourselves.) The truth of the matter is that he is doing other things also, including, most likely, already preparing a response to what we are im-

parting. So the messages we are so desirous of delivering are only partially heard, partially understood, partially agreed with, and often not responded to at all.

Our starting point is with the message's sender. Man is a demanding animal. On this point economists, psychologists, and spouses all agree. He communicates because there is something he wants. This may be companionship or understanding (the spouse and the psychologist) or it may be more material things (the economist). He may even want to help others to perform a duty or fulfill a responsibility. All of his wants, however, involve communicating, a science and an art.

Not being perfect, man reflects his imperfections in his communications. Much of the time he is not even aware of this By the time he reaches maturity, he has acquired many habits. Some of these are culturally induced, some are personal. Much of his communicating involves these habits. He gives orders or he says "pretty please" according to habit. Or he mixes the two depending on time, circumstances, and those he addresses. He uses slang in this situation, but not in that. He writes out some of his messages, he delivers others orally, and he uses different methods for still others. He persistently misinterprets, misjudges, misunderstands, and misstates—he does not communicate.

Let us see how this happens. Here are some of

the more important of the microbarriers to good communications:

- The sender's view of the situation.
- The sender's view of the receiver.
- The message.
- The choice of medium.
- Related and associated messages.
- Interference.
- The views of the receiver.
- Receipt and translation.
- Feedback.

THE SENDER'S VIEW OF THE SITUATION

The subject, and how the sender views it, is as much a part of the communication process as is the message itself. After all, it is what the message is about. "A way of seeing," John Dewey has reminded us, "is also a way of not seeing—a focus upon Object A involves a neglect of Object B."

A communicator who has misjudged a situation, like a weatherman misreading the portents, can never communicate accurately concerning it. If one sees the sky as red and it is actually blue, the best of linguists cannot produce a satisfactory message. He may temper it; he may say "I believe" and "I feel," but insofar as this improves his communication, it will compromise his credibility.

There is no substitute in communicating for accurate observation, for validity and for reliability. Many (most?) of our communications suffer because we are casual and careless observers. What we say will be tested—and so will we. The doubt that the receiver feels is sufficient to discompose the process. So it is that the *subject* of the communication is as much a part of it as the machinery. Surely this makes sense.

THE SENDER'S VIEW OF THE RECEIVER

The sender, if he gives thought to it, will recognize that he also has a view of the receiver and that this view colors the form, nature, and content of the communication. We talk differently to a dog than we talk to a person because we must make allowances for what it can understand. Correspondingly, we talk differently to different adults. If we think a person slow or stupid, we shape our communication to him so that a slow person will get it. If we find him biased, we talk to him so as to offset his biases.

One of the difficulties with this, of course, is that the receiver often perceives what we are about and gives more of his attention to the message's form than he does to its contents—which means he receives one message when we want him to receive another. Another difficulty is that of the self-fulfilling prophecy. The sender is fooled because, believing something of someone, he seeks evidence that it is so. Ordinarily he has no trouble finding such evidence.

THE MESSAGE

Many (the majority?) of our ideas suffer because they are difficult to express. We discover that words have many different meanings and that these meanings vary still further depending upon the manner in which they are expressed, their context, and the like. Many ideas, in fact, are not conveyable at all. This does not mean that they cannot be learned, only that they *must* be learned.

We cannot tell someone how to put down a disturbance satisfactorily, what responsibility is, how to adjust a motor, or what must be done to get someone to change his mind. If you doubt this, try explaining to John something you do know—why you don't like him. Not only will you have difficulty getting the idea into words, but you will surely have trouble saying it so that it conveys—as the Red Queen would have it—precisely what you mean, no more, no less. It is useful in this context to remember that certain ideas are not easily translated from one language to another, and some are not translatable at all.

Not only, of course, may the sender's view of the situation be open to error, but his remedy for it may be even more in question. Honorable men can agree on the nature of a situation but disagree strongly on what to do about it. The receiver is entitled to his own ideas, and he will have them anyway. Having some, he will ordinarily want to make them known. Thus further opportunities for misunderstanding arise.

We noted among the macrobarriers that the complexities of today's society burden additionally the communicative processes. Complexities add also to the difficulties of conceptualizing what we want or think best. Unfortunately, one of the problems with present day "communicology" is that we are led to believe that more will fit into the message than is the case, and so we overload the system from the start.

THE CHOICE OF MEDIUM

The medium we use greatly affects what we want to convey. In fact, each of us as receivers has strong preferences for certain media over others, which means that we tune in and tune out as our preferences indicate. We complain, for example of "stilted language" or—the opposite—of slang. Putting something in writing may help understanding, but it may also be seen as indicating distrust. We heartily dislike the use of particular terms. The willingness of certain people to use vulgarisms insults more conservative listeners. And so on.

Knowing all of the intended receivers of a message, of course, does not automatically make us better communicators. There is still that "ol' debbil," habit, who is so stern a taskmaster. Most of us when in the same room with someone will ordinarily use the spoken word in communicating because it is more convenient to do so. Indeed, talk is so cheap—and often so pleasurable—that we use it when other media may be more effective.

We know that we remember more of what we see than what we hear. Confucius's advice that "I hear and I forget, I see and I remember, I do and I understand" hasn't much more effect on most of us than some of his other observations are having on the contemporary Chinese. Actions may speak more loudly than words, but we often fail to use them in a positive communicative way. In fact, they usually undercut what we say, which is what the aphorism above is suggesting.

RELATED AND ASSOCIATED MESSAGES

Messages are rarely unitary, although we may intend them to be so. Along with our words, we use inflections, constructions, gestures, expressions, body movements, actions, and the like. Even when our intentions are honest, the multiple messages thus sent may have different meanings for the receiver. "It isn't your eyes that trouble me," someone has said, "but how you look through them." The receiver often has a choice of what to believe and usually takes it.

So much for the multiple messages. Now, assuming that we are able to eliminate these, the single message will still probably contain multiple meanings. This is in part what diplomacy is about. Different readers can find in the same concordat what each wants to find there. Thus communist and democratic states can sign the same piece of paper in Russian, English, or Chinese, and all of them can save face. What is functional in diplomacy, however, may be dysfunctional elsewhere, and the communicator is put on notice. This is another barrier to be surmounted.

INTERFERENCE

Interference of one kind or another is always present when Mr. A talks to Mr. B. The father who sought to be interference-free for a talk about sex with his son felt that he had resolved the problem by taking the boy on a fishing trip and then into a boat in the middle of the lake before broaching the subject. Once more, however, he was foiled. The interference he avoided was the likelihood others would break into the conversation, an approaching meal, cars in the street beyond, and so on. What he had not anticipated, and did not avoid, was the lure of the fish to be caught, the rocking of the boat in the waves, the hotness of the sun, and the son's disinclination to listen whatever the situs. All messages must be able to get past the interference, internal or external, to which they are subjected to be successful. Some make it, but others do not.

THE VIEWS OF THE RECEIVER

If the sender has a filter system, the receiver can be expected to have one also—which he does. And if the sender's system can—by his views of the receiver—affect the nature of the message, the receiver's—by his views of the sender—can also distort it. As the message is being sent, he can speculate as to its purpose, the sender's real as apart from his professed meaning, his perceptivity, and the like. Thus attention waivers from message content. Thus what is received is colored by views held by the receiver of sender, subject, media, and of the receiver himself.

RECEIPT AND TRANSLATION

This may be a part of the filter process or it may be one of the "mechanicals." Whichever it is, its effect is much the same. The receiver (the person) is also a receiving set. The message must be received. It must be decoded and translated. It must be examined for content. The situation to which it refers must be examined. Judgments must be made concerning the subject area. That this may be done in a nearly instantaneous way does not mean that it is an error-free process. In fact, it has many elements to it and like any process with many parts is clearly error-prone.

FEEDBACK

The message circuit is not complete until the sender learns that his message has been received in the form intended, that it is acknowledged, and, it is hoped, understood. Feedback is the signal that this has happened.

Feedback occurs in many ways and takes many forms. It is, of course, a communication itself and subject to all of the vagaries of other communications. What is important to note here is that the sender must also be a receiver, and that he must actively seek assurance of the receipt and appreciation of his original message.

A dialogue, for example, will result in a great mixture of sending and receiving signals. The multiplicity of ways in which we give feedback adds further to our problem. So do our honorifics. It is sometimes a miracle that useful feedback—even acknowledgements—get through at all. Many a message has, in fact, been delivered in garbled form and honestly receipted without either sender or receiver for some time being the wiser.

IN SUMMARY

Good communication is at best a difficult process, made more so by many things. Almost any serious effort to improve it will have beneficial results. Perhaps one of the most useful starting points is an awareness of the problems that beset it.

These articles have sought to divide these into two major areas. The macrobarriers are those that are part of the larger environment, the characteristics of the forest. The microbarriers are the specifics, those of the individual trees. Both, however, greatly influence the communication—or lack of communication—which takes place.

When Mr. A talks to Mr. B, the process is affected by both macro- and microfactors. If they cannot be avoided, they at least can be dealt with. Some people are better communicators than others because they have learned how to be. Some are better under certain circumstances than under others because their styles are better adapted to one set of conditions than to another. Messages, after all, do get through. The effective communicator understands the hazards his message faces and is prepared to do some of the kinds of things that the situation may require.

8
MANAGEMENT BY OBJECTIVES

Of the various management approaches or systems that have emerged in recent years, Management By Objectives (MBO) has been held by many to be one of the most theoretically complete. It has been shown to be successful in a wide variety of organizations—for example, business firms, nonprofit organizations, educational organizations, and governmental organizations.

MBO's success or failure seems to be contingent upon its implementation. More specifically, it has been argued that the major difficulty with MBO has been acceptance in ignorance and implementation in haste. Nevertheless, MBO, or results-oriented management approaches that are spin-offs from MBO, continue to be popular in management research, theory, and practice. Consequently, a close look at various aspects of MBO is warranted. In this chapter we examine two major areas: the fundamentals of MBO, and implementing MBO.

Discussing the fundamentals of MBO is an article by William Reif and Gerald Bassford entitled "What MBO Really Is." The authors sketch out the particulars of the MBO process, and discuss in detail the four basic components of MBO: setting objectives, developing action plans, conducting periodic reviews, and annually appraising performance.

The emphasis of the following articles is on implementation aspects of MBO. Heinz Weihrich introduces this section with a piece on "MBO in Four Management Systems." Weihrich illustrates what MBO might look like in various organizational settings ranging from an exploitative–authoritative system to an extremely participative system. He argues that MBO may fail if it is superimposed on the organization without understanding the existing climate.

Bruce Jamieson closes out this section with an examination of "Behavioral Problems With Management By Objectives." Problems that he addresses include those relating to managerial style, adapting to change, interpersonal skills, setting objectives, measurement, and MBO quality control. The author concludes with some criticisms of the current state of MBO research.

Though literally hundreds of articles have been written on MBO, we feel this sampling will provide the reader with a respectable overview of the fundamentals of and implementation difficulties associated with this popular management-initiated system of thought.

WHAT MBO REALLY IS
Results Require a Complete Program

WILLIAM E. REIF
GERALD BASSFORD

In talking with managers about management by objectives (MBO) it is disconcerting to discover how many versions (the authors regard them as misconceptions) there are of the concept. Quite often MBO is viewed as an objective-setting process, and no more. At other times it is interpreted to be an approach to performance appraisal. Some practitioners regard MBO as essentially a management development program. Others have construed MBO to be a tool that is useful in determining executive compensation. Still others consider the concept to be synonymous with manpower planning.

MBO is none of these, or, more appropriately, is all of these—and more. The common error is to define the concept too narrowly and consequently practice, in the name of MBO, only a part of it. Follow-up studies of firms that have reported unsuccessful experiences with MBO have revealed that they were not practicing MBO but one of the limited programs described above. In such cases, the failure was not due to some limitation inherent in MBO, but to a lack of understanding of the concept and its application.

The purpose of this article is to clear up the confusion and misunderstanding that enshroud the concept and allow the real MBO to emerge. As a means of achieving this objective, the authors will describe in some detail the MBO concept and the basic components of its system. As managers become more knowledgeable about the concept and more experienced in developing and implementing sound MBO programs, the greater will be the payoffs, or organizational benefits, that the firm will receive.

THE CONCEPT OF MBO

What is management by objectives? One approach is to view MBO as a systematic way of incorporating into a more effective framework the things that managers do, or should be doing. Stated more formally, MBO is a way of practicing the five basic management functions—planning, organizing, staffing, leading, and controlling. In other words, *management by objectives is a way of managing*. It is not just a part of, nor is it something in addition to, the manager's job. It is not a secondary program or procedure attached to some other process or function. It is the essence of a results-oriented management system.

Peter Drucker, a well-known author and consultant, has referred to management by objectives as a philosophy of management.[1] He states that it is soundly based on a concept of human behavior and human motivation, and that it applies to managers at all levels, in all functional areas, and to any kind and size of organization. He believes that its success in improving managerial performance is due to its ability to convert objective (corporate) needs into personal goals.

Results Orientation

There are two basic tenets of the MBO concept that should be described. One is its results orientation and the other is the concept of human behavior and motivation mentioned by Drucker. The distinguishing characteristic of MBO is its emphasis on results—on achieving objectives. The importance of sound objectives for any organized endeavor has been recognized for some time; in 1945, for example, Marshall Dimock stated that objectives provide the cornerstone of any organization:

> The first step ... is the clear determination of objectives, for you cannot make valid detailed plans for either your program or your strategy until you know just where you are going. The determination of objectives influences policy, organization, personnel, leadership, and control. Fixing your objectives is like identifying the North Star—you sight your compass on it and then use it as the means of getting back on the track when you tend to stray.[2]

More recently, George Odiorne has said that objectives often explain behavior better than any other contributing factor in a managerial situation, and that the understanding and control of objectives provide the main energizing and directive force for managerial action.[3]

A number of well-known cliches express the need for a manager to be results oriented:

> The clearer the idea you have of what it is you are trying to accomplish, the greater are your chances of accomplishment.

> If you know where you want to go, you increase your chances of getting there. Or the opposite, if you don't know where you are going, any road will take you there.

> It's not what you do, but what you get done that counts.

> You don't tell the man what he is supposed to do; you tell him what he is responsible for getting done.

All of these statements emphasize the fact that the most important consideration in a managerial situation is getting results. Furthermore, results cannot be evaluated without some prior expectation (standards) against which to measure them. Management by objectives satisfies both requirements in that it concentrates first on setting objectives and determining the means to achieve them, and then seeing to it that results are forthcoming. In firms practicing MBO, all available resources and managerial talent are directed to achieving the objectives of the organization.

HUMAN BEHAVIOR AND MOTIVATION

Several theories support the second basic tenet of management by objectives, its concept of human behavior and motivation. The first of these is Abraham Maslow's hierarchy of needs theory of individual motivation. According to his theory, all people have five levels of needs that must be satisfied in ascending order. The most basic human needs are physiological, such as the desire for food, rest, and protection from the elements. They are survival oriented. Second order needs represent man's desire for safety and security, both physical and psychological, and include such factors as protection from a threatening environment, stable employment, satisfactory income, and some assurance that the future will provide for personal and family well-being.

Third order, or social, needs include man's desire for love and belonging, social activity, and membership in groups. Psychological or esteem needs refer to man's desire for recognition, status, prestige, competence, independence, and freedom. The highest order need, self-fulfillment, concerns the individual's desire to be master of his fate, to become all that he is capable of becoming, to become actualized in what he is potentially.

If the desire to fulfill these needs motivates individuals and, as a result, conditions their behavior, then management must provide for satisfaction of them within the work environment. Money, the traditional motivator, can satisfy quite well the two most basic needs. However, the higher order needs—social, psychological, and self-fulfillment—are more complex, and it is generally agreed that monetary incentives alone cannot satisfy them for long.

Another general theory of motivation is concerned primarily with the attitudes of managers toward workers. Management's traditional view (many contend it is still the most popular view) of the employee is that he is lazy, has an inherent dislike for work, and must be coerced, closely supervised, and threatened with punishment in order to get him to make any sort of contribution to the achievement of organizational objectives. The more enlightened view, and the one taken by managers practicing MBO, is that work is natural for most employees. If properly motivated, employees will exercise a high degree of self-control, actively seek responsibility, be creative, and generally behave in a manner supportive of goal achievement.

One of the significant aspects of these two sets of assumptions of human behavior is that they tend to be self-fulfilling prophecies. Treat a man as if he were lazy and dislikes work and he will respond accordingly. Encourage him to be responsible and help him to develop and grow on the job, and he will become a highly productive employee.

Further insight into worker motivation is provided by Frederick Herzberg, who focuses his attention on certain factors within the work environment. Herzberg's two-factor theory emphasizes that all job factors can be divided into two rather distinct groups. In the first group are such factors as working conditions, salary, fringe benefits, company policy, and administrative practices. He refers to these as maintenance factors. In the second group are factors such as achievement, recognition, responsibility, advancement (based on merit), opportunity for growth, and others that are considered intrinsic to the job. He calls these factors motivators since he feels these contribute the most to job satisfaction.

These theories of motivation have played an important role in the development of the MBO concept and are responsible for the assumptions it makes about human behavior. MBO recognizes the desire of most managers to satisfy their higher level needs on the job, and takes the position that they are eager to assume responsibility, are achievement oriented (that is, have a desire

to get results), and if given the opportunity can exercise a high degree of self-control in job performance.

MBO places great emphasis on participation. The basic approach taken in practicing MBO is to directly involve employees in the planning, direction, and control of their jobs. The underlying assumption is that involvement leads to commitment, and if an employee is committed he will be motivated to perform in a manner that directly contributes to the achievement of organizational objectives. MBO develops a framework for participation; most decisions that affect a person's job are made jointly by him and his superior.

One might say that if results orientation is the heart of MBO, participation is the blood that flows through it. These two aspects (results and participation) of MBO are not just complementary, but are directly supportive of one another. An MBO program cannot be successful in the long run *unless both are present and an integral part of it.*

THE MBO SYSTEM

MBO is a process by which the members of an organization jointly establish its goals. Each member, with assistance from his superior, defines his area of responsibility; sets objectives that clearly state the results expected of him; and develops performance measures that can be used as guides for managing his unit and that will serve as standards for evaluating his contribution to the organization. There are four basic components of the MBO system: setting objectives, developing action plans, conducting periodic reviews, and appraising the annual performance.

Setting Objectives

Setting objectives is actually a three-step process. The first is concerned with identifying the areas of responsibility or activities that are considered critical to the long-run success of the organization. These are frequently referred to as key result areas and may include market position, profitability, productivity, innovation, personnel development, physical and financial resources, and social responsibility. Key result areas also are identified for each functional area and each unit in the organization.

Once key result areas have been defined, the second step is to determine performance measures for each area. For example, the key result areas for a production operation may be output, as measured by quantity, quality, and time; cost performance, as measured by direct and indirect expenses; and resource utilization, as measured by return on investment, turnover of inventories, and equipment utilization. The third step is to set objectives, which serve as standards against which performance is measured.

As an illustration of the process, a firm may identify one of its key result areas as market position, a key area for most marketing oriented firms. Second, one of the performance measures commonly used to indicate relative status in the marketplace is market share as measured by sales. Third, the firm may set an objective to increase its market share from 12 to 14 percent during the next twelve months.

In setting sound objectives for the organization and in turn for each individual unit, several principles should be followed:

Objectives should be related to the needs of the business and should support organizational goals.

Objectives should be clear, concise, and realistic.

Objectives should be measurable and quantified whenever possible.

Objectives should be guides to action; they should state what to achieve, not how to achieve it.

Objectives should be ambitious enough to offer a challenge so that a man can be proud when he achieves them.

Objectives should take into consideration internal and external constraints, that is, factors not subject to control by the man responsible for results.

Setting objectives is a joint undertaking, and they should be mutually agreed upon by the responsible individual and his superior.

Developing Action Plans

The planning function is concerned with setting objectives and developing the strategies, policies, and programs to achieve them. One of the problems most frequently encountered in firms that are practicing MBO is the lack of attention given to the development of action plans. Firms recognize the importance of sound objectives but, all too often, they lose sight of the total system. Although objectives provide the basis for planning and all of the other primary management functions, it is objectives and the plans for their achievement that give the organization the sense of direction and unity of purpose that are essential for long-run effectiveness.

The *first* concern of the manager in developing action plans is to divide into steps all of the necessary tasks and activities. This allows the manager to give attention to each phase of the plan. He should define the purpose of each step, state what is required to perform it, and set forth the results expected.

Second, the manager should note the relationships among steps, being especially careful to identify any sequences. Sequential steps tend to lengthen the time required for completion of the plan since the next step cannot begin until the previous one has been performed. Scheduling can be improved considerably if steps can be overlapped, and the time required to achieve objectives can be reduced if there is no need to delay one action until another has been completed.

Third, the manager decides who is responsible for each step. *Fourth*, he determines the resources needed. *Finally*, he estimates the time required to perform each step, and assigns specific dates for their completion. Once this has been done a schedule is set up showing the starting and completion dates for all steps. Firms practicing MBO commonly refer to this as targeting and specify a date for the accomplishment of each objective as well as set a time for the completion of each phase of the plan designed to achieve it.

Having completed the first two steps in the process of managing by objectives—setting objectives and developing action plans—the manager should have established a solid base, a position of strength, from which he can readily take advantage of any opportunities that may arise. He should also be able to deal successfully with obstacles that otherwise might reduce his ability to achieve predetermined objectives. Many practitioners contend that one of the major benefits of MBO is the change it brings about in managerial attitudes toward conditions (internal as well as external) that tend to reduce organizational effectiveness.

Under a well-conceived MBO system, the prevailing attitude is that a manager's job is to achieve his objectives, not change them. If for some reason it becomes difficult to achieve a given objective, his first job is to develop new plans (or modify existing ones) that take into consideration the difficulties encountered. The strategy is to change or modify plans, not objectives, unless conditions have changed in a way that makes achieving them unnecessary, irrelevant, or impossible.

The process of anticipating potential problem areas and tentatively deciding what might be done to overcome them is called contingency planning. Developing contingency plans forces managers to foresee situations that might affect their operations and prepare in advance for dealing with them if they occur. In doing so, managers become more flexible and able to cope with change in a positive manner.

The MBO system enables managers to respond more readily to deviations from standards and to overcome obstacles that may arise while they are carrying out their responsibilities. Managers learn not to just anticipate change but actually to incorporate it into the planning process, which greatly increases their ability to get results.

Conducting Periodic Reviews

Once objectives have been set and plans of action have been developed, the next step in the MBO process is to establish a control system that will monitor performance and determine if action being taken will result in achievement of stated objectives. The two basic components of a good control system are standards against which to measure performance and feed-back information that keeps organizational members apprised of progress toward objectives and reports significant deviations from standards.

A clear understanding of what constitutes good performance is fundamental to effective control. For firms practicing MBO, objectives serve as standards against which the individual can measure his performance. Good performance is de-

fined as the individual's ability to get results, and he is evaluated on the basis of progress being made.

The importance of the second basic component, feed-back information, is reflected in the principle that "motivation to accomplish results tends to increase as people are informed about matters affecting those results." In other words, people in an organization can be expected to perform with maximum effectiveness only if they are aware of the objectives sought, the purpose of their work, and how well they are doing in relation to those objectives.

Annual Performance Appraisal

The fourth basic component of the MBO system is annual performance appraisal, which has a twofold purpose: to review and evaluate what has been done, and to begin preparing for the next year. As the following figure indicates, performance appraisal, in addition to completing one MBO cycle, is responsible for initiating the next:

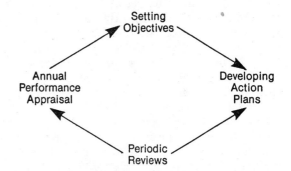

The review part of annual performance appraisal concentrates on the most important consideration in any managerial situation—results. The annual review is similar to that of the periodic reviews; the primary difference is the breadth and depth of treatment given to all aspects of the MBO program, and the totally integrated, holistic approach taken in the appraisal process.

Whereas periodic reviews are conducted for the most part on an individual basis, between superior and subordinate, the annual review incorporates all individual contributions into a composite for the organization. This requires more than just an evaluation of personnel; it necessitates finding out how well each organizational unit (for example, department, division, staff, and group) has performed, and combining all of these to ascertain the progress the organization has made.[4]

Whether it be of an individual or an organizational unit, the appraisal process is the same: review the mutually agreed upon objectives that the individual is responsible for; determine actual results; measure results against predetermined performance standards; and note any significant deviations from the standard that require further attention by the accountable individual.

If objectives have not been met, the accountable individual and his superior should concentrate on finding out why. Numerous studies have shown that there are a number of frequently encountered reasons for poor performance: the subordinate does not know what is expected of him; he does not know how he is doing in terms of the results expected; he cannot do what is expected because of inadequate training and education; he will not do what is expected because he is not motivated to perform efficiently; he lacks the organizational support necessary for effective performance; and he has a poor relationship with his boss. A sound MBO program is designed to greatly reduce—hopefully eliminate—most of these problem areas; however, they should not be ignored during the review process.

Two other factors may account for what would appear to be poor performance. The first is unrealistic objectives. In his desire to excel, a subordinate may set objectives that are too high, thus reducing his chances of accomplishment. The proper time to deal with this problem is when the objectives are being established by the subordinate and his superior, not during the annual performance appraisal.

The second consideration is poor performance caused by factors not under the control of the responsible individual. An individual should not be held accountable for results that become unrealistic due to situations over which he has no control. This does not mean that a manager has no obligation to try and solve problems that may prevent him from achieving his objectives. Solving problems is a part of his job. It does mean, however, that if the problem *and its solution* lie outside his area of responsibility, his performance appraisal should take this into account.

Developing the proper attitude toward performance appraisal can be a major contributor to a successful MBO program. The principal point is that identification of poor performance, especially the reasons for it, is a necessary step in the appraisal process, but it is not done for the purpose of punishing those who have failed to measure up. Rather, such information is valuable as input to the design of a development program that will provide the individual with the knowledge and skills necessary to improve job performance. Under MBO, the concept of appraisal enables the responsible individual to learn from past mistakes, not be punished for them.

The basic idea behind the annual performance appraisal is that the organization should know where it is before it begins planning for where it wants to go. The first step, which reviews objectives and evaluates performance, becomes the basis upon which next year's planning decisions are made. The organization takes what it has learned about its present status and the performance of its managers and uses the information to set new objectives and develop new action plans. In the process of completing this year's program the organization has begun planning for next year's without interruption and without any loss of continuity or purpose.

ORGANIZATIONAL BENEFITS OF MBO

The value of any management system should be measured by its contribution to organizational effectiveness. MBO has been proven effective in getting results, and many firms have found that it plays the leading role in the managerial process of achieving corporate objectives. Its contribution perhaps can best be appreciated by reviewing the major benefits that an organization can expect from managing by objectives.

Improved Management Performance. The best way to increase organizational effectiveness is to improve managerial efficiency—to improve the way managers manage. MBO provides a means of measuring the contribution of a manager. It is a manager's commitment to achieving objectives, his own and those of the organization, that determines long-run effectiveness.

Commitment comes as a result of the strong emphasis MBO places on participation in setting objectives by the managers who are responsible for achieving them; the importance of communication, especially between superior and subordinate; and fast and accurate feed-back of results to the individuals who are responsible for corrective action. Performance also improves when each manager knows precisely what he is responsible for in terms of results.

Improved Planning. Planning is more complete. Not only does the manager know what his objectives are, but there is mutual agreement on how they will be achieved. Discussion includes the subject of the resources that will be needed to support programs and the assistance required from those outside the manager's responsibility area.

Improved Coordination. Effective coordination has been referred to as "the essence of organization," and it cannot be achieved without a common purpose and a sense of direction. Well-defined objectives help to integrate the activities of complex organizations and to elicit the voluntary cooperation of those whose contributions are essential to their achievement.

Improved Control. MBO produces a dramatic shift of control over people to control over operations —in other words, a shift from evaluating the man to evaluating how well he manages. The organization practicing MBO judges the man on the basis of his ability to get results, and provides him with sufficient knowledge, skills, and information so that he can exercise individual control and not have to depend on his superior for the inputs needed for making sound control decisions.

Improved Flexibility. MBO fosters a more immediate response to deviations from standards be-

cause the manager knows his objectives and their order of priority. He has developed plans for achieving them, including the establishment of control measures that specify acceptable levels of performance.

As part of the process of developing action plans, the manager also is encouraged to anticipate potential problem areas and to develop contingency plans for dealing with them. He learns and acknowledges that he is operating in a dynamic environment and, in order to be successful, must take an active, not passive, interest in the future. He develops as a result of this thought process a positive attitude toward change and actually incorporates change into the planning process.

Improved Superior-Subordinate Relationships. Under MBO, the subordinate moves from a position of dependence to one of independence. He experiences greater freedom, is directly involved in decisions that affect him and his job, and receives more open communication about the organization and his role in it. The subordinate views his relationship with his boss as supportive, and, for the help he receives in satisfying his needs, he is willing to commit his best efforts to meeting the requirements of the organization.

Personal Development. Inherent in MBO are several features that contribute directly to personal development and growth as a manager. MBO encourages the manager to assume responsibility for his own performance; at the same time it provides the opportunities for increasing his knowledge, skills, and experiences so that he can perform well. Management development programs are no longer ends in themselves, but the means by which the manager gains the competence, confidence, and motivation to manage effectively.

Peter F. Drucker, in his classic *The Practice of Management*, stated the conditions that he considers essential to organizational effectiveness:

Any business enterprise must build a true team and weld individual efforts into a common effort. Each member of the enterprise contributes something different, but they must all contribute toward a common goal. Their efforts must all pull in the same direction, and their contributions must fit together to produce a whole—without gaps, without friction, without unnecessary duplication of effort.

Business performance therefore requires that each job be directed toward the objectives of the whole business. And in particular each manager's job must be focused on the success of the whole. The performance that is expected of the manager must be derived from the performance goals of the business, his results must be measured by the contribution they make to the success of the enterprise. The manager must know and understand what the business goals demand of him in terms of performance, and his superior must know what contribution to demand and expect of him—and must judge him accordingly.[5]

In evaluating any management system, these are the conditions that should be met. The evidence would suggest that the MBO system meets them exceedingly well.

NOTES

1. Peter F. Drucker, *The Practice of Management* (New York: Harper and Row, Publishers, 1954), Chapters 11 and 12.

2. Marshall E. Dimock, *The Executive in Action* (New York: Harper and Brothers, 1945), p. 54. For a general review of objectives in management, see Dalton E. McFarland, *Management: Principles and Practices,* 3rd ed. (New York: Macmillan Company, 1970), Chapter 7.

3. George S. Odiorne, *Management by Objectives: a System of Managerial Leadership* (New York: Pitman Publishing Corporation, 1965).

4. Performance appraisals may be held other than annually. For instance, a firm operating under the project or program management concept may want to conduct performance appraisals at the completion of each project. For most firms, however, annual performance appraisals are appropriate, and as a result most MBO programs operate on a twelve-month cycle.

5. Drucker, *Practice of Management,* p. 121.

MBO IN FOUR
MANAGEMENT SYSTEMS

HEINZ WEIHRICH

*This process may fail when it is superimposed
on the organization without understanding
of the existing climate.*

Many of the largest companies in the United States now use management by objectives (MBO), yet only a few have realized its full potential. As currently practiced, MBO frequently is superimposed on the existing organization without sufficient effort to evaluate the organizational climate and make changes so that the managerial system is congruent with the MBO philosophy. For most organizations, MBO requires a change in managerial style—a new way of managing. Rensis Likert and his associates have developed a model of four systems of management which facilitates the assessment of the existing organizational environment.[1] The purpose of this article is to approximate the relationships between these four managerial systems and the steps in the MBO process.

The practice of MBO not only differs widely among companies, but the MBO concept itself has changed and evolved over the years. In the early stages of its development, MBO was viewed primarily as an appraisal tool to overcome the weaknesses of the traditional appraisal approaches that focused on personality traits rather than performance.

Heinz Weihrich, "MBO in Four Management Systems," pp. 51–56, *MSU Business Topics,* Autumn 1976. Reprinted by permission of the publisher, Division of Research, Graduate School of Business Administration, Michigan State University.

The motivating power of MBO soon became evident. Participation facilitates the integration of personal and organizational objectives. The individual derives satisfaction by contributing to the aims of the organization. In addition, individuals are encouraged to set personal development objectives. Consequently, managers—and also nonmanagers—recognize that MBO facilitates professional growth and self-development.

In the earlier stages of the development of the MBO concept, emphasis primarily was on short-term objectives, which seldom included aims that went beyond one year. (The terms *aims, goals,* and *objectives* are used interchangeably.) This, of course, can have negative consequences because the short-term focus may result in undesirable managerial behavior. In an effort to meet this year's objectives, long-term opportunities may be ignored. Recognizing these limitations, some firms have included long-range and strategic planning in their approach. This certainly is a step in the right direction, but it should not be the end in the development of MBO. To be fully effective, MBO must become a comprehensive system of managing that integrates MBO in the total managerial process. This does not mean generating a lot of paperwork; rather, MBO must become a way of managing.[2]

The focus here will be on the essentials of the MBO process. Simply stated, MBO involves the steps of (1) setting objectives, (2) developing action plans, (3) implementation, and (4) controlling of organizational performance and appraising individual results. These steps will serve as a framework for this discourse.

FOUR SYSTEMS OF MANAGEMENT

Likert and his associates thoroughly studied many organizations and their effectiveness. Managerial styles and their related organizational factors were identified and grouped into four systems. Likert named System 1 *exploitative-authoritative;* System 2, *benevolent-authoritative;* System 3, *consultative;* and System 4, *participative group.*

System 1 is highly autocratic with little trust and confidence. Motivation is through fear, threat, and punishment. Communication is downward and decisions are made almost entirely at the top of the organization.

System 2 is marked by a condescending approach to management. Motivation is through rewards and some punishment. Communication is still mostly downward. Although there is some delegation, policy control is at the top.

System 3 management is characterized by substantial, but not complete, confidence in subordinates. Motivation is through rewards and involvement; but there is also some punishment. Communication flows down and up, and subordinates are generally consulted in decisions related to their jobs.

System 4 management is highly participative, with a great deal of confidence and trust in subordinates. This system is marked by effective teamwork and individuals feel motivated to achieve the goals of the organization. Communication is downward and upward, as well as with peers. Decision making is well integrated at all levels of the organization. Goals are set primarily by the group, with little or no resistance to the aims.

It is evident that these different systems of management will have an impact on the steps in the MBO process; this is the focal point of the following conjectural discussion.

MBO IN THE FOUR SYSTEMS

Management by objectives is a process that requires interaction among superior, subordinate, and peers. It involves managerial leadership, effective motivation, open communication, decision making, and measuring of performance.

MBO in System 1: Exploitative-Authoritative

In this system, management has no trust in subordinates, uses mainly threats and punishment, has very little real communication, makes decisions basically at the top, issues orders to lower levels, and concentrates control at the top. This environment leaves a distinct mark on the way the steps of MBO are carried out.

Step 1: Setting Objectives

In this kind of organization, objectives are set at the top, or by the superior in an autocratic manner. Subordinates, therefore, have little or no opportunity to set their own objectives. Nor do they provide any inputs to the departmental aims. In general, top management determines objectives, which may or may not be communicated down the organization structure. The set of objectives is rather limited and only a few alternative aims are considered. If some objectives are set by organizational units, they seldom are coordinated with other departments.

The set of individual objectives usually pertains to performance only and does not include personal development objectives. Because managers do not see how they personally benefit from MBO, there is a great deal of resistance to writing down objectives and making commitments.

Step 2: Action Planning

As in the goal-setting process, superiors are very directive. They determine the tasks and develop action plans for their subordinates. There is little awareness that in most situations there are alternative courses of action that can be taken to achieve objectives. Also, the superior establishes the time-frame for the tasks with little input from those who have to carry out the activities. Consequently, there are often severe problems in coordinating and timing the tasks of the various organizational units, especially when the activities are interdependent. And even if extensive action plans are developed, they are not communicated to all who contribute to them or who will be affected by them.

Step 3: Implementation

Top management and superiors determine the implementation of plans. Subordinates are simply required to follow orders. Thus, subordinates may be indifferent to MBO or they may even boycott the efforts of upper management. The program is mechanistic and rigid, with heavy emphasis on filling out forms and meeting the bureaucratic requirements. There is an emphasis on activities and on busy work, rather than on results. Individuals overtly or covertly resist MBO and take little initiative to utilize the potential benefits of the system. It is evident that such an organization does not manage in a way that is congruent with the MBO philosophy, which places responsibility on the subordinate and encourages initiative.

Step 4: Controlling and Appraising

Organizational control is rigid and concentrated at the top. Moreover, control standards are externally imposed on departments and individuals. Consequently, inappropriate standards—that is, those that measure the wrong things—may be set and pursued.

Performance appraisal provides little opportunity for self-control or self-development. Instead, the superior is viewed as a judge who acts in a punitive manner. Subordinates, of course, have a low degree of trust in their superiors. In the appraisal meeting, attention is given only to past performance, although the past cannot be changed. Feed-forward control, which is designed to prevent undesirable deviations from occurring in the future, is completely ignored. Yet, it is the future that provides opportunities for individual as well as organizational growth and development.

MBO in System 2: Benevolent-Authoritative

In a System 2 environment, management has a condescending confidence in subordinates. Rewards and some punishment are used to motivate individuals. The flow of information is still primarily downward. Although there is some delegation, policy decisions are made at the top. Comments are invited when establishing objectives. Control is exercised to a great extent at the top.

Step 1: Setting Objectives

There is a condescending use of authority. Objectives are usually set by the superior, but some inputs from subordinates are invited. There may even be some participation in setting objectives. But objectives are still communicated from the top of the organization downward with only limited upward information flow. There are some alternative objectives considered and some effort is made to coordinate the objectives of different organizational units. If personal development objectives are considered, they are set mostly by superiors.

Step 2: Developing Action Plans

Tasks and responsibilities are determined mainly by the superior, although subordinates provide some inputs to the plans to achieve the objectives. But the information flow is mostly downward, and some problems in the coordination of plans may develop. In such an organization there may even be some plans for contingencies.

Step 3: Implementation

The implementation of MBO is characterized by a benevolent attitude on the part of superiors. Subordinates, then, largely follow direction without a real commitment to the MBO program. Because of the limited amount of upward and horizontal communication, some difficulties may develop in the coordination of activities within the organizational unit as well as among departments. Some covert resistance to MBO also may be encountered. If MBO is accepted, it is only with superficial commitment.

Step 4: Controlling and Appraising

Control is still primarily at the top and upper management, with insufficient responsibility placed on subordinates. Inappropriate standards for control may be set and pursued. During appraisal, the superior plays an active part, using rewards and punishment. There is little participation by subordinates in the evaluation of their own performance. In such an environment, self-appraisal is usually not feasible.

MBO in System 3:
Consultative

System 3 is characterized by considerable trust, rewards, and occasional punishment, an up and down information flow, and a moderate amount of teamwork. Although top management makes general decisions, more specific ones are made at lower levels. The control function is moderately delegated to lower levels.

Step 1: Setting Objectives

Subordinates are consulted on important matters, and there is considerable participation in setting goals. Also, objectives are fairly well communicated, both vertically and horizontally. Consequently, there is usually a good coordination of objectives. Goals are set in several crucial areas. Besides performance goals, personal development objectives are set by subordinates in consultation with their superiors, who may, however, reserve the right to make changes.

Step 2: Developing Action Plans

Subordinates are consulted in developing the action plans. Moreover, there is considerable participation in deciding on the course of action. Plans are quite well communicated to those who need to know. Consequently, there is a fairly good coordination of tasks as well as responsibilities. Plans for contingencies are developed in consultation with subordinates.

Step 3: Implementation

In the implementation phase, subordinates are consulted and there is a moderate commitment to MBO in most parts of the organization. The information flows reasonably well, both vertically and horizontally. In operational decision making, inputs from peers as well as subordinates are given serious consideration.

Step 4: Controlling and Appraising

Controls are installed at different points in order to measure performance. The standards give a moderately accurate picture of organizational accomplishments. There is considerable participation by subordinates in the evaluation of their own performance, and some problem solving occurs during the appraisal meeting. Although the focus is on past performance, some attention is given to preventing undesirable deviations of performance in the future.

MBO in System 4:
Participative Group

In System 4 there is extensive trust and confidence in subordinates. Moreover, people at all levels feel responsible for results and share the control function. With a great deal of teamwork and free flow of information, decisions at various levels are well integrated.

Step 1: Setting Objectives

The supportive environment is conducive to real participation in setting objectives. This results not only in an integration of personal objectives and organizational demands, but it also elicits commitment toward the achievement of aims. Before the set of objectives is finalized, many alternatives are considered. Also, objectives are not set in isolation, rather they are communicated to all who have a need to know. The effect is a well coordinated network of goals throughout the organization, resulting in a synergistic effect. The organizational climate encourages individuals to set high performance standards that are congruent with the aims of the team.

Step 2: Developing Action Plans

In almost all situations, alternative courses of action can be taken to achieve the objectives. System 4 fosters creativity and is conducive to identifying, evaluating, and deciding on the tasks and activities necessary to achieve results. Individual and organizational plans are integrated; system optimization is accomplished through the team effort of individuals whose tasks are seen as being interrelated.

Step 3: Implementation

Managers—and even nonmanagers—at all organizational levels are committed to the achievement of common goals. With the goals set, individuals can use their creativity in finding better ways of doing things. Consequently, there are many opportunities for personal and professional growth. The organization is seen as an interlocking system. If conflicts occur—and they do in any organization—they are effectively resolved through open communication based on trust and confidence. Rather than individuals pursuing their own—sometimes conflicting—goals, it is a true team approach that results in synergistic effects.

Step 4: Controlling and Appraising

In the System 4 environment, control of performance is at critical points in the organization. Deviations from standards are analyzed and steps are taken to prevent undesirable ones from reoccurring in the future. In fact, the focus is on forward-looking controls that attempt to prevent deviations rather than to correct them.

During appraisal, the superior does not sit in judgment over his subordinates. Instead of acting as a judge, the superior is like a coach interested in helping subordinates to improve their performance. Appraisal, then, is primarily self-appraisal aimed at promoting professional development, and the free flow of communication results in a fair evaluation of individual performance.

Implications

While management by objectives is one of the most widely used approaches to managing, not all organizations have been successful in implementing it. The MBO approach may fail when it is superimposed on the organization without proper understanding of the existing climate. It is, for example, unrealistic to expect that managers who have operated for many years under System 1 can suddenly become participative team members (System 4). In fact, forcing these drastic changes without coaching may disturb the organizational equilibrium in a way that results in undesirable consequences.

To effectively implement MBO, it must be understood that MBO is a process as well as a philosophy of managing. If this philosophy is completely incongruent with the organizational climate, problems will occur. What is needed is a systems approach to organizational development that focuses on both the organizational climate and the MBO steps of setting objectives, action planning, implementation, as well as control and appraising.

An alternative to the traditional "try and hope for the best" approach to implementing MBO is *data based organizational development*. This involves the measurement of critical organizational characteristics such as suggested by Likert. The data derived by using his questionnaire facilitate the grouping of organizational factors into System 1 (exploitative-authoritative), System 2 (benevolent-authoritative), System 3 (consultative), and System 4 (participative group). Likert and his colleagues found that over a period of time organizations that moved *toward* System 4 also became more effective. Similarly, the author suggests, most organizations will become more effective when the steps in the MBO process are carried out in ways approximating those described in System 4. But this change will have to come gradually and must be accompanied by changes in the organizational environment. The framework of the four systems and the relationships to the steps in MBO as discussed in this article can facilitate this change process.

The practicing manager, of course, is interested in operationalizing this new approach to the implementation of MBO. Although there are different ways, the focus here is on the *action research model* that may involve: (1) Collection of data and diagnosis of the organization. Based on this information, a profile of organizational characteristics can be developed and grouped into Systems 1 to 4. (2) Discussion of these findings within the organization and a comparison with the characteristics of the four steps in the MBO process. (3) Joint planning of actions to change the organization and the MBO process in the direction of System 4. This also requires the teaching of the MBO concepts as well as MBO philosophy. (4) A repetition of these three processes is then repeated until MBO becomes an integral part of dynamic organizational development.

The approach suggested here differs substantially from traditional ones that often superimpose MBO on the organization. There are several advantages of this new approach for implementing MBO. First, it is a systems approach that recognizes many critical organizational variables. Second, it is data-based, starting with the existing organization and moving toward an ideal one in a planned manner. Third, it is dynamic, flexible, and tailored for a particular organization. Fourth, the emphasis is on collaborative management with a great deal of team effort. Fifth, it is an ongoing process that continuously aims at improving the organization.

In conclusion, to be effective, MBO must be congruent with organizational characteristics. It is suggested that the manner in which the steps in the MBO process are carried out will differ for the four management systems. The wise administrator will collect data on the existing managerial system and develop a change strategy that takes into account both MBO and the organizational environment. Effective implementation of MBO requires time and effort, but the results can be rewarding.

NOTES

1. Rensis Likert, *New Patterns of Management* (New York: McGraw-Hill Book Company, 1961); also, Rensis Likert, *The Human Organization* (New York: McGraw-Hill Book Company, 1967).

2. Heinz Weihrich, "A Study of the Integration of Management by Objectives with Key Managerial Activities and the Relationship to Selected Effectiveness Measures" (Ph.D. diss., University of California, Los Angeles, 1973).

BEHAVIORAL PROBLEMS WITH MANAGEMENT BY OBJECTIVES[1]

BRUCE D. JAMIESON

In the last few years a growing body of MBO literature has been emerging. At the moment, this consists largely of a number of case histories and "do-it-yourself" approaches, and, unfortunately, all too few critical analyses and reports of empirical research. While claims and counterclaims concerning the merits and disadvantages of MBO are common in contemporary management writings, because of the paucity of carefully designed and well documented field studies, it is difficult to obtain a balanced perspective concerning MBO as a technique of management. MBO is no managerial panacea, but unfortunately some of the published material has presented it in this light, albeit unintentionally.

As a result, some companies may have been attracted by the claimed advantages of MBO, and may even have begun installing systems without being fully aware of the concomitant organizational and individual problems which can and will arise. When these have subsequently occurred, the organization may not have been prepared sufficiently well to deal with the difficulties, and the success of the scheme has been placed in jeopardy.

While attention has been given to some of the major problems associated with the installation and maintenance of MBO programs, one class of

Reprinted with the permission of the *Academy of Management Journal* and Bruce D. Jamieson.

problems has not received sufficient detailed examination, although some mention has been made by writers *en passant*. These are what may be termed the behavioral problems associated with the practice of MBO. They arise largely from the way individual managers behave, or the ways in which they react to MBO, rather than from factors where the behavioral content is of less importance, as e.g., with the identification of corporate objectives, costs of installation, integration with budgetary control, and so on.

The distinction is a relative one. In management, one seldom meets a problem which is completely behavioral, but similarly one seldom meets a management problem which does not have some behavioral aspects to it. This observation is true of particular aspects of MBO, each of which, while not strictly behavioral, certainly has definite behavioral consequences. Thus an organizational survey and feasibility study, which is a desirable, if not necessary, preliminary stage to introducing MBO, can be shown to have very definite behavioral consequences. Similarly important behavioral consequences can be seen to stem from decisions concerning the level of entry (12), the time scale of introduction (5), the recommended time period between goal setting and appraisal (16), and the amount of paper work and time involvement, necessitated by the scheme (14).[2]

To date Levinson (9) has produced the only

major critique of MBO from a behavioral perspective. In his article, appropriately entitled "Management by Whose Objectives?", Levinson argues that MBO schemes, as currently practiced in most organizations, are self defeating because they are predicated on a reward-punishment psychology which serves to increase the pressure on the individual. Levinson, whose focus is very much on the appraisal and counselling phases of MBO, notes several major problems in actual practice, including the static nature of job descriptions, the lack of weight given in job descriptions to areas of discretion open to the individual, the failure to acknowledge the interdependence of managerial work and the total managerial situation, the brief time period for objective setting which prevents necessary interaction among peers and the difficulties superiors experience in appraisal. The thrust of Levinson's article is on actual practice as he believes it operates, and he states that he does not reject either MBO or performance appraisal out of hand. One of his suggestions for improvement, namely group appraisal and goal setting, has been suggested elsewhere (4, 15). Levinson also rightly stresses the importance of considering the personal goals of the individual—a feature which this writer would consider to be fundamental to any approach which claims to be management by objectives.

Observations that MBO in practice may fall well short of the ideal, or even fail completely, in spite of detailed planning and careful organization, suggest that such systems give rise to critical behavioral problems. It is this writer's belief that there are several such problems which must be resolved or controlled if an organization is to achieve a fully viable MBO system.

MBO PROBLEM AREAS

Management Style

Writers such as Likert (10) have demonstrated that the managerial style prevalent in an organization has a direct effect on many performance indices. MBO may well involve considerable innovative behavior and some degree of interpersonal risk taking. It therefore requires a supportive managerial style. If, however, the organization

is characterized by authoritarian management, highly centralized decision making, and simplistic motivational assumptions, then MBO is unlikely to succeed until the climate is modified. As Levinson says, "If the organization ethos is one of rapacious internal competition, back-biting and distrust, there is little point in talking about motivation, human needs or commitment" (9).

Top Management Support

Closely related to the previous problem is that of top management support. The active involvement and support of top management and the chief executive in particular appear to be essential, regardless of whether MBO is introduced at corporate or divisional levels or in a subsidiary company (6). Their role is of vital importance in the analysis of the organization's current status, in long-term planning and the setting of corporate objectives. And without these factors MBO at best approximates appraisal by results.

Adapting to Change

Organizational change is an inevitable consequence of MBO. This typically is recognized and accepted by those responsible for the design and introduction of the program. It can also often be predicted by those who will operate within the new framework, and this possibly accounts for some of the resistance to MBO displayed by some managers, particularly in the introductory stages. Implicit, then, in any decision to implement MBO is the assumption that managers will need to make some adaptation. Three specific problems of adapting to change do occur:

Changes in Organizational Structure—MBO can uncover (and even create) problems of organization within jobs, within units, or at a corporate level. The net result may involve a not inconsiderable upheaval, as units are restructured, responsibilities re-assigned and authority levels altered (17). This should not necessarily be regarded as a negative concomitant of MBO although the consequences for a given individual may sometimes be so. In fact, organizational change should be regarded as not only a probable, but also a functional consequence of the introduction of

MBO—certainly if a longer time perspective is adopted.

Changes in Authority and Control—MBO increases the degree of self-control which can be exercised by individual managers. It should be recalled that Drucker's original concept was "management by objectives and self-control" (3). While top management initially may welcome the principle of such job enrichment, the eventual consequences may not be appreciated. To operate with this degree of self-control, managers need both objectives and feedback. This suggests that a manager, regardless of his level, will require adequate relevant information, in order to participate fully in setting useful objectives and subsequently participating in evaluating his own performance. This often requires the organization to provide more information at lower levels—information which previously may have been restricted to higher level executives (17). This may include, for example, providing information to lower levels concerning company-wide and divisional objectives and performances. One consequence of this increased information flow, in an effective MBO program, may be an increase in the amount of evaluation and criticism senior managers receive from their subordinates. Thus it is desirable that managers, particularly senior executives, should examine the long term functional and dysfunctional effects of an increased information flow and decide how best to adapt to a modified pattern and type of authority and control.

Managers Who Do Not Adapt to MBO—This problem deals specifically with managers who do not adapt to a MBO system, once it has become organizational policy. Pascoe (13) found in his study that managers could be classified roughly into three groups, with respect to their responses to MBO.

• Those who are enthusiastic about MBO.

• Those who see advantages but are not convinced—the mild skeptics.

• Those who participate because they have to. They may dislike aspects of MBO or even consider it a waste of time.

His impressions suggested that each group contained about a third of the managers involved, all of whom came from a naval service unit in the British Ministry of Defence. The incidence of failure to adapt may well be quite high in the third group. Certainly MBO represents a substantial change in management behavior. Any large scale change is going to face resistance and some individual cases of failure, and the executive suite is no different from the shop floor in this respect.

Managers who accept the philosophy but lack the essential skills can usually be trained to a satisfactory level of performance but managers who reject the philosophy are a more difficult problem. An organization which has committed itself to MBO, but faces intransigence among some managers, may face a series of "shape-up or ship out" situations, or at least a series of trade-off decisions concerning the future of such executives.

Interpersonal Skills

The superior-subordinate appraisal and goal-setting interview can be considered as one of the two major elements in the total MBO process, the other being the setting of corporate objectives. It is also the point at which the MBO process is most vulnerable. Many managers are not skilled interviewers and the MBO type of interview, which is essentially a counselling process, is technically more demanding than the fact gathering and decision making of, say, a selection interview. It is in fact a complex social interaction, where the paths to desired outcomes cannot always be clearly seen nor formulated in advance, and where structure usually is lacking.

Ideally, these interviews should take a problem-solving approach (11) where both subordinate and superior participate in appraisal and goal setting. If practice is to approach this ideal, it is the opinion of this writer that considerable training for all managers in counselling and interviewing skills must be carried out. There appears to be no alternative. Managers involved with MBO may obtain some benefit from reading texts on interviewing and MBO; they may gain some idea of superior-subordinate interaction from transcripts of MBO interviews (15). But these are supplementary aids—there is no substitute for directed, controlled and supervised training in MBO interviewing with concentrated role-play practice of the essential inter-personal skills required, if the negative aspects of the appraisal situation are to be avoided. Such training can be handled by small workshop groups of managers and MBO advisers where there is a balance of theory and directed practice. Attention in such a setting can also be given to problems such as:

• MBO interviewing with employees whose performance is unsatisfactory.
• MBO interviewing and the employee who is performing well (possibly in a necessary routine job), and has no wish nor need to set improved goals.
• Problems arising from superior-subordinate incompatibility.
• Dealing with conflicting organizational and individual needs.
• Planning and preparation for interviews.
• Relating salary to performance.

One cannot stress too strongly how important a problem area this is. Yet in the opinion of this writer it is a problem area which can be largely overcome—at least to the point where MBO interviewing is effective and beneficial to both superior and subordinate alike.

Job Descriptions and Key Results Analyzed

An adequate approach to MBO demands that comprehensive job descriptions be available and kept fully up to date. Yet experience indicates that many job descriptions can be rightly criticized as static and of limited utility. A job description should be constantly revised, and indeed, each MBO appraisal session could well include a consideration of the adequacy of the subordinate's current job description and possible needs for revision. Humble approaches the problem by beginning with a Key Results Analysis (6). The K.R.A. essentially consists of those aspects of the manager's job description which are seen as critical in the performance of his job. This is prepared by the subordinate and the

MBO adviser or analyst working together, and is then discussed with the subordinate's manager, and finally approved by the manager's manager.
Some particular problems can arise:

• The time need for a K.R.A.—this cannot be hurried, and may take several hours.
• Difficulties in identifying the particular key results—this is where the expertise and analytical skill of the adviser is important.
• Differences of perception between the manager and his superior with regard to what aspects constitute the subordinate's key results.
• The defensive reactions of some managers who dislike the notion of detailed analyses being performed on their jobs.

Setting and Framing Objectives

The setting and framing of objectives often causes some difficulty particularly when managers are inexperienced in MBO techniques (8). Specific difficulties such as the following occur:

• Phrasing objectives with clarity and precision.
• Obtaining "measurable" objectives.
• Relating individual unit to divisional and corporate objectives.
• Setting challenging but realistic objectives.
• Avoiding the setting of "comfortable" objectives.
• Avoiding an overemphasis on more easily measured production goals.

As was suggested with interpersonnel skills generally, mastery of this aspect requires directed practice, preferably using a workshop format. The use of worksheets which systematize this aspect may aid the process. These can assist the subordinate and manager by providing a systematic plan for working from corporate objectives relevant to the subordinate's job, through his job description and/or key results analysis, to the specific objectives to be met. Details on actions to be taken to meet objectives, precisely how performance will be measured or assessed, barriers to goals, costs, some expression of priority of goals, date deadlines, and additional factors involved, can be included.

The Difficult Problems of Measurement

The success of a MBO scheme depends in no small measure upon the development of reliable and valid indices of performance. Essentially, this provides the answer to the question—has the goal been achieved?

In many areas, such as production and sales, relatively unambiguous criteria may be obtained:

units made per time period
cost levels
per cent delay time
sales levels
scrap levels
inventory levels, etc.

These are usually amenable to raw data or ratio quantification even if some situational correction is necessary. In other areas, particularly in staff functions (e.g. personnel, R and D, planning) such clear-cut measures may not exist. Numerical or verbal rating scales may be used. A goal or objective tied to a completion date is verifiable and can provide the same benefits in a program of this type as an apparently more precise production goal.

Levinson (9) considers the problem of objectivity and notes that a heavy subjective element necessarily enters into every appraisal and goal-setting experience. This is true and it should be accepted by managers. After all, a considerable part of management involves subjective behavior in that judgment is involved. But the exercise of judgment does not inevitably lead to error, and indeed, in some cases, a considered rating or judgment of performance may be more valid and accurate than a simple quantifiable measure. However, Levinson does very rightly stress that too much emphasis on quantification per se, may lead to the subtle and important nonmeasurable elements of the task being sacrificed.

In the writer's experience, measurement is the single problem which managers working with MBO most often raise. It seems less troublesome to managers who have had prior experience with a well-designed performance appraisal scheme. With managers lacking this experience some attention given to basic scaling and ratings during MBO training workshops seems to help.

Personal Objectives

Levinson (9) states that the MBO process ignores the individual's personal goals in attending solely to organizational objectives and that if this is the case the goal setting will lack any significant incentive power. He suggests that the organization's task is one of first understanding the man's needs, and then, with him, assessing how well they can be met in the organization, which is attempting to meet its own objectives. While this writer is in substantial agreement with Levinson's position, it should be accepted that the MBO process should actively take account of and consider personal goals only if the subordinate wishes. If this occurs, then some focus will need to be given to the inter-relationship of personal and organizational goals. To expect to achieve complete identity between the two sets of goals, is naive. Rather the aim should be, at best, to maximize compatibility. It seems to this writer that a MBO approach is more likely to achieve such a goal and to be able to evaluate the significance of and take action on personal-organizational goal discrepancies, than an approach where the goal-setting is solely the responsibility of the superior.

Inevitably some conflicts will emerge where organizational and individual goals are incompatible. If some degree of compromise is not possible, then the organization or the individual faces a decision situation concerning whether or not the incompatibility is too serious to be offset by the other need satisfactions present. Certainly no organization can permit the widespread satisfaction of personal goals at the expense of organizational goal-achievement.

Control of the Means of Goal Achievement

A problem which is commonly met occurs when a manager, to achieve a goal, must rely partly on the behavior of others (i.e. work as a member of a team), or be supplied with materials or help from others, factors over which he may have little or no control. It has been suggested that MBO procedures should recognize this problem and allow for the interdependent nature of many managerial jobs (1). MBO programs, therefore, should include group goal setting, group definition of tasks, group appraisal of contribution to the group's effort, and where appropriate, shared compensation based on group performance. Furthermore, allowances must be made where goal achievement is going to be dependent upon factors quite beyond the manager's control. The essential element is that of flexibility. Goal setting and appraisal may be group or individual, and goals need to be considered as subject to modification should external factors intrude.

MBO Quality Control

There is a danger that objective oriented systems may have only a short term impact. Enthusiasm and support may wane, and the need to cope with the procedural demands and interpersonal complexities of some MBO systems may force managers into compliance with only minimal formal requirements or, at best, superficial support. Certainly in this situation, there is little hope of identification with, or internalization of the system (7). As a result the standards of MBO performance deteriorate sharply and one can observe symptoms such as:

• Repeated postponement of goal setting and appraisal sessions.
• Increase in authoritarian goal setting.
• Overemphasis on easily measured goals.
• Falling off of top management support, e.g. during difficult trading periods.
• Reverting to personality and trait appraisals.
• Static job descriptions which take no account of organizational changes.

To maintain the system and to make it become part of the continuing management process, two ingredients seem essential:

• The continuing support of top management, particularly of the chief executive.
• A continuing "quality control" check on MBO procedures and skills by, for example, the MBO advisers or Personnel Staff.

This latter aspect will involve these specialists in a continuing MBO training role, by providing initial training for new employees and remedial and review training, where necessary, for the remainder of the staff who are involved.

These are the core behavioral problems associated with MBO, particularly involving the appraisal and goal setting processes. There are others but they tend to arise due to the nature of the organization rather than from the application of MBO per se. For example, Wickens (16) notes that the informal organization can have a significant influence on the outcomes of a MBO system.

While structural and design problems are generally corrigible, even if the solution proves expensive, the behavioral problems are much more resistant to solution and continue to re-appear. It should be noted, too, that many books on MBO either pay lip service to problems of this sort or ignore them completely. Yet it is probably not an exaggeration to say that any one of these problems has the potential to wreck a MBO program.

CONCLUSION

It is still difficult to gain a clear perspective on the efficacy of MBO in terms of corporate and individual performance. There is a distressing lack of well-documented and well-controlled research using a before-after measurement design. Partial field experiments, case studies and survey reports of reactions to MBO have been published, but these, together with the available case studies, are not enough to provide sufficient evidence.

Certainly one would be surprised if the setting of corporate objectives, the identification of key results areas, the flexible approach to objective setting, the involvement of managers in planning and their participation in decision making did not collectively have some positive effects on unit, divisional, or corporate performance. What is still not clear is how much, if any, each aspect contributes to the final improvement. It is possible that the improved performance, generally claimed, is largely a function of what can be termed the rationalization of planning resulting from detailed and coordinated corporate unit and individual objectives, and that the second major element—individual participation in appraisal and goal setting—is largely superfluous. At least one study provides some evidence for such a viewpoint (2). On the other hand, it is possible that both elements are necessary, if the effectiveness of objectives oriented systems is to be maximized. The only means by which this situation can be clarified appears to be by way of large scale field experiments.

Should it be shown subsequently, as this writer believes it will, that the individual participation element is critical to maximizing the outcomes of MBO, it is clear that such schemes, particularly those which emphasize the superior subordinate goal-setting and appraisal process, will still face very real problems. Carefully designed training programs, with emphasis on workshop sessions to teach the necessary skills, may help to improve the participants' handling of MBO. Giving attention to such problems will not guarantee success; ignoring them, however, will make failure almost certain.

NOTES

1. The author wishes to express his appreciation to Professor A. M. Bourn of the University of Liverpool for his helpful suggestions on the original draft of this paper.

2. It has been suggested that the effectiveness of MBO is inversely related to the number of forms used, see Howell (5).

REFERENCES

1. Brandis, J. "Extending M.B.O. Down the Line," *Management by Objectives,* Vol. 1, July (1971), 32–38.

2. Carroll, S. J., and H. L. Tosi. "Goal Characteristics and Personality Factors in a Management by Objectives Program," *Administrative Science Quarterly,* Vol. 15 (1970), 295–305.

3. Drucker, P. F. *The Practice of Management* (New York: Harper, 1954).

4. Gill, J., and C. F. Molander. "Beyond Management by Objectives," *Personnel Management,* Vol. 1, August (1970), 18–20.

5. Howell, R. A. "Managing by Objectives: A Three-stage System," *Business Horizons,* Vol. 13, No. 1 (1970), 41–45.

6. Humble, J. W. *Improving Business Results* (Maidenhead, U.K.: McGraw-Hill, 1967).

7. Kelman, H. C. "Processes of Opinion Change," *Public Opinion Quarterly,* Vol. 25 (1961), 57–78.

8. Lasagna, J. B. "Make Your M.B.O. Pragmatic," *Harvard Business Review,* Vol. 49, No. 6 (1971), 64–69.

9. Levinson, H. "Management by Whose Objectives?", *Harvard Business Review,* Vol. 48, No. 4 (1970), 125–134.

10. Likert, R. *The Human Organization* (New York: McGraw-Hill, 1967).

11. Maier, N. R. F. "Three Types of Appraisal Interview," *Personnel,* Vol. 34, No. 2 (1958), 27–40.

12. Odiorne, G. S. *Management by Objectives* (New York: Pitman, 1965).

13. Pascoe, B. J. "The Introduction of Management by Objectives into the Royal Naval Supply and Transport Service of the Ministry of Defence," *O. and M. Bulletin,* Vol. 24, August (1969), 139–152.

14. Tosi, H. L., and S. J. Carroll. "Managerial Reaction to Management by Objectives," *Academy of Management Journal,* Vol. 11 (1968), 415–426.

15. Valentine, R. F. *Performance Objectives for Managers* (New York: American Management Association, 1966).

16. Wickens, J. D. "Management by Objectives: An Appraisal," *Journal of Management Studies,* Vol. 5 (1968), 365–379.

17. Wikstrom, W. S. "Management by Objectives or Appraisal by Results," *Conference Board Record,* July 1966, pp. 27–31.

9

ORGANIZATION DEVELOPMENT AND CHANGE

In this chapter we examine the broad concept of organizational development (OD). The concept of OD refers to planned and systematic changes initiated by management to make the organization more effective in its present environment or prepare the organization for some future change. The readings in this section pose a variety of methods for changing and improving skills, attitudes, and behavior, in order to render members of an organization more effective in their respective organizational roles. Of great importance in any OD effort is the need to integrate individual objectives and goals with organizational objectives and goals. The changes attempted with OD can sometimes result in conflict, and for that reason we have devoted attention to the topics of change and conflict. The two major divisions in this chapter are organizational development (OD), and managing change and conflict.

In the first article, "A Comprehensive View of Organization Development," Richard Selfridge and Stanley Sokolik attempt to conceptualize the integration of various change strategies. Their model (the organizational iceberg) identifies both the overt and covert components of the organization. They maintain that managers frequently make decisions regarding organization development without considering covert organization dimensions.

The article, "Patterns of OD in Practice," by W. J. Heisler, reports the results of a survey that examines current OD methods and practices. The survey examined such topics as use of outside consultants, implementation level within the organization, and specific OD techniques.

Under managing change and conflict, we examine some approaches that are available to the manager as he attempts to deal with these two major consequences that frequently flow from the OD effort. In the article, "An Interactive Approach to the Problem of Organizational Change," Robert Shirley develops a framework to facilitate the management of change from a total firm perspective.

Richard Beckhard in "Strategies for Large System Change," describes a model of change planning applicable to large and complex organizations. The article focuses on five specific intervention strategies and concludes with an examination of where in the organization to begin the change effort, as well as how to maintain the change once it has been successfully initiated.

"The Fifth Achievement," by Robert Blake and Jane Mouton presents a conceptual basis for analyzing situations of conflict. They suggest the Conflict Grid as a useful approach to managing conflict in the organizational setting.

A COMPREHENSIVE VIEW OF ORGANIZATION DEVELOPMENT

RICHARD J. SELFRIDGE
STANLEY L. SOKOLIK

An operational model serves as a useful tool to bridge the gap between practitioner and manager.

During the past decade a number of behavioral science-based methodologies have found their way into practical organization application. The objective of each has been in varying degrees to facilitate change toward greater effectiveness and growth in individual, subgroup, and intergroup relationships—that is, to help the organization develop. This article provides a start toward a more useful conceptual integration of various change strategies—an integration which will be useful to both practitioners of organization development and organizations seeking formal organizational change.[1]

One way of conceptualizing the fullest possible scope of major targets of organizational change is to view the organization as an iceberg composed of two major components (see Figure 1 for the characteristic features of each).[2] The iceberg analogy is used widely and is helpful here to stress the existence of the two major levels of possible organization development targets as well as the systemic relationships which exist in actual practice.

As with any iceberg, there are *overt* compo-

Richard J. Selfridge and Stanley L. Sokolik, "A Comprehensive View of Organization Development," pp. 46–61, *MSU Business Topics,* Winter 1975. Reprinted by permission of the publisher, Division of Research, Graduate School of Business Administration, Michigan State University.

nents which physically stand out and are easily observable, and there are *covert* components which remain obscure and often hidden from the observer's eye. To the novice traveler, only the overt dimension of the iceberg seems to exist. A seasoned sailor, in contrast, seeks to account for the hidden part below the surface as well as that readily apparent to the eye. The waterline of the iceberg, which seems to separate the two components, actually serves as only an inexact, jagged, and quite artificial perceptual boundary. On closer inspection both components are found to be inextricably connected.

Similarly, in analyzing the organizational iceberg, the uninformed manager very often seeks organizational change and makes decisions regarding organization development (we shall refer to it as O.D.) without adequately considering the covert organizational dimension. He visualizes only the overt, formal organizational components and acts on the basis only of what he sees—the overt components. Such managers, although they see themselves purposefully engaged in O.D., are making limited and short-lived changes. When efforts are focused entirely upon overt components of the organization, both the O.D. practitioner and the client may be at fault. Because of their inability to see the whole, they may turn to a limited developmental strategy and minimize the risks essential to comprehensive change. How-

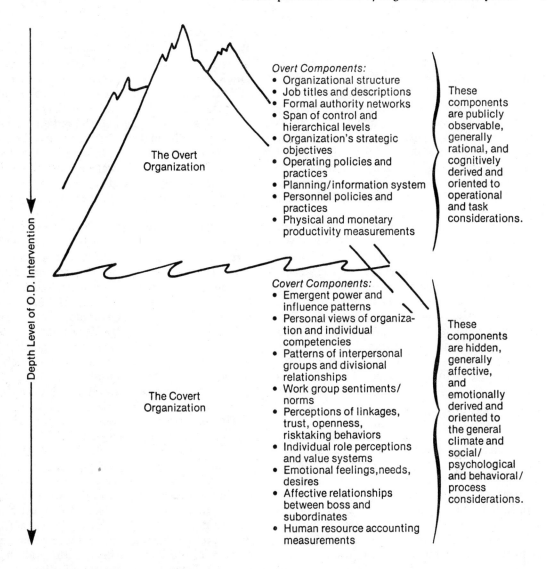

Depth Level of O.D. Intervention

The Overt Organization

Overt Components:
- Organizational structure
- Job titles and descriptions
- Formal authority networks
- Span of control and hierarchical levels
- Organization's strategic objectives
- Operating policies and practices
- Planning/information system
- Personnel policies and practices
- Physical and monetary productivity measurements

These components are publicly observable, generally rational, and cognitively derived and oriented to operational and task considerations.

The Covert Organization

Covert Components:
- Emergent power and influence patterns
- Personal views of organization and individual competencies
- Patterns of interpersonal groups and divisional relationships
- Work group sentiments/norms
- Perceptions of linkages, trust, openness, risktaking behaviors
- Individual role perceptions and value systems
- Emotional feelings, needs, desires
- Affective relationships between boss and subordinates
- Human resource accounting measurements

These components are hidden, generally affective, and emotionally derived and oriented to the general climate and social/psychological and behavioral/process considerations.

FIGURE 1. The organizational iceberg

ever, if they are able to see and to discuss alternatives available in a comprehensive organizational development model, they can fit their effort into (1) what they have accomplished before, (2) where they are now, and (3) what they plan in the future.

It is essential to see both the overt and covert components of an organization—regardless of how extensive the O.D. effort is intended to be. Only in this way can client and practitioner anticipate and account for the intimate relationships that exist within the organization. While this view is consistent with recent research in systems theory, it differs in one important respect. To be truly integrative, a comprehensive O.D. model should visualize organizations as more than systems composed of two or more semi-static dimensions. Instead, both the overt and covert components must be viewed as dynamic and interacting in an open system.

Operating in open-system terms, any O.D. effort will be directed away from a limited perspective toward a more comprehensive perspective of the fundamental nature of change. Comprehensive O.D. requires the development of a capability within an organization to become increasingly more open and adaptive. Each intervention needs to be seen as moving it towards this end. Our model stresses the usefulness of developing an organizational capability to adapt and respond to creative changes regardless of where organizational change is initiated or what particular kind of intervention is attempted.

When O.D. is undertaken with an open-systems approach, a desired change accomplished within the overt dimension of the organization can be sought in ways which influence and trigger (in functional and enhancing ways) corresponding changes in the covert dimension, and vice versa. With a comprehensive O.D. view, such an effect is intended, not left to chance, and specific conditions are established and sustained to ensure the greatest possible impact upon some or all variables in either or in both components.

DEPTH AND BREADTH AS DIFFERENTIATING QUALITIES

Another helpful means of outlining the nature of a comprehensive O.D. model is to differentiate particular intervention strategies as they appear on a continuum of (1) depth of penetration into organizational performance[3] and (2) the operational/task versus behavioral/process nature of the developmental concern (see Figure 2). Central to such a conceptual framework is the depth to which the primary target of the change effort involves an individual worker's confrontation of his own behavior. At increasingly deeper intervention levels, the concern is with the individual's affective and emotionally derived feelings and attitudes. Specifically, those change strategies—which confront the hidden aspects of the individual and his interpersonal relationships—are viewed as falling toward the deeper end of the continuum. At the deeper levels, too, the O.D. efforts deal more specifically with the organization's social/psychological aspects critical to interpersonal behavior.

In contrast, strategies which deal with the more structural, external aspects of the individual and focus upon his more formal (that is, task) and public relationships are seen at the shallow end of O.D. activity. These more surface strategies are easily observable, treating as they do the cognitive level of learning and the more rational aspects of individual performance and behavior. Consequently, strategies conducted at the shallow end typically are technical or operational, task-oriented interventions. They are, in the main, cognitively based and influenced more by reason than by feelings.

We should emphasize again that we are using the concepts of organization development and *intervention* in a somewhat different sense than is usual. Our model visualizes change methodologies as complementary subcomponents of the larger O.D. intent. Using such a frame of reference, any one methodology or intervention strategy is *not* the same as organization development. Rather, O.D. connotes a collective or synergistic effort over time. The various strategies provide choices for dealing with an organization at any one time, whether these choices are exercised independently or in a complementary or sequential manner.

The effectiveness of any single intervention methodology is a necessary but insufficient condition for the success of comprehensive O.D. Rather than any one intervention performing basically the same function as some other one, each different intervention methodology has the potential to contribute a unique, timely impact upon the organization. Some methodologies, for example, reinforce past influences; others directly change one or more of the interdependent structural and behavioral dimensions of the organization; and still others afford feedback about the existing capacity of the organization for realizing further change through other types of intervention.

The two major O.D. targets—the structural and process dimensions of an organization—are substantially different but not wholly separate. Each deals with a different set of organizational variables and different combinations of people. The emphasis upon one or the other often is a function of differing assumptions about the nature of people at work, and certainly each differs as to the primary objective of the change effort. High-

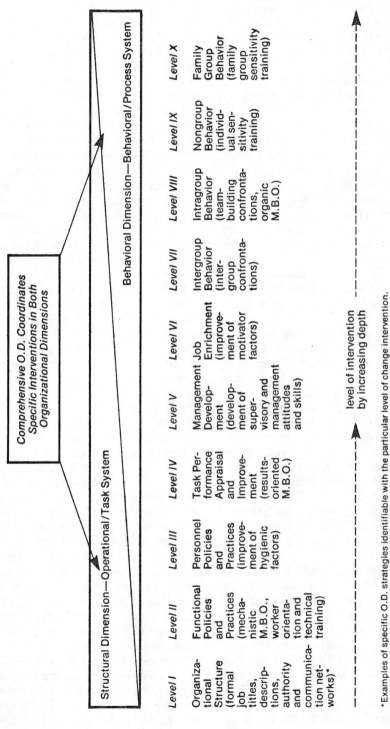

Comprehensive O.D. Coordinates Specific Interventions in Both Organizational Dimensions

Structural Dimension—Operational/Task System

Behavioral Dimension—Behavioral/Process System

Level I	Level II	Level III	Level IV	Level V	Level VI	Level VII	Level VIII	Level IX	Level X
Organizational Structure (formal job titles, descriptions, authority and communication networks)*	Functional Policies and Practices (mechanistic M.B.O., worker orientation and communication-technical training)*	Personnel Policies and Practices (improvement of hygienic factors)	Task Performance Appraisal and Improvement (results-oriented M.B.O.)	Management Development (development of supervisory and management attitudes and skills)	Job Enrichment (improvement of motivator factors)	Intergroup Behavior (intergroup confrontations)	Intragroup Behavior (team-building confrontations, organic M.B.O.)	Nongroup Behavior (individual sensitivity training)	Family Group Behavior (family group sensitivity training)

level of intervention by increasing depth

*Examples of specific O.D. strategies identifiable with the particular level of change intervention.

FIGURE 2. An integrative model of O.D. change targets

lighting the differences between these targets can help to maintain the necessary broader framework and at the same time provide the means for differentiating between the focus of specific intervention strategies. The result will be that seemingly independent interventions are made in a manner which better reflects the relationship of all the organizational changes.

We do not mean to imply that effective change intervention within the process dimension will be of greater importance to organizational change than one within the structural dimension. No organization can be materially improved unless individuals (both in their involvement with the task and in their process interactions with each other) are consciously changed and developed where they are. Interventions undertaken within the structural dimension generally are less complex and easier to sustain. This suggests again the limited depth of behavioral confrontation in interventions focused upon change in formal job assignments.

Looking further at the implications for maximizing the breadth and comprehensiveness of any organizational change effort, we see differences in the roles played by a consultant at the various levels of organization development. For example, when the consultant concentrates upon gathering information and facilitating changes in individual attitudes or interpersonal behavior processes, his intervention occurs at the deeper levels of the continuum. On the other hand, when the consultant's role is one of seeking information and effecting change in public and objectively observable organizational components, his intervention is at surface levels. There is much to be gained when the O.D. consultant can make this clear to his client.

Furthermore, in a continuing O.D. relationship, it is rarely desirable that the contract between consultant and client remain rigidly fixed. Although the consultant's role may be specifically set forth in the initial contract and clearly understood by and acceptable to both parties, the consultant may find it helpful to move from this agreed-upon role to deal in different ways with the different targets and problems which surface during changes and development in the organization. At these times our model offers a functional reference in both parties' efforts to be sensitive to and to deal with the need for role flexibility. Both client and practitioner are more likely to assert themselves in a responsive manner and to understand the possible risks whenever intervention moves beyond the original agreement.

Another important relationship in our comprehensive model is the nature of the primary need system focused upon in a particular O.D. intervention. Two different need systems are significant here: the organizational and the personal. The organizational need system is composed of the organization's unique values, norms, and objectives. Over time this need system becomes "the way we do things here" and generally reflects top management's basic philosophical predispositions whether they are consciously perceived or not.

The personal need system, though less specifically formulated, is at times equally influential. It relates to those unique values, norms, and personal aspirations and objectives of individuals within the organization. This personal need system is rarely explicitly expressed. Yet, its consequences upon the organization's emerging performance are generally considerable and often deleterious when ignored or undermined by the organizational need system. In a comprehensive O.D. change effort, both need systems are openly confronted, the emphasis upon one or the other varying with the depth of O.D. intervention.

A final quality which characterizes the varying depths of O.D. intervention is the differing degrees of dependency the client system exhibits in its relationship with its O.D. consultant. At the surface levels, the client system is reliant upon the consultant only in the initial phases. Generally, the relationship is expected to be short-lived and subject to termination whenever either party's testing finds it wanting or when the agreed-upon objectives are substantially realized. Emphasizing its preexisting cognitive abilities, then, the client group often quickly acquires the more surface outcomes and exerts increasingly greater independence of the consultant—the very basis anticipated for ending the particular intervention. At the surface levels also, transfer of learning is more readily facilitated by the consultant, just as it is more readily measurable.

At the deeper levels, in contrast, there is a more dependent, even interdependent, relationship between the client system and the consultant. With the primary concern here upon behavioral/ process issues, it is more difficult for the client group to acquire the desired intellectual understanding, let alone move on to integrate it into its management practices. Moreover, the nature of such learning is more specifically a function of the consultant's personal skills and style.

Client members are typically unfamiliar with the new behaviors under consideration at the deeper levels. They tend to rely heavily on the consultant as both a behavioral model and a catalyst in developing their new behaviors. At these levels, too, the mere acquisition of an intellectual understanding is not thought to be a sufficient condition for the client's acquiring and perpetuating the desired interpersonal competence. Consequently, it is not uncommon for deeper O.D. interventions to be prolonged; nor is it uncommon for the consultant to leave before the client system has adequately developed and frozen the new, more fundamentally changed behavioral patterns.

Since it is not easy to measure organizational changes at the deeper levels, the decision to terminate such an O.D. intervention is rarely based on objective data. Instead, it is very often a highly subjective decision, one commonly left to a mutual agreement of both parties. For this reason, in many cases, the consultant departs with a sense of frustration that more could have been accomplished. However, in the absence of having specific and measurable indicators of change, the consultant must settle for a sense of reassurance from his client. Regardless of how long he remains or how much is accomplished, there is always a strong likelihood that the learning experience may be transient and recidivism to former behavioral patterns may well occur. To be confident about his progress towards helping the client group, he needs to know that the key members of the client system have achieved some measure of skill in analyzing and altering their own behaviors and are able to facilitate the growth of others.

Numerous O.D. practitioners have attributed this dependency at the deeper levels to the neces-

sity of the client group's making increasingly greater psychological commitments and assuming the risk of more and more uncertain experiments if it is to acquire and reinforce new behaviors. It is for this reason that some practitioners have suggested that success at the deeper levels is a direct function of the client's psychological commitment and willingness to experiment with his organization. Indeed, at the deeper levels, the client system cannot avoid itself becoming the target and the agent of the change effort.

Correspondingly, the consultant at the deeper levels undergoes a clear shift in his role in the learning process. He is no longer an external learning control agent and technical expert. He becomes a facilitator of greater internal control and, ultimately, self-control on the part of the client. Since the shift toward greater internalization of the learning process is so primary to the successful outcome of organizational change at the deeper levels, the consultant cannot avoid the risk of his creating a dependent relationship with his clients. Indeed, his task (and the measure of how well he performs at the deeper levels) is to help his client to reduce the dysfunctionality of this dependency, that is, to make it transactional and interdependent.

CHARACTERISTICS OF SPECIFIC CHANGE INTERVENTIONS

Level I—Organizational Structure

At the top or surface end of the O.D. continuum we see the interventions having the primary concern of changing the organizational structure. The objective of such a strategy is to manipulate and redistribute individual roles and relationship configurations so as to create more effective formal arrangements between the task, the resources, and the authority responsibilities within the organization. The consultant and client are engaged in rationalizing the organization into more functional roles, in terms of both individual and overall organizational performance.

Level I types of interventions presume that (1) organizations can be beneficially dealt with in entirely mechanistic terms and (2) structural elements play a considerable part in shaping individual and interactive behavior. The people themselves are seen as substantially interchangeable parts. Analysis here, as well as the changes that typically result, is generally confined to the development and design of specific, formal positional relationships involving both physical and mental tasks—all of which can be expressed through an organization chart.

Level II—Functional Policies and Practices

A somewhat deeper target often routinely emerges from a Level I O.D. effort. The consultant reviews and recommends changes in the functional policies and practices used to administer and coordinate the organization. His intervention frequently leads to logically deduced changes in the methods of organizing and directing functional units and individual workers. The primary objective at this level of intervention is to develop more rational planning and control.

Organization development, when limited to this level, commonly proceeds from the assumption that organizations can best be operated by tightly administered control systems directed from the top down. Changes made here are often based on the assumption that people need externally imposed controls and artificially administered techniques to stir them to action. The consultant's role is to help formulate these better controls. Without them, it is believed, the organization's members will remain less capable and less willing to work effectively toward organizational goals.

An increasingly popular methodology employed at this second level is the use of a "mechanistic" management by objectives (M.B.O.) program, distinguishable from both the "results oriented" and "organic" M.B.O. attempted at deeper levels of organization development. Mechanistic M.B.O. views the organization as a hierarchy of subunits, each of which can be better directed by measurable objectives. The aim is for better coordinated, organization-wide direction through a unified control mechanism regulating the planning and, in turn, the performance of the organization's members. With specific objectives established for each, it is argued, the organizational subunits are more easily managed. Not only are the activities prescribed and coordinated through the alignment of

explicit goals, but higher management can isolate and deal with results on an exception basis, that is, those which do not meet the previously agreed-upon objectives.

Mechanistic M.B.O., like all management acts, is expressive of the user's values and assumptions about human behavior. When introduced as a Level II intervention, M.B.O. can be little more than a directive effort whereby management seeks to enlarge its capacity to control its subordinates. Management by objectives at Level II is thus at one with Douglas McGregor's Theory X assumptions about the nature of people at work.[4] The orientation is heavily slanted toward the maintenance of organizationally required goals, needs, and values.

Also appropriately identified with Level II organization development are the continuing and periodic efforts taken to orient workers and to provide them with greater technical understandings and skills. There is a renewed interest in such an intervention, sometimes in connection with Level VI job enrichment efforts. The need is also a function of the employment of younger and disadvantaged workers where the aim is to override their prior antiwork conditioning as well as to help them and others avoid some of the dysfunctional impact of the workers' emergent system. Too, the needs of changing technology and accelerated efforts to undo the effects of past racial and sexist discrimination have led to greater technical training. In many of these interventions use is made of new training technologies such as those which enable programmed, individualized learning.

Level III—Personnel Policies and Practices

A still deeper strategy is the organized review and improvement of the ways in which an organization's workers are collectively treated. The focus here is upon the nature and effectiveness of the policy-procedure system and the management of its human resources under the assumption that greater uniformity and fairness of employee treatment will be both more satisfying and more productive. Typical interventions of this kind result in changes in management practices—in particular, those which affect the development and utilization of individual workers. The view remains a collective one insofar as it is the prescribed methods and techniques and the guidelines for using them which are changed, not the behavior of individual workers.

Developments at this level are programmed to set up formal conditions whereby employees come to expect certain treatment from the organization in return for certain investments on their part. Some authors have described this focus as the organizational reward/punishment mechanism (the R/P system). In terms of Frederick Herzberg's model, such systems are characterizable as environmental or hygienic in nature.[5] Changes made here affect principally those factors which surround the job itself, rather than the work done by the workers.

Level IV—Task Performance Appraisal and Improvement

At the fourth level of intervention direct attempts are made to improve task effectiveness. The major concern is with realizing a more effective task module. In the Frederick Taylor tradition of "scientific management," the changes that result from interventions at this level are typically more task-specific than individualized or humanistic in nature. Direct attempts are made to reduce a task to the lowest modicum of mental and physical effort and to pre-program performance in terms of rational and easily measured components. Through the use of motion/time studies, formal communication network analysis, and work flow studies, for example, the consultant intervenes by recommending alterations in the methods by which particular tasks are to be performed. The assumption made here is that the worker will become more productive when he can devote his attention and energies to a specialized function.

A similar purpose is sought through an M.B.O. program which focuses upon helping managers to participate in clarifying the end results expected of them. In contrast to Taylor's emphasis on the rational programming and administration of the processes and methods of operative employees, "end results" M.B.O. is concerned with improving managerial work through more formalized planning and review of the managers' results.

Both approaches are thus similar in the change target addressed, but differ largely in the character of what is measured and analyzed. In both cases, the O.D. strategy is to enhance performance by making it more subject to administration, primarily through performance appraisal based on publicly observable measurements determined in advance.

Level V—Management Development

Management development is an effort intended to directly help the individual manager by upgrading his conceptual understanding and skills as a manager. This strategy assumes that meaningful organization change can result through helping individual managers to consciously improve their management performance by acquiring and using insights concerning delegation, communications, effective use of time, budgeting, control, problem-solving, and decision making—to name only a few. An O.D. practitioner serves here, as at the more surface levels, in the capacity of a technical expert charged with the basic responsibility of facilitating cognitive learning.

There are variations in the subject matter introduced at this level. Due to recent trends in content and methodology in management development, we find this kind of intervention at the half-way position on our O.D. depth continuum. In many current management development programs, for example, the O.D. practitioner is open to the discussion of issues that emanate from the dynamics of the managers' respective socioemotional systems. This is particularly true where the managers are a "family" group drawn from the same organization and where such topics as motivation theory, leadership theory, value systems, and role theory occupy major portions of the training schedule.

It is in these terms that we see management development as increasingly becoming a vehicle for creating greater awareness of and thereby receptivity for dealing with those issues which have in the past been treated only at deeper levels of intervention. So prevalent is this practice that many organizations now view their management development programs as synonymous with organization development. The adverse consequences introduced by such an exaggerated view of management development (no matter how unintended) are significant to an appreciation of the broader view of O.D.

There are good reasons for experientially dealing with behavioral/process issues of the organization only with the use of deeper O.D. interventions. The "there-and-then" handling of such matters in terms of generalizations made in a management development program is really too far removed from the manager's reality to assure adequate understanding and skill for subsequent application in his back-home situation. In addition, it can be argued that behavioral science-based models are best treated in the context of on-the-job experimentation where the manager is helped to apply them to the very people and ongoing problems that are faced day in and day out.

The practice of sending individual managers off to management development programs so that they can be independently introduced to abstract behavioral concepts may indeed be dangerous. Should the training transmit false understandings of the complexities of human behavior or set up unreal expectations, the manager's short-term change efforts may be dysfunctional, no matter how positive his motivation. Moreover, results from such changes are likely to deteriorate quickly when the management development effort is not supported by other interventions, particularly of the type found at the deeper levels. At best, management development provides individual managers with a cognitive map or model with only a beginning understanding of the specific back-home organizational variables against which the model needs to be reality-tested and applied.

Level VI—Job Enrichment

Interventions of the type just described often lead to a focus upon changing task modules through efforts described by Herzberg, M. Scott Myers, and Robert N. Ford as *job enrichment.*[6] The uniqueness of an effort at job enrichment lies with the nature and sequence of the change process it employs. More specifically, the job enrichment approach assumes that task changes are best made in accord with the psychological needs of the employee affected and, as much as pos-

sible, involve the worker himself in the redesign of the job.

Changes in the content and nature of the task are made only after an analysis has revealed the psychological factors most critical to a particular group of workers. It is to the satisfaction of these needs that the job redesign is aimed. When the job is thus enriched, it provides the workers with a more rewarding and psychologically attractive experience.

The job enrichment approach operating at Level VI is thus significantly different from the more surface level interventions. Whereas its initial focus is upon what is needed by the individual, it can be remembered that at Level IV the focus is upon requiring the worker to accommodate himself to the one best way of doing the job. Here, the concern for satisfying the needs of individual workers is direct and intentional, something just not so at the more surface level.

Level VII—Intergroup Behavior

The O.D. concern at the seventh level is with changing those attitudinal and behavioral factors which contribute to functional (or dysfunctional) working relationships between different groups or divisions within an organization. The process target is one of confronting issues which emerge in the groups' respective communicating or withholding of information, in the competition or collaboration which takes place between them, the presence or absence of coordination, and so forth. The aim is to help the groups develop greater effectiveness by means of concentrating on their intergroup working relationship, that is, improving their ability to deal with these issues and thereby work better together toward the achievement of shared organizational goals. Organizational growth is sought through changing intergroup attitudinal perceptions, particularly internal orientations held regarding the "relevant other" groups.

The managerial grid approach developed by Robert Blake and Jane S. Mouton is an example of one of these interventions aimed at analyzing and improving intergroup behavior.[7] The grid intervener chooses his tactics from such alternatives as precipitating bargaining and seeking multiple trade-offs, compromise, and even modification of organizational arrangements. In general, the grid focus is upon bringing about constructive confrontation through first better understanding of the conflicts which stand between two or more linked subgroups.

Similar in its intent is the *confrontation meeting* used by Richard Beckhard.[8] In such meetings, members of each group are instructed to compile lists of adjectives (both positive and negative) which they feel best characterize the other group. These lists are shared with the aim of helping both groups to come to a fuller understanding of their respective perceptions. This process is repeated until specific steps are mutually perceived and agreed upon as a reasonable basis for moving on to resolving remaining differences. Each group's latent images of the "relevant other" having been openly shared, the ensuing dialogue leads almost automatically to trying to resolve the crucial issues still remaining.

The differentiation-integration concept developed by Paul R. Lawrence and Jay W. Lorsch provides still another example of Level VII methodology.[9] When applied to transactions occurring at the group-to-group interface, its objective is to create an appropriate balance between the simultaneous needs for differentiation and integration between two or more functioning groups. The O.D. interventionist is concerned primarily with facilitating a choice on the part of the groups— a choice which can lead them to strive for a better "fit" between the organizational subunits and the various demands placed upon them by organizational goals and environmental influences. The consultant's emphasis is upon helping to identify and then mediate those natural forces which make for conflict between specialized, differentiated subunits that must work cooperatively toward supraordinate goals.

Level VIII—Intragroup Behavior

The strategy of intervening to effect change in the actual behavior of members within a functional work group is commonly termed *teambuilding, process analysis,* or *action research.* It focuses upon directly improving those interactions necessary to facilitate effective joint activity and problem solving by members of a work group. Interventions here typically confront such issues as those arising from worker interdependence, shared problem solving, participative behavior in decision making, supportive leadership styles, informal power and group norms. The direct target is improving the interpersonal processes whereby the individuals who make up the small task group actively contribute to making their group a more cohesive one.

One O.D. approach at the intragroup level is the help given group members in achieving a clearer understanding of the functional roles that individual members of the group assume in making decisions and jointly performing their tasks. Using a model like that developed by Kenneth D. Benne and Paul Sheats, the interventionist helps group members to understand existing role patterns (and their dysfunctionality) as a basis for agreeing to work toward role experimentation and thereby role flexibility congruent to the situation.[10] Another conceptual scheme for describing group behavior is that developed by A. N. Turner using the dimensions of "required" and "emergent" behaviors as a way of helping group members to jointly describe and subsequently change their individual behaviors.[11]

The most prominent objective at this intervention level is to develop each group member's internal capacity to base his actions upon more carefully collected and analyzed data about his and others' behavior within the group. According to L. P. Bradford, K. D. Benne, and R. Lippitt, such interventions are "designed to help some unit of human organization assess its need for change and to support that unit in inventing and testing ways in which change may be achieved."[12] That is, the data collection and analysis is part of the change process.

It is for this reason that, though the methods they use vary, O.D. practitioners who rely upon self-generated data are known as "process consultants." They intervene largely by providing (and generating from the group members themselves) nonevaluative feedback, supporting the members' experimentation with their individual and collective behavior in terms of the way the data "stack up" against the previously agreed-upon models. Recently, the work of Edgar Schein and others has specified categories or patterns of behavior that are easily quantified and systematically diagnosed in such types of O.D. intervention.[13]

At some point in an intragroup intervention, the feedback is simultaneously generated as group members increase their capacity to deal with their behavioral processes. Aiming for greater congruent spontaneity through constructive use of immediate feedback, the interventionist increasingly turns the responsibility for such behavioral processing over to the group members themselves. As this shift occurs each group member comes to serve not only as a learner but also as an interested input source for the potential learning of others within this group.

Another variation of this method is called *action research*. According to Newton Marguiles and Anthony Raia, the aim here is "creating research data which can be incorporated into learning and which will result in social change."[14] Although the process consultant initially serves as the primary analyst, he seeks at later stages of their development to involve group members directly in the fact finding and analysis.

The focus in intragroup behavior remains with helping the members of a task group to achieve specified end results for the better functioning of the group. This emphasis is in contrast with that of the deeper T-group development which is based upon facilitating personal growth. The intragroup strategy seeks more self-regulated performance, but largely within the functional context of the work-group or team. When used in conjunction with an organization-wide management by objectives approach to managerial work, intragroup behavioral interventions substantially expand the potential of M.B.O. Such efforts can be described as "organic" and deserve identification as a Level VIII intervention.

Level IX—Nongroup Behavior (Individual Sensitivity)

The nongroup intervention has as its target the unprogrammed, open social situation rather than either a person's behavior within his work group or the behavior between two or more groups. This distinction is a central one.

The nongroup intervention derives its substantive direction from each individual's own perceived growth needs, rather than from the group's maintenance or task-performance needs. The objective of change here is the individual *qua* individual and it is generally sought through helping an individual develop an existential self-awareness in the areas of: (1) increased personal autonomy (discovery of one's own personal attitudes and feelings); (2) personal ability to focus upon "here-and-now" experiential data; and (3) self-expression of one's internal feelings and attitudes.

Nongroup strategies are not generally concerned with facilitating interpersonal relationship skills which can be specifically transferred to the actual problem-solving activities within the "back-home" situation. This limited focus is intentional. Each person is encouraged to experiment with new and, at times, unusual behaviors in a way that leaves him free to be nonproductive, if he so chooses. The participants are not made self-conscious of an overriding need for specific activities to strengthen their organizational relationships.

Since the development of more functional inter-relationships is not a specific goal of the nongroup change effort, some practitioners see this very atmosphere of independence as itself leading to more authentic relationships. It is further assumed that authentic relationships are a direct function of independence of thought and action, not of preexisting organizational arrangements or the wishes of others.

In nongroup interventions, both the trainer and participant characteristically focus upon reporting to each other their impressions of the other's spontaneous actions. Rarely are attempts made to relate these interactions in terms of their impact upon group relationships or task performance. Nongroup interventions do not therefore require that the consultant serve as a process expert. Instead, he sets out to facilitate individual self-actualization and gives far less attention to those requirements which are critical to the task or formal organizational basis of most other O.D. interventions. Indeed, group or organizational norms themselves often become an issue insofar as they might be perceived as repressive to individual growth and autonomous development.

Throughout, there is the assumption that insights and psychological developments of advantage to the individual will also be of advantage to his organization's well being.

Some practitioners have suggested that this fundamental assumption must be made if the nongroup intervention is to be effective, even though it may not be appropriate universally. Bernard Bass, however, has cautioned that, though the nongroup training methodology may be a necessary component of comprehensive O.D., by itself it is not a sufficient methodology.[15] He suggests that an overemphasis upon individual sensitivity may have dysfunctional effects to the organization over the long run if introduced and applied independently of other types of changes.

The development of individual sensitivity and a healthy personal identity are sufficiently worthwhile as subobjectives of a larger O.D. effort that nongroup interventions are seen as playing a critical part in comprehensive O.D. An exclusive emphasis on nongroup objectives, however, may limit the learning experience. Conditions should not be so established that the individual's actual organizational task performance becomes negatively related to his success in personal sensitivity and self-awareness, as is the risk when nongroup interventions are used exclusive of other kinds of O.D.

Level X—Family Group Behavior (Family T-Group Development)

Over the past decade Chris Argyris has been an early pioneer and continuing source of leadership in the development and testing of T-group methods.[16] His work serves well as a frame of reference for describing intervention activities undertaken at the tenth level of the depth continuum. According to Argyris, there are three primary objectives in using T-group methodology within a family or task group setting: (1) to establish a climate wherein valid information is generated; (2) to provide the client system opportunities to make free and informed choices based on the in-

formation generated therein; and (3) to maintain the client's continuing internal commitment to learning and improving interpersonal processes.

Central to Argyris's intervention strategy is the concept of facilitating interpersonal competence in terms of realizing a growing ability on the part of the task group's members to: (1) own up to and accept responsibility for their own individual thoughts and feelings; (2) be open to the thoughts and feelings of others; (3) experiment with new thoughts and feelings; and (4) help others to own up to, be open to, and experiment with their own thoughts and feelings. The T-group aims to create greater organizational effectiveness only as an indirect goal or independent variable. The focus here is primarily upon the development of the family group's internal capacity to establish open and supportive communications channels among all of its members. In a sense, then, the T-group is more assuredly humanistic and normatively oriented than are other more surface interventions. The T-group procedure begins by recognizing every individual's basic need for valid information exchange and behavioral confirmation, and it is assumed that organizational effectiveness *will* result to the extent that these needs are met.

Beyond exemplifying interventions at Level X the Argyris model helps to illustrate the outline or outer boundaries of any O.D. effort. When administered with such consistency and singleness of purpose as Argyris would require, the T-group effort is surely the deepest intervention activity possible in any O.D. effort. Let us look at some of the reasons for viewing family T-group interventions as the deepest possible change effort in an organizational setting.

First, the development of those skills which enhance interpersonal competence requires that organizational members *communicate with minimal distortion and evaluative information*. Certain personal and organizational preconditions may need to be met before the client system can maximize these qualities through a strategy of confrontation.[17] Individual members already should have demonstrated a high degree of personal self-awareness and self-acceptance. The client system group as a whole accepts each member's self-concept, having demonstrated the ability to deal nonevaluatively with his interpersonal and task behaviors. Not all family groups can meet these preconditions. For this reason, in many instances sensitivity training or self-awareness training needs to precede the family T-group effort. Even then, these preconditions may not be fully met.

Psychological predispositions of the individual members may either limit or enhance their ability to benefit from either the family T-group or the more individualistic nongroup experience of Level IX. Argyris has suggested that individuals who are describable as exhibiting a "growth motivation" hold the greatest potential for benefiting from T-group interventions.[18] Such individuals are motivated by those self-actualizing needs that operate at the higher levels of Maslow's need hierarchy and they generally possess an openness and willingness to explore and improve their interpersonal effectiveness.

On the other hand, there are individuals who can be described as "survival oriented," operating primarily from a deficiency motivation. Being basically defensive and closed, such individuals are less likely to contribute to or share in the benefits of the T-group experience. Should such individuals be confronted by others, there is a great likelihood that they will construct elaborate psychological defenses against such experiential data inputs, thereby minimizing the objectives and benefits of the experience. This is not to say that "survival oriented" persons cannot benefit from more surface levels of O.D. intervention. At the deeper levels where the overriding need is for interpersonal openness, however, their sense of threat may well make it impossible for them to engage in the intervention.

A second feature of the T-group that serves to differentiate it from other interventions is its attempt to operationalize the notion that *individual sensitivities, once exposed, must somehow be integrated into more viable and functional interpersonal relationships.* In contrast to the nongroup approach, the family T-group approach further assumes that the pursuit of pure autonomy can be destructive to the organization if pursued independently of the organization's need for unified action.[19] Sheldon Davis, another T-group practitioner, has suggested that

there is no real growth—there is no real development —in the organization or the individuals within it, if they do not confront and deal directly with their problems. They can get together and share feelings (for example, sensitivity training) but if that is all they do, it is merely a catharsis. While this is useful, it has relatively minimal usefulness compared with what can happen if they start to relate differently within the organizational setting around task issues.[20]

In this respect, then, the family T-group is more complete and wholistic in its recognition and handling of both organizational *and* individual considerations. With this broader individual and organizational focus, the real payoff in the family T-group is the integration of individual awarenesses into more effective relationships with others within the work group. At this deepest level, the O.D. intervention seeks—far more than possible at any other level—to reconcile the complex forces that exist between group maintenance needs and basic individual needs and feelings. Moreover, it directly seeks shared group norms and behavioral skills which the group members see as having the greatest potential for realizing and sustaining an adequate balance between these conflicting needs systems.

A third feature of family T-group activities that sets them apart from other interventions is their focus upon generating a *shared group commitment in support of the development of interpersonal competence through collective endeavor.* Interpersonal competence, as Argyris has described it, must after all be viewed as a synergistic phenomenon.[21] That is, through the intervention, each individual comes to rely upon "relevant others" for their helpful feedback, just as they in turn rely upon him. In this way, each group member contributes to the reeducation of all others. When seen in this way, the family T-group effort aims at the greatest degree of "giving" behavior (that is, cooperative and supportive) that individuals can muster in a work-related endeavor. To a far greater degree than most other interventions described here, there is open recognition and dramatic exploration of the inevitable interdependence and mutual influence people have upon each other.

The O.D. practitioner at Level X assumes that

anyone working within an organization is to some degree a victim of historical organizational influences and is unable to achieve many of his most basic needs, that he is powerless to confront and solve his most critical problems without the assistance and support of others. The family T-group intervention thus dramatically emphasizes what is essentially a quality of all organization development but one not as perceptible in interventions made at more surface levels: the immediate performance of workers is influenced more by the social and environmental nature of behavioral conditioning than by their psychological capacities. Level X interventions are seen as providing the necessary support system to overcome man's psychological incompleteness and thereby enable him to gain wholeness through meaningful interaction.[22]

A fourth and final Level X feature is its *emphasis on the analysis of individual perceptions and personal values concerning effective human relationships.* In a family T-group intervention, more so than at any other level, there is an attempt made to question and challenge some fundamental societal values and organizational norms. The actual targets of change are often the basic organizational norms which obstruct the generation of "valid information." The focus is upon the more highly normative aspects of organizational behavior. There is an intentional confrontation of "what is" (that is, the accepted and entrenched behavioral practices) and an outline of activities which will move individuals and groups toward more effective behaviors—what "should be." By experientially demonstrating the impact which traditional behavioral practices have upon personal growth, family T-group participants confront values they hold about themselves and about what is desirable interpersonal social behavior. Basic cosmologies about people are put to the test far more certainly and directly than with any other intervention methodology. Indeed, it is to a large degree the extent to which other O.D. interventions avoid this fundamental reality testing that they are seen as dealing with more surface focuses rather than with the more substantial kind of organization development attempted in family T-group efforts.

CONCLUSION

In looking at the numerous types of interventions and methodologies we have illustrated, the value of a comprehensive view of organizational change is substantially reinforced. In essence, we need to differentiate between isolated or parochial changes (for example, changes initiated in either the task or process dimension) and the larger-scale, cross-dimensional changes which begin to take on the character of family T-group interventions and thereby hold out the greatest hope for providing a quantum jump in the quality and effectiveness of organizational life. To do this, practitioner and client alike will need to recognize the limited benefits possible when a fragmented or separatistic approach to organization development is employed.

The ten levels of O.D. intervention we have described must come to be seen as separable parts of a total process, not as end results in and of themselves. Any single intervention may initiate the process. Single interventions, however, will remain incomplete until they are systematically applied within the context of the outcomes possible with other kinds of interventions, whether at more surface or deeper levels. Indeed, an intervention at several levels beyond an organization's most recent O.D. effort is likely to succeed only if it is designed in terms of the lack of the intermediate changes and a careful probe of the organization's readiness for the deeper intervention.

In effect, a comprehensive O.D. effort constitutes the creation of a substantially new force field in the organization—an effort which must be continuously monitored and periodically readjusted to assure long-term benefits. With such an approach, each intervention is likely to uncover within the organization both driving and restraining forces that must be confronted head-on. Those factors which are identified as driving forces may, at the particular moment, need strengthening and reinforcement by management, and those factors identified as restraining forces may need to be somehow diminished or removed. Whatever the appropriate intervention, the practitioner and client group need to be aware of the current state and longer-term movement of all organizational components or dimensions, not just those being treated at the moment. The comprehensive view afforded by our model can facilitate this consideration and thereby enhance the choices made as to the most appropriate types of O.D. interventions.

In this view of the O.D. process, organizational equilibrium is approached but rarely realized. The practitioner and client group come to anticipate a continuous disequilibrium—one more productive and healthy than that which would otherwise exist, but one nevertheless fraught with imperfection, ambiguity, and uncertainty. The ongoing comprehensive program of organization development becomes the means for facilitating flexibility and growth as the organization attempts to deal systemically with change in its structure and process.

It is our view that many current O.D. efforts can produce only indefinite and limited results. It is not that the particular intervention is inadequate or even that it has been poorly planned. Rather, too often there is a failure to go beyond the specific intervention and look more comprehensively at additional variables, the organizational focus implied, and the appropriateness of the methodology itself—in terms of both the broader consequences of the single intervention and the comparative advantages of blending several into one organization development effort. When the latter is done, the scope and impact of O.D. within any organization are sure to be broader. The client group is sure to sense a greater control of its development, not necessarily by expending greater resources or dealing with more of the organization at one time, but by exercising the more informed choices available to it.

In the past, elaborate word definitions for organization development have been promoted as the means of integrating characteristic features. In our view, the need for definition must go beyond words to an operational model which allows for the specific incorporation of all those concepts and methodologies which can be intentionally used to change organizations. We believe the comprehensive model presented here satisfies this need, both in outlining those components of the current state of the art and in serving as a point of departure for additions and deletions as new techniques and understandings become available. At the very least, the components of such a model should provide a more tangible definitional framework for identifying what constitutes organization development in the broadest sense.

We believe, too, that our conceptualization provides the framework for an analysis of alternatives not otherwise possible. With this model there can be choices between various strategies, between specific levels or targets for intervention, and in the appropriate adaptation and timing of different kinds of organization development. With it, too, these choices can be made in a manner sensitive to the possible synergistic or gestalt effects and inevitable trade-offs—all the while keeping in mind the unifying, though changing, purpose and overall direction intended for a particular organization's development.

NOTES

1. This need for a more comprehensive view of organization development has been felt for some time. It is our view that W. L. French and C. H. Bell, Jr., *Organization Development* (Englewood Cliffs, N.J.: Prentice-Hall, Inc., 1973), pp. 105–11, is the most notable attempt to constructively differentiate and classify O.D. by intervention methodology. While this also is our intention, we will differ with regard to the model used to illustrate the concept.

2. This illustration is an elaboration of the organization iceberg model originally developed by Stanley M. Herman in "What Is This Thing Called Organization Development?" *Personnel Journal,* August 1971, pp. 595–603.

3. The concept of depth of intervention and the rationale for its use were originally set forth by Roger Harrison in "Choosing the Depth of Organizational Intervention," *Journal of Applied Behavioral Science* 6, no. 2 (1970): 181–202. This paper will draw heavily upon his work but will serve as a further elaboration and integration of additional methodologies in current use.

4. Douglas McGregor, *The Human Side of Enterprise* (New York: McGraw-Hill, 1960); also Harry Levinson, "Management by Whose Objectives?" *Harvard Business Review,* July–August 1970, pp. 125–34.

5. Frederick Herzberg, B. Mausner, and B. Synderman, *The Motivation to Work* (New York: John Wiley & Sons, Inc., 1960).

6. Frederick Herzberg, "One More Time: How Do You Motivate Employees?" *Harvard Business Re-*

view, January–February 1968, pp. 53–62; M. Scott Myers, "Every Employee a Manager," *California Management Review,* Spring 1968, pp. 9–20; also Robert N. Ford, *Motivation Through the Work Itself* (New York: American Management Association, 1969).

7. Robert Blake and Jane S. Mouton, *Managing Intergroup Conflict in Industry* (Houston, Texas: Gulf Publishing Company, 1964).

8. Richard Beckhard, "The Confrontation Meeting," *Harvard Busines Review,* March–April 1967, pp. 149–55.

9. Paul R. Lawrence and Jay W. Lorsch, *Organization and Environment: Managing Differentiation and Integration* (Boston, Mass.: Division of Research, Harvard Business School, 1969).

10. Kenneth D. Benne and Paul Sheats, "Functional Roles of Group Members," *Journal of Social Issues,* Spring 1948, pp. 42–47.

11. Arthur N. Turner, "A Conceptual Scheme for Describing Work Group Behavior," in *Organizational Behavior and Administration: Cases, Concepts, and Research Findings,* ed. Paul R. Lawrence and J. E. Seiler (Homewood, Ill.: Richard D. Irwin, Inc., 1965), pp. 154–64.

12. L. P. Bradford, K. D. Benne, and R. Lippitt, "The Laboratory Method," in *T-Group Theory and Laboratory Method,* ed. L. P. Bradford, J. R. Gibb, and K. D. Benne (New York: John Wiley & Sons, Inc., 1964), pp. 15–44.

13. Edgar H. Schein, *Process Consultation: Its Role in Organization Development* (Reading, Mass.: Addison-Wesley Publishing Company, 1969).

14. Newton Marguiles and Anthony R. Raia, "Action Research and the Consultative Process," *Business Perspectives,* Fall 1968, pp. 26–30.

15. Bernard Bass, "The Anarchist Movement and the T-Group: Some Possible Lessons for Organization Development," *Journal of Applied Behavioral Science* 3, no. 2 (1967): 211.

16. Chris Argyris, *Intervention Theory and Method: A Behavioral Science View* (Reading, Mass.: Addison-Wesley Publishing Company, 1970), pp. 16–18.

17. Chris Argyris, "Conditions for Competence Acquisition and Therapy," *Journal of Applied Behavioral Science* 4, no. 2 (1968): 150.

18. Ibid., p. 163.

19. Chris Argyris, "On the Future of Laboratory Education," *The Journal of Applied Behavioral Science* 3, no. 2 (1967): 153–83.

20. Sheldon A. Davis, "An Organic Problem-Solving Method of Organizational Change," *The Journal of Applied Behavioral Science* 3, no. 1 (1967): 4.

21. Argyris, "Future of Laboratory Education," pp. 154–55.

22. McGregor, *Human Side of Enterprise.*

PATTERNS OF OD
IN PRACTICE

W. J. HEISLER

The acceptance of organization development (OD) as a way of improving organizational performance is now widespread. This study delineates some of the more common patterns in practice.

Organization development (OD) is the name generally applied to an emerging behavioral science discipline; this discipline seeks to improve organizational performance and effectiveness through planned, systematic, long-range efforts focused on the organization's culture and its human and social processes. During the past decade, this discipline has gained increasing attention among management theorists and practitioners. Among the numerous indicators of OD's accelerated growth are those cited by W. Warner Burke and Wendell L. French and Cecil H. Bell:

More than 1,500 people currently hold membership in some organization devoted to OD. The OD network of National Training Laboratories (NTL), which began in 1964, now has over 200 members; an OD division of the American Society for Training and Development was started in 1968 and had close to 800 members toward the end of 1970; in 1971 the Academy of Management established a Division for Organization Development.
A number of universities have established academic programs specializing in OD.
The number of applications to the NTL Institute program for specialists in organization development doubled during the three-year period, 1969–72.[1]

The volume of literature related to OD has increased commensurately. As Burke points out, "Within the past four years over 15 books have been published which deal with OD and a wide variety of others have recently been published or are on the way." While OD research abounds as well, only a few studies have examined the actual features and dimensions of the discipline in practice. This study is intended to analyze many relevant issues that have not yet been fully explored.

PRIOR STUDIES

Some of the earliest data indicative of the extent of OD activity was provided by William F. Glueck.[2] Surveying the presidents of companies listed in *Fortune's 1966–67 Plant and Product Directory* of the 1,000 largest U.S. industrial corporations and 250 largest nonmanufacturers, Glueck found that:

Company size and growth are major factors influencing the establishment of organizational planning and development departments.
These departments tend to have been established relatively recently.
OD departments typically conduct studies and recommend changes in existing organization structure and climate; recommend methods and programs to improve interpersonal and intergroup relations, effec-

tiveness, and company work climate; and develop methods and programs to strengthen leadership and managerial skills, and provide for managerial succession and compensation plans.

The managers of organizational planning and development departments typically report to top management and head relatively small departments consisting of seven or fewer professionals.

Organization authorities observe a significant shift toward more people oriented, behavioral activities in organizational planning and development departments.

More recently, studies by the American Society for Training and Development (ASTD) and the Conference Board have provided more comprehensive information about the status of OD practice. In general, the ASTD survey of practitioners indicated the following:

OD work makes up less than 50 percent of the total work effort of most OD practitioners within their respective organizations.

OD practitioners feel that top priority in OD activity should be placed in building mutual trust, changing the organizational climate, encouraging operation by goals and objectives, reducing barriers to communication, and promoting optimum use of individual contributors.

The processes and techniques most frequently reported by OD practitioners as being of significant value to them in their OD efforts include team building programs, MBO, third-party consultation, and survey/questionnaire feedback.

Most OD practitioners purport to measure the effectiveness of OD efforts. However, a majority of respondents indicate that they rely heavily on highly subjective methods such as personal or staff observations and participants' verbal evaluations.

While group processes and techniques are emphasized by OD practitioners, the individual and his effectiveness are still prime targets in OD effort.[3]

The Conference Board study of 147 companies (45 of which were identified a priori as "OD companies") yielded some more specific operational patterns:

Systematic measurement of organizational climate through attitude surveys occurs in 71 percent of OD companies.

Participative methods of problem identification and problem solving are used by 98 percent of the OD group; however, 47 percent of the non-OD group also report using similar practices.

OD companies report more frequently than non-OD companies the following activities: special attention to problems of communication; the use of task forces, ad hoc groups, and temporary organization structures; job design; and joint objective setting.

Evaluation and measurement of the effectiveness of the various strategies to improve the organization is the least prevalent component of OD programs. Among the OD companies, 40 percent report using objective measures of effectiveness; 7 percent of the non-OD companies report similar measures.[4]

THE SURVEY

A variety of topics were selected for examination in this study to provide new insight into the status of OD awareness and application:

Extent of the CEO's (chief executive officer's) knowledge about OD and his major sources of OD information

Extent of use of internal and external consultants and the factors affecting their selection

Organizational level initiating suggestions for an OD effort and decisions to implement such programs

Major reasons for the initiation of OD programs

Major foci and targets of OD programs

Primary information sources and techniques used in OD programs

Satisfaction with and expectations concerning OD programs

Major criticisms of OD efforts.

Questionnaires to assess the status of OD practice were mailed to the CEOs of 225 companies or major corporate divisions selected at random from the ten largest city listings in the *Indiana Industrial Directory*. While the directory lists well over 10,000 firms, most are extremely small (less than 100 employees). For this reason, the sample was selected so that approximately the same number of companies were represented within each of the directory's size categories. (The four smallest size categories were combined into one—less than 100 employees—for purposes of this survey.) All organizations in the directory's largest size category (more than 5,000 employees) were included in the sample. This number served as the basis for determining the number of organizations to be selected from each

TABLE 1. Characteristics of respondents

| 1a. Industrial Classification | | | 1b. Distribution by Size of Firm | | |
Industry	N	No. Employees	N	1972 Net Sales	N
Manufacturing	45	Less than 100	12	Less than $100,000	2
Public utility	5	100–250	9	$100,000–$500,000	1
Insurance	3	250–500	6	$500,000–$1 million	21
Banking and financial	3	500–1,000	10	$1 million–$10 million	12
services		1,000–2,500	10	$10 million–$50 million	8
Construction	1	2,500–5,000	5	$50 million–$100 million	13
Health services	1	5,000–10,000	7	$100 million–$500 million	2
Other (nutrition, publishing,	5	Over 10,000	4	Over $500 million	4
TV, and so on)					
Total	63	*Total*	63	*Total*	63

of the other size categories. Sixty-three organizations, or approximately 28 percent of those surveyed, completed and returned the questionnaire.

The sixty-three companies participating in the study are categorized by industrial type and size in Table 1. Because of the relatively small size of the sample, raw data frequencies are presented rather than percentages. Although all major industrial types are represented in the sample, manufacturing firms predominate (about 70 percent of the sample returns). This fact should be kept in mind when interpreting the results of the study. In addition, it should be noted that the sample is restricted to relatively small organizations. That is, the majority of the firms represented in this survey have annual net sales between $500,000 and $100 million. In comparison, the net sales of the majority of companies comprising *Fortune*'s 500 largest industrials range from $250 million to more than $10 billion.

THE FINDINGS

Knowledge of OD

Despite the widespread attention OD has received in recent management literature, only 39 percent of the CEOs responding to the survey felt that they had a "substantial" or "good" knowledge of the discipline; 35 percent felt their knowledge was "fair"; 26 percent felt that their knowledge was "weak" or "poor."

The CEOs further indicated a wide range of sources from which they first learned about OD.

Sources external to the organization such as trade journals, books, professional meetings, and university courses were most frequently cited. Members of one's own staff were mentioned as sources by only 16 percent of the respondents.

The personal sources of OD information (staff members, professional acquaintances, friends, and so on), although mentioned infrequently as original sources of OD information, were cited far more often as contributors expanding the CEO's knowledge about OD. However, three of the more formal sources remained most frequently cited (books, trade journals, and professional meetings). University courses apparently were not a major source of subsequent or continuing information, their frequency of citation declining from 27 percent to 20 percent.

Use of Consultants

The use or need for outside consultants in OD interventions has been the subject of controversy. Most theorists agree, however, that third-party interventions are useful and necessary—at least in the early stages of an OD effort. Nevertheless, half of the organizations reporting their present or past involvement in OD stated that their effort involved the use of internal consultants alone. The other half of the companies reported the use of both internal and external consultants. Only one firm reported using only external consultants.

Those companies employing external consultants in conjunction with their OD program overwhelmingly cited "referrals by respected others," the consultant's "personal reputation," and the "reputation of the consulting firm he represents" as the dominant factors influencing their selection of external consultants. Other potential factors—such as university affiliation, doctoral degree, appearances as a speaker, personal friendships, and the publication of articles—were infrequently mentioned as influences in the selection process.

In contrast to the findings for OD companies, nine of the companies who have never instituted an OD program and are not now engaged in one stated that they would rely solely upon external consultants were they to undertake an OD program; seven would use internal consultants alone; five would use a combination of both. Despite a lack of consensus regarding the use of external consultants, these companies overwhelmingly noted that, were they to use an outside consultant, their selection would be most influenced by the referrals of other companies who had engaged in OD.

Level of Program Origination

Of the 63 firms responding to the survey, over half (38) reported that their organization was presently involved in an OD program. Since the term "organization development" has come to mean many things to many people, respondents were asked to answer this question assessing their involvement in OD only after the term had been defined for them in the following way:

OD is a major, long-term, planned effort to change some part of an organization's culture (its values, attitudes, reward systems, procedures of work, structure, processes, and so on) so that the organization can increase its present effectiveness and health, and can better adapt to new technologies, markets, challenges, and other forms of change in the future.

An overwhelming plurality of respondents (20) stated that the suggestion for their OD program originated at the presidential level, as did the decision to implement the program. Division managers were second most frequently cited in both instances, followed by the board of directors and vice-presidents. In only 8 percent of the cases did suggestions for the OD effort originate with the personnel manager; in no instance did the decision to implement the OD program rest with him.

Impetus for OD Program

OD programs are usually initiated in response to some perceived organizational problem or need. Therefore, the CEOs in the study were asked to indicate whether the impetus for their program came from external forces (forces which emerge in the larger environment and are principally beyond the CEO's control—for example, actions of competitors and legislators) or internal forces (forces which operate inside the firm and are generally controllable to some degree by management—for example, certain costs and absenteeism). Twenty-one of the companies indicated that their programs were started in response to internal forces; sixteen said the impetus came from both areas. Only one firm cited external forces alone as the underlying cause for installation of an OD program.

Respondents were asked to break down their responses into more specific internal and external sources. Companies indicating that all or part of the impetus for the program came from external forces cited market factors (competitors' actions, sales, resource markets, and so on) most frequently as the underlying causal forces (70 percent of response total). Social and political changes were rated second in importance. Changes in technology were cited least frequently (31 percent of response total). Process forces (breakdowns in decision making, communication, and so on) were cited most often as the specific internal forces leading to the initiation of OD efforts (60 percent). Cited nearly as frequently, however, were behavioral forces (for example, morale, absenteeism, and turnover).

Focus of OD Effort

Using a classification schema similar to that presented by French and Bell, respondents were asked to indicate the organizational process which was the target of their OD intervention. Since OD programs frequently have multiple process objectives, responses to this question usually were not limited to a single process target. In fact, the average number of responses per organization was 3.2.

Those areas most often cited as major intervention targets were decision, problem solving, and goal setting processes. Communication problems, interfacing relations (relations between personnel from different groups, departments, plants, and so on), and planning methods were second in importance. Creativity, superior-subordinate relations, and conflict resolution were ranked last in terms of their selection as process targets.

OD Techniques

A number of data sources are available to organizations for assessing the present status of their organizational processes and for diagnosing problem areas. A list of the more commonly used information gathering techniques was presented to the CEOs with instructions to check the methods that had been used in their OD efforts.

Companies most frequently reported using direct observation as their principal data gathering method. Nearly as frequently mentioned were interdepartmental group meetings. A number of companies reported the use of interviews and departmental group meetings, while a few cited the use of questionnaires and confrontation meetings.

A significant majority of the companies (29 of 38) felt that the techniques they used had been "moderately" or "very effective" in obtaining a true picture of the current status of their organization. Eight firms felt that their data collection techniques were only "fairly effective." None of the respondents, however, felt that the techniques they used were ineffective.

In addition to various information gathering techniques, companies have a wide variety of OD interventions potentially available for use in improving their organizational effectiveness (for example, job enrichment, MBO, and team building). Of the numerous interventions available, team-building activities and management by objectives were by far the most widely reported in use. Systems analysis and job enrichment/enlargement are also widely employed.

Surprisingly, grid training and sensitivity training, despite their widespread popularity in man-

agement lore, were mentioned only infrequently as applied interventions. This finding is similar to results previously cited by Patten and others. In their survey of OD practitioners, they found that sensitivity training and grid theory were ranked lowest among potential interventions in terms of perceived value to the organizational improvement effort.[5]

While these techniques can be used by organizations without a formal OD program, they nevertheless were reported by respondents as component parts of their OD designs. A breakdown of the frequency of use of these various interventions is presented in Table 2.

TABLE 2. Interventions used in OD programs

Technique	No. Reporting Use
Team building	33
MBO	30
Systems analysis	20
Job enrichment/enlargement	20
Seminars	20
Mechanization/automation	17
Survey-feedback	13
Confrontation meetings	13
Lectures	12
Career planning	12
Grid training	8
Sensitivity training	5
Other	3

Satisfaction and Criticism

About half of the companies (17) currently engaged in OD programs were "quite satisfied" with their programs to date. However, 18 others were only "somewhat satisfied" and two were "somewhat dissatisfied." For the long-run, however, CEOs were somewhat more optimistic. Ten companies felt their program would be "very successful"; 20 felt it would be "quite successful"; and 7 felt it would be "somewhat successful." No respondent felt that his firm's efforts would ultimately prove to be unsuccessful. Perhaps this is to be expected, considering the investment that these firms will make in their programs.

Most respondents' dissatisfaction with their

OD programs centered around the problem of evaluation. Almost half of the survey participants reported that the effectiveness of their program was difficult to evaluate. Time and knowledge requirements were second most frequently mentioned. Surprisingly, costs were cited only twice in their critiques. Other problem areas and their incidence are presented in Table 3.

TABLE 3. Criticisms of OD programs

Major Criticism	No. of Citations*
Effectiveness difficult to evaluate	18
None	8
Too time consuming	7
Insufficient knowledge of OD on part of company personnel	7
Results or potential benefits too uncertain at time program undertaken	6
Objectives too vague	5
Costs too uncertain at time program undertaken	5
Too expensive	2
Insufficient knowledge of OD on part of external consultant	1
Other	3

* Multiple responses possible.

Other Trends

While no attempt has been made to break down the data for specific hypothesis testing because of the relatively small sample of organizations participating in the study, the data suggest trends in several areas. *First,* decisions to implement OD programs appear to be related to company size (total number of employees, net sales, and size of personnel staff). Larger firms are more frequently involved in OD efforts than smaller firms. Although the firms in this study were significantly smaller in annual sales volume than those participating in Glueck's study, similar trends were observed.

Second, general satisfaction with the OD effort is negatively related to the general educational level of the CEO, but positively related to his knowledge about OD. CEOs who had four-year college degrees tend to be less satisfied with their programs than those without college degrees; however, the more the CEO feels he knows about OD, the greater his satisfaction with the program.

Satisfaction is also related to the CEO's area of expertise. Respondents with degrees in engineering tend to be more satisfied with their programs than those with backgrounds in business administration. CEOs with degrees in liberal arts tend to be the least satisfied with their programs (the number of respondents in the latter category, however, was extremely small).

Third, CEOs' feelings regarding the degree of ultimate success they expect from their programs also vary with company size. The larger the firm (as measured by its net sales and number of employees), the less optimistic is the CEO regarding the program's chances for ultimate success.

Fourth, there appear to be no major or significant trends regarding the differential effectiveness of various data collection methodologies or OD interventions. Firms using confrontation meetings, however, are somewhat more satisfied than the average with their data collection efforts, while firms employing questionnaires are somewhat less satisfied than the average.

Similarly, while overall perceptions of the effectiveness of various intervention techniques do not vary widely, firms employing a systems approach and job enrichment/enlargement as part of their OD program are somewhat more satisfied with their results to date. They also tend to be somewhat more optimistic about the likely degree of ultimate success of their program than firms using other types of interventions.

It is apparent from the CEOs' responses to this survey that diversity exists both in expectations concerning the outcomes of OD and in the range of data collection and intervention technologies that are employed. Among the most frequently cited targets of OD programs are organizational communication and decision and problem-solving activities. Less common targets are innovation and creativity.

Direct observation and interdepartmental group meetings are the most commonly used data collection techniques, while questionnaires are cited about only one-third as often. Team building and

MBO head the list of most frequently used interventions; sensitivity training and grid training are reported only infrequently as components of ongoing OD programs.

While CEOs, for the most part, are quite satisfied with their OD efforts to date and are optimistic about the potential of their programs, one major criticism emerged; an overwhelming proportion of the CEOs in the study feel that the effectiveness of their program is difficult to evaluate. Several also feel that the process is too time consuming. Some trends between satisfaction/effectiveness and particular OD methodologies have also been suggested. However, the successful development of more effective OD programs awaits definitive, large-scale investigations which more clearly identify the objectives, situations, and conditions for which these diverse methodologies are best suited.

NOTES

1. W. Warner Burke, "A Look at Organizational Development," in W. Warner Burke, ed., *Contemporary Organization Development: Conceptual Orientations and Interventions* (Washington, D.C.: NTL Institute for Applied Behavioral Science, 1972), pp. 1–3.

Wendell L. French and Cecil H. Bell, *Organization Development* (Englewood Cliffs, N.J.: Prentice-Hall, 1973), p. xiv.

2. William F. Glueck, *Organization Planning and Development* (New York: American Management Association, 1971).

3. Thomas H. Patten and others, *Characteristics and Professional Concerns of Organization Development Practitioners* (Madison, Wis.: American Society for Training and Development, 1973).

4. Harold M. Rush, *Organization Development: A Reconnaissance* (New York: The Conference Board, 1973).

5. Patten, *Characteristics and Professional Concerns.*

AN INTERACTIVE APPROACH
TO THE PROBLEM OF
ORGANIZATIONAL CHANGE

ROBERT C. SHIRLEY

Organizational change is a term of many and varied meanings. At one extreme of a continuum, the term is used to refer to very basic changes in individual beliefs, values, and attitudes within an organization. At the other extreme, it has been applied in a holistic sense to total organizational shifts in objectives, policies and general modes of operation. In between the two extremes, the term has been applied to changes in almost all conceivable facets or dimensions of an organization. Consequently, the body of knowledge generally considered relevant to the management of organizational change is extremely broad and ill-defined. The net result of this general state of ambiguity is confusion—confusion not only about what is meant by the term 'organizational change,' but also about the purposes and areas of applicability of the numerous and varied approaches to change which exist today. The purposes of this article are to 1) provide a perspective on change which will help to clarify its meaning and its systemic properties insofar as organizational activities are concerned and 2) develop a framework to facilitate the management of change from a total firm perspective.

Reprinted by permission from Robert C. Shirley and *Human Resource Management,* Volume 14, No. 2, Summer 1975, pp. 11–19, Graduate School of Business Administration, University of Michigan, Ann Arbor, Michigan 48109.

To gain a clear perspective on the notion of organizational change, it is helpful to first define the term 'organization.' Although there are at least as many definitions as there are writers on the subject, the prevailing orientation is that of a systems view. Regardless of precise wording, an organization is usually (and very abstractly) described as *a complex system of mutually dependent parts.* It follows that the term 'organizational change' would logically refer to *an alteration or modification of one or more parts of the system.* This definition is not sufficient, however, insofar as operationalizing the notion of change in organizations. What is needed is an operational scheme of organization 'parts' so that (a) the focus and direction of change sought may be clearly identified for any given situation and (b) the extended and interactive effects of a change in any one part of the system on the other parts may be anticipated and traced. The next few paragraphs present such a scheme as a necessary background for subsequent consideration of change causes, goals, targets, and techniques.

THE PARTS OF AN ORGANIZATION

It is useful to view any organization as comprising six interdependent dimensions: environment, strategy, technology, program, structure and behavior. These six dimensions, in turn, may be subdivided into their component parts to provide a comprehensive scheme for organizational analysis. Each major dimension is discussed more fully below.

The Environmental Dimension

The particular external conditions faced by any firm may be classified into one of four major (although obviously interrelated) sectors of the environment: economic, social, technological, and political/legal. The economic sector includes phenomena such as characteristics and structure of the industry, competitor strengths and weaknesses, market trends, and other forces which are primarily economic in nature and have external origins. The social sector encompasses larger societal values, ethical customs, consumer psychology, minority group influences, demographic information of concern to the firm, and the like. The technological sector includes technological developments in the firm's industry or elsewhere which are relevant for new product development and/or improvement of production processes. Finally, the political/legal sector encompasses applicable legislation, regulatory agencies, court decisions, executive acts, foreign policy, and other forces which may present either new opportunities to the firm or act as constraints on its operations. As is evident, the environmental dimension is viewed as a part of the organization itself, thus reflecting the open system notion that organizational analysis solely confined to 'internal parts' falls short of providing a complete understanding of the total system.

The Strategic Dimension

This strategy dimension of an organization refers to its basic product(service)/market scope, competitive emphasis, and objectives (performance criteria). Strategic decisions define the basic relationship of the organization to its environment and require determination of the following: product(or service) mix, customer mix, geographic limits of the markets to be served, competitive emphasis, and objectives related to profitability, growth, market share, and survival. Such deci-

sions thus 'bridge the gap' between the environment and the remaining organizational dimensions, providing a set of constraints to guide lower-order decisions concerning technology, programs (e.g., production, marketing), structure, and behavioral requirements. Strategy decisions emerge from an iterative assessment of environmental opportunities and constraints in relation to internal resources, capabilities and values; insofar as total system functioning is concerned, these decisions determine the overall requirements for interactions among the operational parts of the organization.

The Program Dimension

The program dimension of an organization comprises the major implementation programs developed by a firm to achieve its strategy. Included here would be technical plans developed for marketing (distribution, sales, promotion, and market research), production (schedules, inventory management, quality control, operations), research and development, engineering, purchasing, personnel administration, and other major task areas of the firm. This dimension refers to the *technical specifics* of programs in terms of objectives, processes, and techniques utilized in each area to accomplish the overall strategy and objectives of the firm.

The Structural Dimension

The structural dimension of a firm refers to the formal arrangements which have been established to coordinate the total activities required to implement a given strategy. In a sense, this dimension reflects the "anatomy" of a firm via its focus on mechanisms and processes which *link* (both vertically and horizontally) the various parts of an organization. For purposes of analysis, it is useful to classify the major elements of organizational structure as follows:

• Distribution of functions throughout the organization (includes definition of functions to be performed, groupings of functions, and the vertical and horizontal task relationships among functions).

- Vertical and horizontal authority relationships (who has the authority to do what).

- Communication/decision processes (the manner in which formal decisions are made and by whom, supporting informational inputs, and the information systems established to provide the inputs to decision makers).

- Policies (the decision rules or guidelines established in finance, marketing, production, personnel, purchasing, research and development, and other areas; these guidelines serve to tie the performance of specific functions to the overall strategy and objectives of the firm).

- Formal incentive systems (compensation plan characteristics, fringe benefits, incentive or bonus plans, promotion criteria and other features of the formal reward system used by the organization).

Taken together, these six parts of the structural dimension establish the basic conditions under which organizational members perform their various roles.

The Behavioral Dimension

The behavioral dimension is composed of four major parts:

- The individual (includes phenomena such as individual beliefs, values, and attitudes, as well as overt behavior; also includes considerations of abilities, satisfaction, personalities, and other behavioral phenomena which are of an individualistic nature).

- Interpersonal relationships (whereas the above focus was on the individual, the focus here is on interactions between two persons in accomplishing tasks).

- Group behavior (this part refers to the group as a unit of analysis, including consideration of the presence or absence of group cohesiveness; informal group goals, leaders, and members; influence of the group over individuals; group norms; and other behavioral phenomena which are of a group nature).

- Intergroup behavior (whereas the immediately preceding focus was on the single work group, this category relates to the interactions of two or more groups in accomplishing tasks).

The Technology Dimension

Finally, the technology dimension refers to the technology of production, plant and equipment, materials, and other 'physical' parts of an organization.

Overview

Table 1 presents a summary overview of the dimensions and their component parts. This scheme serves to partially operationalize the earlier definition of organizational change. Thus organizational change occurs when one or more of the parts outlined in Table 1 are altered or modified in some fashion. This is only a starting point, however. The utility of the scheme may be proven only through demonstration of how it can facilitate the management of change via a systematic and orderly view of the process.

The First Step: Recognizing the Need for Change

Organizations, of course, are constantly changing. Although the causes of change are numerous and varied, it is useful, for analytical purposes, to group them into two basic categories: external forces and internal forces. External forces creating the need for change in other parts of the total system emerge from the environmental dimension of the organization, in the form of extra-firm technological developments, changing societal values, changing market trends, competitors' actions, anti-pollution legislation, and the like. Although external forces obviously impinge on all dimensions of the firm, the most frequent point of interface is with the strategy dimension. Strategy shifts (e.g., in product or customer mix) in response to changing environmental forces then signal the need for further changes in the program, structure, technology, and behavior dimensions of the organization, creating an almost endless chain of reverberations throughout the system.

It is somewhat obvious that the sole function of many formal departments is to (a) identify external forces toward change and (b) analyze their implications for needed changes or adjustments in other parts of the organization. Market

TABLE 1. Summary listing of organization parts

I. Environmental
  A. Economic
  B. Technological
  C. Social
  D. Political/Legal
	IV. Structure
	  A. Distribution of functions
	  B. Distribution of authority
	  C. Reporting relationships
	  D. Communication/decision processes
	  E. Policies (decision rules)
	  F. Incentive system

II. Strategy
  A. Product mix
  B. Customer mix
  C. Geographic limits of market
  D. Competitive emphasis
  E. Objectives
	V. Behavior
	  A. The individual
	  B. Interpersonal relationships
	  C. The group
	  D. Intergroup relationships

III. Programs
  A. Marketing
  B. Production
  C. Financial
  D. R & D
  E. Engineering
  F. Purchasing
  G. Personnel
  H. Other
	VI. Technology
	  A. Technology of production
	  B. Plant and equipment
	  C. Materials
	  D. Tools

Each of the major organization parts comprise numerous sub-parts which are not explicitly ide t'fied in this Table. For example, the marketing program may be further subdivided into distribution, sales, promotion, and market research. In a similar vein, numerous sub-parts of the individual could be listed (e.g., his values, sentiments toward work, abilities, desires, overt behavior) to provide a more detailed focus for analytical purposes.

research, long range planning, and R & D departments fall in this category. Yet what we often fail to recognize is that the response made to external forces necessarily 'disturbs' the internal system equilibrium. This is in contrast to the case where internal forces themselves create the need for change. Internal forces may be generally considered synonymous with the term 'organizational stress'—stress in sentiments, activities, interactions, or performance results. Such forces toward change thus represent conditions of equilibria which are *already* upset within one or more parts of the organization. For example, a conflict in interactions may exist between R & D and production because of a disagreement over the proper tolerance levels required in precision manufacturing —such disagreement possibly emanating from the differing goals, orientations, and values of the two departments. Or, organizational stress may arise as a result of negative sentiments or feelings on the part of employees about their work. Numerous other familiar varieties of organizational stress could be cited. The essential point is that

tension *always* exists in an organization undergoing change; however, the tension may be either consciously created by individuals or groups (in response to environmental forces) or it may *itself* create the need for change (in the form of organizational stress). Consequently, recognition of the source of the tension makes for a more informed assessment of probable reactions to change by those affected. If internal tension creates the need for change, then those affected should welcome relief; on the other hand, if the response to external forces disturbs some 'comfortable' equilibrium internally, then change is more likely to be resisted by affected employees.

The Second Step: Responding to the Need for Change

Regardless of whether the forces creating the need for change in some part of the system are external in origin or internal or both, the form of organizational response most commonly observed is that of analysis—however thorough or hasty. In the case of extra-firm technological developments, for example, analysis must be conducted to determine the feasibility of application to existing facilities and compatibility with existing skills. This analysis will then determine, for example, whether or not the formal change goal "to utilize new process A in the production of product X" may be established by the organization (whether explicitly or implicitly), with its associated implications for required structural and behavioral changes. In the case of perceived economic or market opportunities which may be achieved via alternative growth routes, the feasibility of merging with another organization may be analyzed in depth, as might be the feasibility of growth through internal expansion and/or diversification. In the case of internal organizational stress, diagnostic analyses directed toward determining the *causes* of such stress would ideally be the first response by managers before any steps were taken to deal directly with the stress.

The scheme of organizational parts developed earlier can serve as a useful tool at this stage for the manager of change. Whether he/she alone is trying to develop some sort of action plan for responding to 'disturbing forces' or whether he/she is evaluating analyses (written or verbal) prepared by others, the scheme provides a handy reference for truly systematizing the approach to the problem. A proposed change in the technology dimension e.g., (utilization of some new equipment or process), for example, may be subjected to an evaluation of its extended consequences for other parts of the system. What will be the effect of such a change on individual skill requirements and/or attitudes (see V, A in Table 1)? What will be the effect on task interactions (see IV, A in Table 1)? What will be the effect on production scheduling (see III, B in Table 1)? What will be the effect on the current piece rate scheme (see IV, F in Table 1)? In general, what other parts of the total organizational system will be affected by this change in technology (see all of Table 1)? Have the costs and benefits of these *extended* effects of the proposed change been calculated?

The Third Step: Establishing Change Goals

Once the manager has completed the analytical process described above and has become cogni-

zant of the extended implications of any proposed change, he/she is ready to formally establish the goals of the proposed change. The analytical process of assessing consequences thus *precedes* goal-setting in order to ensure feasibility of the goals. Illustrative goals include:

- To diversify into product-markets X, Y, and Z (as a result of analysis of changing market opportunities and/or poor economic performance results in existing markets).

- To merge (horizontally) with ABC Corporation (as a result of poor performance results perceived as being caused by lack of volume production necessary to achieve economies of scale in existing facilities).

- To install specified anti-pollution devices on products D and E (as a result of a new legal constraint requiring such installations).

- To move decision levels downward (as a result of organizational stress perceived as being caused by authoritarian decision making at the top levels of the organization).

- To eliminate interdepartmental competition and foster collaboration (as a result of perceived stress in departmental interactions, e.g., the production and R & D conflict noted earlier).

- To change the structure of distribution channels currently being utilized (as a result of increased middle-man costs which have contributed to poor performance results).

Although the illustrative goals obviously cover a broad spectrum of change situations, they (and all other possible change goals) generally have one thing in common: their successful accomplishment ultimately depends greatly on the extent to which necessary *structural* and *behavioral* changes are carefully implemented within the organization. Reflecting for a moment on the differences in the types of goals, however, it is possible to broadly classify them in a fashion consistent with the scheme of organizational parts developed in Table 1:

Strategic—those change goals concerned with altering the relationship between the firm and its environment (e.g., revised objectives, new product/market scope). Examples of change goals of this type include 1 and 2 above.

Technological—those goals directly related to changes in the technology of production, plant and equipment, and the like. An example of this type is goal 3 above.

Structural—change goals which are concerned with alterations in reporting relationships, location of functions and authority, communication/decision processes, spans of control, formal incentive programs, and similar aspects of an organization's "anatomy" fall in this category. An example is goal 4 above. Structural change is elaborated upon in the next major section below.

Behavioral—those goals which aim initially at changing values, attitudes, beliefs, norms, interpersonal relationships, group behavior, intergroup behavior, and similar "humanistic" phenomena. An example is goal 5 above. Behavioral change is also elaborated upon in the next major section below.

Program—those change goals which focus on altering the objectives or structure of the technical implementation plans developed for marketing, production, R & D, and other task areas. An example is goal 6 above.

With respect to the above classification, it should be noted that the goal types are *not* mutually exclusive, as two or more types may be operative simultaneously. Changes in organizational structure and behavior may be pursued in and of themselves, but, and as noted above, changes in strategy and technology also necessitate changes in structure and behavior for their successful accomplishment. For example, the strategic change goal of "merger" will usually require structural change (e.g., consolidation of some administrative functions) and behavioral change (e.g., some transplanting of sole identification with one organization to that of a newly merged concern) for its successful accomplishment. On the other hand, structural change may be deemed appropriate given an *unchanged* strategy or technology in order to increase administrative efficiency or effectiveness. The above classification should permit the practicing manager to pinpoint just what type of change he/she is ini-

tially attempting to accomplish, as well as its relationship to the other types.

A great deal of research on various change programs and situations has been conducted, the results of which are very useful to the manager who has diagnosed his/her firm's problems and formulated appropriate goals. Most of the work has been done in the area of behavioral change. The field of organizational development (OD) is an emerging discipline which focuses on educational strategies "employing experienced-based behavior in order to achieve a self-renewing organization."[1] OD is based on behavioral science findings and theories and generally seeks to help employees to remove barriers which prevent the release of human potential within the organization. Some specific change goals sought with OD are: creating an open, problem-solving climate; building trust; reducing inappropriate competition and fostering collaboration; increasing self-control and self-direction for organizational members; and supplementing the authority of status with that of competence.[2]

The field of corporate strategy is currently in its infancy insofar as the availability of useful research results is concerned. Several excellent conceptual schemes and guides are available for the top manager, however, most notably those developed by Ansoff, Katz, and Learned *et al.*[3] These schemes provide reference material on the various factors and influences involved in the changing of strategy, as well as recommended processes for strategy formation. In the area of structural change, several excellent empirical studies are available,[4] and a few classic studies focus on the impact of introducing technological change.[5]

The Fourth Step: Determining Change Targets and Techniques

As noted earlier, the initial adjustment or modification of any organizational part in response to external or internal forces creates reverberations throughout the total system. It was also noted that *any* of the types of change goals identified, when acted upon, eventually necessitate some subsequent change along the structural and behavioral dimensions. This partially explains why most of the literature labeled 'organizational change' tends to focus on these two dimensions, particularly on the latter. What is frequently overlooked, however, is that the ultimate results of a change effort are greatly influenced by which of the two (structure or behavior) is changed *first* in any given situation. The following paragraphs seek to clarify this notion for the manager, first by examining the two 'philosophies' of target priority which now exist, and secondly by proposing a means for determining which area should receive initial attention.

The *structural approach* to change, as the name implies, is predicated on the assumption that one improves task performance by clarifying and defining the jobs of people and by setting up clearly defined job relationships, lines of authority, and accountability areas. Adherence to this philosophy implies that, no matter what forces create the need for change, the initial change target will be one of the six major parts (or sub-parts thereof) of the structural dimension listed in Table 1. Thus, if the change goal is to encourage the practice of participative management (a behavioral goal), the change target would be the formal distribution of authority in the organization (a structural target) as opposed to, say, the authoritarian personalities of current power figures. This is not to say that the problem of authoritarian personalities would be ignored; rather, it is assumed by structuralists that the negative consequences of such personalities may be better alleviated via a restructuring process (formal realignment of authority relationships) than via an attitudinal or personality change process (relying on behavioral modification to result in their subsequent voluntary delegation of authority).

The second philosophy, labeled the *humanistic approach,* is predicated on the assumption that one improves task performance ultimately by focusing on individual, interpersonal, group, and intergroup behavior. The 'organizational change discipline,' as currently documented and practiced, subscribes primarily to this approach. Its difference from the structural approach may be clarified by considering, again, the behavioral change goal of encouraging participative management. The initial change target under the humanistic approach would be the authoritarian personality, with reliance placed on voluntary delegation of authority; no initial restructuring

would be thought necessary to achieve a realignment of authority relationships within the organization. This approach comprises the field of organizational development and such well-known approaches as T-groups, sensitivity training, and other variations of the general theme of laboratory training.[6] These and similar educational approaches focus *initially* on one or more of the behavioral change targets listed earlier in Table 1. Desirable changes in structure and performance are seen to follow behavioral change, with the implicit assumption being that a better atmosphere for problem-solving (e.g., more cooperation, open acknowledgment and handling of conflict) will have been inculcated in organizational members. A frequent criticism of this approach has been its relative neglect of structural and technological processes in organizations and its consequent overemphasis on behavioral processes.[7]

INTEGRATION OF THE APPROACHES

The structural and humanistic approaches are frequently viewed as 'either-or' approaches. The major point to be made here is that both approaches are useful in a situational approach to change target selection. The key to integration of the approaches appears to lie in recognizing the *uniqueness* of particular change situations. Leavitt notes that the differentiation of change approaches lies in "... (a) points of entry into the organization, (b) relative weightings, and (c) underlying values..."[8] To provide a means for integrating the two approaches, it should first be noted that the 'point of entry' in a change situation will depend on whether or not accomplishment of a given change goal, as discussed above, involves changing *both* structure and behavior. It should be emphasized that *any* change in organizational structure will have ramifications for individual and/or group behavior, yet the reverse is not necessarily the case. The key point is that where structural change must occur, the associated behavioral change desired cannot be effectuated *with direction* until and unless the desired structural changes have been identified. Consider, for example, the case of a desired change in authority relationships between a superior and his/her subordinate. Until each knows his/her role both within the organization and in relation to each other, it is difficult to meaningfully implement any techniques designed to change attitudes or interpersonal relationships. This is to be contrasted to the situation where changes in behavior are necessary to better perform an *unchanged* role within the organization. In the latter case, behavioral targets logically reflect the initial "point of entry" into an organization for purposes of change, whereas the former situation would call for a structural target (definition of authority relationships) as the initial focus.

It thus appears useful to classify behavioral targets as (a) those derivative of structural change targets and (b) those unrelated to structural change. If a change is desired in one of the six structural parts listed in Table 1, then that represents the initial point of entry in order to provide direction for subsequent attitudinal/behavioral change; if there is to be no structural change, and the problem is purely attitudinal or behavioral in nature, the behavioral targets should constitute the initial points of entry.

In order to clarify the preceding notions, let us consider the case of merger (strategic change) as a final example. Both structural and behavioral changes are required as a result of merger; structural changes emanate from an upsetting of the activities and interactions equilibria, while behavioral changes are required to cope with the new structure and to achieve self-maintenance, growth and social satisfactions. The key to determining which to attack first in accomplishing, for example, the "centralization of X, Y, and Z functions" lies in the fact that, for this particular situation, *role content and relations must change*—and this is initially a matter of structure. The behavioral change required to accomplish the new activities and interactions cannot be effectuated until the new activities and interactions have been identified, i.e., unless the structural changes have been pinpointed and agreed upon. Therefore, the structural approach logically reflects the initial "point of entry" in this particular situation, insofar as the *target* of change, while the humanistic approach (and its associated group of techniques) may be necessary to ensure that concomitant attitudinal/behavioral changes move in the desired direction

—acceptance of new roles, role relations, and organizational identities.

That structural changes are necessary in a merger situation to provide some degree of coordinated effort is rather obvious. The fact that behavioral targets are derivative of structural targets is not so obvious, however, and deserves further explanation. It is generally the case that structural realignments resulting from a merger occur primarily at the managerial and supervisory level. Necessary changes in formal authority distribution, differentiation and integration of administrative functions, and communication-decision processes may have little or no effect on the content and method of performance of lower-level operative and technical jobs; thus, behavioral change strategies should be distinctly different between the managerial and operating employee classes, as the type and extent of behavioral changes necessary are *primarily a function of the extent of change in task performance methods and interactions*. The behavioral change targets might be segmented according to hierarchial level in this instance, as a greater degree of behavioral change will be required of those individuals experiencing role (structural) changes. Of course there may be instances in a merger situation where behavioral changes unrelated to structural changes are also necessary. For example, there may be a perceived need to shift (at least partially) organizational identities and loyalties to the parent organization surviving the merger. No structural changes may be called for in this particular case, and behavioral targets logically constitute the appropriate initial focus insofar as change is concerned.

The 'relative weightings' assigned to the structural and humanistic approaches and techniques should also be greatly influenced by the dictates of the situation. It is entirely plausible, for example, that structural change will have such tremendous and far reaching consequences for human behavior that much emphasis should be placed on humanistic approaches and techniques. This is a question of method or technique, however, and not a question of targets. The two are frequently confused. The 'attacking' of structural targets does not automatically mean that an authoritarian or unilateral 'decree' approach is utilized without consideration for the individual(s) affected. Thus structural change targets can be acted upon under conditions of mutual goat setting, deliberation, and equal power distributions (as developed by Warren Bennis) or via a shared approach (as noted by Larry Greiner) to better assure identification with change outcomes. The philosophies underlying methods or techniques of change are well developed by Bennis and Greiner.[9]

Bennis' typology of change processes is often erroneously associated only with humanistic approaches to change (probably because of his leanings in that direction); it can more properly be viewed, however, as a "philosophy of implementation" rather than a philosophy of target selection. His paradigm of change processes provides several key considerations related to the implementation of change, primarily via its emphasis on the nature of goal setting (mutual versus nonmutual), power ratio between the parties involved in change, and the extent of deliberation involved in change processes. Greiner takes an approach similar to Bennis' as he views various approaches to change in terms of their position along a "power distribution" continuum. At one extreme are those approaches which rely on unilateral authority; more toward the middle of the continuum are the shared approaches, and finally, at the opposite extreme are the delegated approaches. Greiner arrives at an interesting conclusion when he notes that "we need to reduce our fond attachment for both unilateral and delegated approaches to change." His reasoning concerning the predicted failure of completely delegated approaches to change is that such an approach removes the power structure from direct involvement in a process that calls for its strong guidance; it appears that a completely unstructured approach to change, and the associated ambiguities, lead to feelings of anxiety on the part of affected employees and thus impede the process of implementing change.

CONCLUSION

This article has attempted to clarify the notion of 'organizational change' and its systemic properties. A paradigm of organizational 'parts' was presented to aid the manager in tracing the inter-

active and extended effects of any change goal contemplated for the organization. Particular attention was devoted to the interactive nature of structural and behavioral change—two primary target areas which are always affected no matter what type of change goal is at work. As a final note, it should be recognized that the intent of this article was to present a framework for structuring one's thinking about change causes, goals, targets, and interactive effects. Issues such as "how to overcome resistance to change" and "the best methods for effecting change" purposefully were not addressed; numerous (and useful) articles exist on these subjects. Yet, the fact is that change is both a highly situational and complex phenomenon which is always characterized by 'process ambiguities,' i.e., individual differences and unforeseen events always crop up to distort our best-laid plans for implementing change. The *attitudinal* thesis of this article is that it is better to initially approach such an ambiguous process with some structure for analysis of causes, goals, and targets than with none at all. Perhaps the best we can hope for is 'structured ambiguity' rather than 'ambiguous ambiguity' in our approach to change—the former at least holds the promise of our being able to anticipate and identify the forces underlying and causing the ambiguity! The paradigm presented herein has hopefully provided a means for anticipation and identification of such forces by utilizing a systems approach to the problem.

NOTES

1. Daniel L. Keegan, "Organizational Development: Description, Issues, and Research Results," *Academy of Management Journal,* December, 1971, p. 456. For an additional summary of techniques and issues in this area, see Anthony P. Raia, "Organizational Development—Some Issues and Challenges," *California Management Review,* Summer, 1972, pp. 13–20.

2. Keegan, "Organizational Development," p. 456.

3. H. Igor Ansoff, *Corporate Strategy,* New York; McGraw-Hill, 1965; Robert L. Katz, *Cases and Concepts in Corporate Strategy,* Englewood Cliffs; Prentice-Hall, Inc., 1970; Edmund P. Learned, *et. al., Business Policy: Text and Cases,* Homewood, Ill., Richard D. Irwin, Inc., 1969.

4. Gene Dalton, *et al., The Distribution of Author-*

ity in Formal Organizations, Boston, Harvard University Division of Research, 1968; Eli Ginzberg and Ewing W. Reilley, *Effecting Change in Large Organizations,* New York, Columbia University Press, 1957; Robert H. Guest, *Organizational Change: The Effect of Successful Leadership,* Homewood, Ill., Richard D. Irwin, Inc., and The Dorsey Press, 1962; Harriet O. Ronken and Paul R. Lawrence, *Administering Changes,* Boston, Harvard University Division of Research, 1952; Floyd Mann, "Changing Superior-Subordinate Relationships," *The Journal of Social Issues,* Vol. VII, No. 3, 1951, pp. 56–63; Kilburn LeCompte, "Organizational Structures in Transition," in *Some Theories of Organization,* ed. by Albert R. Rubenstein and Chadwick J. Haberstroh, Homewood, Ill., Richard D. Irwin, Inc., and The Dorsey Press, 1966; S. E. Seashore and D. G. Bowers, *Changing the Structure and Functioning of An Organization,* Monograph No. 33, Ann Arbor, Mich., Survey Research Center, 1963.

5. F. E. Emery and J. Marek, "Some Socio-Technical Aspects of Automation," *Human Relations,* February, 1962, pp. 17–25; Floyd C. Mann and Lawrence K. Williams, "Observations on the Dynamics of a Change to Electronic Data-Processing Equipment," *Administrative Science Quarterly,* Sept., 1960, pp. 217–56; E. L. Trist and K. W. Bamforth, "Some Social and Psychological Consequences of the Long-Wall Method of Goal-Getting," *Human Relations,* Vol. IV, No. 1, 1951, pp. 3–38.

6. The following sources describe and explain various approaches which focus on behavioral phenomena as initial targets for change: R. Lippet *et al., The Dynamics of Planned Change,* New York, John Wiley and Sons, 1958; A. Bavelas, "Some Problems of Organizational Change," *Journal of Social Issues,* Summer 1948, pp. 48–52; Warren Bennis, "A New Role for the Behavioral Sciences: Effecting Organizational Change," *Administrative Science Quarterly,* Sept., 1963, pp. 125–165; R. T. Golembiewski and A. Blumberg, "Laboratory Approach to Organization Change: Confrontation Design," *Academy of Management Journal,* June, 1968, pp. 199–210; Chris Argyris, *Organization and Innovation,* Homewood, Ill., Richard D. Irwin, Inc. and The Dorsey Press, 1965; W. Bennis, *et al., The Planning of Change,* New York, Holt, Rinehart, and Winston, 1968. Also, see various articles in *The Journal of Applied Behavioral Sciences,* the major journal dealing with "people-changing" approaches.

7. Raia, "Organizational Development," p. 18.

8. Harold J. Leavitt, "Applied Organizational Change in Industry: Structural, Technological, and Humanistic Approaches," *Handbook of Organizations,* ed. James March, Chicago, Rand McNally, 1965, p. 1145.

9. Warren Bennis, "A Typology of Change Processes," *The Planning of Change,* eds. Warren Bennis *et al.,* New York, Holt, Rinehart, and Winston, Inc. 1961; and Larry Greiner, "Patterns of Organization Change," *Harvard Business Review,* May–June 1967, pp. 119–122+

STRATEGIES FOR
LARGE SYSTEM CHANGE*

RICHARD BECKHARD

INTRODUCTION

The focus of this article is on assisting large organization change through consultative or training
interventions. As used below, "client" refers to an
organization's leader(s) and "consultant" refers
to the intervenor or change facilitator. Note that
the consultant can come from within or from outside the organization.

Intervention is defined here as behavior which
affects the *ongoing social processes* of a system.
These processes include:

1. Interaction between individuals.
2. Interaction between groups.
3. The procedures used for transmitting information, making decisions, planning actions,
   and setting goals.
4. The strategies and policies guiding the system, the norms, or the unwritten ground rules
   or values of the system.
5. The attitudes of people toward work, the organization, authority, and social values.

* This article is adapted from a chapter by the author in *Laboratory Method of Changing and Learning*, Benne, Bradford, Gibb, and Lippitt, editors,
forthcoming Spring 1975 from Science and Behavior
Books, Palo Alto, California.
Reprinted by permission of the *Sloan Management
Review*; an article by Richard Beckhard, *Sloan Management Review*, Winter 1975, pp. 43–55.

6. The distribution of effort within the system.
   Interventions can affect any one or several of
   these processes.

The first part of this article describes a model
of diagnosis and strategy planning which has had
high utility for the author during the past several
years. The second part examines a number of
actual strategies in organization and large system change and the issues of where to begin
change and how to maintain change.[1]

A MODEL FOR CHANGE
PLANNING

The following model is far from perfect. However,
its use seems to enable one to ask the "right"
questions and to obtain answers that yield a basis
for relatively trustworthy judgment on early interventions into the large system. For convenience
the model will be discussed under four headings.

Defining the Change Problem

When a change effort is initiated, either the client
and/or the consultant, or some other part of the
system has determined that there is some need for
change. An initial diagnostic step concerns analyzing what these needs are and whether they are
shared in different parts of the system. For example, let us suppose top management in an orga-

nization sees as a major need the improvement of the supervisory behavior of middle management and, simultaneously, the personnel staff in the organization sees as a *prior* need a change in the behavior of the top management and a change in the reward system. These are two very different perceptions of the priority of need for initial change, but a common perception that there is a need for change in the organization does exist. As a part of determining the need for change, it is also useful to collect some information from various parts of the system in order to determine the strength of the need.

There are two distinct ways of defining the change problem. The first considers the *organization* change needed or desired. For example, does the need concern changing the state of morale, the way work is done, the communication system, the reporting system, the structure or location of the decision making, the effectiveness of the top team, the relationships between levels, the way goals are set, or something else? The second considers what *type* of change is desired and what the hierarchy or rank-ordering of these types is. One should ask whether the primary initial change requires a change:

1. Of attitudes? Whose?
2. Of behavior? By whom and to what?
3. Of knowledge and understanding? Where?
4. Of organization procedures? Where?
5. Of practices and ways of work?

Rank-ordering the various types of change helps to determine which early interventions are most appropriate.

Having defined the change problem or problems from the viewpoint of both organizational change and change process, one can look at the organization system and subsystems to determine which are primarily related to the particular problem. The appropriate systems may be the organizational hierarchy, may be pieces of it, may be systems both inside and outside of the formal structure, or may be some parts of the formal structure and not other parts. A conscious identification of those parts of the total system which primarily affect or are affected by the particular change helps to reduce the number of subsystems

to be considered and also helps to clarify directions for early intervention.

Determining Readiness and Capability for Change

Readiness as stated here means either attitudinal or motivational energy concerning the change. Capability means the physical, financial, or organizational capacity to make the change. These are separate but interdependent variables.

In determining readiness for change, there is a formula developed by David Gleicher of Arthur D. Little that is particularly helpful. The formula can be described mathematically as $C = (abd) > x$, where C = change, a = level of dissatisfaction with the status quo, b = clear or understood desired state, d = practical first steps toward a desired state, and x = "cost" of changing. In other words, for change to be possible and for commitment to occur there has to be enough dissatisfaction with the current state of affairs to mobilize energy toward change. There also has to be some fairly clear conception of what the state of affairs would be if and when the change were sucessful. Of course, a desired state needs to be consistent with the values and priorities of the client system. There also needs to be some client awareness of practical first steps, or starting points, toward the desired state.

An early diagnosis by the consultant of which of these conditions does not exist, or does not exist in high strength, may provide direct clues concerning where to put early intervention energy. For example, if most of the system is not really dissatisfied with the present state of things, then early interventions may well need to aim toward increasing the level of dissatisfaction. On the other hand, there may be plenty of dissatisfaction with the present state, but no clear picture of what a desired state might be. In this case, early interventions might be aimed at getting strategic parts of the organization to define the ideal or desired state. If both of these conditions exist but practical first steps are missing, then early intervention strategy may well be to pick some subsystem, e.g., the top unit or a couple of experimental groups, and to begin improvement activities.

The following case illustrates these ideas. A general manager was concerned that the line managers were not making good use of the resources of the staff specialists. He felt that the specialists were not aggressive enough in offering their help. He had a desired state in mind of what good use of staff by line would be. He also had a practical first step in mind: send the staff out to visit the units on a systematic basis and have them report to him after their visits. The manager sent a memo to all staff and line heads announcing the plan. Staff went to the field and had a variety of experiences, mostly frustrating. The general manager got very busy on other priorities and did not hold his planned follow-up meetings. After one round of visits, the staff stopped its visits except in rare cases. Things returned to normal. An analysis showed that the general manager's real level of dissatisfaction with the previous state of affairs was not high enough to cause him to invest personal energy in follow-up reporting, so the change did not last.

Capability as defined here is frequently but not always outside of personal control. For example, a personnel or training manager may be ready to initiate a management development program but have low capability for doing it because he has no funds or support. The president of an organization may have only moderate or low readiness to start a management development program but may have very high capability because he can allocate the necessary resources. Two subordinates in an organization may be equally ready and motivated towards some change in their own functioning or leadership skills. One may have reached the ceiling of his capabilities and the other may not. Looking at this variable is an important guideline in determining interventions.

Identifying the Consultant's Own Resources and Motivations for the Change

In addition to defining the client and system status, and determining with the client the rank-ordering of change priorities, it is necessary for the consultant to be clear with himself and with the client about what knowledge and skills he brings to the problems and what knowledge and skills he does not have. One of the results of the early dependency on a consultant, particularly if the first interventions are seen as helpful or if his reputation is good, is to transfer the expertise of the consultant in a particular field to others in which his competence to help just is not there.

Concerning motivations, one of the fundamental choices that the consultant must make in intervening in any system is when to be an advocate and when to be a methodologist. The values of the consultant and the values of the system and their congruence or incongruence come together around this point. The choice of whether to work with the client, whether to try to influence the client toward the consultant's value system, or whether to take an active or passive role is a function of the decision that is made concerning advocacy vs. methodology.

This is not an absolute decision that, once made at the beginning of a relationship, holds firm throughout a change effort. Rather, it is a choice that is made daily around the multitude of interventions throughout a change effort. The choice is not always the same. It is helpful to the relationship and to the change effort if the results of the choice are known to the client as well as to the consultant.

Determining the Intermediate Change Strategy and Goals

Once change problems and change goals are defined, it is important to look at intermediate objectives if enough positive tension and energy toward change are to be maintained. For example, let us suppose that a change goal is to have all of the work teams in an organization consciously looking at their own functioning and systematically setting work priorities and improvement priorities on a regular basis. An intermediate goal might be to have developed within the various divisions or sections of the organization at least one team per unit by a certain time. These *intermediate* change goals provide a target and a measuring point en route to a larger change objective.

One other set of diagnostic questions concerns looking at the subsystems again in terms of:

1. Readiness of each system to be influenced by the consultant and/or entry client.

2. Accessibility of each of the subsystems to the consultant or entry client.
3. Linkage of each of the subsystems to the total system or organization.

To return to the earlier illustration concerning a management development program, let us suppose that the personnel director was highly vulnerable to influence by the consultant and highly accessible to the consultant but had low linkage to the organization, and that the president was much less vulnerable to influence by the consultant and the entry client, here the training manager. Then the question would be who should sign the anouncement of the program to line management. The correct answer is not necessarily the president with his higher linkage nor the personnel man with his accessibility and commitment. The point is that weighing these three variables helps the consultant and client to make an operational decision based on data. Whether one uses this model or some other, the concept of systematic analysis of a change problem helps develop realistic, practical, and attainable strategy and goals.

INTERVENTION STRATEGIES IN LARGE SYSTEMS

The kinds of conditions in organizations that tend to need large system interventions will now be examined.

Change in the Relationship of the Organization to the Environment

The number and complexity of outside demands on organization leaders are increasing at a rapid pace. Environmental organizations, minorities, youth, governments, and consumers exert strong demands on the organization's effort and require organization leaders to focus on creative adaptation to these pressures. The autonomy of organizations is fast becoming a myth. Organization leaders are increasingly recognizing that the institutions they manage are truly *open* systems. Improvement strategies based on looking at the internal structure, decision making, or intergroup relationships exclusively are an incomplete method of organization diagnosis and change

strategy. A more relevant method for today's environment is to start by examining how the organization and its key subsystems relate to the different environments with which the organization interfaces. One can then determine what kinds of organization structures, procedures and practices will allow each of the units in the organization to optimize the interface with its different environment. Having identified these, management can turn its energy toward the problems of integration (of standards, rewards, communications systems, etc.) which are consequences of the multiple interfaces.

The concept of differentiating and integration has been developed by Paul Lawrence and Jay Lorsch.[2] In essence, their theory states that within any organization there are very different types of environments and very different types of interfaces. In an industrial organization, for example, the sales department interfaces with a relatively volatile environment: the market. The production department, on the other hand, interfaces with a relatively stable environment: the technology of production. The kind of organization structure, rewards, work schedules and skills necessary to perform optimally in these two departments is very different. From a definition of what is appropriate for each of these departments, one can organize an ideal, independent structure. Only then can one look at the problems of interface and communication.

Clark, Krone and McWhinney[3] have developed a technology called "Open Systems Planning" which, when used as an intervention, helps the management of an organization to systematically sharpen its mission goals; to look objectively at its present response pattern to demands; to project the likely demand system if no proactive actions are taken by the organization leadership; to project an "ideal" demand system; to define what activities and behavior would have to be developed for the desired state to exist; and finally to analyze the cost effectiveness of undertaking these activities. Such a planning method serves several purposes:

1. It forces systematic thinking.
2. It forces people to think from outside-in (environment to organization).

3. It forces empathy with other parts of the environment.
4. It forces the facing of today's realities.
5. It forces a systematic plan for priorities in the medium-term future.

This is one example of large system intervention dealing with the organization and its environment. Another type of intervention is a survey of organization structure, work, attitudes and environmental requirements. From this an optimum organization design is developed.

There is an increasing demand for assistance in helping organization leaders with these macro-organization issues. Much current change agent training almost ignores this market need. Major changes in training are called for if OD specialists are to stay organizationally relevant.

Change in Managerial Strategy

Another change program involving behavioral science oriented interventions is a change in the *style* of managing the human resources of the organization. This can occur when top management is changing their assumptions and/or values about people and their motivations. It can occur as a result of new inputs from the environment, such as the loss of a number of key executives or difficulty in recruiting top young people. It can occur as females in the organization demand equal treatment or as the government requires new employment practices. Whatever the causes, once such a change is planned, help is likely to be needed in:

1. Working with the top leaders.
2. Assessing middle management attitudes.
3. Unfreezing old attitudes.
4. Developing credibility down the line.
5. Dealing with interfacing organizations, unions, regulatory agencies, etc.

Help can be provided in organization diagnosis, job design, goal setting, team building, and planning. Style changes particularly need considerable time and patience since perspective is essential and is often lost by the client. Both internal and outside consultants can provide significant leadership in providing perspectives to operating management. Some of the questions about key managers that need answers in planning a change in managerial strategy are:

1. To what degree does the top management encourage influence from other parts of the organization?
2. How do they manage conflict?
3. To what degree do they locate decision making based on where information is located rather than on hierarchical roles?
4. How do they handle the rewards that they control?
5. What kind of feedback systems do they have for getting information about the state of things?

Change in the Organization Structures

One key aspect of healthy and effective organizations is that the structures, the formal ways that work is organized, follow and relate to the actual work to be done. In many organizations the structure relates to the authority system: who reports to whom. Most organizations are designed to simplify the structure in order to get clear reporting lines which define the power relationships.

As work becomes more complex, it becomes impossible in any large system to have *one* organization structure that is relevant to all of the kinds of work to be done. The basic organization chart rarely describes the way even the basic work gets done. More and more organization leaders recognize and endorse the reality that organizations actually operate through a variety of structures. In addition to the permanent organization chart, there are project organizations, task forces, and other temporary systems.

To clarify this concept, we examine a case where a firmly fixed organizational structure was a major resistance to getting the required work done. In this particular consumer-based organization there was a marketing organization that was primarily concerned with competing in the market, and a technical subsystem that was primarily concerned with getting packages designed with high quality. Market demands required that the organization get some sample packages of new products into supermarkets as sales promotions.

The "rules of the game" were that for a package to be produced it had to go through a very thorough preparation including design and considerable field testing. These standards had been developed for products which were marketed extensively in markets where the company had a very high share. The problem developed around a market in which the company had a very low share and was competing desperately with a number of other strong companies. Because of the overall company rules about packages, the marketing people were unable to get the promotion packages into the stores on time. The result was the loss of an even greater share of the market. The frustration was tremendous and was felt right up to the president.

Within the marketing organization there was a very bright, technically oriented, skilled, abrasive entrepreneurial person, who kept very heavy pressure on the package technical people. He was convinced that he could produce the packages himself within a matter of weeks as opposed to the months that the technical people required. Because of his abrasiveness he produced much tension within the technical department and the tensions between the two departments also increased. At one point the heads of the two departments were on a very "cool" basis. The president of the company was quite concerned at the loss of markets. He had attempted to do something earlier about the situation by giving the marketing entrepreneur a little back room shop in which he could prove his assertions of being able to produce a package in a short time. The man did produce them, but when he took them to the technical people for reproduction, they called up all the traditional ground rules and policies to demonstrate that the package would not work and could not be used.

The client, here the president, had diagnosed the problem as one of noncooperation between departments and particularly between individuals. Based on this diagnosis he asked for some consultative help with the interpersonal problem between the marketing entrepreneur and the people in the technical department. He also thought that an intergroup intervention might be appropriate to increase collaboration between the groups.

The consultant's diagnosis was that although either of these interventions was possible and might, in fact, produce some temporary change in the sense of lowering the heat in the situation, there was little possibility of either event producing more packages. Rather, the change problem was one of an inappropriate structure for managing work.

The consultant suggested that the leaders of marketing and technical development together develop a flow chart of the steps involved in moving from an idea to a finished promotion package. Then they were to isolate those items which clearly fitted within the organization structure, such as the last few steps in the process which were handled by the buying and production department. The remaining steps, it was suggested, needed to be managed by a *temporary* organization created for just that purpose. The consultant proposed that for each new promotion a temporary management organization be set up consisting of one person from packaging, one from marketing, one from purchasing, and one from manufacturing. This organization would have, as its charter, the management of the flow of that product from idea to manufacturing. They would analyze the problem, set a timetable, set the resource requirements and control the flow of work. The resources that they needed were back in the permanent structures, of which they were also members. This task force would report weekly and jointly to the heads of both the technical and marketing departments. The president would withdraw from the problem.

The intervention produced the targeted result: promotion packages became available in one-fifth of the time previously required. The interpersonal difficulties remained for some time but gradually decreased as people were forced to collaborate in getting the job done.

Change in the Ways Work Is Done

This condition is one where there is a special effort to improve the meaningfulness as well as the efficiency of work. Job enrichment programs, work analysis programs, and development of criteria for effectiveness can all be included here.

To give an example, an intervention might be to work with a management group helping them examine their recent meeting agendas in order to improve the allocation of work tasks. Specifically, one can get them to make an initial list of those activities and functions that absolutely have to be done by that group functioning as a group. Next, a list can be made of things that are not being done but need to be. A third list can be made of those things that the group is now doing that could be done, even if not so well, by either the same people wearing their functional or other hats, or by other people. Experience has shown that the second two lists tend to balance each other and tend to represent somewhere around 25–30 percent of the total work of such a group. Based on this analysis a replan of work can emerge. It can have significant effects on both attitudes and behavior. The output of such an activity by a group at the top means that work gets reallocated to the next level, and thus a domino effect is set in motion which can result in significant change.

Another illustration concerns an organization-wide change effort to improve both the way work is done and the management of the work. The total staff of this very large organization was about forty thousand people. During a six month period, the total organization met in their work teams with the task of developing the criteria against which that team wanted the performance of their work unit to be measured. They then located their current performance against those criteria and projected their performance at a date about six months in the future against the same criteria. These criteria and projections were checked with senior management committees in each subsystem. If approved they became the work plan and basis for performance appraisal for that group.

With this one intervention the top management distributed the responsibility for managing the work to the people who were doing the work throughout the organization. The results of this program were a significant increase in productivity, significant cost reductions, and a significant change in attitudes and feelings of ownership among large numbers of employees, many of whom were previously quite dissatisfied with the state of things. Given this participative mode, it is most unlikely that any future management could successfully return to overcentralized control. Much latent energy was released and continues to be used by people all over the organization who feel responsible and appreciated for *their* management of *their* work.

Change in the Reward System

One significant organization problem concerns making the reward system consistent with the work. How often we see organizations in which someone in a staff department spends 90 percent of his time in assisting some line department; yet for his annual review his performance is evaluated solely by the head of his staff department, probably on 10 percent of his work. One result of this is that any smart person behaves in ways that please the individual who most influences his career and other rewards rather than those with whom he is working. Inappropriate reward systems do much to sabotage effective work as well as organization health.

An example of an intervention in this area follows. The vice president of one of the major groups in a very large company was concerned about the lack of motivation by his division general managers toward working with him on planning for the future of the business as a whole. He was equally concerned that the managers were not fully developing their own subordinates. In his opinion, this was blocking the managers' promotions. The vice president had spoken of these concerns many times. His staff had agreed that it was important to change, but their behavior was heavily directed toward maintaining the old priorities: meeting short-term profit goals. This group existed in an organization where the reward system was very clear. The chief executives in any sub-enterprise were accountable for their short-term profits. This was their most important assignment. Division managers knew that if they did not participate actively in future business planning, or if they did not invest energy in the development of subordinates, they would incur the group vice president's displeasure. They also knew, however, that if they did not meet their short-term profit objectives, they probably would not be around. The company had an executive incentive plan in which considerable amounts of bonus money were available to people in the upper ranks for good performance. In trying to find a method for changing his division managers' priorities, the group vice president looked, with consultant help, at the reward system. As a result of this he called his colleagues together and told them, "I thought you'd like to know that in determining your bonus at the next review, I will be using the following formula. You are still 100 percent accountable for your short-term profit goals, but that represents 60 percent of the bonus. Another 25 percent will be my evaluation of your performance as members of this top management planning team. The other 15 percent will be your discernible efforts toward the development of your subordinates." Executive behavior changed dramatically. The reality of the reward system and the desired state were now consistent.

We have examined briefly several types of organization phenomena which need large system oriented interventions. We will now look at initial interventions and examine some of the choices facing the intervenor.

EARLY INTERVENTIONS

There are a number of choices about where to intervene. Several are listed here with the objective of creating a map of possibilities. The list includes:

1. The top team or the top of a system.
2. A pilot project which can have a linkage to the larger system.
3. Ready subsystems: those whose leaders and members are known to be ready for a change.
4. Hurting systems. This is one class of ready system where the environment has caused some acute discomfort in a generally unready system.
5. The rewards system.
6. Experiments: a series of experiments on new ways of organizing or new ways of handling communications.

7. Educational interventions: training programs, outside courses, etc.
8. An organization-wide confrontation meeting, bringing together a variety of parts of the organization, to examine the state of affairs and to make first step plans for improvement.[4]
9. The creation of a critical mass.

The last concept requires some elaboration. It is most difficult for a stable organization to change itself, that is, for the regular structures of the organization to be used for change. Temporary systems are frequently created to accomplish this. As an example, in one very large system, a country, there were a number of agencies involved in training and development for organization leaders. The government provided grants to the agencies for training activities. These grants also provided funds to support the agency staffs for other purposes. Because of this condition each agency was developing programs for the same small clientele. Each agency kept innovations secret from its competitors.

In an attempt to move this competitive state toward a more collaborative one, a small group of people developed a "nonorganization" called the Association for Commercial and Industrial Education. It was a luncheon club. Its rules were the opposite of an ordinary organization's. It could make no group decisions, it distributed no minutes, no one was allowed to take anyone else to lunch, there were no dues, and there were no officers or hierarchy.

In this context it was possible for individuals from the various competing agencies to sit down and talk together about matters of mutual interest. After a couple of years it even became possible to develop a national organization development training project in the form of a four week course which was attended by top line managers and personnel people from all the major economic and social institutions in the country. Only this nonorganization could sponsor such a program. From this program a great many other linkages were developed. Today there is an entire professional association of collaborating change agents with bases in a variety of institutions, but with the capacity to collaborate around larger national problems.

MAINTAINING CHANGE

To maintain change in a large system it is necessary to have conscious procedures and commitment. Organization change will not be maintained simply because there has been early success. There are a number of interventions which are possible, and many are necessary if a change is to be maintained. Many organizations are living with the effects of successful short-term change results which have not been maintained.

Perhaps the most important single requirement for continued change is a continued feedback and information system that lets people in the organization know the system status in relation to the desired states. Some feedback systems that are used fairly frequently are:

1. Periodic team meetings to review a team's functioning and what its next goal priorities should be.

2. Organization sensing meetings in which the top of an organization meets, on a systematic planned basis, with a sample of employees from a variety of different organizational centers in order to keep apprised of the state of the system.

3. Periodic meetings between interdependent units of an organization.

4. Renewal conferences. For example, one company has an annual five-year planning meeting with its top management. Three weeks prior to that meeting the same management group and their wives go to a retreat for two or three days to take a look at themselves, their personal and company priorities, the new forces in the environment, what they need to keep in mind in their upcoming planning, and what has happened in the way they work and in their relationships that needs review before the planning meeting.

5. Performance review on a systematic, goal-directed basis.

6. Periodic visits from outside consultants to keep the organization leaders thinking about the organization's renewal.

There are other possible techniques but this list includes the most commonly used methods of maintaining a change effort in a complex organization.

SUMMARY

In order to help organizations improve their operational effectiveness and system health, we have examined:

1. A model for determining early organization interventions.
2. Some choices of change strategies.
3. Some choices of early interventions.
4. Some choices of strategies for maintaining change.

The focus of this article has been on what the third party, facilitator, consultant, etc., can do as either a consultant, expert, trainer, or coach in helping organization leaders diagnose their own system and plan strategies for development toward a better state. This focus includes process intervention but is not exclusively that. It also includes the skills of system diagnosis, of determining change strategies, of understanding the relationship of organizations to external environments, and of understanding such organizational processes as power, reward systems, organizational decision making, information systems, structural designs and planning.

It is the author's experience that the demand for assistance in organizational interventions and large system organization change is increasing at a very fast rate, certainly faster than the growth of resources to meet the demand. As the world shrinks, as there are more multinational organizations, as the interfaces between government and the private sector and the social sector become more blurred and more overlapping, large system interventions and the technology and skill available to facilitate these will be in increasingly greater demand.

NOTES

1. For a more detailed explanation of the author's views concerning organization development and intervention, see Beckhard [1].

2. See Lawrence and Lorsch [4].

3. See Krone [3].

4. For one view of this, see Beckhard [2].

REFERENCES

1. Beckhard, R. *Organization Development: Strategies and Models.* Reading, Mass.: Addison-Wesley, 1969.
2. Beckhard, R. "The Confrontation Meeting." *Harvard Business Review,* March–April 1967.
3. Krone, C. "Open Systems Redesign." In *Theory and Method in Organization Development: An Evolutionary Process,* edited by John Adams. Rosslyn, Virginia: NTL Institute, 1974.
4. Lawrence, P. R., and Lorsch, J. W. *Organization and Environment: Managing Differentiation and Integration.* Boston: Harvard Business School, Division of Research, 1967.

THE FIFTH ACHIEVEMENT

ROBERT R. BLAKE
JANE SRYGLEY MOUTON

A great new challenge to the American way of conducting its national life is taking shape. Conformity with older patterns is breaking down. Yet creative definitions of new patterns are not forthcoming, or at best are coming at a snail's pace. Unless the challenge of finding new patterns that can serve to strengthen society is successfully met, some of the nation's most cherished human values may very well be sacrificed. If we can meet it, however, our deeply embedded beliefs as to the role of men in society may not only be reinforced but may find even richer and more extensive applications in the society of tomorrow.

What is this challenge?

We widely acknowledge the objective of an open and free society based on individual responsibility and self-regulated participation by all in the conduct of national life. That men will differ in the ways they think and act is accepted as both inevitable and desirable. Indeed, this is one hallmark of an open society. Differences are intrinsically valuable. They provide the rich possibility that alternatives and options will be discovered for better and poorer ways of responding to any particular situation. Preserving the privi-

Reprinted by special permission from *The Journal of Applied Behavioral Science*. "The Fifth Achievement," by Robert R. Blake and Jane Srygley Mouton, Volume 6, Number 4, pp. 413–426. Copyright 1970 NTL Institute.

lege of having and expressing differences increases our chances of finding "best" solutions to the many dilemmas that arise in living. They also add the spice of variety and give zest to human pursuits.

When it is possible for a man to make a choice from among several solutions, and when he can make this choice without infringing upon another man's freedom or requiring his cooperation, there is genuine autonomy. This is real freedom.

But in many situations not every man can have his own personal solution. When cooperation and coordination are required in conducting national life—in government, business, the university, agencies of the community, the home, and so on —differences that arise must find reconciliation. A solution must be agreed upon and embraced which can provide a pattern to which those involved are prepared to conform their behavior. Yet efforts to reconcile differences in order to achieve consensus-based patterns of conduct often only serve to promote difficulties. When disagreements as to sound bases for action can be successfully resolved, freedom can be retained and necessary solutions implemented. Dealing with the many and varied misunderstandings that are inevitable in a society dedicated to preserving the privilege of having and expressing differences is the challenge. As individuals, we find this hard to do. As members of organized groups, we appear to find it even more difficult.

FOUR CLASSICAL SOLUTIONS
FOR RESOLVING CONFLICTS

In the conduct of society there are at least four major and different kinds of formal, structural arrangements which we rely on for resolving differences. They are the scientific method; politics; law, with its associated police powers; and organizational hierarchy.

Of undisputed value in finding the objective solution to which agreement can readily be given are the methods of science. A well-designed experiment confirms which of several alternatives is the most valid basis of explanation while simultaneously demonstrating the unacceptability of the remaining explanations.

Our political mechanisms are based on the one-man-one-vote approach to problem solving. This provides for the resolution of differences according to a weighting approach, and the basis is usually that the majority prevail. By this means, decisions can be made and actions taken even though differences may remain. Simply being outvoted, however, does not aid those on the losing side in changing their intellectual and emotional attitudes. While it ensures that a solution is chosen, the fact that it is often on a win-lose or a compromise basis may pose further problems when those who are outvoted resolve to be the winners of the future. Often the underlying disagreements are deepened.

Legal mechanisms apply only in resolving differences when questions of law are involved and other means of reaching agreement usually have met with failure. With application of associated police powers, the use of force is available to back up legal mechanisms when law is violated. But this constitutes a far more severe solution to the problem. The ultimate failure of law which invites the use of military power is in effect a court of last resort.

Within society's formal institutions such as business, government, education, and the family, organizational hierarchy, or rank, can and does permit the resolution of differences. The premise is that when a disagreement arises between any two persons of differing rank, the one of higher rank can impose a solution unilaterally based on his position. In the exercise of authority, sup-

pression may also sacrifice the validity of a solution, since there is no intrinsic basis of truth in the idea that simply because a man is the boss of other men he is ordained with an inherent wisdom. While this arrangement provides a basis for avoiding indecision and impasse, it may and often does have the undesirable consequence of sacrificing the support of those to whom it is applied for the solution of the problem, to say nothing of its adverse effects on future creativity.

These classical solutions to dealing with differences—science, politics, law, and hierarchy—represent real progress in learning to conduct the national life. Where it can be applied, scientific method provides a close to ideal basis for resolving differences. That politics, courts of justice, and organizational hierarchy, though more limited, are necessary is indisputable. But that they are being questioned and increasingly rejected is also indisputable. Even if they were not, none of these alone nor all of them together provide a sound and sufficient basis for the development of a truly problem-solving society.

WHAT IS THE
FIFTH ACHIEVEMENT?

There is another essential ingredient. It is a sharply increased understanding by every man of the roots of conflict and the human skills of gaining the resolution of differences. The acquisition of such insight and skill by every man could provide a social foundation for reaching firm and sound understandings on a direct man-to-man basis of the inevitable disagreements that arise in conducting the national life. This kind of deepened skill in the direct resolution of differences could do much to provide a realistic prospect that the antagonisms, cleavages, or injustices real and imagined in society today can be reduced if not eliminated. It offers the promise that the sicknesses of alienation and apathy, the destructive aggressions, and the organization-man mentality can be healed.

The Fifth Achievement, then, is in the establishment of a problem-solving society where differences among men are subject to resolution through insights that permit protagonists themselves to identify and implement solutions to their differences upon the basis of committed agreement. That men ultimately will be able to work out, face to face, their differences is a hoped-for achievement of the future. Extending their capacity to do so could reduce the number of problems brought before the bench or dealt with through hierarchy. At the same time, scientific and political processes could be strengthened if progress were made in this direction. Even more important, it could perhaps lead to the resolution of many conflicts on a local level that block the development of a creative and committed problem-solving community. Success in meeting this challenge in the period ahead is perhaps the surest way to preserve and strengthen the values of a free society while protecting and even strengthening the privilege of having and expressing differences.

HOW TO INCREASE SKILL IN MANAGING CONFLICT

Why do men rely on these other four approaches to conflict settlement while placing lower value on the resolution of differences in a direct, man-to-man way? One explanation for this might be that they do not hold in concert a conceptual basis for analyzing situations of disagreement and their causes. It should be said that conceptual understanding, while necessary for strengthening behavior, is clearly not in itself a sufficient basis for learning the skills of sound resolution of conflict. Personal entrapment from self-deception about one's motivations is too great. Insensitivity about one's behavior and the reactions of others to it is too extensive. To connect a conceptual analysis to one's own behavior and conduct in ways that permit insight and change seems to require something more in the way of personal learning.

Classroom learning methodologies that could enable men to gain insights regarding conflict and acquire skills for resolving it seem to be impoverished. To aid men in acquiring both the conceptual understanding for managing conflict and the skills to see their own reactions in situations of conflict, man-to-man feedback seems to be an essential condition. A variety of situations involving laboratory learning that permit this have

been designed (Bach & Wyden, 1969; Blake & Mouton, 1968; Bradford, Gibb, & Benne, 1964; Schein & Bennis, 1965). They set the stage for men to learn to face their differences and find creative and valid solutions to their problems.

Success in mastering this Fifth Achievement will undoubtedly require reconception of the classroom in ways that permit the study of conflict as a set of concepts and the giving and receiving of feedback in ways that enable men to see how to strengthen their own capacities and skills for coping with it directly.

Conceptual Analysis of Conflict

This paper concentrates upon a first step toward this Fifth Achievement by presenting a conceptual basis for analyzing situations of conflict. The Conflict Grid® in Figure 1 is a way of identifying basic assumptions when men act in situations where differences are present, whether disagreement is openly expressed or silently present (Blake & Mouton, 1964; Blake, Shepard, & Mouton, 1964).

Whenever a man meets a situation of conflict, he has at least two basic considerations in mind. One of these is the *people* with whom he is in disagreement. Another is *production of results,* or getting a resolution to the disagreement. It is the amount and kind of emphasis he places on various combinations of each of these elements that determine his thinking in dealing with conflict.

Basic attitudes toward people and toward results are visualized on nine-point scales. These form the Grid in Figure 1. The nine-point scale representing concern for producing a result provides the horizontal axis for the Grid. The phrase "concern for" does not show results produced but rather denotes the degree of emphasis in his thinking that the man places on getting results. The *1* end represents low concern, and the *9* represents the highest possible concern. The same applies on the vertical or concern-for-people axis. Considering the interactions of these two scales, there are 81 possible positions. Each describes an intersection between the two dimensions.

The following pages discuss strategies of managing conflict according to the five basic theories

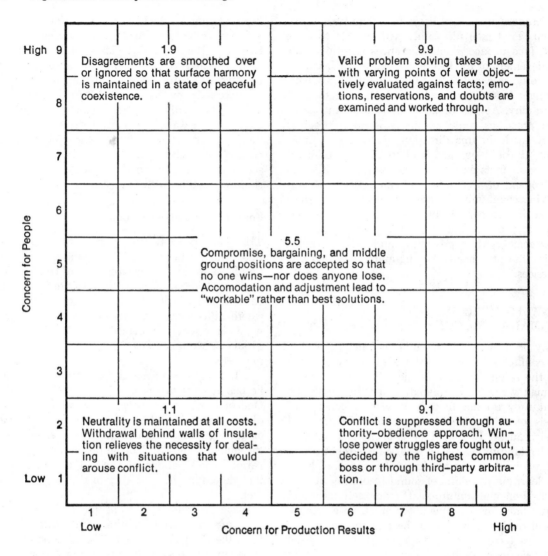

FIGURE 1. The conflict grid

—those appearing at the four corners and the center of the figure. When these basic styles are understood, one can predict for each how a man operating under that style is likely to handle conflict. There are eight additional important theories composed from various mixtures of these five, but basic issues of conflict resolution can be seen in dealing with these "pure" theories.

No one style is exclusively characteristic of one man in comparison with another, although one style may be dominant in a man's actions. Furthermore, even though one may be dominant for a time, it may be abandoned and replaced by another when the first has been ineffective in achieving resolution.

What are some of the ways of dealing with conflict?

Conflict can be controlled by overpowering it and suppressing one's adversary (9,1 in the lower right corner of the Grid). An ultimate expression of this is in the extremes of police power and military action. Extracting compliance by authority-obedience is possible when rank is present. The conflict can be cut off and suppressed in this way, "Yours not to question why!" When rank is not available, a win–lose basis expresses the same set of assumptions. Winning for one's own position predominates over seeking a valid solution.

Another strategy is to smooth conflict by cajolery, by letting a man know that with a little patience he will find that all is right (1,9 in the upper left corner). The assumption of sweetness and light often leads to resolution by people's retracting from previously held positions, preferring personal acceptance to solution validity. This can promote accord and harmony, but it sacrifices conviction and insight into differences, while decreasing the likelihood of achieving valid solutions. Staying out of situations that provoke controversy or turning away from topics that promote disagreement represents a set of assumptions about how to live in a conflict-free way (1.1 in the lower left corner). Then one need not be stirred up even though the issue may need resolution. A man can remain composed if he does not let himself be drawn into controversy; he avoids it by remaining neutral. This kind of "see no disagreement, hear no disagreement, and speak no disagreement" represents a withdrawal from social responsibility in a world where the resolution of differences is key to finding sound solutions. It is the ultimate in alienation.

A third set of assumptions leads to a middle-of-the-road solution to differences through accommodation and adjustment. Disagreement is settled through bargaining a compromise solution (5,5). The assumptions underlying compromising of one's convictions are at the root of this approach. It means agreeing so as to be agreeable, even to sacrificing sound action; settling for what you can get rather than working to get what is sound in the light of the best available facts and data.

The mental attitude behind the one-man-one-vote approach often leads to the endorsement of positions calculated to get majority support even though this means giving up a solution of deeper validity. The same assumptions often prevail behind the scenes in out-of-court settlement.

Outside the sphere of industrial management, solutions to major political and international problems of recent years provide classic examples of 5,5 splitting. One is the "separate but equal" approach to solving what is seen as the race problem. The cessation of hostilities in Korea by the establishment of the thirty-eighth parallel as a line of demarcation between North and South in the early Fifties is another. This set a precedent for setting up the "Demilitarized Zone" between North and South Vietnam. The Berlin Wall is probably the most significant symbol of the East–West split. The 5,5 attitude is reflected daily by news reporters and commentators who quote "unidentified but high-level sources" or hide their sources by attributing their facts merely to "usually reliable sources."

Under a 9,9 approach, disagreement is valued as an inevitable result of the fact that strong-minded people have convictions about what is right. A man says, "Nothing is sacrosanct. What are the facts? What are the causes? What are the conclusions?" Reservations and emotions that interrupt agreement based on logic and data are confronted through candid discussion of them directly with the person involved in the disagreement. Insight and resolution are possible but involve maturity and real human skill. This approach may be time-consuming in the short run but time-conserving over the long term. It permits men to disagree, to work out their disagreements in the light of facts, and ultimately to understand one another. Such problem-solving constructiveness in conflict situations is the fundamental basis for realizing the Fifth Achievement.

Conflict, Conformity, and Creative Problem Solving

How does effective conflict management interrelate with other social processes of seemingly equal or greater significance in strengthening society? Indeed, it might be maintained that the challenge to society seen today is in nonconformity with its norms, rather than in faulty management of conflict.

In what ways are conflict and conformity interdependent (Blake & Mouton, 1961)? Men in everyday life do conform to the expectations of others and the patterns of their institutions. This readiness to conform reduces conflict and is what permits regularity, order, and predictability. To adhere to common norms provides a basis for organized effort. From conformity with conventionalized social and organizational practices can come a sense of identification, belonging, and *esprit de corps*. On the other hand, failure to conform may stir conflict with one's colleagues and associates so that the nonconformist is rejected. Indeed, anxiety about rejection can be so overwhelming that, for many, conformity becomes an end in itself rather than a means to cooperation through interdependence. Under these circumstances, the capacity to challenge outmoded traditions, precedents, and past practices is lost. With sound ways of approaching and resolving conflict, outmoded patterns can successfully be challenged and upgraded by replacement of them with agreements which themselves can promote problem solving and creativity. In this way, finding new and better ways to accomplish personal, organizational, national, and perhaps even international objectives becomes possible.

Just stimulating people to challenge and contest status quo conformities, however, is likely to do little more than provoke disagreement and controversy, increase polarization, and ultimately end in win-lose, impasse, compromise, or chaos. Yet the status quo requirements must continuously be challenged in a problem-solving and creative way, not in a manner that pits man against man to see who can win or, even worse, in a way that ends in anarchy.

The Conflict Grid is useful in seeing the more subtle connections among conflict and conformity and creative problem solving. Conformity to the 9,1 authority-obedience demands that are involved in hierarchical rank is exemplified by the boss, teacher, or parent who gives the orders to subordinates, students, or children who are expected to obey. The exercise of initiative which produces differences is equivalent to insubordination. Conformity under 9,1 may produce the protocol of surface compliance, but the frustrations of those who are suppressed are often evident. Ways of striking back against the boss, teacher, or parent appear. Such acts may be open ones of resistance and rebellion or disguised ones of sabotage, cheating, or giving agreement without following through. Each of these in a certain sense involves reverse creativity, where ingenuity is exercised in attacking or "beating" the system. It is creativity in resentment of the system, not in support of it.

In another type of conformity, the rules of relationship are, "Don't say anything if you can't say something nice" (1,9). Togetherness, social intimacy, and warmth engendered by yielding one's convictions in the interests of personal acceptance are certainly objectionable solutions in a society where having and expressing differences is relied on as the basis for finding sound courses of action. It can produce a quorum of agreement but smother creative problem solving in sweetness and love. The kind of disagreement that might provoke resentment is avoided. The opportunity for creative problem solving to emerge is absent.

Another kind of conformity relates to adhering to the form and not to the substance of life. Here people conform by going through the motions expected of them, treadmilling through the days, months, and years (1,1). In this way, survival is accomplished by being visible without being seen.

Organization-man conformity (5,5) entails positively embracing the status quo with minimum regard for the soundness of status quo requirements. Yet, even here, as new problems arise, differences appear and disagreements become evident. There are several kinds of 5,5 actions that on shallow examination may give the appearance of approaching problems from an altered, fresh, and original point of view. Pseudo-creativity may be seen when new approaches, even though they constitute only small departures from the outmoded past, are recommended on the basis of their having been tried elsewhere. Under these circumstances a man is forwarding actions taken by others rather than promoting examination of actions on the basis of his own convictions. In this way, he can suggest, while avoiding the challenge or rejection of his own convictions. Deeper examination of 5,5 behavior leads to the conclusion that imitation rather than innovation is the rule.

In other instances, solutions which are proposed as compromise positions can give the impression of "flexibility" in thought. When adjustment and accommodation, backing and filling, twisting and turning, shifting and adapting take place in the spirit of compromise, the motivation behind them is usually to avoid interpersonal emotions resulting from confrontation. Behaving in this manner is a reaction to disagreement, and it means that personal validity is being eroded.

Flexibility is a highly valued component in mature and effective behavior. But is it not contradictory to advocate flexibility on the one hand and to forewarn against compromise on the other? This question is important to clarify.

Flexibility calls for deliberate examination of options and alternatives. It means having back-up tactics that permit swift resolution of unforeseen circumstances, a climate that permits people to move back and forth and in and out from one situation to another, but based on facts, data, and logic of the situation as it unfolds. These are the characteristics of creative problem solving that permit gains to be made as opportunities arrive; that permit opportunities to be created, threats to be anticipated, and risks that result when people fail to react to be reduced.

Thus there are actions to adjust a difference to keep peace and actions to adjust to altered circumstances for better results. It is most important to distinguish between the two kinds. Flexibility for better results is likely to have a stamp of 9,9 on it; "flexibility" to keep peace by avoiding clash of personalities is in the 5,5 area. One is enlivening and promotes creativity. The other leads to the perpetuation of the organization-man mentality of status quo rigidities.

In the final analysis, conformity is to be valued. The problem is to ensure that the thinking of men conforms with sound purposes and premises. Conformity which means adherence to premises of human logic so that decisions reached are furthering growth capacity in sound and fundamental ways is what every individual might be expected to want. It is what man should want in the underpinnings of his daily interactions. It is conformity at this level that promotes the pursuit of creative and innovative solutions. Only when the values of a nation stimulate experimentation and promote a truly constructive attitude toward discovery and innovation is the full potential from creative efforts available as a source of thrust

for replacing outmoded status quo conformities with more problem-solving requirements (9,9).

What Men Want—Transnationally

Though varying widely in their ways of *actually* dealing with conflict, studies show that leaders in the United States, Great Britain, the Middle and Far East all indicate that they would *prefer* the 9,9 approach of *open confrontation* as the soundest way of managing situations of conflict, particularly under circumstances where outmoded conformities are under examination (Mouton & Blake, 1970). Though extremely difficult, it appears to be the soundest of several possible choices. This is not to imply that every decision should be made by a leader through calling a meeting or obtaining team agreement. Nor for a crisis situation does it imply that a leader should withhold exercising direction. But a 9,9 foundation of interdependence can build a strong basis for an open, problem-solving society in which men can have and express differences and yet be interrelated in ways that promote the mutual respect, common goals, and trust and understanding they must have to achieve results in ways that lead to personal gratification and maturity.

POSSIBILITIES OF THE FIFTH ACHIEVEMENT FOR STRENGTHENING SOCIETY

This challenge to America, the need for men to learn to confront outmoded status quo requirements and to manage the resultant conflict in such ways as to promote creative problem solving, promises much for the decades ahead, if we can meet and master it.

Consider for a moment the possibility of success in mastering this Fifth Achievement. What might it mean?

1. Enriched family life rather than the steady rise in the divorce rate.

2. Sounder child rearing, evidenced in teen-age youngsters capable of expression and action in dealing in a problem-solving rather than a protest way with adults and the institutions of society who are capable of interacting in an equally sound way.

3. The conversion of academic environments from subject-oriented learning centers to ones that expand the capacity of individuals for contributing creatively to the evolving character of society.

4. The betterment of communities in ways that more fully serve human wants.

5. The more rapid integration of minorities into a more just society, with the reduction and eventual elimination of disenfranchised, alienated segments.

6. Fuller and more creative use of human energies in conducting the organizations that serve society.

7. A greater readiness to support and utilize science for approaching problems when evidence, facts, and data come to have an ever greater value as the bases for gaining insight.

8. A strengthening of politics by readiness to advocate positions on the basis of statesmanlike convictions rather than to adopt positions for political expediency.

9. Reliance on knowledge rather than rank in the resolution of differences and disagreements in organization situations.

10. A stronger basis for mind-meeting agreements rather than resorting to legal actions to force a resolution of disputes.

If erosion of social institutions has not already become too great, all of these aims can perhaps be forwarded over time by our classical institutions for settling conflicts. But surely men capable of resolving their conflicts directly would forward human progress with a dramatic thrust—and on a far more fundamental and therefore enduring basis.

If this **Fifth Achievement** is to be realized, it is likely that greater use of the behavioral sciences will be essential. For in the behavioral sciences may well lie the key to a more rewarding and progressive society in which men can share and evaluate their differences, learn from them, and use conflict as a stepping stone to the greater progress that is possible when differences can be resolved in a direct, face-to-face way.

Will this challenge be met, or will the cherished freedom of having and expressing differences be sacrificed?

REFERENCES

Bach, G. R., & Wyden, P. *The ultimate enemy.* New York: Morrow, 1969.

Blake, R. R., & Mouton, Jane S. The experimental investigation of interpersonal influence. In A. D. Biderman & H. Zimmer (Eds.), *The manipulation of human behavior.* New York: Wiley, 1961.

Blake, R. R., & Mouton, Jane S. *The managerial grid.* Houston: Gulf, 1964.

Blake, R. R., & Mouton, Jane S. *Corporate excellence through grid organization development: A systems approach.* Houston: Gulf, 1968.

Blake, R. R., Shepard, H. A., & Mouton, Jane S. *Managing intergroup conflict in industry.* Houston: Gulf, 1964.

Bradford, L. P., Gibb, J. R., & Benne, K. D. (Eds.) *T-group theory and laboratory method: Innovation in re-education.* New York: Wiley, 1964.

Mouton, Jane S., & Blake, R. R. Issues in transnational organization development. In B. M. Bass, R. B. Cooper, & J. A. Haas (Eds.), *Managing for task accomplishment.* Lexington, Mass.: D. C. Heath, 1970. Pp. 208–224.

Schein, E. H., & Bennis, W. G. (Eds.) *Personal and organizational change through group methods: The laboratory approach.* New York: Wiley, 1965.